Controversies in Media Ethics
Third Edition

Controversies in Media Ethics offers students, instructors and professionals multiple perspectives on media ethics issues presenting vast "gray areas" and few, if any, easy answers. This third edition includes a wide range of subjects, and demonstrates a willingness to tackle the problems raised by new technologies, new media, new politics and new economics. The core of the text is formed by 14 chapters, each of which deals with a particular problem or likelihood of ethical dilemma, presented as different points of view on the topic in question, as argued by two or more contributing authors. Chapter 15 is a collection of "mini-chapters," allowing students to discern first-hand how to deal with ethical problems.

This edition has been thoroughly updated to provide:

- Discussions of issues reflecting the breadth and depth of the media spectrum
- Numerous real-world examples
- Broad discussion of confidentiality and other timely topics
- A companion Web site supplies additional resources for both students and instructors.

Developed for use in media ethics courses, *Controversies in Media Ethics* provides up-to-date discussions and analysis of ethical situations across a variety of media, including issues dealing with the Internet and new media. It provides a unique consideration of ethical concerns, and serves as provocative reading for all media students.

A. David Gordon retired from the University of Wisconsin-Eau Claire in 2002, where he taught mass media ethics and law as well as journalism and media/society courses.

John Michael Kittross is editor of *Media Ethics* magazine. He retired from Emerson College, where he served as provost and vice president for academic affairs. He is managing director of K\E\G Associates, an academic consulting group.

John C. Merrill is professor emeritus of journalism at the University of Missouri.

William A. Babcock is senior ethics professor at Southern Illinois University, Carbondale.

Michael Dorsher teaches mass media ethics at the University of Wisconsin-Eau Claire.

Third Edition

Controversies in Media Ethics

A. David Gordon
John Michael Kittross
John C. Merrill
William A. Babcock
Michael Dorsher

with contributions by
John A. Armstrong
Peter J. Gade
Julianne H. Newton
Kim Sheehan
Jane B. Singer

Routledge
Taylor & Francis Group
NEW YORK AND LONDON

Second edition published 1999
by Addison-Wesley Longman

This edition published 2011
by Routledge
711 Third Avenue, New York, NY 10017

Simultaneously published in the UK
by Routledge
2 Park Square, Milton Park, Abingdon, Oxon OX14 4RN

Routledge is an imprint of the Taylor & Francis Group, an informa business

© 2011 Routledge, Taylor & Francis

The right of A. David Gordon and John Michael Kittross to be identified as authors
of this work has been asserted by them in accordance with sections 77 and 78
of the Copyright, Designs and Patents Act 1988.

Library of Congress Cataloging in Publication Data
Controversies in media ethics / A. David Gordon ... [et al.]. — 3rd ed.
    p. cm.
1. Mass media—Moral and ethical aspects. I. Gordon, David, 1935–
P94.C585 2011
175—dc22   2010050712

ISBN 13: 978–0–415–99247–3 (hbk)
ISBN 13: 978–0–415–96332–9 (pbk)
ISBN 13: 978–0–203–82991–2 (ebk)

Typeset in Times New Roman and Futura
by Keystroke, Station Road, Codsall, Wolverhampton

Printed and bound in the United States of America on acid-free paper
by Edwards Brothers, Inc

SUSTAINABLE FORESTRY INITIATIVE
Certified Fiber Sourcing
www.sfiprogram.org

Contents in Brief

Part 4 HOT TOPICS IN MEDIA ETHICS   **331**

Contents

issues that go beyond those faced by professionals working in traditional media environments. (*Jane B. Singer*)   216

B. Ethics transcends media technologies and methods, so developments such as convergence journalism, citizen journalism, blogs, and multimedia mobile phones require little if any rethinking of long-standing ethical principles or guidelines. (*Dorsher*)   227

Commentary (*Merrill*)   233

7 Digitally Manipulated Content

A. There is no ethical mandate to authenticate digital material, especially in the persuasive and entertainment realms, and news operations can rely on corrections if they find they have disseminated erroneous material. (*Babcock and Gordon*)   238

B. The ability to "doctor" visual images and audio content digitally and undetectably will not go away so we must live with it, and newsrooms should verify digital materials even at the risk of not being "first." (*Kittross*)   245

Commentary (*Merrill*)   252

8 Media Ethics and the Economic Marketplace

A. The economic marketplace is at best irrelevant, and at worst counterproductive ethics and the marketplace of ideas. (*Kittross*)   257

B. The evolving economic marketplace can still help to hold the media responsible for their actions, with help from nonprofit organizations, knowledgeable media consumers, and farsighted privately owned media companies. (*Gordon*)   280

Commentary (Merrill)   299

9 Access to Media: Equity in Receiving and Disseminating Information

A. Mass media must guard against practices that isolate some groups in society from access to information they need. (*Gordon*)   308

B. Market forces are sufficient safeguards against any groups in society being deprived of access to necessary information, or of expressing themselves. (*Babcock*)   318

Commentary (*Merrill*)   325

I do not Twitter—yet—because I have never believed that my first thought on a subject is always my best thought.

—E. J. Dionne, columnist for *The Washington Post*, at the Ann Devroy Memorial Forum, University of Wisconsin-Eau Claire, May 4, 2011

Preface

THIS book is about questions, which we hope will enable you to work on the answers with increasing confidence. What it *doesn't* deal with might be easier to consider than what it does—or tries—to do.

Media ethics isn't an oxymoron—a contradiction in terms—nor is it a fixed set of rules or laws, as in medicine or theology. Neither is it a clear list of "do's and don'ts" or "blacks and whites." Instead, we believe that media ethics is an essential *process* that evolves with the world in which media operate, and on which the media report—a seemingly endless array of gray areas, where issues and appropriate courses of action aren't always obvious.

In other words—and it would be a lot easier not to have to tell you this—there are no fixed "right answers" in media ethics. Sometimes it is even hard to compose the questions! As philosophers Thomas Cathcart and Daniel Klein (2006) said in their popular *Plato and a Platypus Walk into a Bar . . .* (New York: Abrams Image, 2006, p. 4), "Questions beget questions, and those questions beget another whole generation of questions." And because ethical decision-making is a process without firm rules, it also is the subject of continual discussions—sometimes heated arguments—among media ethicists and practitioners, and media users, about what will make media content of all kinds—information, persuasion or entertainment—better and more valuable. The purpose of this book is to help with that process.

Because there are a wide variety of ethical dilemmas and conflicts of values, there are no answers that are consistently correct. Some alternatives, though, are always better than others and we can often find them by following principles and guidelines that have been developed by media ethicists to assist practitioners (and their audiences) come to grips with moral and ethical problems that confront them every day. Finding the better alternatives, though, is not an easy process and may become uncomfortable at times. But as John C. Merrill writes in his commentary for Chapter 11, "there is simply no clear and completely satisfying answer. But there is no reason for us to discontinue the search" (p. 407).

Even in this free-form environment, and sometimes even without its inhabitants knowing, media ethics tends to follow—or can be explained by—a number of traditional philosophical concepts: Aristotle's Golden Mean; Bentham's and Mill's utilitarian principle of the greatest good for the greatest number; Kant's categorical imperatives of treating every moral rule as if it were a universal law, and of treating people as ends rather than as means to an end; Rawls's "veil of ignorance;" and others that you will encounter in the pages that follow.

At the same time, the news, entertainment, and persuasive media operate under time pressures that are rarely matched—except probably by surgeons in an operating room. As a direct consequence of dealing continually with new events, concepts, technologies and techniques, conditions, and opinions, the mass media are continually faced with decisions that must be made with limited and imperfect data, amid competing goals and purposes, and with a societal leaning toward *ad hoc* situational ethics. It is little wonder that media ethics has so many controversies!

And that is another reason for this book. We don't want to leave this kind of decision to the flip of a coin, or an assumption that if we personally benefit then we can assume that our audiences and the public at large also will benefit.

But, one may ask—in a newsroom, an integrated marketing office, an editing suite, and even a required media ethics course—does anyone pay attention to ethics guidelines? Do people—in the media, or in the general population—even care? Isn't it easier just to go with the flow, and with what "feels" right or expedient, and let the chips fall where they may without regard for the most ethical course of action?

We believe that people *do* care, both within the various media industries and among their actual and potential audiences. As we see it, media ethics *isn't* a meaningless contradiction but, rather, offers various ways for practitioners to improve both their media and their society (not to mention themselves, as moral agents). To paraphrase slightly a century-old political commentary:

> There is no force so potent . . . as a moral issue. Politicians may scorn it, ambitious men [and women] may despise it or fight shy of it, newspapers may caricature or misrepresent it; but it has a way of confounding the plans of those who pride themselves on their astuteness and rendering powerless the most formidable [economic, social or political forces].
>
> (*The Nation* 86 (2242), June 18, 1908, p. 549)

Our goal is to provide both students and practitioners with a carefully constructed set of opposing arguments focusing on more than a dozen major controversies facing mass media practitioners today—at all levels. The table of contents shows that we are dealing with *real* and *current* problems and controversies in media ethics. Several chapters are new to this edition, bringing in such varied factors as the economic upheaval which erupted in 2008, policy changes by a new presidential administration, and the introduction of several new technologies for communication between and among groups and individuals. Virtually every page that was written for earlier editions of *Controversies in Media Ethics* has undergone major updating or clarification—and, in some instances, deletion. The additional ethical dilemmas affecting advertising, public relations, and entertainment as well as journalism—stemming from developments that range from digital manipulation of content to the explosion of online ethical problems to revolutionary changes in media industry structures—have been incorporated into this edition.

Because we are dealing with still-active controversies, the reader cannot assume that *either* half of a given chapter is automatically the "correct" one. The ordering of half-chapters is random, and the various authors are willing to defend vigorously their positions in these arguments. Many of the specific cases or situations in media ethics that you will face in the future—as either a communicator or member of the public—will be informed by one or more of these arguments. Because *you* will encounter a large variety of such dilemmas in the future, we saw no reason to select examples from the past or invent hypothetical ones, although we certainly refer frequently to ethical problems current as we were writing this book, as well as to older cases that remain relevant. We hope that these illustrations of ethical dilemmas will stimulate your thinking, so that you will be prepared when you encounter similar situations in your own lives and careers. Although practice in media ethics may not make perfect, it is certain to be helpful. But we again caution against using past situations as inflexible blueprints for resolving current or future ethics problems.

Each of this book's 15 chapters deals with a specific controversy and has at least two contrasting points of view, written by different authors. These arguments are accompanied by a short introduction, John C. Merrill's brief commentary that highlights some of the points in each controversy and provides Merrill's opinion of the arguments themselves, and a number of references. These commentaries, by a scholar and former newsman who has produced some three dozen books over a long and distinguished career, are not summaries of each issue, but rather an independent view that is intended to promote additional discussion with your peers, co-workers and instructors.

Because our purpose is to stimulate thought and discussion, the authors often have taken relatively extreme positions in their arguments. This is a common pedagogical approach: start at extremes in order to define alternatives clearly, and then work toward a viable middle ground, if one can be found. However, we stopped in many chapters before coming to this "viable middle ground," in order to leave to you the experience of defining that ground. We hope that you will consider, modify, and merge our different points of view, and apply them to the media ethics problems that face each of us every day. Remember: there is rarely a single clear or easy solution. But you may come closer to one if you think about these issues *before* you have to make a decision in the teeth of deadline pressures.

We recommend reading each chapter completely before going back to the individual positions (or "half-chapters") for analysis. You will notice that, contrary to the linear nature of most books, the authors of the first segment of each chapter will occasionally refer to points made in the second half. This occurs because, in writing the book, we had the opportunity to exchange our work more than once (in one instance, more than half-a-dozen times), allowing us to refine our positions and to comment as appropriate on the opposite side of the argument. As mentioned earlier, the selection of which author's argument is presented first is arbitrary. This give-and-take approach, while potentially confusing, allows you the opportunity to give each argument equal weight while reading.

Similarly, you'll find that a particular author, at times, may embrace an argument that runs counter to something that she or he wrote in a different chapter. That doesn't indicate inconsistency or hypocrisy! It simply illustrates that these complex media ethics questions have many uncertain (or "gray") areas and usually can be argued cogently from different perspectives rather than lending themselves to simple and easy answers. In some instances, it reflects the possibility that one author persuaded another of something. None of the authors was ever required to take a position that he or she strongly opposed, but neither was anyone urged to defend to the death any personal favorites among the traditional ethical theories we discussed—and yes, we all have personal favorites (see the biographies on pp. xxi–xxiii).

Also, please do not think of these arguments as legal briefs. Our discussions are very different from arguments presented during court trials, which are organized to come to a firm conclusion and decision. Even though logic, principles and verifiable data are parts of both systems, the rapid changes in the nuances of each ethical dilemma and the lack of agreed-upon statutes and precedents mandate a different and more intense approach to ethical problems. They must be looked at afresh, and with even fuller consideration of facts, theories and principles than are found in most law trials.

As you read through the book, keep in mind that law and ethics are two sides of the same coin. Proscriptive law, as practiced in the U.S. system, tells us what we are prevented from doing—in reality, it tells us we can *get away with* doing everything else. Ethics, by contrast, tells us what we *should* do, sometimes regardless of what the law says.

Although you'll notice different writing and reasoning styles, as well as different levels of "heat" in our arguments, each of the authors has tried to present his or her position with evidence and reason, and with respect for the opposing points of view. Each of us recognized that the various sides of each issue have some validity. In preparing our arguments, we had the luxury of time—unlike practitioners who are suddenly faced with ethical problems—to flesh out fully the various arguments we used, do some research (we provide full source citations for the benefit of the reader), consider opposing points of view and respond to them. Indeed, one of the major benefits of dealing with topics such as these in a classroom, rather than on a professional "firing line" or even sitting at home with some form of media, is the opportunity to ponder them, discuss them with fellow students, instructors or others, and begin to draw some conclusions about how to "do" media ethics—a skill that will serve you well throughout life.

As mentioned earlier, although we each have a favorite ethical theory (or theories), and methods of analyzing problems, none of us takes a particular philosophical position and runs its logic out to the end in any given chapter. Instead, after the problem or controversy has been spelled out, we have tried out a number of ethical principles and theories in a variety of ways. So, while *Controversies in Media Ethics* is not "case study oriented," we do treat each major ethical controversy that we deal with as something unique and worthy of considering as a fresh problem rather than as an opportunity to demonstrate blind adherence to a particular ethical theory.

Controversies in Media Ethics also aims to arm today's media practitioners with different points of view. In a time when many media and associated industries (such as marketing) are reducing staff and expenses, those working in such organizations may be called upon to become "one-man (or woman) gangs," doing several tasks at once, unlike the situation in yesterday's more specialized organizations. If one is called upon in this manner, one needs to understand the ethics and purposes of this new job, as well as its techniques and procedures. We hope that this book will help practitioners to optimize the very limited time available for discussing ethical problems (and their possible solutions) with professional colleagues and help everyone make good decisions—even while a deadline is looming. These opportunities can be expanded if top management brings in an "ethics coach" to lead periodic discussions on issues that raise ethics concerns. Another approach is to remember that everyone is part of a team of some sort, and—regardless of individual ambitions—people must work together in order to preserve the organization that provides their pay-checks. Accordingly, it would be worthwhile to use every opportunity—driving to location, having a meal together, interacting socially, coffee breaks—to discuss these concerns and "what if" scenarios *before* deadlines loom—as well as conducting a post mortem on what was done, *after* the crisis ends and *before* the next one starts.

We hope that the issues presented and argued here, and the various ways we have analyzed and individually resolved them, will produce spirited discussion—and further arguments—among our readers. Like defensive driving practice, it is important to become familiar with what one might do in a given situation *now*, without the need for snap judg-ments. This will help you make appropriately ethical decisions when snap judgments are required . . . and consequences are real. And, as we say throughout this book, we are convinced that media ethics is indispensable for the media to serve appropriately the society, culture, and body politic of which they are an essential part.

It is impossible in a single book to cover every current media ethics issue, let alone predict—from economics, technology and sociology—what will face us in the future. The world—and the media—are constantly evolving, as are the relationships between law and ethics. We have tried in this volume to focus on larger issues that, so far as we can tell, most people interested in the mass media, particularly American mass media, consider important. But we are sure that there are other—and very different—ethics issues that we could have used as the basis of chapters. Some might be obvious or subject to a published rule or code, such as how one relates to whistleblowers and their needs for confidentiality. But others might have more subtle nuances, such as how a foreign correspondent should balance the behavior expected of a visitor and the responsibility to his or her audience at home.

The 14 main chapters, each devoted to a single controversy, are not the entire book. Chapter 15 consists of a number of topics that are less thoroughly discussed here (and may be expanded on this book's Web site), sometimes from only a single point of view, leaving it up to the reader to think of a contrasting position.

In this edition, there are three broad essays. John C. Merrill's "Theoretical Foundations for Media Ethics" has been joined by John Armstrong's "Taking Aristotle to Work—Practical and Moral Values" and a three-author treatise on "Tools for Ethical Decision-Making." Merrill's commentaries for each chapter and his Postscript on "Some Questions without Answers and Answers without Questions" are integral sections of the book. The reader will also have available a glossary (compiled by John Armstrong), a bibliography and an index, as well as the many tools presented by Michael Dorsher on the Routledge *Controversies in Media Ethics* webpage (www.routledge.com/textbooks/9780415963329).

So, we urge the reader *not* to consider these sections and chapters as absolutes, traditions, or isolated concepts. We have tried to provide some theoretical frameworks that can be applied to analyze one's own positions both with regard to the issues presented in this book and others that will unfold for you. We have at times deliberately avoided providing the reasons *why* we selected a particular ethical or philosophical theory in a given situation or controversy—and hope that you enjoy selecting your own theory and making your own decisions. After all, the entire field of ethics and altruism is now burgeoning, and is on occasion incorporating social science research in psychology and even animal biology in ways that are shedding light on theology and philosophy. It is quite possible to do "good" things for "bad" reasons and "bad" things for "good" reasons, and we want to give our readers ample opportunity to think this conundrum through for themselves.

We want to repeat: *there are no "always correct" answers* to many of the questions or problems presented in *Controversies in Media Ethics*. Issues that *do* have simple answers—for instance, the wrongness of Jayson Blair's fabrications in "reporting" the news—don't merit space in a discussion of multi-sided issues. We do, however, believe that there are correct *methods* of analyzing problems and making ethical decisions, using the facts of each case and knowledge of past (and present) philosophical thinking. *Why* and *how you* reach a particular conclusion is probably much more important to your ethical development than exactly what that conclusion is. Reaching ethical decisions is *your* job, now and in the future—and you have to live with the consequences of what *you* decide. We hope that this book will help you while you reach those decisions—and avoid unfortunate consequences.

A. David Gordon
John Michael Kittross
John C. Merrill
William A. Babcock
Michael Dorsher

Acknowledgements

"ACKNOWLEDGEMENTS" published in any book usually are positive expressions of gratitude directed to those who have helped with a project, and this section is no exception—even in a book about controversies.

A great many individuals have helped us in the evolution of this book, directly and indirectly, recently or in the past. Some have mentored us over the years (formally, informally and sometimes unwittingly) about the principles, standards and methodologies of ethics and different ways of "doing ethics." Some have been colleagues and exemplars in ethics and in life, in the classroom as well as in our various and varied stints working in the mass media. Some have played direct roles in making sure that this book evolved from a very different edition a dozen years ago to a much more thorough look at what has become a complex and ever more important tangle of media ethics problems and (at least partial) answers—or ways of pursuing answers.

Any listing such as this one will inevitably omit some names that belong there and, to those people, we say only that you know who you are and how much in your debt we (as individuals and, in some cases, collectively) remain.

But this particular list of those to whom we are indebted has an unusual aspect—the author of the commentaries in this volume also is one of the giants in our field, and the other four of us join in thanking John C. Merrill for his guidance, his example, his innumerable contributions to the media ethics field, and his friendship over many years. Merrill has never forgotten that journalism is a field with responsibilities as well as privileges, and that the effects of this synergy are global.

There also are other colleagues, teachers and exemplars who have helped shape the media ethics landscape—and our own thinking—over several decades. In no particular order, we would like to mention five whose influence still helps guide the field, recognizing that they represent a much larger group whose contributions have been and remain valuable both to us and to media ethics more generally:

Clifford Christians, prolific scholar, creative and deep thinker and one of the key people in creating wide awareness that media ethics is an area very much worthy of academic attention and effort. Cliff has always been willing to share his approaches to all aspects of this field, to philosophy in general, and—at the same time—to the nitty-gritty details of ethical decision-making.

Donald M. Gillmor, founding director of the Silha Center for the Study of Media Ethics and Law at the University of Minnesota and an eminent First Amendment scholar, produced ground-breaking work examining the intersection of media ethics and law. Never too busy to offer support to colleagues in need of it, Don taught generations of students that the law can be a moral agent.

Jay Black, not only the founding editor (with Ralph Barney) of the *Journal of Mass Media Ethics*, but also an original and seminal contributor to the fabric of media ethics. To realize the scope of Jay's thought, one need look only at two of his (many) ideas that are discussed in the pages that follow—his 1994 thoughts about cyberspace ethics which came well before most people were aware there was such a topic; and his 2011 model for "doing ethics" which—typically—he was more than willing to share with us and the readers of this book.

Edmund Lambeth, who more than two decades ago began a series of annual seminars on the teaching of ethics in journalism and mass communication that helped to shape the way this subject matter has been transmitted ever since. Ed's vision greatly expanded the rigor of and expertise in the media ethics field, and those seminars were highly useful to at least two of this book's authors—and, in one case, gave that author both the knowledge and the confidence to get involved in media ethics in the first place.

Louis Hodges, Knight professor emeritus at Washington and Lee University, who has focused much of his interest and energy on the study of ethics across the professions. An ordained minister, Lou has always maintained that ethics trumps law. His understanding of the broad concept of "profession" informs his own impressive, yet thoroughly grounded, research and writing.

We, as authors and you, as readers of this book also are indebted to Carol Reuss, professor emerita at the University of North Carolina, whose major contributions to the first edition of this book extended into the 2nd edition. In some cases her ideas withstood the test of time so well that they are found in this 3rd edition.

We are also indebted to Ralph B. Potter, Jr., whose "Potter Box" model has contributed to many college and university ethics courses, and which we have gratefully adopted and included in this book. That inclusion owes much to material drawn from a videotaped lecture by Clifford Christians, explaining some important aspects and implications of Potter's graphic model, which was graciously—and typically—made available when David Gordon requested it a decade ago. We also appreciate greatly that Mitchell Land and William Hornaday gave us permission to reproduce their "Point of Decision" model, which we see as building on and complementing the Potter Box approach to doing ethics. Our thanks go also their graphic artist, Nola Kemp, whose illustration of that model provides the basis for ours.

We are all indebted to Sharon S. Kessler, who compiled most of the Index for this edition in addition to inspiring Michael Dorsher daily with her professional journalistic ethics and matrimonial compassion. Michael notes that he also owes other unpayable debts to his first ethics professor, the late Rev. James Whalen of the University of St. Thomas; his mentors at the University of Maryland, Katherine C. McAdams, Maurine H. Beasley, and Douglas Gomary; his Fulbright hosts at the McGill Institute for the Study of Canada; and those he calls his "guiding lights" at the University of Wisconsin-Eau Claire, David Gordon and James Oberly.

Dorothy Merrill, John's wife, gave her husband both support and a wonderful line to use when he was pushing us repeatedly to finish the work and get the book published. She wondered aloud whether John (the most senior of those working on this volume) would still be around when the book (finally) came out. Merrill also wishes to thank Sue Schuermann, associate librarian at the Missouri Journalism School Library, for her tireless and courageous aid in his computer-related "incessant technology problems"—assistance that others of us would also have found quite helpful.

William Babcock wishes to thank Carol Perruso, the journalism reference librarian at California State University, Long Beach, and Delwar Mohammad Hossain, his graduate research assistant at Southern Illinois University-Carbondale, for their help in unearthing materials he needed. Bill also thanks his wife Kathryn and his daughter Lillian for their support even when he abandoned them to hunker over his laptop.

Sally Kittross, unfortunately, became lost to us—except in memory—in 2002, although as Mike's severest critic, she was instrumental in setting high standards for the 2nd edition which, together with much of her sage advice, carried over to the 3rd. Sue Gordon provided her usual encouragement and support, as well as sustenance and conversation about something other than "the book" during a pair of joint working sessions in Wisconsin.

We are fortunate to have contributors such as John A. Armstrong, Peter J. Gade, Julianne H. Newton, Kim Sheehan and Jane B. Singer. Each of them did everything we requested, quickly and with care, and the book is greatly strengthened by their efforts. Armstrong's work on the Glossary went well beyond the call of duty, and merits a special "thanks."

We also want to thank students in several of Mike Dorsher's mass media ethics classes at the University of Wisconsin-Eau Claire for the feedback they provided on various parts of the manuscript as the 3rd edition took shape, including their suggestion that we add the "Key Points" at the end of each half-chapter. Several of David Gordon's UW-EC classes provided useful feedback on the 2nd edition as the 3rd was being planned, and one of William Babcock's ethics classes at California State University, Long Beach also helped with reactions to parts of the 3rd edition. One UW-EC student merits special mention here: research assistant Olivia Jeske, who drafted several of the case studies that you'll find on this book's Web site.

We doubt that we would have completed this project without the help and encouragement of the almost-always patient Linda Bathgate, originally with Lawrence Erlbaum Associates and now Publisher, Communication and Media Studies, at Routledge. Mhairi Bennett, Deputy Production Editorial Manager for Routledge, has refused to allow the eight time zones difference between the western United States and her base in the United Kingdom to interfere with her gentleness and efficiency. Also in the UK, Maggie Lindsey-Jones and the team at Keystroke, as well as copyeditor Christine Firth and proofreader Rictor Norton caught everything from major errors to minor inconsistencies and made the copy and resulting production process flow more smoothly than otherwise might have been the case. Gareth Toye created the book's cover.

Working with Linda in New York were Katherine Ghezzi who, before she left Routledge, spent a great deal of time and energy on details—notably the cover. Marketing assistance was provided by Joon Won Moon and Julia Sammartino in Routledge's U.S.

operation, and by Carla Hepburn and Christine Stead in the UK. We appreciate all of their efforts.

Reviewers often add much to a final product, and we had three who reviewed our manuscript with great care, and in the process improved it markedly: Andrew Cline of Missouri State University, Randy Covington of the University of South Carolina and, especially Fred Vultee of Wayne State University. We also received guidance from Chris Hanson at the University of Maryland, and from a fifth person who wished to remain anonymous.

The people listed previously are, of course, not responsible for any errors that have slipped through the lengthy production and editing process. That responsibility rests with us.

This book wasn't written in a vacuum. We believed that a third edition of *Controversies in Media Ethics* was needed not only because the media landscape has changed so greatly since 1999, but also because fallible human beings keep finding new ways (or repeating old ways) to ignore ethical standards . . . or, in some cases, to reject such standards deliberately in a Machiavellian effort to achieve their goals by any means possible. We won't name names here, but you'll find some of them in the succeeding chapters. So, to some degree, we must also acknowledge those whose poor ethical decision-making has affected their readers, listeners and viewers and made this book necessary.

A. David Gordon
John Michael Kittross
John C. Merrill
William A. Babcock
Michael Dorsher

About the Authors

A. David Gordon taught mass media ethics and law and a varied menu of other journalism and media/society courses during his 34-year academic career. He retired from the University of Wisconsin-Eau Claire (UW-EC) in 2002, having also taught at Northwestern University, the University of Miami, Emerson College and Northeastern University. He chaired departments at Miami, Emerson and UW-EC, was acting dean at Miami and master of a residential college at Northwestern. Before entering academia, he was a newspaper reporter and mayor's administrative assistant. He is the author of *Problems in Law of Mass Communication* (1978) and articles on media law and ethics. His approach to media ethics is usually from a utilitarian perspective, with touches of Rawls's and the feminist "ethics of care."

John Michael Kittross is editor of *Media Ethics* magazine and edited the *Journal of Broadcasting* for a dozen years. He is co-author of *Stay Tuned: A History of American Broadcasting* (1978, 1990, Routledge: 2002), and has written, co-authored, or edited approximately a dozen other volumes and a variety of scholarly and professional articles. He has taught at the University of Southern California, Temple University, and Emerson College, where he also served as provost and vice president for academic affairs. He has had professional experience at several radio and television stations, in both on-air and non-air capacities. He is managing director of K\E\G Associates, an academic consulting group, and now lives in Seattle. As a media ethicist, he says he is a "conservative anarchist"—toward the left side of the libertarian spectrum.

John C. Merrill is professor emeritus of journalism at the University of Missouri, and now lives in Birmingham, Alabama. He has half a century of journalism and journalism teaching behind him. He has been a prolific writer, having written at least 33 books and more than 200 journal articles. His main scholarly interests are in international communication and journalism ethics. His first book was *A Handbook of the Foreign Press* (1955) and his most recent were *A Call to Order: Plato's Legacy of Social Control* (2009) and *Viva Journalism! The Triumph of Print in the Media Revolution* (co-authored, 2010). He is a World War II veteran, having served in both the Atlantic and Pacific. Merrill has earned degrees in English and history, journalism, philosophy, and mass communication. He has traveled widely, having lectured and taught in some 75 countries. Married, with 15 descendants in three generations, he calls himself a libertarian and a conservative in politics.

William A. Babcock is senior ethics professor at Southern Illinois University, Carbondale. In past years he chaired the Department of Journalism at California State University, Long Beach, directed the University of Minnesota's Silha Center for the Study of Media Ethics and Law, and served on the Newhouse School's faculty at Syracuse University. He has worked at *The Christian Science Monitor* as senior international news editor and was founding chairman of the Association for Education in Journalism and Mass Communication's (AEJMC) Media Ethics Division. He directs AEJMC's annual media ethics teaching workshop. He has degrees from Principia College, American University, and Southern Illinois University. When pressed, he admits to being a Kantian—with an American Indian "walk a mile in another person's moccasins" twist.

Michael Dorsher teaches mass media ethics—online and in the classroom—along with several journalism courses at the University of Wisconsin-Eau Claire. He was a 2008–09 Fulbright Scholar in Media at McGill University in Montreal, and he taught in 2008 at Harlaxton College in England. He capped a 20-year journalism career as one of the founding editors of washingtonpost.com from 1996 to 2000. He is the author of several entries in *The Encyclopedia of Journalism* and many conference papers on new media. He sees himself as a Rawlsian ethicist, intent on improving society by protecting its most vulnerable members.

John A. Armstrong teaches courses in mass communication, media law, and broadcast journalism at Furman University. He is a former television news producer and executive producer. He has worked at CNN in Atlanta and at network affiliates in Denver and Salt Lake City. Much of his research focuses on the historical impact of law and regulation on the television industry. He takes a communitarian approach to media ethics and believes that it is the responsibility of journalists to nurture social and political communities.

Peter J. Gade is the journalism area head and a Gaylord Family Endowed Professor at the University of Oklahoma. He worked for newspapers in New York state as a bureau chief, assignment editor and reporter. He is co-author of *Twilight of Press Freedom* (2001), and is co-editor of *Changing the News* (2011), exploring the confluence of technical, social and economic forces impacting journalism norms and practices. His research has appeared in *Journalism and Communication Monographs*, *Journalism and Mass Communication Quarterly*, *Journal of Media Business Studies* and *Newspaper Research Journal*. Gade believes ethical development is nurtured by freedom, intellectual curiosity, rationalism and individual accountability.

Julianne H. Newton is associate dean for undergraduate affairs and professor of visual communication, University of Oregon School of Journalism and Communication. She is author of *The Burden of Visual Truth: The Role of Photojournalism in Mediating Reality* (2001) and co-author of *Visual Communication: Integrating Media, Art and Science* (2007). Her publications span scholarly, professional, and public forums, and her documentary photographs have been exhibited internationally. She has worked as a reporter, editor, photographer, and designer for news and public affairs media. She is a "pragmatic idealist" who believes combining intuitive reflection with rational processes can foster ethical balance among the diverse "selves" and "others" of a global society.

Kim Sheehan is a professor of advertising and Director of the Strategic Communication Master's program at the School of Journalism and Communication at the University of Oregon. She is the author or co-author of several books that focus on ethics and digital technology, including *Using Qualitative Research in Advertising: Strategies, Techniques, and Applications* (2002) and *Controversies in Contemporary Advertising* (2003). Sheehan has published articles on new technology, ethics and public policy in the *Journal of Advertising*, the *Journal of Public Policy and Marketing*, *The Information Society*, and *First Monday*.

Jane B. Singer is an associate professor in the University of Iowa School of Journalism and Mass Communication. From 2007 through 2009, she was the Johnston Press Chair in Digital Journalism at the University of Central Lancashire (England). Her research explores digital journalism, including changing roles, perceptions, and practices. Before earning her Ph.D. from the University of Missouri, she was the first news manager of Prodigy Interactive Services, as well as a newspaper reporter and editor. She is a past president of Kappa Tau Alpha, the national journalism honor society. She is especially fond of existentialist philosophy, with its dual emphasis on individual freedom and responsibility.

Part One

The Basics

Overview

Theoretical Foundations for Media Ethics

John C. Merrill

MEDIA ethics concerns right and wrong, good and bad, better and worse actions taken by people working in the field of journalism and mass communication. Media themselves, of course, cannot be ethical or unethical—only workers in the media can. When we deal with *media ethics*, we are really concerned with standards media people have and the kinds of actions they take.

Because this book is designed largely as a textbook for students considering the complexities of media ethics as well as for those who want an introductory view of the moral problems and dilemmas of mass communication, it is well that we use this rather long introduction to build a framework or a foundation from which to attack the specific ethical controversies that we discuss later on. Ethics is a nebulous subject. All a person has to do is to pick up almost any book or article on ethics to see that disagreements and contradictions arise almost at once. The great moral philosophers of history have not agreed on many aspects of ethics or on its main theories and subtheories.

One thing we do know: ethics is the study of what we ought to do. Some of us (followers of Immanuel Kant) try to follow predetermined rules and treat others as ends and not means. The intuitivists get help from some kind of instinctive, metaphysical or mystical sense. The egoists think of self first and the transvaluation of the person. The altruists put self last and the community first in making ethical decisions. The existentialists are devoted to freedom, courage, action, and personal responsibility. The communitarians seek group conversation, harmony, social stability and security. The utilitarians want to maximize happiness and goodness. The Machiavellians desire pragmatic success in achieving desired ends, by any means necessary.

Ethics has to do with duty—duty to self and duty to others. It is private and personal, although it is related to obligations and duties to others. The quality of human life relates to both solitude and sociability. We do right or wrong by ourselves in the private or inward part of our lives where we are acting and reacting in a context of others. This duality of individual and social morality is implicit in the very concept of ethics, and the reader of this book will notice how these two aspects affect core arguments on each side of various issues.

For example, a journalist (or for that matter, a person who writes a television drama) is not simply writing for the consumption of others. He or she is writing as self-expression and self-gratification, and the self is developed by the very act of expression. The processes of deciding to do a story, selecting what will be used, and expressing this material all impinge on ethics and affect the moral character of the media person. What all media people communicate is, in a very real sense, what they are. They please or displease themselves, not just those for whom they are writing. What they do to live up to their personal standards affects not only the beliefs and activities of others but also, in a very real sense, the very essence of their own lives. Through their actions, they existentially make their ethical selves.

ETHICAL CONCERN: STARTING POINT

A concern for being ethical is the starting point. If media people do not care whether what they do is good or bad, then they will have little or no interest in, or consideration of, ethics. For the average person working in the communications media, however, ethics is an important concern that permeates the entire professional activity. A sense of right conduct does not come naturally; it must be developed, thought about, reasoned through, cared deeply about. In short, it must be nurtured. Unless journalists, for example, see themselves as blotters, soaking up news-reality, how they collect this news and what they do with it is the essence of their professional life.

In recent years, an interest in making ethics relevant to the professions has become firmly entrenched. Books, articles, seminars, conferences, and workshops have stressed the need for practical ethics. Professional ethics courses have developed in many areas, especially in business, law, medicine, and journalism. Books for such courses have followed; a good example of an ethics book encompassing several professions is Serafini's (1989) *Ethics and Social Concern*. Journalism and mass communications academics and practitioners have written a great number of ethics books in the last several decades. Media organizations, subject to increasing criticism from the public, have encouraged their staff members to become more concerned with moral issues.

Mass communicators are right in the middle of all sorts of ethical problems in the daily work environment. Such people must decide what is the right (or at least the best) thing to do at every turn. At the core of media ethics are certain key questions: What should I consider worth publishing, broadcasting, or disseminating in the first place? How much should I publish? Which parts should I omit? These and other questions spin out of a decision to bring a story, program, or advertisement to the public's attention. The media person works in the realm of ethics, whether or not he or she gives any thought to it as *ethics*.

Ethical concern is important, for it forces the media person to make commitments and thoughtful decisions among alternatives. Ethical concern leads the media person to seek the *summum bonum*, the highest good in professional practice, thereby heightening self-respect and public credibility and respect. The reader who expects this book to answer every question about what to do (prescriptive ethics) or not to do (proscriptive ethics) will be disappointed. In fact, as the very nature of the book attests, ethical determinations are *debatable*. What we hope to do is to serve as ethical thought-provokers and moral consciousness-raisers, and to raise significant ethical controversies in various media contexts with which readers can grapple. The purpose of this book is not to answer once and for all the basic questions of media morality, but to raise significant questions worthy of continuing concern.

Although concern with media ethics may be growing, it is still underdeveloped. Marvin Kalb, former NBC reporter who went on to Harvard's Kennedy School of Government, maintains that American journalism is "mean-spirited," having a "desire to tear down rather than build up" (Budiansky, 1995, p. 46). In the same article by Budiansky in *U.S. News & World Report*, Kathleen Hall Jamieson of the University of Pennsylvania says of today's journalists that "everyone operates out of cynical self-interest" (p. 46). Newton N. Minow, who called television "a vast wasteland" in 1961, reappraised the medium in 1995 and found it still lacking in quality. He writes that TV has had a "distorting influence" (Minow, 1995, p. 6) and has failed to serve four main needs: properly supporting education, meeting the needs of children, adequately providing serious public programming, and supporting the political system during campaigns. Minow maintains that television has not "fulfilled our needs and will not do so in the next 30 years" (Minow, 1995, p. 6). There seems to be no doubt that ethical awareness among media people is not what it ought to be.

> Ethical concern is important, for it forces the media person to make commitments and thoughtful decisions among alternatives.

Two Main Ethical Emphases

Ethical concern can manifest itself in two main emphases: (1) the mass communicator can be concerned mainly with taking ethical cues from the society, from colleagues, and from the community, or (2) he or she can emphasize personal ethical development and put community priorities second. The first emphasis is today called *social* or *communitarian* ethics, the second is called *personal* or *individual* ethics. In both cases, the media person is concerned with ethics and wants to do the right or best thing. It is simply a matter of emphasis—one relying on group-driven ethics, the other on personally determined ethics. One stresses other-directed ethical action, the other inner-directed ethical action.

Actually, these two emphases are not mutually exclusive, although the proponents of each often seem hostile to one another. The communitarian does not ignore individuality; the individualist does not disdain cooperative or social concerns. It is simply a matter of emphasis. A good book that gives the communitarian perspective is *Good News*, by Clifford Christians et al. (1993), which proposes that journalists forget the Enlightenment concepts of individualism and libertarianism touted by such liberal thinkers throughout history as Locke, Voltaire, Constant, Adam Smith, James Mill, John Stuart Mill, and Kant. Communitarians see individual or liberal ethics as dysfunctional to the community and generally based on personal quirks rather than on group-determined standards.

Today, communitarian ethicists such as Amitai Etzioni, Alasdair MacIntyre, Christopher Lasch, Joseph de Maistre, and Michael Sandel would have journalists publish things that would bring people together, not fractionalize them. Christians et al. (1993) ask for a universal ethics, saying that journalists should realize that "universal solidarity is the normative core of the social and moral order" and that journalists should throw out the old concepts of journalistic autonomy, individualism, and *negative freedom* (Christians et al., 1993, pp. 14 and 42–44).

The other emphasis or ethical orientation is the liberal or libertarian one, which asks for maximum personal autonomy in ethical decision-making. It does indeed stress the values of the European Enlightenment thinkers and puts the individual at the center of the ethical system. One of the best books upholding the liberal or individualistic emphasis and criticizing the communitarian perspective is Stephen Holmes's (1993) book *The Anatomy of Antiliberalism*. This University of Chicago political theorist explains both communitarianism and libertarianism, but mainly provides a critique of what he calls antiliberalism (communitarianism).

Communitarians	Libertarians
Groupists Egalitarians Altruists	Individualists Enlightenment liberals Existentialists
Traits Restrained freedom Civic transformation Normative ethics codes Selflessness Cooperation Social influence on policy Bonding/conformity Group-progress "Other-directed" Like-minded worldview Positive, cohesive news Social guidance Universal solidarity Agreement on common ethics Universal-legalistic ethics Media professionalism	**Traits** Maximum freedom Self-transformation Personal ethical codes Self-concern Self-enhancement Personal influence Autonomy/diversity Competition/meritocracy "Inter-directed" Diverse worldviews Total spectrum news Social information Universal competition Disagreement on ethics Relative-situation ethics Anti-media professionalization
Exemplars Confucius, Plato, Marx, Etzioni, Bellah, Lasch, Hutchins, MacIntyre, Niebuhr, Buber, Jonas, Sandel, Christians	**Exemplars** Lao-tzu, Socrates, Aristotle, Locke, Jefferson, Madison, Voltaire, Constant, Tocqueville, Mill, Thoreau, Camus, Jaspers, Rand, Nozick, Hayek, Merrill

FIGURE 0.1 | Two ethical mega-emphases

Another defender of individualism and critic of egalitarianism and other forms of communitarianism is *Time* magazine's former media critic, William A. Henry III. In his book *In Defense of Elitism*, Henry (1994) describes the growth of the "community" emphasis, which leads to a deprecation of the individual, and of "elitism" or meritocracy—the idea that some people are smarter than others, that some ideas are better than others. Explaining the kind of elitism he supports, Henry (1994) writes:

> The kind of elitists I admire are those who ruthlessly seek out and encourage intelligence and who believe that competition—and, inevitably, some measure of failure—will do more for character than coddling ever can. My kind of elitist does not grade on a curve and is willing to flunk the whole class. My kind of elitist detests the policy of social promotion that has rendered a high school diploma meaningless and a college degree nearly so. . . . My kind of elitist hates tenure, seniority, and the whole union ethos that contends that workers are interchangeable and their performances essentially equivalent.
>
> (Henry, 1994, p. 19)

To Henry, the contemporary emphasis on community desires is taking precedence over individual preferences to the degree that the marketplace of ideas is being threatened. Even in education, which Henry believes should foster individualism, there is an "academic echo of Marxism [as] administrators join activists in celebrating the importance of 'community' over the importance of individual thought and exploration" (Henry, 1994, p. 108).

Another book, George Morgan's (1968) *The Human Predicament*, is also anticommunitarian in its thrust; it extols the individual person and bemoans the drift toward standardization of social activities. In a chapter called "Dissolution of the Person," Morgan warns that increasingly one's everyday activity is modeled after the machine: standardized, automatic, and repeatable. "In all departments of life," he writes, "unceasing efforts are made to avoid, or render unnecessary, the judgments, decisions, and even the presence of the individual man" (Morgan, 1968, p. 61). He continues:

> This situation is so taken for granted that few are aware of it or can see its true nature. Once recognized, however, its manifestations are found everywhere. Let it be epitomized here by a development that reaches into the core of the person: the ever-spreading assumption that a person's life need not be shaped through his own search, understanding, and decision—aided by the experience and wisdom of others.
>
> (Morgan, 1968, p. 62)

We can see that these two emphases are important: the libertarian holds fast to individualistic ethical development and the communitarian seeks to enhance the community and take ethical nourishment from the group. The first would improve society by stressing self-improvement and individual decision-making; the second would improve society by sublimating personal concerns to community wishes and cooperatively making decisions that are designed to eliminate friction.

THE IMPORTANCE OF FREEDOM IN DISCUSSIONS OF ETHICS

It is good that we think seriously about press freedom and its relationship to media ethics. Freedom, or a large amount of it, is necessary even to consider ethical action. Positive freedom (freedom from outside control) must be present for the actor to be able to decide between or among alternative actions. If there is no freedom, then the ethical debate is moot—the media person is acting in accordance with a controlling agent and cannot really be making an individual ethical decision.

In the United States and throughout Western society, journalists—and people generally—put their trust in the owners and managers of their media. And, therefore, this loyalty affects their concept of ethics. But in many non-Western countries—e.g. Singapore, Saudi Arabia, and Iran—the main loyalty is to a political or religious authority. Social order there is often more important than individual pluralism or a private media system. Many in the world feel that Western journalism is irresponsible, biased, greedy, imperialistic, and harmful to nation-building. Therefore, it is natural that they see Western media morality as intrinsically bad.

So, in discussing media ethics there are really two main paradigms of the press in the world—(1) the Western freedom-centered one that has grown out of the European Enlightenment and (2) the non-Western authority-centered one that prevails in most of the world. The first type of press system is designed for maximum freedom and consequently permits excesses in journalistic activity, while the second type is designed to bring about an increasing degree of social order.

In the social-order (authoritarian) countries the media system is not much concerned with *ethics* per se, but with guiding principles and controls placed on the press by the political authority. Journalists in these countries have their guidelines and rules; what is the proper thing to do is determined for them *a priori*, so there is no real need for any serious consideration of ethical behavior. So it should be remembered that when we talk about countries having less and less press freedom, we are at the same time decreasingly concerned with ethics. Yet there are exceptions, for example Venezuela in mid-2007, when the opposition television channel was ordered off the air by the government. It moved its content to the Web and defied government efforts to silence its point of view (James, 2007).

Since the controversies in this book mainly relate to ethics in the United States, it is helpful to assume that those making the ethical decisions are virtually free. Of course, we know that there are freedom-limiting factors such as political correctness, editors and publishers, news directors, advertisers and others that impinge on complete freedom. But by and large, U.S. journalists are free and cannot really escape their freedom (and necessity) to make ethical decisions.

It is paradoxical to some degree that a growing concern for ethics can *diminish* press freedom. Being ethical in journalism often results in compromise, pulling punches, circumlocutions, self-censorship, biasing stories for "ethical reasons," being "fair," or trying to bring about "good" consequences.

So freedom and ethics are closely connected, and this connection can be seen as basically good by some and basically bad by others. It is little wonder that the controversies presented in this book provide a problematic view of media ethics in the U.S. context. And often what is at issue in these controversies is the importance the different commentators give to freedom as compared to order and a concern for "responsibility."

INTRODUCING THE FIELD OF ETHICS

Before getting to the controversial issues in the succeeding chapters, it is well to provide an introduction to the field of ethics, to talk *about ethics*—the need for ethics and some of the theories and subtheories of ethics. Actually, this discussion deals with what moral philosophers call *theoretical* normative ethics—the theories philosophers have developed to explain moral behavior. The rest of the book considers what is called normative ethics (what ought to be done in specific situations and cases). This introductory part, along with the *pro* and *con* arguments (and the commentaries) throughout the rest of the book, provide a rather broad perspective on ethics as it relates to the problems of media people as they face real decision-making.

Media ethics is a branch of philosophy seeking to help journalists and other media people determine how to behave in their work. In its practical application, it is very much a normative science of conduct, with conduct considered primarily self-determined, rational, and voluntary. It must be remembered that without freedom and sanity, ethics is meaningless to a person and impossible to take seriously as a subject of discourse. To have the option of being ethical, I must know what I am doing and I must have the freedom to decide among alternatives of action.

Many workers in the media might say that they have very little freedom because they are employees—that they must follow orders, not make their own ethical decisions. They point to the fact that jobs are scarce and that they must make a living. Indeed, there is much pressure on media employees to conform, to give up their freedom and their integrity; to be sure, there are authoritarian bosses who give little or no leeway to the individual worker. But media people cannot adopt the defense used by the Nazis at the Nuremberg war crimes trials, and disclaim their responsibility for the actions they take. Although journalists and other media people in the United States may not have all the freedom they might want, they have a great deal—enough at least to have the force of ethical sanctions fall on them.

A media person concerned with ethics, like anyone else, goes through a process of moral development. It is generally thought there are three main levels in such a moral progress, each one more sophisticated than the last. The first level is based on *instinct*, in which right conduct is determined by the person's fundamental needs and instincts. On this primitive level, ethics comes from innate tendencies. The second level is based on *custom*— what seems right to the person is conduct that is in accordance with the customs of the various groups to which he or she belongs. The third and highest general level of morality is based on *conscience*. Here, conduct that appears right is that which is approved by the agent's own personally developed judgment of what is right or wrong. The conscience is developed by the person's own reasoning, building on custom and instinct.

Regardless of the particular theory or subtheory of ethics used, the third level of moral development is the media person's goal. Here, moral standards are actively chosen by the individual after deliberation; they are no longer accepted passively as a natural part of group-assigned conduct, although they may rely to some extent on social expectations. The person at this level senses a new personal interest in morality, recognizing that *at the level of conscience* to be good is essentially an individual matter. At this third level of moral development, which William Lillie (1961, pp. 51 ff.) calls "pure morality," the agent leaves a level of ethics based on institutional or group-approved actions and enters a level where right and wrong become a matter of individual determination. James Q. Wilson (1993), in *The Moral Sense*, deals at length with this more personal kind of ethics, and his approach will be discussed later.

It is probably true that most media morality today is largely stuck at the level of custom. But there are those in the media who reflect on moral matters and, guided by conscience, refuse to follow the customs of their particular media institution or professional society. It is undoubtedly beneficial to the group or society that most people accept the group standards without question; if all journalists constantly asked questions about the rightness and wrongness of the rules of their newspaper, there would be a breakdown of stability and traditional principles would not be passed on.

It should be noted that many of the ethical principles found at the custom level actually *began* with the thoughts of some person in the past. How else could a custom get its start? So it is not true that all custom-based ethical principles are wrong. Generally, however, the level of custom in ethics is more non-rational and inflexible than the level of conscience. It is more ritualistic and conformist, making morality less likely to progress, develop, and adapt to the special needs of the individual or the particular situation. Being a group-determined morality, it is more absolutist and often insensitive to the thoughtful individual who finds a need for exceptions to rules. Such a thinking individual is often considered, on the level of customary ethics, to be a danger to social stability and harmony. (Lillie (1961) discusses this in Chapter 3, "Development of Morality," of *An Introduction to Ethics*.)

Later we shall consider various theories of ethics that fall in all three of these levels of moral development—instinct, custom, and conscience. We shall see that the custom level (including various versions of social or communitarian ethics) and the conscience level (including the more individualistic, egocentric, and existential ethical inclinations) seem to manifest themselves as moral adversaries. It might be said that the two strands of moral emphasis have their genesis in the moral thinking of Plato (more aligned to communitarian, social ethics) and Aristotle (more aligned to individualistic ethics), although the ideas of both philosophers were quite complex and there are bits of both strands in each of them. At any rate, it will be interesting to keep these *levels of ethical development* in mind as we consider broad and narrow theories of ethics.

THREE CLASSES OF ETHICAL THEORIES

Theories of ethics abound, but we shall try to keep our explanations here as simple as possible and focus primarily on two main or mega-theories of ethics: *deontological*, those that base ethical actions on *a priori* principles or maxims that are accepted as guides for such actions, and *teleological*, those that base ethical actions on a consideration of their consequences. Here we shall expand this binary typology, placing several subconcepts under a third heading, which we shall call *personalist* or *subjective theories*, which provide more instinctive guidance theories.

The following sections offer brief descriptions of these three main classes or types of ethical theory: *absolutist/legalistic theories*, which are deontological (including Aristotelianism, Confucianism, Kantianism, and the divine command theory); *consequence theories*, which are teleological (including utilitarianism, altruism, egoism, the social contract theory, and the pragmatic or Machiavellian); and *personalist theories*, which are predominantly subjective and individualistic (including the instinctual, emotive, antinomian, and existential).

Deontological Ethical Theory

The first of the mega-theories, the *deontological*, has to do with duty, with following formalistic rules, principles, or maxims. If you follow them (e.g., *always* give sources of quotes in a news story), you are ethical; if you don't, you are unethical. In this sense, it is clear-cut and simple. And it has a great appeal for many people in the media. Just tell the truth. Be consistent. Have no double standards. Be forthright and full in your reporting. Let the chips fall where they will. Don't worry about consequences; just do what you are supposed to do.

Probably history's leading *deontologist* in ethics was Immanuel Kant (1724–1804), a German philosopher who provided the fullest arguments for a duty-bound system of ethical behavior. He believed that *only* an action taken out of self-imposed duty could be ethical, and he formulated what he called the *categorical imperative*, which said that what was ethical for a person to do was what that person would will that everyone should do. Another version of the famous imperative (a kind of supermaxim from which ethical principles can be formulated) was that no person should be treated as a means to an end, but only as an end. Together, these two formulations make up the core of Kant's duty-to-principle ethics— guidelines a person can have ahead of time to guide ethical decisions.

Teleological Ethical Theory

The *teleological or consequence-related* mega-theory says that the person trying to decide what to do attempts to predict what the consequences will be if *A* is done instead of *B*. The object is to choose the action that will bring the most good to the party the actor deems most important. The altruist thinks of good to others; the egoist considers good to the self, with perhaps some benefits spinning off to others.

At any rate, the *teleological* approach to ethics is a popular one and will recur in most of the arguments found in the controversy discussions in later chapters of this book. The theorist most commonly associated with this thinking is John Stuart Mill, the 19th-century British philosopher who formulated the theory of *utilitarianism*—whose aim it was to bring the greatest happiness (or pleasure) to the greatest number (see Merrill's (1994) *Legacy of Wisdom*, profile 16). Many versions of teleological ethics, other than the altruistic one just mentioned, were propounded by such thinkers as Mill, Bentham, and Hume. For example, there are *egoistic* teleologists who consider consequences mainly to one's self, rather than to others. Twentieth-century writer Ayn Rand (see Merrill, 1994, profile 22) is a good example of an egoistic teleologist.

Personalist or Subjective Theory

The *personalist* or *subjective* mega-theory subsumes many subtheories lending themselves to intuitive, emotive, spiritual, and other highly personal moral factors. Unlike the deontological and teleological theories, this personal-subjective theory is non-rational. It is more spontaneous, motivated by instinct or a spiritually motivated will. The person has a kind of moral sense that nudges him or her toward right action—call it conscience, instinct, or spiritual guidance. For the Christian moralist, this ethical sense may be directed by a deep-rooted concern often called *agape* (God-centered love). Such spiritual-religious overtones are exemplified by the *religious* or *faith* level—the highest level of Kierkegaard's moral progression. It is also related to Joseph Fletcher's (1966) *situation ethics*, where one's actions in any situation are directed by a love (deep concern) that flows constantly through the agent and is projected to others. *Agape ethics* serves as a kind of underpinning for such a social ethical stance, in one of the domains of communitarian ethics. Personalist or subjective ethics does not have to be God-centered, however; ethical direction can also be found through various forms of meditation, mystical experiences, and existentialism.

One type of the *personalist* or *subjective* mega-theory we should mention is what C. S. Lewis in *Mere Christianity* (1952, esp. Book III, ch. 3) and others call *conscience* and James Q. Wilson (1993) calls the *moral sense*—something genetic or biological, something, as Wilson (1993, p. xii) says, that is "intuitive or directly felt . . . about how one ought to act when one is free to act voluntarily." Wilson says that it is impossible to define such a subjective concept any more clearly than that, and he mentions British philosopher Henry Sidgwick's (1956) struggle with the concept of "ought" through six editions of his great ethics treatise; Wilson (1993, p. 30) concludes that the concept "is too elementary to admit of any formal definition."

It seems that gender may have something to do with the moral sense Wilson talks about. Harvard's Carol Gilligan (1982) has concluded that childhood experiences coupled with innate or genetic differences may lead to the existence and development of a moral sense. She also believes that much of it is gender based. For example, her research indicates that men are more prone to stress such concepts as fairness, justice, and duty, whereas women stress such moral attributes as assistance, care, and sympathy. It should be noted that these gender-based inclinations are based on what people *say* they are concerned about, not what they *do* in a real situation.

Because this third cluster of theories is personal and subjective, it is hard to make generalizations beyond the kind made by Gilligan which are applicable to the mass communicator.

At this point we shall leave this subjective macro-theory and briefly consider two perspectives that can be considered professional indicators of a journalist's basic allegiance: to norms or rules, on the one hand, and to consequences on the other. For the journalist, these legalistic and consequence theories often collide.

For example, does the journalist who claims to have some predetermined *deontological* principle (for example, to be truthful and full in the report) on occasion break with these beliefs when consequences seem to warrant it? The answer usually is yes. For instance, many rule-based journalists would omit the name of a rape victim from a story, even though it would be required for a full account. Thus, deontology and teleology intermingle in the decisions and actions of most media practitioners.

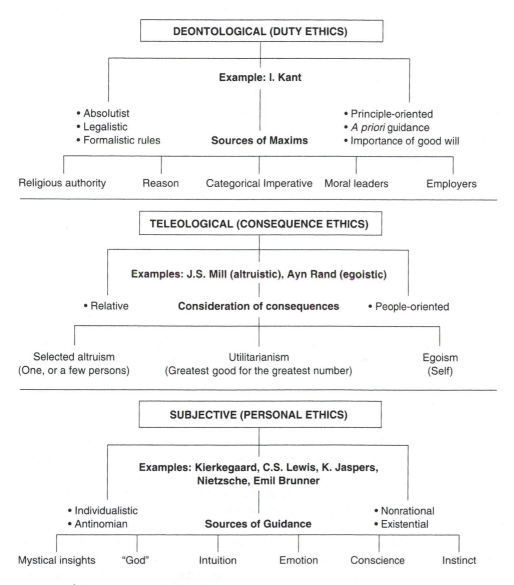

DEONTOLOGICAL (DUTY ETHICS)

Example: I. Kant

- Absolutist
- Legalistic
- Formalistic rules

Sources of Maxims

- Principle-oriented
- *A priori* guidance
- Importance of good will

Religious authority   Reason   Categorical Imperative   Moral leaders   Employers

TELEOLOGICAL (CONSEQUENCE ETHICS)

Examples: J.S. Mill (altruistic), Ayn Rand (egoistic)

- Relative   **Consideration of consequences**   • People-oriented

Selected altruism   Utilitarianism   Egoism
(One, or a few persons)   (Greatest good for the greatest number)   (Self)

SUBJECTIVE (PERSONAL ETHICS)

Examples: Kierkegaard, C.S. Lewis, K. Jaspers, Nietzsche, Emil Brunner

- Individualistic
- Antinomian

Sources of Guidance

- Nonrational
- Existential

Mystical insights   "God"   Intuition   Emotion   Conscience   Instinct

FIGURE 0.2 | Three classes of ethical theory

THE PROFESSIONAL AND HUMANISTIC STANCES

We are faced with a real conundrum in ethics—two perspectives that might be called the *professional* stance and the *humanistic* stance. The professional stance, for example, is that of reporters who are dedicated to "the people's right to know," who feel an ethical obligation to let them know. They might do so without worrying about consequences and, perhaps, without considering as important the *means* of getting the story. The driving principle would be providing a truthful and full account. Neither the means of achieving this end nor the consequences would be important. For example, a reporter who publishes the name of a rape victim, believing this to be good, full, accurate, and truthful reporting, could be described as taking the "professional" stance (Merrill, 1985). The corresponding *Machiavellian* principle would be that the information needed to make a full and accurate story may be obtained by any means necessary (Merrill, 1998).

The *humanistic* stance, on the other hand, is more relativistic and more teleological or consequence motivated. It is not tied to any one professional objective, however important it might be. Of course, a person taking this stance would make exceptions to general principles, consider consequences to people involved in the situation, use ethical means to achieve desired ends, and put human sensitivities and humanistic concerns above the job of simply providing a full and truthful account or meeting some other goal.

A BRIEF LOOK AT SUBTHEORIES

There are many ways to look at ethics and its many theories and subtheories. The main three have been presented as teleological, deontological, and personalist. We now proceed to some of the more restricted or specific ways philosophers have classified conceptions of ethics. This is not an exhaustive list, and some concepts do not fit neatly into only one of the three basic theoretical types. We can certainly see in each of the following the genesis of many interesting controversies, some of which manifest themselves throughout the rest of this book.

Acquired-Virtue Ethics

Many ethicists actually consider *virtue ethics* one of the macro-theories, not a subtheory. At any rate, Aristotle (384–322 B.C.) can probably be called the father (or at least one of the fathers, along with Confucius) of this kind of ethical theory, which is elaborated on in his *Nicomachean Ethics*. Such an ethics is built mainly on the concept of virtue and on the habitual practice of actions that foster harmonious relations among people. Aristotle saw ethics tied to character, principles, and good will (see Merrill, 1994, profile 5). Self-esteem was important to Aristotle and the practice of virtue was the key to self-development. He would have people concentrate on character building and the formation of intellectually sound habits, for he believed that moral virtues arise within us as a result of habits. We are not born with them. In fact, the Greek word *ethos* (habit) is similar to *ethike*, from which we get our word "ethics."

For Aristotle, virtue is a state of character concerned with choices of a moderate nature, a kind of balance determined by a rational person possessing practical wisdom. This *Golden Mean* is the midpoint between two vices, one excessive (too much) and the other defective (too little). Avoid extremes in action, he seems to say; seek a moderate and rational position in ethical decision-making.

In journalism, Merrill (1989) has related Aristotle's Golden Mean to Hegel's synthesis of the dialectic and has proposed this middle-way ethical stance as a worthy one for media people. Personal needs clash with societal needs; the resulting synthesis is moderated action. James Wilson (1993, p. 93) says that, according to Aristotle, most people become temperate as they begin to value "deferred pleasures" such as friendship, respect, and lasting happiness that come as they "subordinate their immoderate passions to moderate habits."

Many journalists feel that seeking some kind of Aristotelian mean is not very useful in journalism. Some issues, such as freedom of expression, do not lend themselves to a Golden Mean position; a journalist, they say, cannot be a "little free." However, compromise in ethics is indeed possible, and the fact that one does not have complete freedom does not keep that person from having a great degree of freedom. It seems that one can indeed be a "little free." Some media people—and entire media systems—can be freer than others.

As Anthony Serafini (1989) points out, Aristotle's approach to ethics is empirical, similar to the approach taken later on by the utilitarians and by their 20th-century followers who have modified and adapted their ideas. A person, in acquiring virtues and making them habitual in practice, brings happiness to others—and to oneself at the same time. Through *reason*, and through following the practices of respected people deemed virtuous in their society, one develops good habits and a moral character. That person's morality can be observed by others in everyday activities; ethics, for the person who enthrones the development of character, is not a matter of simple belief, but a matter of empirical reality where the virtuous person habituates actions on the basis of thinking, has good motives, and does nothing in excess.

Another ancient sage who proposed a variant of *acquired-virtue ethics* is Confucius (Kung Fu-tzu, 551–470 B.C.). This Chinese thinker was, in many ways, similar in his ethical outlook to Aristotle. When we think of Confucian ethics (see his *Analects*, many editions), we are mainly considering ceremonial activities, manners, and the like. In short, in Confucius we see a stress on Aristotelian habitual virtuous actions (see Merrill, 1994, profile 1).

In the ethics of Confucius, manners are extremely important; in fact, they play a key role. Life would be brutish and graceless, Confucius believed, without human ceremony. Ceremony, he said, can transform a person's life (Dawson, 1932). It can check depravity before it develops, and cause the individual to move toward what is good, keeping him or her from wrongdoing without consciously realizing it. This kind of ceremonial ethics is largely culture bound. Moral habits come, in large degree, from community expectations and are "habits of the heart" (a term coined by Alexis de Tocqueville and discussed at length by Bellah et al., 1985).

Virtues can be learned and developed. They then become part of the person, and come into play automatically when they are needed to keep the person on the moral road. The virtues of work and courage and the graces of courtesy, civility, consideration, and empathy are all central to Confucian ethics. Henry Hazlitt (1972, pp. 76–77) has called this kind of ethics "major ethics," in the sense that it is an ethics of everyday life. Codes of manners, according to Hazlitt, set up an unwritten order of priorities such as the young yielding to the old, the able-bodied to those who are ill or have a disability, the gentleman to the lady, the host to the guest. How we act toward one another was very important to Confucius. He even proposed (four centuries before Christ) what is called the Negative Golden Rule: do not do unto others what you would not wish others to do unto you. Confucius believed that an internalized code of ethics is the foundation of morality and tends to reduce or eliminate life's irritations and traumas.

Confucius recognized the importance of such an everyday morality and gave less attention to what might be called "crisis" morality and its focus on big issues. For this Chinese thinker, what was important was having good manners, being polite, being considerate of others in all the details of everyday life. The big crisis issues would tend to disappear in the presence of the continuous practice of the "little virtues."

By and large, Confucian ethicists believe that the person who is considerate and thoughtful in little things will also be so in big things. Of course, rational morality (with the possible exception of Kant's) concedes that there are exceptions to any ethical path. For example, a person can evidence perfect manners and outward manifestations of concern for others while also being cunning, devious, and scornful of others. But generally, according to Confucian thought, this is not the case; the habit of good manners and consideration casts the person in an ethical mode from which he or she seldom deviates. In a sense, we have here a kind of morality where actions (manners and ceremonial actions) destine a person to be ethical. It is the ethics of acquired virtues, habitually put into action. It is the ethics of habitual virtue, the concept of "do and you will be"—a trait of cultural morality often found in Eastern cultures.

> Confucian ethicists believe that the person who is considerate and thoughtful in little things will also be so in big things.

For Confucius, the whole social order is preserved by customs (*li*, which can be defined as imperatives of conduct). Karl Jaspers (1957) summarizes the importance that Confucius gave to *li*:

> Confucius drew no distinction between custom, morality, and justice. . . . His vision embraced the whole world of Chinese customs: the right way of walking, greeting, behaving in company, always in accordance with the particular situation; the rites of marriage, birth, death, and burial; the rules of administration; the customs governing work, war, the family, the priesthood, the court; the order of the days and seasons, the stages of life.
>
> (Jaspers, 1957, p. 45)

Cultural Relativism

Many thinkers believe that different cultures have different moral codes, thus generating a system of cultural relativism. A good example of such theories can be found in anthropologist Ruth Benedict's (1934) popular book *Patterns of Culture*. What one believes and does depends simply on where you are, according to Benedict. For example, in Mexico a journalist may well moonlight for a politician in the evenings, and there is nothing unethical about it, whereas in the United States such a practice would be considered unethical. The believer in ethical *cultural relativism* would claim that there is no objective standard by which we can call one societal code better than another, that different societies or cultures have differing ethical codes, that one's own moral code has no advantage over others, that there is no universal truth in ethics, and that it is nothing more than arrogance for us to judge the conduct of other peoples. Cultural relativism is closely related to contextual (sometimes called situation) ethics.

Ethical Subjectivism

Ethical subjectivism is the view of ethics that says that our moral opinions are based simply on our feelings. No objective right or wrong exists. When we say that a reporter should keep personal opinions out of a story, we are not stating a fact that putting personal opinions in the story is bad or wrong; we are only saying that we have negative feelings about doing so. If I am an ethical subjectivist, I am only recognizing that my opinions represent my own personal feelings and have nothing to do with "the truth" of the matter.

Subjectivism is by far the most common form of relative ethics. Fundamentally, the subjective ethicist who is saying that a certain action is right is simply expressing personal approval or disapproval of an action. Serious moral philosophers through the ages have not found subjectivism very convincing as an ethical theory, seeing it more as a psychological manifestation than a rational view of morality. This theory is also known as *emotivism*. It is closely related to ethical intuitionism, antinomianism, and even existentialism.

Religious Morality

Theologian Emil Brunner offered the well-known statement that doing good means always doing what God wills at any particular moment. This expresses the core idea of the ethics of religion. The problem for the media person and for anyone else, however, is knowing what "God wills" at any one moment in the decision-making workday. Holy books such as the Bible, the Talmud, and the Koran can give only general guidance, not specifics, about the will of some higher being or spirit. For many, a solution is found in the *divine command theory*, where "ethically correct" or "morally right" means "commanded by God" and "morally wrong" means "forbidden by God." But many problems are connected to this theory. For instance, such a theory would be of no help to the many people who are atheists. Also, as Plato asked four centuries before Christ: is conduct right because the gods command it, or do the gods command it because it is right? Of course, there is also the basic problem of receiving specific guidelines for professional decision-making via a transcendental channel.

This is nevertheless a real and important theory for many religious media people. They believe that they can take divine guidance in general things and adapt it to specific decisions; it is a matter of belief, faith, and interpretation. For them, this is sufficient ethical guidance. Related to this theory is what is often called the *theory of natural law*, which states that moral judgments are "dictates of reason," and that the best thing to do in any case is what seems most reasonable.

Natural law, which is not really in conflict with religious ethical theory, also includes the person who is not religious. There are natural laws that prescribe our behavior just as there are "laws of nature" by which nature operates. Reason, it may be said, is congenial with the idea of a rational divinity who created the world as a rational order peopled by rational creatures.

Ethical Egoism

The core of ethical egoism was well expressed by Ayn Rand (1964, p. 37) when she stated that the "achievement of his own happiness is man's highest moral purpose." Rand's version is a kind of egoistical utilitarianism that many see negatively as a form of ethical hedonism. Thomas Hobbes (1950) defended ethical egoism by connecting it with the Golden Rule. One considers the self first by thinking that if he or she does good things for others, they will do good things in return. In one way, the theory is a common-sense view of ethics, saying that we should look out for our own interests and that at least we should balance our interests against the interests of others. Whereas psychological egoism says that we do pursue our own interests, *ethical egoism* goes further and says that we *should* pursue our own self-interests.

Certainly it is a theory that challenges some of our deepest moral beliefs. Ethical egoism is a radical theory that says that one's *sole* duty is to promote one's personal interests. The theory does not forbid one from aiding others; in fact, it often sees such aid as an effective way of helping oneself. The ethical egoist believes that what makes an act ethical is the fact that it is beneficial to oneself. It should also be noted that ethical egoists do not always do what they want to do, or what might give them short-term pleasure. What a person should do is what will be the best for that person *in the long run*. It does indeed recommend selfishness, but it doesn't advocate foolishness.

Writing of the rational self-interest of Ayn Rand, Leonard Peikoff (1983) stresses that moral selfishness does not mean a license to act as one pleases or to engage in "whim" ethics. What it does mean is a disciplined defining and pursuing of one's *rational* self-interest and a rejection of all forms of sacrifice, whether of self to others or others to self. The theory upholds the virtues of reason, independence, justice, honesty, productiveness, self-pride, and integrity (Peikoff, 1983, pp. 308–309).

Despite a stress on such virtues, ethical egoism seems rather cold and uncaring. Maybe it is the word *egoism* that makes it hard to accept as an ethical theory. Can there be any real arguments for such a theory? There are some. For example, if we are always concerned for others, we may intrude into their privacy; it may be better for us to mind our own business. Besides, giving charity may well be degrading to others, robbing them of individual dignity and self-respect. Altruistic ethics regards the individual as sacrificial for the good of others, whereas ethical egoism permits a person to view his or her life as being of ultimate value. It seems, however, that these two contrasting ethical stances are really not "pure," for there is considerable overlap. A person living in a social situation *must* have some consideration for the welfare and progress of others—although, it may be said, this consideration stems from a selfish motivation.

Egoism is more ethically substantive than people usually think. For example, if we think of the moral end as self-perfection, then it is likely that we can do very little for the perfection of others. Egoism holds that the only contribution a person can make to a good world is to maximize his or her own goodness. One of the significant arguments against ethical egoism, however, is that it does not conform with moral intuitions. The moral sense or conscience (the highest of the development stages of morality) tells us to seek the good of others rather than our own, and it is impossible to have a meaningful ethics that goes against basic instincts.

Somewhere between egoistic ethics and the ethics of altruism is what some have called *mutualistic ethics*. Most of us are not really against the pursuit of self-interest; what we feel uncomfortable with is the pursuit of self-interest at the expense of others. Are we like the egoist (even a rational one) of Ayn Rand who would act only out of self-interest? Or, on the other hand, do we act solely out of the interest of others? For most of us, or perhaps all of us, the answer to both questions is *no*.

A society in which all people worked only for the good of others would be hard to conceive. A society in which everyone acted purely egoistically would certainly not be workable. What is important to recognize is that egoism and altruism are not mutually exclusive. What we really have as ethical motivations might be called mutualism—a kind of synthesis of symbiosis. This ethical stance shows that what promotes the well-being of the individual also promotes the well-being of society generally, and what is good for society is good for the individual. As a theory, this mutualistic ethics may seem reasonable, but in all probability each person will remain intrinsically—or mainly—an egoist or an altruist, motivated either largely by concern for self or concern for others.

Machiavellian Ethics

A variant of egoistic ethics is one that might be called *pragmatic egoism*, or *Machiavellian ethics*, and its leading exemplar was Niccolò Machiavelli (1469–1527), a Florentine historian and political consultant who championed the achieving of predetermined ends. Success was his guiding principle. Use conventional ethical standards, he said, when they will work for you, but don't refrain from using *any* means if they are needed to achieve your ends. His was certainly a very pragmatic, flexible, relativistic, ego-centered *teleological* system of ethics (Merrill, 1998), predicated on personal achievement of desired ends.

Machiavelli might well be considered the father of modern propaganda and, many might say, of modern advertising and public relations. Certainly he would represent the competitive, get-the-story-at-all-costs philosophy of many modern hard-nosed investigative reporters. Machiavelli's ethics is success-driven and egoistic.

It is not hard for today's media viewers to see media-Machiavellians at work. One is hardly surprised at the invocation of the old saw that "the end justifies the means." Hidden cameras have been used by television programs such as ABC's *20/20* and CBS's *60 Minutes*—is that unethical? They were used in the Academy Award-nominated documentary *The Last Truck* (2009), and many local news investigations have used them over the years on the basis that the ends justified the deceptive means. CBS's Don Hewitt, legendary producer of *60 Minutes*, said in 1992 that using hidden cameras bothered him somewhat, but he saw it as "a minor crime versus the greater good" (*Washington Post National Weekly Edition*, 1992, pp. 31–32). (See Chapter 3, p. 105, for additional discussion of Hewitt's position on the use of hidden cameras.)

Journalists have been at this undercover reporting sting business for a long time. One of the most widely discussed cases was in the late 1970s, when the Chicago *Sun-Times* and the Better Government Association set up a Chicago bar called the Mirage, secretly photographing local inspectors seeking bribes. Was this entrapment? It has been argued both ways. However, since then U.S. newspapers have avoided such operations, although similar stings have appeared on television.

Mike Wallace of CBS admits he does not like to lie or to mislead, but says it depends on your motive; each case, for Wallace, "must be weighed separately as to the cost-benefit ratio" (*Washington Post National Weekly Edition*, 1992, p. 32). Machiavelli would have been happy with that statement. I have no doubt that many leading journalists subscribe to such Machiavellian or pragmatic ethics. Some ethics scholars even question whether such deceptive journalistic tactics as hiding one's identity as a journalist or surreptitiously taping are wrong, or whether some ends can indeed justify the means.

Others are more certain of the unethical nature of such activities. Tom Goldstein, long-time journalist, media critic, and journalism educator (including 13 years as a dean, first at the University of California-Berkeley and then at Columbia University's Graduate School of Journalism), said bluntly: "I think it is wrong. Journalists should announce who they are. I'm uncomfortable living in a world where you don't know who you're talking to" (*Washington Post National Weekly Edition*, 1992, p. 32). Despite voices such as Goldstein's that rise emphatically from time to time, I fear that the spirit of Machiavelli pervades the ranks of serious investigative reporters, who often seem to put professional expediency before traditional ethical concerns.

One thing is certain: the public does not respect or trust the media, thinking the national press is politically biased, inaccurate and unwilling to admit its mistakes. A 2009 survey by the Pew Research Center for the People and the Press reported that 63% of the respondents thought that news stories frequently were inaccurate, while only 29% thought they were accurate. In a similar 1985 survey, those percentages were 34% and 55%, respectively. Only 26% of the people agreed that news organizations take care to avoid political bias; only 20% said that the news media are independent of powerful people or institutions, and 21% said that they were willing to admit mistakes—both matching all-time lows in this series of surveys ("Press Accuracy Rating . . .," 2009).

It is hardly a new phenomenon. In 1995, Everette Dennis, former executive director of the Freedom Forum Media Studies Center in New York, was quoted as saying today's journalists have a sense of superiority: "I think a lot of journalists think they could do a better job of running the country than anyone in office" (Budiansky, 1995, p. 46). Much of the hatred and mistrust of the press stems from its Machiavellian penchant to succeed, to have power, to get the story by any means necessary (see also Merrill, 1998).

Utilitarian Ethics

Now we come to *utilitarianism*, a theory that is quite different, being happiness-oriented and altruistic. This is probably the most influential of ethical theories. It belongs to the consequence, or *teleological*, class of theories, one of the great moral systems we discussed earlier. Utilitarianism in some form has profoundly altered the thinking about morality and pushed ethics into a new direction that emphasizes the importance of means and ends. Utilitarians (such as David Hume, Jeremy Bentham, and John Stuart Mill of 18th- and 19th-century Britain) began thinking differently about ethics. For example, Bentham (1823) said that morality was more than loyalty to abstract rules and even more than pleasing God; it was nothing less than an attempt to maximize the happiness in the world. This is one variant of *teleological ethics*, or consequence-oriented ethics.

What this means for the media person making an ethical decision is that he or she would determine which of several possible courses of action would bring about the most happiness or the greatest good to the greatest number of people. Then this ethical course could be taken. John Stuart Mill, in his *Utilitarianism* (1863), states that the primary ethical rule is following this happiness-producing theory which he called the Greatest Happiness Principle. The end would justify the means if the end were the greatest happiness for the greatest number.

Often, the words *pleasure, value*, or *good* are substituted for *happiness* in the utilitarian model. Mill believed that pleasure is the only desirable end, and the only proof that something is desirable is the fact that people actually desire it, and every person's pleasure (or happiness) is a good to that person, so the general happiness is the largest good of all. The name of this theory, utilitarianism, is somewhat misleading, for it emphasizes utility or usefulness rather than happiness or pleasure. But the term has stuck and has taken on a meaning consistent with the slogan "the greatest happiness to the greatest number."

> Often, the words *pleasure, value*, or *good* are substituted for *happiness* in the utilitarian model.

In the field of mass communication, such a theory is often professed by media people. The journalist, for example, may consider consequences when the story is written, and certain liberties then may be taken with presentation of the facts in the name of happiness-production or justice-production. This is the teleological approach, as we have said earlier; the journalist who would reject the utilitarian approach would be the *professional* type who would see happiness of others as irrelevant, and even damaging, to the truth of the story. Even for the utilitarian journalist, one of the main problems of using such a theory would be the difficulty (many would say the impossibility) of predicting which action would bring greater future happiness.

According to the theory of utilitarianism, a person is considered ethical if the motivation is to bring about happiness—not only to the agent, but also to the greatest number of people. (Note: such a will or motive to do good reminds us, rather strangely, of Kant, one of utilitarianism's opponents.) Most utilitarians, however, would dismiss motive and place the emphasis on the results or the actual consequences of the action. Also, such a concept has been refined through the years by substituting "good" for "happiness." But this enlargement of the concept has not done very much to obviate the problems with utilitarianism.

In fact, in many ways, trying to bring about "good" to the greatest number is as troublesome, if not more so, than trying to bring about "happiness." Semantic problems abound everywhere in ethics, but with utilitarianism they are legion. Today's journalist is in a peculiar situation: a member of a *minority*—intellectually and morally seeking after high quality—wanting to push society to high levels, while at the same time facing a largely indifferent *majority* (the masses) that wants no more than superficiality and entertainment. What then is the journalist's moral goal: satisfy the masses or try to reform and transform them? Here is one of the paradoxical aspects of the philosophy of John Stuart Mill and later utilitarians. When one tries to merge "good" (mainly a moral term) with "happiness" (mainly an emotional term), there arises an inherent conflict if not an outright contradiction.

Jeremy Bentham (1748–1832), utilitarianism's founder, enthroned happiness but seemed to equate it with pleasure and contrast it with pain. This, of course, could include intellectual and moral pleasure and not only emotional happiness. J. S. Mill, in revising Bentham's utilitarianism in the direction of quality rather than quantity, seemed to read into "happiness" something deeper than mere physical or emotional well-being.

In spite of its troublesome nature, utilitarianism is probably the most popular ethical theory. It is both rational and freely chosen. It is both individualistic and socially concerned. It is concerned with actions and consequences, not just lofty rhetoric or ideas. Sissela Bok (1978), a Harvard philosopher, in her book *Lying*, has called utilitarianism the "common-sense" approach to ethics. By contrast, Edmund Lambeth (1992) noted the difficulty of predicting the effects of an action and warned that "journalists may hobble themselves in pursuit of the truth if they allow themselves to become preoccupied with the effects and beneficial results of their work. To concentrate on effects can interfere with the gathering of facts." He also expressed concern that under "utilitarianism's loose standards, too much that is shabby can be justified under the journalistic mantle of watchdog of the public interest" (Lambeth, 1992, pp. 20 and 44). And there is also the very real concern that in maximizing the "good" for the majority, utilitarianism makes it easy to overlook harmful effects that the minority may experience.

In spite of the positive concepts that surround utilitarianism, especially the expansion of the meaning of happiness and good into more aesthetic and intellectual levels, there is one theory that contradicts it: the absolute or legalistic ethics of Immanuel Kant that we will look at next. For Kant sees this "consider-the-results" stance of Mill's philosophy as a surrender of principle, an abdication of moral responsibility, and an invitation to personal aggrandizement and rationalization. Certainly it is a theory worthy to contend with utilitarianism.

Ethical Absolutism

The foremost spokesman for the formalistic approach to ethics theory was Immanuel Kant (1724–1804). It is a species of what is called *deontological ethics*, and it is the opposite of such theories as utilitarianism. According to Kant, consequences are not to be considered. The essential ingredient of this ethical theory is *duty* to principle. Have some *a priori* maxims, principles, rules and feel a profound *duty* to follow them. These are absolute principles that one imposes rationally on oneself and which will serve as a guide to ethical behavior. The person who follows them, is ethical; the one who does not follow them is unethical, according to Kant (see Merrill, 1994, profile 12).

An ethical maxim, for Kant, implied obligation. You should do such-and-such, period. These duties are called *categorical*, as contrasted with hypothetical, which hold that if you want to achieve some desire, then do such-and-such. A categorical duty is one that, *regardless of your particular desire*, you would do. These categorical "oughts" bind rational people simply *because they are rational*. These "oughts" stem from what Kant called his *categorical imperative*, a principle that he believed every rational person would accept. This supermaxim, or imperative, went like this: "Act only according to that maxim by which you can at the same time will that it should become a universal law" (Kant, 1959).

Being an ethical person, in Kant's view, entails being guided by absolute rules, universal laws, and moral principles that hold, without exception, everywhere. Kant also enthroned people as people, and his second formulation of the categorical imperative insisted that every person should be treated as a person and not as a means to some end. A basic respect for people and a deep valuation of their human dignity were the foundation of Kant's ethics. He was saying, in effect, "Don't *use* people." Pragmatists or Machiavellians could never be Kantians. Perhaps we can summarize the essence of Kant's ethical theory in this way: have a deep respect for human dignity and act toward others only in ways you would want everyone to act. Not a bad formula for the media person trying to make ethical decisions.

Many media people try to be Kantians, having strongly held beliefs about what to do and what not to do. Tell the truth, for example. Always give the source for quotes. Don't ever change direct quotes. Don't misrepresent a product. On the other hand, many media people who believe in human dignity, or say they do, find nothing wrong with "using" people to garner information or to put together an eye-catching ad. This Kantian ethical road is a difficult one to travel, and most media people seem to wander from it from time to time, thereby exposing many double standards, exceptions, and contradictions in their overall moral demeanor. But Kantian ethics is a good starting point for media people, and many of the maxims found in codes of ethics seem to reflect a proclivity for this formalistic absolutism.

Antinomian Ethics

The ethics of law, of duty, of absolute obligation such as Kant recommends is a little strong for most media workers. This legalistic stance is often confronted by its opposite—what has been called *antinomianism*. Some rebels against Kantian legalism have accepted what might be considered an extremely reactionary stance called by many a non-ethics—a completely open kind of morality that is against any *a priori* rules, laws, or guidelines.

The antinomian has, by and large, tossed out all basic principles, precepts, codes, standards, and laws that might guide conduct. Just as the legalist tends toward absolutist or universal ethics, the antinomian tends toward anarchy or nihilism in morality. In many ways, antinomian ethics is a modern variety of what might be called Freudian ethics. Some people consider this ethic really an anti-ethical, or at least a non-ethical, system. Freud at various times evidenced a hostility to self-restraint and self-discipline and showed a tolerance for self-indulgence and irresponsibility. Richard LePiere (1959) has gone deeply into this antinomian aspect of Freudian ethics.

In brief, such an ethic says that people must be socially supported and maintained and they cannot be expected to be provident and self-reliant. Support for this type of moral philosophy has been spread in the United States through a steady growth of permissiveness and avoidance of personal responsibility. There is a tendency to blame others or social institutions or conditions for any kind of immoral actions one may take. The person who might be said to act unethically is simply a victim of "society," limited by its rigorous moral code.

This "hostility to moral laws" ethical system places non-rational freedom above self-restraint and assumes that what comes naturally is the ethical thing to do. Such a view is based on psychology rather than moral philosophy. The antinomian clashes with the legalist. And such a clash, as Joseph Fletcher (1966) has asserted, has resulted in a synthesis that is often called "situation ethics."

Another version of this kind of "non-ethical" system might be that which has been suggested by analytical philosophers who have truly abandoned morality. In essence, they say that moral judgments are no more than personal preferences and not much different from a taste or distaste for apple pie. A. J. Ayer (1946), for example, maintained that because moral arguments cannot be verified scientifically, they are no more than commands or pure expressions of feeling that have absolutely no objective validity.

Situation Ethics

The basic tenet of *situation ethics* is that we must consider the particular situation before we can determine what is ethical or not ethical. This concept has been around in some form for a long time, but it was Fletcher (1966), in his *Situation Ethics*, who planted this term firmly in the public mind. He was talking about a special Christian concept of situationism that applied a kind of God-induced love (agape) to any moral dilemma. Love would be the guide to ethical action *in any situation*. Much of the philosophical (or theological) basis for this theory—in its Christian sense—comes largely from the writings of German theologians Dietrich Bonhoeffer, Rudolf Bultmann, and Paul Tillich.

In this Christian sense, situationism is just another variant of religious ethics, but one that eschews specific moral principles to be applied on every occasion. It certainly is different from the divine command theory of ethics. The only guide for the Christian situationist is to act out of love. *Simply apply love in every situation and you will be ethical.* Of course, this poses some problems because love can be defined differently and lead to a wide variety of destinations in ethical thinking and behavior.

These religious versions of situation ethics were, however, somewhat different from an earlier and more prominent idea of situationism in morality. More common was the idea that the situation determines the ethics—no more than a form of moral relativism that said there are no universal ethical principles that can be applied in every situation. These situation ethicists believed that only non-rational moral robots would try to adhere to an absolutist ethics.

Thus, situationism is really a type of relativistic ethics focusing on the particular set of circumstances. For Fletcher and other Christian ethicists, love determines action in each situation; for general relativists, each situation requires a special and different kind of ethical decision-making, using whatever standards they think best.

An extreme approach is what Leonard Peikoff (1983) called the new relativism—a theory based on the belief that truth is unknowable, that there is no objectivity, that reason is not as reliable as passion. It dismisses values and sees society as diminishing the individual. It denies that virtue is possible, it hates standards, it despises quality and excellence, and it attacks achievement, success, and beauty. And it believes that one person's sense of morality is as good as another's.

Intuitive Ethics

Intuitive ethics is perhaps the oldest moral doctrine. It is the theory that we know what is right and what is wrong without having any *a priori* rules or without doing a lot of thinking before we act. Intuitionists give many answers when asked how they know what to do. Theorists like James Wilson (1993) say that God plants in each person a certain *moral sense*. Others call the immediate guide to ethical action *conscience*, a kind of inner voice that directs each person. At any rate, most intuitionists believe that rightness and wrongness are self-evident—simply a matter of intuition. *Conscience*, of course, means many different things, from the repressive superego of Freud (1930), to the God-given moral implantation of C. S. Lewis (1952), to the "disinterested spectator" theory of Adam Smith (1759).

Although there are philosophers who believe in ethical intuition, the doctrine does not have a wide following. Usually one who points to intuition is someone whose intuition is based on past experiences and who has thought about consequences of varying kinds of action. Or, and this perhaps is even more plausible, such an intuitionist is a person who has habituated certain actions and does certain things spontaneously. Therefore, the actions *seem* to flow from mere instinct or intuition.

Intuitionism is closely related to what has been called common-sense ethics, which draws on wisdom gleaned from large numbers of particular cases. We use traditional moral rules that have seemed to satisfy moral conditions throughout the ages. Taken together, these traditions and rules tend to crystallize into a body of practical wisdom (as found in the philosophies of Aristotle and Confucius). This is nothing more than common sense that respects precedent. Common-sense morality, and also perhaps so-called intuitionism, recognizes the need to abide by general rules that have proved to be useful.

Having such general rules in ethics is very close to what Immanuel Kant proposed as duty ethics. Each person develops rules, maxims, or principles to which she or he is dedicated and obligated. Unlike Kant, however, modern common-sense ethicists are flexible, being willing to follow moral rules except when there are clear reasons for not doing so. It is important that exceptions be made carefully and infrequently—with the burden of proof being on the exception or on the alternative ethical innovation.

Although there may not be any ethical intuitions per se, there may be certain ethical principles or maxims that are self-evident. For example, a rule that journalists should not fabricate news stories is self-evident in that the whole concept of news and the media's credibility would disappear if it were not so; besides, no reasonable journalist would ever feel the need to ask the justification for such an ethical rule.

Social Contract Theory

Another theory or subtheory of ethics we should mention is one that links morality to the state or to society. It is a kind of citizen-volunteerism to accept socially enforced rules of conduct; because this social enforcement is by the state, it is a kind of people–state agreement or contract for a common morality. The state exists to make possible social living through external enforcement, whereas ethics deals with overarching voluntary rules that enhance social living.

This theory says that only in the context of the social contract can people be moral agents. Why? Because the contract creates the conditions necessary for us to care about other people. As the state organizes society generally, it organizes social and moral expectations of society specifically. In short, a state makes it possible for us to have civilized relations with others, giving rise to the very concept of ethics.

The Harvard philosophy professor John Rawls (*A Theory of Justice*, 1971) built on the social contract in the development of his theory of justice. In this theory, Rawls stresses that free and rational people must assume a position of equality in determining the terms of their association. These people agree on, or contract, the basis of their social cooperation. Rawls proposes what he calls the *veil of ignorance* in order to ensure that the principles agreed on will be just. Participants in such a contract, according to Rawls, are situated behind this veil of ignorance, not knowing how the decisions they make will affect their own lives. In short, they must put aside their own identities and make decisions by adopting the identities, in turn, of the other people affected by their decisions. Nobody behind this veil of ignorance knows for sure what their identities will be when the veil is lifted. This, according to Rawls, will ensure fairness and justice in the contractual situation (Rawls, 1971, pp. 136–142).

Thomas Hobbes (1588–1679), also an espouser of ethical egoism, and Jean-Jacques Rousseau (1712–78) are most closely identified with the social contract theory. Somewhat related to this theory is one that is sometimes called the *socialist* or *Marxist* theory stressing a kind of classless utopianism in which people are bound together by a sense of community veering in the direction of egalitarianism. In the various versions, the objective is to eliminate discrepancies among people, level out material benefits and opportunities, and permit the state to play a more important part in making a fair and equitable system, after which presumably it would wither away. Probably the earliest proponent of such a theory was Plato, who saw a person's ethical duty as supporting the authority of the state and working for the public good.

The social contract theory requires people to set aside private, self-centered desires and inclinations in favor of principles that impartially promote the welfare of everyone. Of course, a person can do this only if others have agreed to do the same thing—in effect, by entering into a kind of unwritten contract. For the advocate of this theory, ethics consists of rules dealing with the way people will treat one another—rules reasonable people will accept for their mutual benefit. This is the basis of the theory in a nutshell.

Actually, a media organization—not necessarily a state or total society—can subscribe to a social contract theory. The members of the staff of a broadcast station, a public relations agency, or a newspaper can agree to follow certain institutional moral rules because it is to the advantage of each person to do so. It would not be to anyone's advantage if people violated the rules at any time. The main point of such a theory of ethics is that people must be able to *predict* what others will do; we must be able to count on one another to follow certain rules, at least most of the time.

One advantage of the social contract theory is that morality is simply a set of rules that reasonable people agree to accept for their mutual benefit. We don't need to worry about the objectivity or subjectivity of moral principles, about relativism or absolutism around the world. What we have is a socially based theory; we have socially established rules, and if we deviate from them we are being unethical. Period. It seems, in many ways, a theory akin

One advantage of the social contract theory is that morality is simply a set of rules that reasonable people agree to accept for their mutual benefit.

to that of Kant—certainly a deontological one—but, unlike Kant's theory, it is socially rather than individually determined and enforced.

It is not difficult to see this social contract approach as spawning what today is often called the *social responsibility* media theory. The media and the people, in a sense, contract with one another to bring about certain mutual expectations, such as adequate and pluralistic information, truthfulness, reliable and credible social exposition, and a meaningful context, with social good as a guiding ethical principle.

Existentialist Ethical Theory

In one sense, there is no real ethical theory of existentialism; existentialist ethics is so individualistic that many feel the term is oxymoronic. Jean-Paul Sartre (1905–80), perhaps the best known existentialist, said he would write on this subject of ethics specifically, but never got around to it. However, he did deal with ethical problems to some extent. For example, Sartre (1957, pp. 42–43) stresses that we cannot decide *a priori* on an ethics that will guide us in a specific action; he is certainly not a Kantian in this respect. Ethical considerations, of course, permeate the writings of all existentialists from Kierkegaard onward. At the heart of any existentialist ethics appear to lie personal authenticity, integrity, honesty, deep concern with freedom, and the acceptance of personal responsibility. One may be free to be unethical, but according to American philosopher Hazel Barnes, an authority on existentialism, the person who chooses to be unethical rejects the positive benefits of freedom. Barnes's (1978) *An Existentialist Ethics* makes the overall point that ethics and freedom are both needed for a rich, fulfilling, productive life that benefits both the individual and society.

Ethics, for the existentialist, must be personal if it is to contribute to the authenticity of the person. As I pointed out in *Existential Journalism* (Merrill, 1995), for a media person to follow some group-designed code or traditional manner of action, either out of blind submission or thoughtless habit, is inauthentic and depersonalizing. The basic point is that there is no blueprint for what an individual media person can become or what he or she should do. The individual must decide, for the essence of each person is self-determined.

Many see existentialist ethics as a form of egoistic ethics, and to some degree they are right. But no major existentialist philosopher has ever suggested extreme individualism and the fulfillment of all one's desires. Always there is some control. A kind of reasonableness, for instance, that keeps personal freedom in bounds, is quite common in existentialist literature. Or, as Kierkegaard believed, Christian love and a concern for others keep personal freedom under control. Or, as Sartre held, control is exercised by a person's notion of responsibility. He also said the anguish of personal choice arises from the fact that, in making the choice, a person is committing not only him- or herself but, in a certain manner, all humankind. This existentialist statement is almost Kantian: we choose only the things we would be willing to see universalized.

Also, for the existentialist, an ethical demeanor is necessary because of the necessity of accepting personal responsibility for actions. This imposes a kind of ethical restraint on a person; for example, existentialist media people would never try to escape the consequences of their freely determined actions. Media workers have superiors—and colleagues, sources, and audience members—who are affected by the workers' actions. Media people know this, understand this, and must decide whether to take certain actions. It is the ethical restraint of individual integrity.

For the existentialist, there is also the restraint of human dignity. Such dignity places just limits on action for the simple reason that a person does not live isolated in society, and all members of society have this same human dignity. Moral people have such dignity. And who are moral people? Those who do not succumb to instincts or passions, who do not change opinions without justification, who are not flatterers or falsifiers, who constantly attempt to transcend self and traditional morality.

This concept of transcendence was important to Friedrich Nietzsche, an important existentialist voice. He would have us say "yes" to life, therefore becoming more noble and heroic, always rising to our highest potential. Nietzsche sounded a common note of the existentialist concept of ethics: that the individual person is extremely valuable and worthy, more so as that person determines his or her own destiny and does not submit to any authority that restricts personal freedom or makes the person inauthentic.

One variant of existentialist ethics might be a kind of "superior person" ethics, where through existential progress an individual "transcends" normal morality and, in a sense, becomes a superior ethical person. Nietzsche, who espoused in *Beyond Good and Evil* (1866) what he called the *Übermensch* (*Overman*, usually translated as the *Superman*) and talked of a "master-morality," is probably the best example of such an ethicist.

Nietzsche drew heavily on Greek philosopher Thrasymachus, who believed that justice is no more than the interest of the stronger. Nietzsche would interpret stronger not only in terms of physical or military strength but also in terms of a full spectrum of intellectual and moral strength that transcends physical power. Nietzsche is rather vague as to how these superior people will manifest themselves. His ethical theory is a close relative of the egoistic ethical theory, but is different in that Nietzsche's Superman draws on subjective and mystical insights for transforming moral progress. Egoistic theory is based more on rationality.

Communitarian Theory

A theory of ethics that is concerned with "the community" and with "civic transformation" and retreat of the individual into the comfortable and cooperative warmth of the group is known as *communitarianism*. This theory, espoused by people such as Amitai Etzioni, a sociologist, and Clifford Christians, a communications scholar and ethicist, would shift the purpose of news from unbiased information transmission to what Christians calls "an agent of community transformation." Community impact journalism, it might be called. Consistent with postmodernism, communitarianism considers the tenets of 18th-century European Enlightenment to have failed and the tradition of objectivity unprepared to deal with the complexities of modern communities and morality.

The spirit of communitarianism has always been with us. Communitarians contend generally that their theory permits ethical discussion to focus on social altruism and benevolence and to have them treated on equal footing with the more traditional concepts of loyalty and truth-telling. A rejoinder to this might be that ethical discussions have always considered altruism and benevolence and certainly traditional theories (e.g., utilitarianism, intuitionism, legalism) have gone far beyond concern only with truth-telling and loyalty.

Communitarianism stresses cooperation. The good cooperator with the group is the ethical person, reminding us of the German philosophers Georg Hegel and Gottlieb Fichte who would have people sacrifice their individualism to their state or community. What is good for the community is the moral imperative. Confucius, the great sage of ancient China, was probably the first communitarian, stressing social harmony, loyalty and love of family and allegiance to elders and superiors in government. His philosophy is usually contrasted to that of Mo-tzu, a more individualistic thinker, and even more meritocratic. And, of course, the "democrats" of ancient Greece (who condemned Socrates to death) were community oriented. Plato, in a way, was even more group oriented, structuring his ideal republic into "groups," each knowing exactly what was expected of them.

In Medieval Europe the Church was *the community*, although modern communitarians would say that it was not a democratic one. Nevertheless, it was a voluntary one that fostered not only obedience to religious norms, but also to the virtues of selflessness, altruism, temperance and honor. It was a cooperationist era. But with the Renaissance of the 14th and 15th centuries, a spirit of individualism began to make its mark on Europe. And the 17th and 18th centuries brought in very strong individualism and reason, and a stress on personal liberty that had been missing.

Communitarians believe that this Enlightenment emphasis on freedom has been misused and has spawned much of modern immorality. So they recommend cooperation and community values over personal freedom and competition. The free press under the direction of elite media owners is seen by communitarians as ineffective and even a negative institution—one that has been tried and found wanting. Communitarianism has become a strong force in the public-media debates.

The journalist dedicated to communitarianism finds his or her role shifting. No longer an observer of the passing scene, the communitarian journalist attempts to *change or transform the scene*. In a sense this journalist disdains neutralism and objectivity and seeks only the social good. This is defined by some kind of "conversation" (perhaps drawing on Jürgen Habermas' "ideal speech situation") where consensus emerges based on the participants' tolerance of one another, their interest in the problem, their abilities as communicators, and their knowledge of the issue. The communitarian journalist thus becomes a kind of social worker, rather than emulating the old-time journalist. More important than public information are public cohesion, public interdependence, public involvement, and shared moral values.

CONCLUDING REMARKS

Now that we have taken a quick trip through many of the paths of ethics and ethical theory, we are ready to consider some specific examples of troublesome ethical problems facing people who work in mass communication. We will do so in the chapters that follow. These chapters are in the form of informal debates (or better, opposing contentions) on a variety of today's controversial ethical issues.

As we stated earlier, there are no hard and fast answers to such ethical questions, and the varying ethical positions on the issues that follow attempt to provide only some of the most

this is . . . not a textbook of normative ethics intended to provide concrete answers to these many difficult moral problems.

salient arguments on either side. Of course, there are always *more than two sides* to these complex ethical questions, but the basic format of the chapters deals mainly with the most common two sides of the issues. Other ethical positions are mainly left to each student to grapple with. Some are suggested by questions posed by the opposing positions, or in the commentary that follows each debate; others will probably come up in class or other discussion. The important point is that this is a book of basic *positions and commentary* on some important ethical issues in the field of media studies; it is *not* a textbook of normative ethics intended to provide concrete answers to these many difficult moral problems.

We hope that you will weigh the evidence presented by each debater carefully, consider the commentaries, and resolve the controversies as rationally as possible. But what is truly important is that the reader realize that, in a real sense, nobody *wins* or *loses* in such controversial ethical discourse. The smart reader takes what is most meaningful, useful, and helpful from *all of the positions* presented here, integrates it into an already developing personal morality, and makes it useful in present and future relationships and activities.

Media people can progress ethically—becoming ever more consistent and sensitive to the moral environment that encompasses them. Many moral development theories are available to the serious person desiring to mature ethically. Except for the three main theories discussed early in this Overview, we have not dealt with them, but they are important and indicate that there are many levels or stages through which a person may proceed on an ethical journey. Books such as Ronald Duska and Mariellen Whelan's (1975) *Moral Development: A Guide to Piaget and Kohlberg* will acquaint the student with development models. And, of course, books by Jean Piaget (1932) and Lawrence Kohlberg (1981), both important developmental theorists, will get the reader into the intricacies of moral development theories.

The important point here is that a person does not one day just become "ethical" and that is the end of the moral story. Individuals grow ethically just as they grow physically and intellectually. Whatever ethical theory—or combination of theories—drives them through the brambles of moral choices, there is always the possibility of maturing further and making even better ethical decisions.

We hope that the controversial discussions that follow will give you the opportunity to think about ethical quandaries facing a person working in the media. By accepting or rejecting the arguments put forth by the debaters, and by considering the remarks made in the commentaries, we believe you can improve your moral reasoning and reach a higher level of ethical consciousness. But remember: there are always higher levels to strive for. The ethical journey is never over.

REFERENCES AND RELATED READINGS

Aristotle. (Many editions). *Nicomachean Ethics*.

Ayer, Alfred J. (1946). *Language, Truth and Logic*. New York: Dover.

Barnes, Hazel. (1978). *An Existentialist Ethics*. Chicago, IL: University of Chicago Press.

Bellah, Robert N., Richard Madsen, W. M. Sullivan, Ann Swidler, and Stephen M. Tipton. (1985). *Habits of the Heart: Individualism and Commitment in American Life*. New York: Harper & Row.

Benedict, Ruth. (1934). *Patterns of Culture*. Boston, MA: Houghton Mifflin.

Bentham, Jeremy. (1823). *An Introduction to the Principles of Morals and Legislation*. Oxford, UK: Clarendon Press.

Bok, Sissela. (1978). *Lying: Moral Choice in Public and Private Life*. New York: Pantheon.

Budiansky, Stephen. (1995). "The media's message: The public thinks the national press is elitist, insensitive and arrogant." *U.S. News & World Report*, January 9, pp. 45–47.

Christians, Clifford G., John P. Ferré, and P. Mark Fackler. (1993). *Good News: Social Ethics and the Press*. New York: Oxford University Press.

Cooper, J. M. (1975). *Reason and the Human Good in Aristotle*. Cambridge, MA: Harvard University Press.

Cooper, Thomas W., Clifford G. Christians, Francis Forde Plude, and Robert A. White. (1989). *Communication Ethics and Global Change*. White Plains, NY: Longman.

Dawson, Miles M., ed. (1932). *The Wisdom of Confucius*. Boston, MA: International Pocket Library.

Duska, Ronald, and Mariellen Whelan. (1975). *Moral Development: A Guide to Piaget and Kohlberg*. New York: Paulist Press.

Etzioni, Amitai. (1993). *The Spirit of Community: Rights, Responsibilities, and the Communitarian Agenda*. New York: Crown.

Fletcher, Joseph. (1966). *Situation Ethics: The New Morality*. Philadelphia, PA: Westminster Press.

Freud, Sigmund. (1930). *Civilization and its Discontents*. New York: Norton.

Gilligan, Carol. (1982). *In a Different Voice*. Cambridge, MA: Harvard University Press.

Haselden, Kyle. (1968). *Morality and the Mass Media*. Nashville, TN: Broadman.

Hazlitt, Henry. (1972). *The Foundations of Morality*. Los Angeles, CA: Nash.

Henry, William A., III. (1994). *In Defense of Elitism*. New York: Doubleday.

Hobbes, Thomas. (1950). *Leviathan*. New York: E. P. Dutton.

Holmes, Stephen. (1993). *The Anatomy of Antiliberalism*. Cambridge, MA: Harvard University Press.

James, Ian. (Associated Press). (2007). "Venezuelan TV channel turns to the Web." *The Burlington* (VT) *Free Press*, June 2, p. 13A.

Jaspers, Karl. (1957). *Socrates, Buddha, Confucius, Jesus: The Paradigmatic Individuals*, edited by Hannah Arendt. San Diego, CA: Harcourt Brace Jovanovich.

Kant, Immanuel. (1959). *Foundations of the Metaphysics of Morals*. Indianapolis, IN: Bobbs-Merrill.

Kohlberg, Lawrence. (1981). *The Philosophy of Moral Development: Moral Stages and the Idea of Justice*. New York: Harper & Row.

Lambeth, Edmund B. (1992). *Committed Journalism: An Ethic for the Profession*, 2nd ed. Bloomington and Indianapolis, IN: Indiana University Press.

LePiere, Richard. (1959). *The Freudian Ethic*. New York: Duell, Sloan & Pearce.

Lewis, C. S. (1952). *Mere Christianity*. New York: Macmillan.

Lillie, William. (1961). *An Introduction to Ethics*. New York: Barnes & Noble.

Machiavelli, Niccolò. (Many editions). *The Prince*.

MacIntyre, Alasdair. (1966). *A Short History of Ethics*. New York: Random House.

Merrill, John C. (1985). "Is ethical journalism simply objective reporting?" *Journalism Quarterly* 62(2), pp. 391–393.

——. (1989, 1993). *The Dialectic in Journalism: Toward a Responsible Use of Press Freedom*. Baton Rouge, LA: Louisiana State University Press.

——. (1994). *Legacy of Wisdom: Great Thinkers and Journalism*. Ames, IA: Iowa State University Press.

——. (1995). *Existential Journalism*, rev. ed. Ames, IA: Iowa State University Press.

——. (1998). *The Princely Press: Machiavelli on American Journalism*. Lanham, MD: University Press of America.

Mill, John Stuart (Many editions). *On Liberty*.

———. (Many editions). *Utilitarianism*.

Minow, Newton N. (1995). "How vast the wasteland now?" *Media Studies Journal* 9(1), pp. 3–8.

Morgan, George W. (1968). *The Human Predicament: Dissolution and Wholeness*. Providence, RI: Brown University Press.

Newman, Jay. (1989). *The Journalist in Plato's Cave*. Rutherford, NJ: Fairleigh Dickinson University Press.

Nietzsche, Friederich. (Many editions). *Beyond Good and Evil*.

Patka, Frederick, ed. (1962). *Existentialist Thinkers and Thought*. New York: Citadel.

Peikoff, Leonard. (1983). *Ominous Parallels*. Briarcliffe Manor, NY: Stein & Day.

Piaget, Jean. (1932). *The Moral Judgment of the Child*. Glencoe, IL: Free Press.

Postman, Neil. (1985). *Amusing Ourselves to Death*. New York: Viking.

"Press accuracy rating hits two decade low." (2009). Washington, DC: The Pew Research Center for the People and the Press, September 12. Retrieved from http://people-press.org/reports/pdf/543.pdf (March 15, 2010).

Rachels, James. (1986). *The Elements of Moral Philosophy*. New York: Random House.

Rand, Ayn. (1964). *The Virtue of Selfishness*. New York: New American Library.

Rawls, John. (1971). *A Theory of Justice*. Cambridge, MA: Belknap.

Sartre, Jean-Paul (1957). *Existentialism and Human Emotions*. New York: Philosophical Library.

Serafini, Anthony. (1989). *Ethics and Social Concern*. New York: Paragon.

Sidgwick, Henry. (1956). *The Methods of Ethics*, 7th ed. Indianapolis, IN: Hackett.

Siebert, Fred S., Theodore Peterson, and Wilbur Schramm. (1956). *Four Theories of the Press*. Urbana, IL: University of Illinois Press.

Smith, Adam. (1759). *The Theory of Moral Sentiments*. Oxford, UK: Clarendon Press.

Washington Post National Weekly Edition. (1992). December 14–20, pp. 31–32.

Wilson, James Q. (1993). *The Moral Sense*. New York: Free Press.

Chapter 1

Ethics and Freedom

Mass Media Accountability

FREEDOM and responsibility are two sides of the same coin when one looks at the U.S. mass media system. But there often are major differences of opinion as to which side society most needs to have facing up.

This is a problem that faces all mass communicators. It could be a journalist considering whether to exercise the freedom to destroy a reputation, preferably for a useful purpose. Or it could be the head of an advertising agency pondering the appropriate creativity limits in regard to an anti-abortion ad—one that could well offend sensibilities on both sides of the issue at the same time it catches the attention of millions of television viewers. In both cases, is freedom to publish or broadcast the overriding value, or should the journalist and advertising executive take other factors into consideration and stop short of exercising the full freedom they have?

Similar concerns have emerged in regard to cyberspace communication. To take just one example, how much freedom should online advertisers have in regard to behavioral targeting—the practice of sending ads to people based on the interests displayed in their Web-surfing history. Does the freedom to use new methods of advertising trump an individual's right of privacy—the "right to be let alone"?

To some degree, it's a chicken-and-egg situation. Freedom of expression is guaranteed by the First Amendment to everyone, and that gives the mass media "ethical breathing room" to make their own decisions to be responsible or irresponsible. But if their decisions are seen as continually irresponsible, the result has often been public (or government) pressures to curtail media freedom in favor of requiring increased responsibility. This is a potential problem for the news media, but an existing one for the advertising and entertainment industries which are already regulated more than are news media.

These competing values are the crux of the arguments that follow. Each author agrees that both freedom and responsibility are important if the mass media are to function properly in society. Julianne H. Newton maintains that the media cannot be allowed to hide behind the First Amendment in order to justify irresponsible behavior. David Gordon argues that freedom of expression must be protected at almost any cost, regardless of whether the media are ethical or responsible.

One other aspect of this dilemma also merits some consideration, although it is not discussed directly in the following material. That's the question of to whom or what the media should be responsible or accountable, assuming that some level of responsibility is expected. Is it to society as a whole—that is, to the general public? To specific audiences or subaudiences? To their owners and stockholders? To their peers, or perhaps to some general notion of "ethics" appropriate for the mass media? To more than one of these groups, or perhaps to some others as well? These questions are well worth further thought, as you ponder the different perspectives on the freedom/responsibility relationship presented here.

GORDON: Freedom of expression in news, entertainment or persuasive communication must be zealously defended regardless of whether it is exercised ethically.

Inroads on freedom of speech and of the press in the United States were part of the reaction to the 9/11 attacks on the World Trade Center and Pentagon. These incursions were advocated and implemented in the name of national security, perhaps most notably in the USA PATRIOT Act of 2001. Although relatively few voices opposed these developments at the time (only one senator, Russell Feingold of Wisconsin, voted against the Act), more opposition has been expressed with the passage of time and further analysis has raised concerns about what core values are threatened by a knee-jerk devotion to "national security" concerns. Some changes were made in the statute during the reauthorization process in 2005–06 but critics continued to express concern about the law's damage to rights of expression.

Prof. Geoffrey Stone of the University of Chicago Law School made a strong argument in 2004 for robust protection of First Amendment freedoms and values, perhaps especially in times of national crisis. He argued that curtailing free speech, even in wartime, winds up endangering national security because it undermines the democratic process to which freedom of speech is essential (Stone, 2004).

Freedom of the press is arguably at least as important to democracy as is freedom of speech, as we move headlong into the complexities of the Information Age. Together, as a pair of First Amendment scholars (Sanford and Kirtley, 2005) noted, these two freedoms protect both individuals in expressing their opinions and beliefs, and the ability of news and information outlets to provide "citizens with the knowledge they need in order to govern themselves and to use their votes wisely." The First Amendment, of course, also protects communications of far lesser importance but it nonetheless "remains the heart of American democracy" (Sanford and Kirtley, 2005, pp. 267 and 263).

Back in 1974, writing for a unanimous Supreme Court, Chief Justice Warren Burger noted that the First Amendment guarantees a free press but does *not* require a responsible press. That comment, in *Miami Herald Publishing Co.* v. *Tornillo* (418 U.S. 241, 1974), was part of the Supreme Court's rejection of a Florida law that *required* newspapers to provide specific reply space to political candidates whom they had attacked on their editorial pages.

The decision epitomizes the position taken by those who believe that we dare not even *begin* to limit freedom of expression in the service of requiring responsible use of that freedom.

There is no doubt that giving the media this degree of freedom inevitably leads to considerable discomfort in some segments of society, and sometimes to potentially difficult or even dangerous situations. But that's really no different from the risks we accept by embracing democracy as our chosen form of government. In a democratic society, the people are given the ultimate power to decide and they retain that power even when a large minority of the people think the decisions are wrong. The antidote for wrong or even foolish ～ Gordon or dangerous political decisions is to rejoin the political battles and convince enough people to make the right decision the next time. It is *not* to impose restrictions on the political dialogue or the political process in order to prevent "wrong" decisions.

But legal restrictions aren't the only threats to the media's First Amendment freedoms. Ethical considerations can also be invoked as a vehicle for curtailing various types of expression. And if it's crucial to protect the legal underpinning of the First Amendment in the face of national security concerns, as Stone (2004) argues, then certainly it follows that ethics arguments also should not be allowed to erode freedoms of speech and of the press.

The ideal situation, of course, would be to have *both* freedom of expression and responsible exercise of that freedom. However, human nature being what it is, there will always be people who abuse protected freedoms of expression. That, I believe, is simply a cost of doing business in a society that values the right to express oneself freely—a right that must be zealously protected against all incursions, even those attempted in the name of ethics.

Leonard Pitts Jr., a *Miami Herald* columnist, put it well in mid-2009 in decrying the use of the word "Nazi" in connection with that summer's bitter debate over health care reform. The First Amendment, he wrote,

> says we can say whatever we want. It doesn't say it has to be intelligent.
>
> And, yes, you are even protected if you liken [President] Obama or [ex-President] Bush to Hitler. Yet every time I hear that, it makes me cringe for what it says about our collective propensity for historical amnesia.
>
> (Pitts, 2009)

Regardless of the "cringe factor" in some freely exercised speech, any efforts to legislate or otherwise require ethics at the expense of the First Amendment will aim for a cure that is worse than the disease—and, as will be noted later, run the risk of preventing change in society's moral values.

Theodore Glasser, writing in the mid-1980s, made an eloquent argument for coupling First Amendment freedoms with requirements for responsible use of those freedoms, taking issue with what he called "an essentially libertarian construction of the First Amendment, [in which] questions of responsibility are effectively reduced to questions of conscience" (Glasser, 1986, p. 81). Glasser proposes instead an "'affirmative' theory of the First Amendment," in which the press is not just free *from* government control, but is free from it in order to *do* or *accomplish* something—for example, to "accommodate and disseminate a broad range of expression" (Glasser, 1986, p. 90) or otherwise to provide what democracy requires from a free press.

Glasser (1986) argues that the press must somehow be made "as free from the whims of the marketplace as it is free from the authority of the state," so that it "is at all times free to conduct itself in accordance with its highest ideals." He suggests some first steps that journalists can take (individually and collectively) "to challenge the unabashedly self-serving view of the First Amendment that equates press freedom with property rights," but eventually concludes that only government "can restore confidence in the press by insulating the press from influences inimical to the highest ideals of American journalism" (Glasser, 1986, pp. 93 and 96).

And that's where I have to part company with Glasser. His argument is appealing, particularly in light of the way that economics have negatively impacted the amount and quality of journalism being practiced. But Glasser's conclusion must be resisted in order to protect the First Amendment values which are a necessary condition for communicators' freedom to make personal ethical choices. It's those personal choices, instilled and sharpened (it is hoped) over the years in individuals, that should hold the press—and the persuasive media—to their own highest ideals.

To attempt to *require* ethical conduct in connection with the First Amendment would be to allow the regulatory camel to get its nose into the tent of free expression. And once that nose is in, the issue becomes not *whether* some curtailment of free expression is permissible, but rather *where* to draw the line, *how far* to extend the regulations, and *who* gets to make those decisions. I suspect that's why Chief Justice Burger—no zealot in supporting many aspects of the First Amendment—drew a sharp line in the face of Pat Tornillo's attempt to force his way onto the *Miami Herald*'s front pages in response to a pair of editorials attacking his political candidacy.

Although elementary fairness might have dictated that the *Herald* give Tornillo such a prime opportunity to respond, Burger made it clear that this was not something the state government could mandate, even though the Florida legislature had tried to do just that via the law (passed six decades earlier) that Tornillo attempted to invoke. Burger was willing to let the *Herald*—which had, in fact, followed its usual procedures in offering Tornillo reply space inside the paper—determine the conditions under which Tornillo could respond. Government interference with this process, Burger wrote, would impinge on the paper's freedom to determine its own contents.

And that's as it should be for all of the mass media, with government prohibited from imposing requirements for responsible use of free speech, because any such requirements would limit that freedom. This prohibition is a major reason why efforts to establish a broad legal right of access to the media have gone nowhere. Attorney Jerome Barron, in his unsuccessful argument in the *Tornillo* case as well as in an earlier book (Barron, 1973), urged the establishment of such a "right of access" rather than leaving access decisions to the media. But the unanimous *Tornillo* decision effectively foreclosed such a *legal* requirement and left the question of providing access (or "fairness") as *ethics* issues to be determined by the media themselves.

Such responsibility in communication should, by definition, be an ethical rather than a legal concern. And, because ethics involves choice, people are free (and likely) to make some "wrong" decisions about communicating responsibly, and, if they choose, to cater to those audience segments that enjoy various types of "less ethical" media content or practices. In our society, mass media ethics must be based on a "first principle" that ensures zealous protection for freedom of both informational and persuasive expression while leaving us fallible mortals free to chart our own ethical (or unethical) courses, guided by our own principles (let's hope by something more concrete than the "conscience" that Glasser doesn't fully trust) regarding responsibility.

I could be persuaded that private individuals ought to retain some rights to sue the media for irresponsible communication that damages their reputation in an unwarranted manner. But I much prefer Justice Hugo Black's position that the best response to libelous material is not a lawsuit but rather the opportunity to respond and set the record straight. The value of such an approach, as the remedy for defamatory publications or broadcasts, is borne out by a study reporting that *libel* plaintiffs—especially those allegedly damaged in connection with public rather than private matters—were far more concerned with correcting false statements about themselves than they were in recovering monetary damages (Bezanson et al., 1987, pp. 4–5 and 79–81).

Such an approach, invoking "more speech" rather than monetary damages, would also help avoid the problem of media self-censorship that has cropped up in response to large libel verdicts. This "chilling effect" of large verdicts, not to mention the cost of defending a libel suit even if you win, is a very real consequence (particularly for smaller, less affluent media outlets) of the law's goal of providing remedies for the more irresponsible instances of defamation. It illustrates well one type of problem that can follow the camel's regulatory nose into the free expression tent.

LEGAL LIMITS ON FREE EXPRESSION

Of course, some governmental limits or regulations on the exercise of free speech have received Supreme Court sanction and help delineate the context within which ethical choices must be made. Restraining publications that are obscene or directly incite violence (see *Near v. Minnesota*, 283 U.S. 697, 1931) or that *clearly* threaten "national security" (see *New York Times Co.* v. *U.S.*, 403 U.S. 713, 1971—the *Pentagon Papers* case), is permissible, the Supreme Court said. In both cases, however, the Supreme Court ruled that the conditions required to permit prior restraint were *not* present. Another area where expression is regulated by the government is in the federal requirements imposed on broadcasters (see especially *Red Lion Broadcasting Co.* v. *FCC*, 395 U.S. 367, 1969, which held that enforcement of the Federal Communications Commission's now-terminated Fairness Doctrine did *not* violate broadcasters' First Amendment rights). Other examples are potential restrictions on expression that could threaten a criminal defendant's right to a fair trial, and the limits that still remain on some non-political aspects of "commercial speech" (i.e., advertising) that fall outside the First Amendment's protection.

None of these, except perhaps some of the "commercial speech" restrictions, are likely to be undone by the courts, although the Fairness Doctrine was repealed in the 1980s by the Federal Communications Commission. Such law-based ethical notions as broadcasters serving the "public interest, convenience and necessity"—required by the Communications Act of 1934, as amended by the Telecommunications Act of 1996 (47 U.S. Code)—are unlikely to be scrapped entirely, and the repeal of the Fairness Doctrine has certainly not ended an ethical allegiance to the general principle of fairness on the part of many broadcasters.

"Hate speech," discussed below, is another area where courts have upheld some restrictions as not violating First Amendment protections. Rodney Smolla (1992), a First Amendment scholar, put it very well in discussing the protections afforded hate speech under the First Amendment and the ethical balance that is needed. He noted that society should consider "the feelings of victims with humility and with respect for the integrity of their assertions" that hate speech damages them. Indeed, he wrote, the "issue is whether this pain must be endured as part of the cost of freedom of speech, or whether the actions of [hateful speakers] crossed the threshold from protected expression to unprotected infliction of harm" (Smolla, 1992, p. 168).

All of this leads to two key points: first, the short-run need to make sure that the government imposes no further limitations on freedom of expression (for you and me, as well as for the media) in the name of *mandated* responsibility—or even accountability; and, second, the longer-run need to develop the ethics-based arguments supporting a strong presumption of protection for *everyone's* freedom of expression, regardless of whether it is used responsibly.

Restrictions on freedom of expression can come from private parties as well as from the government, and these are no less dangerous to societal health if they are successful. The brief and quickly abandoned attempt in late 2007 by Verizon to prohibit an abortion rights group from sending text messages to its supporters brought immediate waves of criticism, which led to the policy reversal (Liptak). The incident occurred while the U.S. Congress and others were first considering so-called net neutrality laws, which would prohibit Internet access providers from barring messages because they disliked their content or from providing lesser levels of service to some people, again depending on factors such as whether the providers approved of the content. (See Chapter 8 for further discussion of the "net neutrality" concept.)

One final comment in regard to legal limits on free expression—I am *not* arguing that existing limitations should all be scrapped, though you might think so at times when you come to Julianne Newton's side of this discussion (see pp. 44–55). As I noted above, the legal boundaries of protected speech form the context *within which* ethical decisions must be made, and it's those boundaries that must, I believe, be protected from further encroachment. Newton's implication to the contrary, I'm not *justifying* "reckless, negligent or harmful" mass media behavior. Rather, I'm arguing that it exists despite our wishes to the contrary, and it can't be allowed to become the basis for additional restrictions on freedom of expression.

"HATEFUL SPEECH" IN THE REAL AND VIRTUAL WORLDS

Let's look at hate speech as an example of why *more* speech rather than restricting speech is the route to follow, when dealing with irresponsible uses of freedom of speech. U.S. Court rulings in hate speech cases have held that only very precise provisions prohibiting such speech in specific, narrow circumstances can overcome the First Amendment protections for speech in general. Words that present a clear threat of violence, or that involve speech on "private" topics totally removed from the arena where public issues should be debated, are among the very few types of hate speech that might properly be subject to regulation (Smolla, 1992, p. 167).

This approach differs from some other countries—Germany, for example, where there are stronger prohibitions on anti-Semitic and other hate speech. But because hate speech in the United States is (in most instances) legal, we need to come to grips with the damage that it can do to the fabric of society. And we need to consider whether there should be some sort of extra-legal mechanisms used to encourage responsibility even if it can't (or shouldn't) be enforced. As is, our general willingness to put up with it most certainly fails to discourage, much less prevent, various kinds of "hateful" speech that may be legal while still being highly offensive and perhaps damaging.

This approach, though, makes sense in regard to free expression in general, throughout a democratic society. The antidote for wrong, dangerous, or offensive speech should be *more* speech by those who disagree, rather than restrictions on the original statements. The key here is that we must be willing to provide protection even for speech that offends us, and even if that speech offends us greatly. To quote Justice Oliver Wendell Holmes's dissent in *United States* v. *Schwimmer*, we must safeguard "freedom for the thought that we hate" (279 U.S. 644, at 655, 1929) every bit as much as freedom for words we find agreeable. Or, as Massachusetts Congressman Barney Frank said much more recently, "the First Amendment protects hateful people's right to be hateful."

The antidote for wrong, dangerous, or offensive speech should be *more* speech by those who disagree,

A classic example of the complexity of trying to control hateful speech—and how that can backfire—is the 1978–79 controversy surrounding the attempts of the National Socialist Party of America (a small, Illinois-based Nazi organization) to march in the Chicago suburb of Skokie, a community with a large Jewish population, including many concentration camp survivors. The village proceeded to enact three ordinances aimed at creating conditions under which this and future requests of this type could be denied. One of the three required proof of $350,000 in liability insurance, to cover possible costs to the village if the parade led to any kind of disorder or damage. And the first group to be denied a parade permit because it couldn't post that bond? A group of Jewish war veterans who wanted to demonstrate, a few months later, *against* the Nazi group (Hamlin, 1980, pp. 77–79)!

Protecting offensive speech clearly runs counter to various contemporary efforts to deal with so-called hate speech, among them campus speech codes that aim to prohibit or punish such speech. The problems with such codes, as with all attempts to regulate "irresponsible" communication, are the questions of who gets to decide what "irresponsible" really means and what criteria can be used to provide consistency from one situation to another. The fact that linguistic and political fashions change from one generation to another further complicates the attempt to answer these questions, because what is seen as derogatory or offensive speech today may become much more acceptable a decade or two hence, much as calling one a socialist during the Cold War would have been seen as highly damaging to one's reputation, while today it's at most a very mild epithet.

Perhaps more central to this discussion is the issue of whether "hate speakers" should be given free rein on cable television's public access channels or in the various venues available on the information superhighway. The cable access issue has arisen in a number of cities, and the usual response has been to allow the hate speech to air and then seek opposing groups to provide the "more speech" antidote. One danger in this approach has been that city councils, if they don't agree with an open access policy, can cut or eliminate funding for public access channels, or simply abolish the channel, as happened in Kansas City in the late 1980s after the Ku Klux Klan—a white supremacist group—sought to use the channel.

An analysis of four cities where controversies over hate speech access erupted in the 1980s is relevant to the Internet today. That analysis demonstrated "that the most prudent, responsible, and ethical course is to permit outrageous speech and counter it with positive messages" (Harmon, 1991, p. 146). It examined ethical theory and concluded that approaches suggested by John Milton's *Areopagitica*, John Stuart Mill's espousal of the societal benefits of doctrinal competition, "the 'free expression as utilitarian' view espoused by David Hume" (Harmon, 1991, p. 152), John Locke's social contract approach, and John Rawls's distributive justice theory all supported the "more speech" remedy to this problem. So, I would add, does the "free marketplace of ideas" concept inherent in the social responsibility model for the mass media.

As Harmon (1991, p. 153) concluded: "regardless of whether one views free expression as a natural right, a utilitarian tool, or a component of the social contract, one comes to exactly the same conclusion about the [Ku Klux Klan's] use of cable access."

In other words, hateful speech should not be restricted because it too is entitled to the freedom guaranteed by the First Amendment. And even hateful speech may contribute in some marginal ways to the dialogue necessary for an informed, democratic society. But it should most certainly be countered by opposing viewpoints in a marketplace of ideas that remains open even to hateful ideas.

If this is the best solution to hate speech on cable access channels, it also will be the best approach to combating irresponsible use of freedom of expression wherever it occurs in the mass media (or more generally throughout society, although that's a broader discussion than is appropriate here). If freedom of expression is zealously guarded for everyone, it is available for the speech we agree with as well as for speech we find offensive. And it will help safeguard society—and us—by having hateful ideas out in the open rather than forcing them to fester underground because they can't get access to media channels.

Hate speech, though, has the capability of running rampant on the Internet far more than on public access TV, potentially regulated only by federal law and—on moderated lists or chat rooms—by the criteria set up in regard to participation (if they are enforced). Bloggers may or may not feel constrained to avoid speech that others will find hateful; those that are under the umbrella of a news organization or a similar entity can be reined in by the organization's guidelines, but independent unaffiliated bloggers can spout hateful language freely, if they choose. But they can also be countered by others who have access to the various cyberspace forums where such blogs appear.

This "more speech" approach is going to do less damage in the long run, on the Internet as elsewhere, than trying to craft restrictions that are narrow enough to avoid the risk of also preventing speech that is relevant (even if only in peripheral ways) to a self-governing society. There is some logic behind attempts to prohibit patently "obscene" speech (however the courts define that term) on the Internet, especially where children are concerned, but in other situations I'd argue that attempts to make communication on the Internet more "responsible" by prohibiting certain kinds of content are, themselves, inherently unethical. That's equally important whether the prohibitions are mandated by the government or by private parties and countenanced by the government. The latter possibility is why the net neutrality legislation mentioned elsewhere in the book is so important.

This "more speech" approach is not likely to sit well with people who are concerned about "responsible" behavior on the Internet, which they see as having fairly minimal controls—not to mention the minimal inhibitions that sometimes show up there. But I believe it makes sense here in the same way that I suggested it does in regard to public access channels—that "more speech" rather than restrictions should be the answer. The Internet, after all, is a platform that's open to anyone with access to a computer and the knowledge to erect a "soapbox" in cyberspace, and hateful speech can be answered fairly easily and, equally important, in the cyberspace forum where it occurred.

SOME FURTHER CONSIDERATIONS

If the "more speech" remedy is the best way to deal with hate speech on cable access channels and the Internet, it seems logical that it is also the best approach to combating irresponsible use of freedom of expression wherever it occurs. It is worth stressing again that, if freedom of expression is zealously guarded for everyone, it is available for the speech we agree with as well as for speech we find offensive. That is a necessary safeguard for a self-governing society.

This approach also protects each of us individually, if those in power find *our* ideas offensive or hateful. It's well worth recalling that such political and social movements as abolition, women's suffrage, civil rights, and opposition to the Vietnam and Iraq wars all started out as unpopular positions within the body politic. Had those in power been able to suppress the upstart opposition, American history would be vastly different.

When political positions, ideas, or social philosophies clash, as Mill would point out, the only way to modify "erroneous" ideas short of force or violence is to subject them to the test of competing opinions. Mill would also note that even the most wrongheaded ideas may have a grain of truth in them, and that grain will be lost if they are silenced. In other words, we must rely on the guarantees of the First Amendment, forbidding government interference—even to mandate "responsibility," as Newton (and Glasser) would do—so that we can come, sooner or later, to an appropriate societal consensus forged from unfettered, robust, and wide-open discussion and debate. Newton's contention that we can protect free expression while also facilitating responsible expression is true to some degree, but there are times when we have to choose between freedom and responsibility. Favoring one over the other always has trade-offs. But when push comes to shove, I have to come down on the side of freedom and take my chances with responsibility simply because people can't choose to be responsible without the freedom to make that choice.

In the second half of this chapter, you will see that Newton is concerned about the "more speech" formula because not everyone has equal access to mass media or equal expressive ability. There's not much that can be done about the latter, but the former concern can be dealt with by increasing the channels that are available for expression—public access TV channels and access to the Internet, among other possibilities. As to the idea of everyone attending to everyone else's ideas, that's beyond what's possible even in an ideal society.

I certainly would encourage various efforts (including education) to convince people—in the traditional media, on public access channels and online—to act responsibly. But if they choose not to do so, I believe that a utilitarian perspective works best for a democratic society. Some people or groups within the society may be damaged by various kinds of "irresponsible" speech, but this is one of the prices that utilitarianism requires that we pay in order to achieve the greatest benefit for the society as a whole.

Followers of John Rawls would disagree, and argue that those most directly attacked by hate speech are the people most in need of protection. They would be willing to scale back the First Amendment in order to provide that protection, thereby sacrificing at least some of the freedom necessary for an open and informed society, in order to protect the relatively few victims of hate speech. Utilitarians, by contrast, would preserve the First Amendment freedoms that benefit us all in both the short and long runs, at the short-term expense of the victims of hate or other irresponsible speech.

In the last analysis, this is one situation where Kant's categorical imperative is worth following if we believe in the benefits of absolute freedom of expression. Even stopping short of espousing an absolutist position, we could frame a general proposition that freedom of expression should be protected regardless of whether it is used responsibly or irresponsibly. Using a rule utilitarian approach, we can argue that giving the widest possible latitude to freedom of expression will, on balance and in the long run, always produce the greatest amount of good and perhaps even "happiness" for the greatest number of people in the society. I believe this is true whether one focuses on the news media, whether one is concerned with the legal and ethical dimensions of entertainment content, advertising or public relations materials, or whether one is dealing with broader issues such as hate speech.

British ethicist H. L. A. Hart (1963) argued that it is not morally desirable to legislate ethical behavior:

> The use of legal punishment to freeze into immobility the morality dominant at a particular time in a society's existence may possibly succeed, but even where it does it contributes nothing to the survival of the animating spirit and formal values of social morality and may do much to harm them.
>
> (Hart, 1963, p. 72)

In other words, enforcing responsible communication behavior ("morality," in Hart's terms) may well not succeed. Even if it does, such enforcement may damage both the underlying value of free expression and the societal change it can help bring about. Mill would support the latter argument, in his concern that any moment's "truth" should continually be tested rather than allowed to become unchallenged dogma.

American ethicist Deni Elliott (1987) argued that First Amendment freedom is an inadequate basis for defining media responsibility. The law, she wrote, is "problematic as a basis for moral responsibilities because one cannot derive duties from rights" (Elliott, 1987,

p. 7). In other words—Theodore Glasser's arguments to the contrary—we cannot use protected rights of expression to impose duties and responsibilities on a speaker without risking serious damage to those protected rights.

Let's take an example from the news realm—the 2006 publication by several newspapers of stories exposing a secret government program to "monitor the financial transactions of terror suspects" ("Story on secret program. . . .", 2006) I hope I have convinced you that the papers had to be left free to make their choices, whether you consider their decisions to be unwise and damaging to national security, or ethical and necessary for an informed society. Or, think for a moment about whether or not it's irresponsible for the entertainment industry to produce programming that unreasonably invades people's privacy, or makes them look ridiculous. And go back to the example in the introduction to this chapter, of the anti-abortion ad that is likely to offend greatly the sensibilities of a lot of people while succeeding in getting the attention of the audience. I hope you'll agree that government should let these industries make their own decisions on such matters rather than trying to define and mandate "responsibility," thus leaving to the public the final decision on whether to pay attention.

The important issue for our purposes is to protect free expression as fully as possible. An Aristotelian balance between freedom and responsibility will not work here. If freedom is used irresponsibly (immorally, in Hart's terms), we can certainly use our own freedom of expression to argue for more responsibility, in either the news or the entertainment and persuasion sectors of the media. But we may well fatally threaten our own freedom of speech, as in the Skokie march example noted earlier, if we try to legislate or otherwise impose what we consider to be ethical, responsible communication standards as part of our traditional freedom of expression.

KEY POINTS

- People can't choose to act responsibly without the *freedom* to make that change.
- The antidote for "wrong" or dangerous or hateful speech should be a Kantian or rule utilitarian approach supporting *more* speech (and access to channels through which to deliver it effectively), *not* restrictions on speech.
- Restrictions on "the thought we hate" are very hard to craft narrowly enough to prevent their impinging—down the road—on expression that we would agree with.

NEWTON: Freedom of expression cannot be allowed to become an excuse for irresponsible media conduct—in news, entertainment, public relations or advertising.

When early humans developed ways to communicate consciously, they probably were more concerned about food, shelter and impending danger than whether they were free to express themselves as they wished. Nevertheless, their lives depended on how they responded to each other and to their environments.

We 21st-century humans would do well to acknowledge that our lives also depend on how we communicate. As a species, we evolved the ability to integrate and express intuitive and rational mental processes to formulate wise decisions about how best to live our lives—individually and collectively. And as 21st-century participants in a world with global communication capabilities, we have more resources for large-scale and wide-reaching communication than preceding generations.

I agree with David Gordon's core position that free expression must be "zealously defended." However, I also believe that almost anything—including the defense of free expression—can be taken to such an extreme that it actually negates its original purpose. As Veronica A. Shoffstall (1971) wrote, "After a while you learn that even sunshine burns if you get too much." My point is that people—and the messages and media systems they create—sometimes fall back on the principle of freedom of expression to excuse their bad behavior rather than take responsibility for the consequences their behavior engenders. Support of ethical and responsible conduct in the development and dissemination of media messages must be core to the determination of what is and is not protected as free expression. Unethical and irresponsible conduct is not acceptable in media messaging. However, the concept "cannot be allowed" requires careful consideration and substantively differs from wholesale advocacy of legal restrictions against free expression.

A BIG-PICTURE PERSPECTIVE

One way to gain perspective on the proposition that "freedom of expression cannot be allowed to become an excuse for irresponsible media conduct" is to place it within the contexts of everyday life and the long-term sustainability of our species and planet. Mass-mediated communication begins and ends with individuals. In everyday life, we communicate with friends, family, acquaintances and even strangers in face-to-face encounters through one-on-one or group interaction, through handwritten letters via snail mail, and through such electronic technologies as phones, e-mail and social networks in cyberspace. The quality of those communications varies according to our individual physiological and psychological abilities to interact meaningfully with others, the amount of time and thought each of us contributes, and the extent to which we consider the potential positive or negative effects of our communications.

Parallels can be drawn between individual communication and community, national and global levels of communication across mass-mediated news, entertainment and persuasive genres. In a packed movie theater one person shouting "Fire!" can incite panic among hundreds of people, perhaps injuring many as they flee in panic. An example that is more than hypothetical is Orson Welles's 1938 radio adaptation of H. G. Wells's *War of the Worlds*, which incited reactions ranging from alarm to panic in the minds of many listeners. The potential benefits and consequences of our communications expand with geographic and temporal boundaries. For example, an international audience watching the Super Bowl perceives a carefully constructed image of American might and wealth, an image that overflows entertainment boundaries and creates lasting images and perceptions of reality that guide future behavior and opinion beyond U.S. borders.

In theory, it is tempting to argue simply that each of us should communicate—whether individually or collectively, interpersonally or via mass media—in ways that do no harm. An ethical idealist might argue that individuals should not lie or say hurtful things to one another, that news magazines should not use misleading computer-manipulated images on their covers, that movie producers should not make films that model violent actions, or that television advertisers should not use enhanced visuals that misrepresent reality to entice viewers to buy products. One also can argue that communication, as a broadly conceived human activity, should enhance our lives individually and collectively while doing no harm.

> In theory, it is tempting to argue simply that each of us should communicate . . . in ways that do no harm.

Of course, "shoulds" do not always translate into "doings." We do not live in an ideal world. We live in a real world in which real people help and harm, attend to and ignore one another. So, how do we protect the ideal of free expression by encouraging responsible free expression without undermining the very concept we want to protect—freedom?

DEFINITIONS

Let's define key concepts to make sure you're reading and interpreting the words the way I am in this chapter.

Freedom is the core concept for which we need to establish meaning—and the most problematic. In the United States, freedom is associated with the "right to life, liberty and the pursuit of happiness." In the Western tradition, discussions of free will, or the ability, without restriction, to choose for oneself how one should live and act, have occupied great philosophical and legal minds for more than 2,000 years. In Eastern traditions, freedom often encompasses inner enlightenment, a state of existence one can reach regardless of external physical or legal circumstances, and responsibility to community. On the other hand, in both Western and Eastern traditions, the idea of freedom can threaten personal and societal security. One might argue, for example, that a society without laws or restrictions to insure a basic level of general safety would lead to a state of untenable chaos. Without traffic lights at busy intersections, navigating city streets would be far more dangerous than it already is. Traffic lights regulate comings and goings so people take turns moving through intersections. If we ignore a red light and speed through an intersection, because we believe we should be free to do so, we risk getting a ticket or worse—physically harming ourselves or others. So we agree to restrict our freedom of expression—using "driving" as a metaphor for "expression"—to establish laws that facilitate order and safety.

People still are "free" to disobey, but consequences discourage the likelihood that people will disobey. Does this same line of reasoning apply to other forms of expression? Must we agree, for example, to restrict free speech to decrease the likelihood that the language we use does no harm?

Expression refers to the outward conveyance of information, ideas or sending forth of thoughts, emotions and behaviors beyond the mind (through expressive gesture and other actions) into the air, onto paper or canvas, through the Internet, or by any other means, including all forms of mass media. Yet communication does not necessarily occur each time we express ourselves. Communication, or shared meaning, requires a degree of reception, interpretation and understanding of an expressed message.

Freedom of expression, then, is quite complex. Do we refer to the ability to say or do whatever we want in the interest of self-fulfillment and inalienable rights? Or do we refer to the ability to explore our ideas and interests without restriction as long as we are not harming someone? Does that someone include oneself?

Believing in absolute freedom of expression, with no accountability, could mean we believe it is acceptable to lie and to defame someone for personal gain. Gordon advocates more expression to counter expression with which we disagree. Yet research indicates that negative press, advertising and rumor, even if quickly and publicly proven untruthful through more expression, can permanently damage a political candidate or other individual.

Consider the example of the Swift Boat Veterans versus presidential candidate John Kerry during the 2004 campaign. No amount of "more expression" and positive discourse—including multiple publications in major newspapers, news magazines and television news broadcasts—will erase the doubt about Kerry's military heroism planted in some voters' minds by misleading and erroneous political ads. In a controlled experiment of reader perception, Zillmann et al. (1999) determined that one-sided photographs result in distorted reader memory of news items, even when the one-sided photographs were published alongside accurate and balanced verbal reports.

Although libel and slander laws cannot entirely discourage people from intentionally trying to hurt others with untrue statements, they at least provide a framework for protecting most individuals against malicious verbal and visual attacks in news media and beyond. So, we have learned that legal penalties that restrict free expression sometimes are necessary to guide responsible exercise of free press and speech and to protect individuals and the broader public from false information. Restrictions on certain types of advertising fall into a similar category.

Let's define other terms in our proposition. The meaning of *allow* seems straight-forward: "permit" or "tolerate." Yet those terms are passive, and an effective democracy requires active participation. Active interpretations of the term allow are "agree to" or "consent to." So, if we knowingly allow something to happen, in theory, we are agreeing that it is acceptable. A friend once asked me—as we sat quietly in front of a campfire—"Isn't doing nothing doing something?" Realistically, however, it is not within the power of every individual to prevent all actions he or she believes should not occur. The important point for our discussion is that individual and group expression—and non-expression (as a form of expression)—can effect change in ways that both enhance and harm.

An *excuse* is a reason or explanation. Again, however, a more active interpretation of the concept "excuse" is "pretext" or "justification" for behavior. Saying a behavior is excused can mean we are willing to accept that behavior for a particular reason regardless of whether our decision is justified in the sense that the behavior enhances rather than harms.

Irresponsible carries a similar range of implications. Dictionaries include "immature," "careless" and "foolish" in the definition of irresponsible, implying a lesser degree of culpability that can more easily be forgiven than can deliberate intention. On the other end of the definitional continuum are the words "reckless" and "negligent," which imply a degree of wrongful, often aware and potentially harmful behavior.

Media are environments through which signals are conveyed. Each medium has characteristics that influence the signal conveyed via that environment. In everyday use, the word *media* often refers to mass media, which convey messages to varying numbers of people. One problem with discussing "mass media" is that people often think of them as organizations and corporations—vague "its" or "theys" "out there" somewhere that somehow send us content of all forms. It is important to remember that mass media are comprised of groups of individuals who own the organizations and corporations, gather and produce content, and disseminate content to a variety of users in a variety of forms. These individuals are capable of being responsible in ways that enhance rather than harm and they can be held accountable for their actions. Also important to remember is that the Internet makes possible mass communication by a wider range of individuals—both professional and non-professional—than ever. Anyone who can access the Internet can distribute content of almost any variety to global audiences.

The proposition we are exploring in this half of the chapter characterizes media by their functions, or "purposes": news (information), entertainment (amusement) and persuasion (influence). Each function can be fulfilled via a number of media, ranging from signs to newspapers to television and the Internet. The functions also overlap. Advertising can inform and entertain in the service of influencing consumption. News can entertain as it informs and influences opinion. Entertainment can inform and influence behavior as it evokes pleasure. Consider, for example, the Oscar-winning film *Philadelphia* (1993), which not only entertained millions of people but also informed them about the AIDs crisis—and helped bring AIDs to the forefront of the public agenda, thus influencing opinion and possibly behavior. The popularity of blogs and online publications has expanded the ability for anyone to write and publish about almost anything.

Conduct refers to behavior—the performance of actions and deeds.

So, where are we, now that we have clarified meanings and use of concepts? We might restate the proposition in the following way. *The fact that we value and protect free expression does not justify reckless, negligent or harmful behavior by practitioners of media communication.* I believe in this interpretation of the proposition with which we began. It suggests that there may be a place for carefully considered guidelines that encourage socially responsible expression and discourage socially irresponsible expression by media.

GORDON'S ARGUMENT

Here are the key points I take from Gordon's discussion:

1   Freedom of expression primarily refers to free speech and press.
2   Limiting free speech and press threatens democracy.
3   Irresponsible use of freedom is unethical.
4   Having the government try to enforce ethical speech and press conduct will not succeed (because there always will be some people who will find ways to abuse freedoms) and will cause more damage than good (because it limits those who are ethical as well as those who are unethical).
5   The best response to unethical expression is more expression by those who disagree.
6   Balancing freedom and responsibility will not work because we should not use rights to impose responsibilities.

Let me address Gordon's line of reasoning. Freedom of expression takes many forms. The First Amendment to the U.S. Constitution protects the forms of expression known as religion, speech, press, assembly and petition by requiring that "Congress shall make no law" abridging those freedoms. Through the years since 1791, when the first ten amendments (the Bill of Rights) were enacted, U.S. courts have extended the meaning of the term "Congress" to include the federal government and the states. The courts also have extended what we might normally consider "speech" to include activities such as flag burning. The issues are so complex that even First Amendment scholars have found them perplexing.

I believe that individual free expression is central to this discussion. Individuals create and perceive the expressions conveyed by media. The range of media—especially new media—increasingly facilitate individual expression through participation in media expression. Even a mass audience of viewers, readers and users is comprised of individuals who perceive and potentially respond to mediated messages, which emphasizes the importance of individual free expression.

Does freedom of expression also extend to sexual freedom, clothing, dance and art, burning the flag, gestures, smoking in public places, telling or showing lies in advertisements, praying in public, or luring children into dangerous encounters via Internet personae? An absolutist might say "yes" to all of these expressive forms. However, Gordon rightly notes policies and court rulings that regulate publications that are obscene, incite violence or threaten national security, threaten an individual's right to fair trial, use false "commercial speech" or inflict harm through "hate speech." Some of these policies and court rulings that do limit freedom of expression are excellent examples of the "responsible" conduct I support. Others, as Gordon also notes, raise problems even as they try to solve problems. That potential, in turn, leads Gordon to assert that "freedom of expression should be protected regardless of whether it is used responsibly or irresponsibly."

As a general principle, Gordon's assertion makes sense—especially in a society that values differences of opinion as a path to ultimately wise and well-informed decision-making for the majority of those in that society. However, when I weigh my deeply held passion for free expression against equally deep passions for respecting others and for socially responsible citizenship that does no harm, I conclude that democracy is better served with carefully considered guidelines for responsible conduct. Indeed, a number of the regulations that Gordon describes are such guidelines. Furthermore, contrary to his suggestion that I favor silencing unpopular opinion, I favor free and open expression, regardless of its popularity. Key to my argument, however, are the concepts of *responsibility* and *accountability*.

At this point more clarification of terms will help. By *ethics*, I refer both to the study of right and wrong and "to the human pursuit of a beneficent life" (Newton, 2004, p. 433). Right generally is associated with "correct" or "good." Wrong generally is associated with "incorrect" or "bad." Beneficent refers to helpful. (Its opposite, maleficent, refers to "harmful.") The problem, as Gordon notes, is determining who gets to set the standard for right and wrong? What happens if one person's "right" is another person's "wrong"?

An example of this dilemma is whether news media should publish the name of a rape victim. Although it generally is legal to do so, traditional policy in many news organizations prohibits publishing names in such circumstances. The policies were created in order to avoid doing more harm to the victim, someone many people consider vulnerable and in need of protection from embarrassment, shame or reprisal—which might further victimize the already-harmed individual. One feminist-based argument, however, states that rape is a crime of violence rather than a sexual act and that not naming someone who was raped implies the victim has indeed been shamed by what happened, thus further victimizing and disempowering that individual. Another argument, one that influenced the *Winston-Salem* (NC) *Journal* to enact its long-standing policy of naming rape victims, stressing fairness to the person accused of the crime. (This topic is discussed further in Chapter 10.) In this example, then, one person's "good" is another person's "bad." The point of such policies—whichever way they go—is that those who run the newspaper organizations weigh the plusses and minuses of naming rape victims and determine policy based on careful thought about potential consequences. That is responsible free expression.

Ethics, which usually refers to high standards for living one's life, often forms the basis for laws establishing safety within and among groups of individuals: as a general principle, killing another person is considered wrong and is against the law. Yet killing someone in self-defense or as an act of war can be a legal act. In a democratic society, people elect government officials to help make laws. Laws are regulations, usually with clearly stated consequences for violating them, that in effect become minimum standards for living in that society, rather than higher codes for living. Laws have to be obeyed or disobeyed.

Ethics, on the other hand, can be innate, cultivated, discovered and chosen. Cognitive neuroscientist Michael Gazzaniga (2005) argues that we "instinctively react to events," that our brains interpret our reactions, and "out of that interpretation, beliefs emerge about rules to live by." He adds, "Sometimes they have a moral character; sometimes they have an utterly practical nature" (Gazzaniga, 2005, pp. 144–145). The First Amendment is itself a rule that emerged out of the nation's founders' reactions to their experiences, their interpretations of those reactions, and the beliefs that emerged.

I agree with Gordon that ethics cannot be enforced through laws. However, to some extent, the responsibility that supports ethical behavior can be encouraged, if we define responsibility as answerability or accountability. And ethical behavior can be encouraged or discouraged by policies and guidelines that stimulate discussion and educate about potential consequences. When news organizations weigh consequences of publishing or not publishing the names of rape victims, and subsequently adopt formal policy, they encourage responsibility and accountability among their staffs and the reading community. Similar considerations have led to the formulation of policies about the posting of comments concerning online stories.

Consider the free-speech dilemma of deciding whether to publish information that police prefer to keep out of the public eye? Melinda Kletzok (2008), public information office for the Eugene (Oregon) police department, described a situation in which a local television station obtained exclusive information about a widely publicized crime. The station had the legal right to scoop other Eugene stations by airing the information in its evening newscast. Yet the station made an ethical decision against airing the information—because it agreed with the police's contention that doing so would tip off the perpetrators and impede investigation. Airing the information would have been irresponsible—and the station decided not to use the First Amendment as an excuse for doing so.

> The First Amendment protects free expression even as it restrains government. By enacting [it], we, as a democracy, assumed responsibility for protecting freedom of expression.

Following this line of reasoning, we might argue that the First Amendment, as a legal document, is grounded in ethics and assigns responsibility. It defines perimeters beyond which our government may not extend itself, establishing a prohibition against laws abridging free expression. In Gordon's words, this keeps "the regulatory camel" from getting "its nose into the tent of free expression." Yet the First Amendment is itself a regulation that requires "the regulatory camel to get its nose into the tent" in order to protect freedom of expression. The First Amendment protects free expression even as it restrains government. By enacting the amendment, we, as a democracy, assumed responsibility for protecting freedom of expression. See where this leads? We began our system of government with a mandate restraining that same government in order to insure freedom. Is it so big a leap to consider that guidelines may be needed in order to make sure free expression itself is not abused under the guise of protecting that very freedom?

Some may call this argument tautological, meaning it comes back on itself and is therefore invalid. I do not see it that way at all. I usually do not support either/or oppositions. Issues seldom are clearly right or wrong: they are dynamic, with nuances and complexities that do not have absolutely right or wrong resolutions. In other words, we can protect free expression while also facilitating responsible expression.

Note that the proposition with which we began this half chapter uses the phrase "cannot be allowed. " To me, the use of that phrase does not mean that we should enact laws and regulations to limit free expression. Rather, it means that we who hold truly free expression dear must create ways to facilitate responsible and beneficent expression and communication and to discourage irresponsible and harmful expression. It is a matter of ethics and responsible citizenship. Here, Gordon and I agree.

But what about Gordon's position that the best response to unethical expression is more expression by those who disagree? That works quite well in an ideal society in which, first, everyone has equal power, equal access to media for expression, and equal expressive ability; second, everyone waits his/her turn to "express;" and third, everyone attends to everyone else with equal, fair, truthful and respectful consideration. As I noted earlier, and as Gordon notes, we live in a real world, not an ideal one, although it often is tempting to live in media worlds rather than corporeal worlds.

Nevertheless, the fact that humans have not yet succeeded—though some have tried—in establishing such a society is a specious rationale for dismissing the value of contemplating and working toward such a society as a goal in the quest of freedom. On the contrary, it is unethical—especially given the existence of countries such as the United States with its bountiful resources—to accept a laissez-faire perspective about free expression. Those who hold financial, social, political, institutional and physical resources too often dominate discourse, not only in the United States but also in other countries. In particular, those given legislative, judicial and policy-making power in a democratic society have responsibilities to those they represent and govern, including those whose voices are drowned out by the more powerful. One can also make an ethical argument that those who "have" should share with those who do not. An example of individuals seeking to correct the imbalance of access to computers and the Internet—and thus the imbalance of voices—is MIT Prof. Nicholas Negroponte's One Laptop Per Child Project, which gives laptop computers to children in developing countries. The project's educational goal is "to provide children around the world with new opportunities to explore, experiment and express themselves" (One Laptop Per Child, 2008). Leaving the children's participation in the global dialogue to chance would essentially bar them from exercising free expression in cyberspace and be a grossly irresponsible misuse of freedom of expression as an excuse to do nothing.

An example of responsible media conduct is the Canadian Film Board's Filmmaker-in-Residence program. One project seeks to help pregnant homeless teens improve their lives by putting cameras in the girls' hands. Given wider and more powerful voice via media technology and distribution through the Internet and exhibitions, the girls have gained access to the public and to political leaders who can help mobilize support systems.

A nuanced but significant point regarding these two examples is important here. In the first example, good intentions have not always resulted in good consequences. The introduction of laptops to a few children in a community shifts family hierarchies in unpredicted and sometimes negative ways. The laptops usually go to the oldest child, who gets to go to school, leaving younger children behind. One has to ask, however, should those few children not gain voice via access because all children are not given access?

In the second example, a key to the program's success is empowerment of individual girls to communicate with one another as well as with public audiences. Stories that would not be told to outside adults are told to peers with cameras, thus enriching the depth and validity (and thus the freer the expression) of the visual and verbal information exchanged and disseminated.

Finally, I disagree with Gordon's last point—that we cannot derive responsibilities out of rights. I believe rights encompass responsibilities. Rights empower those to whom they are extended. Rights make freedom possible—and rights can be abused, as the proposition at the head of this half chapter argues. Rights deserve to be protected through responsible use; irresponsible use of rights often results in the opposite of freedom: loss of rights.

SO, WHAT DO WE DO?

Although absolute freedom of expression may be a right that people value and desire, absolute freedom can be akin to absolute power. Without checks on power—and carefully considered guidelines for responsible exercise of freedom—we are neither free nor powerful. We have to be free to say "No" before we are truly free to say "Yes."

Is there any such thing as completely "free expression"? Do you tell your significant other, always, what you think about his or her hair or lovemaking? Do you always tell the rude person behind you in line what you think? Do you always strike out verbally at someone you really want to hurt, or yell at the police officer who has just stopped you for speeding, or picket your boss's office because you feel you've not been dealt with fairly?

Gordon probably would argue that even though the above scenarios present situations in which people are less likely to express themselves freely, protecting free expression means still having the right to say exactly what you want, even if it is irresponsible to do so and regardless of the consequences. The issue, for me, is that humankind has come a long way since we developed conscious means of expressing (and not expressing) ourselves. Even though we still are capable of barbaric behavior, we have learned to value civility, a characteristic of interaction based on mutual respect and good will, rather than on purely self-fulfilling behavior. In fact, well-considered civility can be in an individual's and society's best interest because it can help prevent unwise statements and actions that might be harmful or even threaten life.

Power and freedom can go both ways—toward those who are reasonable and good and toward those who are not. Aristotle and Confucius carry the day for me. For Aristotle, the best path was to seek the middle ground between extremes, a principle he called the Doctrine of the Mean. "Every knowledgeable person avoids excess and deficiency, but looks for the mean and chooses it," Aristotle wrote in his *Nicomachean Ethics*, Book Two (*circa* fourth century B.C.E., 1106a20–b9, p. 100 in Tredennick, ed.). In regard to "self-expression," Aristotle posited "Truthfulness" as the mean between "Boastfulness" and "Understatement." Confucians believe that humans are relational beings and that respecting one's community in the interest of the common good is key to living a good life. This communal-based understanding of rights includes the "duty to speak frankly when the violation of propriety and justice is in question," writes Confucian ethicist David B. Wong (2004, p. 35). Wong argues for "the interdependence of [individually grounded] rights and community" (2004, p. 33)

Also following the wisdom of Alexis de Tocqueville, Wong (2004) stresses "the dangers of an atomistic individualism that leaves citizens isolated, pursuing their purely private interests, and quite ineffective in making their voices heard in the political sphere because their voices are single." The consequence "is not enough community . . . to support effective democracy" (Wong, 2004, pp. 41 and 42). Another way to think about this point of view is that if we say anything at any time, we may relate to no one. Moderation and compromise encourage us to consider both possibilities and consequences, while also attending to core principles in which we believe—such as freedom of expression. Conversely, strict adherence to principle or duty (deontological ethics) at the expense of goal or consequence (teleological ethics) too easily results in absolutist positions that may be neither ethically congruent nor tenable.

Gordon applies utilitarianism and the categorical imperative to support his position. I favor the theory of universal ethics proposed by media ethicist Clifford Christians, who grounds his argument in "the sacredness of human life" as a universal value, or protonorm, that "will either flourish or whither," depending on individual and group action (Christians, 2005, p. 12). Christians writes: "The ethics of human sacredness is a people's manifesto, calling us to fulfill our duty to honor life, while insisting with credibility that the big-time media symbol-makers and government elite fulfill their specialized obligations too" (Christians, 2005, p. 12). In this way individuals, both alone and collectively, move beyond the norms of specific cultures and nations to embrace a sustainable ethic that enhances life. And media act in socially responsible ways.

To address our core proposition—that "freedom of expression cannot be allowed to become an excuse for irresponsible media conduct"—I have developed a four-track, integrative model that facilitates ethical decision-making about issues related to free expression. The model reviews the purposes, platforms, practices and potentials of expressive conduct and supports ethical expression and communication:

1   Consider the *purpose* of a particular expression to understand intentions and motivations. Why is someone saying this? Why might they be feeling this way? What thinking might be behind this expressive action?
2   Examine the *platform* of an expression to become aware of the potential audience for, as well as the form of, the expression. Who is likely to view, hear or read this expression? Will the form keep the expression among a few individuals or will it be conveyed around the world?
3   Review *practices* to comprehend the process of creating the message form and its content. How was this expression determined? Is there a more responsible way to express this message and convey it to those who need to hear it?
4   Envision *potentials* to focus attention on possible or probable effects or consequences of conveying an expression. What might happen if I say this? Will it hurt or help someone? Is the hurt justified because it will help others? To what extent will this message harm someone and is it worth the harm?

Applying the model to the Skokie scenario described in Gordon's half of the chapter offers an excellent example of how the model will help prevent implementing a harmful policy without fully considering the range of issues.

- *Purpose:* Did Skokie leaders want to protect their community from physical damage and violence, or did they want to stop the Nazi group? Did the Nazi group want to express its opinion through lawful assembly, incite violence or make a point about free expression?
- *Platform:* Was the platform the Nazi group chose one of effective expression, or one calculated to cause pain and distress?
- *Practices:* Did the Nazi group determine the most effective means for conveying its message? Was this an issue of free expression or of intent to harm? Did the community leaders determine the most effective means for handling a potentially violent situation?

- *Potentials:* Did the Nazi group consider the consequences of inciting hatred toward themselves by expressing hatred for others? Did the community leaders consider the consequences of setting policy that would prevent all those without financial resources from marching in their community?

Applying the model to an ethical dilemma such as the Skokie march requires only that we evaluate to the fullest extent possible how each component might be addressed while honoring universal ethics and social responsibility. The model requires no laws or regulations. It does, however, require education about the nature of human communication, free expression and ethical decision-making, and it requires implementation through the exercise of free expression. "Not allowing" irresponsible conduct can be as simple as changing the channel or as complex as beginning a campaign to change the dominant content of a local television station—or challenge a court ruling. The more we carefully consider purposes, platforms, processes and potentials, the more likely we are to hold ourselves—and others—accountable.

IN CONCLUSION

Humans evolved expressive abilities as part of their means of survival. In a world in which differences sometimes outweigh similarities, we need every form of expression we can muster in order to understand one another. It is important to remember, however, that one reason we have survived and evolved as a species is because we also evolved the capacity for knowing when and how best to express what we think and feel. Our conscious and nonconscious reactions to events and ideas and subsequent interpretations of our reactions are the very thoughts and feelings that lead us to express ourselves—for good or for bad.

Make no mistake: I am passionate about protecting freedom of expression. Gordon and I agree more than we disagree. Indeed, free expression must be zealously protected as a fundamental right in what First Amendment scholar Prof. Kyu Ho Youm terms the "great laboratory of experiment" that is the United States (personal communication, November 3, 2007). However, it took legal action in the form of a constitutional amendment restraining government to guarantee the freedom to experiment with open expression. It takes legal action to protect private individuals from the publication of damaging lies and to protect children from Internet stalkers. We need guidelines that facilitate socially responsible citizenship—by individuals and mass media alike.

We must remember that individuals create, compose and act as the government, and individuals create and consume media and their content. Individual disagreement, civil disobedience, codes of ethics, policies and regulations all have their place in protecting our freedom of expression. Freedom itself is an ethic the United States agreed to support, a right through which we seek to accomplish the democratic goal of equality for all.

We owe it to the ethic of freedom to protect free expression by exercising our right responsibly.

KEY POINTS

- Unethical and irresponsible conduct is not acceptable in media messaging, and unlimited freedom can threaten personal and societal security.
- Laws are regulations that in effect become minimum standards for living in a society, rather than higher (ethics) codes for living.
- By enacting the First Amendment, we assumed the responsibility to protect freedom of expression, and to restrain our government in order to insure that freedom. We need guidelines to make sure that free expression is not abused under the guise of protecting it.
- Following Aristotle's "middle ground" approach and Christians' (2005) theory of universal ethics, we can protect free expression while also facilitating responsible expression.

MERRILL: Commentary

What a great chapter to begin this book of controversies! Both David Gordon and Julianne Newton have pulled out all the stops in defending their positions. Their presentations are solid, well-written, articulate, and thought-provoking. This is perhaps the most complex—and basic—topic that a book about ethics can confront. The authors have done it well.

But, sad to say, they have left the question open. No satisfactory answer—at least not a simple, direct one—is given by either. However, this is a perennial dialectic—freedom versus responsibility—that has troubled philosophers throughout the ages. It lies at the very foundation of ethics. We must be free in order to be responsible—or at least to aspire to responsibility. But this very freedom opens the door to unethical actions or irresponsibility.

Gordon takes more the radical libertarian position on this controversial issue. It is the position I prefer, although I realize that it permits ethical misbehavior. It puts the onus directly on the ethical agent whose freedom propels him or her into an existential personal commitment.

A more moderate—and perhaps more rational—position is taken by Newton, whose controlled-freedom position supports the legacy of Plato. Or, as she says, the legacy of Confucius or Aristotle. At any rate she contends that freedom of expression cannot be allowed as an excuse for irresponsible media action. Freely determined media expression that is irresponsible simply is not acceptable. Period. She does recognize that freedom is "the core concept" and the most problematic. Freedom is certainly problematic, but for me it is no more troublesome than "responsibility." In fact, if one does not denude "freedom" from its pure meaning, it is actually a very meaningful concept. Responsibility, on the other hand, is subjective and relative and, in any context, filled with powerful semantic noise.

Gordon comes close here to being a freedom purist, a strict libertarian. For him, freedom of expression is to be protected *even when exercised unethically*. That's a strong statement.

It finds an uncomfortable spot in a book like this one—on ethics. But not really—not for the libertarian who sees freedom as anterior to, and more important than, ethics. Saying one is for freedom is not the same as saying that one is against ethics. In the U.S. context, Gordon notes that the First Amendment requires a free press but not a responsible one. Responsibility, says Gordon, must be left to the press itself.

Quoting Theodore Glasser (1986), Gordon invokes what is often called "positive freedom"—freedom to accomplish something. So, says Glasser, freedom *requires* something of the agent: to accomplish something. This view Gordon rejects, as do I. If I am an editor and I want to "sit on my freedom," doing nothing positive, then so be it. Freedom includes the freedom to do nothing as well as to be negative, harmful, and—yes—even unethical.

Newton is almost as pure in her legalism as Gordon is in his libertarianism. Irresponsible media conduct is not acceptable. Period. The media, like all of society, need rules, controls, limits, and guidance. Just who these "philosopher kings" of the media will be, Newton never says. But presumably they would be in the judicial branch of government. The old "internal" controls of the media simply have not worked, she says, and little empirical evidence is needed to agree with her.

But the question remains: if ethics is not legalism, and morality not law, therefore, when we get outside forces handing down ethical standards, is that still in the realm of ethics?

Since my concept of ethics is quite different from law by being self-determined and self-enforced, I must fall back on Gordon's position of libertarianism. As Gordon insightfully says, ethical arguments can and do erode freedom by curtailing or eliminating many actions. The corollary is, of course, that freedom can and does erode ethics by, in essence, circumventing "the right" action whenever desired. This is one of the weaknesses of utilitarianism: that it provides a rationale for pragmatic action rather than for ethical action. And freedom, unless self-controlled, loses its essence and turns into a kind of authoritarianism.

> my concept of ethics is quite different from law by being self-determined and self-enforced,

A bothersome point in Gordon's argument: if an action is forced upon someone, it cannot be responsible (ethical). Why is this? If I am forced to be ethical, am I not still ethical? Do I have to act from self-realization of moral values? If I am stopped by a traffic light, is this any less ethical than if I stop myself at a lightless intersection? The results are the same, and Newton's position reasserts itself in this controversy. But then Newton argues that the First Amendment is grounded in ethics. I am puzzled again. The amendment says that Congress shall make no laws abridging press freedom. Does this mean that laws are unethical? That free press actions are ethical? Where is the "grounding" Newton mentions?

Interestingly, Newton prescribes a "four-track model" revolving around Christians' (2005) call for us to fulfill our "duty to honor life"—what he regards as the ethics of "human sacredness." In spite of its vagueness, this humanistic admonition is immune to criticism. But one wonders, if there is a sacredness about human beings, why we would need to worry about being unethical. And, we might wonder also just what is meant by "honoring life." The journalist who takes a trip on a government airplane or who prints the name of a youthful offender or who exposes the crimes of another person—this journalist may honor life. Does this make such actions ethical? The concept is so full of semantic noise that it falls into the pit of meaninglessness.

People who mainly side with Gordon, and I am one of them, see any limitation of freedom of expression (by outside forces) as dangerous. It is dangerous for several reasons: it opens the door to any would-be determiner of "right" or "correct" expression; it assumes that media people cannot make their own decisions; it propagandizes a monistic concept of responsible communication, and it is nothing more than incipient authoritarianism in the guise of ethical communications behavior.

Those siding with Newton in this controversy contend that morality dictates such limitations on freedom. Unlimited freedom, they say, is socially harmful, counterproductive to the development of a moral sense, unintelligent, and potentially disruptive to social harmony, and perhaps even to national security. A strong—and basically rational—argument. Underneath our contentious exteriors, it seems that we are automatically enjoined to place ethics ahead of freedom, the community good ahead of individualistic proclivities. Most of us seem to be quite willing to place ethics in the hands of someone or some body outside ourselves—but then we get into the realm of law. Law, of course, can give more stability to society than can individual ethics. This is the slippery slope of the freedom–ethics dialectic.

Now if Newton means that free expression may be limited in some ways (meaning self-control or self-limitation), I agree with her. But if she condones an outside person or entity doing the limiting, even in the name of morality, I cannot agree with her, although I must admit I am increasingly prone to. This is a topic ever-open to discussion and refinement, and it is hoped that these two thoughtful persons have stimulated you to further and vigorous consideration of it.

REFERENCES AND RELATED READINGS

Aristotle. (4th century BCE/1976). *The Ethics of Aristotle: The Nicomachean Ethics*, rev. ed., edited by Hugh Tredennick, trans. James Alexander Kerr Thomas, intro., Jonathan Barnes. New York: Penguin.

Barron, Jerome A. (1973). *Freedom of the Press for Whom?* Bloomington, IN: Indiana University Press.

Bezanson, Randall P., Gilbert Cranberg, and John Soloski. (1987). *Libel Law and the Press: Myth and Reality.* New York: Free Press.

Boller, Paul F., Jr. (1964). "Freedom in the thought of William James." *American Quarterly* 16(2), Part 1, pp. 131–152.

Christians, Clifford G. (2005). "Ethical theory in communications research." *Journalism Studies* 6(1), pp. 3–14.

Elliott, Deni. (1987). "Creating conditions for ethical journalism." *Mass Comm Review* 14(3), pp. 6–10.

Gant, Scott. (2007). *We're All Journalists Now: The Transformation of the Press and Reshaping of the Law in Internet Age.* New York: Free Press.

Gazzaniga, Michael. (2005). *The Ethical Brain.* New York and Washington: Dana.

Gillmor, Dan. (2006). *We the Media: Grassroots Journalism by the People, for the People.* Sebastopol, CA: O'Reilly Media.

Glasser, Theodore L. (1986). "Press responsibility and First Amendment values." In Deni Elliott, ed., *Responsible Journalism.* Beverly Hills, CA: Sage, pp. 81–98.

Hamlin, David. (1980) *The Nazi/Skokie Conflict: A Civil Liberties Battle.* Boston, MA: Beacon.

Harmon, Mark. (1991). "Hate groups and cable public access." *Journal of Mass Media Ethics* 6(3), pp. 146–155.

Hart, H. L. A. (1963). *Law, Liberty and Morality.* New York: Vintage.

Kletzok, Melinda (2008). Presentation to Advanced Photojournalism, School of Journalism and Communication, University of Oregon, February 12.

Linder, Laura R. (1999). *Public Access Television: America's Electronic Soapbox*. Westport, CT: Praeger.

Liptak, Adam. (2007). "Verizon reverses itself on abortion messages." *The New York Times*, September 27. Retrieved from www.nytimes.com/2007/09/28/business/28verizon.html?_r=1&scp=1&sq=Verizon%20Reverses%20itself%20on%20Abortion%20Messages&st=cse (March 24, 2008).

Newton, Julianne H. (2004). "Visual ethics." In Kenneth Smith, Gretchen Barbatsis, Sandra Moriarty, and Keith Kenney, eds., *Handbook of Visual Communication*. Mahwah, NJ: Lawrence Erlbaum Associates, pp. 429–443.

One Laptop Per Child (2008). "Mission." Retrieved from www.laptop.org/vision/index.shtml (March 24, 2008).

Pitts, Leonard, Jr. (2009). "Nazi invasion." Column from *The Miami Herald*, reprinted in the Eau Claire, WI *Leader-Telegram*, August 23, p. 3F.

Sanford, Bruce W., and Jane E. Kirtley. (2005). "The First Amendment tradition and its critics." In Geneva Overholser and Kathleen Hall Jamieson, eds., *The Press*. Oxford, UK, and New York: Oxford University Press, pp. 263–283.

Shoffstall, Veronica A. (1971). "After a while." In Robert J. Ackerman, ed. (2002). *Perfect Daughters: Adult Daughters of Alcoholics*, rev. ed. Deerfield Beach, FL: Health Communications, p. 68.

Smolla, Rodney A. (1992). *Free Speech in an Open Society*. New York: Knopf.

Stone, Geoffrey R. (2004). *Perilous Times: Free Speech in Wartime from the Sedition Act of 1798 to the War on Terrorism*. New York: Norton.

"Story on secret program riles critics of N.Y. Times." (2006). Eau Claire, WI *Leader-Telegram*, June 29, p. 7C (story by *The Washington Post*).

Wong, David B. (2004). "Rights and community in Confucianism." In Kwong-loi Shun and David B. Wong, eds., *Confucian Ethics: A Comparative Study of Self, Autonomy, and Community*. Cambridge, UK: Cambridge University Press, pp. 31–48.

Youm, Kyu H. (2001). "Assessing an interdisciplinary approach to freedom of speech." *Journal of Broadcasting & Electronic Media* 47(3), pp. 487–490.

Zillmann, Dolf. (1998). "The psychology of the appeal of portrayals of violence." In Jeffrey H. Goldstein, ed., *Why We Watch: The Attractions of Violent Entertainment*. New York: Oxford University Press, pp. 179–211.

Zillmann, Dolf, Rhonda Gibson, and Stephanie L. Sargent (1999). "Effects of photographs in news-magazine reports on issue perception." *Media Psychology* 1, pp. 207–228.

Chapter 2

Individual Values, Social Pressures, and Conflicting Loyalties

THOSE who study the principles that ought to shape human behavior—we call them ethicists—generally have agreed that unless an individual is free to choose what courses of action to take, there is little point in discussing ethical decision-making. However, that does not allow individuals to ponder ethics decisions in a vacuum, without reference to external influences. Inevitably, various real-world factors enter into the decision-making process.

All of this doesn't invalidate the idea of individuals as moral agents, able to determine their own ethical criteria, directions and behavior. It also does not mean that individuals are *controlled* by any or all of those real-world factors. But it does mean that some of those factors may well have an influence on some people's ethical decisions, either in general or in specific circumstances. Applied, as contrasted with theoretical, ethics often revolves around the tensions created by the clash of individual moral autonomy and organizational, cultural, or societal pressures.

In 2000, capping a four-year research project that included 20 forums around the United States and a national survey of journalists, the Committee of Concerned Journalists identified nine principles that, in their judgment, form the underpinning for journalism. The last of these, which is particularly relevant to this discussion, specifies that practitioners of journalism "must be allowed to exercise their personal conscience" and goes on, in part:

> Every journalist must have a personal sense of ethics and responsibility—a moral compass. Each of us must be willing, if fairness and accuracy require, to voice differences with our colleagues, whether in the newsroom or the executive suite.
>
> (Committee of Concerned Journalists, 2000)

While this principle was developed in a journalism context, the idea of a personal sense of ethics which can be maintained in the face of differences with colleagues is a useful one for those in advertising, public relations and entertainment as well. But the omitted questions in the statement of this principle ask whether it is possible to preserve that personal sense of ethics and responsibility in the face of outside pressures that all mass communicators face in one way or another.

This chapter focuses on those unasked questions: how much influence is exerted on the individual moral agent, under what circumstances may outside factors become important, and whether—and how far—those factors may constrain the individual? John Michael Kittross argues that the individual values of media people are by far the most potent forces in shaping ethical decisions and, thereby, the contents of the mass media and that media people should stick to their ethical principles despite outside pressures. David Gordon responds that economic and other forces in society influence severely the ethical decisions made by media practitioners, even though they may well *believe* that their moral compass remains independent.

KITTROSS: Stick to your personal values in making ethical decisions, despite the various pressures that you encounter in the workplace, such as those from media owners, government or advertisers.

"To whom are you responsible?" is paradoxically one of the most common, most simple-appearing, and yet most difficult-to-answer questions that we frequently run into. Much like the also commonly heard "Do you love me?" one should beware of giving a quick answer. Shakespeare advised, in *Hamlet*, "To thine own self be true, and it follows, as the night the day, thou can'st not then be false to any man." But, in practice, what does this mean?

Among other things, it means that we must repeatedly test for logic and relevance in our own lives those values we have acquired over years. John Merrill (2007) has written that the

> student of media ethics picks up ethical concepts from . . . sociology, psychology, English, economics, biology, et al. And from parents, friends, teachers, television, radio, music lyrics, movies, the Internet, newspapers and magazines, the church and other organizations.

> (Merrill, 2007, p. 9)

Such factors have shaped—and continue to shape—the beliefs to which we as ethical actors should remain true.

RESPONSIBILITY

"Responsibility" is a very strong, important word. It covers the higher creative functions of the film director and the social impetus of the industrial or governmental whistleblower. It isn't identical to the meanings of "obligation" or "debt" or "requirement," but it overlaps all of them. It differs primarily in its internal aspects: being responsible requires thought, decision-making, and action, not just obeying orders. In the feature film *The Hospital* (1971), the hero—chief of medicine in a large dysfunctional hospital—turns away from the opportunity to live a full life with a beautiful woman in a remote village and a last chance "to practice medicine again" in order to return to his paper-shuffling post and an existence that is slowly destroying him and everything he once believed in. But as he says to the hospital administrator, as they march back into the hospital through a gauntlet of protestors, striking employees, patients waiting to be admitted to the emergency room, reporters and police, "*someone* has got to be responsible."

I believe that the key to responsibility is altruism, that is, a regard for the benefit of others without an expectation of reward; in a word, being *unselfish*. "Women and children first" was the generally understood standard of moral behavior when the ocean liner *Titanic* collided with an iceberg. Such priorities made sense when it was impossible to save everyone because of a lack of lifeboats. The survival of a family's young, and women who might nurture children in the future—in a way, giving priority to the continuation of the human race—was placed above the individual male's life.

How do doctors, men on sinking ships, and most of the rest of us develop those personal values that enable us to do the "right thing," even if others might be benefiting at our expense? Do we pay income taxes solely because there are legal penalties if we don't? Why do soldiers decide to throw themselves on a hand grenade to save comrades? Do we vote solely in our own personal interest? Do we help others solely in the expectation of reward? I don't think so—and reject the idea that the only purpose in life is to boss others, have fun, collect more "toys," and accumulate wealth.

Ethics has been construed as virtuous behavior and a component of "what constitutes a good life." A world in which competition is the only goal wouldn't be one in which most of us would want to live, even if we were equipped with claws and fangs.

What separates humans from animals, whatever we call it—a soul, a spirit, or something else—seems to be a form of conscious altruism that can look forward into the future. Naturally, like other species, we gain many of our values from our parents and from others whom we observe and otherwise learn from. But humans also can absorb the wisdom others have constructed or collected over the millennia, in religious teachings and dogma, and through both oral tradition and the written word—a medium unavailable to other species.

We can make it easy—the Ten Commandments and the Boy Scout Law ("a scout is trustworthy, loyal, helpful, friendly, courteous, kind, obedient, cheerful, thrifty, brave, clean and reverent") are extremely useful as we learn the values of our society during childhood—even though these words can be very ambiguous. We can make it hard—and spend a lifetime studying a single concept. For example, one of the United States' most important independent journalists, I. F. Stone—whose *I. F. Stone's Weekly* was required reading among those who needed to understand power during the middle decades of the 20th century—retired so that he had the time to learn Ancient Greek in order to continue his personal study into the philosophical basis of democracy.

Even if one's immediate goal is to become or train inquisitive reporters or persuasive publicists, thoughtful people understand how these skills can fit within a larger, altruistic framework, that is, the watchdog role of the press or the marketplace of ideas. Such frameworks, in turn, serve notions of human fulfillment such as political participation, individual freedom, or intellectual engagement. This is a mission to be proud of and it can be informed by long traditions of rationalism and humanistic thought (Armstrong, 2007).

The framework as well as the touchstone of this chapter is responsibility. One level of this concept may be found in the day-to-day habits of obeying orders, accepting the rules of whatever game is being played in home, school, workplace, or the larger society. Another level looks to the goals and penalties of whatever more important or larger game is being played; ultimately the game of life. An employee who shows up on time, does her job, and doesn't interfere with the jobs of other employees is being responsible to employer, co-workers and, presumably, customers. But if she was working for a marketing firm that was busily selling a fraudulent product or service, or with a gang of rogue "celebrity reporters" actually engaged in blackmail, the victims would be hard pressed to find praise for her otherwise responsible behavior. Her responsibility to the society that nurtured and protects her would be missing.

This sort of conflict, between the goals and ethics of an institution, or organization or profession and the morals of an individual or society, is common. An example is that of an officer in the U.S. armed services, who is part of a rigid hierarchal command structure, but nevertheless took a personal oath to support and defend the Constitution of the United States. History tells us that these two levels of responsibility sometimes are in conflict—does obedience to one's superior officer trump the plain language of the Constitution? Or vice versa? The consequences of such conflicts can be severe on the individual, but shouldn't the officer's attention be paid to both obligations?

The interaction between individual values (regardless of how they developed) and social pressures (regardless of how much they have been internalized) are particularly problematic for communications practitioners.

Take a typical reporter, regardless of medium. He has responsibility to, or owes a debt of allegiance to, his supervisors at the station, newspaper, or magazine. They, in turn, have some responsibilities to the reporter—although all too frequently employers seem to think that providing paychecks is all that they owe their staffs (and in a time of economic stress, perhaps not even that—see Chapter 8). Obligation—debt—responsibility all rely on *someone's* value structure.

But the reporter—or editor, account executive, manager, "talent," salesperson, director, camera operator, producer, public relations professional, political operative, blogger or any other job title—is a part of a communications organization that also has responsibilities on a higher level. ("Izzy" Stone was a rare exception, and most bloggers also operate independently and with little reward.) So, whatever ethical decisions are made, by whoever is working anywhere in the mass media, have implications in higher (i.e., more consequential) planes.

For example, while business managers and sales directors tend to think mostly in terms of the "bottom line" for their company (and, likely, themselves), or the fortunes of the advertisers who support that media company, they—and everyone else—need also to consider the beneficial or harmful consequences of their decisions insofar as they affect others. These "others" include the readers and viewers in the audience, the community whose needs for information and entertainment (and jobs) are served by that media outlet, as well as specific groups that are directly involved in the in the situation or event the message is about. To paraphrase John Donne, no media organization is an island; it has its vendors and suppliers, advertisers and subscribers, workers (from star copywriters to janitors), audiences, and many other connections to the larger society.

This book hasn't ignored the differences between ethics and morals—two words that are often used interchangeably, except by philosophers and others to whom the precision and nuances of language are very important. These words often are defined in terms of one another; "ethical" refers to moral action, motive or character as the first definition in one popular collegiate dictionary. But they can be distinguished: the ethical student says that cheating is wrong, but the moral student just doesn't cheat. To some extent, then, ethics deals with the science of morals or ideal human behavior (especially with respect to conforming to professional standards of conduct). Morals are concerned with both the broader practice and the science of good conduct, with moral behavior being what is right, proper and, to use an older word, virtuous.

These terms have much in common, although in practice ethics usually refers to the purview of a specific group or profession involved, and morality, being the broader or universal approach to behavior, is usually both within the purview of the individual and, to a great extent, the entire society in which she lives. I'm sure that, at the end of a long day, accepting the responsibility of acting *either* ethically or morally isn't easy.

Fortunately for mass communicators in the United States, the information and opinion media have the usually overriding concept of press freedom to provide support for professional behaviors, ethical or moral and occasionally unethical or immoral. As discussed earlier in this book, freedom is only part of the equation that faces each of us with every decision.

What are some of the other aspects of this equation? Responsibility, obligation (different from responsibility in that it is voluntarily adopted rather than imposed from without), authority (the power to do things, or get others to do them), and reward (which may be anything from wealth and power to "feeling good" about something) (Kittross, 2007).

WHAT IS A CONFLICT OF INTEREST?

Conflicts of interest are one of many triggers for the need to make ethical choices. What are we talking about? The primary interest of the journalist should be to inform the public. But communicators in public relations or advertising have persuasive as well as informational interests to satisfy, and few entertainers would make a living if they didn't entertain an audience. For all of them, however, competing goals—money, fame, associations, ideas—might well lead to a conflict. But if we are lucky, upon honest and sober reflection, we might decide that the conflict is inconsequential—and, better yet, the public (if they learn about it) will feel the same way.

A business reporter who provides valid information to the public that might result in a rise or fall in the price of a particular security is doing her job, but if that reporter also engages in "insider trading," buying or selling the stock for her own account before publishing the story, that is a clear conflict of interest—as well as being illegal. The path that this reporter should take is well signposted.

There are many definitions of "conflict of interest." One of the easiest to work with is that of Louis W. Hodges: "A conflict of interest in journalism exists when a journalist's professional (and professed) duty to serve audience interests is weakened, or risks being so, by the journalist's self-interests or any interests or obligations other than those of her audience" (Hodges, 2007, p. 113). That definition can easily be adapted to the entertainment and persuasion fields, as well.

Although it isn't hard to find and use a dictionary definition of both "conflict" and "interest," these words have more than one meaning. Also, there are at least two major connotations of "conflict" and "interest" applicable to the mass media that may not be found in the dictionary.

First, conflict of interest becomes tied to credibility whenever it comes to the public's attention. Credibility is nothing more than a reputation for honesty, and is related to the entire question of truth, accuracy, and fairness that is discussed in Chapter 3. (I do not believe that a strict mathematical balance of points of view is a legitimate goal of the media. Among other things, it is rare that there are only two sides to a given question, topic or dilemma, and it is the job of the professional journalist to do much of the weighing of these points of view, not merely to relay them.) Second, as mentioned earlier, the communicator always has a primary responsibility to the audience and the society of which the listeners, viewers and readers are a part, regardless of whether one is serving a national network audience or a few acquaintances via Twitter.

David Gordon and I have argued for years where the conflict-of-interest line should be drawn, but we both agree that there *is* a line—and that it is important. For example, we both agree that there is no excuse for the public harm that results from either extortion or the prostitution that occurs when one lies to the audience about something in exchange for money or other favors. The now-illegal practice of "payola," where disk jockeys accepted money (and sometimes drugs and sex partners) from music record companies in exchange for playing certain records or tracks, violated the public trust that disk jockeys implicitly or explicitly advertise: that they are using only their best professional judgment and consider only the public interest (or, perhaps, what the public is interested in—unfortunately, a very different phrase) when choosing which records or performances to air. "Plugola"—using one's access to media production to plug a product or service in the hope and expectation of receiving something tangible in exchange—is similar.

One of the most obvious conflicts arises, day in and day out, when one's internalized personal values clash with actions stemming from one's professional position that can produce monetary or personal benefits (or damages). The business reporter who invests in companies he is reporting on. The sports reporter who needs some extra game tickets for her visiting relatives. It is easy to think of other examples where professional roles conflict with personal ones.

The roles of citizen and media professional may often be in conflict—for example, shouldn't a statehouse reporter be able to run for office in her child's parent-teacher association (PTA), or a reporter on the police beat become a trustee of the town library? Should news gatherers and processors have *any* public role in politics, including the citizen's duty to vote? Some would say "No." Some would ask "Why not?"

These conflicts of interest may be more apparent than real, because a true professional will always give priority to his or her prime professional responsibility—the audience, in the case of the media. Just because there have been occasions when media owners allowed their non-media financial interests (or civic boosterism) to warp content, doesn't mean that everything published or aired is automatically biased. Indeed, the biases of management might well be balanced by those of the editorial staff—and, even more likely, both are aware of the impact that a known conflict of interest can have on both content and credibility.

But not always. Sometimes the conflicts *are* real and are kept below the surface. In 2007, the Cowles Company was developing a large downtown mall project in Spokane, Washington, and was also publisher of the Spokane *Spokesman-Review*. The Washington News Council—one of the few news councils in the United States—found that the paper, over a ten-year period, didn't investigate thoroughly or in a timely manner the financial structure of the development, and suppressed financial information of importance to decision-makers and the public at large that was potentially unfavorable to the developers. Officers of the company (including legal counsel) and editors of the paper both were involved in protecting the financial interests of the company. (It is, however, to the credit of *The Spokesman-Review* that it helped sponsor and cooperated fully with the Washington News Council's investigation, and published the entire report; see Hamer, 2007.)

Nowadays, when one reads the medical and scientific literature, one sees announcements attached to professional articles that spell out any financial arrangements that helped pay for the research or otherwise might have affected the published results. Disclaimers noting common corporate ownership often appear in some general news media (particularly broadcast news), in situations such as when ABC News reports on something at Disney World (owned by ABC's parent company) or CNN reports on some development at its corporate parent, Time-Warner.

It used to be a bad joke among journalists that they could be bribed by a cup of bad (but free) coffee. Good journalists used to take the cup, but write the story the way it should be written. And they wouldn't accept more expensive gifts—or, to be more exact, bribes. Some employers, media organizations such as the Society of Professional Journalists (SPJ) and the Radio Television Digital News Association (RTDNA), and codes of ethics writers—perhaps mistaking the symbol of free coffee for the reality of bribery or just thinking about the reputation and credibility of their media outlet—have spent many hours debating whether ballpoint pens or free key chains containing advertising should be handed out at journalism conventions. This is akin to debating how many angels can dance on the head of a pin—or, more precisely, where the line should be drawn between social intercourse and prostitution.

It isn't easy to deal with such questions and conflicts of interest, particularly when the temptation to do what is best for one's career is always present. Should one have to flip a coin to choose between being rewarded monetarily, or losing part of one's reputation? This book comes down solidly on the side of a third alternative: don't react without thinking about the issue you are facing. You have responsibilities other than supporting the interests of any group or institution—including, sometimes unfortunately, your employer, your sources, and your family. Think first, analyze the situation, consider the long-term implications of your choices, select the ethical guideline(s) that will best help you navigate through the dilemma—and you will find that even the most complex problems usually become manageable.

DOING IT RIGHT

In addition to avoiding conflicts of interest, people in the media need to meet other standards. Some of these are journalistic standards, some are dictated by society at large, some are traditional, and—particularly for those who are constructing newscasts, articles and other non-fiction works—some are variations on the age-old question of scholars: "How do we know what we know?" The answer to that question can affect the credibility of the medium as well as of the individuals involved—and have major implications for audience members who act upon the information they receive from the media

Although some reportage or research is dismissed *solely* because of the obvious "smoking gun" of financial or other support—even when the research was done properly— this can be a mistake. If valid and reliable evidence has been collected using honest and transparent methods, and we still dismiss it because we automatically mistrust the people involved because of their connections or past reputation, it creates a dilemma in regard to providing information and ideas to the audience. On the one hand, we can accept information from *any* source and obtained in *any* manner as long as the information itself is valid and reliable—even if obtained from experiments performed on unwilling prisoners or slave labor (as was true under the Nazi regime) or by individuals whose honesty might be questioned, but without proof. Or, on the other hand, we can throw out the baby with the bathwater if there is even the slightest question about the procedures used in getting the information. To make this sort of decision is difficult—but essential. Reporters are not bound by the legal rules of evidence, but this doesn't give them *carte blanche* to accept information just because it (or the source) is plausible; neither are they expected to mistrust information because of something in the past. The answer? Pay attention to the evidence itself.

DECISION-MAKING

Each individual working in the mass media needs to consider *all* of those whom our decisions affect, *all* the time. In the media, our output is certain to affect many different groups (news sources and subjects, those seeking entertainment, advertisers and their competitors, the general public, governments, colleagues, etc.)—and, in turn, they affect (or attempt to affect) what the media say and do.

Advertisers are very glad to sponsor popular programs on television, even though from a strict short-term dollars-and-cents viewpoint it often is cheaper for advertisers to buy commercial "spots" rather than actually sponsor a program. As long as any form of advertising is the economic backbone for a medium there will be both conscious and unconscious striving to avoid biting the hand that feeds it. To accept this fact of economic life does not mean that we must always accept the values of those who have their own axes to grind. Consider them, yes—but if, for example, a supervisor tries to impose duties on you in violation of your own standards, your best course may be to resign. (Whether one goes beyond resigning—e.g., going public, whistleblowing, bringing a lawsuit—depends on the situation and your personal values.) This raises other questions: some of the information you possess may legally belong to your employer, others may be affected by your decision, and the complexity of media operations often renders decision-making very difficult. If you want simplicity, it won't be found in the media's operations!

Although numerous pressures are focused on the decision-maker—the needs, desires, and plans of spouses, family and co-workers, for example—I believe that it would result in chaos if we tried to satisfy at the same instant the goals of *every* group to which we belonged. Indeed, it might be impossible even to list them! We never asked to belong to some groups—family, age cohort, gender and race, for example—although we may be pleased to be part of them. Other groups to which we may belong—based on education, occupation, professional associations or unions, even religions and nationalities—are more under our control. And make no bones about it—*all* of these groups can, do and want to influence those who produce and distribute messages.

Being a journalist or other communicator seems to be like making love to a porcupine—you do it *v-e-r-r-r-y* carefully.

CONSEQUENCES

Suppose your supervisor/boss/employer tells you to do something that seems immoral or unethical to you after you've thought about it and have applied the "how to" instructions provided in "Tools for Ethical Decision-Making" at the end of Part II. Your response may well depend upon such varied factors as how easy it would be to find a new job should you be fired, whether you think the employer is or isn't making sense, who will be affected by your decision and how, the advice you receive or a myriad of other factors. If you won't be able to put food on the table for your family if you decide against the interests of those who control your paycheck, you will be under a great deal of pressure to decide the other way.

Once we are faced with decisions, it is up to us, as individuals, to use our own knowledge, skill, ability, *and ethical standards* to ensure that we are acting ethically. By the time the reader has finished this book, we hope that he or she will have a pretty good idea of whether Kantian rule-based logic or utilitarian consequence-based logic—or some other of the ethical systems discussed by John Merrill in his overview of the "Theoretical Foundations for Media Ethics"—is most useful in a particular situation. In other words, ethical standards and concepts are very useful "moral tools," helping people with their decisions—but rarely dictating them. As future media decision-makers, as audience members, communicators, regulators, citizens and part of a society, it is up to each individual to make decisions whenever a situation arises that has ethical connotations.

But, at the same time, you have to look at yourself in the mirror every morning—and you must remember that you are a moral agent, intentionally or not, and any consequences of your decision are on your shoulders. Not only your reputation, but also your own sense of self-esteem, of integrity, is at stake.

PRESSURES

If there is a chance that intelligence agents or the police will swarm over your newsroom, office, or home, you might decide that discretion is the better part of valor and decide to publish only what the government or the most powerful organizations in town apparently desire. This problem of deliberate pressure from those with power affects advertising, public relations, and creative personnel in all media fields who need to have an audience. If the powers that be, or public opinion, are clearly pushing in one direction, it isn't easy—in spite of one's training, additional knowledge, and thought—to advocate (or even mention) other possible avenues of action.

Your supervisor or employer, as a supervisor or employer rather than as a human being faced with the same dilemma you are facing, can easily fall back on the easy answer: *Whatever will make the stockholders in the company happy is good.* This is an ethical point of view, isn't it? The stockholders have invested the money that created the company and your job, and have the right to expect that their investment's return will be maximized.

But there are other people with a stake in that company, and in the actions that you must take when you make the decision. For a public relations agency, these stakeholders include, at a minimum, clients, suppliers, news media contacts, other clients, employees, delivery people and the government. For a public service, such as a newspaper or broadcasting station, there are certainly the readers, listeners and viewers who pay attention to what is aired or printed. For everyone, there is the nation in which they reside, the community or communities served by the media outlets, and the general public or humanity at large. In some cases, as our ability to destroy ourselves or the planet increases, humanity itself is a stakeholder in what is printed or broadcast.

We might expect to be fired or condemned for doing the wrong thing, but how about being fired (or blamed, or attacked) for doing what usually has been thought of as the right thing? Some things as traditional as a news "scoop" must be weighed against the potential consequences. There can be problems when individual considered news judgments are contrasted to the judgments of peers, whether in "pack journalism" (see Chapter 15-H) or examining what the competition has featured that day. Since the same action can be interpreted in different ways, and "right" and "wrong" may depend on the perspective from which an action is viewed, criticism for doing the "right" thing is always a possibility. An "enterprising reporter" to some may be just a "sneaky eavesdropper" to others. You need either to be ready to accept criticism even when it is unwarranted or else to think carefully—ahead of time—about how your actions may be interpreted.

> criticism for doing the "right" thing is always a possibility.

THE INDIVIDUAL AND THE STATE

Some stories currently have "legs"—they have been in the public eye for years—but every week can bring new ones. Arguments still rage over Watergate, the Pentagon Papers, treatment by the United States of prisoners at Abu Ghraib in Iraq and Guantanamo in Cuba, warrantless wiretapping by the National Security Agency (NSA), and President George W. Bush's military service record. On one side, there is the administration exercising executive power in Washington at the time. On the other side, there are those who published information about these events. In the background, are national divides over political parties, the Vietnam War and the post-2001 "war on terrorism."

Things change, of course. Germany was a totalitarian state under Hitler, and a democracy today. This means that governmental powers, privacy, and the rule of law were very different during the Third Reich. Few nations have been unaffected by time.

An American reporter is both an American and a reporter and, if working in another country, a resident alien. In each role the reporter must decide what is acceptable conduct based on the set of ethics that he or she believes must be followed.

This is also the case in other countries. The head of the news division of the Liaoning (China) provincial Propaganda Department was quoted as saying:

> For some social issues, reporters can do their own investigations. But in cases of serious incidents, government departments should do the work. If reporters can do investigations on everything, then what is the use of government departments?
>
> (Cody, 2007)

In the United States, interpretations of the First Amendment abound, but there is a continuing struggle between government and the media. In the United Kingdom the system is different, with an Official Secrets Act and strict rules against publishing most news (or speculation) before criminal trials. In fact, not only are the more than 150 countries in the world different, so too are the 50 states in the United States with respect to matters such as privacy. Laws, while powerful, are not universal.

It is awfully easy to ignore ethics from both ends of the matter. As mentioned above, one method is to bear in mind only the written or unwritten goals of those higher in the hierarchy—one's employer or the government, for example. To use a lesson from the Christian Bible, we should "render unto Caesar the things that are Caesar's, and render unto God the things that are God's"—although, unfortunately, there are few guideposts for determining which are which.

Another approach is to join with one's peers, colleagues, or neighbors in whatever is happening. The first alternative abandons all pretenses of individual responsibility to think about ethics, and the latter leads to everything from lynch mobs to the "Blue Flu" excuse for job absences by forbidden-to-strike-by-law police officers when arguing for higher wages. *Neither* of these approaches, followed rigidly, is likely to improve the society at large.

CONTENT

The fact that President Franklin D. Roosevelt's mistress was staying with him in Warm Springs, Georgia when he died just before the end of World War II, wasn't covered as part of the story of the death of the longest serving president. By contrast the Monica Lewinsky affair led to the 1998 impeachment of President Bill Clinton and occupied front pages, network newscasts, and cable talk shows for many months. (It should be noted that when a television newswoman reported in 2007 that the Los Angeles mayor and his wife had split, it turned out that one reason for the separation was an affair the mayor was having with that reporter, who was promptly suspended and later left the station. The mayor remained in office.) The physical effects of President Roosevelt's polio were generally ignored by the press, but, in recent years, information about the health of every president has been disseminated in the most excruciating detail by the avid media.

Today—helped by Members of Congress, governors, and others whose sexual dalliances inform the discussion of their "character"—there is almost no detail that is off limits in news, entertainment, and advertising. Former presidential candidate Sen. Bob Dole, after he left the Senate, appeared in Viagra television advertisements containing medical details that would have been taboo in "family media" only a few years earlier. Sen. Hillary Clinton's cleavage still had the power to create a political furor in the media early in the 2008 presidential campaign, and a little later Gov. Sarah Palin's sexual "hotness" became a staple of news coverage.

NEWSGATHERING

One journalistic standard deals with the ethics of reporting. This standard is analogous to the strict adherence of some courts to the "fruit of the poisoned tree" principle that encourages police to follow the Constitution: if a search warrant or reason for an arrest were invalid, any information gained as a direct or indirect result would be inadmissible in court. In recent years, if a reporter should do something considered improper in reporting an important story, some newsrooms might refuse to carry the story, no matter how important it is. These examples of self-regulation (which aren't universal) are sometimes the result of fear of legal action and sometimes a consequence of the growing number of attacks on the press by politicians, commentators and members of the public.

Nellie Bly (the pseudonym of one of the earliest female news correspondents) in 1897 lied her way into a mental institution, and her paper published a scathing—and avidly read—expose of conditions "from the inside" that led to much-needed reforms. By contrast, in the late 1990s, the courts and the public agreed that it was unfair for two ABC reporters to get jobs inside a food processing plant in order to expose unsanitary conditions. This story (the Food Lion case) was aired—but most of the benefits went to the lawyers. In another case, the public never got the full story about President Bush's Air National Guard service because one source was invalid in CBS's coverage of Bush's record. News producers and supervisors were fired, and long-time CBS anchor Dan Rather "retired." But the important result was that the public, supplied with pages and hours of news about CBS's peccadilloes, had few details of how the Bush family had pulled strings to get George W. Bush into the Air National Guard when he might otherwise have had to go to Vietnam, that he hadn't fulfilled all of the normal requirements for service, that all sorts of records were missing, and so on. (*The Boston Globe* was an exception: it did its own extensive reporting of Bush's military record.)

Similarly, Procter & Gamble's efforts to secure the supposedly "private" telephone records of several million people in the Cincinnati area were completely overshadowed by outrage (stimulated by P&G, of course) over a reporter's successful attempt to gain access to P&G's internal e-mail. Unlike the Bush story, which was straightforward reportage using interviews and government documents, P&G owned the e-mails in question and there was no inherent right of the reporter to obtain and publish them. It is ironic that P&G's desire for the telephone records was to discover which employee whistleblower had alerted the news media about a corporate decision of public interest. (See Chapter 10.)

It is interesting how simplistic, even erroneous, views are adopted. For example, many lawyers, including some of those specializing in libel cases, are surprised when told that the media do not have an iron-clad rule that all facts supplied by anonymous sources must be verified by a second source. They probably think this because they generalized from such a rule adopted by Bob Woodward and Carl Bernstein (and their editors) when reporting the Watergate break-in and cover-up that had massive ramifications for the Nixon administration—and led to a best-seller book and a major motion picture, *All the President's Men* (1976).

Other oversimplifications and errors probably have worse consequences. Large and small newsroom managements alike are arguing that reporters should avoid even the most innocuous appearance of impropriety, and consider the acceptance of small, inexpensive gifts or even a cup of coffee or a beer from potential news sources to be evidence of serious wrongdoing.

STANDARDS

Each media practitioner needs to develop her or his own moral standards, and simple and easy actions and answers aren't likely to be the best ones. The photojournalist who snatches a photo from a suspect's home because the police allowed the photographer to be present while a search or interrogation was being conducted is guilty of theft—regardless of whether his or her editor is pleased with the result.

Practitioners should also consider (and possibly adopt) those ethical standards that have been promulgated by professional associations such as the National Press Photographers Association or constructed in bull sessions held with colleagues who collectively know many of the problems that a filmmaker or videographer or reporter or other media person will surely face. But these are created by committees or informal groups, and the resulting camel may not look like much of a thoroughbred racehorse. Clifford Christians and others have been working on a description of basic "protonorms" that can be applied to the media. Whether general (Kantian) rules—do not lie, cheat, steal, etc.—may work in this field is uncertain. Each of us has to walk this road by ourselves.

There are many techniques for developing one's own set of ethical standards. Barbara Brotman (1993) once posed some very simple questions starting with "Is it ever acceptable. . . ." For example, is it ever acceptable for media people to deceive potential sources about one's professional identity or intentions; to steal documents, photos or other material, or to copy them without first asking permission; to re-create or stage an event; to accept gifts, tickets, or other freebies; to seek or give special treatment for themselves, their families or causes they favor; to violate laws such as speeding and parking regulations? Some might say that the answer to all of the above questions is that it *never* is acceptable to do such and so. But such an overly simplistic answer sometimes may make little sense. Suppose the only way one can review a sold-out concert is to be given a ticket? What if it is necessary to overstay at a parking meter to cover an important story? Or to blend into a crowd by pretending to be a member of it? Remember: most reporters—and the authors of this book—believe that their primary responsibility is to provide the public with the information it needs in order to make rational decisions in a democracy.

Obviously, the answers to Brotman-type questions require some thinking about each individual instance, because reporters probably would be remiss if they couldn't dream up at least one case where the simple answer is inappropriate. And people in the entertainment industry routinely re-create events. But behavior such as blocking fire department access by parking next to a fire hydrant is placing a story above protection of the public. The standards used by media people might come from their schooling, their reading, or informal chats with colleagues—one of the advantages of belonging to a professional association—or their parents, religious upbringing, or other source. We all can learn life's lessons by being observant. But to be useful, the ethical standards to be employed in responding to a question involving ethics must be internalized to the point where they can be drawn from one's memory without difficulty. When faced with a deadline, there isn't much time for further study of ethical principles.

Many years ago, in an award-winning television program, *The DuMont Show of the Week*, a long documentary about two underpaid and overworked members of the New York Police Department ended with the voice-over narrator reminding us that, in spite of having to do all the "dirty jobs" in their precinct (such as picking up dead bodies because they drove a station wagon rather than a squad car) and filling in where others might find a reason for not doing a cold, boring task, "they sleep well nights, and never have to ask why they were put on this earth." With those words, even an unobservant viewer realizes that every-thing that these policemen did—from directing traffic, to helping an old lady home with her groceries—was to help someone else.

Sleep well.

KEY POINTS

- Media practitioners need to develop their own set of moral standards, and simple answers aren't likely to be the best ones.
- Altruism (unselfishness) is the key to responsible action.
- True professionals will always give priority to their primary professional respon-sibility in instances of conflicts of interest.

GORDON: Sticking to your personal values is a worthy but unattainable ideal, in view of the social, economic, and political forces that often run counter to individuals' ethics.

In the abstract, I agree completely with John Michael Kittross that media practitioners should ignore all outside forces and remain true to their personal sense of ethics and responsibility. I just don't believe this is possible in view of the myriad pressures that impinge on decision-making in the media industries.

People working in the entertainment, persuasive and news media may think they are acting independently in determining the content they produce. But in fact, experience argues that those individual decision-makers are *not* free to act based only on their own ethical values (or lack of them). There is considerable evidence—both anecdotal and empirical—to the contrary. It appears that decisions at key points are influenced heavily—and, in some cases, are dictated—by various cultural, political, social, audience and, especially, economic forces whose operation prevents individual communicators from exercising anything resembling complete moral autonomy.

The most powerful and important of these economic forces are discussed in detail in Chapter 8, so I will mention some of them here only briefly. Instead, I will focus more on the social, political and other constraints that can become at least as important as ethical beliefs and guidelines in determining how an individual will act or react, and to whom or what that individual ultimately feels responsible. To take just one possible factor, ponder the possible impact of demands for "political correctness" in the ads you're being paid to create, or in the film you want to make, and how those demands might impinge on the way your ethical values influence your work.

AUDIENCE, ORGANIZATIONAL, AND SOCIETAL CONSTRAINTS

One need look no further than problems posed by "getting too far out ahead of your audience" to realize that mass communicators are rarely able to act with complete moral autonomy. This is true whether one looks at the news and information component of the mass media, the persuasive communication segment, or at entertainment content. Gatekeepers in all of those areas must take into consideration what their intended audience will pay attention to, not just some idealized version of what that audience "needs." The concerns of various subgroups within the general target audience can complicate even further the question of to whom those gatekeepers owe responsibility.

I'm not endorsing a "lowest common denominator" approach to content, but when the interests of the audience—or major components of it—don't match what *you* think is important or necessary, you'd better take a gradual approach toward persuading the audience that they *should* pay attention to content you think matters. Otherwise, you'll find yourself without an audience, and all the autonomy in the world won't help you—or your media organization—then.

Kittross advocates an altruistic approach and suggests that it is the key to being a responsible mass communicator, indeed, a responsible human being. But no matter how altruistic journalists—or anyone else in the media—may be, they must pay attention to the size, interests and reactions of the audience and the many types of people and groups that it includes. Ratings, subscriptions and circulation, single-copy or single-play sales, and movie attendance all have a direct impacts in our primarily profit-driven media system on how media content turns out, as does such direct feedback as complaints to the editor, general manager, or advertiser. If an altruistic approach to the media product engenders serious resistance from the intended audience, either the altruism or the individual exhibiting it is likely to be gone quite soon. What often happens is that the ethical framework of media workers takes second place to the likes and dislikes—and on some issues, the ethical concerns—of the media audience, the advertisers trying to reach them, and at times the media decision-makers who are keeping the advertisers' concerns in mind.

Altruism isn't the only quality in media people that may be severely constrained by outside forces. Independence is another, particularly as economic factors become more and more important in all aspects of the media business. Autonomy is reduced in large media organizations, and economic factors are increasingly producing such large media organizations. As Weaver et al. (2006) note, many journalists have left chain-owned or group media organizations because they didn't want to see their independence and autonomy threatened. But what of the media people who don't or can't make such a career change? It is reasonable to conclude that by opting to stay rather than to leave such situations, they are giving up some of their moral independence in trade for the benefits derived from their job.

Internal organizational norms and customs may exert negative as well as positive influences on individual moral autonomy. A classic early study by Warren Breed (1955) found that the newsroom culture was usually sufficiently strong to socialize new reporters into the established way of doing things, at least on the medium-sized papers included in his study. Nearly 20 years later, an in-depth study of the overall operation of a major newspaper—widely believed to be *The New York Times*—indicated that an organization's internal dynamics might be at least as important as economic pressures in regard to impacting individuals and their ethical independence (Argyris, 1974).

I'd suggest, though, that the internal structures and organization of media institutions are still important factors that can muffle individual moral autonomy and responsibility. Bill Kovach and Tom Rosenstiel of the Project for Excellence in Journalism put it very well in a book that grew out of the 1997–2000 research study by the Committee of Concerned Journalists:

> Routines become safe havens. This occurs because news organizations—with their business, community, production, and other interests—are complex and hierarchical. It becomes easy to fall into a process of what might be called cascading rationalization, which can undermine and discourage acts of individual conscience.
>
> (Kovach and Rosenstiel, 2001, p. 189)

Although the authors were focusing on journalism, their observation would seem to have considerable validity for almost any mass media organization. Certainly, all but the smallest public relations agencies could fall victim to the same cascading rationalization, for the same reasons, as could larger entertainment-oriented companies and advertising agencies.

Another type of internal pressure can come from technological changes. Throughout media history, new technologies have put pressure on the gathering and dissemination of news. The "deadline every minute" competition between wire services was an early example, and is echoed by pressures for instantaneous news on the Internet. The quicker and more frequent deadlines mean less time for ethical concerns to surface and more need to "go by the book"—or by "how it's always been done here"—in putting stories together, rather than allowing journalists to make ethical awareness part of their story preparation process. The same concerns about deadlines trumping ethics are reflected in the growth of 24/7 cable and radio newscasts and their insatiable appetite for current stories—and those capable of reporting them.

This situation can lead to repeating and sensationalizing stories that, on later reflection or with time to weigh ethics questions before deciding to publish or air a story, might have merited much less play than they received. This has exacerbated the news media's fascination with human-made and natural disasters, ranging from hurricanes and earthquakes to particularly gruesome accidents to the 2009 news coverage devoted to swine flu. The coverage has often given such events more exposure than their actual impact on the public would warrant.

Admittedly, it is difficult to strike a "proper" balance in covering these kinds of stories. But keeping in mind Rawls's concern for protection of the weakest parties and Aristotle's "middle ground approach" would serve journalists well, perhaps seasoned with a dash of the utilitarian focus on the greatest good for society.

POLITICAL AND GOVERNMENTAL PRESSURES

Although the First Amendment theoretically guarantees the American mass media the freedom to operate without political interference, the specter of government regulation or influence can't be ignored. Kittross makes this point very well for me with his example of federal agents potentially swarming over a newsroom, an occurrence that could well influence the denizens of that newsroom to follow the government line.

Broadcasting has historically been regulated far more than print, going back to the early decades of radio. The Federal Communications Commission's late (and occasionally lamented) Fairness Doctrine, adopted in 1949 (13 FCC Reports 1246), exemplified how governmental and political systems can impinge on mass media ethics and values. Most broadcasters would certainly have agreed, at least in the abstract, with the idea of "fairness" as an ethical principle. But their ability to interpret what "fairness" means and how it should be implemented were constrained when the FCC adopted and applied—"enforced" would certainly overstate what actually took place—a fairness principle on all broadcasters in regard to "controversial issues" and personal attacks.

Content rating systems have long had a similar impact on several mass communication industries. The first film code, dating to the early 1930s, resulted from a combination of public concern over perceived immorality in Hollywood itself and in its films; fear of possible federal regulation; and pressure (including boycott threats) from the Catholic (National) Legion of Decency. This movie code was followed by more recent examples in the television and recording fields. These industries have generally (though not always) agreed to follow the codes' dictates in part because of their fear that the government might step in with stronger measures if these "voluntary" codes were disregarded—clearly, an external influence insisting that someone other than media people exercise moral autonomy and define what "responsible" means.

PRESSURES DURING THE MCCARTHY ERA . . .

Among the most frightening and most effective examples of (heavily) "raised eyebrow" governmental and political constraints on media gatekeepers were the results of the investigations by the House Un-American Activities Committee (the infamous HUAC) of alleged Communist influence in Hollywood, in 1947, and again in 1951–52 when Sen. Joseph McCarthy's anti-Communist crusades were at their height. The climate of fear these Cold War era investigations engendered sent a clear message to the entertainment industries (particularly film) that certain subjects were not fit topics for loyal Americans to feature in their productions.

HUAC also sent the message that anti-Communist films *were* appropriate to the political climate, and the film industry responded with more than 50 such movies between 1947 and 1954, even though most of them were box office failures (Sayre, 1978, pp. 79–80). This "interplay between American film and politics" (Doherty, 1988, p. 15) illustrates how government can replace the individual moral agent in making decisions with ethics overtones.

. . . AND MORE RECENTLY

The aftermath of the terrorist attacks of September 11, 2001 is a much more recent and vivid example of how government and political pressures can become more important than individual media decision-makers and their values. The U.S. government's call for across-the-board support for its efforts both to calm the country and to fight the threat of terrorism produced immediate and enthusiastic news media compliance. Perhaps the most visible symbol of that response was the wearing of American flag lapel pins by several network TV news anchors, an action that generally drew approval but which was questioned in some quarters as giving the appearance that the news media might be retreating from their traditional Fourth Estate role of questioning the government. Indeed, with the benefit of hindsight, it seems clear that, as *Bill Moyers Journal* on PBS concluded in April 2007, "in the rage that followed the Sept. 11, 2001 terrorist attacks, the media abandoned their role as watchdog and became a lapdog instead" (Shales, 2007).

Similar criticism was leveled at the media—mainly in retrospect—for its failure to question the administration's arguments for invading Iraq in 2003. Rex Smith, editor of the Albany, New York *Times Union*, analyzed the situation well in a mid-2004 column that was prompted by a lengthy editors' note in *The New York Times* several days earlier. The paper, Smith wrote,

> conceded that its coverage of the events leading up to the United States invasion of Iraq was "not as rigorous as it should have been," and that controversial information presented to reporters "was insufficiently qualified or allowed to stand unchallenged."
>
> (2004)

Smith noted that it was not just *The New York Times* that failed in its watchdog role. Other "highly regarded reporters and editors, handling some of the most important stories of their careers, didn't do their jobs well enough" and let into print various articles that "supported President Bush's rationale for invading Iraq," based on bogus information.

> More than any other story in recent times, the reporting leading up to this [Iraq] war demanded what might be called "prosecutorial editing." Nothing should have gotten into the pages of the newspaper that the reporter couldn't defend against questioning by an editor as aggressive as a tough D.A. Every source needed to be, in effect, cross-examined for bias.

Smith criticized his newspaper colleagues for failing to exercise "the skepticism that is a hallmark of American journalism." But he noted that in the aftermath of 9/11 the United States "seemed eager to find scapegoats and enemies" and added that journalists "are not immune to the mind-set of their friends and neighbors." In essence, he was saying that in the stresses following 9/11—perhaps prompted by the government's calls for support—both good journalistic practice and some key ethical values gave way to "second-rate reporting and editing".

Some seven months after President Barack Obama's election, conservative columnist Cal Thomas (2009) raised similar concerns about the news media's failure "to question much of what he [Obama] does." Thomas also criticized the media for not pushing the administration for specifics on its claims in such areas as jobs saved or created by the economic stimulus funding, and for what amounted to hero worship of the new president, and noted that this paralleled criticism of the media in the early years of George W. Bush's presidency (i.e. the media abandoned their adversarial "watchdog" role in both instances).

Regardless of Thomas's ideological perspective, his concerns are valid ones no matter which party is in power. And the fact that such concerns have been raised about recent presidents from both parties should be a clear reminder to journalists that it's easy to fail (or to be perceived as failing) their adversarial role because they are unable to separate their reporting from a popular consensus in support of an incumbent president (or any other office-holder, for that matter). To use Bill Moyers' words in a different context, this illustrates anew how media can become lapdogs rather than watchdogs—a lapse that's indefensible under any ethics theory except perhaps ethical egoism (or overdoing the practical concern to maintain access to sources).

Pressure to abandon the adversarial role of the press can also come in much more mundane guises. For, example, the Attorney General in Wisconsin pressured news media in that state to refrain from asking questions about a 2007 mass killing in a small town northwest of Green Bay. The state official, who said he was merely expressing the wishes of the victims' families for privacy, suggested that members of the community refuse to talk to reporters. Many followed that advice and some "told reporters to go home" (Associated Press, 2007).

PRESSURE GROUPS

Another example of political (and social) influences on media decision-making is the pressure from various quarters to reduce considerably violence and sexual content in TV programming (a topic discussed in detail in Chapter 14). Organized groups—for example, the American Family Association and the Parents Television Council (PTC)—have fueled this concern, as have congressional hearings going back not only to the 1990s but also as long ago as the Kefauver hearings in the 1950s. Political candidates ranging (recently) from Hillary Clinton to Joe Lieberman to John McCain and Sam Brownback also have criticized the media for too much content dealing with sex or violence or both. Groups such as the AFA and the PTC are also concerned about content dealing with gay rights, and any material that can fall into the somewhat nebulous area of what they (if not the FCC and the courts) regard as "indecent."

The Parents Television Council has been the source of numerous indecency complaints filed with the Federal Communications Commission and covering a wide range of network programming. The roster of targets in the first nine years of the 21st century included *That '70s Show*, *Father of the Bride*, *Without a Trace*, *Friends*, *The Simpsons*, *Two and a Half Men*, *Family Guy* and even the morning *Today* show. (The notorious Janet Jackson incident involving brief partial nudity because of a "wardrobe malfunction" during a Super Bowl halftime made its way to and from the Supreme Court, with the PTC cheerleading for heavy fines.) Such complaints require a major expenditure of broadcasters' time and money to defend against the potential fines, and tend to shift the emphasis in programming decisions from ethics to whether the program may produce a formal complaint.

Even when such complaints are eventually dismissed by the FCC (as many of these were), the prospect of needing to spend time and money defending against this particular brand of activism will, I believe, give broadcasters some second thoughts about venturing off tried-and-true (and perhaps trite) paths of program content.

Although all of this has led only to minimal changes in program content, and to a "voluntary" TV content rating system begun in 1997, threats of organized social and political action, economic boycotts, and potential government regulation can put major pressures on the gatekeepers both within the television industry—including the made-for-TV movie producers who supply sizable portions of TV programming—and elsewhere. Decision-makers in advertising agencies and television advertisers also have to decide whether to sponsor programs with high violence quotients, or sexual or other "indecent" content, and are at times directly constrained by these pressures. Some have dropped their sponsorships in the face of them.

ECONOMICS AND INDIVIDUAL AUTONOMY

Economic pressures on individual autonomy are increasingly common in media conglomerates, where top management may have little familiarity with traditions that historically have been important to their media subsidiaries.

James Squires, former editor of the *Chicago Tribune*, discussed this issue extensively back in 1993 in his book, *Read All About It!* He provided—well ahead of the news industry's more recent recession-compounded problems—examples of the economic forces that increasingly are taking content decisions away from the people who formerly used journalistic criteria to make them. A major factor, he said, was the increase in the number of companies whose stock is owned by members of the public, especially those with heavy investment from pension funds and other institutional investors whose only concern was to maximize profits (Squires, 1993). Stockholders, of course, can't take traditional journalistic standards to the bank, and thus may put relatively little emphasis on the traditional role of news media as the vehicle through which a self-governing society becomes more informed.

Thus, bottom-line pressures to maintain and increase profit margins (discussed more fully in Chapter 8) can take away the autonomy and independence that Weaver et al. (2006) found to be something that journalists value. It is worth noting that these authors' "typical" 21st-century journalist works for a group-owned paper, most likely a local monopoly paper that could survive quite well without diverting potential profits to improve quality. Furthermore, this group-owned paper is likely to be part of a conglomerate where the parent firm may have interests that differ greatly from traditional journalistic values—for example, the Disney empire noted below.

Corporate pressures to produce profits thus greatly limit journalists' freedom to make decisions based on their own ethical frameworks. Kittross reinforces this point with his comment that company managers might have an ethical leg to stand on if they act on the maxim that making the stockholders happy is good. It is thus no longer correct, if it ever was, to say that news media content is determined mainly through the decisions made by various individual journalists. Of course, those decisions are still made and do influence media content, but increasingly, they are being made within a profit-driven context that removes important choices from the realistic options available to individual practitioners.

Nor is this limited to newspapers. The Time-Warner conglomerate—a merger which turned out to be much less profitable than anticipated—illustrates how management can be much less influenced by ethics and values issues than by the need to return the greatest possible profit to its shareholders and creditors. Soon after the merger, Time-Warner representatives praised "the 'artistic integrity' of the racist and sadistic outpourings of the rappers Ice-T and 2 Live Crew" (Harwood, 1992)—recordings produced and distributed (surprise!) by a Time-Warner company.

In another area of the mass media, we should ask whether conglomerate owners of advertising agencies are likely to give free rein to employees' creativity if the economic results are decidedly less certain than profits previously produced by less imaginative, "tried and true" ad campaigns? I wouldn't bet on ethics overcoming economics in this case, either.

ETHICAL FRAMEWORKS

If external pressures and bottom-line considerations are more important than individual values and long-standing customs in the mass media, are there any useful ethical frameworks other than the pragmatic ends-justify-the-means approach of Machiavelli? Edmund Lambeth (1992) warns against using utilitarianism as a guide because it may be "ever so easy and often tempting to choose as a 'maximizer of the good' the path that suits the individual [practitioner's] or media organization's interest rather than the course [an individual], as a moral agent, would decide" (p. 57). Ethical egoism might be a viable alternative in a context where rational pursuit of self-interest is the accepted approach. However, it might not be useful if one looks at long-run self-interest while the corporate bean-counters are trying to maximize short-term profits.

Unless you are going to rely on "gut feeling" (or on John Merrill's notion of a "moral epiphany"), the most practical personal ethical guideline for many of these situations comes from Aristotle's Golden Mean. That approach might suggest staying in a job as long as you can live with the ethical constraints imposed by outside forces. When things get too bad, then it's time to leave, a move that may be possible if you have built up from the early days of your employment what might be called a "go-to-hell fund"—one that enables you to tell that to your boss when you're asked to step across a line that takes you too far from your basic ethical principles.

Squires used the pragmatic, Machiavellian approach in dealing with the head of the business operations at the *Chicago Tribune* and in Florida at the *Orlando Sentinel*. He struck what he later came to view as a Faustian bargain. He would control what went into the paper, its editorial opinions, when it went to press, and the face it presented to its community; in return, he would "run the tightest ship in the business. It was a deal designed to deliver both prizes and profits" and did deliver considerable success for a while (Squires, 1993, pp. 57–58).

Even if this approach were to work, attaining one's goal at any cost is not comforting to people concerned with ethics. Similarly, executives responsible for making television programming decisions are increasingly likely to be constrained by economic factors. For example, if a potential program isn't expected to appeal to viewers in a desired niche of the overall audience, it is unlikely to be seen on a national network no matter how good it is or how much "good" it might bring to a large number of viewers.

the very structure of American media industries is increasingly creating conditions in which media traditions, individual ethical values and concerns about responsibility are less important than economics.

Conglomerate ownership has produced relationships—and the potential for decisions about the media—that extend well beyond the mass media gatekeepers. For example, the tie-ins between the Disney Corporation's various media activities, including ABC, and its ownership of theme parks and pro sports franchises, could easily produce media content decisions based on marketing considerations benefiting these non-media activities rather than traditional gatekeeping criteria.

Thus, the very structure of American media industries is increasingly creating conditions in which media traditions, individual ethical values and concerns about responsibility are less important than economics. When the actual and potential influence of government, politics, technology and the social system are added to the equation, the constraints on individual ethics, values, and autonomy should be obvious, as should the need for a go-to-hell fund.

KEY POINTS

- Aristotle and Rawls provide useful guidance in the face of political, cultural, social and economic pressures that can deter individuals from acting as independent "moral agents."
- Among the factors limiting individual moral autonomy are pressure groups, the internal culture of media organizations, and constant Internet and 24/7 news cycle deadlines.
- Media people should build up a "go-to-hell" fund so they can quit their jobs when the alternative is to violate their own ethical principles.

MERRILL: Commentary

David Gordon is right when he maintains that ethical decisions in the media are greatly influenced by forces operating in the larger society. Certainly it would be simplistic to believe that individual media people make their decisions based *solely* on their own ethical values. Media policy, peer expectations, and social pressures of many kinds inevitably have an impact on individual ethical determinations. Journalists, for example, often can avoid ethical decision-making if they are willing to follow the traditional media or social expectations. Sociologists would not quarrel with this; it is well known that people tend to conform to the policies of the institutions they work for.

Although such a position is not too bothersome in most areas of social activity, when it comes to ethics the concept of social conformity is rather worrisome, at least to those who feel that the individual should have the courage to carry the moral burden independent of external expectations. Even an immoral person can conform to the group, as we know. Like Kant, some believe that the "principled" media worker would be guided by a reasoned duty to do the right or the better thing—regardless of the social sentiment and pressures of the day. This is the position supported in this chapter by John Michael Kittross.

Certainly we shouldn't go too far in such thinking, however. We know that a meaningful ethics is not isolated from society, that in reality there is no ethics that is not social. At least this is what a large segment of ethicists—especially communitarians—tell us. Religious, political, economic, and other forces, as Gordon argues, have their impact on media ethics. Organized social and political action, boycotts, and government regulation do indeed make independent ethical determinations difficult, if not impossible—or so it seems. But the question persists: *should* they?

Gordon gets very close to saying that the free-market capitalist economy, with its normal pressures, keeps journalists from making their own ethical decisions. It is incorrect, he maintains, to attribute significant media content to editorial decisions; he argues that such decisions are frequently influenced by outside social or governmental factors, or are made in a profit-driven context that largely omits moral considerations from the model. If this is true, then it is indeed a sad day for media morality. Journalists become no more than slaves to forces outside themselves, mere functionaries operating in an institutional environment without morals. Like Machiavelli (and American journalist James Squires) Gordon seems to see pragmatism replacing the individual values of media people.

Taking issue with Gordon, Kittross puts considerable stress on the importance of individual moral values and decisions. Question your own ethical premises, think out your own ethical problems, act out your own moral strategies, take responsibility for your own ethical action: These are individualistic mandates, according to Kittross, that fall on every media functionary. But Gordon is right there with his counter-position: sticking to personal ethics is unattainable.

These collective and individual expectations may or may not be in conflict, but it would seem that if they are, the journalist would have to come down on the side of individual expectations. Why? Because morality is not determined by a majority vote or even a desire to do what the crowd or social pressures require.

Gordon is correct in noting that many forces influence journalistic ethics, such as audience expectations, the wishes of the editors, and the importance of the advertisers. He quotes Kovach and Rosenstiel about "cascading rationalization" as discouraging acts of individual conscience. All right. That is what the situation *is*. But we're talking about ethics—about what *should be*.

Aristotle's "Golden Mean" is the best ethical guide for Gordon, the middle-ground between extremes. But besides being semantically difficult, the Golden Mean may not accomplish another of Gordon's aims—the utilitarian consequences of John Stuart Mill.

Kittross, reflecting a proclivity for Kant's ethics, stresses a need for a rational, personal code of journalistic conduct. Kittross would prefer a code individually formulated, and not one based on a special concern for consequences. Basically a self-determined principled ethics, devoid of teleological expectation.

Of course, out of such discussions as this comes the inevitable question: why should I individually feel any ethical mandate placed on me? If I do, does it perhaps come from the expectations of my colleagues in the media or from those in the audience I serve? These are good questions, and ones that are usually avoided in media ethics books. I'm not sure that I can answer them—or that I really want to relieve you of this obligation, at this point. But I will say that a concern with being ethical must always precede any wrestling with moral dilemmas and any systematic concern for doing the right or best thing.

Many would say that a moral consciousness, with its determination to be ethical, derives from a deep-seated selfishness, a kind of doing unto others as you would have them do unto you. (Others might say it is the exact opposite, stemming from a desire to improve how society functions—to help "repair the world," if you will.) Be honest with others because you want them to be honest with you. Don't lie, said Kant, unless you would be willing to say that everyone should be allowed to lie. This is ethical reasoning, all right, but it is built on a foundation of selfishness. It makes sense, no doubt, but does it make moral as well as logical sense? Perhaps I should not lie even though everyone else, indeed, does lie.

Is it possible that I should have a desire to be ethical simply for the sake of being ethical—and for no other reason? Just because I sense that it is good to be ethical? No consideration of Gordon's Millian consequences here. And no dedication to Kittross's concern with Kant's universalizing principle here. Just a deep-seated, personal commitment to doing right, regardless of what others might do or think, or what the social repercussions might be. This would free me from the formalistic ethical strictures of Immanuel Kant and also from the altruistic consequentialism of John Stuart Mill. It would throw me, existentially, into the moral maelstrom and force me momentarily to make ethical decisions and accept responsibility for them.

This might be called a kind of motivation ethics. It is somewhere between the social determinism of Gordon's argument and the personal autonomy of Kittross's position. My motive is simply to do what I think is right, or what I feel or intuit is right. The simple motive of doing good, of following the righteous path as I see it in the existential context of the moment and situation: this is the reasonless stimulant to ethical concern that may well lie at the foundation of much moral motivation.

This will not appeal to everyone; in fact it will probably not appeal to very many. It has Kierkegaardian overtones that rise to a kind of religious apex of faith, intuition, and personal spontaneity. Not to be found here is an overriding concern with moral reasoning, or with "doing ethics." It is not exactly the philosopher's way; it is perhaps more the theological or the mystical way. It is coming at ethics from the subjective, not the objective, side.

It is unfolding ethics from the inside out, not from the outside in. It is more feeling-ethics than thinking-ethics. Of course, when we talk like this we are getting into the religious sphere, but it is a sphere that many philosophers (such as Kierkegaard, Nietzsche, Schopenhauer, and Jaspers) and many religious figures (such as Buddha and Jesus) have endorsed whole-heartedly.

I have departed considerably from Gordon's and Kittross's main arguments, perhaps. But maybe not. Such an inward-motivational stance is certainly an individualistic one, based not on social conformity and peer expectations and pressures but rather on a personal, almost transcendental moral consciousness. That consciousness rises from spiritual aware-ness of what is better or worse, right or wrong, not from worldly reasoning. It derives from a kind of subjective inflation of one's sense of being human, a form of flooding the spiritual aspects of personhood with mystical positive overtones, and it results in a moral epiphany quite different from the purely philosophical reasons for being ethical.

The arguments of Gordon and Kittross deal with much less spiritual matters. They present their arguments cogently and stay far away from the mystical moral epiphany that I have just suggested. But they are facing the same sort of question, an old question with which many thinkers have grappled: is ethics mainly individualistic or social? Many agree with Hegel, who saw each of us as insignificant, no more than an expression of the grand forces of society and history, believing that an ethical sense must flow from the needs and wishes of society. The modern communitarians, under the leadership of sociologist Amitai Etzioni, are busy reinforcing the appeal of a socially endowed and concerned ethics.

Others, like Kierkegaard and Nietzsche, see the individual as of more importance than society, and make the case for personal moral accountability. Kittross would be supported by psychiatrist Carl Jung and philosopher Karl Jaspers, who believed that the individual matters more than the system, thus reversing the idea of Hegel, Marx, and other "groupist" thinkers. Contemporary Harvard philosopher Robert Nozick, an individualist, would support Kittross, and his colleague John Rawls would support Gordon in his concern for social happiness and benefits.

What is clear is that the individual is essential to ethics, but at the same time others are also needed. The individual cannot be ethical in a vacuum. Without a doubt, media people must consider the human environment in which they function. Of course, this will lead to a certain moderation of action and to a certain conformity. But such moderation is self-determined. At the same time, it is necessary to recognize that the media person—regardless of field—must often be willing to make ethical decisions in a courageous and independent manner regardless of social expectations.

REFERENCES AND RELATED READINGS

Argyris, Chris. (1974). *Behind the Front Page*. San Francisco, CA: Jossey-Bass.

Armstrong, John. (2007). "More philosophy means more relevance." *Media Ethics* 19(1), pp. 1, 16–18.

Associated Press. (2007). "Media rip attorney general for remarks." AP story printed in the Eau Claire, WI *Leader-Telegram*, October 15, p. 10A.

Bagdikian, Ben. (1989). "The lords of the global village." *The Nation*, (June 12, 1989), pp. 805–820.

Breed, Warren. (1955). "Social control in the newsroom." *Social Forces* 33(4), pp. 326–335.

Brotman, Barbara (1993). "When conscience fails to guide." *The News & Observer*, March 7, Raleigh, NC, pp. 1E, 5E.

Committee of Concerned Journalists (2000). *Principles of Journalism*. Retrieved from www.journalism.org/resources/principles (May 11, 2009).

Cody, Edward. (2007). "Freedom to suppress." *The Seattle Times*, article from *The Washington Post*, August 12, p. A3.

Doherty, Thomas. (1988). "Hollywood agit-prop: The anti-Communist cycle, 1948–1954." *Journal of Film and Video* 40(4), pp. 15–27.

Endres, Fred F. (1985). "Influences on the ethical socialization of U.S. newspaper journalists." *Newspaper Research Journal* 6(3), pp. 47–56.

Ford, Frederick W. (1963–64). "The Fairness Doctrine." *Journal of Broadcasting* 8(1), pp. 3–16.

"Gartner shares lessons he learned from NBC years." (1993). *SNPA Bulletin*, June 1, pp. 8–9.

Hamer, John (2007) " 'Unprecedented.' 'Groundbreaking.' 'One of a kind': How the Washington News Council studied the Spokane *Spokesman-Review*." *Media Ethics* 19(1), pp. 3, 18–19.

Harwood, Richard. (1992). "Knights of the Fourth Estate." *Washington Post*, December 5, p. A23.

Hodges, Louis W. (2007). "Conflict of interest." In Donald W. Hatley and Paula F. Furr, eds., *Freedom Fighter: A Festschrift Honoring John C. Merrill on his Six Decades of Service to Journalism Education*. Natchitoches, LA: Northwestern State University Press, pp. 111–129.

Kittross, John Michael. (2007). "Some thoughts on John C. Merrill, responsibility and professionalism." In Donald W. Hatley and Paula F. Furr, eds., *Freedom Fighter: A Festschrift Honoring John C. Merrill on his Six Decades of Service to Journalism Education*. Natchitoches, LA: Northwestern State University Press, pp. 169–186.

Kovach, Bill and Tom Rosenstiel. (2001). *The Elements of Journalism: What Newspeople Should Know and the Public Should Expect*. New York: Three Rivers Press.

Lambeth, Edmund. (1992). *Committed Journalism: An Ethic for the Profession*, 2nd ed. Bloomington and Indianapolis, IN: Indiana University Press.

Mentzer, Robert. (2009). "Did media cry swine? Flu coverage heavy, and some say overblown." *Wausau Daily Herald*, May 10. Retrieved from www.wausaudailyherald.com/article/20090510/WDH06/905100344#pluckcomments (May 11, 2009).

Merrill, John C. (2007). "Academic media ethics courses: Factors for frustration." *Media Ethics* 19(1), pp. 9, 24.

Sayre, Nora. (1978). *Running Time: Films of the Cold War*. New York: Dial Press.

Shales, Tom. (2007). "A media role in selling the war? No question." *The Washington Post*, April 25, p. C01.

Smith, Rex. (2004). "Checking—facts, as well as the faces." Albany, NY *Times Union*, May 29, p. A9.

Squires, James D. (1993). *Read All About It!: The Corporate Takeover of America's Newspapers*. New York: Times Books.

Thomas, Cal. (2009). "Media worship the god Obama." Syndicated column in *The Burlington* (VT) *Free Press*, June 12, p. 9B.

Weaver, David H., Randal A. Beam, Bonnie J. Brownlee, Paul S. Voakes and G. Cleveland Wilhoit. (2006). *The American Journalist in the 21st Century: U.S. News People at the Dawn of New Millennium*. Mahwah, NJ: Lawrence Erlbaum Associates.

Reflections

Taking Aristotle to Work—Practical and Moral Values

John A. Armstrong

IN his Overview of ethics and ethicists (see pp. 3–32), John Merrill helps us appreciate the classical, philosophical roots of ethics. However, this systematic approach to media ethics may suggest a heavier dose of philosophy than many students—and media professionals—prefer. Media people are pragmatic, and what does Aristotle (or Kant, or Mill, or any ethicist) have to do anyway with getting and keeping that first job in journalism, public relations, or marketing?

In fact, immersion in ethical philosophy *can* help students become more skillful and effective (as well as more ethical) media professionals. Ethical reasoning should not be confined to a media ethics class or to the occasional controversy in the workplace. Media studies and media careers are shot through with questions that are, at their roots, ethical problems. Ethical philosophy and the critical faculties it engenders are invaluable for the workplace and for life itself.

To grasp the importance of ethical reasoning, it is necessary to understand a particular notion of ethical philosophy and its implications. Ethics is here construed as *virtuous behavior* and as a component of the larger notion of what constitutes a *good life*. But this notion of ethics should be only the starting point for a rigorous, and—I will argue—beneficial, process of reasoning and self-examination. The practical reasoning of ethics and virtue is grounded in our personal valuations of such qualities as happiness, freedom, autonomy, duty, and rationality. At least since Socrates (c. 470–399 B.C.), the definition of virtue has been a persistent question in Western philosophy; so too has the question of what constitutes a life well lived. Aristotle (384–322 B.C.), for example, begins his *Nicomachean Ethics* with an analysis of human happiness, which he suggests should be the aim of virtuous behavior.

This is not to say that traditional Western philosophy and "dead white males" such as Socrates, Aristotle, and their heirs are the only sources of ethical wisdom. But their thinking on ethics and the nature of the individual is a powerful application of reason to questions about our lives, our actions, and our purposes. Socrates and Aristotle placed virtue and other fundamental human questions at the forefront of their thinking, and they used a line of inquiry employing rationality to attack "received knowledge," assumptions, and prejudices.

Many students and professionals are aware of the humanistic possibilities of media work: to serve human values, and fulfillment. The altruistic framework of media work includes, for example, fulfilling the watchdog role of the press or engaging in the market-place of ideas. Such frameworks, in turn, promote components of human fulfillment such as political participation, individual freedom, and intellectual engagement. This is a mission to be proud of and it can be informed by long traditions of rationalism and humanistic thought. However, you may also have seen this impulse crowded out by career anxiety and appetite for "practical" skills. The humanistic mission is not necessarily in conflict with these imperatives. There are even some convincing arguments for this from the "real world" of the marketplace.

In a strikingly blunt essay, Matthew Stewart (2006) argues that much of management theory is inane and that those who wish to succeed in business would be better off studying philosophy. Stewart is well positioned to make such judgments. He has a doctoral degree in philosophy and was a principal founder of a management consulting firm that eventually employed 600 people. His case for philosophical education is twofold: it stimulates clearer, more robust reasoning and it introduces a humanistic approach to activities that are often perceived as taking place in their own, discrete regions (frequently that of the marketplace) that apparently operate on internal rules. Stewart's claims apply to the media business, where marketplace logic often has ethical implications.

Stewart also makes a second, more fundamental claim about philosophy, ethics, and the workplace:

> Beyond building skills, business training must be about values. As I write this, I know that my M.B.A. friends are squirming in their seats. They've all been forced to sit through an "ethics" course, in which they learned to toss around yet more fancy phrases like "the categorical imperative" and discuss borderline criminal behavior, such as what's a legitimate hotel bill and what's just plain stealing from the expense account, how to tell the difference between a pat on the shoulder and sexual harassment and so on. But, as anyone who has studied Aristotle will know, "values" aren't something you bump into from time to time during the course of a business career. All of business is about values, all of the time.
>
> (p. 87)

As examples of how values permeate management decisions, Stewart suggests that seemingly straightforward strategies to promote worker productivity and teamwork (drawn from classic management studies) in fact have strong ethical dimensions that have been overlooked. How many tons *should* (as well as *can*) a worker be required to lift in a certain amount of time? How much of a worker's sense of identity and well-being does a business have a right to harness in order to build teamwork (p. 87)?

Students and teachers of mass communication will attest that Kant's "categorical imperative" also appears frequently in media ethics textbooks and case studies, sometimes offered in contrast to utilitarian ethics. Typically, these philosophies are applied to problems of journalism: what are the reporter's obligations for telling the truth, for protecting sources, or for balancing other societal interests against unrestrained reporting? The ethical frameworks of both rule-based deontological reasoning or consequence-based "greatest-good-for-the-greatest-number-of-people" utilitarian (or teleological) reasoning are germane to such questions and they encourage systematic thinking about them. However, Stewart's claim about the pervasiveness of values in business poses a challenge to media students and professionals: can we, too, identify ethical questions throughout *our* field? Can we address ethical questions that arise outside of journalistic practices?

Media deregulation is an example of a topic that is seldom analyzed as an ethical issue. Discussions of U.S. media policy often focus on questions of diversity and concentration in media ownership and the related question of the proper role of markets in shaping the mission and structure of mass media. These are substantial questions that deserve the attention that they receive. It is also possible, however, to explore more thoroughly their ethical underpinnings and implications. Here again, a particular notion of ethics comes into play: virtuous behavior that is defined and animated by a concept of human fulfillment.

An ethical critique of media policy can emphasize the explicit and implicit values inherent in arguments about deregulation. Critics point to giant media conglomerates that have arisen from deregulation and argue that they focus relentlessly on profits; the result is often shoddy journalism and other content that lacks quality and taste. Concerns about deregulation energize citizen groups such as the National Conference for Media Reform, which reports that attendance at its national conventions surged from 1,700 to 3,500 between 2003 and 2007 (Free Press, 2007). Kuttner (1997) asserts that market ideology casts individuals as consumers to the core, beings whose fulfillment hinges on material gain. The implication for media conglomerates is that "good" content is simply anything that people will buy or watch.

It is also possible, however, to understand some pro-market arguments as grounded in values more profound than a materialist caricature of human needs. With its emphasis on self-interest and private property, market ideology still has echoes of Enlightenment values of individual rationality and freedom. Whether or not contemporary scholars and students find them compelling, these values are more fundamental than simple assertions about market efficiency. Locke (1690), in particular, defined labor—and its byproduct of property—as an inviolable possession of the autonomous person. Do contemporary media markets, through the mechanisms of subscription, advertising, and audience ratings, actually serve the Enlightenment values of individual autonomy and of rational, self-interested choice?

Conversely, what notions of human fulfillment justify media regulation that purports to serve a common good? Dewey (1927), for example, argued that we should value "publicity" because of its role in cultivating democratic communities. His view of media also contains an ethical idea: Dewey believed that participation in a democratic community is, in itself, a form of human fulfillment. This notion, as well, may or may not be convincing to contemporary media students and scholars, but it is one worth considering. Former *New York Times* reporter Douglas McGill (2008) asserts that, with regard to civic-mindedness, journalists are among the most ethical people one could imagine. "Why else," he asks, "would someone choose a profession with such long hours and poor pay, if not for the chance to improve the world a little bit?" Yet, McGill asserts, norms of objectivity prevent journalists from discussing ethics in the newsroom. To McGill, their silence is "similar to, say, environmentalists who work for lumber companies."

Journalists, other media professionals, and students are likely familiar with another issue whose ethical implications are often overlooked: the debate over copyright law. The collision of intellectual property law and new technologies has already shaken the entertainment industry. It has fought bitter legal battles with Internet users who download (for free) copyrighted songs, TV programs, and films. In 2005, the United States Supreme Court ruled that even the producers of the file-sharing software (such as Grokster) used by individual downloaders are themselves liable for copyright infringement (*Metro-Goldwyn-Mayer*). Some legal experts criticize the decision for extending ownership power over creative works so far as to prevent the public from fully benefiting from them.

Mass media's intellectual property struggle is often portrayed as an economic contest. The music industry provides the best known example. On one side are the record companies, who may or may not be gouging the public with overpriced CDs. Sometimes, they are supported by artists who depend on record companies and CD sales for their livelihood. Pitted against them are Internet "pirates," individuals who sometimes claim to use free downloading to fight the monopoly of greedy record companies. In some cases, the "pirates" are supported by other artists who want to bypass the recording industry and create a better way of sharing and marketing their music.

With their conflicting notions of property rights, virtuous behavior, and human fulfillment, intellectual property debates can also be analyzed as ethical quandaries. Again, the music downloading provides a useful example. Under current law, free downloading of copyrighted music is both illegal and common. Whether they are conscious rebels against corporate control of music, or casual exploiters of a cheap and easy method of obtaining music, downloaders might well consider the ethical implications of their behavior.

Mill (1864), in *Utilitarianism*, provides a theory of justice that seeks human happiness— and avoidance of misery—as its outcome. An essential need for happiness, Mill asserts, is that of security. Laws are a means to mutual security and our support for common justice flows from a desire to protect our own persons and property from arbitrary assaults (p. 54). Despite their anger (or apathy) toward public laws restricting the use of copyrighted music, downloaders might well weigh how their noncompliance with one law undermines a broader legal system from which they derive other benefits. Mill also suggests that there are instances when a social duty (e.g. saving a human life) is so strong as to outweigh general laws of behavior (pp. 63–64). Music downloaders might consider whether their grievance against the recording industry genuinely rises to this level of significance.

> downloaders might well weigh how their noncompliance with one law undermines a broader legal system from which they derive other benefits.

Citizens and (especially) media professionals can also extend their ethical analysis to the "ought" of copyright law: in what direction should intellectual property laws now move? In recent decades, the U.S. Congress and courts have lengthened the duration of copyrights and strengthened the grip of copyright holders. Critics argue that this increased control goes far beyond what is necessary to encourage creativity on the part of artists and entertainment companies. Instead, such controls serve to keep copyrighted materials out of the hands of the public, and to prevent other artists and entertainers from drawing on them for their own creations.

When intellectual property law is analyzed as an ethics issue, the paramount question becomes how the ownership of intellectual property serves—or fails to serve—human fulfillment. For example, intellectual tastes figure prominently in the notion of human happiness encompassed by utilitarian philosophy (Mill, 1864, p. 10). In a famous formulation, utilitarianism seeks the greatest happiness for the greatest number of people (Bentham, 1781, p. 31). If intellectual property rights are instrumental to this end, rather than an end in themselves, we might consider how the law would best serve the general welfare, rather than just protect property rights or economic interests.

These ethical questions about intellectual property and media deregulation are not offered because they are susceptible to easy answers. Rather, they exemplify the ethical complexity that we can find throughout media studies, including areas that are seldom viewed through an ethical lens.

Philosophers honor Socrates because he put humans and virtuous behavior at the forefront of inquiry. Media work confronts some of the same problems that engaged Socrates. Mass media present many questions that are essentially ethical, philosophical puzzles. These questions can help students and professionals sharpen their minds for the workplace. Better still, they can challenge them to examine their own ethical systems.

REFERENCES AND RELATED READINGS

Aristotle. (Many editions). *Nicomachean Ethics*.

Bentham, Jeremy. (1781). *The Principles of Morals and Legislation* (reprinted, 1988). Buffalo, NY: Prometheus.

Dewey, John. (1927). *The Public and its Problems* (reprinted, 1991). Athens, OH: Swallow Press.

Free Press. (2007). "NCMR: 2007, National Conference for Media Reform." Retrieved from www.free press.net/ncmr07=previous07 (February 26, 2008).

Kuttner, Robert. (1997). *Everything for Sale: The Virtues and Limits of Markets*. New York: Knopf.

Locke, John. (1690). *Second Treatise of Government* (reprinted, 1980). Indianapolis, IN: Hackett.

McGill, Douglas. (2008). "The true promise of citizen journalism." *The Burleigh Lecture on Media Ethics*, Marquette University (online posting of cancelled program scheduled for February 6, 2008). Retrieved from www.mcgillreport.org/truepromise.htm (February 26, 2008).

Metro-Goldwyn-Mayer Studios, Inc. v. Grokster, Ltd., 545 U.S. 913 (2005).

Mill, John Stuart. (1864). *Utilitarianism* (reprinted, 2001). Indianapolis, IN: Hackett.

Stewart, Matthew. (2006). "The management myth." *Atlantic Monthly*, June, pp. 80–87.

Part Two

Roles and Pressures

Chapter 3

Gatekeepers and Manipulators

Truth, Fairness, and Accuracy

THE reader may occasionally wonder if the authors of this chapter were writing on two different topics. Like trains going in different directions that pass in the night, there are few collisions—but a great deal of latent power—in this controversy. Among other things, David Gordon worries about "filters" that are self-imposed by members of the public, whereas John Michael Kittross goes more deeply into the nitty-gritty questions of gatekeeping and manipulation and asks the age-old question: What is truth? And both try to assign responsibility where they think it is due.

Much—perhaps most—of the content of the media is intended to manipulate. Drama, humor, and music evoke emotions even while they illuminate the human condition; persuasion evokes changes in attitude or promotes specific purchases or behaviors; and information that goes beyond titillation or infotainment is bound to have often-unpredictable consequences. Everyone in the communication process—from the creator of a message through the media gatekeepers to the audience—has some responsibility for the effects of that message. Gordon and Kittross may disagree in this chapter about the apportionment of responsibility in that process, and about the ethics involved. But both are firmly aware of the importance of what *everyone* in the communication process must do and that each of them shares the responsibility for infusing ethics into the process.

Lies are usually "bad." Truth is usually "good." But, in addition to it frequently being difficult to distinguish one from the other (particularly if the lies are due to omissions), these aphorisms probably are not Kantian absolutes. Even without a utilitarian orientation, sometimes a lie is necessary, sometimes a truth is harmful.

In the mass media field, however, it is rare that one can argue that an untruthful message is ultimately going to be "a good thing." During wartime, in virtually every nation, there are those who would argue that—in the interests of winning the war—truth is relatively unimportant. Those who remember how the United States got involved in the invasion of Iraq are aware of this. Those strongly in favor of that war and those strongly opposed considered that the "greater truth" of their position was more important than the lesser truth of what actually occurred. This led to emphasis on exaggeration, false assertions (such as the claim that there was a strong connection between the destruction of the New York World Trade Center and Saddam Hussein of Iraq), and appeals to ideology, slogans, and over-simplification rather than facts, logic, and reasoning.

Unfortunately, it becomes a goal of those who believe that the people "can't take the truth" and need to be manipulated for their own good to—intentionally—distract the citizenry from considering such distinctions as "greater" or "lesser" truths. Other concepts in the same family—accuracy, objectivity, validity, reliability, fairness, balance (which Kittross rejects), and the like—are discussed at some length in Kittross's half of this chapter, while Gordon discusses the self-imposed filters that create audiences wrapped in their own "informational cocoons," in addition to his focus on truth and the interplay between public relations and journalism.

Words can have very powerful consequences. While we all are aware that complex issues or assertions may be hard to understand, oversimplification also may lead to confusion, even when a "larger truth" or principle is being sought. Furthermore, the "greater truth" may be the result of distilling many verifiable, valid, and reliable facts into knowledge, which gives us what is needed to make future decisions of benefit to ourselves and our society.

The chapter that follows probably has as many ideas and disagreements per page as any in this book. Organization may zigzag, but each author has concentrated on those aspects of the process of gatekeeping of content and manipulation of audiences that he considers most important. That, of course, doesn't preclude the reader from drawing his or her own conclusions, making her or his own assertions, testing them, perhaps disagreeing with one or both authors, and determining the necessary ethical course or courses.

GORDON: Mass media are inevitable targets for those seeking to manipulate how content is presented, but truth and the need for exposure to new ideas remain as key principles.

The relationship between the news media and public relations practitioners is important for media ethicists to consider, as are the truth-fairness-accuracy concerns discussed in this chapter by John Michael Kittross. But before turning to those topics, I want to examine what I regard as the other side of the gatekeeping coin: whether individual members of the public are too insulated against perspectives they might find uncomfortable but still informative and useful.

One example of this concern, as Kittross will note, is the popularity of some radio talk shows that reinforce their listeners' various prejudices and stereotypes rather than provide information or new ideas that might help the audience look at the world differently. Overall, I agree with Kittross's concern about the public's need for multiple points of view, even when the audience might prefer entertainment programming. But I shudder a bit at his apparent willingness to have the government exert some control over the media to ensure that they will provide information we "need" to have, even (and perhaps especially) if this were restricted to "times of crisis"—a phrase that can always be defined by those in power to suit their own ends.

If audience members can construct an effective "informational cocoon," they will be able to block media gatekeepers at least as effectively as any "traditional" media manipulator can. For such consumers, the purpose is to cut off exposure to information and opinion that might unsettle them. This power—to avoid contact with new (but important) ideas and information—is a serious threat to *informed* self-government. And the media need to ask if there's anything they might do about it.

Cass Sunstein, a law professor at the University of Chicago and Harvard University until he was confirmed in 2009 as head of the Federal Office of Information and Regulatory Affairs, has expressed concern about technological "filters" on the Internet that enable individual consumers to customize what they download. He feared that this would allow people to avoid *encounters with* material that might clash in some way with their beliefs or expose them to new perspectives. Carried to the extreme, he wrote, you could wind up with a downloaded and highly customized "Daily Me" that would never force you to confront new ideas or information about unfamiliar topics (Sunstein, 2007).

Ralph Barney has expressed some of the same concerns. He wrote that a democratic society needs to provide a variety of information sources that people can draw on in their decision-making processes. This pluralism is needed both across the media spectrum and perhaps especially within the narrow, specialized spectrum of media outlets that many individuals restrict themselves to using (Barney, 1986, especially pp. 77–79).

In 1971, Tom Wicker of *The New York Times* noted a related problem, with his criticism of reporters who rely too heavily on sources representing established institutions (Wicker, 1971). Such institutional news sources usually have well-developed public relations arms and use a wide range of techniques to influence what eventually appears in the news media. The result too often is an "establishment" point of view put forward as "the way things are," rather than the pluralism that Barney (1986) advocates. If media gatekeepers adopted a pluralistic approach, they would help ensure that all points of view, mainstream or fringe or somewhere in between, would be open to challenge from all corners of society.

Any limitations on the availability of voices or ideas necessarily reduces or eliminates debate in an open "marketplace of ideas" where ideas can clash, be tempered, and perhaps refined by argument or discussion. Sunstein (2007), focusing specifically on the Internet, called for electronic "public spaces" where such debate can occur, rather than the individualized and fragmented communications spheres that would result from a "Daily Me." His approach can be seen as a cyberspace updating of the "public sphere" advocated by Jürgen Habermas—a location or "space" (or, better, an opportunity) where rational people could deliberate and attempt to reach a mutual understanding that might serve as a check on governmental power (Habermas, 1962).

Sunstein (2007, p. xii) argues that the ethical use of freedom of expression—not to mention the needs of effective democratic self-government—requires that people be exposed to competing perspectives rather than having "like-minded people speak or listen mostly to one another"—a point that recalls arguments in Chapter 1. He contends that "there are serious dangers in a system in which individuals bypass general-interest intermediaries and restrict themselves to opinions and topics of their own choosing" and listen primarily "to louder echoes of their own voices." Free societies, he argues, need "a set of public forums, providing speakers' access to a diverse people, and ensuring in the process that each of us hears a wide range of speakers, spanning many topics and opinions" (Sunstein, 2007, pp. 13 and 22).

The late television journalist Tim Russert, in his last public speech, stressed the same need for public exposure to differing opinions and added an admonition that should be a central credo for journalists:

> It's not enough to simply confirm your political views by only watching or accessing outlets that reinforce your views and do not challenge them. . . .
>
> It will not be enough in a democratic society to simply have those on the left or right who are the pamphleteers and unwilling to challenge the views of people they support. Tough questions need not be the loudest or the most sensational or the most theatrical, but rather probing and, hopefully, incisive.
>
> A case in point is the war in Iraq . . . and whether the appropriate questions were asked of our leaders [beforehand].
>
> (Russert, 2008, p. 8)

BROADENING PERSPECTIVES VIA TV AND THE INTERNET

Another example—this one in a crisis situation—of exposing the public to a very different perspective comes from the ongoing Israeli–Palestinian conflict where an Israeli human rights group distributed video cameras to Palestinians living in the West Bank. The cameras were used "to document injustices and the violence of the occupation from within—pictures that were then screened on Israeli television over and over again. This, in turn, gave rise to investigations and charges" (Be'er, 2009).

> People engaged in protracted national conflict tend to reject, ignore and deny the narratives of the enemy. Television can help achieve the opposite. By broadcasting the tragic truth of conflict we personalise and humanise the other. Television coverage of this sort can increase tolerance, empathy and heightened awareness.
>
> (Be'er, 2009)

(For further discussion of the tendency to view the enemy as "the other" and of the "we–they syndrome" more generally, see Chapter 4.)

The results were similar to those after heavy Israeli TV and newspaper coverage of a Palestinian doctor whose three daughters were killed by Israeli fire during its 2008–09 invasion of Gaza.

> Never before had a Palestinian received such empathetic coverage by the mainstream media in Israel. His was the figure of a modern day Job: a pacifist, a doctor who speaks Hebrew and a human being who continues to speak the language of peace even after his daughters were killed.

. . . The change in atmosphere was tangible even in the media. Reporters and pro-gramme hosts began challenging military spokesmen with tougher questions. Some people argue that this brought about an early end to the war.

. . . the bottom line is that the story of Dr. Abuelaish humanised the suffering of the Palestinians in Israeli eyes more than anything else in this war.

Television made this phenomenon possible. The nature of the medium is that it leaves editors with little choice. In an era of competition between television stations, no editor can afford to miss out on such dramatic coverage.

(Be'er, 2009)

Sunstein (2007) suggested that various means can be used to force people to confront new perspectives and ideas. Such isolation must be ended, he wrote, if there is to be any hope of reaching common ground on such important but divisive issues as climate change, welfare reform, genetic engineering of food products, or others where rational discussion is required. This will be extremely difficult "if people do not know the competing view, consistently avoid speaking with one another, and are unaware how to address divergent concerns of fellow citizens" (p. 57).

Sunstein also suggested several ways to enrich the mix of ideas and perspectives to which the public is exposed. These could include extending the "public forum" concept to specific locations on the Internet (perhaps with some public subsidies); voluntary agree-ments among traditional media outlets to give their audiences the broadest possible range of views; and the creation of "deliberative domains" online, "where people of very different views are invited to listen and to speak" (p. 193).

Perhaps his most creative suggestion is that Internet "providers of material with a certain point of view might also provide links to sites with a very different point of view"—for example, reciprocal links between *The Nation* and the *Weekly Standard* or between partisan sites. "The icon itself would not require anyone to read anything. It would merely provide a signal, to the viewer, that there is a place where a different point of view might be consulted." And "public-spirited bloggers" might use a similar approach to expose their readers to opposing perspectives and "reflect a healthy degree of mutual respect" (Sunstein, 2007, pp. 208 and 210)—and maybe, just maybe, lead to more civil dialogue on some controversial issues.

Maintaining a functioning, heterogeneous republic requires not just a ban on govern-ment censorship, but also

some kind of public domain in which a wide range of speakers have access to a diverse public. . . . It also demands not only a law of free expression, but also a culture of free expression, in which people are eager to listen to what their fellow citizens have to say.

(Sunstein, 2007, p. 222)

The 2009–10 health care reform brouhaha both illustrated Sunstein's concern all too well and demonstrated how far we still have to go to create that "culture of free expression" where people actually listen to opposing opinions. The underlying goal, of course, is to enable Mill's concept of ideas competing against each other to become a source of progress and of truth for society as a whole.

THE NEWS–PUBLIC RELATIONS RELATIONSHIP

pluralism is meaningless if people "are isolated from alternative messages by the velvety cocoon of special interest and come into contact only with advocate-type messages"— Ralph Barney

Barney (1986) reflects concerns similar to those of Sunstein, Wicker, and Russert when he notes that the concept of pluralism is meaningless if people "are isolated from alternative messages by the velvety cocoon of special interest and come into contact only with advocate-type messages" (see Chapter 4 for more on Barney's advocacy of pluralism). Teaching journalists to be open at all times to weighing new evidence rather than believing they have all the answers—in essence, teaching them the "scientific method"—would help "immunize them from the inevitable persuasive rhetoric of the special pleader" and help them "generate and present messages presenting alternatives to those of organized, special pleading individuals" (Barney pp. 74, 76 and 79).

Which brings us to the news–public relations (PR) relationship. *Attempts* to manipulate the news media raise no ethical problems per se, since that's an appropriate aspect of public relations practice. What matters is whether journalists are able to maintain their independence, make their own news judgments, and hold fast to their traditional gatekeeping role—and, as noted below, whether they are *perceived* that way. As any reporter knows, a good public relations practitioner can frequently be a lifesaver in providing information, or access to information, that the reporter needs. Among thoughtful reporters and PR people, there's an understanding that they need to work together on many things, but that each must remain an independent agent and that, in the last analysis, they must make their decisions without being influenced by their symbiotic relationship. That's the way it should work, in an ideal world.

But, of course, we don't live in an ideal world, so some PR practitioners *do* try to influence reporters (or their bosses) in inappropriate ways, and sometimes they succeed in that manipulation. And some journalists are lazy (or overworked, in this time of staff cutbacks, which poses a different genre of ethics issues) and will use press, audio, or video news releases without vetting them. Some news outlets have been known to run that material without indicating that it came from a public relations source, which adds another layer of ethical transgression. And some public relations people *try* to get the news media to use their material *without* identifying the source, which violates most recognized PR standards. Worse yet, some have tried to strike deals with media outlets to use only sources from the PR practitioner's organization. (For an egregious example of portions of newscasts that were almost "sold" for that kind of PR purpose, see Chapter 12.)

Responsible public relations practitioners know that their job is to present as good a face for their company or institution as they can, to and through the media. But they also know that the journalist's job is to consider what PR people have to offer and then make up her or his own mind as to whether the material is worth using and, if so, how to use it. The only serious concern in this system would be the damage to the credibility of both journalists and public relations people if there is a public *perception* that undue influence is being used to get some item into the news channels.

GRASS ROOTS AND OTHER PUBLIC RELATIONS EFFORTS

Professional public relations people are not the only ones trying to manipulate the media. Ordinary citizens, in a variety of roles and for a variety of reasons, try to do the same thing. Publicity chairs of PTA organizations, the local choral society, someone who grew a record-setting watermelon last summer, and all sorts of other people try to get information on their causes past the media gatekeepers. Politicians, pressure groups, and educational institutions sometimes do this without professional PR guidance, though that becomes less common as institutions increase in size—or at the higher levels of politics. (If you check on how many people work for the News Bureau, or whatever it's called at your college or university, the results may surprise you.)

These various efforts occur because many organizations need media exposure to accomplish their goals. In addition, the different levels of government have also developed huge publicity arms to get their own messages through the media to the public. All of these groups are simply trying to use the media system to get the attention of the public or to make sure that their particular point of view on an issue or a story receives at least equal prominence with any others. The danger, of course, is that without proper gatekeeping, the news media could become mere conduits for the equivalent of junk mail or spam.

When the news media become overly reliant on manipulative sources, news accounts can become weighted too heavily toward sources with their own agendas, and thus become slanted. A second, less obvious, result is that information and points of view provided by would-be media manipulators can crowd out information and points of view from people and groups who lack the money, skill, or status to make their voices heard. PR professionals are much more likely than is John Q. Citizen to use higher technology to achieve their goals, and the media must be alert to this.

People without access to institutionalized public relations efforts are thus at a major disadvantage when it comes to getting their ideas or concerns into the mainstream media. They can post that material on the Internet, but it won't get the same size audience that is available to PR practitioners who succeed in getting their material past mainstream media gatekeepers. This becomes even more of a concern when individuals are criticizing established institutions, whose PR people can command much greater media attention in response. This problem could be balanced somewhat if media gatekeepers would follow Wicker's (1971) suggestion to draw on a wider range of sources.

DOES TECHNOLOGY TRUMP ETHICS GUIDELINES?

There is a very real danger that technology can trump relevance, or even truth, as PR people deal with traditional media gatekeepers. Those with the resources to put out well-crafted and executed audio, video, and written press releases will often secure an improved opportunity to get their point of view past the media gatekeepers, unless—as Barney (1986) suggests—those gatekeepers retain a measure of concern and even skepticism about what their sources are telling them. The increasing Internet presence of public relations wire services—which blend a traditional news source with a PR tool—makes it more likely that lazy, careless, overworked or penny-pinching news media can be easily manipulated. In too many news operations, there is little independent evaluation of what comes in from media manipulators. If there is space or air time to be filled, and if the news release is smoothly done, it all too often goes right into the paper or onto the air waves. Internet technologies and techniques only increase those possibilities.

The 24/7 news operations on cable TV and the Internet have insatiable appetites for content. This increases the likelihood that the media will serve as a conduit rather than perform a gatekeeping function. So do the widespread staff reductions that affected the news industry as the economy worsened after 2007. This problem is intensified by two factors: constant deadlines that allow little time to check out and revise news releases; and the bottom-line benefits if the news staff acts as a conduit for material rather than producing from scratch a smaller stream of on-air, print, or online news stories. These developments may enhance profits, but they can also run roughshod over ethical concerns.

Left unchecked, all of this can violate virtually every major philosophical guideline for news media ethics. Both of Kant's categorical imperatives (acting on a particular principle that you would like to see as a universal law, and not "using" people in order to achieve your ends) are ignored when media manipulators succeed in getting self-serving messages to the public without appropriate scrutiny from the media gatekeepers. The utilitarian ideal of the greatest good for the greatest number of people is in serious danger when the good of the manipulators is served at the expense of the public as a whole.

John Rawls's concern for protecting the situation's most vulnerable participants fares no better in such circumstances. Even Aristotle's Golden Mean approach is in danger if the manipulators become more skilled at presenting their messages than media gatekeepers are at screening and evaluating them, as—arguably—happens regularly in some smaller (and even some larger) news operations. This trend makes a travesty of the social responsibility ideal.

About the only ethical system that can be applied to successes achieved by media manipulators is Machiavelli's contention that any means are justified if they are needed to reach one's goal, and that brand of ethics holds up only from the perspective of the media manipulators. The steady growth of the government agencies' public relations apparatus (called—for PR purposes—its "public information" function) has on occasion exemplified a successful Machiavellian approach. Technology now enables government bureaucrats and office-holders alike to bypass traditional media gatekeepers to get their messages to the public—for example, by using the Internet to make speeches, or making the text of proposed bills, or video clips, available to anyone who is plugged in.

Bypassing traditional journalistic news values and moving Washington news coverage "toward the politics of image and away from the politics of policy" (McKay, 1992, p. 15) may benefit both office-holders and news directors with tight budgets, but I doubt that sharing—or bypassing—the media's gatekeeping function benefits the public. And there is no question that the public doesn't get what it needs when material produced by and for elected officials is used by local news outlets without identifying the source. That becomes Machiavellian on both sides. (In regard to Machiavelli and the news media, see Merrill, 1998.)

SOME ETHICAL GUIDELINES FOR THE JOURNALISM–PUBLIC RELATIONS RELATIONSHIP

Which ethics, then, *should* guide news media practitioners in dealing with sources who would manipulate the media for their own ends? On the other side of that coin, what ethical standards are most appropriate for those who are trying to use the media to spread their messages and points of view?

Let's take the second question first; most public relations practitioners would profess a much higher set of standards than the Machiavellian code of conduct. If they follow the Public Relations Society of America's code of ethics, they would agree that outright lying and deception exceed the limits of acceptable conduct, and that respect for the news media and the public are both pragmatic and ethically sound. Although they are almost certain to reject Kant's stricture against using people (both those in the media and the public more generally) to accomplish their ends, many PR people would maintain that their craft, when practiced properly, helps to provide needed information for the good of the overall society— a utilitarian approach, if somewhat roundabout.

Public relations practitioners also must consider how far they will go on behalf of a client whose demands raise ethical concerns. In essence, they need to decide which of their loyalties take precedence: Are they most loyal to their clients, or do they place that loyalty lower than their responsibility to the public at large, or to themselves and their own values? To use a high-profile example from the George W. Bush administration, should former White House press secretary Scott McClellan have become a public whistleblower when he first learned of the administration's dishonesty regarding the Valerie Plame "outing" (i.e., her CIA connection), or various aspects of the Iraq War, or how the aftermath of Hurricane Katrina was mishandled? Or was he right to decide that his first loyalty remained with the administration that employed him?

Hill & Knowlton, one of the United States' largest and most politically well-connected PR firms, apparently had no concerns about where its loyalties lay when it was hired by a front group for the government of Kuwait to generate support for U.S. military action against Iraq in the 1991 Gulf War. The firm, which was paid well for its work, led a successful effort to manipulate public opinion in support of U.S. intervention, highlighted (or, perhaps, "lowlighted") by false testimony before the congressional Human Rights Caucus about supposed atrocities committed by Iraqi troops in Kuwait (see MacArthur, 1992, especially pp. 46–68). While public relations practitioners are free to represent foreign governments, whether or not they agree with their client's positions and actions, I believe it would have been better for the country, the public relations industry (and Hill & Knowlton's reputation) if this decision about whom to take on as a client—and what tactics to use—had been made in a context where ethics, as well as financial considerations, played a part.

Tom Bivins (2004) has pointed out that ethics standards *should* be different for news, PR, and advertising practitioners, in large part precisely because these industries have different goals and demand different loyalties. "Ultimately, the dicta of truth and minimizing harm should apply to all mass media, but in differing doses and for decidedly different reasons" (Bivins, 2004, p. x)—a standard that Hill & Knowlton's representation of Kuwait failed to meet even at a "lower dosage." Anticipating the McClellan situation neatly, Bivins added that the priority given to conflicting loyalties will depend largely on whether the practitioner is acting more as an advocate or as a counselor. An "advocate usually acts as an agent of the client, performing some service on the client's behalf or representing the client's interests," and because advocates are expected to be subjective, this brings with it "an implicit understanding that one's first allegiance is to the client" (Bivins, 2004, p. 17).

By contrast, I'd stress that in dealing with sources who want to manipulate them, journalists must maintain the *autonomy* that scholars such as Edmund Lambeth and John Merrill see as a crucial ingredient of news media ethics. As I noted earlier, even the *appearance* of anything else can damage journalistic credibility, which is the lubricant that keeps the system running properly. At the same time, it would be a mistake to overlook the useful symbiotic relationship that must exist between journalism and public relations when both are practiced as they should be.

None of this lends itself to easy answers. But it would be useful for media practitioners in both news and PR to think a bit more about the ethical dimensions of these concerns before confronting them and being forced to retreat into a situational ethic for lack of any more structured approach.

> it would be a mistake to overlook the useful symbiotic relationship that must exist between journalism and public relations when both are practiced as they should be.

TRUTH . . . AND BEYOND?

Ah, yes . . . truth! Kittross raises some interesting points about the need for fairness, accuracy, and the definitionally elusive concept of objectivity, in addition to truth. I don't disagree that some elements beyond truth are *useful* to the media and that *searching* for truth may be a more realistic goal than finding it. As Jim Willis (1991) and others have pointed out, truth is an ideal that is hard to attain and doesn't always reflect all of "reality."

If journalism and public relations practitioners choose to concern themselves with additional matters of ethics, that's all to the good. Edmund Lambeth (1992), in his excellent treatise *Committed Journalism*, provides an extremely useful discussion of some of these other principles in a chapter that begins to develop "a framework of principles for journalism ethics" (p. 23). He suggests there the principles of truth-telling, justice, freedom, humaneness, and stewardship. More recently, Patrick Plaisance (2009) omitted a specific mention of truth in listing six key principles as the basis for media ethics: transparency, justice, harm, autonomy, privacy, and community. Although only one term is duplicated between the two lists, there clearly is some overlap in how the terms are applied.

I have no quarrel with the value of any of these principles, nor with others that people have stressed over the years. But—pushed to the wall—I'd argue that truth-telling is a first principle in journalism and, if choices must be made, truth must be given primacy over any other ethical concerns. Ideally, of course, as Kittross will argue, those truths should be told within a context of accuracy and fairness.

There may well be circumstances where people working in advertising and PR can have allegiance to something other than the "whole truth." Those in the entertainment industry obviously have some license to deviate from, or embellish, the literal truth of settings drawn from history. In fact, the constraints of the narrative form may often require this. But when this is done, I take the Rawlsian position that the audience should be made aware of the changes and whether they are major or minor ones.

Public relations people must determine how forthcoming they will be in regard to the truth of a situation where something less than 100% of the truth may be beneficial to their clients. A "middle ground" approach might work well here: being completely truthful if asked, but not volunteering information that might put a client in a bad light. Sissela Bok (1978), while advocating strongly the need to respect veracity and tell the truth, rejects Kant's absolutist position against any or all lies. She acknowledges that there are some situations where a lie would be warranted, especially "those where innocent lives are at stake, and where only a lie can deflect the danger" (p. 45). But the question of whether one may ever lie and still be ethical is a topic for a different discussion, which could well start with Bok's insightful work.

Here, my focus is on whether other ethics standards than truth-telling are important. I believe that truth is a *sufficient* condition for media practitioners to claim to be acting ethically and, furthermore, that being truthful is almost always *necessary* for ethical practice in the mass media. Telling the truth as fully as possible should be a "first principle" in both journalism and public relations, in the spirit of Kant's categorical imperative even if one agrees with Bok that a few exceptions are needed to that absolutist stance.

For journalists in particular, Walter Lippmann's approach in the early 1920s still has an immense amount to recommend it as an ideal. In his ground-breaking book *Public Opinion*, Lippmann wrote that the "function of news is to signalize an event, the function of truth is to *bring to light the hidden facts*, to set them into relation with each other, and make a *picture of reality*" (Lippmann, 1922, p. 271, emphasis added). The telling of truth—especially in Lippmann's suggested framework—should be the crux of the ethical focus, despite Kittross's concerns about how fragile truth really is or how many different truths can be brought to bear on a particular set of events.

Objectivity, even if it could be defined succinctly, doesn't come close to reaching that level of primal importance, even for journalists. I disagree strongly with Kittross's argument that objectivity is one criterion for good journalism, in part because I believe that it is a more complex concept than his overly simple definition of it as "reporting without bias." It has also been defined as embodying fairness and impartiality, or an absence of interpretation or analysis or even of facts that would correct deliberate distortions. Joseph Turow, for example, defines it as recounting "a news event based on the facts and without interpretation, so that anyone else who witnessed the news event would agree with the journalists' recounting of it" (Turow, 2009, p. 306). By contrast, Christiane Amanpour, speaking about reporting on Bosnia, said that "neutrality" isn't possible in all situations, "because when you are neutral you are an accomplice. Objectivity doesn't mean treating all sides equally. It means giving each side a hearing" (Alterman, 2010).

Stephen Ward (2004) has traced the roots of objectivity back to Greek philosophy and early modern science and developed a theory of "pragmatic objectivity" that goes well beyond "the traditional idea of objective reporting as a neutral description of 'just the facts.' " That traditional approach to objectivity, he wrote, "is indefensible philosophically" and is being abandoned as "more and more newsrooms adopt a reporting style that includes perspective and interpretation." (p. 4) "Pragmatic objectivity," by contrast, seeks to provide "reasonable judgment in a context" (pp. 4 and 263). Ward draws on John Rawls's "reflective equilibrium," a continual process of "mutual adjustment of principles, rules, facts, and judgments" (p. 279) to develop what he calls a "rhetorical theory of journalism truth . . . [which may] help public argumentation be rational and objective" (p. 291). In brief, Ward says, "pragmatic objectivity in journalism is a holistic, fallible, rational evaluation of reports" (p. 300) and that adopting it as an ethical standard "is one of the most important choices that we can make, as individuals and as a society" (p. 318).

Objectivity by whatever definition may or may not be a difficult goal, but it certainly goes well beyond "reporting without bias." As Everette Dennis (1990, p. 8) has pointed out, objectivity is an approach "that almost always valued official sources over ordinary people" and that has contributed to "the straitjacket of unelaborated fact." (For John Merrill's further discussion of objectivity, see Chapter 15-A.)

Kittross and I may be closer to agreement about the importance of fairness than on any other point in this argument. But I totally reject his assertion, below, that I think journalists should merely provide their audience "with all available ideas without evaluating or choosing between them." In fact, I *agree* with him that reporters must evaluate material—i.e., exercise their news judgment—rather than acting only as conduits for information provided by others. But my rationale differs from his; any other approach would greatly weaken reporters' ability to function as tellers of truth. Indeed, for me, everything starts with an emphasis on truth—which certainly must include some context as well as "unelaborated fact." If proper attention is paid to truth-telling as the key ethical principle, the other ethical concerns will resolve themselves.

TRUTH IN PREPARING AND PRESENTING NEWS AND ENTERTAINMENT

The goal of reporting the truth is so important that it also overcomes any concerns about what some people call deception in the gathering of news. So, using hidden cameras or undercover reporting, or even false identities, should not be at issue as long as these techniques produce truthful reports on topics that are (or should be) of importance to the public.

On the other hand, Bob Steele (1993), of the Poynter Institute and DePauw University, has expressed misgivings about *any* kind of deception in reporting, noting that "anything that hides the truth contradicts journalism's basic mission: to seek the truth." Whether this takes the form of "outright lying, misleading, misrepresenting, or merely being less than forthright," he argues that it can damage the necessary level of trust in the truthfulness of shared information, which he regards as vital to a democratic society (Steele, 1993, p. 3).

Black, Steele, and Barney (1995, p. 120) suggest criteria that can be used to weigh whether any type of deceptive information gathering is ethical. For them, *all* of these guidelines must be met to justify lying or any other deceptive tactics that may be necessary to unearth information and report the full truth:

■ The information must be vitally important to the public, or it must prevent profound harm to individuals.

■ Every alternative to obtain the information must have been exhausted.

■ The journalists involved must be willing to disclose publicly the type of deception used and the reason for using it.

■ The harm prevented by obtaining the information must outweigh whatever harm is caused by deception.

■ The individuals and their news organization must be willing to commit time and money to pursue the story fully and to use a high degree of "craftsmanship" in presenting it.

■ There must be a full examination, by the journalists involved, of their motivations, the consistency of their decision, the consequences on those being deceived, the deception's impact on credibility, and the legal implications of the action.

Perhaps ironically, deception in order to get at the truth is something on which Kant and Machiavelli might agree, possibly even without this list of qualifying criteria. Kant—if he could get past his absolutist opposition to lying—might well argue that reporting of "the truth," or perhaps even a full account of different "truths," is the kind of universal law he had in mind in formulating his first categorical imperative. Machiavelli would agree that the end—here, providing accurate information on matters of public importance—certainly justifies even deceptive means of acquiring that information. As Don Hewitt, the longtime producer of *60 Minutes* put it, "If you can catch a thief with lies and deception, . . . 'that's a pretty good trade-off' " (Harwood, 1992, p. A23). Hewitt, however, came to regard hidden cameras as *in*appropriate tools for most investigative reporting and rarely let his reporters use them in his later years with the program. (*60 Minutes*, CBS Television, August 23, 2009).

> Perhaps ironically, deception in order to get at the truth is something on which Kant and Machiavelli might agree,

Machiavelli would see no problem with docudramas or films that take considerable and unnoted liberty with historical fact; he would argue that those liberties are justified because they enhance the entertainment value of the presentation. To the degree that the audience realizes that the film or docudrama is a fictionalized account of real events, the question of truth is much less important than it is in the nonentertainment portions of the mass media sphere. But are the audiences that sophisticated?

As an extreme example, consider the television docudrama that portrayed a completely fictitious court-martial of General George Armstrong Custer *after* the Battle of the Little Big Horn, where Custer and his command were killed. Did this realistic depiction of a trial *that never took place* leave viewers with the belief that this is what really happened? A somewhat less extreme example, from the film world, involves the changes made to civil rights history for dramatic purposes in the film *Mississippi Burning* (1989). Many of those changes made the white Federal Bureau of Investigation (FBI) agents seem more heroic and downplayed the real 1964 roles and actions of blacks in Mississippi.

How many people in these audiences wound up accepting the revised history as being the literal truth of what happened? And, even if most people were generally aware that liberties had been taken with historical fact, would it not have been more ethical for the audiences to know how "true" such accounts were, in much the same way that movies edited for TV must indicate that this has been done? If entertainment media are to be accepted as accurate sources for history—and there is some evidence that they are—shouldn't this impose an ethical requirement on them not to rewrite that history in ways that deceive their audiences? I believe these questions raise some major ethical concerns for writers and producers of docudramas, although entertainment media normally need not be anywhere near as concerned with truth as are the news media.

One possible cure for the specific dilemma posed by changes made for entertainment purposes would be to apply the third Black-Steele-Barney (1995) guideline. Under this approach, there would be full disclosure of whatever changes were made in the historical record for the sake of increased entertainment values and *why* those changes were made, thus placing on the audience the burden to use or to ignore that information.

In the news and information area, Dennis (1990, p. 10) has proposed fuller disclosure by media organizations about how they operate—a plea for *transparency* that fits nicely with an emphasis on truth as the key ethical concern. He suggested that the news media tell their audiences how many people cover major stories and, more important, provide information about their backgrounds, interests, and ideological preferences, if any.

DIFFERING PERCEPTIONS OF THE TRUTH

One important question that arises regarding the news and information media is *whose* truth or whose version of the truth are we referring to? Or, to approach this another way, does telling the truth require us to reveal every single fact we have learned?

Answers to those questions are perhaps easier to provide for public relations than for journalism. Public relations practitioners are concerned with presenting as positive an image of their clients as is possible. For a practitioner concerned with ethics, that requires telling the truth in the sense of presenting no material that is untrue, as well as answering questions truthfully or avoiding uncomfortable questions without lying.

I believe that it also requires one to avoid using truthful information—either selectively or in a slanted manner—to paint an overall picture that is untrue. Any departures from this general approach, which would equate to lying on behalf of a client, should come only after applying an adaptation of the six Black-Steele-Barney (1995) criteria noted earlier. If these overall general principles are adhered to, there is no need for the public relations practitioner to volunteer additional facts that might detract from the client's overall image or lead reporters or the public to raise questions about the client. It is perfectly appropriate for PR practitioners to emphasize the good points of their clients, as long as the truth is acknowledged about any warts that also exist. This approach should also be part of the counseling and guidance that public relations practitioners provide to clients. The only exception would have to do with credibility, which might sometimes be enhanced (as Kittross says) by providing information that casts the client in a less favorable light. In this case, the end—enhanced credibility— would justify the means, and Machiavelli would be happy.

credibility in public relations depends first and foremost on telling the truth.

But I believe that credibility in public relations depends first and foremost on telling the truth. Neither the public nor journalists should be so naive as to expect public relations practitioners to be objective or even fair all of the time. That's not what the business is about. However, they should be expected to tell the truth if they hold themselves out to be ethical and effective practitioners.

For journalists, the issue is frequently more complex. Let's focus here on privacy, where courts have held that if the appropriate criteria are met, monetary damages may be awarded for publication of embarrassing facts that an individual has a right to keep private, *even if* those facts are *true*. (See also Chapter 10.) This legal guideline is one that the news media may want to take into account in their considerations of how much of the truth to tell—to reduce their risk of exposure to legal liability, if not for ethical reasons.

But the courts have also generally held that where information is legitimately newsworthy, it can be published even if it is embarrassing. This brings us back to ethics—specifically, the need to publish truthful reports, but only on newsworthy topics (i.e., those of concern and interest to the public). If you do that, the rest of the potential ethical issues will take care of themselves, as will most of the legal ones.

However, the legal guideline fails to provide sufficient help when invasion of privacy is not a potential legal danger. For example, in political campaign coverage, is there a need to think twice about reporting material that is true, potentially embarrassing to a candidate, but only marginally relevant to the story at hand?

If the material is clearly *ir*relevant, it shouldn't be included whether it's embarrassing to the candidate or not. That seems not so much an ethical guideline as simply a principle of competent news judgment and reporting. If the material falls into the gray area of *possible* relevance—as so many items seem to do—I believe that once a reporter has verified its accuracy, the material should be reported, and the audience members should be given the privilege of making up their own minds about its relevance. To handle the situation any other way smacks of an elitist approach, with the reporter determining what her or his audience should be allowed to know. Reporters have long been cautioned against trying to play God by including or withholding various types of information, and that admonition seems highly appropriate in this situation.

Journalists who provide as much truthful information as is relevant, and report the material in context, serve the public well and need not worry about additional ethical concerns. Conversely, reporters do not serve the public well if they tailor a story to avoid a possible negative impact on some of the people mentioned in it, provided the material at issue is both relevant and important to the public.

This puts a considerable burden on journalists to determine when any particular item of information is so crucial to the public that it justifies the risk of personal harm resulting from its publication, a possibility that can't be brushed off lightly. This becomes very much a situational ethics issue, because one must weigh the importance against the likelihood of harm. In addition, one must decide whether the story could be told fully without this particular item.

To me, if the material is highly relevant to the story, and if the story is one the public needs to be aware of, it would require an almost inevitable likelihood of a human life being lost to justify even considering the withholding of truthful information. Even then, the best approach in some circumstances might well be to withhold the information only temporarily. Kittross's upcoming query about running a kidnapping story that could endanger the victim's life raises this question, and I'd respond—in advance—that if releasing the story would truly endanger (rather than just embarrass) the victim, there are strong ethical reasons for telling something other than the whole truth, at least for the moment. (Whether to withhold information merely to avoid embarrassing someone is a different discussion—but one that is worth pursuing elsewhere.)

I can't, however, justify an outright lie, in print or on the air, even to avoid endangering the victim, but this is based more on the credibility issue than on Kant's categorical imperative (mentioned earlier). Withholding information would fall short of an absolutist Kantian position to tell the whole truth under all circumstances. Thereby, it would recognize preventing serious harm to a fellow human being as another overriding ethical principle that merits consideration along with truth-telling.

A RULE UTILITARIAN PERSPECTIVE

This whole argument is framed in utilitarian terms. This isn't surprising because, as John Merrill notes in his "Overview: Theoretical Foundations for Media Ethics" (starting on p. 3), utilitarianism is probably the most influential ethical framework in general, and the ethical approach most often professed by mass media practitioners. But the utilitarian perspective used here is somewhat different from the one Merrill outlined. He emphasized the aspect of utilitarianism that focuses on the greatest happiness for the largest number of people, thus requiring an attempt to *predict* the consequences of a specific act or decision.

In contrast to that *act utilitarianism* approach, my focus requires agreement that truthful and complete reporting—and truthful public relations—as a general *rule* will produce the greatest good (or "happiness," in at least a loosely defined sense) for the greatest number of people; that is, that it will provide a greater service to the public than any other option. This approach to utilitarianism holds that predictions of specific consequences are unimportant because the general results are *assumed* when one follows the relevant guideline—in this case, truth-telling. In a sense, this approach lets one use the strengths of both the Kantian and utilitarian approaches while avoiding some of their pitfalls. (For further discussion of linkage between Kant and utilitarianism, see Merrill's discussion in Chapter 15-A.)

Such a *rule utilitarian* perspective requires one to reject alternative ethical principles if they interfere in any way with this greatest good of providing the largest amount of (relevant) truthful information to the audience. If there is no such interference, complying with additional ethical principles would be perfectly appropriate, even though they are not *necessary* to meet the threshold definition of ethical behavior.

However, information provided to the public should have context. One part of meeting this need is to provide historical perspective along with reports on breaking news, thereby viewing "news stories not as single, isolated events but rather as links in a longer chain" (Willis, 1991, p. 11). Such an approach demands that the media devote enough time and resources to gathering information so it will reflect the historical context—and enough space or air time to present it to the public. It certainly will raise costs for the news media, but the result will be a more complete truth in the information provided to the public. Ethical news reporting should require this kind of investment but, unfortunately, journalism's economic problems have accelerated the trend to cut these kinds of costs.

Computer-assisted reporting, with its access to huge amounts of information that can be retrieved from a wide variety of databases, provides new opportunities for telling "the whole truth" and doing so more easily than was possible for earlier generations of reporters. But these opportunities also raise concerns regarding information overload, beyond what the audience can or will absorb. Kittross's reference to the horde of topics and details that might provide appropriate context for the report of Hurricane Katrina or an earthquake seems excessive, for the same reason. With too much context and too many details, audience members can too easily become distracted from the essence of the news, or be led to misinterpret what happened.

However, I don't want to denigrate the need to give the audience a complete picture—within reasonable limits—of what took place or of a product being advertised. That's implicit in my stress on truth-telling as the prime principle for the news, information, and persuasive media. Incomplete reporting or ad copy can create "shortages of truth" that lead to serious problems for the community in general and/or for the media's credibility. The slogan used by *The Capital Times*, the afternoon paper in Madison, Wisconsin, until 2008 (when it went exclusively online), would be a good reminder here: "Let the people have the truth and the freedom to discuss it, and all will go well."

KEY POINTS

- Media audiences will be better served if media gatekeepers are able to ensure that they, not would-be manipulators of the media, are really in control of content; even the appearance of anything else can damage journalistic credibility.
- Truthful and complete reporting—and truthful public relations—as a general *rule* will produce the greatest good (or "happiness") for the greatest number of people.
- It is ethically appropriate for public relations practitioners to emphasize the good points of their clients, as long as they also acknowledge the truth about any warts that also exist and avoid uncomfortable questions without lying.

KITTROSS: Social values of mass communication require practices reflecting ethical considerations extending beyond truth to include both fairness and accuracy.

David Gordon's assertion that "individual members of the public are too insulated against perspectives they might find uncomfortable" is one with which I agree. But I hold different ideas with respect to the responsibility for this unfortunate situation. In most instances, it is the individual's own biases and prejudices that select certain ideas for attention. In other cases, it is the government (for example, the Chinese government's "pulling the plug" in mid-2009 on Twitter and thousands of Web sites, ahead of the 20th anniversary of the 1989 Tiananmen Square demonstrations and their bloody crushing by military action). Or it might be the overwhelming but narrow public focus on something (such as the "patriotic" after-math of the 9/11 terrorist attack on New York and Washington), or self-preservation on the part of the media, as represented by decades of the major media "keeping the lid" on discussion of interracial dating and marriage, abortion, and other uncomfortable topics in order—I believe—to pave a smoother, blander way for advertising messages.

So, although I agree with Gordon that new, unfamiliar or even disturbing ideas and their dissemination are important, I believe that the *quality* of *all* ideas—new and old—must be considered by the public and by the media that serve them. The logic and the applicability of ideas are more important than their numbers, their ages, or their sources. I focus on that aspect of the overall topic in this half of the chapter. I recognize, however, that this kind of analysis isn't easy, and am disturbed that the news media have—over the years—found it more profitable to present a new or exclusive story, or an unedited PR release, catering to the public desire for novelty or resulting from the media's own inertia, rather than pay attention to the quality of ideas.

Gordon creates a false problem with his argument that the failure of new ideas to gain a public foothold is due to the technological "filters" on the Internet that are supposed to enable the public to customize what they download from the vast flow of ideas. My position is that stemming the flow of ideas depends more on the personal filters—biases—of individuals and groups that determine which technological filters are employed and how they are set.

Nobody (except spammers) objects seriously to spam filters. But if such filters are controlled even in part by the government (as is true in many countries), or if they are used merely to avoid paying attention to ideas that someone in charge doesn't want to bother with, they can be harmful to the free flow of ideas, since they can be employed to ban *any* specific content—a technique employed for political purposes in many countries.

Furthermore, individuals who consider a particular idea—such as abortion, or even sex education—inherently evil are not noted for their willingness to pay attention to other points of view, or their willingness to allow others to be so exposed. Sometimes this rejection is associated with politics—or with religion—or with the leaders of either. But in virtually every case, there is an intolerance of ideas that make someone—anyone—uncomfortable, such as sex and violence on television. I am not saying that everyone who is against something is a fanatic, or that everyone in favor of something is unreasonable. Many parents, with the best interests of their children in mind, try various means to "protect" them from topics that the parents either find uncomfortable or don't feel ready to discuss. My complaint is with those who would prevent all others (including children) from being exposed to different ideas and different views at an age-appropriate time. After all, when such filtering and gatekeeping is done at the media source (rather than in the family home), it prevents *everyone* from having access to these ideas or information.

And, of course, there are *institutional filters*, it is a rare person who will sort through the biases of both MSNBC and Fox News in a search for a middle-ground truth. It doesn't matter if people lie to us, or try to manipulate our thinking, because most of the success of such activities stems from the fact that we allow ourselves to be manipulated, and we decided a long time ago what we wanted to believe: "Don't confuse me with facts, my mind's made up."

Gordon goes further in one sense and says that "*Attempts* to manipulate the news media raise no ethical problems per se" if journalists retain their independence. But is "independence" an end that simply benefits the journalist, or an altruistic condition that will aid journalists to serve the public good? Such a rhetorical question is analogous to asserting that although the theoretical goal of adversary law is justice, the role of a trial lawyer is "to win" at all costs (within the rules), which frequently has little to do with justice.

L) problem W
Gordon

UNFAIR PERSUASION

Similarly, giving automatic acceptance to our manipulation by those who do it as a function of their economic and persuasive roles seems unjustified—and harmful. Do the media have particularly important responsibilities in this arena? Yes. Does the public have the final responsibility? Also yes. But can we really expect the public to go beyond the definitions that distinguish between advertising, public relations, propaganda, and brainwashing?

Many years ago, I proposed a definition for propaganda that said that it was "getting an idea from the brain of 'A' to the brain of 'B'—with the best interests of 'A' at heart." Advertising could be defined similarly, but the ideas would be restricted to those involved in the sale of goods or services. Education, presumably, would have the best interests of "B" at heart. What is often overlooked is that these definitions say nothing about the best interests of "B" (in the case of propaganda) or the best interests of "A" (in the example of education). Hence, because we frequently don't know what the intention is of those trying to persuade (or inform) us, it is incumbent upon the public, as well as upon gatekeepers and manipulators, to examine *all* messages (and their sources) to identify those messages that do not have the best interests of the public—or the society of which they are a part—at heart.

So, to an extent that may surprise him, I accept much of Gordon's reasoning; but, just as I don't believe that "truth" is sufficient (even though it may be necessary), I don't believe that one can justify ignoring the special and specific obligations of the media—particularly as they exercise a "gatekeeper" function for content—and thus place all responsibility upon individual members of the audience. Hence, I agree with Gordon that the provision of Internet links to opposing views is a responsibility of the media. But I'm also aware that the decision to actually click on those links is still a responsibility of the audience member. In this instance of decision-making, as in so many others, when authority divides, responsibility multiplies.

THE REAL PROBLEM

When someone takes an oath in a court of law, he or she swears to tell "the truth, the whole truth, and nothing but the truth." Not an easy task, when required to answer only "Yes" or "No" to the specific questions asked by attorneys who have their clients' interests to serve. But it is much easier than being asked to be both *objective* and *fair* at the same time, all the time, as journalists always are expected to be—and also as we sometimes hope for from the persuasive and entertainment sides of the media.

For many journalists, the concept of truth has become a deontological standard—requiring specific rules of or obligations for ethical conduct: *Thou shall speak or write only the truth*. But it isn't so simple, as the prevalence of lying and fictionalizing in mass media content illustrates.

Are truth and objectivity *adequate* standards for the news media? Indeed, are they *attainable*? Would a teleological or "consequence" approach (dealing with results rather than principles or rules) be better? It is questions like these that lead to constant rounds of argument among journalists, ethicists, and members of the public over whether the concept of "objectivity" is definable, attainable, or even desirable.

Or, expanding this argument, is it too easy to use traditional journalistic standards of truth and objectivity as a smokescreen to hide what really may be less than the whole truth, or inaccuracy—maybe even dishonesty and falsehood? Don't we need to be *fair* as well as truthful, *accurate* as well as objective?

If the media are, as is traditionally held, surrogates for the citizens in a democracy, providing information that is necessary for the citizenry to make valid and reliable decisions, then standards of truth and evidence even higher than those of the courtroom may be inadequate. Hence, I believe that truth alone is not—despite Gordon's opinion—sufficient "media for practitioners to claim to be acting ethically."

"Balance" is not an adequate substitute for truth. I hold that balance is not a substitute for either fairness, accuracy, or truth, although Aristotle might find it in accord with his Golden Mean. I think that balance in the media—in spite of all those who count words or seconds or adjectives to "prove" that one side in an argument got more attention or more brickbats than another—is more than vastly overrated. I believe it usually is harmful. It isn't the amount of time or space or the number of advocates of a particular view that dictate how useful that presentation is to the viewer, reader, or listener. It is in the *quality* of the position being expressed and the *data*, *evidence*, and *logic* that back it up.

To demand a strict "balance" is similar to a small child demanding equal time in expressing her or his views to an adult gathering, even if the child knows nothing about the subject. Certainly, it is up to the audience to choose between viewpoints, but it is a real putdown to provide the basis for those choices in terms of how many minutes each side will have. In the day-in, day-out hurly-burly of political argument, many participants don't know the rules or, indeed, if there are any. And it takes time to come up with a cogent, organized statement unless one is trained for that task. If these shortcomings affected only those doing the arguing, it wouldn't be very important. But the ideas themselves are important to the media's audiences—readers, viewers, listeners—and it is up to the media to ensure fairness and accuracy. "Balance" is merely a worthless straw figure.

Although this chapter deals largely with the journalistic function of the mass media, almost all of what is said also applies to such persuasive communication as propaganda, advertising, and public relations. After all, truth is usually, but unfortunately not always, more credible than fiction produced either by commission or omission, and one must be credible in order to persuade and inform.

(margin note) Don't we need to be *fair* as well as truthful, *accurate* as well as objective?

TRUTH

At the very best, truth is "truth as we know it." Griffiths (1996, p. 85) maintains that "journalists seek the truth and public relations professionals never lie." Some reporters have another definition: As long as we got someone to say it on the record, it must be true, or at least reportable without cautionary notices. The definition of truth is not self-evident, despite Gordon's attempts to wiggle out of this basic problem. Fairy tales, legends, and even psychological studies show us how fragile the concept of truth may be.

The film *Rashomon* (1950) portrays an event as perceived very differently by different characters in the drama, and there is no single "correct" view of the event. Prosecutors in criminal trials are well aware that witnesses' memories of events are often faulty. When we tell a story among friends, we tend to polish off its rough edges and reduce its complexities. When talking with children, we simplify as much as we can. We often forget—or try to forget—unpleasant memories.

These are normal human traits. Good reporters are aware of them and are constantly looking for additional objective evidence to back up the accounts of those they interview. But often, reporters are unaware of their own perceptual biases or motivations. A reporter, like a pollster, may unconsciously seek to interview only those who are well dressed, seem rational, appear to be articulate, of their own race—or who are conveniently located. It is easier to get a story from such a person than from someone who seems to be homeless, who may appear irrational or inarticulate or just "strange," or who must be sought out.

A 1940s study on rumor dissemination and stereotyping—what Walter Lippmann (1922) called "the world inside our heads"—found that, when a *description* of a picture of a white man holding a straight razor during an apparent confrontation with a black man was relayed orally through two or three people who hadn't seen the picture, then the razor—a "stereotypical symbol of Negro violence"—migrated in the final telling to the hand of the black man, even though the original picture clearly showed it in the white man's hand (Allport and Postman, 1945, p. 75). Similar stereotypes or expectancies are part of what each of us learned unconsciously as we grew up.

This happens over and over again in all sorts of newsmaking situations. If it doesn't make sense according to our stereotypes, it may not be reported. During the Cold War, the Soviet Union was the enemy of the United States, and it was always a shock when a report of cooperation or agreement or laudable behavior came along. During the civil rights marches of the 1960s in the South, Northerners rarely heard about the many police officers in Dixie who did *not* attack the black marchers. Could the film *Schindler's List* (1993), which portrayed a Nazi Party member who saved hundreds of Jews from the Holocaust, have been understood—or even made—immediately after World War II?

Hollywood understood early on that people were complex and that many of its most popular and potent characters were the "good bad girl" or the "bad good man." But such complexity is almost never shown in television news or on the pages of American newspapers. We stereotype and simplify the news without even thinking about it.

Another assault on the absolutist conception of truth is the "little white lie," where an untruth is told because we believe that it will benefit the listener or reader more than the truth will—the "Yes, Virginia, there is a Santa Claus" syndrome, where the media have the arrogance to assume that they have the right to prevent harm to the audience. Additionally, but with less concern for the recipient of a message, we have the relatively harmless spin put on a political or other utterance by a public relations practitioner, or the puffery created by an advertising agency.

Worse yet, it isn't unknown for a reporter or an advertiser to lie deliberately, by omission or commission. Any reporter who lies deliberately in expectation of some sort of acclaim or other reward, isn't a reporter, of course, but a journalistic whore. Lying is unacceptable and unprofessional behavior because, among other things, it misleads the publics whom the reporter serves and challenges every justification for the news media's existence.

Even more delicate may be the situation where a source is lying, and the reporter knows it. Does this give the reporter the right to report that "this is a lie"? Perhaps, at least in the state of Washington, where the Supreme Court said in 2007 that it is permissible for a candidate for high political office to lie, and that scrutiny and reporting by the media was a better corrective than governmental prohibitions against lying. But suppose, rather than a political figure, it was a land developer who was lying, and then suppose that developer happened to own the newspaper or station (or both)?

Then there is what may be the biggest unconscious bias of all: The reporter has a mental picture of a specific audience and wants to satisfy them. Bias can also creep in because reporters and advertising copywriters use simplification as a useful tool. This is like the parents who simplify bedtime stories so there is no possibility of the children misunderstanding the main points, by taking out most of the potentially confusing detail, contradictions, and complexity that are part of any "real" story.

Reporters and editors, for the same reason, often simplify the stories they cover and present to their readers, listeners, and viewers. Telling the "whole truth" is rarely an option, although reporters often use this idea as an excuse for covering too much. Frankly, there aren't enough rolls of newsprint or feet of videotape ever to present "the whole truth."

OBJECTIVITY

Many journalists and journalism teachers become uneasy at the very mention of objectivity, for the same reasons that they find truth to be such an elusive concept: It may be impossible to be 100% objective about anything. The reason is simple: We are human beings. Is this any reason not to try—whether we succeed or fail? Fortunately, Rawls's veil of ignorance allows us to achieve a form of objectivity, defined here as reporting without bias (or at least with "detachment") more easily than achieving more complex ethical goals, such as truth. (For another point of view, see Chapter 15-A.)

Most of what was said earlier in the section on truth dealt with what might be called honest untruths. But reporters, like everyone else, have their own axes to grind. A reporter, after all, lives a life outside of the newsroom. He or she may be a liberal, a conservative, a feminist, an environmentalist, or a racist. Background—urban/suburban, white/black, old/young, fundamentalist/agnostic, male/female, poor/rich—may control much of the reporter's value system. On any given day, a reporter may get up on the wrong side of the bed and may allow personal impressions of events or subjects to color what and who is reported.

Reporters are trained to stand outside of controversies, although this is hard to do and still report fully. How can someone sitting in an auditorium know what is happening backstage? How can someone reporting from the police station under siege during a riot, or from one party's election headquarters during a campaign, be fully objective? Can a foreign correspondent, reporting on a country where the language, the customs, and the politics are strange, ever get beneath the surface? If only superficial reports are prepared, is this really an objective or a truthful view of that person, event, situation, or country?

Is journalism's function and purpose to produce "a truthful, comprehensive, and intelligent account of the day's events in a context which gives them meaning" (Commission on Freedom of the Press, 1947, p. 21), or is journalism merely a conduit, carrying whatever happens to get inside, without context, comprehensiveness, or intelligence? Is the provision of context, or using the writer's intelligence to accept or discard data and opinion, ever truly objective?

It is this need for context that makes it so necessary for reporters and editors to be widely read and curious about almost everything. Otherwise, it is truly impossible to interpret what is going on, and the news media become, at best, merely a channel for the words of those who want to say something (and who are selected by the media to say it).

Photographs frequently are selected mostly for immediate reward—titillation—rather than information. Of course, there is nothing intrinsically wrong with titillation or trying to gain the audience's attention. In fact, for any of the other mass media effects (such as attitude change, opinion formation, or overt behavior such as shopping, voting, or demonstrating) to take place, one must first gain attention.

But news must go beyond titillation and gossip to be of any lasting value. It is history in the making; it enables the public to make better decisions. The choice of stories is important. Watergate dealt with misconduct by President Nixon while in office, but the now-largely forgotten Whitewater scandal originally dealt with a time before President Clinton took office and with events in which he was passive, not active—events that had nothing to do with his obligation to support and defend the U.S. Constitution. Often, political figures are considered fair game by reporters because, we are sanctimoniously told, their mistakes reflect their character—and we wouldn't want a person of bad character in the White House, would we? In a similar vein, why do mobs of reporters try to photograph or interview those who are relatives or friends of disaster victims in the name of "news"—as when photographers cornered the emotional children in Christa McAuliffe's classroom after the spacecraft *Challenger* exploded with her aboard in 1986? (See Chapter 15-H p. 523.)

To prevent one's own feelings from affecting the story in some way probably is impossible, but to prevent them from affecting the story grossly is not difficult. If eternal vigilance is the price of liberty, as John Philpot Curran said in 1790, it is also the price of the journalist's objectivity.

Reporters covering the 2005 flooding in New Orleans caused by Hurricane Katrina had to know more than the script for the isolated flooding that occurs even in deserts. The magnitude of the New Orleans disaster required a reversion to the days of the great Mississippi floods before the flood control projects of the 20th century. It mandated that the good reporter have a background in the meteorology of the storm, the hydrology, ecology and even geology of Louisiana, the engineering of the levee system, the demographics of the police force, the planning (or lack of it) by medical and rescue organizations, the race relations in this part of the world, and the bureaucracy of the city, the state, and federal agencies such as the Federal Emergency Management Agency (FEMA). True, they could interview "sources" for this information, but unless source names and numbers are in the

Rolodex or cell phone *before* the event, they will be hard to find in a crisis, and the media still have the responsibility of pulling it all together.

Similarly, coverage of the 1994 Los Angeles earthquake needed more than the ability to paraphrase lines from a steamy movie ("the earth shook at 4:31 A.M."). Those reporters and editors needed—or needed to obtain—a background in Southern California geography, politics, transportation, history, demography, and many other matters, in addition to a general knowledge of government, technology, and geology.

While I've listed here a great many things that a reporter covering a disaster such as a major earthquake or Hurricane Katrina should be familiar with, it isn't just to construct a more complete story. Rather, this kind and amount of detail enables members of the audience to understand fully what occurred, and, more importantly, enables them to use that knowledge to plan how to avoid harm in some future disaster. (See the discussion of "delayed reward" news on p. 121.)

With adequate context, reportage may be quite "objective." But it still has to assume a point of view: that of the temporarily (or permanently) homeless, the politicians, the technocrats, the opportunists, the victims, the predators, the altruistic, the ignorant, or the uncaring. The reporter's location and view of the scene often determine what the audience sees and hears and, as a result, thinks. Television journalism, in particular, tends to select stories with dramatic pictures rather than those that give a comprehensive and intelligent context for the day's events. Although a picture may be "truthful" in the sense of not having been staged or digitally manipulated (on the latter, see Chapter 7), this is not sufficient for the citizen who must make decisions on the basis of the *available* news.

This point is illustrated by the folk story about the blind men and the elephant: The first feels the tusks and describes them, the second feels the ears and describes them, and so on. But none of them is able to describe the elephant until, or unless, all of the smaller pictures are put together and given context. It might be argued that in many instances the connections are far more important than what is being connected.

But if, as posited above, neither truth nor objectivity are fully realizable, on what shall we base our professional journalistic standards?

First, I do not propose that we just surrender, whining that because entertainment communication isn't usually expected to be truthful (although such production techniques as documentary and cinéma vérité are intended to look that way), we should classify media by their entertainment function and ignore the entire concept of truth. (As John Stossel, then a ABC investigative reporter, arrogantly said at an Investigative Reporters and Editors convention, "Once *we* decide who the 'bad guy' is, it's show biz.")

Instead, I suggest that journalists must meet two other standards or factors, interwoven with but distinct from truth and objectivity: Accuracy and fairness, with fairness being the more important.

ACCURACY

One of the most entertaining and useful books on research methods is Darryl Huff's (1954) *How to Lie with Statistics*. Among the many fallacies illustrated in this book is that of "false accuracy." To say that "33.333% of the female students at Such-and-so University in 1890 married members of the faculty" may be true, but it may mean that there were only three women in the student body that year, and one married an instructor. You can't generalize from that year or institution to another. Other statistical or logical fallacies or errors that may seem to be technically accurate but are actually incorrect abound in journalism, as they do in scholarly or commercial research.

The careful researcher distinguishes between validity (something measures what we say it does, based on its ability to predict or otherwise demonstrate logical reasoning), reliability (repeated measurements of the same phenomenon have the same result), and precision. This approach is something we should all follow. Journalists need to know enough about statistics and research methods to assess validity and reliability of data from any source, and they may find it wiser to omit a piece of information unless they can do so. But the journalist up against a deadline often tends to ignore these distinctions and is concerned only with a somewhat fuzzy concept of "accuracy"—which itself often takes a back seat to getting the story published or aired. This can be serious. It is possible to infer from Gordon's half of this chapter that he believes that journalists should provide their readers, viewers, and listeners with all available ideas without evaluating or choosing between them. But if the reporter doesn't use carefully defined standards for evaluating information, it is unlikely that the audience will be provided with ideas of high quality.

Even the "small stuff" that has a large effect on credibility can lead to similar problems. Traditionally, embryonic reporters—whether they eventually went into journalism or public relations—were taught that "it doesn't matter what you call someone as long as you get the name right." But we all know that there is a declining standard, even of spelling proper names. The use of tape recorders hasn't helped much, and if a newspaper reporter hears one thing being said at a presidential news conference and millions of viewers and listeners hear something else, what happens to the paper's credibility? If one has selected the wrong words, no spell-check program will help. These computer programs may be reliable (they spell the word the same way each time), but may not be valid (they are checking the wrong word). Words that sound the same but have different meanings (wrap and rap, for example) are even worse to deal with, and when early Kindle reading machines pronounced President Obama's name incorrectly, it should have served as a warning.

Furthermore, if a reporter is "accurate" but doesn't give the whole story, the overall effect is one of inaccuracy. This is one of many reasons for transparency with respect to data no less than to potential conflicts of interest. The old advertising slogan that "four out of five doctors prefer" a particular product may be accurate and truthful as far as it goes, but suppose that only five doctors were asked and all of them worked for the firm producing the product?

To achieve accuracy is one reason that we have editors; the shortsighted money-pinching of some media chief financial and chief executive officers (CFOs and CEOs) with respect to copyediting and fact-checking is a major factor leading both to loss of credibility and damaging libel suits. I was an expert witness in one libel case where a magazine's top management bragged about its almost universal fact-checking, an editor said that there was some fact-checking, but the reporter involved testified to complete ignorance of this stage in the process. The judgment against the magazine was for $6 million.

FAIRNESS

The media are not merely a conduit; they have an obligation to assess the validity or truth of the information they disseminate.

Fairness is the act of keeping an open mind, of suspending individual judgment until enough information is available so that judgments or decisions can validly be made. It is impartiality, but not ignorance. The media are not merely a conduit; they have an obligation to assess the validity or truth of the information they disseminate. Of particular importance is the need to provide sufficient valid and reliable information that will allow readers, listeners, and viewers to reach their own conclusions.

One must continually assess whether something is fair. Is "one man, one vote" inherently fair if it excludes women? Or is it fair if the effect is to give all power to 51% of the electorate and none to the other 49%? Is it fair to select an obvious "kook" as a spokesperson for a position frowned on by the reporter? Should the names of rape victims be published? How about the names of accused (but not yet convicted) rapists?

Some of the categorical imperatives discussed by Gordon may have unforeseen pitfalls. For example, is it fair (or truly ethical) to publicize names of victims of crime? Arguably, it is not—if they might be further damaged by the story. (Victims of sexual assault are particularly vulnerable). But is it fair (or truly ethical) to publicize accused rape suspects regardless of whether they ever are convicted?

In the United States, unlike the United Kingdom, suspects—particularly ones for whom the police are searching—will be named, described, their photographs shown and previous encounters with the law listed in the media. (Although if they are minors, they usually are "off limits," no matter how heinous the crime, unless there is tremendous public interest, when rules get broken). However, it can be argued that the practice of naming adult suspects is elitist and unfair to various groups and individuals who are often stereotyped. To counter this complaint, some newspapers (such as *The Seattle Times*) will not name suspects until they are arraigned and formally charged. Most of the time, at any rate. (People in the public eye may be exceptions.)

The now-defunct FCC Fairness Doctrine, which dealt only with personal attacks and controversial issues, often got confused with the statutory requirement (47 U.S.C. 315) that *bona fide* candidates for political office were entitled to equal *opportunity* to be seen or heard on the air during a campaign. The public has picked up this idea and tends to believe that opposing views on all sorts of matters should have "equal time," regardless of the medium. Allied with this is a belief that all views are equally valid. This, obviously, is nonsense, and deciding that "freedom of speech" excuses any fibs or falsehoods is equally nonsensical, if only because the First Amendment applies to government interference with individual rights rather than everyday behavior. (Another acquired belief appears to be that all quotations are sacrosanct, and there is no need to provide valid and reliable proof of what someone says; see Chapter 15-I.)

To a certain extent, we can think of fairness in terms of what *not* to air or publish. Should a mass murderer have as much attention as the victims? During the first Gulf War, should the ruler of Iraq automatically have rated "equal time" or "equal space" with the combined leadership of the coalition arrayed against him? Was the situation different before the U.S. invasion of Iraq in 2003? Should a spokesperson for an unpopular view or other controversial position—perhaps one favoring pornography or on either side of the abortion, gun control, or smoking issues—automatically have exactly the same attention from the media as those on the opposing side? What about someone who wants to place restrictions on the news media? Should advertisers always (or never) be given priority when soliciting quotes and interviews? Should a station run a story about a kidnapping when it has been warned that it may put the victim's life in danger, or should it hold the story for a while and give the police some room to maneuver?

During an unpopular war, such as Iraq, should the office of President of the United States be allowed to use his office as a "bully pulpit" from which to argue continuation of the conflict, even if the rationales for invasion (such as the assertion that Iraq possessed weapons of mass destruction) have been disproved? Is there a civic need for the media to provide additional points of view after political events, even though the audience would much rather have gone back to entertainment programming instead of being forced to watch anything more on this subject (or to make the effort to change the channel)? Would it have been even more important to have sought out opposition views *before* the final decision to commit troops to Iraq had been made? Should the news media have learned this lesson from the Vietnam War?

Fairness can be complex, as are other ethical questions. If ethics involves what we *ought* to do, then fairness asks, "For whom?" It isn't a game. Identifying oneself as a reporter may be morally correct and truthful, but doing so may mean that the public doesn't get the information it needs. On a pragmatic level, libel and privacy law cases often involve questions of fairness, and most juries with which I'm familiar see it that way. Some day libel law might be tweaked to require any disseminator of information—including bloggers—to demonstrate that what they were publishing was of public concern. This could well require those in the information-mongering business (including amateurs using new technologies) to rely on fairness and ethics, quite aside from legal concerns or advice.

Although reporters may start to feel as if they are playing God, they must concern themselves with individuals as well as with a mass or general audience. "Playing fair" has not yet achieved the status in law that injuries to reputation (libel) and the right to be let alone (privacy) have. Indeed, because our legal system tends to be proscriptive ("thou shalt not") rather than prescriptive ("thou shall"), it may never reach that status. But invasion of privacy became a tort only after it was described in the late 19th century (Warren and Brandeis, 1890). I believe that fairness may well become a similar requirement later in the 21st century. It certainly would ease friction as the population burgeons and competition for resources and amenities increases. Civilized nations substituted the rule of law for dueling to satisfy those injured by torts such as libel; if we don't want the results of private revenge or other action cluttering our streets, public demand for fairness may well require finding a way to legislate it.

GATEKEEPING

A gatekeeper (and we are all gatekeepers to some extent, unless we are in an isolation chamber) acts like a judge. A column by Ellen Goodman (2009) commented that "I've never been sure why Lady Justice wore a blindfold as part of her wardrobe. Yes, it's supposed to be a symbol of impartiality, but it does limit her vision a bit."

One of the most sensitive and important tasks of the media is to make decisions as to what is aired or printed or transmitted in some other physical or electronic form. Although it is easy to think of this as the domain of some editor or producer, it goes well beyond one job description or responsibility. It starts with an assignment editor, or a tipster, or a PR person, or an observant reporter or videographer noticing "a story" somewhere in the "real world." As that story is covered, similar decisions are made throughout the process.

Someone must decide that story "A" is more important or more interesting than story "B." Someone must decide which person—which "talent"—should read, write, or edit the story. Someone must decide which elements of a story are to receive emphasis and which are to be deleted—and this applies to ideas as well as to events or quotes. Someone must decide that the words and pictures used to describe or illustrate an event or development are better than other choices that might have been made. Someone has to buy that paper or magazine or tune to that station or channel. Decisions, decisions, decisions. And they can't be made ethically by merely flipping a coin or throwing a dart.

None of the mass media are common carriers, open to all without discrimination, although to some extent the Internet—if true "net neutrality" comes to pass—might be thought of in this way. For one reason, there are limits as to how much traditional mass media can carry. On a single channel, a radio broadcaster can program 24 hours a day (at about 150 words a minute), no more. A newspaper is limited by economics as well as the capacities of a press room, although it has more flexibility than broadcasting. Since audience members need to sleep and eat as well as pay attention to the media, no one pays attention to even their favorite channel for all 24 hours in the day. There must be some control over entrance to a media channel, and there is a tremendous need for fairness during this process. But fairness is sought by media professionals for the benefit of the audience more than for the source of information and opinion. This means something more than taking the easy way out by trying to achieve a balance or equilibrium of space or time. That kind of "balance" is merely a way to make the gatekeeping job easier. It is not a public interest goal in its own right.

This applies to more than the dissemination of current information—journalism. Managers decide what kinds of people are hired by the media; those in the persuasive media are aware of limitations imposed by law, societal pressure, or the human foibles and prejudices of their clients and bosses. Throughout the creative process the entertainment media must make gatekeeping decision after gatekeeping decision. The process is much the same regardless of the reason for standing guard at the media gate. Can there be errors in this process? Certainly. Some (people, ideas, quotes, descriptions, words, etc.) are prevented from entering the communication process even though they should have been allowed through. Others are given a chance to be heard but have little or nothing of value to say to the audience. More decisions.

There are many reasons for the errors mentioned here. Yes, gatekeepers can be ignorant, stupid, or biased. But they can also be knowledgeable, intelligent, and impartial—and still make mistakes because of habit, false perceptions, or fatigue. Sometimes they are required to act in certain ways because of the economics of the media, or even by a desire for order amid information chaos. To some, using any gatekeeper at all is inherently unfair. The media should be open to all, on equal terms. But to avoid being swamped by raw information or shouted conclusions with or without evidence or analysis, we rely on media institutions to make a selection that will enable each of us to make sense of an increasingly data-overloaded world.

Both Gordon and I want to expand rather than limit the audience's vision, and we are both aware that complete impartiality by conscientious gatekeepers is an unrealizable ideal. But the very practice of media gatekeeping (and content manipulation inside the gates) logically *must* lead to restriction and limitation of what is made available to the public. Whether this is something we desire or not, it *is* going to happen. The questions of *how* the media perform this role and what *standards* they employ are not simple ones.

BEYOND THE STANDARDS

None of the elements discussed earlier—balance, truth, objectivity, accuracy, fairness—are much good unless there is an audience to pay attention to the news story, public relations release, advertisement, or other message. The first problem, of course, is getting the potential audience to pay attention. There is an old joke about how to deliver a message to a mule: First, get its attention by hitting it over the head with a 2×4—much as headlines, titles, and graphics are designed to "grab" the audience's attention. Some headlines, graphics, and lead sentences are designed for this purpose alone, rather than for the more complex purposes of imparting information or affecting attitudes, opinions, or actions such as voting. Lorenzo Milam's (1975) *Sex and Broadcasting* is an excellent book about how to start a radio station—but it may have sold many copies (or, conversely, lost potential sales) solely because of the author's choice of a title.

There are two kinds of reward that people can receive from the media. "Immediate-reward" information such as contest results or weather-related events or even "there but for the grace of God" thrills and titillation can relatively easily get an audience's attention. Sometimes, this is because of self-selection; those who watch MSNBC are almost certainly going to have different political views and general outlooks than those who watch Fox Cable News. But news of crime, sports, and weather will be much the same in all media that make a pretense of covering "the news." To some extent, immediate-reward news is like the tree that falls in the forest that nobody notices—or needs to notice. And yet, we pay attention to it for various reasons, from expressing loyalty to the local sports team to being told what had caused the house to shake in the middle of the night (to verify our own guess).

"Delayed-reward" news is different. It is much more important—but in the long run, not the short run. The difference between immediate-reward and delayed-reward news is like the difference between short-term weather and long-term climate change. Delayed-reward news requires us to pay attention to both form and content that we might (in the short run) prefer to ignore. In other words, it isn't "fun." With really important "delayed reward" news such as that dealing with economic or ecological trends that we would do well to anticipate, we must rely in part on others—primarily the mass media—to provide early warning of trends and events. Delayed-reward news is keeping our eyes open as we walk through the forest, and becoming aware of the tree that might fall on us—or the cougar hiding in the underbrush.

It may be that newer communication techniques, such as blogs, can fill in the gaps—but will they? Should there be some control of all media, so that collectively they will provide information that somebody—the government media executives?—believes will be important for members of the public to know, particularly in times of crisis. Will the lack of control over communications practitioners entering into practice, as well as lack of transparency (that is, the public has no way to know the biases—actual or potential—of a given blogger or other communicator), make the general public decide that these lacks mean that new media shouldn't deserve any credence? Or, just as scary, will the novelty of new media make the public turn to them rather than to media in which professionals have demonstrated some ethical and other education and training?

Most serious students of the mass media—including those still in school and their instructors—like to think of the serious roles of the media, such as transmitting culture (education, in the broadest sense), providing surveillance for the environment (news in the broadest sense), and the like. But P. T. Barnum, the circus magnate, probably was correct when he pointed out that nobody had ever gone broke underestimating the tastes of the American public. For example, the popularity of radio talk shows, providing support for some listeners' political or other prejudices rather than information and ideas that may allow listeners to change their minds, should have been easy to predict. Although we may decry sensationalism, opinion-mongering, misinformation, and low-level tasteless performance, the public at large usually gravitates to that which entertains them. Social psychological research has demonstrated time and time again that we tend to associate with the familiar, with those whose ideas and other attributes are "like ours." When this happens, the old joke (noted earlier), "Don't confuse me with facts; my mind's made up," becomes very real.

Psychology, sociology, and other social sciences often are ignored when considering the ethics of mass media. The fact that, for example, more than one candidate participates in a political debate doesn't mean that all candidates actually are heard by all viewers or listeners. We mentally "tune out" those whom we dislike, whose views we disapprove of, or with whom we are unfamiliar. Merely providing a "balance" of opposing sound bites will not achieve the theoretically desirable result of helping the public make rational decisions.

Furthermore, another psychological effect of multiple messages is a "tuning out" of *all* messages. Theoretically, it is great that Mothers Against Drunk Driving can seek media attention, and it is even better that so can the Tobacco Institute, the National Dairy Council, the National Rifle Association, MoveOn, and the Moral Majority. Each of these organizations, and thousands of others, has a purpose or a cause that someone believes will be useful to the public. But these groups, in the aggregate, lead to sensory overloads in members of the public. Because most of these appeals are to our desire to help those less fortunate—we could even label this as "guilt"—we must deal with that emotional overload as well. Finally, even without paying attention to these "worthy causes" that are scrabbling for our money and time, many feel overloaded merely by the number of channels on cable, the number of stations that can be heard or seen in their vicinity, and the number of gadgets in our pockets or purses that beep, buzz, chirp, play music, and otherwise demand our attention.

Do these cautionary tales mitigate against the good deeds that the media can perform in the everyday nature of things? Of course. But that doesn't mean that the media aren't doing or shouldn't do good things for their own sake. We just need to do them better.

CONCLUSIONS

Now that I've set up balance, truth, objectivity, accuracy, and fairness as straw figures to be knocked down, what touchstone do I believe media people should adopt? And why?

The second question is the easier, and it may be answered in two ways. Journalists and public relations specialists should do what is "right," or what will help them to sleep well nights; and they should do what will create the greatest credibility for the media. The "public good" principle fits in on both levels. That which is "right" will benefit the greatest number of people, in a utilitarian sense, but without credibility the media will not be believed even when acting strictly for the public good. With respect to affecting public opinion, credibility is much more important than truth, which may not be believed. For example, most of the people in the world would find incredible and unbelievable the fact that the vast majority of homes in the United States have a television set, a flush toilet, a working telephone and bathing facilities. Public relations and business communication practitioners are particularly aware of the need for credibility, and today some public relations groups (including the Public Relations Society of America) are among the few professional communications associations to offer a form of accreditation or certification intended to provide additional credibility for practitioners whose education and standards measure up.

So, one should try to meet the highest standards for truth, objectivity, accuracy, and fairness that one can and, beyond that moral approach, use any other techniques that will at least mitigate any unfairness, untruth, inaccuracy, or lack of objectivity.

One technique, used rarely, for improving the media's credibility is to state in advance any connections or conditions that might lead the reader or the viewer to suspect bias (particularly if unsuccessfully concealed). An example of this transparency approach was Peter Arnett's reminders, in his CNN broadcasts from Baghdad during the first Gulf War, that his material was subject to censorship by the Iraqi government. Another example is that of Jeffrey Schmalz, an editor and reporter on *The New York Times*, afflicted with AIDS, who nevertheless was assigned or allowed to report on AIDS and similar health matters—but with full disclosure to his readers in every column ("The Changing Times," 1992).

Another method that encourages reader trust is the prominent use of corrections whenever a publication has been in error. There are at least 19 other kinds of "media accountability systems" used in various countries (Bertrand, 1993, p. 9), including opinion surveys, accuracy and fairness questionnaires mailed to people mentioned in the news, ombudsmen, and press councils.

A technique often reflected in journalistic and public relations codes of ethics might be thought of as the "Caesar's wife" technique: be above reproach. To achieve this status, however, often requires that one become a political and social eunuch. Reporters are often required to forgo political activity, although most publishers consider that it is permissible for themselves.

Finally, there is the "I must be doing a good job" logic of the beleaguered journalist when both sides to a controversy accuse the same media outlet (or individual) of bias and dishonesty. After all, we must convince ourselves that we are the "good guys" because we tell the truth—which is more than just conveying "facts"—and that we are fair, accurate, and objective. This, of course, is a teleological (and perhaps theological or tautological) argument: our strength is the strength of ten because Our hearts are pure.

In all of this, I am definitely not advocating that the reporter should be ignorant as well as unbiased, as trial jurors (in contravention of any rational principle) are expected to be today. Rawls's veil of ignorance concept does *not* advocate the common meaning of the word "ignorance"—that is, "not knowing the facts." It merely points out that we should make an ethical decision as though we are unaware of which side we are on; such "ignorance" allows us better to evaluate whether the outcome of that decision was fair.

In the long run, if we go beyond rules or codes that are unreliable and impossible to follow, into the realm of morality—and try to do the best job we can—our reputations will become so high that we will gain credibility even as we provide our readers, viewers, and listeners with the information they need. To some extent, this is "doing well by doing good" because the only way the media can be successful—financially, journalistically, personally— is to maintain a reputation for honesty, which goes far beyond the copout of saying that we are attempting merely to be "truthful" and "objective" or, heaven forfend, "balanced."

KEY POINTS

- Truth-telling is essential, but it may not be sufficient. The news media, in particular, need to be truthful, but they also need to be fair and accurate.
- Opinions—whether belonging to news media personnel or those whom they interview—always need to be distinguished from facts. Such transparency is essential.
- The need to meet the standards of truth applies to persuasive communication as well as to news and information media. Not only is it the ethical thing to do, but also, truth usually is more credible than fiction, and one must be credible in order to persuade or inform.

MERRILL: Commentary

Gordon and Kittross really get at it in this chapter. They are dealing with the weightiest topics in journalism (e.g., truth, objectivity, accuracy, and fairness) and relate these to the equally heavy topic of ethics. Readers should be able to have fun with this controversy.

Both antagonists accept the same basic assumption: Truth and fairness compose the mission or purpose of journalism. This assumption itself can be questioned and that would knock this controversy askew. Who says that truth is the prime purpose of journalism (except Gordon and, to a lesser extent, Kittross)? Journalism, even traditionally, has gone in many directions—toward fiction, entertainment, analysis, humorous subjectivity, even propaganda, and pornography. Especially in relatively free societies, journalism (or at least individual media organizations) has been, and should be, free to accept *any* mission it desires. If it wants to try to be unbiased, it can. If it wants to try to be accurate or fair, it can. But it has no imperial metaphysical commander specifying its mission outside its temporal venues.

Some similar concerns exist regarding truth and fairness in public relations. But, of course, in this book we're talking about *ethics*. In a sense, that eliminates or at least obviates the *idea that anything goes*. We must assume here that ethics takes precedence over freedom.

ethics takes precedence over freedom.

Let's look a minute at fairness. In this specific controversy one might ask if Kittross is being fair to Gordon. We could measure how much space each uses for his arguments. But maybe fairness has no quantitative measurement. And it might be asked if I, in this commentary, am being fairer to one writer than I am to the other. I doubt it, but who knows? Actually, I doubt if I am being fair to either one. Fairness, unlike truthful, accurate and unbiased content, is non-measurable. In reporting, it is strictly teleological—certainly semantically empty—and avoids any kind of Kantian legalistic imperative. However, if one worships the "truth," as Gordon does, he might contend that a reporter can be fair—if this is *fairness to the truth*, not worrying about the consequences to other people. This would mean that if I am truthful, I am fair. It could then be a maxim that could be universalized, thus bringing it in line with Kant's Categorical Imperative. To be ethical, then, would be telling the truth—period.

Again in this controversy I think Gordon takes the high (or at least the more traditional) road by enthroning truth in journalism. Kittross seems to take more the utilitarian approach, seeing a lie as sometimes necessary (apparently accepting Sissela Bok's perspective) and the truth as sometimes harmful.

This is indeed a controversy that is especially important to anyone concerned about the ethics of journalistic reporting. But it is likewise important to those who are in the field of public relations. Gordon especially wants to place the PR practitioner under the same truthful obligation as the news reporter. For me, this gets us into a central dilemma of ethics: the importance of truth as contrasted with something-less-than-the-truth. And it gets us to the differing traditional missions and purposes of PR and a news medium. The medium's purpose is to give the news as neutrally and objectively as possible. For the PR firm or practitioner, it is to present the client in as favorable light as possible. Quite a contrast in purpose.

Many hard-nosed reporters, in both the print and electronic media, come at ethics from a mainly deontological (principle-bound) perspective. This is basically the one championed by Gordon in this chapter. A dominant principle for them is the presentation of a true, unbiased, and thorough account of an event. They believe that it is not only their professional duty but also their ethical duty to do so. These are the reporters who report; they do not distort, hide certain things, tamper with quotes, or in other ways provide a "report" that is flawed intentionally to fulfill some personal or corporate agenda. This is consistent with Gordon's view of ethical reporting.

And then there are other ethicists, who agree with Kittross and take the more teleological ethical stance (consideration of consequences) in making decisions that might well go beyond a concern for the truth or objectivity. Actually, in journalism I believe these practitioners probably outnumber the truth-oriented ones, and in public relations almost everyone accepts this consequentialist (or utilitarian) philosophy.

I think it is important to remember here that both types of practitioners can be thought of as ethical. The hard-nosed, full-disclosure types feel ethical when they provide an account that's as truthful as possible. Their reportorial ethics are based on a belief that the people must know the truth, and in revealing this truth, such reporters consider themselves as also being fair. The other type of journalist—the consequence ethicists—would feel ethical when they, through purposely tampering (if necessary) with the facts in some way, bring about fairness to some principal in the story. This type of reporter, for instance, might withhold the name of a rape victim while knowing that the integrity of the story is being compromised. The possible consequences, for this reporter, outweigh the full disclosure of relevant facts in the story. Fairness, then, is more important than truth.

Now let us look a moment at the public relations enterprise. Truth, though important as Gordon contends, is not the main concern of the PR practitioner, at least, not *all* the truth. The main objective in PR is to provide the most positive image possible of the client or institution. This may necessitate manipulating the facts, stressing some and deemphasizing others, revealing some and omitting others. The loyalty here is to the client, not to the general public. One hardly expects a public relations person (or an advertiser) to have the same dedication to truthful information as a news reporter should have.

A conscientious journalistic medium will question the accuracy and honesty of news releases it receives. This is the natural thing to do, just as the medium would question its own reportorial accuracy and honesty. One might say that ethics places this responsibility on the medium. In fact, both Gordon and Kittross would subscribe to this when it comes to dealing with PR. In reality, however, years of empirical observation convinces me that seldom, if ever, do editors "check out" the validity of information sent them.

If the editor decides to accept a news release blindly, without verifying the accuracy of all details, does this mean that he or she is unethical? Might it not simply be a case of carelessness, or laziness, or simply having a trusting disposition? Can carelessness be equated with a lack of ethics? The reader will note that when we get into areas of content selection (gatekeeping), we are dealing with what most media workers think of as extra-ethical and as skills related more to effective work habits than to morality. Nevertheless, even the most prosaic media practices do, indeed, have ethical overtones. A good case can be made that sloppy quoting of a source is both poor reporting and bad ethics—poor reporting because it distorts reality and bad ethics because it misleads the audience and portrays the source erroneously.

The idea of "news management" being unethical is very problematic. Journalism *is* news management. All through the process of selecting a story, determining what will go in the story, how it will be organized and edited—the whole process is managing the news. Everyone connected with this process will, in specific instances, be faced with some ethical decision. But the overarching idea of "managing the news" is a professional necessity, not an unethical practice.

Gordon gets onto an interesting side road as he notes the problem with audience members being too insulated against perspectives with which they are uncomfortable. He refers to this as an "informational cocoon" and proposes that it is a way consumers can manipulate media and sources. Many people, he maintains, are mainly interested in getting information that reinforces their views and prejudices. He quotes Cass Sunstein (2007) as pointing out that the Internet provides a way for consumers easily to avoid encounters with materials that clash with their beliefs, turning the news into a highly customized "Daily Me." Of course, this is nothing new; we have long known that people seek out self-aggrandizing information, that liberals are mainly ignorant of conservative thought, and conservatives rarely expose themselves to liberal thinking.

Kittross agrees with Gordon on this, but places the blame on the individual audience members, not on the media. He locates the problem with "the individual's own biases and prejudices that select" certain types of information and ideas. Instead of stressing technological "filters" imposed by the Internet as does Gordon, Kittross believes that what stems the flow of ideas are "personal filters—biases." He makes the very perceptive point that rarely will a person "sort through the biases of both MSNBC and Fox News in a search for a middle-ground truth." A person could do it, of course, but closed-mindedness is not the fault of the media but rather of the individual person. As Kittross sees it, we permit ourselves to be manipulated. In short, in order to get a more comprehensive worldview, Kittross would have us change ourselves, whereas Gordon would have us change the media.

While Kittross makes some significant points, he does present some problematic ideas. One of these is his questioning if truth and objectivity are "*adequate* standards for the news media." Would not, he asks, consequences (dealing with results rather than principles or rules) be a better approach? With one fell swoop, Kittross attempts to abolish the traditional (at least since the Enlightenment) dedication to truth with his provocative belief that we need to be *fair* as well as truthful. He maintains that really there is no truth, no single "correct" view of an event. He can fall back here on Kant's contention that we as human beings can see only the "phenomena" (the surface, insubstantial, and incomplete) things around us, not the "noumena" (the real, complete, metaphysical) perfection of the things. This is similar to Plato's "ideas" or "form" contrasted to his physical representations or shadows on the cave wall. So Kittross is right: There is no "truth" that we can fully find, but this does not obviate Gordon's desire to see communicators constantly attempt to find it.

While *postmodernism* is still a rather vague concept to me, I would say that Kittross exemplifies it in several ways: his denial of objectivity, and his strong dedication to relativity. Gordon seems more tied to the more formalistic absolutism of Immanuel Kant—or at least to a less relativistic moral philosophy. Perhaps Gordon swings a little too much between a kind of Kantian idealism and an ethics based on success. At least he pays considerable attention to Machiavelli and the ethics of success. This, of course, is a long-standing ethical quandary, having good ends brought about through less than ethical means. There are, certainly, what might be termed "moral Machiavellians" and "immoral Machiavellians." The former would use any means to avoid a huge, catastrophic disaster—a kind of Millian utilitarianism aimed at bringing the most good to the greatest number of people, even if it means subjecting certain people to immoral acts of torture or even murder. The latter type of Machiavellian would be one who, for no beneficial or utilitarian reason, would do immoral acts simply for personal, egocentric, selfish, or institutional purposes.

Gordon seems worried about Kittross's "apparent willingness" to see government have some control over the media so that the people will have information they "need." The idea of government interference in media affairs is always worrisome in a free-press country. But when the subject turns to "ethics," as it is in this book, is there any reason to think that government cannot, through its power, bring about helpful ethical changes in media operations? Kittross may feel that private owners of the press have failed to make such changes and that a "democratically formed" government may be able to rectify the situation. But why should elected government officials have more concern for ethics than private, profit-making media managers? Or less, for that matter?

Gordon would say, I'm sure, that there is the matter of the First Amendment. Government should keep out of the press business (at least Congress should). Question: What if the privately owned press were to act in a completely harmful way, even threatening the viability of the nation? Would the First Amendment still offer protection? For Gordon's ideal press there would be no need for government interference if truth were the only ethical requisite. "Truth" for Gordon is the key aspect of ethics, and being fair, public-spirited, balanced, pluralistic and all such things, are not *essential*. My main question about Gordon's position is this: Who would determine the truth of all the media accounts?

Both Gordon and Kittross, in this chapter, have done admirable jobs of making their arguments and providing catalytic thoughts and questions. Gordon contends that media audiences are better served if media gatekeepers take effective steps to ensure that media, rather than the would-be manipulators, really control. Although there is something a little strange about one institution (the media) being in control rather than the more democratic idea of the people sharing power with the media establishment, Gordon's statement is given in the spirit of the First Amendment and the traditional American concept of an autonomous media system.

This is a difficult topic, one with which the reader could wrestle for a long time. It gets us into the areas of power, power-sharing, journalistic purpose, conflict of interest, the public's right to know, the right of public access to the media, and the basic meaning of press freedom in our society. It is certainly a topic in which broadcasters, print media people, bloggers, advertisers, and public relations practitioners all have a vital and vested interest. It should stimulate considerable discussion.

REFERENCES AND RELATED READINGS

Allport, Gordon W., and Leo J. Postman. (1945). "The basic psychology of rumor." *Transactions of the New York Academy of Sciences Series* 2(8), pp. 61–81. (Reprinted in numerous collections.)

Alterman, Eric. (2010) "Will ABC let Amanpour be Amanpour?" *The Nation*, April 12, p. 10.

Barney, Ralph. (1986). "The journalist and a pluralistic society: An ethical approach." In Deni Elliott, ed., *Responsible Journalism*. Beverly Hills, CA: Sage, pp. 60–80.

Be'er, Yizhar. (2009). "Human tragedy as a catalyst for change." Common Ground News Service, April 9. Retrieved from www.commongroundnews.org/article.php?id=25249&lan=en&sid=08&sp=0 (October 4, 2009).

Bertrand, Claude-Jean. (1993). "Media ethics in Europe: Media accountability systems." *Media Ethics* 6(1), pp. 7–9.

Bivins, Thomas H. (2004). *Mixed Media: Moral Distinctions in Advertising, Public Relations, and Journalism*. London: Taylor & Francis.

Black, Jay, Bob Steele, and Ralph Barney. (1995). *Doing Ethics in Journalism: A Handbook with Case Studies*, 2nd ed. Boston, MA: Allyn & Bacon.

Bok, Sissela. (1978). *Lying: Moral Choice in Public and Private Life*. New York: Pantheon.

Christians, Clifford G., Mark Fackler, Kathy Brittain McKee, Peggy J. Kreshel, and Robert H. Woods, Jr. (2009). *Media Ethics: Cases and Moral Reasoning*, 8th ed. Boston, MA: Allyn & Bacon.

Commission on Freedom of the Press. (1947). *A Free and Responsible Press*. Chicago, IL: University of Chicago Press.

Curran, John Philpot. (1790). Speech upon the Right of Election of the Lord Mayor of Dublin (July 10, 1790). Quoted in Bartlett, John and Kaplan, Justin (eds) (1992) *Bartlett's Familiar Quotation* 16th ed. Boston: Little, Brown & Co., p. 351

Dennis, Everette E. (1990). "In allegiance to truth: News, ethics and split-personality journalism." New York Gannett Center for Media Studies. Speech delivered March 6, Honolulu.

Fink, Conrad. (1988). *Media Ethics: In the Newsroom and Beyond.* New York: McGraw-Hill.

Goodman, Ellen. (2009). "No sympathy for empathy." *The Seattle Times,* May 22, p. A16.

Griffiths, David. (1996). "Teaching journalism skills courses to new public relations majors." *Journalism & Mass Communication Educator* 51(1), pp. 82–86.

Habermas, Jürgen. (1962). *The Structural Transformation of the Public Sphere: An Inquiry into a Category of Bourgeois Society,* translated from the German in 1989, by Thomas Burger and Frederick Lawrence. Cambridge, UK: Polity.

Harwood, Richard. (1992). "Knights of the Fourth Estate." *The Washington Post,* December 5, p. A23.

Howard, Jennifer. (2008). "'Libel tourism' puts British and American defamation standards in the spotlight." *The Chronicle of Higher Education,* July 4, p. A9.

Huff, Darryl. (1954). *How to Lie with Statistics.* New York: Norton.

Kinsella, James. (1989). *Covering the Plague: AIDS and the American Media.* New Brunswick, NJ: Rutgers University Press.

Lambeth, Edmund B. (1992). *Committed Journalism: An Ethic for the Profession,* 2nd ed. Bloomington and Indianapolis, IN: Indiana University Press.

Lippmann, Walter. (1922). *Public Opinion.* New York: Macmillan.

MacArthur, John R. (1992). *Second Front: Censorship and Propaganda in the 1991 Gulf War.* Berkeley and Los Angeles, CA: University of California Press.

McKay, Floyd J. (1992). "Filling the gap: Congress increases its video as TV news cuts budgets." Paper presented at the annual convention of the Association for Education in Journalism and Mass Communication, Montreal, August 5–8.

Merrill, John C. (1998). *The Princely Press: Machiavelli on American Journalism.* Lanham, MD: University Press of America.

Milam, Lorenzo. (1975). *Sex and Broadcasting.* (3rd edition) Los Gatos, CA: Dildo Press.

Plaisance, Patrick Lee. (2009). *Media Ethics: Key Principles for Responsible Practice.* Thousand Oaks, CA: Sage.

Rawls, John. (1971). *A Theory of Justice.* Cambridge, MA: Belknap.

Russert, Tim. (2008). "When politicians meet the press." The Red Smith Lecture in Journalism, University of Notre Dame, April 14. Published by the John W. Gallivan Program in Journalism, Ethics & Democracy. South Bend, IN: University of Notre Dame.

Steele, Bob. (1993). "Lying to tell the truth: Is it ever OK?" *Poynter Report,* Winter, p. 3.

Sunstein, Cass. (2007). *Republic.com 2.0.* Princeton, NJ: Princeton University Press.

"The changing times." (1992). *The New Yorker,* October 5, p. 63.

Turow, Joseph. (2009). *Media Today: An Introduction to Mass Communication,* 3rd ed. New York: Routledge.

Ward, Stephen J.A. (2004) *The Invention of Journalism Ethics: The Path to Objectivity and Beyond.* Montreal: McGill-Queens' University Press.

Warren, Samuel D., and Louis D. Brandeis. (1890). "The right to privacy." *Harvard Law Review* 4(5), pp. 193–220.

Wicker, Tom. (1971). "The greening of the press." *Columbia Journalism Review,* May–June, pp. 7–12.

Willis, W. J. (Jim). (1991). *The Shadow World: Life Between the News Media and Reality.* New York: Praeger.

Chapter 4

The Ethics of "Correctness" and "Inclusiveness"

ALL media—informative (including news), persuasive, or entertaining, and regardless of the technology they employ—inevitably contribute to society's expectations of what is "usual" or "normal," often to an extent the public doesn't fully realize. This is a complicated process, since the mass media simultaneously reflect and define the society and culture(s) in which they operate, as Lee Loevinger (1968) pointed out in an oft-quoted article.

However, the media do not always carry out these socialization functions in ways that all groups in the society consider inclusive—or even adequate. The criticisms are many. They range from charges that the media simply ignore non-mainstream groups to complaints of distorted representations of various groups and points of view. Concern about such omissions and distortions may refer to media content, to ownership of media companies, and to the fact that most key decisions in the media of many nations are still made by males from the dominant ethnic group.

Arguments against media shortcomings in these areas have been recounted for decades. Although many people would agree that large segments of the media have shown improvement during this period, there still is considerable concern that their pace is slow, uneven, and uncertain. Therefore, some say, additional efforts are required if the media are to serve a diverse society well.

On the other side of the argument are those who believe that additional efforts can skew the equation too far the other way and bog the media down in what is often referred to as "political correctness." They maintain that it is far better to aim for fairness and balance than for "representation" of each of the many diverse groups in some sort of "equitable" manner.

In this chapter, David Gordon supports the need for special efforts by the media to become more inclusive of society's diversity in their news, advertising and entertainment content and in their employment practices. John Michael Kittross argues against simplistic, or "quota," approaches to such issues as race, gender, and ethnicity. He is more concerned with individuals than with groups and holds that no special efforts are necessary—that the media belong to society at large more than to any one part of it.

GORDON: Mass media must make special efforts to deal with race, gender, culture, and ethnicity in their personnel, news, advertising, and entertainment functions.

People in the media bring their own experiences and perceptions to the advertising, public relations, news, and entertainment tables. For that reason alone, special efforts are needed to ensure that the media are *inclusive* rather than *exclusive*.

John Michael Kittross makes this point well in his comment in Chapter 3 that "We stereotype and simplify the news without even thinking about it" (p. 113). Others have also voiced serious concerns about what is excluded or distorted in the media's accounts of "the news" and the various ideas, opinions, and people who are part of it (see Stephens and Mindich, 2005). News—and persuasive communication, as well—is inevitably shaped by the perspectives, ideologies, and life experiences of the gatekeepers. We each bring our own baggage to our communication efforts, and ideas or groups that lie outside our experiences and beliefs may never make it past the "gates" that screen the communications we produce.

If the mass media omit minorities, or even majorities without substantial financial or other power, from their portrayals of society—or if they misrepresent those groups because they don't understand them—the result is unfair and damaging to more than just the ignored or misrepresented parts of society. Such an inaccurate mediated picture also harms the many people who know little or nothing about their fellow citizens with different backgrounds—about the so-called "others" in their society.

Media that deal realistically with society's diversity are thus important to members of all groups in society, both majority and minority, not to mention the society as a whole. It has been argued that media portrayals and news coverage of the society influence what takes place between individuals and groups in their *un*mediated social, political, and economic interactions. If this is at all valid, ignoring minorities or regularly portraying them negatively rather than as contributors to, and participants in, the society will make it hard for anyone (majority or minority) to view them—or interact with them—as if minorities have a real stake in society and its institutions.

There certainly has been progress toward including a diverse portrait of society in news and entertainment media. Still, a great deal of further effort—and sensitivity on the part of media people—is required. Two knowledgeable observers of the media diversity scene noted in 1994 that many minorities who were still outside society's mainstream had good reason

to think their perspectives are at best warped by the media or, worse, not heard at all. In the year that saw a black man elected president of South Africa, there is irony in the fact that apartheid still rules the information age in America.

(Dates and Pease, 1994, p. 90)

Fifteen years later, very shortly after a black man was elected president of the United States, *The New York Post* reignited some of the same concerns about perspectives, with a cartoon depicting a chimpanzee shot by the police, with the caption, "They'll have to find someone else to write the next stimulus bill." There was an immediate outcry, arising partly from the belief that the cartoonist was comparing President Obama (whose first legislative success following his inauguration was an economic stimulus package) to a chimp or, worse, suggesting that he deserved assassination. This cartoon, and the *Post*'s initial clueless response that it saw nothing for which to apologize, illustrated all too vividly the failure to understand how the "other" may view the world.

As part of the ensuing national discussion, syndicated columnist Leonard Pitts—after listing half a dozen examples of newspaper stories published between 1899 and 1940 that referred to African Americans as beasts or wild animals—noted that it took almost a week for *Post* owner Rupert Murdoch to issue a "no strings attached" apology.

> That it took so long to do the obvious speaks volumes.
>
> Let's be clear on one thing: The Post has a right to provoke and even offend. That is absolute and sacrosanct. But it is difficult not to be troubled by a suffocating cluelessness that allows it to provoke and offend without knowing it or meaning it or even, apparently, caring about it . . .
>
> The paper's attitude . . . is fed by the fact that in recent years too many African Americans have found it convenient to "cry wolf" where race is concerned. But if arrogance on the one end and disingenuousness on the other are our only alternatives, we're in trouble.
>
> Fittingly, this all unfolds in the wake of . . . contentions that we need to become better and braver in talking about race. Take the Post's self-satisfied ignorance as Exhibit A.
>
> The paper didn't know that it didn't know.
>
> (Pitts, 2009)

From a more conservative perspective, syndicated columnist Kathleen Parker criticized the cartoon because its

> images carry too much free-associative weight. . . . The mind's eye sees a dead chimpanzee and . . . strays off course, away from the news of the animal attacking a woman [in Connecticut shortly before] to a history of dehumanizing blacks.
>
> It may be subliminal, but it's there. And dehumanization is never funny.
>
> (Parker, 2009)

One of the mandates presented to the news media in 1947 by the Commission on Freedom of the Press is to provide a representative picture of society's various groups. I believe this is equally applicable today to the entertainment and persuasive media. To provide this picture to a broad cross-section of the United States' pluralistic society, the mass media must first—to follow the prescription from Pitts and Parker—be aware of what they *don't* know, and be sensitive to how their words and images may be perceived by people who are "not like them." The "special efforts" that I'm advocating are nothing more than first aiming to recognize and overcome this lack of knowledge and of sensitivity. Only then can the media strive both to be inclusive and to reflect that the total society is made up of diverse groups and individuals—even if that isn't immediately obvious in some geographic (or economic) areas.

Don Heider, a television journalist turned academic, wrote from his own experiences in the 1980s

> that journalists didn't generally sit around the table and say: "how can we exclude (insert: Blacks, Latinos, Asians or Native Americans) today?" Yet, if you watched our 5 p.m. shows, it was as if that's *exactly* what we had done.
>
> (Heider, 2000, p. 2)

When Heider went into two TV newsrooms (in Albuquerque, New Mexico, and Honolulu, Hawai'i—both of them "diverse, except at the top") for five weeks of participant observation in the late 1990s, he still "found consistently inadequate coverage of communities of color" (Heider pp. 81 and 82).

Given U.S. society's increasing pluralism—and the heightened recognition of it—a "representative picture" requires the media to go beyond casual recognition and portrayal of society as a so-called melting pot. That somewhat dated metaphor uses an assimilationist perspective that expects different groups to blend into the majoritarian culture and modify it with their own subtle flavors. In recent years, various people have suggested that a more appropriate metaphor is the salad bowl or the pizza, in which the different groups in our society retain a great deal of their own identity while adding their unique flavors to the larger culture.

It may require a new perspective for the media to focus on the "salad bowl" type of diversity so as to reflect—and help define for their audiences and therefore for society—the *legitimacy* of different traditions, perspectives, and values. This is needed whether one is concerned with news, persuasive, or entertainment media, because all of them in various ways help to reflect and transmit the society's cultures and values.

This certainly does not mean—as Kittross points out—that editors of particular genders, sexual orientations, races, or political perspectives should be given veto power over content intended for a mass audience. It does require a heightened sensitivity to diversity concerns that go well beyond just opening the doors to equal-opportunity hiring or general ethical behavior. It is important to remember that such special efforts as trying to increase one's sensitivity to, or empathy for, others are not "special treatment." They simply implement John Rawls's concern for the weakest party in any given situation, and they might well focus most strongly on *un*intentional insensitivity, which can be just as damaging—though arguably easier to overcome—as intentional disrespect for those who are "different."

I'm puzzled by Kittross's concern (p. 147) that "'representation' often means content and employment quotas, diversity tends to mean divisiveness, and plurality is a code word for separatism." I believe that it's possible to be "representative" without coming anywhere near "quotas"; that "plurality," in society as in elections, says nothing on its face about closeness or separation; and that "diversity"—done *properly*—celebrates the societal unity that Kittross advocates.

The problem is that the media have *not* handled properly the job of being representative and portraying diversity, and that's why I'm concerned. Too often, the media have *not* followed the Hutchins Commission directive that Kittross quotes but, rather, have failed to recognize the values, aspirations, or even the common humanity of groups outside of society's mainstream. Or groups that are outside the circles frequented by mainstream media people. While we're focusing here mainly on non-whites and women, there are many other groups with ongoing concerns about how they are (or are not) portrayed in the media—for instance, gun owners, evangelicals, and various types of "conservatives" (who, among other things, are often portrayed as a monolithic group).

I'll leave it to the reader to decide—as this discussion unfolds—whether Kittross is putting words in my mouth and is ascribing to me ideas that are mutant interpretations of what I believe. Obviously, I think he is, throughout much of his argument in this chapter. For example, my citation of some unsettling statistics does *not* equate to support of quotas. Those data are not a prescription for what should be, but rather a *reflection* of the missing shades of color in what has too often been a mostly white landscape. Any single statistic that I've cited proves absolutely nothing on its own. Let me repeat that point—any *single* statistic proves absolutely nothing *by itself*.

the media portrait of the various hues that make up our human race has too often been flawed, or monochromatic

But when the pattern of minority absence keeps repeating and repeating (and repeating), it takes a remarkable set of blinders to miss seeing the reality that this reflects. (Or, perhaps, a wonderful pair of rose-colored glasses to imply that since we all belong to the human race and the human race is well represented, then everything is fine.) In fact, the media portrait of the various hues that make up our human race has too often been flawed, or monochromatic, as has the composition of the humans who have served as media gatekeepers.

Robert Entman and Andrew Rojecki (2000, p. 211) seem to suggest the need for special efforts when they note that "conventions of objectivity, the relatively simple techniques used to ensure balance and avoid bias, are not up to the task of covering issues in a racialized culture." Heider (2000) says much the same thing in noting that (white) reporters too often lack knowledge of the history and context of topics affecting people of color and many such stories—even when they draw on minority sources—"still reinforce existing beliefs about people of color individually and collectively" (p. 81). Kittross indicates (below) his agreement with this statement but extends it with a gratuitous attack on reporters' news-gathering skills and thought processes in general—a topic for a different debate.

Aside from outright racism, sexism, and other prejudice, three points sum up succinctly, if in somewhat oversimplified fashion, why special efforts are needed:

■ Stereotypes (those "existing beliefs" that Heider referred to).
■ The human tendency to view the world from familiar perspectives and to be insensitive—often without even knowing it—to those who view things from different perspectives
■ Simple ignorance about cultures, groups, and traditions that are different from one's own.

Thus, men may see nothing out of line or offensive in a newspaper column that refers to someone who, "like you and me, has to look himself in the mirror every morning when he shaves." Women's reactions could range from simply tuning out an irrelevant message to anger or feeling belittled or otherwise offended. And what about blacks who read in the late 1960s, in *The New York Times*, about the several hundred "well-dressed Negro officials and their wives" who attended a White House function in Washington. Was it really news (i.e., worth noting) that people invited to White House functions dress up for the occasion? Or was it simply a manifestation of an old stereotype in the mind of the white reporter who wrote the story (see Smith, 1969)?

Even an entertainment program as sensitive as the original *Star Trek*—which regularly tackled issues of "being different" with sensitivity—didn't escape the insensitive use of language. At the beginning of each episode, the mission of the *Enterprise* was clearly stated: "to boldly go where no man has gone before." It was not until the sequel *Star Trek: The Next Generation*, with its considerable increase in the number of women in the ship's crew, that this male perspective was eliminated and the gender reference was changed from "no man" to "no one." Even such a minor bow toward greater sensitivity apparently didn't occur to the creators of the original series.

One way in which the mass media have contributed strongly to public acceptance of society's diversity is TV's coverage of integrated sports events. In the mid-1970s, a decade or so after Governor George Wallace "stood in the schoolhouse door" to prevent blacks from entering the University of Alabama, its basketball team, with five black starters, was applauded enthusiastically by its (predominantly white) fans during introductions before a National Collegiate Athletic Association (NCAA) tournament game. Similar attitude change has been aided by increasing TV coverage of women's college, professional, and international sports. In these instances, the media have portrayed realities of participation by women and African Americans, and some parts of society have learned more about these groups. Other factors (e.g., Title IX) have also played important roles. But the impact of media portrayals shouldn't be ignored.

THE ENTERTAINMENT MEDIA: DIVERSITY AND STEREOTYPING

This issue's complexity is compounded when the entertainment media are considered. First, there is the question of what characters are chosen to be portrayed. Because many of those decisions have been made by white men, it's not surprising that the TV version of our society over the years has lacked significant numbers of women over 35, people with a disability, and minorities. Numerous studies over recent decades have documented the absence of these and other groups within our diverse society. To list just a few illustrations:

■ The disparity between male and female roles (about two to one) in cable and over-the-air TV programming didn't change much in the nine years between the 1982–83 and the 1991–92 television seasons (Gerbner, 1993); and a 2006 study (of more than 1,000 TV shows aimed at children, and some 400 movies) indicated about the same ratio, which existed "not only in lead speaking roles, but even in crowd scenes" (Nagel, 2008).

■ In *daytime* programming in the decade after 1982, a time when women are a prime target audience, women had 45% of the roles (Gerbner, 1993).

■ Hispanic characters filled only about 1% of prime-time roles on major network television in 1992 (Gerbner, 1993), and the percentage rose only to 6% in prime-time roles by 2002 (National Association of Television Program Executives (NATPE), 2003)—figures far below Hispanics' 13.5% presence in the general U.S. population. And, as noted below, when Hispanic characters did appear, it was often in negative roles.

■ Small numbers (1–2%) of Asians and Asian Americans were cast in 2002 prime-time programs, and those portrayals were generally positive (Kim, 2003). By 2007, performers of South Asian descent—primarily Indian—were breaking some stereotypes as they established a small presence in TV and film roles (Keveney, 2007). And, of course, *Slumdog Millionaire* (2008) won the best picture Oscar with a largely Indian cast.

■ People 60 and older accounted for only 4% of the major characters in 2002–03 prime-time TV programs, although in those years this age group made up 18% of the American population (Lauzen and Dozier, 2005). Statistics for African American characters were much closer to their numbers in the general U.S. population. Gerbner (1993) found that they had nearly 11% of the prime-time roles on the major networks—fairly close to their population percentage. Ten years later, African American roles were up to 15.5% (NATPE, 2003), slightly above their general population percentage.

Both the real Ellen DeGeneres and the lead character she played on television came "out of the closet" in 1997 (during the May ratings sweeps, amid great hype), though the appearance of the first gay character on a network series was in a short-lived comedy back in the early 1970s (Graham, 1997). Gay and lesbian characters gradually began to show up after that in leading or supporting roles in other series, though the numbers remained small—just over 1% of the roles in the 2005–06 and 2006–07 seasons, according to the Gay & Lesbian Alliance Against Defamation ("Study: Gay characters' television presence . . .," 2006). Still, when one considers that the modern gay rights movement in the United States really dates only from the late 1940s, there has been considerable progress in how the various media have dealt with these groups (see Gross, 2001).

There has also been progress in television advertisements, where African Americans and Hispanics have appeared with increasing frequency after being largely invisible until recent decades. An early and unfortunate exception to that invisibility was the "Frito Bandito" ad campaign for four years in the 1960s, featuring "a portly, animated mouse . . . [who] revived the old stereotype of the Mexican bandito who stole whatever he wanted, while speaking in broken English" (Lichter and Amundson, 1994, p. 4). Some Asians have also become visible, but very few identifiable Native Americans have been seen in TV ads, although one famous public service spot showed Chief Dan George weeping over what was being done to the environment. The increased visibility of ethnic characters in ads is a clear sign that advertisers see the Hispanic, African American, and Asian American markets as potentially profitable ones and want the people in those markets to feel comfortable while watching their commercials.

Despite the progress, media still have a long way to go in acknowledging diversity, and that it extends beyond the question of numbers. When Hollywood did start including blacks in the cast, the portrayal was often unflattering. Black characters in early films were usually portrayed with negative stereotypes—in some cases, outright caricatures—if they appeared at all. Early television programming had similar problems, with blacks appearing mainly in subservient roles or in sitcoms. Heavy criticism of the *Amos 'n' Andy* television series was directed at the stereotypical caricatures of blacks presented by the program's white producers. (The African American community had mixed reactions to the original radio program, with the criticism reaching its height in 1931 as the result of a campaign led by the editor of *The Pittsburgh Courier*, a black weekly newspaper; see Dates and Barlow, 1990, pp. 180–181.)

Similar problems have existed for other groups. A study of prime-time television series back to the 1950s (Lichter and Amundson, 1994) reported that although Hispanic characters appeared rarely on TV, they committed many more TV crimes per person, and were cast as "heavies" more often, than was the case for either African American or non-Hispanic white characters. "Their depictions are notable for the high proportion of criminals and violent characters . . . and the absence of starring roles and successful role models" (p. 2). By early in the 21st century, however, Jimmy Smits did portray a successful Hispanic presidential candidate in *The West Wing*, a program that gave leading roles to a lot of people who didn't portray typical white male—usually WASP—characters.

Even a diversity of positive roles is no guarantee that society will be reflected realistically. Minority groups have often been portrayed—by both entertainment and news—as monolithic. Lichter and Amundson noted that the "cultural diversity *within* the Latino community is almost completely absent from prime time" (1994, p. 16, italics added). Consider, for example, that the term *Hispanic* is sometimes applied indiscriminately, without regard for the fact that it can include people with roots in Cuba, Mexico, Puerto Rico, the rest of Latin America, and Spain. In the United States, relatively few non-Hispanics distinguish between Spanish slang words that identify those of Mexican or Puerto Rican ancestry, but such distinctions are important to many Hispanics.

> Even a diversity of positive roles is no guarantee that society will be reflected realistically.

This really isn't a surprising phenomenon. In movies or TV programs, time is limited and it is far easier to ignore or gloss over the nuances of the various characters. Therefore, rather than developing them fully, writers and producers find it much easier to rely on stereotypes. These were defined by Walter Lippmann (1922) as the "pictures inside our heads," which necessarily have a major impact on our perceptions of "reality" (or of the *various* social realities). Such mental pictures act as a shorthand or shortcut to developing film or TV characters, and the writers and producers of necessity rely on the ones in their *own* minds, which often are oversimplified and fail to portray fully or accurately the groups to which the characters belong.

Stereotypes often offend members of the audience who see themselves as differing from the blanket description applied simplistically to their group. In arguing against using this kind of categorized description for men and women, Deborah Tannen (1990) explained the dilemma concisely:

> We all know we are unique individuals, but we tend to see others as representatives of groups. It's a natural tendency, since we must see the world in patterns in order to make sense of it; we wouldn't be able to deal with the daily onslaught of people and objects if we couldn't predict a lot about them and feel that we know who and what they are.
>
> (pp. 15–16)

But this also means that, to be ethical—perhaps particularly in regard to Rawls's "veil of ignorance"—the media must work seriously, and unceasingly, to *transcend* stereotypes, especially those originated by and relevant to only the majority groups in the audience. Otherwise, there is little hope of portraying society's real complexity and diversity.

The majority/minority distinction used here itself oversimplifies—stereotypes, if you prefer—a situation that is in considerable flux. A mid-2008 estimate by the U.S. Census Bureau projected that American "minority" groups—African Americans, Hispanics, Asians, Native Americans, and others—would outnumber non-Hispanic whites in the United States in 2042 and would be 54% of the total population (up from about 33% in 2008) by mid-century. The size of the Hispanic population will nearly triple between 2008 and 2050, according to this estimate, and Hispanics, at 30%, will become the United States' second largest population group (U.S. Census Bureau, 2008).

Worldwide, of course, non-Hispanic whites have always been a minority, as is also the case in several major American cities. And females have outnumbered males in the United States for some time now. Thus, we may be overdue in reconsidering just who is in the "majority," and different terminology may well be warranted.

OTHER DIMENSIONS OF DIVERSITY

News coverage of "minorities" has often been criticized either for its almost total absence, or for its focus on violence and crime. Even that focus frequently emphasized black-on-white crime, while the much more prevalent instances of black-on-black crime rated considerably less attention.

Hispanics have also had problems with coverage. In 2001, when Hispanics were about 12% of the U.S. population, the three major TV networks plus CNN aired an average of only 1 in 160 stories about members of this group, according to the National Association of Hispanic Journalists (NAHJ). And, the NAHJ said, most of those few stories about Hispanics were both stereotyped and negative (BBC, 2002b). Nor is this a problem only in the United States. Another 2002 study, of British entertainment programming, concluded that it provided an unrealistic picture of ethnic minorities in the United Kingdom, using negative stereotypes or ignoring and oversimplifying issues important to minority communities. One example: British TV was portraying arranged marriages inaccurately, using outdated customs as if they were still current (BBC, 2002a). In France, then-President Jacques Chirac called for French TV networks to do more to reflect France's diverse population, threatening tougher broadcasting laws to accomplish that goal (James, 2005).

With a little thought, and some sensitivity to groups that are often seen as outside the mainstream, a broad spectrum of potentially newsworthy stories might well be developed about African American, Latino, Asian, and Native American communities, *along with* continued coverage for those of European descent. Similarly, with some thought and a reasonable amount of research, entertainment programming could avoid a reliance on stereotypes and grapple meaningfully with the complex realities of minority communities and the various issues that arise within them.

Children's programming—and ads aimed at children—have provided a different prism through which to consider diversity and status. Gerbner (1993) found that women filled just under 25% of the roles in children's programming in his 10-year study. Other researchers have pointed out the domination by white males of TV commercials on Saturday morning children's programming. A 1991 study of Boston's ABC, CBS, Fox, and NBC affiliates found that 95% of the characters in those commercials were white, that males outnumbered females by about two to one, and that female characters were more likely than not to be children. This study updated two earlier ones from the 1970s and found that relatively little had changed in the interim (Pecora, 1993). A broader study that examined how women are portrayed in prime-time TV commercials found that in 2001, younger girls still appeared less often than did boys of the same ages. It also found that in almost all age groups, female characters were less likely than their male counterparts "to work, have authority, be shown outdoors, and be associated with non-domestic products" (Stern and Mastro, 2004, p. 233).

Commercials aimed directly at children are more than just pitches for products. They are also subtle messages about the societal importance of different genders and races. Even if unintentional, such messages still may indicate to young viewers that different races and genders should have different positions in society and exercise differing amounts of control. (It's also noteworthy that girls usually appeared in toy ads playing with dolls while boys were shown with toy cars, in the 1970s and again in 1991.) All of this is part of the socialization process for children and, if stereotypes are prominent in that process, they are likely to be perpetuated as the children take on adult roles in society.

The 1989 "Central Park Jogger" case illustrates how greater sensitivity to women's perspectives might have raised public awareness of an important social issue. Most media reports of that attack emphasized the racial angle of a white female victim and black and Hispanic teenagers accused of gang-raping and beating her. Some analyses tried to deal with the larger question of why *anyone* would commit such a vicious crime. Very little of the coverage looked at the general question of rape in the context of society's attitude toward women. Helen Benedict, a Columbia University journalism professor who studied the case, concluded that only female columnists and non-mainstream papers and magazines (such as *The Village Voice*, *The Nation*, and *Ms.*) raised the issue of societal attitudes toward women.

Benedict (1992) interviewed many (primarily male) editors and reporters and learned that most were almost totally ignorant of the phenomenon of gang rape. Nor had it apparently occurred to them that they might fill in that ignorance by calling a rape crisis center or looking at some of the studies on the subject of gang rape (Benedict, 1992). To borrow Leonard Pitts' (2009) comment about the *New York Post*, these journalists also "didn't know that they didn't know."

It's hard to dispute the view that coverage of this story would have been more useful to the news consumers had it included diverse perspectives and a wider range of background information. And, despite Kittross's dismissive approach later in this chapter, there certainly can be valid and important differences in male and female perspectives on a town council meeting or the aftermath of an earthquake or any other event that raises concerns about caring for people or interpersonal relations more generally—a point to which Carol Gilligan's (1982) work speaks cogently.

Language choices are another area where greater sensitivity could pay dividends. Richard Lederer (1991) has noted that English is "a window through which we look at the world"—one which both reflects and influences our culture. He questions whether that window distorts the view by providing built-in language biases against left-handed people, blacks, and women. Lederer (pp. 49–57) offers numerous examples of words that, he argues, indicate directly as well as subtly that these groups are inferior to right-handed people, whites, and males. To cite just one example, he suggests that men might become more aware of these language biases if their first graduate degree was a "mistress of arts" degree (p. 53). Lederer adds:

> We limit and diminish males and females alike when we use sexist language. In doing so, we become prisoners of language and abandon that which makes us human: the capacity to distinguish, discriminate, compare, and evaluate.
>
> (p. 57)

Or, to consider another dimension of the linguistic "we–they" syndrome, as an older Native American put it, in talking to a group of (white) students and faculty members: When the U.S. Cavalry killed huge numbers of Indians, the event was usually referred to as a "battle." When Native Americans killed large numbers of the U.S. Cavalry, he said, the term used by the U.S. government (and others) was "massacre"—though this wasn't always true, such as such as when Gen. Custer's 7th Cavalry was wiped out at the Battle of the Little Big Horn.

EMPLOYMENT STATISTICS

One reason for special efforts on behalf of a multicultural perspective is the relative shortage of female and non-white perspectives among media employees generally, but especially in decision-making positions in the news and entertainment media. In 2008, only 9% of the directors of the top 250 domestic grossing films were women—no percentage change from ten years earlier. Female representation among directors, producers, executive producers, writers, cinematographers and editors on those films was 16%, one percentage point *lower* than 1998 (Lauzen, 2009). Surveys of Hollywood employment in the early 1990s found even lower percentages in many key entertainment industry positions. As one example, only three women (compared to 45 men) held the title of president of any operations of 20 major film and TV studios and about 30% of the middle management positions there were held by women.

In the news media, the numbers are similar—but changing at least a little—regarding women and minority group members in positions of authority. Four decades after the 1968 Kerner Commission (established in the wake of the 1967 racial riots across the United States) strongly urged the news media to train minority group members and promote them to decision-making positions, whites (usually white males) were still the main newsroom decision-makers, though there has been recent progress, particularly in the broadcast media.

A survey (Papper, 2008) for the Radio-Television News Directors Association showed that, in the prior 18 years, while the U.S. minority population was growing 8.1% (to a total of 34%), minority employment rose only 5.8% in TV news and just 1% in radio. The 2007 proportion of all minority employees was 23.6% in TV news (but 3.5% lower when TV stations aimed at Hispanics are removed), well above the 11.8% (up just 1% from 1990) in radio news. (Papper also noted that minorities comprised just 13.5% of newspaper newsroom employees in 2007.) On a more positive note, 15.5% of TV news directors in 2007 were minorities, and female news directors comprised 28.3% of the total—both all-time-high percentages. But 17.5% of U.S. TV stations and 90% of U.S. radio stations had *no minority* personnel on their local news staffs! So much for the Kerner Commission's exhortation.

The picture is less encouraging in the newspaper industry. In 2005, data from the American Society of Newspaper Editors (ASNE) indicated that only 13% of U.S. print journalists were people of color (Meyer, 2006, p. 61) compared to 11% in the mid-1990s. And many newspaper newsrooms—especially those in smaller markets—had no minority journalists at all: depending on which survey you trust, anywhere from about 25% to over 40%, well above the comparable figure for TV newsrooms. Even a $5 million commitment by the Freedom Forum and ASNE to fund minority recruitment and development (Freedom Forum, 2000), had only minimal impact.

While more women are working their way into upper-level print media jobs, male editors are still the norm. The 2005 ASNE survey reported that newspapers with 21% of the nation's daily newspaper circulation had female editors, up fourfold from the 5% figure in 1982 (Meyer, 2006, p. 65). But publishers still need to meet the challenge of making newsroom working conditions—for editors and lower-ranking staffers alike—more compatible with the needs of women who are trying to juggle a career with the responsibilities of motherhood. One effort in that direction is the American Press Institute (2002) "survival guide" aimed at helping female editors. This publication provides advice from 50 editors (45 of them female) about how to navigate the shoals of the newsroom and their lives outside it. Male staffers, too, may need more consideration than they're getting across the board, to balance their professional and family responsibilities; this really is an ethical issue that has far too often been ignored by news media executives (not to mention those in other industries).

If decisions about what to cover and how to cover it are made mainly by white men, and if that coverage is mainly guided and edited by white men, it's not surprising that operative news values reflect mainly white male perspectives and sensitivities. One result is that some people or groups are measured by a different scale in determining their newsworthiness. Another is the frequent reliance on white men as experts in news stories, and even as non-experts who are quoted in stories. Similarly, if white men are the gatekeepers for TV and films, those vehicles are likely to reflect a mostly white male perspective. Such messages paint an increasingly inaccurate picture of society, send both subtle and direct signals about who and what society really values, and raise ethical concerns that the mass media must acknowledge and address.

ETHICAL FRAMEWORKS

Media that purport to serve a diverse, pluralistic society—and have First Amendment protection to do so—have an ethical obligation to provide a spectrum of perspectives reflecting that pluralism. This obligation can be based on the overall balance required by the Aristotelian Golden Mean or on utilitarianism's dictum of the greatest good for the society as a whole.

> Media that purport to serve a diverse, pluralistic society . . . have an ethical obligation to provide a spectrum of perspectives reflecting that pluralism.

This same obligation can also be grounded, strongly, in the social and journalistic pluralism for which Ralph Barney (1986) has argued eloquently. Barney's concerns about pluralism were directed more at the need for a variety of information sources in a participatory society than at ensuring diverse perspectives about race, gender, culture, and ethnicity—or, for that matter, age, lifestyle, sexual orientation, religion, or economic status. Nonetheless, they are highly applicable to those issues. Barney (p. 76) discussed the need for journalists to work under an ethic of pluralism and "distribute views that may be personally repugnant," while avoiding the trap of falling under the spell of whoever may be in positions of power and authority (that is, to avoid blindly extending the status quo).

Extrapolating from those concerns, a more general approach to pluralism would require the news and entertainment media to distribute "pictures" of the society that may be personally unfamiliar to the media gatekeepers but nevertheless portray real and important aspects of the society. A media pluralist, to paraphrase Barney, would almost automatically have empathy for many societal perspectives, and would introduce as many of them as possible into both professional media messages and private conversations.

One technique for this was tried in the Minnesota Public Radio newsroom, where reporters were told to spend one day a month cultivating "diverse" sources (i.e., sources from groups or cultures they were unfamiliar with). An alternative was to schedule coffee or tea once a week with such sources, and the goal was to let these sources tell their own stories and, eventually, to cover more stories that the diverse communities *themselves* considered important (McCallum, 2010).

Clifford Christians (1986), among others, has stressed the social responsibility theory of the press put forward in 1947 by the Commission on Freedom of the Press and amplified in *Four Theories of the Press* (Siebert et al., 1956) as a guiding ethic for the mass media. Christians also has suggested a communitarian approach in which the news media have a responsibility to report thoroughly on the powerless segments of society and to give voice to their needs. To do this, he wrote, requires the media to overcome their middle-class ethnocentrism (and he might well have added *white* and *male* to his middle-class reference).

That, of course, is the crux of the problem we have been discussing here. Christians (1986) relies heavily on John Rawls's veil of ignorance approach to ethics, where fairness is the cornerstone of social justice, and where the weaker, more vulnerable parties must be protected to the same degree that everyone else is. If this approach is applied to the current deficiencies in mass media representations of society, the need for special efforts to redress these shortcomings and portray all portions of the social spectrum seems both logical and obvious.

ETHICS PLUS ECONOMICS

For the mass media, this matter has become much more than just an ethical issue. It is increasingly a matter of long-term economic survival as well. As non-white groups become a greater and greater proportion of the population, diversity relates to sound long-term economics as well as to the media's social responsibility. Media outlets that fail to cultivate an audience among growing minority groups in their market may well find themselves with a much smaller audience when those groups become the majority.

Even if we all were to agree that some special efforts are needed to make American mass media more pluralistic, we must face some valid questions as to *what* should be done. Some suggestions have already been noted. Others probably come down to the need for empathy and sensitivity toward the perspectives and experiences of all groups, not just the ones we grew up in or the circles we now move in.

But at the least, we can get a greater diversity of people (and therefore, additional perspectives) involved at the decision-making levels so that previously ignored subjects can be considered for mass media content. For example, the increase in the number of African American filmmakers has added some very different, if sometimes controversial, perspectives to American cinema. A capsule newspaper review of Mario Van Peebles' *Posse* in mid-1993 called it a "revisionist Western [that] makes room for the historically real but cinematically invisible African American cowboy." The fact that movies have often ignored black cowboys is just one illustration of how non-mainstream groups have been disenfranchised by the media over the years, and thereby kept from the consciousness of both majority and minority members of society. Consider that it took until 1993 for mainstream Hollywood filmmakers to release their first movies dealing with AIDS. And it took until 2005 for *Brokeback Mountain* to come to grips with the existence of gay cowboys in the Old West, and that there might be marketable film plots drawn from them.

Another fairly basic approach would require greater efforts to eliminate the more subtle sexism and racism from the mass media's language. This might be something as simple as being sensitive to language that says women "giggle" while men "chuckle." It might mean omitting physical descriptions of women—or their clothing—when none is needed, or provided, for men. It could mean being sensitive enough to realize that phrases such as "black reputation" or "yellow coward" can be very offensive to members of non-white groups. And it means being sensitive enough not to use a historically loaded phrase like "They're circling the wagons" to describe how a high school athletics department was reacting to criticism from parents and community members; the phrase, as Kittross will argue, has historical validity but can also conjure up images of "savage" Indians attacking wagon trains of whites.

Possibly the simplest way to raise our consciousness about language use is to be aware of what has been called the "we–they syndrome." This is simply the human tendency to see the world as made up of two groups: people "like us" and "others." It shows up most readily, perhaps, in news reports (or in everyday conversations) about "the enemy" in wartime, whom we refer to in pejorative language as subhuman forms of life. During World War II, Americans demonized (in very different ways) Japanese and Germans, who have since become allies of the United States. In the 1960s, news media mentions of the North (and

South) Vietnamese didn't hesitate to refer to them as "gooks." And descriptions of the Iraq War in the 21st century—in the media and elsewhere—frequently referred to Iraqis (and, at times, to Muslims in general) in highly unflattering terms.

At the same time, there is a need to weigh carefully where inclusiveness or pluralism becomes the thicket of "political correctness." For example, was it appropriate, or overreacting, for the Minneapolis *Star Tribune* and *The Oregonian* in Portland to drop the use of American Indian team nicknames—such as "Redskins"—on their sports pages, as they did in 1993, even though the teams retained those nicknames (Fitzgerald, 1994; Jensen, 1994)? (This concern has been picked up by the NCAA and in some state high school athletic associations, which have encouraged or even forced various teams to drop mascots or team names referring to concepts that might offend.) The question of whether refusing to report such team nicknames is overreaction can be argued both ways, but suffice it to say that a realistic picture of a diverse society requires that details about all elements of that society be included, even if some of them make some people uncomfortable or unhappy.

The media need to be inclusive in portraying their society as fully as possible—warts and all, but without focusing unduly on the warts. It's not an easy task, and it's certainly not one that can be accomplished without making use of the multiple backgrounds, experiences, and perspectives that abound in this country. You may remember the story (which Kittross mentioned in Chapter 3) of the group of blind men who touched different parts of an elephant and argued heatedly over what it was they were touching. Pamela Creedon (1993), then an Ohio State journalism professor, raised the intriguing question of what would have changed had this parable been based on blind women—or blind women of color. Would that have added other perspectives to the argument? "Would they notice its smell?" she asked. "Would they feel its body heat?" She concluded by asking

> how much richer, more complete would the whole be if the touching were done by many different people from many different standpoints—men and women—of different classes, races, sexual preferences or ethnicities?
>
> (pp. 73–74)

This creates a striking analogy to the mass media and their attempts to portray for their audience a realistic picture of a world that media people, as well as their audiences, may be familiar with only through the societal equivalent of the elephant's trunk or ear. Too often, media portrayals have come from middle-class white males, without the richness and the texture that could have been added "by many different people from many different standpoints." The challenge facing the mass media is to take the necessary steps to add those diverse perspectives both in their professional workforces and in their content. But that content must truly reflect society's real diversity, not shaped to some artificial "content quota" formula, as Kittross tries to paint my argument.

What's really needed is an awareness that if the news and entertainment media continually overlook minorities in general or portray them negatively (for example, as violent criminals) beyond what reality dictates, such snapshots of society will become part of the pictures inside the heads of the audience. Such incessantly negative stereotypes will inevitably influence how members of the media audience act toward people who are different from themselves in some way and, perhaps, how those "others" regard themselves and act in return.

Meeting this challenge won't be easy, but it's necessary if U.S. society is to become truly inclusive. Anything less will fall well short of meeting the mass media's responsibilities as major players in U.S. society, both in reflecting it and in helping to shape its present *and* its future. Although this concern rests firmly on the grounds of media ethics and societal need, it also makes very good business sense in view of the evolving composition of the United States' actual and potential media consumers. It is an approach that melds Rawls's philosophy with a utilitarian perspective and in the process heightens an appreciation of true societal diversity.

KEY POINTS

- Individuals bring their personal "baggage"—perceptions, experiences, and beliefs—to communication efforts, and unfamiliar ideas or societal groups may never be included in those communications unless individuals make special efforts to transcend the limitations of their own backgrounds.
- Efforts to increase one's sensitivity to, or empathy for, others isn't "special treatment" but rather is an attempt to implement John Rawls's concern for the most vulnerable or weaker party.
- With some effort and sensitivity, news stories and entertainment programs could focus on non-white communities, *along with* those of European descent and, instead of using stereotypes, could portray meaningfully the complex realities of minority communities.

KITTROSS: No special efforts are required on the part of the mass media to deal "correctly" with race, gender, sexual orientation, culture, religion, age, and ethnicity.

We each are unique. No doubt about it. Human beings have not (yet) been cloned. But all of us are members of the same overall human community. We have more similarities than differences. The very fact that we are of one species ensures this. Regardless of our racial, religious, ethnic, gender, age, sexual orientation, and other differences, I doubt that anyone disagrees with the precept that we humans live in a global community and that the mass media link this community.

Indeed, the very phrase "mass medium" implies a community of attention—a number of people united by attention to a particular medium, if by nothing else. This is true, even though "political correctness" seems to be demanding that we dismiss much of our common intellectual heritage, such as a literary canon by "dead white males" (e.g., Shakespeare and the Bible; see Bloom, 1994) in favor of more modern or demographically diverse intellectual efforts. We also seem to be losing our common sense of history (major events or developments such as the American Revolution, the Civil War, the Great Depression) formerly familiar to every person with a smattering of schooling. Trying to talk with a college student today about the battles of Lexington and Concord, the First Amendment, or Lady Macbeth, often is a fruitless exercise. But here's the important thing: If the United States is to be a nation or a functioning community, we must have many, many things in common.

Today, what we do have in common is network television and mass circulation magazines, the Internet with all of its resources and distractions, and, to some extent, pop culture in general. And yet now, for a single network television program to reach a quarter of the population is a rare event. Even the largest circulation magazines, such as *AARP The Magazine* (formerly *Modern Maturity*), *National Geographic*, *TV Guide* and *Reader's Digest*, reach only perhaps one-tenth of U.S. homes. And, in so doing, these "mainstream" media really are trying to appeal to a varied collection of small groups while hoping that other small groups will not turn away.

William Butler Yeats, in his poem *The Second Coming*, laments: "things fall apart; the centre cannot hold." Nowadays, we have no center, yet it is absolutely necessary that we find one if we are to survive as a political, economic, and cultural entity.

(OVER)SIMPLICITY

One approach to discussing these issues is to concentrate on such simplistic facets of a larger problem as how many members of one group or another are shown on television or movie screens, how many are found in advertisements in a particular medium, and how many are employed at a particular media job level—and whether the number in that group is proportional to its numbers in the entire population. Gordon even provides some statistics about such proportions in managerial ranks in the news media. Such a focus assumes that we are all identical—cogs in the same wheel, no matter what our gender, age, race, or religious belief—which contradicts much of the argument for diversity.

But my position is that we are all individuals, and that this individuality is precious, not to be submerged into a politically correct or stereotypical grouping. Why in the world would we need to classify Tiger Woods as anything other than a superb golfer (though one with marital problems), even with his rich racial/ethnic background? My own age, gender, etc., would call forth a number of stereotypes, few of which are valid in my case. I think too highly of individuality to allow myself the easy approach, and find very disturbing some of today's shortsighted and often selfish attempts to glorify differences between groups rather than similarity between individuals.

Furthermore, Gordon's concentration on our differences seems to be open-ended. In the long run, human differences may become unimportant rather than determinative. People, such as Gordon, who embrace this "differences" approach seem to believe that whether genetic, environmental, or the result of history, they are not only immutable but also desirable. I believe that social development and evolution are different from biological evolution, and that Gordon carries both the "melting pot" and the "salad bowl" analogies too far and overlooks the possibility of humanity-wide change. In other words, emphasis on our present differences may not take into account the (probably remote) possibility of a truly color- and gender-blind society, or allow for other major societal changes.

For example, effective birth control and World War II (when a large proportion of men were in military service) had more to do with the changing roles of women in the 20th century than did all the mass media put together. Today, we need to look at the effects of the overwhelming population growth of the past century, migrations of millions of people, certain to be exacerbated by such factors as climate change and shortages of energy or water, and the changes in family formation stimulated by greater familiarity with other peoples caused by migration, the development of global patterns of higher education—and the mass media. Our awareness of the rest of the world, and our embrace of technology in areas such as transportation and communication, are certain to change society in ways we can't predict.

Those who remember the "Jim Crow" years of American interpersonal and institutional racial separation are amazed at how much change there has been since the early 1960s. Perfection? No. Improvements that benefit the human race? Definitely. Although Gordon and I are discussing the same controversy, we do so from very different philosophical positions and using very different logical and ethical tools to predict the human future.

The 1947 (Hutchins) Commission on Freedom of the Press posed the following five requirements for a free and responsible press:

- A truthful, comprehensive, and intelligent account of the day's events in a context which gives them meaning.
- A forum for the exchange of comment and criticism.
- The projection of a representative picture of the constituent groups in the society.
- The presentation and clarification of the goals and values of the society.
- Full access to the day's intelligence.

                    (Commission on Freedom of the Press, 1947, pp. 21–27)

As an example of our different approaches, Gordon interprets the third of the five Hutchins Commission requirements in a very different way than I do. I believe that where Gordon and others make their mistake is in forgetting that the groups referred to by the Hutchins Commission are constituent groups in a single society—a common humanity.

Throughout this chapter, I express my fear that the societally necessary concepts of unity and cooperation are being replaced. It seems to me that the word "representation" often means content and employment quotas, diversity tends to mean divisiveness, and plurality is a code word for separatism, particularly for those whose political and other ambitions are tied to these code words. I hope that I'm wrong, but I'm afraid that I'm not. Almost any group can claim that the mere act of criticizing a member (or, more importantly, a leader) of that group is an insult to the entire group. A simplistic tactic of not offending *any* group is probably impossible and certainly self-defeating.

This was not the Hutchins Commission's view. In its discussion of this requirement it was concerned about stereotypes and called for publication of "the truth about any social group, though it should not exclude its weaknesses and vices, [including] also recognition of its values, its aspirations, and its common humanity" (Commission on Freedom of the Press, 1947, pp. 26–27). Throughout its publications are found the words "society" (singular) and "community" (singular), without the modifications used today by Gordon and the politically correct.

COMMUNITY

The primary problem reflected in this chapter is that there is little agreement nowadays on what community (or society or culture) means. I believe that a viable society, is both more than an amalgam of groups and less. To say "less" implies that the real building blocks are individuals, rather than merely thinking of individuals as less important than groups.

The expressed need of individuals for identity as members of a group—generally spelled out in terms of membership, roots, or family—may have established an artificial diversity in the larger American society that actually is divisive in its effect. Robert Heinlein (1982, p. 240) argues persuasively that it is a bad sign when the people of a country stop identifying themselves with the country and start identifying with a racial, religious, linguistic, or other group that is less than the whole population. Ethnic strife in Eastern Europe and religious conflict in the Middle East have little to do with the modern Western concept of "nation" or "state," although they are tied closely to history and to older non-geographic concepts of these terms.

> it is a bad sign when the people of a country stop identifying themselves with the country and start identifying with a . . . group that is less than the whole population.

Virtually all psychological, sociological, and physiological research has concluded that there are greater human differences *within* groups than *between* them, as Gordon has noted, and as a careful reading of *The Bell Curve* (Herrnstein and Murray, 1994) will show. Those authors argue that society is becoming increasingly stratified by I.Q. This controversial—largely because of its discussion of race and statistical differences between races—book and the methodology of I.Q. testing have been defended by some scientists and attacked by others, most cogently by Gould (1994, 1995).

As an article by Ivan Hannaford (1994, p. 8) points out, "[g]enuine public life—not to mention a genuine solution to racial problems—becomes impossible when a society allows race or ethnicity to displace citizenship as one's badge of identity."

Certainly, individuals and groups have the right to name themselves, although it may be difficult for outsiders to follow the evolution or the emotional content of such nomenclature. The terms *Negroes*, *colored people*, *blacks*, *Afro-Americans*, *African Americans*, and *people of color* have nuances that the larger community may find confusing, but all agree, I believe, that any of these terms is better than those intended to be derogatory or insulting, such as *nigger*—even though it sometimes may be used jocularly among blacks—or *coon*. Each individual member of any group, even the smallest, has the same right to life, liberty, and the pursuit of happiness. As members of the larger society, they also have the right to be treated fairly, politely, and responsibly. Unfortunately, in the past—and present—the members of some more-easily identified groups have been discriminated against shamelessly, in many ways.

For hundreds of years, this discrimination was sanctioned by the law as well as by custom. Extra-legal, stereotypical discrimination was as bad. *Los Angeles Times* columnist Art Seidenbaum wrote in the aftermath of the riots in the mid-1960s (quoted in an editorial in the spring 1968 *Journal of Broadcasting*, p. 95): "There is nothing wrong with growing up to be a maid. There is a dreadful wrong when one child assumes another child has been born a maid."

To my way of thinking, there also is something wrong when individuals of mixed race are forced to choose between the cultures of their parents, or when arbitrary definitions (such as "Hispanic," which is causing ever more difficulty to the U.S. Census Bureau) are superimposed over large numbers of individuals and are adopted by the media.

In the past half-century in the United States, almost all legally sanctioned discriminatory practices on the basis of race, religion, and gender have, thank goodness, been outlawed. However, many people still feel disadvantaged or discriminated against and believe that they should have redress for perceived past and present discrimination. This includes both blacks whose ancestors were slaves and whites who were looked down upon because of their ethnic origins and culture—or who think that affirmative action is a hurtful form of "reverse racism," whether or not their own ancestors were in this country when slavery was a legalized institution. During the past century we have learned that genuine acknowledgement of wrongdoing, in forums such as reconciliation commissions, apparently is effective. For example, these new institutions went a long way toward avoidance of the bloodbath originally predicted for racially split South Africa.

But many of the less well justified stereotypes that often shape behavior remain, even though much more subtle than formerly, and often part of the subconscious rather than the conscious mind. Much of the heat in discussion of the O. J. Simpson murder case came from stereotypes that can be traced back hundreds of years and have been included in the modern mass media almost since these media were introduced.

For example, one of the earliest feature films was *The Birth of a Nation* (1915), from a book written by a relative of a high-ranking member of the Ku Klux Klan; *Amos 'n 'Andy*, a tremendously popular radio program in the 1930s and 1940s, featured stereotypical black characters (played by white actors) to the enjoyment of most of the United States. The highly publicized 2006 accusations against members of the Duke University lacrosse team, later proven groundless (and leading to punitive actions against the district attorney who brought the charges), were at least partly due to public stereotypes about sex and race. There is considerable evidence that the mass media have been responsible for much of the belief that certain cities—such as New York—are more crowded and more dangerous than they really are.

But is the best solution or remedy for actual or perceived wrongs to seek monetary or other reparations or apologies? Should one group attempt to bring down other groups, in the expectation of being raised as a result (which cavalierly denies the aphorism that a rising tide raises all boats)? Isn't it wrong to use arbitrary definitions to describe the rapidly growing number of people—such as Barack Obama or Tiger Woods—whose parents have come from more than one ethnic group? Or to dismiss the thoughts and wishes of independent individuals who, because of their gender, color, or heritage, are listed as "belonging" to a group only because others believe they so belong? Or to insist on special treatment or special efforts in society's institutions, including the media? Or to laugh at those who list their race as "human"?

More than at any other time during the human history of the planet, we are part of one community. By and large, globally speaking, those of similar ages tend to watch the same kinds of TV, listen to the same kinds of music (Seabrook, 1994), and worry about the same crimes, economic situations, and foreign threats. Coca-Cola is sold almost everywhere. At the height of his popularity the late Michael Jackson was a worldwide entertainment and news media phenomenon. And big business—no matter how battered by global economic crises—is almost synonymous with major multinational or global corporations.

Often this interaction with other cultures is one-way: the rest of the world virtually demanded that Michael Jackson (and the culture he personified) be available to them, and he flooded into their communities, rather than engaging in a two-way exchange. Such interaction, which ignores national or cultural boundaries, is truly global—but one-way. Global interaction has been brought about by unprecedented improvements in communication and transportation since the mid-19th century. In 1914, within the memory span of a few living, the assassination of a little-known archduke in an obscure Balkan town stimulated most of the world, like lemmings, to enter into a great war. What happened then and since in that one little city of Sarajevo—in 1914, during the 1984 Olympic games, or during the bloody consequences of the breakup of Yugoslavia in the 1990s—affected the entire world. We are all interconnected.

SPECIALIZATION AND ISOLATION

A century ago, the United States was proud of its status as a melting pot for immigrants. A strong nation was constructed from many peoples. They came from many different (mostly European) cultures, nationalities, and religions and found America bewildering. Often, they were exploited and discriminated against. Slaves and their "free" descendants were discriminated against the most, unless one counts the virtually complete exclusion of Asians before the past few decades, or Native Americans exiled out-of-sight on reservations.

To help ease the transition of immigrants, many newspapers aimed at particular ethnic groups were established. Even in the early part of the 21st century, New Yorkers could purchase such newspapers as *The Forward* (formerly *The Jewish Daily Forward*, and at one time published in English, Yiddish, and Russian), *El Diario-La Prensa* (in Spanish), the *Ming Pao Daily News* (in Chinese), the *Amsterdam News* (edited for New York blacks), and an ever-changing number of daily, weekly, and published-at-other-intervals newspapers in Chinese, Spanish, Polish, Korean, Greek, Russian, Italian, and as many as 35 other languages. In the 1990s, there were at least seven in Chinese, and there may have been as many as 20 newspapers and newsletters published in the Russian enclave in Brighton Beach, Brooklyn (Remnick, 1994).

But the audiences of these narrowly focused newspapers (and radio stations and, later, cable television channels) started to drop as early as the late 1940s—and many went out of business, cut back frequency of publication (*The Forward* is now a weekly, in English and Yiddish, with roughly only 9% of its enormous early-1930s circulation of 275,000) or otherwise lost audience and influence. Why did this happen? It isn't because there are that many fewer Jews in New York—that number is still very large. But this particular foreign-language media population now is largely assimilated, at least linguistically, or suburbanized into the larger population, or speaks only languages other than Yiddish or English. There is certainly a smaller proportion of *non-English-speaking* first-generation Jewish immigrants in New York. Also, as the children of all foreign language immigrants—including Hispanics—experience public education and develop the need to conduct commercial transactions outside their mono-linguistic apartment house or neighborhood, I predict that in the future there will be even fewer linguistically oriented newspapers with even smaller circulations.

While this all has a negative effect on the financial and cultural importance of these channels, stations, newspapers, and magazines, it remains clear that the inhabitants of the Jackson Heights section of New York City see no great need for mass media catering to all of the 167 tongues spoken on its streets. Jackson Heights will solve its own problems of communication, as it has since I was a child there. So will other metropolitan areas and countries around the globe—even if they have to modify their language habits (e.g., create new languages like Spanglish, develop "pidgin" trade languages, or become fully assimilated in the predominant culture) (Santos, 2010). Remember, the very definition of "mass medium" refers to a relatively undifferentiated—"to whom it may concern"—audience united primarily by the act of paying attention to the same mediated content.

But when, as has happened frequently around the globe, there is little or no assimilation of the young into a larger culture, it can lead to conflict—sometimes violent conflict. In Ireland (because of religious differences), Belgium (with three national anthems in different languages), Canada (English-speaking and French-speaking), and in other large nations and small, a tremendous amount of energy must be devoted to finding ways for groups that are adamant in wishing to retain their identity to nevertheless live with others who occupy the same or adjoining real estate. The alternative? Conflict that could lead to genocide or other forms of "ethnic cleansing," unless there is some investment of social or political capital.

Retaining a myriad of specialized and separatist media outlets may be desired by some of the groups that today complain about the existing mass media; they want their own station or newspaper aimed specifically at and prepared by their own group. This specialization often is welcomed by advertisers, and provides a localized sense of community, although it rejects—or at least delays—the evolution of the melting pot. Such specialization is a fairly well-established idea; for example, cable's Black Entertainment Network, several Spanish-language networks, and service in other languages in appropriate markets. Additionally, there are numerous magazines (including some segregated by gender), a few "minority" daily papers in large cities, and a variety of social media (often on the Internet) that provide the contact that enables a large polyglot nation to survive.

But there are potential drawbacks to such specialization. First, if all of a region's or nation's media are specialized, intended to appeal to or serve a very specific group, it is very likely that the "melting pot" and the "salad bowl" models both will fail. Even a salad needs to be tossed, and for one ingredient to associate with other ingredients. Second, there are logistical difficulties that go along with the linguistic ones: During World War II, it was thought necessary to supervise all foreign language radio programming to prevent it from being used for espionage. Third, some media outlets might believe that their role is to fight for the preservation of their constituency (and obtain a "proper share" of municipal services) rather than contemplate assimilation.

Let's look at these factors more closely. First, it seems that much of the agitation for specialized media outlets comes from entrepreneurs who are anxious to focus on narrow demographic classifications or an opportunity for promoters, politicians, and others to be the big fish in a small pond. Their audiences, many of whom live in large and complex urban or political communities, and who might benefit from gaining their information from more broadly based media, often are thought of solely as potential customers. This is, of course, true of almost any audience in a commercial environment where the term "public interest" has devolved into "what we can get the public interested in."

Second, establishing a newspaper, magazine, or broadcasting station is very risky. Even if we accept the doubtful assumption that start-up capital is available, there still remains the need to develop a revenue stream that can be counted on. In general, mass communication industries are capital- rather than labor-intensive, although the head of the American Association of Advertising Agencies once said that his was the only industry where all the assets go down the elevator at the end of the day

The third drawback is less obvious. Is it a good thing to be talking *only* with one's group? No, not if we wish to participate fully in the economic and political life of the country. As Hannaford (1994) points out:

> The Greeks taught us the importance of living as a community of citizens bound together by law. If we are to rise above our current condition—a national society of ethnic groups cleaving only to kith and kin—Americans, as well as Bosnians and innumerable others, will need to act politically, rethinking the nature of citizenship and of the civic compact.
>
> (p. 12)

No matter how comforting, it isn't very efficient within a society as large and diverse as ours if we restrict ourselves to our own little (or big) groups. We each are in (or claimed by) so many minorities that logically this emphasis on belonging, carried to extremes, eventually might lead to "one-person groups" or—to use the old-fashioned word I prefer—individuals, with groups becoming relatively unimportant, as I think they should be.

The impermanence of present-day groups might seem more likely if we consider how important family dynasties were before the modern nation evolved. With today's space-and-time-defeating communication and transportation technologies, we may be entering another, more broadly and inclusively communitarian phase.

STEREOTYPES

Of course, the media themselves also are stereotyped. Often-heard phrases such as "the liberal media" ignore the conservative leanings of most publishers, licensees, and radio talk show hosts. People can always find something negative in news they don't like, and something positive in news that they do. In a March, 2009 column published in *The Seattle Times* a few days after the rival *Seattle Post-Intelligencer* ceased publication, the paper's executive editor, in an effort to acquire former *Post-Intelligencer* subscribers, attempted to rebut some frequently heard assumptions. The first two of these were "The Times is a right-wing paper" and "The Times is a left-wing paper" (Boardman 2009). As with someone cycling down the centerline of a highway, being in the middle of the road can lead to unhappy collisions in both directions.

Even the most stereotypical male WASP (White Anglo-Saxon Protestant) is in the minority with respect to gender, religion, and ethnic background, in terms of potential economic or political power. White males, as a demographically defined group if not as individuals, are in this position because the combination of all females and male people of color far outnumber white males and because females are the beneficiaries of most of the nation's wealth (partly because they live, on average, several years longer than men).

On the other hand, 2008 U.S. Bureau of the Census data quoted by Gordon projects that today's "minority" groups—African Americans, Hispanics, Asian Americans and others—will not collectively outnumber all non-Hispanic whites in the U.S. population until the middle of the 21st century. It is difficult to see how, on the one hand, Gordon seems to think that the growing number of minority group members deserve special treatment, and on the other hand, that the current majority of whites would not deserve special attention or treatment when they become a minority. Looked at another way, after mid-century, when (unless the projections are wrong, as they may be—see p. 156) Hispanics become the dominant group in terms of numbers, should their majority status then be used to eliminate special programs serving their needs in order to focus governmental funding on the (then) minority whites? I believe that, then and now, even in such a situation, it would be far fairer to consider individuals and individual circumstances rather than groups of *any* arbitrary kind when organizing priorities.

"POLITICAL CORRECTNESS": INDIVIDUALITY, SENSITIVITY, AND PROTECTIVITY

But do the mainstream media, now serving a less-differentiated audience, still have an obligation (since they must serve everybody) to make special efforts with respect to various "protected groups" or others who want additional coverage? Is "sensitivity," in the way Gordon uses it, the *primary* consideration the media should use for hiring, casting, writing, and illustrating? Should we believe that, in light of new and "sensitive" standards, the opening words of the original *Star Trek* series ("to boldly go where no man has gone before") were *intentionally* disrespectful to all women and received that way, and had no legitimacy, despite the hundreds of years of generic use in English of the noun "man" or "mankind" to refer to all members of the human race? We acknowledge that in today's more aware climate, it is good that the opening words of *Star Trek: The Next Generation* are now "where no *one* has gone before." But should we go back and change history, change the words of the first person to land on the moon ("one giant step for mankind") in the interests of giving females a greater feeling of participation? Isn't this analogous to "expunging" juvenile criminal records without the same goal of providing a "second chance"?

Where does this lead us? Since I believe the media have an obligation to be fair and civil only to all *individuals*, I also believe that membership in a group is morphing into a meaningless distinction. If stereotypes of religion, race, or gender overshadow one's personal attributes and accomplishments, then we may devolve into a governmental system of quotas rather than a government of the people. Each of us has—or should have—knowledge of and interest in the broader news of politics, social trends, and economics that help us make the decisions that rule our lives, what Schramm (1949, p. 260) calls a "delayed reward" in contrast to titillation's "immediate reward."

To repeat, I believe that the media's obligations are to individuals and cannot be sloughed off merely because the individual in question is or is not a member of a group. Tony Hillerman, the southwestern mystery writer, could have identified one of his leading characters as a "Native American," "native person," "indigenous person," "Indian," "Navajo," or "Lt. Joseph Leaphorn," but he still is referring to a single (fictional) human being who shares space on the planet and in the U.S. nation with individuals of many other races, cultures, ethnic groups, and religions. Even in our "winner takes all" political system, the key is the votes of the number of individuals, not the number of groups. People with disabilities are to be found in almost any demographic group, as are members of both genders and elderly people. Differences between individuals are, as mentioned in the first paragraph of my argument here, to be expected—but similarities also should be expected, and applauded.

> People with disabilities are to be found in almost any demographic group, as are members of both genders and elderly people.

Unfortunately, there has been a growing dependence on what is pejoratively called "politically correct" language as a cure-all for everything that ails us. Hannaford (1994) says that:

> a new, more "correct" derivative of the orthodoxy is imposing itself upon the literature and language of Western politics, an orthodoxy that vainly seeks to end racial discrimination by identifying pernicious language wherever it appears, in the home, the factory, the school, even the university, and eradicating it entirely from the conversation of humankind.
>
> (p. 33)

Some of the newer language changes make a great deal of sense—*firefighter* is more descriptive than *fireman* and reflects current hiring patterns—but some are merely an awkward genuflecting to the principle, such as "waitpersons" or "wait staff" rather than the equally gender-free "server." However, it is unlikely that any label that implies a subservient relationship will long survive, even though the relationship may. (Think, for example, of the growing use of *associate* to replace *clerk* or *salesperson*.)

The use of "politically correct" language and behavior may be intended to achieve, through constant repetition, a society free of language that may offend, intentionally or unintentionally. A former editor of the *Los Angeles Times* claims that the use of such language promotes "greater clarity" (Coffey, 1994). Stuart Hall (1994) says that to focus on language alone reflects a mistaken belief that calling things by a different name will make them disappear or, in the dialogue Edward Borgers put into the mouth of St. Paul (formerly known as Roman tax collector Saul of Tarsus): "If you don't like something, change the name." Often, the results are absurd, as when the children's book *Thomas the Tank Engine* came under attack for "sexism, sizeism and distorted values" (Lester, 1994).

When Gordon decries use of the "historically loaded" phrase "circling the wagons," he ignores the fact that this defensive tactic has been used for hundreds of years—whenever relatively slow conveyances have been threatened by a more mobile adversary that could attack from any direction. This says nothing, either for or against, native peoples or wagoneers and would-be settlers in the American West. Is Gordon trying to change history by sweeping the story of the use of legitimate military tactics under the rug because some group (and I'm not sure which) might be upset by bringing it up as a metaphor based on American history?

The politically correct approach places the burden of communication solely on the shoulders of the communicator, ignoring the fact that the act of communication requires a receiver as well. Our spam filters do this with every e-mail in our inbox—sometimes to our dismay. Even worse is the use of computer programs not merely to flag, but to modify offending words, such as the (almost certainly apocryphal) reference to "African American holes in space" in an astronomy article. These practices appear to be extensions of the earlier "let's avoid harming the sensibilities of the faint-hearted" use of euphemisms such as *departed* rather than *dead*, *sanitary engineer* instead of *garbage collector*, or similar examples of what Fowler (1965) calls "genteelisms." A buffalo chip by any other name would smell as sweet.

THE PROFESSIONAL APPROACH

I look for the media to be professional, which must include the Kantian need to be ethical and altruistic, and to think of the welfare of others (which itself is utilitarian) and not merely of the financial bottom line. If the media are truly professional, many of the attacks on the media fall from their own weight of selfishness. Any reliance on employment statistics to justify what are, in effect, hiring quotas falls into this trap.

In his part of this chapter, Gordon quotes Heider (2000, p. 81) as noting that (white) reporters too often lack knowledge of the history and context of topics affecting people of color and many such stories—even when they draw on minority sources—"still reinforce existing beliefs about people of color individually and collectively." True enough, but the same reporters, white or black, too often lack knowledge of the history and context of topics affecting the majority as well as minority groups. This entire situation is not a matter of conspiring to ensure "inclusiveness and correctness," but is much more likely to be a matter of unprofessionally inadequate reporting skill and thought during that process.

Essentially my position is a Kantian approach to the problem or challenge of defining community. If everyone acts according to the categorical imperative that what is ethical for a person to do is what that person would want everyone to do, then there is no need for special efforts such as quotas. Equal opportunity would replace affirmative action. Such an approach also could stem from a universal application of the "charter of compassion" (analogous to the Charter of Human Rights) that the United Nations is being urged to adopt by a movement spearheaded by Karen Armstrong—or from the reliance of its supporters on the Golden Rule of "do not do unto others what you would not have done to you." Those—Christians, Muslims, Jews—who are working on this charter have combined the

Golden Rule, Martin Buber's "I . . . thou" concept, and Confucianism. Whether or not it receives UN support, it might become a philosophical school of thought; however, just as new groups and new diseases are identified, so there are certain to be new ways of thinking.

STATISTICS

Statisticians—as a group—have almost as negative a reputation as accountants or lawyers (or those working in the media). Figures don't lie, but many liars can figure. The problem with statistics is that their interpretation lies at the border between mathematical symbols and words. It is awfully easy to bandy about terms such as "significance" and "representation" without worrying about the technical meaning of those terms. For example, if one is dealing with a too-small or too-unrepresentative sample, one cannot legitimately generalize from it.

Just because something has increased "fourfold" doesn't mean that it is statistically significant. The very word "percent" means "of one hundred," and thus shouldn't be used with very small samples (warn your reader by using proportions or ratios instead). Other rules—such as that it is the size (and representativeness) of a sample that is important, not what proportion of the population it represents—can be misleading to those who haven't learned the jargon or technical or mathematical vocabulary involved.

So, when Gordon decries the number of members of minority groups in a newsroom, and employs statistics, he owes it to his readers to spell out his criteria for significance, both statistically and in clear language. Is he saying that newsrooms should have equal numbers of members of each major demographic group, or should they be in proportion to the numbers found in the decennial U.S. census? Should the figures for the market in which the station or paper is produced be used as guides rather than national figures? Should they be in relation only to the numbers of those who meet whatever standards of employment are applied? Is he using "estimates" or "data"? Anyone can estimate, but objectively verifiable data are harder to come by. For example, in 1947 the U.S. Bureau of the Census estimated that there would be nearly 164 million Americans by 1980, but when an actual count was made April 1980, the actual figure was nearly 229 million (there are now more than 310 million). When to this sort of numerical uncertainty is added the voluntary nature of the census when determining race, and the difficulty of defining biracial Americans or, most particularly (since it is a linguistic and cultural grouping, rather than a racial one) Hispanics, Gordon should be very, very careful about drawing conclusions, making assertions, and exhorting action.

QUOTAS

Would it be good if each media outlet or source of news were required to provide material of specific interest to several specific groups? I'd say "No," but that is my unsupported opinion speaking, as I've only heard of one (college) newspaper that tried this. This isolated example, however, might show how such a system could be operated. The University of Massachusetts *Daily Collegian* established a Black Affairs page in 1977 and a Women's

Desk the following year. For the next dozen years, both were guaranteed a certain number of pages each month and an editor's slot—at times with no review of the content by the paper's copy desk. Predictably, other groups (e.g., Jewish students, the gay/lesbian/bisexual group, pro-Palestinian students) demanded similar treatment, and the paper complied at times with some of those demands. The whole situation could be framed as a clash of utilitarianism versus John Rawls, pitting freedom of the press (as the producer of the greatest good) against the concern that the "loss of freedom for some groups is not justified by the overall greatest good" (List, 1991, p. 223).

To carry this concept to an extreme, there probably would need to be special care taken to ensure that women had roughly the same amount of news of interest to them as do men; Hispanics, Asians, blacks, all should have their percentages; young people and elderly people their quotas just as conservatives and liberals have their soapboxes, and so on through the list of those groups that have managed to aggregate enough political clout to be listed as an identifiable "minority" or "interest group." But how would one choose among them if there aren't enough media minutes or column inches in the day? How can one know what would be of interest to a particular group? Editors are individuals, not pollsters, and owe their primary duty to serve the community as a whole or, at least, all of their readers, listeners, and viewers rather than stereotypes or meaningless averages. To say that sports are the domain of men and soap operas the territory of women is to ignore the millions of fans of the "wrong" gender. Not even an honest and objective general report on such a presumably neutral and universal topic as the U.S. budget or a weather-related disaster could be expected to be equally acceptable, even to every one of the major identified groups.

Under such a system, would content-quota obligations also accrue to the few media outlets owned or controlled by the specialized groups themselves? Would a black-owned newspaper have to ensure space for whites? Must *The Sheepherder's Gazette* be sure to provide coverage directed toward cattle ranchers, or would it be permitted to focus on those who have found a career among sheep? Must every mention of breast cancer be balanced by a mention of prostate cancer? How do we determine what is of interest (preferably what is of importance) to each group?

And what about the equally common misrepresentations of and ignoring the interests of some very large, even majority, groups? Although many Americans are religious, this aspect of their lives rarely is given much attention in the mass media. The growing proportion of elderly people, or those with vision or hearing problems, is given similarly short shrift. On the other hand, when possible, the media try to demonstrate their open-mindedness through tokenism and quotas. There seems to be a far greater proportion of black and female judges in TV drama than in U.S. courtrooms, and even as far back as World War II, an army squad in a feature film had to have its quota of one soldier from Brooklyn, one from the Ozarks or Appalachia, and so on.

How could we provide true representation without giving every person his or her own station and newspaper? Since, economically, logistically, and technologically, this would be impossible, we might paraphrase this as "if everyone is talking, who will be there to listen?"

And, although we might try to answer the problem posed by the previous question through selection of staff, we might actually compound it by requiring that the reporters, anchors, editors, publishers, and station owners be present in the media workforce in proportion to the number of each of these groups in the total population, regardless of individual training, talent, or wealth—or even amount of news generated by each population segment. Even now, some call for an instant fulfillment of quotas. It is argued that all the problems of content discussed in this chapter will be solved by a rigorous enforcement of affirmative action rules when selecting staff. This argument seems weak to me, since in practice it almost certainly will focus on groups rather than individuals, but I recognize that discussion of affirmative action can set off the human resources equivalent of an atomic war. Yes, I believe that to overcome past discrimination requires special efforts to make sure that discrimination no longer is an influence, but affirmative action should not be an end in itself, without a statement of the criteria that will let us decide to put it away, sometime in the future, as no longer being needed. In other words, I believe that equality is a desirable goal— not bureaucracy. As with any bureaucracy or set of regulations, arranging for it to go out of business is easier said than done; the aphorism "God (or the devil) is in the details" probably applies.

I keep asking, is there a black view of earthquakes? An Hispanic view of the Iraq War? A male view of the town council meeting (even though some agenda items might not affect both sexes in the same way)? I suggest that the answer is "No," but not always. For example, is a close-up "black view" of earthquake destruction and public reaction less valid than the view of those officials occupying city hall? Again, there is no single correct way to serve the public with the material it needs.

After all, we are individuals and should have the right to select our own representatives, and not be forced to accept those who put themselves forward in that role on the basis of their color, religion, gender, or other attributes. For example, the fact that there are "feminists" who believe variously in beauty contests, no makeup, lesbianism, heterosexuality, running a household, independence, abortion access, abortion bans, equal opportunity, reparations, and dozens of other beliefs explains both the internecine conflicts between one type of "feminist" and another and the difficulty in selecting a single representative spokesperson for feminism or women in general.

Let us not think that the content-quota approach is merely a straw figure, a *reductio ad absurdum* approach to the problem. It has been adopted by a number of advocates. Every year, letters to the editor—as well as content analyses in scholarly journals—draw conclusions about the worth of advertising, entertainment, and news, based solely on counts of the number of people of various groups who are shown on the screen, quoted in the newspaper, or featured in the advertising, and not on the quality of their ideas. In this chapter, Gordon implicitly adopts this approach.

The opposite of specialization is a general service that appeals to *all* groups. This is, of course, subject to some practical limitations. Not all media owners have the financial strength to reach the entire public, nor would they want to; although FM station transmitter subcarriers can provide teletype service to deaf people, by definition they can't provide *the exact same* content that they give their hearing audience. If newspapers are dumbed down and designed for the nearly illiterate, won't the literate stop reading them?

CONCLUSION

In the heyday of the national radio and television networks, universality was their strategy. As fewer and fewer competing newspapers are published, their strategy of appealing to the widest possible audience of readers is similar, although their immediate goal is to avoid losing readers (and consequently, being forced to lower advertising rates). But how is this done without appealing only to baser interests and instincts, by covering sex crimes rather than science, sports rather than foreign affairs, or gossip rather than news? I'm afraid that, in order to appeal to the largest number for economic reasons, the media are finding it increasingly difficult to provide anything other than the "titillate, don't educate," "whatever bleeds, leads" programming and editing mentality that shows little respect for the audience. As a consequence, efforts by some media outlets to be attractive to everybody mean that they may well be attractive to nobody.

> In the heyday of the national radio and television networks, universality was their strategy.

Let's go back to my original thesis: In the mass media the only real obligation we each have (with respect to the matters discussed in this chapter) is to be civil and fair to our fellow humans. As individuals. Regardless of whether we think certain people are overly touchy, or that certain words or phrases (*handicapped=differently abled=challenged=blind or deaf*) are either silly or empowering, our recourse should be through education, not insult. This wasn't true in the past: blacks were mostly ignored in most mainstream papers (unless they were being accused of a crime against a white person), their honorifics (Mr., Mrs., Dr.) were omitted, reporters weren't assigned to stories in neighborhoods frequented by members of minority groups, and no blacks were accepted by the white media as spokespersons for the community. Women, as recently as one or two generations ago, weren't hired for some jobs and rarely took (or were allowed to take) the training that would better qualify them.

There is good evidence, however, that social equality, even if not carried to the extreme of homogenization, requires economic equality. The disgraceful lack of trained journalists familiar with all areas of the geographic and economic community in which they work shows itself every time an important story occurs in a "minority neighborhood"—whether a *de facto* ghetto or merely an inconvenient rural area. Obviously, any job discrimination on the basis of anything other than quality, ability, and potential should be rooted out, including that directed against people with disabilities, elderly people, or the "different."

The fact that the majority of students in mass communication programs now are female, but that the proportion of students who are members of minority groups has shrunk, cannot be explained on the basis of deliberate discrimination. Regardless of the fate of the affirmative action rules, it is in everyone's self-interest that communication schools recruit aggressively and educate all qualified applicants who wish to enter the field, just as the media need to hire those who meet their legitimate qualifications without regard to their gender, sexual orientation, age, religion, race, or ethnicity. We must remember, however, that short of firing all those who are now perceived by some to have too large a slice of the pie, it will take time for new generations to enter the executive suites. The glass ceiling really is composed of human beings who achieved their own level. Neither affirmative action nor fairness can be allowed to mandate specific results or general outcomes, even though most of us would philosophically desire them. Fairness should be inclusive, not exclusive.

So, to construct a simple example, even though it may contain some unsupported assertions, if (and this is a great big "IF") the basic obligation is to follow the Golden Rule and be fair and civil or polite, some implementing rules would be simple. For example, if honorific titles are used for one, they should be used for all. Of course, there is another Kantian rule that could be employed: *not* using honorifics for anyone, which would remove them from whites, and thus treat everyone with the same (lack of) dignity. Would this be the way to achieve some of that inclusiveness that is being called for in this chapter? If we develop ways to hire and promote that are as truly color- and gender-blind as the methods practiced by major symphony orchestras (auditions and competitions with the unidentified contestants hidden behind a screen), we may defuse some of the "My turn!" attitudes in the applicant pool. If the nitpicking of "political correctness" in language and content is abandoned in favor of the use of civil language rather than dogma, as gender-free as understanding and common sense permit, reality may prevail over rhetoric in helping each person to be equal under the law and able to achieve the highest goal of which he or she is individually capable.

Defining *common sense* may not be easy, but it is usually the opposite of the doctrinaire; it is thinking things through rather than reacting, considering an idea on its own merits and not on the merits or demerits of its supporters. If all Americans, as Martin Luther King, Jr. said, are to be judged by the content of their character rather than by the color of their skin, there may be less political satisfaction but a better metaculture and civic polity in the United States—one that doesn't confuse gender, race, age, religion, and ethnicity with economics and politics.

KEY POINTS

- We are all individuals, not cogs in the same wheel, and our individuality is too precious to submerge into a politically correct or stereotypical grouping.
- If religious, racial or gender stereotypes overshadow personal attributes and accomplishments, we may devolve into a governmental system of quotas rather than a democracy.
- My position is a Kantian approach to the challenge of defining community: If everyone acts according to the categorical imperative that ethical actions are what a person would want everyone to do, there would be no need for special efforts.

MERRILL: COMMENTARY

David Gordon in this controversy takes the high road and John Michael Kittross takes the low road—the high being the idealistic one and the low being the realistic one. I am naturally inclined to agree with Gordon in that greater efforts need to be taken by mass media to become more inclusive of society's diversity and that it is unfair for certain groups to get special play. Most people, I think, would not disagree with the media making "special efforts." Well, in a way Kittross does disagree. He contends that the media naturally try to include many groups in their contents. In a capitalistic media system it would be financially unwise not to.

It is harmful to the many who know "little or nothing about their fellow citizens with different backgrounds" to have media that do not give a fair representation to the various constituent social groups. That is Gordon's contention. But I would ask: How does it "harm" me if I know little or nothing about the various Indian tribes in the United States or about the Vietnamese communities along the American Gulf Coast? I might like to know more about some subgroups, but that is different from being "harmed" by not knowing, although Gordon might need to know about the Hmong in Wisconsin (where he lives), and Kittross might have the same need regarding the Chinese and Koreans who are a major part of his Seattle neighborhood.

And it might well be that some minority groups *should* be given little attention—or even portrayed negatively. Truth is perhaps better than balance. Gordon refers to the year that "saw a black man [Obama] elected president." Is President Obama—with a black father and a white mother—any more a "black man" than he is a "white man"? What about dedication to truth, or is this some kind of political correctness that gets in the way of truth, as Kittross contends in his arguments? I think we need more care in using words; for example, "African Americans" as meaning black Americans. That ignores my good friend from South Africa who is an American now—but who is white. And what about referring to the earliest inhabitants of North America as "Indians" or "Native Americans" (Kittross calls them "native peoples," not quite wishing to go all the way to "first nations," the current term in English-speaking Canada)? Gordon, Kittross, and I, as are millions of Americans, are "native Americans." And obviously, all people everywhere are "native people" of somewhere.

Special efforts, says Gordon, need to be made to deal "correctly" with race and other socially important topics. Just what is the "correct" way is not made clear. Balance? I doubt it. Quotas? I doubt it. Perhaps what would help, as Gordon implies, would be a heightened sensitivity and ethical demeanor on the part of media people. One thing that is wrong, according to Gordon, is that there are not enough minorities in the newsrooms. The problem: the definition of "enough." Is the implication here that a minority journalist can write a more objective story? There is no evidence that this is the case.

What "minorities" is Gordon talking about? With respect to religion, should a newsroom have some Muslims, some Catholics, some Protestants, some Jews, some Hindus, and perhaps some Buddhists (and maybe some agnostics or atheists)? And what would be the "proper" proportions?

Gordon endorses the Hutchins Commission's 1947 mandate for the American press to present a "representative picture" of society's various constituent groups. If this is done, Gordon believes, the culture/race/gender problem will take care of itself. Of course, the fact is that the press does not give, nor has it ever given, a representative picture of society's constituent groups. In fact, time and space constraints prevent journalists from even listing the constituent groups, much less providing a reliable picture of them.

Kittross expresses his belief that mainstream media do not have a special obligation to any particular groups; they have only the obligation, he says, to be civil to all *individuals*, recognizing that membership in a group is often a meaningless distinction. For Kittross the media's responsibility is to individuals, not to groups. He goes on to offer some fine examples of how "political correctness" has infiltrated the media and has introduced a plethora of euphemisms, even going beyond earlier terminology such as sanitary engineer instead of garbage collector. But, as Kittross says, a "buffalo chip by any other name would smell as sweet." I prefer Shakespeare's statement about a rose smelling sweet, but Kittross makes the point.

I am prone to agree with Kittross and not Gordon in this political correctness business. Political correctness shows a dismal ignorance of general semantics, rhetoric, and semiotics. Euphemisms often hide, not reveal, essential truths. It is getting very complicated for the media person who wants to understand just who everyone is, what to call social ethnic groups and races, and what should be changed to make everybody happy. Is that the purpose of the media—to make people happy? What we are getting is an increasing concern for "communities" or special segments (or constituencies) in society, all clamoring to be treated equally or "fairly" (or specially) by the mass media.

Such communities as Hispanics, suburbanites, inner-city dwellers, environmentalists, blacks, gays and lesbians, Polish Americans, German Americans, religious fundamentalists, liberal Protestants, American Muslims, Catholics, American and Southern Baptists, lawyers, doctors, skinheads, drug dealers, and on and on: All are constituencies or "communities" that have their particular messages and want to be treated "fairly." Gordon would make special efforts to deal with them; Kittross would not. My position is that there is no need to worry about it; they really cannot be dealt with.

Kittross would not have the media do anything other than what all conscientious media people already do: make content decisions as intelligently as possible, a practice that he contends is the perpetual ideal for the media. Gordon makes some suggestions that would focus more media attention on special multicultural concerns and calls for sociocultural consciousness-raising in media decision-making. It is obvious that he feels the media can do much better than they are doing. And, of course, they can.

We can see certain changes in the direction Gordon is suggesting. Media are demasculinizing certain terms, such as routinely changing "chairman" to "chair" or "chairperson." And they are making sure to use "he and she" and "him and her," or are simply using the plural "they" or "their." I suppose that if the print media take this to extremes, they will be avoiding "man-words" such as "management," "penmanship," and "manipulate." At any rate, it is obvious that media consciousness has been raised, but perhaps, as Gordon says, it can be raised much more. I can only wish that the current problems with media viability were due to a lack of political correctness instead of a variety of substantive news content problems that has emasculated that content and turned the media (especially TV) into a cesspool of triviality and vulgarity.

Kittross makes an interesting point when he says that Kant's categorical imperative (universalizing one's beliefs and actions) will take care of using sensitive ethical language. My newspaper can use the words "nigger" and "faggot" if it is willing that everyone use it? No, no. I can't believe that Kittross meant that. Both Kant and Kittross place rationality at the heart of such a universalizing ethic. Kittross says that he wants the media to be "professional" (ethical and altruistic). Although the word "professional" is semantically troublesome, the concepts of ethics and altruism are somewhat more meaningful and give more substance to Kittross's belief.

Both Gordon and Kittross want the media to be better. And one feels that they are conscientious communicators for a better world. Gordon is more optimistic and hopeful. Kittross is more sanguine and realistic. Kittross's thesis is that the mass media's only obligation is to be "civil and fair." That's a big mouthful, and if taken seriously, encapsulates Gordon's hopes and suggestions. I suppose that being civil and fair is about all that anyone can expect of the media. Can we realistically believe that all classes of society will ever get equal (or appropriate) media treatment? The rational answer is *definitely no*.

My position is that the media can never please everyone. Some person or group will always feel ignored, slighted, misrepresented, stereotyped, or "put down" by some segment of the communication media. Such is the nature of mass communication. It cannot be objective, nor can it ever be truly fair. Its very nature determines that it will ignore some things, minimize or exaggerate others, and misrepresent still others. It's a complex, multifaceted, rather chaotic world out there with its legions of cultures, and the media can only distort it. The various constituencies may not like how they are treated in the media, but they had best get used to it. The media form a giant and multi-sided prism that refracts the light of truth, turning people, constituencies, and realities into murky shadows on the wall of Plato's cave. We may someday emerge from this cave, but it will not be due to the mass media.

REFERENCES AND RELATED READINGS

American Press Institute. (2002). *Survival Guide for Women Editors*. Reston, VA: API.

Barney, Ralph D. (1986). "The journalist and a pluralistic society: An ethical approach." In Deni Elliott, ed., *Responsible Journalism*. Beverly Hills, CA: Sage, pp. 60–80.

BBC News World Edition. (2002a). "Minorities 'let down by TV.' " November 12. Retrieved from http://news. bbc.co.uk/2/hi/entertainment/2448387.stm (September 21, 2004).

——. (2002b). "US TV news 'fails Hispanics.' " December 16. Retrieved from http://news.bbc.co.uk/2/hi/ entertainment/2579371.stm (September 21, 2004).

Benedict, Helen. (1992). *Virgin or Vamp: How the Press Covers Sex Crimes*. New York: Oxford University Press.

Bloom, Harold. (1994). *The Western Canon—the Books and School of the Ages*. New York: Harcourt Brace.

Boardman, David. (2009). "Get to know who we are and who we aren't." *The Seattle Times*, March 22, p. A17.

Borgers, Edward W. (1961). "The credentials argument." (Unpublished dramatic reading of a dialogue between Saint Paul and Saint James.)

Christians, Clifford G. (1986). "Reporting and the oppressed." In Deni Elliott, ed., *Responsible Journalism*. Beverly Hills, CA: Sage, pp. 109–130.

Coffey, Shelby. (1994). "Why newspapers watch their language." Letter to *The New York Times*, April 8.

Commission on Freedom of the Press. (1947). *A Free and Responsible Press*. Chicago, IL: University of Chicago Press.

Creedon, Pamela. (1993). "Framing feminism—A feminist primer for the mass media." *Media Studies Journal* 7(2), pp. 69–80.

Dates, Jannette L., and William Barlow. (1990). *Split Image: African Americans in the Mass Media*. Washington, DC: Howard University Press.

Dates, Jannette L., and Edward C. Pease. (1994). "Warping the world: Media's mangled images of race." *Media Studies Journal* 8(3), pp. 89–95.

Entman, Robert M., and Andrew Rojecki. (2000). *The Black Image in the White Mind: Media and Race in America*. Chicago, IL: University of Chicago Press.

Fitzgerald, Mark. (1994). "Downside of political correctness." *Editor & Publisher*, June 11, p. 9.

Fowler, H. W. (1965). *A Dictionary of Modern English Usage*, 2nd ed. New York: Oxford University Press.

Freedom Forum, The. (2000). "$5 million effort seeks to achieve more diversity in newspaper newsrooms." *American Journalism Review*, May, p. 20.

Gerbner, George. (1993). "Women and minorities on television: A study in casting and fate." (Unpublished report). Philadelphia, PA: Annenberg School for Communication.

Gilligan, Carol. (1982). *In a Different Voice*. Cambridge, MA: Harvard University Press.

Gould, Stephen Jay. (1994). "Review of The Bell Curve." *The New Yorker*, November 28, pp. 139–149.

Gould, Stephen Jay. (1995). "Review of The Bell Curve," *Natural History*, February, pp. 12–19.

Graham, Renee. (1997). " 'Ellen' leaves the closet, and leaves us laughing." *The Boston Globe*, April 30, pp. C1 and C8.

Gross, Larry. (2001). *Up from Invisibility: Lesbians, Gay Men, and the Media in America*. New York: Columbia University Press.

Hall, Stuart. (1994). "Some 'politically incorrect' pathways through PC." In Sarah Dunant, ed., *The War of the Words: The Political Correctness Debate*. London: Virago.

Hannaford, Ivan. (1994). "The idiocy of race." *The Wilson Quarterly* 18(2), pp. 8–35.

Heider, Don. (2000). *White News: Why Local News Programs Don't Cover People of Color*. Mahwah, NJ: Lawrence Erlbaum Associates.

Heinlein, Robert A. (1982). *Friday*. New York: Ballantine.

Herrnstein, Richard J., and Charles Murray. (1994). *The Bell Curve*. New York: Free Press.

James, Alison. (2005). "A diversity mandate." *Variety.com*, November 22. Retrieved from www.variety.com/index.asp?1=story&a=VR1117933400&c=14 (November 24, 2005).

Jensen, Robert. (1994). "Banning 'Redskins' from the sports page: The ethics and politics of Native American nicknames." *Journal of Mass Media Ethics* 9(1), pp. 16–25.

Keveney, Bill. (2007). "Stars of South Asian descent are on the ascent." *USA Today*, April 9. Retrieved from www.usatoday.com/printededition/life/20070409/d_bottomstrip09.art.htm (May 7, 2007).

Kim, Jinhee. (2003). "Model minority: Portrayals of Asians and Asian Americans on U.S. prime-time television." Paper presented to the Minorities and Communication Division at the convention of the Association for Education in Journalism and Mass Communication, Kansas City, MO, July 30–August 2.

Lauzen, Martha. (2009). "The celluloid ceiling: Behind-the-scenes employment of women on the top 250 films of 2008." Retrieved from www.wif.org/images/stories/news/lauzen_2008_celluloid_ceiling.pdf (March 11, 2009).

Lauzen, Martha M., and David M. Dozier. (2005). "Recognition and respect revisited: Portrayals of age and gender in prime-time television." *Mass Communication and Society* 8(3), pp. 241–256.

Lederer, Richard. (1991). *The Miracle of Language*. New York: Pocket Books.

Lester, Gideon. (1994). "Thomasina the Tank Engine stearns into a sex storm." *The Times* (London), October 2.

Lichter, S. Robert, and Daniel Amundson. (1994). *Distorted Reality: Hispanic Characters in TV Entertainment*. Washington, DC: Center for Media and Public Affairs.

Lippmann, Walter. (1922). "The world outside and the pictures in our heads." Chapter 1 (pp. 3–32) in Walter Lippmann, *Public Opinion*. New York: Macmillan.

List, Karen K. (1991) "Guaranteed pages in college newspapers: A case study." *Journal of Mass Media Ethics* 6(4), pp. 222–233.

Loevinger, Lee. (1968). "The ambiguous mirror: The reflective-projective theory of broadcasting and mass communication." *Journal of Broadcasting* 12(2), pp. 97–116.

McCallum, Laura. (2010). Panel discussion on "Diversifying Your News Coverage," at Midwest Journalism Conference, Bloomington, MN, April 17.

Meyer, Philip. (2006). *Newspaper Ethics in the New Century: A Report to the American Society of Newspaper Editors.* Reston, VA: American Society of Newspaper Editors.

Nagel, Jan. (2008). "Gender in media: Females don't rule." *Animation World Magazine*, May 21. Retrieved from http://mag.awn.com/index.php?1type=pageone&article_no=3646 (March 4, 2009). An overview of this and related studies can be found at www.thegeenadavisinstitute.org/downloads/GDIGM_Main_Findings.pdf.

National Association of Television Program Executives (NATPE). (2003). "Blacks, Hispanics get more TV roles." *NATPE dailyLead.* Retrieved from www.smartbrief.com/alquemie/servlet/encodeServlet?issue id=DF2D56E8-D3B1-4568-B589-5C5890BDDB3F&lmid=archives, citing a story from the *Los Angeles Times*, August 8, 2003.

Papper, Bob. (2008). "The face of the workforce." RTNDA *Communicator* 62(6), pp. 10–12. Retrieved (as "Cover story: 2008 Women and minorities survey") from www.rtnda.org/pages/media_items/the-face-of-the-workforce1472.php (April 1, 2009).

Parker, Kathleen. (2009). "Cartoonist has right to be offensive." Eau Claire, WI *Leader-Telegram*, March 1, p. 6F.

Pease, Edward C. (1990). "Ducking the diversity issue." *Newspaper Research Journal* 11(2), pp. 24–37.

Pecora, Norma. (1993). "The environment of children's advertising." Paper presented to the International Communication Association convention, Washington, DC, May.

Pitts, Leonard. (2009). "New York Post has right to offend but not without understanding." *The Seattle Times*, March 1, p. B8. Retrieved from http://seattletimes.nwsource.com/html/opinion/2008794910_opinb01 pitts.html (March 1, 2009).

Rawls, John. (1971). *A Theory of Justice.* Cambridge, MA: Belknap.

Remnick, David. (1994). "News in a dying language." *The New Yorker*, January 10, pp. 40–47.

Santos, Fernanda. (2010). "Capturing the vitality of Jackson Heights and putting it on stage." *The New York Times*, May 5, p. A23.

Schramm, Wilbur. (1949). "The nature of news." *Journalism Quarterly* 26(3), pp. 259–269.

Seabrook, John. (1994). "Rocking in Shangri-La." *The New Yorker*, October, pp. 64–78.

Siebert, Fred S., Theodore Peterson, and Wilbur Schramm. (1956). *Four Theories of the Press.* Urbana, IL: University of Illinois Press.

Smith, Robert E. (1969). "They still write it white." *Columbia Journalism Review*, Spring, pp. 36–38.

Stephens, Mitchell, and David T. Z. Mindich. (2005). "The press and the politics of representation." In Geneva Overholser and Kathleen Hall Jamieson, eds., *The Press.* Oxford, UK: Oxford University Press.

Stern, Susannah R., and Dana E. Mastro. (2004). "Gender portrayals across the life span: A content analytic look at broadcast commercials." *Mass Communication & Society* 7(2), pp. 215–236.

"Study: Gay characters' television presence reduced in coming season." (2006). Associated Press story in the Bloomington, IL *Pantagraph*, August 22, p. D4.

Tannen, Deborah. (1990). *You Just Don't Understand.* New York: Morrow.

U.S. Census Bureau. (2008). "An older and more diverse nation by midcentury." Washington, DC: U.S. Department of Commerce press release, August 14. Retrieved from www.census.gov/Press-Release/www/releases/archives/population/012496.html (April 20, 2009).

U.S. Department of Commerce, Bureau of the Census. (1982). *Forecasts of the Population of the United States: 1945–1975*, Table 27. Washington, DC: U.S. Government Printing Office, 1947 and U.S. Department of Commerce, Bureau of the Census, Current Population Reports, Population Estimates and Projections, Series P-25, no. 921 (October 1982).

Chapter 5

Codes of Ethics

ONE of the hallmarks of a profession (as distinct from an occupation or a trade) or a field with pretensions to professionalism is that it has a code of ethics, often with teeth to enforce it.

Some ethics codes are primarily for the benefit of practitioners in the profession. A good example is the original Hippocratic Oath, which focuses on such things as the medical practitioner's reputation and obligation to avoid harming patients. Codes may also be public relations exercises, intended to make customers or the general public look more favorably on the profession. The injunction against administering poisons in the Hippocratic Oath can be read this way because its concern is for the reputation of all doctors. Finally, codes can form a useful set of guidelines for practitioners, with the best interests of the public—the profession's customers—at heart.

But there is no agreement as to whether codes do (or should) prescribe the highest or lowest acceptable standards of practice. For that matter, there is no consensus on whether they should be prescriptive (exhorting practitioners to high, perhaps idealized and possibly unattainable, standards) or whether they should be proscriptive (specifying what is *not* ethical practice).

There are many codes of ethics in the mass media fields. Various organizations in print and broadcast journalism, such as the Society of Professional Journalists (SPJ), the National Press Photographers Association (NPPA), and the Radio Television Digital News Association (RTDNA), have developed, and argued over, their own codes. Specialized journalism groups (e.g., the Society of American Travel Writers and the National Conference of Editorial Writers) also have their own, specialized codes. In addition, many individual newspapers have ethics codes that apply internally to their employees, and—particularly since the demise of the National Association of Broadcasters' code of practice—so do various broadcast stations, networks, and groups.

Ethics codes also exist in public relations (the Public Relations Society of America, PRSA), business communication (International Association of Business Communicators), and advertising (American Advertising Federation and the American Association of Advertising Agencies). They also are found in technical writing and political campaigns, among other areas. The movie industry's first ethics code was written in 1930, amid strong criticism of their industry that some feared would bring government intervention, and the earliest broadcasting industry codes—in 1930 for radio and 1952 for TV—also were motivated in part by the same concern.

But there is considerable debate about the value of ethics codes—or the lack of it. "For some people, formal codes are a necessary mark of a true profession. For others, codes are worthless exercises in vagueness, irrelevance, and slick public relations" (Johannesen et al., 2008, p. 179). There are concerns that codes may not be fully understood by those for whom they are written, that the practitioners who need them the most are the ones who pay the least attention to them, and that codes are almost by necessity full of ambiguities—fuzzy, imprecise words and statements that can be interpreted in different ways.

Codes of ethics in the mass media can be traced back at least to 1910, when the state press association in Kansas adopted one. By 1929 some newspapers and at least a dozen state press associations had adopted ethics codes, fueled in part by concerns over the re-emergence of newspaper sensationalism and an increasing erosion of newspapers' credibility (Cronin and McPherson, 1995). A code with national dimensions emerged in 1923, when the Canons of Journalism were adopted by the American Society of Newspaper Editors (ASNE).

The early codes and those that have followed tend to be worded quite generally. Almost all are voluntary, without enforcement provisions. One exception, for 41 years, was in the public relations field, where the PRSA's 1959 Code of Professional Standards (until its revision in 2000) allowed complaints to be filed against practitioners who allegedly violated provisions of the code. In a few cases, following hearings, such complaints may have led to the expulsion, suspension, or censure of public relations personnel by the PRSA, but that didn't bar them from continuing to practice public relations.

Arguments for and against media codes of ethics have been made in many forums over the years. Usually, these have focused on the philosophical implications of codes. Johannesen et al. (2008, p. 180) provide a concise summary of arguments against formal codes. Sometimes, these arguments have reflected fears that a voluntary code will be taken over and enforced by government, or that plaintiffs' lawyers in libel or other cases will use the language of the code to argue that their clients were wronged. Occasionally, the arguments have focused on fears that those who adhere to a code may find themselves at a competitive disadvantage to those who ignore it, on specific revisions in a code, or on whether any enforcement provisions should be added. Some of those disputes have reached vitriolic levels.

In the calmer and more reasoned discussion that follows, Michael Dorsher argues that codes are too general and too idealistic to be useful in dealing with real-world dilemmas. David Gordon maintains that ethics codes are valuable both to the mass media themselves and to society.

GORDON: Codes of ethics are useful and necessary, both for the news media and in public relations and advertising, because these codes benefit society.

Media codes of ethics cannot be enforced, unless employers adopt them and make them mandatory for employees. But even unenforceable codes serve an important purpose by setting standards against which conduct can be measured and evaluated. This benchmark function is beneficial to both individuals and employers in the media, but it is perhaps even more worthwhile for the society served by the mass media.

Within the media, codes serve several different purposes. Perhaps the least important is to ensure that standards are set internally, within the media industries, rather than having this done by courts, legislatures, or regulatory agencies. Much more important is the internal benchmark function noted above. Ethics codes can provide ideal standards of excellence, as goals for those in the advertising, entertainment, news, and public relations industries. For individuals who are making conscious efforts to act as "moral agents," these codes provide a baseline against which they can measure their own values and performance, even when they fall short of ideal levels of morality, as all of us human beings do on occasion. Media organizations as a whole can benefit from using the goals set forth in codes to reflect on how their performances measure up. Codes can "act as the conscience of the professional, of the organization, of the enterprise" (Black et al., 1995, p. 13).

Even codes that don't set forth idealized levels of performance can usually provide some worthwhile ethical goals toward which individuals and organizations can aim. As the honorary president of the International Organization of Journalists noted back in 1977, an ethics code can proclaim "the elementary rules of the morality of our profession" (Jones, 1980, p. 12, quoting Jean-Maurice Hermann).

Codes can also serve as a starting point—a threshold, if you will—for debating which principles deserve to be honored by ethical media practitioners. Indeed, because ethics deals with normative behavior as well as philosophy, ethics codes can be a major factor in helping to establish these norms, especially if the codes provoke discussion as to what they should cover and how that coverage should be worded.

As Richard Johannesen et al. (2008) have argued, ethics codes "should not require heroic virtue, extreme sacrifice, or doing right no matter what the obstacles," but rather should aim at people of ordinary conscientiousness (p. 181, citing Kultgen, 1983). Johannesen, a long-time leader in the broad area of human communication ethics, provides 10 other guidelines to overcome what might otherwise be valid objections to ethics codes. Among them are the need to specify which parts of the codes represent *ideal goals* and which are *minimum conditions* that must be met in order to be considered ethical (or to avoid punishment). Other guidelines include clear, specific language; logical coherence; protection of *both* the general public interest and the practitioners covered by the code; and stimulation by the code of "continued discussion and reflection leading to possible modification or revision" (p. 181, citing DeGeorge, 1985, and Kultgen, 1983).

ethics codes . . . should aim at people of ordinary conscientiousness

For our society overall, codes may provide standards and guidelines that help the public discuss, debate, and measure media performance, and assist it in articulating reasonable demands and criticism of the news, persuasive, and entertainment media. If the codes are realistic, they can also help to *protect* the media and individual practitioners from unrealistic or unthinking expectations, demands, and criticism. And they may also be used to help the public understand why certain decisions were made in newsrooms, ad agencies, public relations offices, or film studios. Codes used this way can help make the mass media more accountable to their various publics. If that increased accountability can lead to more dialogue and, perhaps, more understanding between the media and their audiences, the result could be increased public confidence in the media.

All of that, of course, assumes that ethics codes will be made available to the public and that the public will read them. Unfortunately, few organizations (news or other) have gone as far as the *Post Register* in Idaho Falls, Idaho, whose Web site contains an interactive version of a 2005 investigative story to which its ethics code was applied, with explanations of why various decisions were made. The paper has localized the SPJ code and invited its audience to help hold it accountable. As of May, 2010, the Web site material (accompanied by a photo of the editor and publisher) told its readers: "You can also challenge our behavior in a letter to the editor or by reporting us to another media outlet, whose professional standards should include the duty to report on the ethical decision-making of the media." The paper's Web site also lists—though not usually by name, and none more recent than 2005—staffers who ran afoul of various sections of the code and the actions taken by the paper in each case. This applies a Kantian standard: that the paper's reporters and editors should be no more exempt from having their transgressions revealed than are members of the public whom the paper covers when they run afoul of the law (see www.postregister.com/ethics/index.php).

Dean Miller, then the paper's executive editor, wrote in 2006 that making the code easily available to the public can help the audience "learn that your ethics, like theirs, are the starting point for searching conversations, the weighing of alternatives, and the honest treatment of what is known and not known" (Miller, 2006, pp. 82–83). He added that having the code in front of both parties when an irate consumer calls to criticize the paper is a very helpful way of moving toward a reasoned discussion of the reader's concerns. I would add that this degree of *transparency* can only add to the credibility not only of the paper, but also of journalism more generally. (Miller left the paper shortly after writing that article, and the time and effort devoted to the Web site appear to have diminished since then.)

FURTHER BENEFITS OF ETHICS CODES

Codes of ethics do more than help to protect the public from unethical performance and the media from unreasonable public demands. They also provide a reference point that can be invoked to protect media workers from pressures within their own organizations intended to force them to violate their own consciences. Written codes can also help acquaint mass media students, new employees, or anyone new to moral reasoning with some of the key ethical issues and principles they will face in their careers—*if* they pay some attention to them. Codes can increase their understanding of professional values and can sharpen the focus on ethical issues that people in all branches of the media must face regularly, whether they work in advertising agencies, newsrooms, studios, or public relations offices, or whether they are independent bloggers working from their homes.

Codes can be used to anticipate specific ethical dilemmas and reflect on possible ways to deal with them, perhaps most usefully when reasoned discussion *is* possible because no deadline is looming just minutes away. More generally, written codes focus attention in specific ethics issues and provide a context for media practitioners to discuss and reflect on their responsibilities and obligations—as this discussion may do for you as you read through it. An introduction to a 1980 study of ethics codes in some 50 countries noted that voluntary codes can serve "as a lifeline tracing the way back to responsibility and credibility" (Jones, 1980, p. 7), both of which are topics of increasing concern to journalists and public relations practitioners (as well as to their critics).

I will concede without hesitation that written ethics codes generally reflect compromises that fall short of what some people see as an appropriate standard for ethical conduct. Some codes use terminology that is too vague to have much meaning, such as the reference to avoiding material that is "offensive to good taste or public decency" in the 1984 ethics code of the American Advertising Federation (AAF, 1984). Others omit some standards that many observers and practitioners consider important (e.g., the failure of some journalism ethics codes to mention truth, which most people would consider an essential element of the practice as well as of the ethics of the field).

The public relations field—which has had an ethics code since the Public Relations Society of America (PRSA) adopted one in 1950, three years after the organization was chartered—still debates the viability of such a code for its practitioners. Edward Bernays, the legendary public relations pioneer widely regarded as the father of the field, argued repeatedly before his death in 1995 for some form of certification or licensing to denote PR practitioners who have mastered a specified body of knowledge *and* who promise to adhere to a recognized code of ethics.

In a 1992 talk to journalism and mass communication educators, Bernays defined a public relations practitioner ("counsel," in his terminology) as

> an applied social scientist who . . . advises what changes in attitude and action are demanded to reach the highest point of adjustment to meet social goals.
>
> With this definition in mind, it becomes clear that PR also depends on the formation of a strict ethical code. Ethical behavior needn't be spelled out—there is no universal definition. Simply put, standard Judeo-Christian ethics, based on integrity and honesty are necessary for a public relations practitioner to properly practice his profession.
>
> (Bernays, 1992)

Based on his lengthy PR experience and an active lifetime that was then just short of 101 years, he added his belief "that good ethics is good business, and that those practitioners who earn their license and uphold the ethical code will be rewarded with very prosperous and constructive careers in public relations" (Bernays, 1992).

The PRSA adopted a new ethics code in 2000, with the aim of defining "the professional responsibilities of public relations practitioners in the 21st Century" and inspiring "ethical behavior rather than (emphasizing) punishment for unethical conduct" (Fitzpatrick, p. 2). The new code dropped the 1959 emphasis on trying to enforce ethical standards (complete with a quasi-judicial system to deal with violations) in favor of one that relies "on the personal commitments of members to uphold industry standards" as long as they choose to remain members. The change sparked much debate, but was necessary because "PRSA's judicial system simply was not practical for a body that had no legal authority over its members" (p. 1).

That doesn't mean that PRSA and its voluntary code are not serious about ethics concerns. The new code is featured prominently on the organization's Web site, as is information about its Board of Ethics and Professional Standards. PRSA also periodically posts online professional standards advisories that apply the code to specific issues arising in the field, such as the use of video news releases (see www.prsa.org).

Other ethics codes available to public relations practitioners are those of the International Association of Business Communicators (IABC) and the International Public Relations Association's Code of Conduct. Those, along with the PRSA code, stress honesty as a core value, and could be of considerable help to corporate PR people who need to stand up within their organization for the ethical course of action. Interestingly, that ethical course of corporate action frequently turns out to be the best way to maintain a positive corporate image, but that's a discussion for a different class.

The Radio-Television News Directors Association (renamed in 2009 as the Radio Television Digital News Association) code of ethics and professional practice focuses on ethics issues in broadcasting and, like the codes noted in the preceding paragraph, stresses honesty. One of its occasionally issued sets of guidelines includes a provision that broadcast journalists should "clearly disclose the origin of information and label all material provided by outsiders," a standard that isn't always honored, as you will read in Michael Dorsher's half of this chapter.

CONCERNS WITH ETHICS CODES

Generalities are indeed a problem with some codes, as Dorsher points out. So are some apparent conflicts between different statements within codes, as he notes with regard to the PRSA code. But, on a closer look, some of those statements are perhaps less contradictory than he would have us believe. For instance, as he says, the PRSA code states that practitioners should be faithful to their clients, ignoring if necessary their personal interests, while at the same time honoring the obligation to serve the public interest. At first glance, that may seem difficult if not impossible but, on reflection, it's not a bad guideline to follow. What it really exhorts PRSA members to do is to make sure that their clients are also aware of an obligation to the public interest—a point reinforced elsewhere in the code by the provision suggesting that members decline to represent clients who "urge or require actions contrary to this Code." If PRSA members pay attention to their code, it could have an influence not just on them but on their clients, as well.

SPJ also provides online ethics assistance for journalists (see www.spj.org/ethics.asp), to flesh out the language contained in its ethics code. That code has a potential major conflict, between the section that says being ethical requires telling the truth and the one that says being ethical involves minimizing harm, something that's not always easy when telling the truth. But I'd suggest that shortcomings within ethics codes—such as conflicts or generalities—call for more thoughtful and probably more specific writing of those codes rather than dismissing the whole concept of codes out of hand, just because the existing ones aren't perfect.

Johannesen et al. (2008) point out that the tension between different sections of the SPJ code reflects the freedom-responsibility tension that journalists must contend with (and which was discussed in Chapter 1).

The code sensitizes journalists both to the freedom to report the truth and act independently on the one hand and their responsibilities to avoid harm to innocent others and to be publicly accountable on the other hand.

(2008, p. 195)

It is certainly true that codes of ethics *cannot* be Kantian in their approach—that is, they can't be written to apply without exception or to cover every possible situation where a media ethics issue may arise, given human ingenuity in creating unique dilemmas. But they definitely can be useful in dealing with general concerns that many media practitioners may encounter during their careers. In the mid-1960s, a distinguished clergyman responded to one aspect of this problem by arguing that ethics codes governing any aspect of public life must be absolute *and* relative, drawing on the Judeo-Christian tradition that places on humankind the responsibility to avoid both excessive relativism and rigid absolutism (Blake, 1966).

Codes can be used to establish an ethical threshold as a starting point from which individual or group (or corporate) ethics standards can be developed and refined further. Additional institutional policies can be formulated to craft ethical standards exceeding the provisions of a code (internal or external), or localizing them as the Idaho paper has done, so as to deal with unique situations or problems or with matters of personal concern. Individuals can certainly follow the same path, if their personal ethics standards exceed those of a specific organizational or corporate code.

The argument can be made that the lack of "teeth" in codes makes them nothing more than unenforceable, worthless streams of lofty rhetoric. The relatively new PRSA code, although entirely voluntary, does require members to pledge their allegiance to the code's principles annually, when they pay their dues. The code also provides that the organization's board of directors may bar from membership or expel anyone "who has been or is sanctioned by a government agency or convicted in a court of law of an action that is in violation of this Code" (PRSA Code of Ethics, 2000, Preamble). This provision goes beyond the stance taken by SPJ and RTNDA, and I think Dorsher dismisses it a bit too quickly, even if PRSA membership isn't required in order to practice public relations.

SPJ (in which membership for journalists is also voluntary) has gone through several revisions of its code. The most recent one, adopted in 1996, provoked considerable argument during the discussion of proposals for some sort of enforcement mechanism. That approach was not adopted—the same fate that prevailed in an even noisier and more bitter fight in the 1980s when some SPJ leaders suggested that violators should be censured or even expelled. The idea of adding teeth to the code hasn't died, though; it came up again at an SPJ board meeting as recently as mid-2007.

In reality, the whole argument over the enforceability of organizational ethics codes is somewhat specious. Ethics, by its nature, deals with what "*should*" happen rather than with what "*must*" happen according to the law. An enforceable code could raise the specter of the government stepping in to enforce such "threshold" standards. Moreover—because specifics would have to be included to make the code enforceable—it would lose some of the necessary flexibility that a code should have, since ethics dilemmas rarely have absolute answers.

SOME POTENTIAL PITFALLS

It does seem fair to say that if ethics codes get too watered down, or perhaps too vague and general, they might dilute the ethical standards within the medium or field to which they apply. Codes that are too general can also produce ethics standards so closely bound to the existing (majority) culture that they provide little or no useful guidance to individuals who try to think for themselves. Specifics can help make written ethics codes more useful, especially because such language makes it more likely that there will be widespread agreement on what the code really means. But if a code becomes *too* detailed—especially if it becomes a laundry list of prohibited practices—it could stifle the individual reasoning process that is the essence of acting as a moral agent.

Dorsher discusses at some length a case study involving Tim Mahoney, a part-time copy editor who was disciplined by the *St. Paul Pioneer Press* after he marched (on his own time) as part of a church contingent protesting the Iraq War. The problem with this case was *not* either the SPJ ethics code or the internal one at the newspaper. Rather, it was the fact that the paper's management didn't use common sense. Both codes specify that journalists should avoid real or perceived conflicts of interest and avoid situations that might damage their credibility or integrity. The facts of the Mahoney case indicate pretty clearly to me that it wasn't either code that led to Mahoney's suspension, but rather a very extreme *interpretation* of the guidelines about perceived conflicts of interest. It certainly would have sufficed just to remove Mahoney from editing any further stories about Iraq, without any suspension, if the paper's management really was concerned about a (somewhat far-fetched) *appearance* of a conflict of interest. As I said earlier, sensible thought goes a long way in using any code of ethics!

I'd argue that Mahoney's actions were clearly *not un*ethical. Whether or not they represented *ethical* behavior probably depends on your views about the Iraq War and about anti-war demonstrations. But it's certainly stretching things to blame the ethics codes for the fuzzy thinking of the paper's management.

However, if codes are so strict and rigid that no one can realistically live up to them, they can become objects of derision and thus counterproductive. As with so many other aspects of ethics, the Aristotelian/Confucian Golden Mean has much to recommend it in dealing with codes. Striking a balance between specificity and universality, between absolutism and situational ethics, between the ideal and the pragmatic can help produce a highly useful ethics code. One would certainly get into trouble with a Kantian approach, insisting that code provisions must be absolute, formal or universal in order to be worthwhile.

Ethics codes can also be helpful as the various mass media fields move—or grope—their way into 21st-century technology. As these new technologies take the media into uncharted areas with new problems in ethics, there is an increased need for ethics codes to help provide some useful guidelines. For example, how do privacy concerns intersect with the various electronic databases available to marketers, journalists, and others (a topic discussed further in Chapter 10)? Would it be useful for ethics codes to speak directly to the tendency of some reporters or public relations practitioners who grew up with the Internet to regard it as a wholly reliable source for information they're seeking, without bothering to check that information against additional ("real world," if you will) sources?

> As with so many other aspects of ethics, the Aristotelian/ Confucian Golden Mean has much to recommend it in dealing with codes.

Similarly, it could be very helpful to media people working with new formats or platforms to have some type of guidance for what is and isn't appropriate. The negative response in mid-2007 to some of *Dateline NBC*'s "To Catch a Predator" programming might have been avoided (or at least reduced) if some codified approach had existed regarding appropriate ethical boundaries for a televised "sting" operation (here, aimed at potential child-sex predators), and if the program's leadership had stopped to consider them. Such ethics issues as whether or how closely media should cooperate with law enforcement efforts were inherent in this situation, along with (among other concerns) the ethics of entrapment and privacy concerns (Eaton, 2006).

If the producers considered ethics guidelines at all, they might well have concluded that the utilitarian benefit to society overall, by ensnaring potential sexual predators, clearly outweighed any harm that might be caused. Or they could have used Rawls's approach and concluded that a televised sting is too dismissive of individuals' rights of privacy; this position might have prevented the suicide of an assistant district attorney in Texas who shot himself after being ensnared in the sting (Stelter, 2008). This type of programming, and the ethical dilemmas it can produce, is one byproduct of the television industry's emphasis on "reality" programming, which is far cheaper to produce than scripted programs where ethics issues may become more evident *before* a program is aired. I'd suggest that people in the entertainment and infotainment industries should consider these types of ethics dilemmas in advance, rather than relying only on hindsight to analyze the problems after they have played out.

SOME USES FOR ETHICS CODES

As with all efforts to act as a "moral agent," thinking about various ethical dilemmas and how they might be dealt with—*before* they erupt into a crisis—is likely to produce more effective and more ethical responses than dealing with them on an *ad hoc* basis under deadline pressures. An ethics code can be a useful tool in facilitating those types of discussions.

Using codes as a catalyst for non-deadline thought and reflection may be particularly appropriate in light of several studies reporting that "codes rarely determine day-to-day behavior for most journalists" (Keith et al., 2006, citing Boeyink, 1994, 1998, and others). A further indication that this approach could be fruitful is Dorsher's admission that neither he nor his editors ever used the SPJ code during his 20 years as a journalist. That statement makes me wonder if using some *post*-college ethics sources—in addition to the classical philosophy underpinning for his undergraduate ethics course—might have expanded even further his thinking about how to respond to ethical dilemmas.

Karen Lebacqz (1985), writing on codes of ethics in the professions, suggested that they must go beyond prescriptive rules for behavior. Rather, they should describe the "moral character" expected of and needed by practitioners in a particular field. They should illuminate "where stresses and tensions have been felt within the profession and what image of the good professional is held up to assist professionals through those stresses and tensions" (Lebacqz, 1985, p. 68).

Johannesen et al.'s (2008) guidelines for developing useful ethics codes, noted earlier, also suggest that such codes "should go beyond general admonitions against lying and cheating to focus on those facets of the group's functions 'that pose particular and special- ized temptations to its members' " (Johannesen et al., 2008, p. 181, quoting DeGeorge, 1986, p. 342). "Problems" and "concerns" are perhaps more relevant today than are "tempta- tions," although these still occur. For instance, a journalist might be tempted to alter a story by an offer of, say, a free weekend vacation from a resort publicist—a situation that would violate the ethics codes of both PRSA and SPJ. It's worth noting that references to potential conflicts of interest were missing from many of the early journalism codes, but the phrase is now standard in most of them. The codes are also quite—perhaps overly—explicit in defining this term, reflecting increased attention paid to this topic by society in general as well as by the journalism field.

It seems likely that the early journalism codes of ethics, written in the 1920s, were intended at least in part to be public relations tools aimed at enhancing media credibility with the public. Many state press associations formulated codes that focused on such concerns as propaganda in the media, the influence of press agents, and a resurgence of sensationalism. There is also some evidence that the early codes were developed in part as buttresses for many journalists' desire that their occupation be regarded as a profession (Cronin and McPherson, 1995, pp. 892–893). But even if these were the only reasons for writing the pioneering codes—and even if there are still overtones of these goals inherent in today's codes—their purpose and value have evolved and matured. They are particularly relevant in light of the current public concern about mass media ethics.

INTERNAL ETHICS CODES

So far, this side of the argument has not dealt with company codes of ethics. Obviously, a media company that believes strongly in its code of ethics or conduct is in a position to enforce it, so these codes clearly have some teeth. Nor are they unimportant to the employees who could lose their jobs by violating them. The real question here might better be whether company codes really come to grips with ethics issues in a meaningful—or sensible—way.

No blanket assessment of this is possible because media companies deal with ethics in many different ways (or not at all) on a corporate level. One example, though, can drive home the fact that company codes *can* deal head-on with important ethics issues—and can do so meaningfully. In 1991, the U.S. Supreme Court ruled that several Minnesota news organizations were liable for damages (under the theory of a breached contract) because their editors had overridden pledges of confidentiality given to a source by reporters and had published the source's identity (see *Cohen v. Cowles Media Co.*, 1991). Beyond the highly relevant ethical question of whether confidentiality should have been promised at all in this instance, the case focused on the issue of whether a reporter could bind a news organization to respect a pledge of confidentiality regardless of what editors thought about the situation. (For a further discussion of ethics issues inherent in the use of confidential sources, see Chapter 15-D.)

The upshot of this case, in many newsrooms, was a revision of company codes, or clari- fication of what had been hazy guidelines, to require that reporters henceforth must obtain an editor's agreement before promising confidentiality to a source. News organizations taking this approach came directly to grips with an important ethical (and legal) issue in a way that set standards which their employees had little choice but to observe, however adversely it might affect getting sources to talk.

In regard to newsrooms more generally, a 2005 survey by the Ethics Committee of the American Society of Newspaper Editors reported that 77% of the editors who responded said their newspapers had a written code of ethics or set of guidelines, up sharply from the 51% who answered affirmatively in a 1985 survey. Almost the same percentage said they preferred a written code to a case-by-case approach, an increase of some 12% since 1985 (Meyer, 2006, pp. 132–133). That 1985 study also indicated that ethics requirements were being enforced, with at least 78 newspaper journalists dismissed or suspended in the prior three years for ethics violations ranging from plagiarism to outright fabrication of stories (American Society of Newspaper Editors, 1986–87, p. 7).

ARE BLOGGERS EXEMPT FROM ETHICS CODES?

Standards of behavior for bloggers—codes of ethics, if you will—pose a developing area of concern. This may be true for bloggers with their own Web sites, but it is a particular problem in regard to bloggers who write for news sites (either as staff members or as members of the audience). Some of the same concerns exist regarding "citizen journalists" who provide images from their digital cameras (or phones) to news media outlets. Many of them are likely to be engaging in a journalistic enterprise without much, if any, training in journalism or ethics (though many laid-off newspaper staffers are now part of those ranks). Ethics codes could be extremely useful in providing guidance to citizen journalists and bloggers without training in journalism, particularly those who lack experience in dealing with the ethical dimensions of visual imagery and privacy concerns. (For a more in-depth look at these and related concerns, see Chapter 6.)

The introduction to a model bloggers' code, modified by CyberJournalist.net (a Web site of the Online News Association) from the SPJ code, states the need for such codes:

> Since not all bloggers are journalists and the Weblog form is more casual, [some bloggers] argue they shouldn't be expected to follow the same ethics codes journalists are. But responsible bloggers should recognize that they are publishing words publicly, and therefore have certain ethical obligations to their readers, the people they write about, and society in general.

The introduction notes that this code is no more than a guideline and that individual bloggers must "choose their own best practices," but then adds: "Integrity is the cornerstone of credibility. Bloggers who adopt this code of principles and these standards of practice not only practice ethical publishing but convey to their readers that they can be trusted" (www.cyberjournalist.net/news/000215.php, retrieved March 10, 2010).

A comment, posted online shortly after this model code first appeared in 2003, argued that bloggers differ from traditional journalists and that accuracy and fairness (which are emphasized in the SPJ code) aren't central to their mission. Instead, the post offered guidelines for a blogger's code of ethics, and suggested a core standard of *transparency* (Blood, 2003)—e.g., full disclosure of potential conflicts of interest—something that has also been discussed in both mainstream journalism and in public relations. Similar concerns also exist in regard to non-professional creators of online video content for outlets ranging from YouTube to the latest iteration of searches for online talent and content by such giants as Yahoo! and AOL.

It's worth noting, though, that the SPJ ethics code has served as an explicit model for at least one online news publication, the *Minnesota Monitor*, which described itself in 2008 as "a coalition of long-time bloggers, freelance writers, and professional journalists" emphasizing "original investigative reporting" and striving for "truth-telling, fairness, and accountability" (Marty, 2008).

SOME FINAL THOUGHTS

I've already dealt with Dorsher's concerns that the PRSA code is full of conflicts and co-tradictions. In that connection, it's worth noting the argument made by public relations Professor Dean Kruckeberg in the early 1990s, when he contended that a binding code for public relations practitioners, perhaps modeled on one used by Certified Public Accountants and omitting activities protected by the First Amendment, would be "reasonable and suitable—indeed, essential—in contemporary global society" (Kruckeberg, 1993, p. 22). A similar—but voluntary—code has been proposed for journalists (Ellington, 2010).

Two other PR educators, also arguing for a universal code (regardless of enforceability), suggested that codes could provide a mechanism for leaders in public relations (or other communication fields) "to speak out and declare to the public that [inappropriate communication] behaviors are not the norm and are not ethical according to accepted standards" (Hunt and Tirpok, 1993, p. 8). They also noted that some PR firms included "in their client contracts a stipulation that the firm adheres to a certain ethics code and that it will not violate the code on the client's behalf" (p. 3).

Unlike Dorsher, I believe that the code of the American Advertising Federation (AAF) has value even if some advertisers disregard its language discouraging the practice of "puffery." I'd argue that this code—which says advertising and advertisers "shall tell the truth and shall reveal significant facts, the omission of which would mislead the public"—is a useful (if idealistic) standard to have available, both for the ad agency employee trying to convince her/his boss to avoid puffery, and for members of the public who want to hold to the fire the feet of those who do practice puffery.

I also have some problems with a few other aspects of the Dorsher argument that follows. First, the Bergman (2005) article—which he cites in regard to his concern about media trainers teaching company officials how to stick to their message regardless of what questions journalists ask—also argues for making ethics codes more than just threshold standards! More important, I don't understand his conclusion that the SPJ ethics code (or any other one) could have kept the Watergate scandal under wraps. Is it really possible that the information needed to expose the Watergate conspiracy fully would have become available without a promise of absolute confidentiality to "Deep Throat"? It seems clear to me that it was *not* "feasible" to identify the source at the time, and that the language of the SPJ code supports the path chosen by Bob Woodward and Carl Bernstein. Given the importance of this story to the United States, virtually any ethical theory you'd care to name (but especially utilitarianism, and Rawls, if you consider either W. Mark Felt ("Deep Throat") or American society as the weakest actor in this drama) would support the way *The Washington Post* and its reporters handled the situation.

Moreover, it was inappropriate for Woodward to reveal the identity of his "Deep Throat" source—until he received explicit permission from Felt—at any time before Felt died, since the original arrangement was to guard "Deep Throat's" anonymity with no ending date. To me, keeping that promise, even if it meant getting scooped by *Vanity Fair*, was the only ethical course to follow. As to Felt's motives, he seemed to be concerned at least as much about the cover-up and the politicizing of the FBI as about Nixon's passing him over for the top FBI job (see Woodward, 2005, especially pp. 104–107). And even if Felt had only base motives in this situation, a utilitarian approach, with a story this important to the United States as a whole, would have made the decision to use his information obvious.

The bottom line on this whole topic is that ethics codes will never be a total cure for the problems of the news, persuasion, and entertainment media. And they shouldn't be expected to cover—or illustrate—every conceivable ethical challenge that humans can invent. But even if they are well short of perfection and of being a panacea, ethics codes can still be useful in pointing the way to media self-improvement and greater accountability to the public. When codes work well, they can focus attention on key issues and help make those concerns part of the media's general decision-making process. As Lebacqz (1985, p. 83) has suggested, they can also be very useful to individuals concerned about their own moral character and development, because "each choice about what to do is also a choice about whom to be—or, more accurately, whom to become."

A set of three general goals for any code of ethics, developed as part of the transnational study noted earlier, illustrates some basic values of ethics codes and might form a broad philosophical context for codes in all areas of mass communication:

1   Protecting the audience toward whom mass communication is directed "from any irresponsible, antisocial or propaganda use of the media."
2   Protecting people working in the various media "from being forced to act in ways which are irresponsible, humiliating or in any manner contrary to the dictates of their consciences."
3   Keeping "open all channels of communication, both from above and from below," to make sure that the public gets the information needed in a self-governing society, and to ensure that ordinary people can always register their opinions through the media.

(Jones, 1980, p.14)

Of course, those goals would require some agreement on the meaning of key terms such as *irresponsible* before they can be implemented. There are inherent shortcomings in any code of ethics, but that doesn't mean that this approach should be completely avoided. To dismiss ethics codes out of hand as worthless and counterproductive seems to be throwing out the baby with the bath water merely because perfection is beyond our grasp.

> When codes work well, they can focus attention on key issues and help make those concerns part of the media's general decision-making process.

KEY POINTS

■ For individuals who are trying to act as "moral agents," ethics codes provide a baseline against which to measure their own values and performance.

■ Codes can set standards which the public can use to evaluate media performance.

■ Ethics codes can point the way to media self-improvement and greater accountability to the public—in the advertising and public relations areas no less than in journalism.

DORSHER: Ethics codes are too general to apply to many real situations, too black-and-white, and too idealistic in the cases of public relations and advertising.

In this chapter, David Gordon argues that media company codes of ethics are enforceable and therefore important, and they can be meaningful. Let's examine Gordon's argument by applying it to a real-life situation.

A novelist by day, Tim Mahoney worked nights as a part-time copy editor for the *St. Paul Pioneer Press*, Minnesota's oldest and second-largest newspaper. He floated among the business, sports, online and news copy desks, occasionally editing stories about the war in Iraq and writing headlines for them. No reader or editor ever complained about Mahoney's editing of those stories even though, during office discussions, he expressed opposition to the United States' continuing combat operations in Iraq. One weekend when he was not scheduled to work, Mahoney joined nearly 200 other members of his Catholic church in boarding buses, riding overnight to Washington, DC, and marching in an anti-war rally on the Mall. Mahoney, a Vietnam War combat veteran and the author of two novels about Vietnam, avoided appearing in any news coverage of the rally.

When he returned to work at the *Pioneer Press* the next week, Mahoney casually mentioned that he had been at the anti-war rally. A co-worker who overheard him thought Mahoney's participation in the rally represented at least the appearance of a conflict of interest with his occasional editing of stories about Iraq, and she told a supervisor. Mahoney had not sought his editors' approval to attend the rally, because he thought he could do whatever he wanted with his church group on his days off, especially since he wasn't working for a competitor of the paper or doing anything involving a financial conflict of interest. His newsroom supervisor disagreed, citing a portion of the *Pioneer Press* ethics code, based on part of its union contract with the Twin Cities chapter of the American Newspaper Guild (ANG). That provision read, in pertinent part:

Employees of the Publisher shall be free to engage in activities outside of working hours provided such activities do not create a conflict of interest, (and) are not inconsistent with proper and impartial performance of their duties as employees.

In response, Mahoney and the ANG attorney said that portion of the ethics code and contract was exactly what protected him in this instance. He had engaged in this church activity outside of his working hours, he avoided the limelight and did not seek to create a conflict of interest, and no one had accused him of biased performance of his duties—before or after attending the anti-war rally.

Conceding all that was true, Mahoney's supervisors said he had at least created the appearance of a conflict of interest. Readers who found out about his attendance of the rally, they said, might wonder if he were inserting his anti-war bias into the copy and headlines of Iraq stories. Not only the stories Mahoney edited would be suspect, they noted, but also so would all of the *Pioneer Press* stories on the Iraq war. Unlike reporters, copy editors do not get bylines, so readers would not know which Iraq stories Mahoney edited and which he didn't.

JOURNALISM CODES HAVE IT BACKWARD

Thus, we see that the *Pioneer Press* internal ethics code was too general to be of any help in resolving this real-life dilemma. It did not provide Mahoney guidance on how to avert this controversy. It did not direct him to seek a supervisor's approval before engaging in activity outside working hours or define "conflict of interest." Nor did it give examples of conflicts of interest. This bears out the argument that, at their worst, ethics codes are impotent facades, and even at their best, "they leave a lot to be desired in terms of implementation and efficiency" (Nordenstreng, 1995, p. 2).

Gordon argues that internal codes of ethics are neither impotent nor unenforceable, but like all coercive tactics, the editors' attempt to enforce the *Pioneer Press* internal code in the Mahoney case did not increase their authority or unify their staff. Rather, the staff split into factions and morale eroded over the Mahoney case and an earlier one where the *Pioneer Press* editors suspended two reporters who attended a 2004 Bruce Springsteen concert sponsored by the John Kerry presidential campaign. As the *Pioneer Press* learned, if unions, masses of employees and masses of clients and audience members disagree with an internal code of ethics, the company cannot uphold its code, without deeply wounding the company's potency. In the end, the editors suspended Mahoney for three days without pay and forbade him from editing any more Iraq stories. Mahoney and the ANG filed an appeal, but the case died when new owners bought the *Pioneer Press*.

codes should be aimed at news organization owners, not their employees

"Journalism's ethical codes have it backwards," ethicist John McManus says, explaining that codes should be aimed at news organization owners, not their employees, because "journalists are more decision takers than decision-makers . . . their authority to produce high-quality ethical news reports is circumscribed, tightly for some, loosely for others" (McManus, 1997, p. 13).

Gordon says most media codes now define conflicts of interest—"perhaps overly"—but I don't see it that way at all with the Society of Professional Journalists' Code of Ethics. Had the *Pioneer Press* editors consulted this code, it would have been of little help in the Mahoney case. It merely states that "Journalists should avoid conflicts of interest, real or perceived." It, too, does not define conflict of interest or what distinguishes a "real" conflict from a "perceived" one. Nor does it indicate whose perception is most important—the reporter's, the editor's or the audience's.

The SPJ code does go on to say journalists should "remain free of associations and activities that may compromise integrity or damage credibility." But are we to imagine that association with the Catholic Church compromised Mahoney's integrity? Does participation in an anti-war rally automatically damage a journalist's credibility, especially when the SPJ code also exhorts journalists to "be vigilant and courageous about holding those in power accountable"? Does it suddenly become unethical if journalists seek to do that in their non-working hours in addition to their workdays? More to the point here, how does the SPJ code help us determine whether Mahoney's actions were ethical or not?

The SPJ code is equally vague and unhelpful on many other points. "Identify sources whenever feasible," it admonishes, without attempting to define or illustrate when it would not be feasible. Is it enough to say that a source "asked to remain unidentified" or was a "high-ranking official" in Washington? *The Washington Post*'s Bob Woodward had promised not to reveal the identity of his Watergate source "Deep Throat" until that whistleblower died, but was it not "feasible" for Woodward to name him, even after President Nixon resigned from office or after the source left the FBI or, at least, before *Vanity Fair* scooped Woodward and the *Post* in 2005 by identifying Mark Felt? And would Felt, who was upset that Nixon chose L. Patrick Gray to head the FBI instead of him, have even qualified for anonymity under the SPJ code's requirement to "Always question sources' motives before promising anonymity." In other words, how useful or ethical is an ethics code that could have kept the Watergate scandal under wraps and extended a corrupt presidency?

In other places, the SPJ code contradicts itself, at least potentially, it seems to me. For instance, it tries to deal with digital manipulation by advising, "Never distort the content of news photos or video. Image enhancement for technical clarity is always permissible. Label montages and photo illustrations." Where is the line between image distortion and enhancement? In 2003, the *Los Angeles Times* fired one of its award-winning photographers for submitting a composite photograph of a U.S. soldier confronting war refugees in Iraq, without revealing it was a composite until after the *Times* and several other large papers, in its chain or subscribing to its wire service, printed the picture and suspicions about it arose. Had he merely labeled the photo a montage, would the photographer have been acting ethically? Would readers who saw the photo have been satisfied and well served by that?

Elsewhere, the SPJ code says, "Be cautious about identifying juvenile suspects or victims of sex crimes." Two sentences later, with no hint of irony or ambivalence, it adds, "Balance a criminal suspect's fair trial rights with the public's right to be informed." Well, what is the balancing test when deciding whether to inform the public of juvenile suspects' names? And if journalists do not name the accusers in sex crime cases, even after a jury acquits the suspects or prosecutors drop the charges, how is that informing the public, let alone guarding the suspects' fair trial rights or dealing even-handedly with them?

The News & Observer in Raleigh, NC, went against its own decades-old policy of not naming accusers in sex crime cases in April 2007 when the North Carolina attorney general dropped all charges against the three Duke University lacrosse players named a year earlier, when exotic dancer Crystal Gail Mangum said they raped her. "Mangum's claim has been vehemently denied by the three men indicted in the case and by their teammates, who believe they have been damaged by a false accusation," *News & Observer* executive editor Melanie Sill wrote in an explanatory editorial.

> Attorney General Roy Cooper said his office concluded that the three are innocent. Mangum also has been widely identified on the Internet, including on mainstream sites such as Wikipedia. Because of these circumstances, and to more fully report on the case and its aftermath, we decided to publish her name. Also, we will review our standing policy.
>
> (Sill, 2007)

She also invited readers to "weigh in on this decision and the issue of naming sexual assault claimants in criminal cases," asking only that they "be civil" in their comments (Sill, 2007). (See also Chapter 10 in regard to this case.)

VIDEO NEWS RELEASES DEFY CODES

Even the SPJ code's exhortations to act independently and be accountable are not so clear-cut when it comes to TV newscasts' widespread use of video news releases (VNRs). Those two sections of the SPJ code contain language urging journalists to avoid activities that could compromise their integrity or damage their credibility and to clarify and explain their news coverage. Those pretty much go by the board when news broadcasts fail to attribute their sources for the VNRs. What the stations are really doing is stealing time and trust from their audiences, who tuned in to see objective and independently produced information, not a commercial that a lazy or budget-restrained producer has disguised as news.

In September 2007, the Federal Communications Commission fined Comcast $20,000 for airing five unattributed VNRs on its CN8 news channel in Pennsylvania. Rushing to Comcast's defense—on First Amendment grounds—was the Radio-Television News Directors Association (Eggerton, 2007), even though its Code of Ethics admonished its members to "clearly disclose the origin of information and label all material provided by outsiders" (RTNDA, 2007).

Picking apart the SPJ code is not a new sport. SPJ first adopted a code of ethics in 1926 and revised it in 1973, 1984, 1987 and 1996, sometimes amid significant contention. I do not doubt the sincerity of any of those efforts or the intelligence of the code writers. Rather, I think this shows how difficult—perhaps how impossible—it is to compose a code of ethics that anticipates and applies to all the real-world dilemmas facing mass media professionals, especially with new technologies and economic realities rocking their worlds.

My final word on the efficacy of the SPJ Code of Ethics is this: not once did any editor refer me to it in my 20 years as a journalist in newsrooms ranging from the tiny Faribault (Minnesota) *Daily News* to the burgeoning, cutting-edge washingtonpost.com, and not once did I consult it to guide my ethical decision-making. Rather, I navigated dilemmas throughout my career by applying what I learned in one of the first journalism ethics courses ever offered, at a Catholic liberal arts college—an ethics foundation built on complex, classical philosophy, not simplistic contemporary capitalism. Similarly, former *Washington Star* managing editor and *Washington Post* ombudsman Charles B. Seib said he never saw an editor turn to a code of ethics when faced with a journalistic dilemma. "Codes," he said, "do not touch the broader ethical issues confronting today's journalists" (Seib, 1981, p. 6).

PUBLIC RELATIONS CODES

Having said all that about journalists' principal codes of ethics, the SPJ and RTDNA principles seem practical in comparison to the unworkably idealistic and unenforceable codes that public relations and advertising practitioners have purveyed, including those from the International Association of Business Communicators, the Better Business Bureau, and the American Association of Advertising Agencies (Christians, 1985–86; Wright, 1993). The Public Relations Society of America's (2000) ethics code illustrates some of the problems. It is a collection of contradictory prescriptions for acting in the public interest while always keeping the clients' interest foremost.

"We are faithful to those we represent, while honoring our obligation to serve the public interest," the PRSA code says, seemingly subjugating the interests of clients—or at least putting them on equal footing with those of the public. But under the "conflicts" section of its code, the PRSA says, "A member shall act in the best interests of the client or employer, even subordinating the member's personal interests." Yet under its "independence" section, the code asserts, "We provide objective counsel to those we represent. We are accountable for our actions."

Is it always possible for PR practitioners to serve two masters, the client and the public? Even if there are, theoretically, Aristotelian Golden Mean solutions to all such dilemmas in the real world, the PRSA code does not hint at how to reach them. This code, which PRSA adopted in 1988 and revised in 2000, does include helpful real-life (but anonymous) "examples of improper conduct" for each of its six major sections, but they are far from all-encompassing. "Be honest and accurate in all communications," the code commands, adding, "Avoid deceptive practices." That might not cover spin or other lies of omission, I thought, but one of the examples of improper conduct the code lists is, "Lying by omission: A practitioner for a corporation knowingly fails to release financial information, giving a misleading impression of a corporation's performance."

Well, from the Exxon Valdez oil spill of 1989 and the Enron insider trading scandal of 2001 to everyday occurrences now, the history of corporate public relations is rife with examples of practitioners who, at a minimum, did not go out of their way to disclose pertinent information that would tarnish their company. In fact, PR "media trainers" travel the world teaching executives and spokespeople how to spout the company line and stay on message, no matter what journalists ask them (Bergman, 2005). Where is the line in PRSA's ethics code between lying by omission and airing your dirty laundry in public?

Perhaps PRSA's line is the thin blue line of the law. While the Preamble to its 2000 document says, "Emphasis on enforcement of the Code has been eliminated," it goes on to say, "[T]he PRSA Board of Directors retains the right to bar from membership or expel from the Society any individual who has been sanctioned by a government agency or convicted in a court of law of an action that is in violation of this Code." But as every ethicist knows, laws are, at best, a minimum standard for ethics and at worst, an excuse for unethical behavior. Furthermore, if PRSA or the Council of Public Relations Firms has sanctioned one of its members for an ethics violation, they have not disclosed it in any of their press releases over the past five years.

ADVERTISING CODES

Even further divorced from reality is the ethics code of the American Advertising Federation (1984). It starts by stating, "Advertising shall tell the truth and shall reveal significant facts, the omission of which would mislead the public." How does that square with the industry's pervasive practice of puffery, which is the use of empty or unsupported claims, such as "unbeaten" or "award-winning" where no objective competition exists? Puffery is the technique advertisers use to try to manufacture significant distinctions in the mind of audience members between essentially identical products, such as aspirins or soaps (Preston, 1996). Its goal is to mislead the public by omitting the fact that the only true distinction between these products is lower price (which might lead to lower profits). I don't deny that the U.S. economy would suffer and many people would lose jobs in all sorts of sectors if advertisers weren't so good at creating markets for parity products. But for the AAF to claim its members are revealing all significant facts about the products they advertise is a form of ethics code puffery, if not outright hypocrisy.

Furthermore, the AAF code says, "Advertising containing testimonials shall be limited to those of competent witnesses who are reflecting a real and honest opinion or experience." How does this fit with the legions of ads in which actors play homemakers or experts or voters with an ax to grind? Ads with actors playing medical doctors were once such a common outrage that the Federal Trade Commission banned them. Now we instead are bombarded with direct-to-consumer advertising of prescription medicines featuring the disembodied voices of actors fulfilling the Food and Drug Administration's mandate to list all proven side effects. They might not claim to be someone they're not, but isn't it every ad actor's job to convince the audience they are the ideal or everyman or woman in the target market?

Last, the AAF has not updated its ethics code since 1984, which means it is silent on a whole range of new media advertising dilemmas, such as cellular ring tone scams, tracking spam, data surveillance and phishing, especially on Web sites aimed at kids.

CONCLUSION

In his half of this chapter, Gordon argues that codes of ethics can, at least, serve as a starting point—a minimum threshold—for mass media practitioners facing dilemmas. Perhaps that's possible, but show me the one that actually does. I haven't found one, so far, because media codes of ethics tend to be hegemonic exercises in control and obfuscation that relatively small committees of elites write and hand down from on-high. Gordon notes that the percentage of U.S. newspapers with a written code of ethics is at an all-time high. Yet the public's esteem for journalists is at an all-time low. That's correlation, not cause and effect, but it highlights the need for each media ethics code to move beyond empty compromises to become a true golden mean: a win-win consensus that results from lengthy discussions—in person and online—among not only the elites and owners of the media but also their employees and, most importantly, their audiences.

Even then, as with democracy, the codes themselves will not be as important and ethically rewarding as the process by which they are arrived at. Greater interaction—ideally face-to-face—between mass communicators and their audiences will help them better understand each other's goals and constraints, thereby reducing the need to rely on codes or to deploy them as shields. Complex sociological and technological dilemmas such as those facing the media require complex analyses, solutions and consensus building. Media professionals need training and practice in ethics—off- and on-deadline—as do bloggers and every other media provider. Studies have shown that advertising students who study ethics are less likely to choose unethical courses of action (Burnett et al., 2003), and PR practitioners say education is the best way to make public relations more ethical (Huang, 2001; Pratt, 1991). Gordon is right that codes of ethics can play a positive role—if they are the result of ethical analyses and consensus building—but they seldom do now, because it's too much to expect codes alone to incite ethical behavior.

KEY POINTS

- At best, ethics codes are hard to implement and often difficult to interpret. At their worst, they are impotent facades.
- Codes are too often vague and contain contradictory language.
- Journalism ethics codes are rife with problems, but the codes for the advertising and public relations fields are unworkably idealistic and unenforceable, and the AAF code has not been updated since 1984.

MERRILL: Commentary

A very definite sense of *déjà vu* falls over me as I read this controversy related to codes of ethics. I must admit, due to my writing much about this subject through the years, that I am pretty well biased *against* codes of journalistic ethics. Michael Dorsher's position, presented here with a calm, logical treatment, finds substantial and sympathetic lodging in my mind. I must admit, however, that David Gordon's rather extended advocacy of media ethics codes almost—and I say almost—sways me to his side.

Most readers of this book will probably tend toward Gordon's position. Codes of ethics are "in" these days and are said at least to help to clarify the proper thinking and action of mass communicators making moral decisions. Dorsher and many others say "No"—codes of ethics are not helpful. Gordon says they provide "ideal standards of excellence." Dorsher says they are vague and give little in the way of real standards of excellence; in addition, they are often self-contradictory. What's more, says Dorsher, a higher percentage of newspapers have codes than ever before, but public esteem for journalism is lower than ever.

Gordon quotes a president of the International Organization of Journalists as saying that codes proclaim "the elementary rules of the morality of our profession." Beside the point that journalism *is not* a "profession," this man should know that codes are hardly read by journalists and any linguistic analysis will show that they are little beyond broad generalizations and clichés that provide a few personal preferences of the code-writers. Gordon does, I think, make a good point when he says that codes stimulate debate. Indeed they do, but this does not mean that they clarify norms or create rules for journalism's "morality."

Dorsher provides the case of the failure by the *Pioneer Press* to provide reasonable guidance to a copy editor whose anti-war stance might have made him less than objective in his work. But what if reporters took *all* of their corporate and personal loyalties and values as possible interference with objective news reporting? How many stories would be written? It would seem that, as Dorsher sees it, codes of ethics do little or nothing to clarify morality—even in the pursuit of truth. How much truth? And what if it conflicts with "fairness"?

Gordon says that codes can help the public understand the workings of the media. How so? Codes may say what somebody *thinks should be done*, but the "workings" of the media certainly go beyond that. And where I think Gordon really gets into quicksand is when he seems to promote the ideas of PR pioneer Edward Bernays. "Good ethics is good business," said Bernays.

Now that's helpful! Sounds a little pragmatic—or Machiavellian—to me. How can balance and fairness be part of a program of public relations? We do not get a firm answer. And, says Gordon, it is natural for advertising to contain "puffery." Assuming we can agree on a definition, why don't advertising codes simply say: no puffery. Puffery is unethical. Can you imagine an ad agency that seriously had that in its code?

As for bloggers (and Gordon tries to get everybody in), they are simply not trained journalists, and real (or trained) journalists are more ethical than untrained journalists. True? We have no empirical evidence of this. Codes, according to Gordon, must be detailed, but not too detailed. Such a sentence shows what is wrong with the language of codes. If they are too general, they are next to meaningless. And, if they are too detailed, says Gordon, they will stifle individual reasoning. True. But don't *all* codes stifle individual reasoning?

Dorsher, it seems to me, is a little too hard on the Society of Professional Journalists' code. The present one is so far superior to the older one that it seems almost worthwhile. It is still filled with vague concepts and contradictions, but overall it evidences an attempt to provide a more helpful set of norms than most. Dorsher is a tough contender: he calls codes "impotent facades" (about as vague as "helpful freedom"). In fact, Dorsher finds nothing helpful in media codes. I do, however. They can be printed beautifully and framed and hung on the office wall. Something, whether it is read and taken seriously or not, is probably better than nothing. At least it can be considered a form of PR puffery.

The two positions presented in this chapter are catalytic and should provide the reader with some new ideas. Of course, the very fact that such a chapter can be included in a book on *media controversies* indicates that there is something imprecise and unsettled about the whole business of media ethics.

REFERENCES AND RELATED READINGS

American Advertising Federation. (1984). *Advertising Ethics and Principles*. Retrieved from www.aaf.org/default.asp?id=37 (December 13, 2007).

American Society of Newspaper Editors (ASNE, Ethics Committee). (1986–87). "Newsroom ethics: How tough is enforcement?" *Journal of Mass Media Ethics* 2(1), pp. 7–16.

Bergman, Eric. (2005). "The ethics of not answering." *Communication World*, September–October, 22: 16.

Bernays, Edward L. (1992). "The future of public relations." Talk to the convention of the Association for Education in Journalism, Montreal, Canada, August 5–8. Retrieved www.prmuseum.com/bernays/bernays_1990.html.

Black, Jay, Bob Steele, and Ralph Barney. (1995). *Doing Ethics in Journalism: A Handbook with Case Studies*, 2nd ed. Boston, MA: Allyn & Bacon.

Blake, Eugene Carson. (1966). "Should the code of ethics in public life be absolute or relative?" *The Annals of the American Academy of Political and Social Science*, January, pp. 4–11.

Blood, Rebecca. (2003). "Rebecca's pocket." Retrieved from www.rebeccablood.net/handbook/excerpts/weblog_ethics.html (January 10, 2010).

Boeyink, David E. (1994). "How effective are codes of ethics? A look at three newsrooms." *Journalism Quarterly* 71, pp. 893–904.

———. (1998). "Codes and culture at *The Courier-Journal*: Complexity in ethical decision-making." *Journal of Mass Media Ethics* 13(3), pp. 165–182.

Burnett, Melissa, Nancy Keith, and Charles Pettijohn. (2003). "An empirical analysis of factors influencing student reactions to ethical advertising dilemmas." *Marketing Education Review* 13(1), pp. 33–46.

Christians, Clifford G. (1985–86). "Enforcing media codes." *Journal of Mass Media Ethics* 1(1), pp. 14–21.

Cronin, Mary M., and James B. McPherson. (1995). "Pronouncements and denunciations: An analysis of state press association ethics codes from the 1920s." *Journalism & Mass Communication Quarterly* 72(4), pp. 890–901.

DeGeorge, Richard T. (1986). *Business Ethics*, 2d ed. New York: Macmillan.

Eaton, Tim. (2006). "Prosecutor kills himself in Texas raid over child sex." *The New York Times*, November 7. Retrieved from www.nytimes.com/2006/11/07/us/07pedophile.html, September 24, 2009.

Eggerton, John. (2007). "RTNDA asks FCC to rescind Comcast VNR fines." *Broadcasting & Cable*, November 1. Retrieved from www.broadcastingcable.com/article/CA6496474.html?rssid=193 (May 3, 2008).

Ellington, Coke. (2010). "Philip Meyer and expansion of voluntary certification of U.S. journalists." *Media Ethics*, 21(2), pp. 3, 19–23.

Fitzpatrick, Kathy R. (no date) "PRSA Code of Ethics moves from enforcement to inspiration." Unpublished paper. Retrieved from www.prsa.org/aboutUs/ethics/documents/enforcement.pdf.

Huang, Yi-Hui. (2001). "Should a public relations code of ethics be enforced?" *Journal of Business Ethics* 31(3), pp.259–270.

Hunt, Todd, and Andrew Tirpok. (1993). "Universal ethics code: An idea whose time has come." *Public Relations Review* 19(1), pp. 1–12.

Johannesen, Richard L., Kathleen S. Valde, and Karen E. Whedbee. (2008). *Ethics in Human Communication*, 6th ed. Long Grove, IL: Waveland.

Jones, J. Clement. (1980). *Mass Media Codes of Ethics and Councils*. Paris: Unesco Press.

Keith, Susan, Carol B. Schwalbe, and B. William Silcock. (2006.) "Images in ethics codes in an era of violence and tragedy." *Journal of Mass Media Ethics* 21(4), pp. 245–264.

Kruckeberg, Dean. (1993). "Universal ethics code: Both possible and feasible." *Public Relations Review* 19(1), pp. 21–31.

Kultgen, John. (1983). "Evaluating codes of professional ethics." In Wade L. Robison, Michael S. Pritchard, and Joseph Ellin, eds., *Profits and Professions: Essays in Business and Professional Ethics*. Clifton, NJ: Humana Press, pp. 225–264.

Lebacqz, Karen. (1985). *Professional Ethics: Power and Paradox*. Nashville, TN: Abingdon Press.

Marty, Robin. (2006). "About." *Minnesota Monitor*, August 21. Retrieved from www.minnesotamonitor.com/showDiary.do?diaryId=23 (May 24, 2008).

McManus, John H. (1997). "Who's responsible for journalism?" *Journal of Mass Media Ethics* 12(1), pp. 5–17.

Meyer, Philip. (2006). *Newspaper Ethics in the New Century: A Report to the American Society of Newspaper Editors*. Reston, VA: American Society of Newspaper Editors.

Miller, Dean. (2006) "The digital reach of a newspaper's code of ethics." In *Goodbye Gutenberg. Nieman Reports* 60(4). Cambridge, MA: Nieman Foundation for Journalism, Harvard University. Also available online at www.nieman.harvard.edu/reports/06–4NRwinter/index.html.

Nordenstreng, Kaarle, ed. (1995). *Reports on Media Ethics in Europe*. Tampere, Finland: Department of Journalism and Mass Communication, University of Tampere, Series B 41/1995.

Online News Association. (2003). *A Blogger's Code of Ethics*, April 15. Retrieved from www.cyberjournalist.net/news/000215.php (March 10, 2010).

Pratt, Cornelius. B. (1991). "Public relations: The empirical research on practitioner ethics." *Journal of Business Ethics* 10(3), pp.229–236.

Preston, Ivan L. (1996). *The Great American Blowup: Puffery in Advertising and Selling*. Madison, WI: University of Wisconsin Press.

Public Relations Society of America [PRSA] (2000). Code of Ethics. Retrieved from www.prsa.org/aboutUs/ethics/preamble_en.html (December 13, 2007).

RTNDA. (no date). "Ethics: Code of ethics and professional conduct." Retrieved from www.rtdna.org/pages/media_items/code-of-ethics-and-professional-conduct48.php?g=36?id=48 (March 24, 2010).

RTNDA. (no date). "Ethics: Guidelines for use of non-editorial video and audio." Retrieved from www.rtnda.org/pages/media_items/guidelines-for-use-of-non- editorial-video-and-audio250.php (December 13, 2007).

Seib, Charles B. (1981). "Ethics: Many questions, few right or wrong answers." *Presstime*, February, pp. 4–10.

Sill, Melanie. (2007). "N&O's decision to identify accuser was made with care." Raleigh, NC, *The News & Observer*, April 12. Retrieved from www.newsobserver.com:80/1185/story/563049.html (December 13, 2007).

Stelter, Brian. (2008). "NBC settles with family that blamed a TV investigation for a man's suicide." *The New York Times*, June 26. Retrieved from www.nytimes.com/2008/06/26/business/media/26nbc.html?_r=1&oref=slogin (September 24, 2009).

Woodward, Bob. (2005). *The Secret Man: The Story of Watergate's Deep Throat*. New York: Simon & Schuster.

Wright, Donald K. (1993). "Enforcement dilemma: Voluntary nature of public relations codes." *Public Relations Review* 19(1), pp. 13–20.

Tools for Ethical Decision-Making

William A. Babcock, A. David Gordon, and John Michael Kittross

INTRODUCTION

"MEDIA ethics: isn't that an oxymoron?" This question is one that anyone working in this area has encountered numerous times. One is hard pressed to consider media ethics any more of a contradiction, however, than ethics in other professions. The Roman Catholic Church has been plagued in recent years with ethics scandals involving sexual misbehavior by priests. Most law schools have instituted mandatory ethics classes due to the public's perception that lawyers are willing to go to any lengths to win cases without paying much attention to the public welfare. Physicians continue to grapple with a wide range of ethical conundrums, not the least of which is whether the medical profession should condone physician-assisted suicides.

But all of these institutions, including the mass media, are *trying* to act ethically. What makes media (and particularly journalism) ethics muckups appear more egregious than those in other professions stems from the omnipresence of the media, and the fact that the media regularly report—as they should—on their own failings. Even though the worst (e.g., Janet Cooke, Jayson Blair, Stephen Glass) episodes are exceptions to the practice of most journalists, they have been so prominently discussed and covered in the media that these professional missteps take on a life of their own and often overshadow the good work being done by other journalists and media professionals in the United States and around the globe.

When *ethical lapses* occur, the media lose credibility. And when credibility is lost, the media audience is likely to distrust and stop using that media outlet for its news, information or entertainment. When this occurs, the "marketplace of ideas" and a democracy comprised of informed citizens are at risk, and persuasive communication will suffer.

Hence, media professionals of all kinds need to act regularly and systematically in an ethical manner such that the public will have little reason to distrust the media and wish to "kill the messenger" whose credibility has been self-destroyed. How media professionals and mass media students address and deal with ethical issues is key to improving the mass media and to showing the public that the media are responsible. The more consistently media professionals approach ethical issues, the greater the chance that there will be fewer contradictory outcomes, and media audiences will come to see that similar principles and practices are being adhered to in the public's interest.

While there are many approaches that can aid the practitioner by making the ethics decision-making process more consistent, we selected the following models and processes as effective approaches in this regard. They are intended to provide a number of different "how to do it" schemes, applications and interpretations, and to make "doing media ethics" less of a mystery and more of an everyday behavior. Some are complex, and possibly hard to apply when faced with a deadline (game theory, for example); you may already be familiar with others (e.g., the Society of Professional Journalists' code). Any one may possibly turn out to be "just the right model" to use in a given situation—and, just as likely, will be of little or no value in a different situation or to a different person.

We urge you *not* to immediately adopt one of these models and discard the others. Each of them has its own benefits and drawbacks, and we hope that you will find those that seem to "speak" to you. We hope, also, that you won't be afraid to try out and perhaps adopt other models as your ethical understanding matures.

When you are next faced with an ethical problem or dilemma—or an ethics class assignment—try out several of these approaches. We think you'll be glad you did.

POTTER BOX

The Potter Box is a "circular" decision-making process developed by Ralph Potter, a Harvard Divinity School professor of social ethics. The Potter Box has four parts that media practitioners may find particularly useful in deadline situations, while at the same time it is inherently more complex—not only in its specific categories but also in its requirement that any user of this model repeatedly go back and forth between and among its various points. The Potter Box is not limited to journalism, but may be used in a variety of ethics-related scenarios, reflecting Potter's belief that these four categories are inherent in all ethical dilemmas.

The Potter Box approach requires the user to:

1 Define the ethical issue at hand, i.e., the facts that define the ethical situation.
2 Identify his/her personal and general (professional) values.
3 Consider different ethical principles, and choose among them.
4 Choose among loyalties, which may be in conflict.

The Potter Box is a way of going beyond the first level (what John Merrill characterized in his opening Overview as the *instinctive* level) of ethics. It aims at reaching a justifiable conclusion that can take you to the higher ethical levels of *custom* or *conscience*. It approaches issues from a social ethics perspective, where not just individual but also institutional questions must be dealt with.

In the graphic model on p. 192, the top two compartments in the Potter Box (defining the ethical issue and choosing among competing loyalties) are sociological in nature; they deal with what's at stake in external, real-life situations. The bottom two (values and ethical principles) are philosophical and deal with internal, reflective approaches to those external aspects of the analysis. Working through all four compartments should bring together both social and individual ethics concerns and lead to a reasoned conclusion—not by any means the *only* possible conclusion, but certainly one that goes beyond "impressions" or assumptions or "gut feelings" and allows the decision-maker to explain *why* the specific ethics choices were made.

The left side of the Potter Box (definition and values—for our purposes, both personal and *professional* values) deals with "what is" and requires descriptive analysis: what are the facts of the situation, the choices available, and the bases for making those choices? The sections on the right side (principles and loyalties) deal with "what ought to be" and require normative or critical analysis. The key is to go through the process to the "loyalties" box, which should get one thinking about the *implications* of an ethical decision.

Using the Potter Box methodology should help people facing ethics dilemmas—in the classroom or on the job—to recognize issues and frame them coherently. It should assist in developing analytical reasoning processes and in stimulating the "moral imagination" to translate ethical principles into applied ethics decisions. Applied ethics (i.e., relating real-life situations to moral values) *should* result from interplay between sociological factors (the top two boxes in the model) and philosophical ones (the lower two).

At times, it can become all too easy to reach incomplete conclusions by using only the two left-hand boxes—the definition and values quadrants—to analyze a situation as it exists, but ignoring the boxes on the right side (principles and loyalties). This would remove the possibility of looking beyond the immediate situation to consider options that might be suggested by various ethicists ethical principles. In essence, it would put up a roadblock to taking an idealistic "what ought to be" look at the problem.

USING THE POTTER BOX

Once one has carefully defined the facts of the situation, it's time to move on to the values section. We need to determine with equal care what values are included, and *why they matter*. It's important to be explicit at this stage about both our positive values *and* our biases. The values can be professional, and/or very personal ones—aesthetic, social/cultural, religious, familial—and to some degree they pervade everything we do, consciously or unconsciously. It's fine to list several values, and it's a good idea to make sure that you include more than just professional values here, since restricting yourself to them could lead to ethics decisions that wind up making you uncomfortable on a personal level.

For example, think about balancing the professional value of informing the public with the personal value of compassion for vulnerable participants in a situation. Or about balancing the professional value of preventing damage to your PR client's image with the personal value of truth-telling. These pairs of values are not necessarily incompatible with each other—and we suggest that you may be more likely to reach an ethical decision that

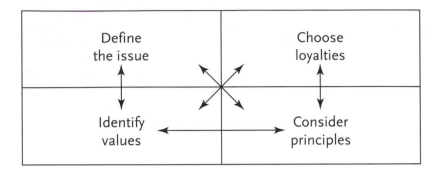

FIGURE 5.1 Potter Box (after Ralph B. Potter, Jr.)

you can live with if neither half of a pair is discarded as you move from the values to the ethical principles quadrant. If you go through the Potter Box process more than once, you may be able to reconcile potentially conflicting values based on which ethical principles you choose to emphasize, and/or which loyalties you see as paramount. (Or, it may become clearer to you which of the conflicting values is really *more* important to you.)

In the third of the four sections, you can draw on one or more of the ethicists and ethical theories that John Merrill discussed in his "Overview of Theoretical Foundations for Media Ethics". Until you gain experience and a feeling of comfort with this process, you may want to rely on one of the more often used theories—Aristotle/Confucius and the harmony/ balance/middle ground approach; Kant's theory of duty; utilitarianism's stress on results and consequences that benefit the most people; the Judeo-Christian "love thy neighbor" approach; or Rawls's rights/justice and "protect the weakest" perspective. As you become more practiced, you may well be comfortable using more than one of these approaches in the same situation, and/or bringing in other ethicists whose focus appeals to you—the feminist "ethics of care" approach of Carol Gilligan and Nel Noddings comes to mind, as does the communitarian perspective. Ethics decision-makers over the years have drawn on a wide range of theories and theorists, as disparate as Lawrence Kohlberg's moral development approach or Ayn Rand's ethical egoism. Be aware, however, that some ethicists believe that Rand's "view that everyone ought to promote his or her own self-interests" lacks "coherence as an ethical theory" and clashes with "the emphasis on social responsibility in the Potter Box model" (see Christians et al., 2009, p. 28, footnote 11).

Finally, in the fourth box (loyalties), the key questions are "who benefits?" or "to whom (or what) are you ultimately loyal?" Or, "who are you trying to serve or be responsible to?" There will almost always be multiple answers to these questions, especially on the first circuit through the Potter Box's four segments. Some of the answers may include the public in general, your immediate audience, your employer, your fellow employees, others working in your field (in this book's context, that would include public relations, advertising, journalism or entertainment), the people you're reporting on, your client(s), *and* yourself and your own moral values. As you sort out the hierarchy of your loyalties, and couple that with your basic personal and/or professional values and with your preferred ethicist(s), some answers may begin to emerge—and the process may begin to become second nature.

LET'S USE AN EXAMPLE . . .

Suppose you work for an integrated marketing PR/advertising agency, which has an automobile manufacturer for a client. You are part of a team tasked with developing a marketing plan for a newly designed convertible. It will be an expensive campaign, and the company plans to piggy-back some institutional (corporate image) messages on the convertible campaign.

One night, a good friend who works for an independent testing organization tells you, as a matter you might find of interest, that each of the three convertibles that his organization tested that week had left some unanswered questions about its handling and safety on rough roads in bad weather, indicating a possible (but not proven) design flaw.

The next day, another friend—a foreman at the automobile manufacturer's assembly plant on the edge of town—mentions how pleased he and his co-workers were at the word from management that they were going to start producing convertibles at a maximum rate, and that there weren't going to be any last-minute design changes to slow things down.

The preceding paragraph contains most of the facts that belong in the first quadrant of your Potter Box. But there's one more. You're also aware that the auto manufacturer is planning to close this plant unless it can be utilized profitably. Are there ethical issues here? Of course! Your firm (and the manufacturer) might find themselves in the PR quagmire that Toyota was in during 2009–10—a concern with pragmatic as well as ethics overtones. You, as a member of the marketing team, will bear some responsibility for your agency's role in selling these cars (which could cost buyers a lot of money at insurance-buying and trade-in time) and, possibly, at least moral responsibility for luring buyers into the showrooms, where (should the convertible prove truly dangerous) they would face an unanticipated risk.

In the second quadrant of the Potter Box, you need to list the *values* you might find at stake. These could range from loyalty to your agency and its client, to not covering up a potential flaw (i.e., truth-telling), to conflicting concerns for the jobs at the assembly plant and for preventing (possible) harm to the buyers of the convertible. Not to mention concern for your reputation, and for your career. (And you can probably come up with a few more values, as well.)

At this point, you can move on to *ethical principles*, and these might include the following, among others:

- Machiavelli would tell you to shut up and sit down.
- Kant, Rawls and others would want to avoid harm to individual humans—even if no causal link to potential danger has yet been proven.
- Utilitarianism wants the most happiness for the most people—but what is that here? Keeping the jobs that the plant provides or making sure that convertible buyers aren't exposed to possible dangers?
- An Aristotelian "middle ground," which would suggest delaying the campaign pending further information.

Finally, where do your *loyalties* lie (and how should that term be defined)? There are many possibilities: Your agency and its employees? Potential customers for the car? The manufacturer, whose reputation and business could suffer from either a premature campaign for a car that proves to have problems *or* a delayed campaign for one that works "as advertised"? The automobile or advertising industries? Your friend who works there? Your family (at least insofar as they need you to bring in a steady income)? Yourself (for instance, a desire to do no harm to individuals and the guilt that would accompany such harm, while also making sure you are attractive to potential future employers)? These are not all mutually exclusive loyalties, and there certainly are other individuals, groups or institutions who could fit in here.

Note that there is no statement here that the car is definitely unsafe. If that *were* the case, how might the entries in the Potter Box quadrants change? Similarly, how would the analysis change if the person who tipped you off had been a paid consultant for a competing auto manufacturer? Or if this person were an experienced automobile expert who "wrote the book" on the safety of convertibles?

You may find it helpful to go through the Potter Box cycle a second or third time, to pare down the lists you've compiled in each of the boxes the first time through. This may be especially helpful—taking your values and loyalties into account—which ethical theory works best in dealing with the various factors in this situation. So might going back and forth among the quadrants. If people within an organization disagree, it may be particularly useful to go through the process more than once. One purpose of the Potter Box is to identify the sources of such disagreements and to pin down from which quadrant they originate. In the process, it may be possible to sharpen the ongoing discussions (or debates) and, at worst, reach an agreement to disagree—with civility and with tolerance for other point(s) of view.

> One purpose of the Potter Box is to identify the sources of . . . disagreements and to pin down from which quadrant they originate.

The final step in the process is what we just did—applying the results of your thought and analysis to a specific case—or perhaps using those results to set institutional policy. Using this circular method carefully should help clarify the thinking process at each step along the way, and help you understand the *reasons* behind your decision.

The Potter Box process can help you recognize and define moral issues clearly, clarify the relevant personal and professional values, choose a useful theoretical approach (or two), and determine which of the many possible loyalties are most important in a given situation. This process certainly may seem artificial at first, but as one becomes more familiar and more comfortable with it, the Potter Box can be a useful analytical tool that helps you reach an acceptable answer to an ethics issue (and realize that there are also other "acceptable" answers). Perhaps most important, it will help you answer (to yourself and to such others as your audience, your colleagues or your supervisors) *why* you reached the answer you did, and will prepare you better to "do ethics," not just think about them.

POINT OF DECISION MODEL

Mitchell Land and Bill Hornaday (2006) have used a variant of the Potter Box to construct a three-dimensional model. Theirs is in the form of a three-sided pyramid, with the bottom being the "philosophic base" and the very top being the "point of decision." It is neither the architectural language nor the pun that gives this model its strength. It is the illustration of the journey from the philosophic base in a "spiral of decision" around and around the three sides

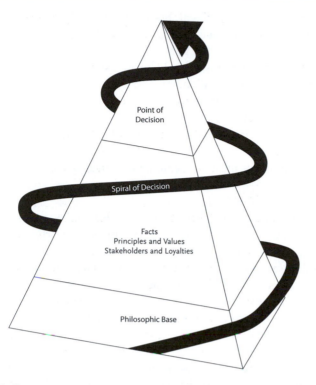

Point of
Decision

Spiral of Decision

Facts
Principles and Values
Stakeholders and Loyalties

Philosophic Base

FIGURE 5.2 Mitchell Land's Point-of Decision Pyramid Model (courtesy of Nola Kemp)

of the pyramid to its apex, climbing higher at every turn. The spiral path of this decision-making process passes along all three of the mid-level faces of the pyramid (one of which, of course, is invisible on this two-dimensional page). In words, we can describe the journey as analogous to a circuit through the Potter Box. The searcher for an ethical decision travels from a base of philosophic knowledge and theory up to and across the "Facts" (of the particular matter in question) mid-level panel and keeps moving (and climbing) along the spiral path through the other two sides of the pyramid ("Principles and Values" and "Stakeholders and Loyalties,") until the actual point of decision is reached—and the decision made. Some climbs may require several circuits of the middle sections of the pyramid, and some only a single (steep!) pass. Indeed, the combination of "Facts" with "Philosophic Base" may permit a short-cut of the entire process when under extreme time pressure—but it would mean that the Base will have influenced principles and values earlier (Land and Hornaday, 2006)."

SOCIETY OF PROFESSIONAL JOURNALISTS (SPJ) ETHICS CODE

Unlike most ethics codes, the SPJ ethics code is *inherently* process-oriented. This four-part code is especially helpful for journalists and journalism students to use in determining whether or not a proposed action is ethical, but it can also help in analyzing and learning from a case after the fact. The four touchstones of this code are:

1 ***Seek Truth and Report It***: Journalists should be honest, fair and courageous in gathering, reporting and interpreting information.
2 ***Minimize Harm***: Ethical journalists treat sources, subjects and colleagues as human beings deserving of respect.
3 ***Act Independently***: Journalists should be free of obligation to any interest other than the public's right to know.
4 ***Be Accountable***: Journalists must be accountable to their readers, listeners and viewers, and to each other.

This ethics code constitutes a "balance-driven" decision-making process that allows journalists and journalism students to weigh the seeking and reporting of truth against the goal of minimizing harm. Also, independence is balanced with accountability. The strength of this journalism-focused model is its inherent simplicity and usefulness under tight deadlines, while its weakness stems from the fact that it is so basic that it may not be well suited for more complex decision-making scenarios and case studies.

Another inherent strength of this model also is its balancing of rights with responsibilities. Items 1 and 3 really are *rights* that have their genesis in the First Amendment, while items 2 and 4 basically are ethics-focused *responsibilities*. For example, journalists have the constitutional right to be truthful in their work and the legal protection to act independently. At the same time, journalists of all sorts have the moral responsibility to minimize harm to the audience and to their sources and the ethical duty to act in an accountable fashion. Media practitioners should never focus solely on telling the truth without regard for the degree to which individuals may be harmed, nor is it an option *not* to report on an issue that could have a major impact on society simply because an individual might somehow be made to feel uncomfortable. If it becomes necessary to cause some harm in reporting on an issue of considerable importance, that decision should never be reached lightly.

In other words, it's not an issue of *either* being truthful *or* minimizing harm, but rather one of balancing the truth that needs telling with being socially responsible. For example, by using Aristotle's Golden Mean, journalists would be urged to use an accurate photo, but not necessarily the most graphic photo, especially if the graphic representation might identify an individual and thus place the subject of the photograph in danger, or if it might cause needless suffering for that individual (or for his or her family).

The SPJ ethics code is likely to be found more frequently in newsrooms than are all other codes and problem-solving models combined (except for the ubiquitous *Associated Press Libel Guide*). In part, this is because SPJ has done a superb job in promoting its model. Too, this code works well in deadline situations, balancing important issues in a quick and dirty fashion that is easily digestible and allows journalists to address a moderate number of ethics issues in any given case.

RTDNA GUIDELINES FOR AVOIDING CONFLICTS OF INTEREST

This is not the code of ethics and professional conduct of the group formerly known as the Radio-Television News Directors Association and now as Radio Television Digital News Association, which is well worth reading, and is discussed briefly in Chapter 5. Instead, this is a "how to do it" set of guidelines for decision-making, in the form of questions and discussions. (Only the questions, slightly edited and shortened, are reprinted below.) These "Guidelines for Avoiding Conflict of Interest" was distributed to the RTDNA membership in late 2008. These questions are particularly good in helping practitioners identify potential conflict of interest situations (or *perceived* conflicts).

1 Will the private actions of a journalist with a news source or newsmaker give the appearance of an unprofessional connection?
2 Will the actions of a journalist's or newsroom manager's family members with a news source or newsmaker give that same appearance?
3 Is it ever acceptable to accept gifts from a source on a story? If so, is there a monetary value limit on that gift?
4 Will you accept free admission to events you are covering even when the general public must pay for the same access?
5 Will you accept free travel from sources? If you do, how do you disclose this to the audience?
6 Will newsroom personnel be allowed to "moonlight" with interests that may be the subject of news coverage? Can on-air personalities do commercial appearances or voice-over work? What about journalists appearing as themselves in comedy movies or television shows?
7 Does the subject matter of (or approach to) a story benefit or harm the reporter, the manager, or the station? Would members of the audience perceive that a story is done for the monetary benefit of the station or any of its employees?
8 Does the station have a policy on if and how employees can participate in political campaigns? Are journalists and their managers treated differently in the policy than other station employees?
9 Is there a system in place to allow journalists and managers to recuse themselves from editorial decisions about stories from which a conflict of interest—real or perceived—may arise? Do reporters and editors have a clear picture of what constitutes a conflict of interest large enough to call for their withdrawal from a story?
10 Finally, is there a whistleblower system in the newsroom that allows anyone to point out possible conflicts of interest so that management can act on them? Should this task and authority be limited to management? Is the review of all work for possible conflicts of interest a regular part of the newsroom culture?

These guidelines go on to discuss more specific conflict of interest problems that arise from the fact that local journalists typically live and work in the community that they cover. They also deal with the possibility that a particular story that affects everyone may create *unavoidable* conflicts of interest. If that occurs, these additional questions could be asked:

1   When and how will you disclose personal connections that could result in perceptions of conflicts of interest even if managers have decided the reporter is able to cover a story? What if those connections are of a very personal nature?
2   Will you disclose connections the owners of your station have with sources and subjects of stories?
3   How will the connections above be inserted in the story? In the introduction, the tag, both, or some other way?
4   Finally, if an employee commits a violation of the station's rules regarding conflict of interest, will that violation be disclosed to the public? If so, how?

Note that most or all of these guidelines *could* produce an answer of "it depends." As mentioned in the organization's further discussion of item 5 of the guidelines, "most journalists will accept a ride in a pickup truck to the local farmer's pumpkin patch, but will they also accept a free ride on an airline showing off a new route?"

Just because these guidelines were written for the use of broadcast journalists doesn't mean that they aren't applicable to those in other media, or that specific rules promulgated by media entities—newspapers, magazines, stations, networks, etc.—don't exist. A business has the legal right to enforce its own rules, even though some of them are subject to negotiation with employees or unions. People in the media tend to have the professional need, as well as the desire, to protect their own reputations to a much greater extent than, for example, workers on a production line or behind a coffee counter.

RTDNA GUIDELINES FOR SOCIAL MEDIA AND BLOGGING

First disseminated in February, 2010, these guidelines, like those for conflicts of interest (above), are in the form of questions and answers. These guidelines also contain numerous questions for discussion in the newsroom. They deal with matters such as:

1   Truth and fairness
2   Critical questions to be asked when using content from social media or blogs
3   Accountability and transparency
4   Image and reputation.

ASK GOOD QUESTIONS

Bob Steele, while he was at the Poynter Institute in St. Petersburg, Florida, helped prepare a system that elaborates on the SPJ model while also being a bit more journalism-focused than the Kidder model (below). Like that model, it is inherently helpful in confronting more complex ethics issues, rather than in situations where there are tight deadlines. This 10-step model, often referred to as "Ask Good Questions to Make Good Ethical Decisions," includes the following:

1   What do I know? What do I need to know?
2   What is my journalistic purpose?
3   What are my ethical concerns?
4   What organizational policies and professional guidelines should I consider?
5   How can I include other people, with different perspectives and diverse ideas, in the decision-making process?
6   Who are the stakeholders—those affected by my decision? What are their motivations? Which are legitimate?
7   What if the roles were reversed? How would I feel if I were in the shoes of one of the stakeholders?
8   What are the possible consequences of my actions? Short-term? Long-term?
9   What are my alternatives to maximize my truthtelling responsibility and minimize harm?
10 Can I fully justify my thinking and my decision? To my colleagues? To the stakeholders? To the public?

(Steele, 2002)

Neither this list nor the SPJ code of ethics' four guiding principles is etched in stone. The Poynter Institute thus recommends proposing, rather than imposing, the use of these questions even as it encourages the "doing ethics" approach.

These questions can be applied equally well to ethical dilemmas in advertising, public relations or entertainment simply by substituting the proper adjective for "journalistic" in Question 2. For example, the aspirational Code of Ethics of the Public Relations Society of America focuses on professional values that include advocacy, honesty, expertise, independence, loyalty and fairness, which dovetail with values inherent in Poynter's ten questions. All of these questions—and perhaps especially numbers 3, 5 and 6—resonate not only with journalists and public relations practitioners, but also with those in advertising. As is the case with PRSA's Code of Ethics, the Advertising Code of American Business and the Standards of Practice of the American Association of Advertising Agencies also focus largely on what advertisers "shall" or "shall not" do. Accordingly, Poynter's 10 questions provide a means of converting *aspirational* codes of ethics to *operational* ones—of putting such codes to work, regardless of whether one is in journalism, public relations or advertising.

That a decision is said to have been "ethically justified" does not mean the decision will be popular. Rather, as Black, Steele, and Barney say, "justified" simply means that ethical principles have been applied in such a way that a disinterested but fully informed public would agree that the decision-maker was careful. And, in the final analysis, these authors say the "key is not to overreact, neither rigidly and blindly following codes or trade practices on the one hand nor amorally pandering on the other" (Black et al., 1999, p. 31)

GAME THEORY

"Game theory" is a much more interesting title than "a method for decision-making"—which is what it is. It is now an important approach to the study and practice of politics, international relations, diplomacy, business, economics, and similar complex fields—some more important than others (most of the recent Nobel prizes in economics have involved the skill set of "game theory"). Author John McDonald (1950) labeled it *Strategy in Poker, Business and War*.

We make many decisions in our lives: deciding on a college and a major, starting and maintaining a family, applying for and changing jobs, engaging in the political process, and dealing with the many constituencies and stakeholders on the job (supervisors, fellow employees or professionals; viewers, listeners and readers; advertisers, and so on). These and other types of decisions can be made easier (and possibly more successful or beneficial) with the use of game theory principles. Those trying to program a station, fight a war, win an election, sell something, get more air time or a byline, convince a client of the merit of an advertising campaign, write an effective story or script, or woo a member of the opposite gender are bound to be using the tenets of game theory, whether they know it or not.

Ethical decisions have much in common with other decisions. Some ("should I throw a ball or try to throw a strike in this situation?") rely on experience; some ("what is the best way to make this product rustproof?") may rely more on education and training; some ("should I bet on this poker hand?") require an ability to calculate odds; some ("should I attempt to play this concerto in the recital?") rely on skill and self-confidence; and some rely on chance or luck ("maybe we should flip a coin"). Many decisions would be better if more than one of these factors were considered. Obviously, it is possible to use experience, education and training, "the odds" (particularly when employing utilitarian principles), skill and even luck when making ethical decisions.

Although practitioners in a variety of fields (including casinos) may have used many of the principles of game theory in the past, it wasn't formally presented until the early 1950s, when John Von Neumann (whose ideas on computer architecture helped shape that field) and Oskar Morgenstern published their seminal book (Morgenstern and Von Neumann, 1953). Part of the utility of game theory is that its concepts can be extremely helpful without using any arithmetic at all—or certainly no more than can be scribbled on the back of an envelope—even though Von Neumann developed an entire branch of probability theory (called Monte Carlo mathematics) to deal with more sophisticated game theory analyses. Game theory requires attention to a checklist of factors or elements. Among them are participants (including actors and those acted upon), coalitions, rules, strategies and rewards.

In a theoretical rational choice process, a participant is confronted by a number of different, specified, mutually exclusive courses of action. To each of these is attached a set of consequences or results which are of differential value to each concerned party. The participant makes his or her choice on the basis of the most desirable (or least undesirable) of these possible consequences, which may not be obvious. There is nothing trivial about determining what consequences (including "unintended" ones) will follow each alternative, and one often is concerned with finding a *satisfactory* rather than the *best* alternative. Usually, one adopts a "minimax" strategy: minimizing one's chances of losing (or how much one could lose) and maximizing one's chances of winning. At the same time, other participants are conducting similar analyses. The devil is in the details.

It is the consideration of *all* of these factors that makes game theory exceptionally useful for making decisions in all sorts of ethical (and political, economic and other) matters. Most are extremely simple: a game has written (or unwritten) rules, and you ignore them at your peril, not only because someone might object, but also because you usually can't "win" if you ignore them. Each game has participants or players, who usually are in competition; but it frequently is useful to ally oneself with others in a coalition that ignores even long-term antagonisms to present a mutual front against a common threat.

Unlike a sporting event, each participant in these more complex games probably has a different goal. What is valuable to one may be worthless to another. Therefore, it is likely that participants will select different strategies. (Sometimes the best strategy is to have *no* strategy, or flip-a-coin chance: your opponents can't predict your behavior that way.) This is almost certainly true if the game is of the "zero-sum" type where one player will win at the expense of the other player(s). There are also "non-zero-sum" games where all can win (a successful "win-win" negotiation) or where all could lose (an atomic war). Knowing what one is facing permits a much more accurate assessment of the differential potentials of each alternative.

> Unlike a sporting event, each participant in these more complex games probably has a different goal. What is valuable to one may be worthless to another.

Although massive computer power is applied to game theory analyses by business and governments, it is possible to analyze important situations without using numbers. For example, a study of television frequency allocation policy in the United States (Kittross, 1979), and *The Politics of Broadcast Regulation* (Krasnow et al., 1982) both relied on game theory in order to deduce the strategies and goals of the various players in historical policy conflicts, and use these findings to predict the optimum strategies for future ones. This has proved to be of considerable predictive value in other issues coming before Congress and the Federal Communications Commission. In the frequency allocation study, inconsistencies in the data and rapidly shifting coalitions could best be explained by a simple (but not easy to uncover) reward structure: those "on top" had good reason for using every technique for seeking delay so as to keep making money, and this was reinforced by the FCC's political-survival (protect your backside at any cost!) ploy of trying not to step on the toes of those already active in inventing, patenting, manufacturing, and programming television. The unintended result was slower telecommunications innovation (adoption) in the United States than in some other nations.

Many media practices have evolved that actually are using game theory without ever thinking about it. Content decisions in every medium are made with the competition and potential rewards in mind. Even mass media ethical decisions often are improved after a game theory analysis, no matter how little time there is to consider the situation in those terms. In the long run, is a "scoop" worth alienating a source, or one's fellow journalists? Will "pushing the envelope" in television program content lead to government crackdowns, or is the game worth the candle in a competitive world? If the only way to get a photo is to trespass, should one violate the privacy of another? Is stretching the truth to create a good ad, or lying to get a source to talk, worthwhile? What are the rewards and penalties if one lies or doesn't lie, in journalism or in advertising? For a good or a frivolous or selfish cause? Both Kantian and utilitarian ethical principles are at play when analyzing questions like these, and they, too, can be factored into the equation.

The more one uses game theory principles, the easier it becomes, and the more valuable they appear. But this brief exposition is intended only to whet your appetite. There is a vast literature about game theory, and a number of works (e.g., McDonald, 1950; Williams, 1954) are fun besides. Try it. It works.

MEDIA ACCOUNTABILITY SYSTEMS

Claude-Jean Bertrand (2000, 2003) described general classes of media accountability systems (MAS or M*A*S) that recognize non-governmental means of inducing media to respect the ethical rules set by their professions, and bring the general public into the process. While these diverse classifications often are mechanisms used by groups rather than "tools" for individual use, they all aim to improve news media, using evaluation, monitoring, education, feedback, and communication. Essentially, the MAS fall into three groups according to their intrinsic natures:

1   Documents (printed or broadcast), including written codes of ethics, correction boxes, letters to the editor, etc.
2   People (individuals or groups), including ombudsmen, those reporting on the media from within, outside critics, etc.
3   Processes (long or short), including higher education, ethics classes, seminars for journalists, etc.

While Bertrand said "news media," he might just as well have said "mass media," as the points he makes are equally appropriate for public relations, advertising and entertainment. For example, ethics codes in the first group, outside critics in the second, and the entire third group resonate with non-journalistic mass media.

RUSHWORTH KIDDER MODEL

Rushworth Kidder's (1995) *How Good People Make Tough Choices* has produced an ethics decision-making model that is useful in analyzing mass media dilemmas and those in other fields. A more complex process than the SPJ code or the Potter Box, Kidder's model does not lend itself to ethics situations that are either inherently rather basic or where there is severe deadline pressure. When examining more complex cases in a situation with fewer time constraints, the Kidder model can be a useful mechanism that encourages the user to answer very pragmatic questions while at the same time examining ethical theories and philosophies.

The steps (or "checkpoints") suggested by Kidder (1995) include:

1   Recognizing that there *is* a *moral* issue (as distinct from issues in such other areas as aesthetics or economics), a step that requires people to *identify values* that may be in conflict.
2   Determining the actor—more specifically, is it an issue that obligates *you* to seek an ethical course of action?
3   Gathering the relevant facts, including the context.
4   Testing for right-versus-wrong issues, to make sure that this is an ethics rather than a legal issue—and if it is, asking (among other things) what your moral intuition tells you and what your mother (or any other respected moral example) would do.
5   Testing for right-versus-right paradigms—scenarios where deeply held values clash and neither one is "wrong."

6   Applying ethical principles that seem most relevant and persuasive in leading you to resolve the dilemma (utilitarian, Kantian, Rawlsian, or others).
7   Investigating the "trilemma" options—i.e., might there be a middle ground or some other third alternative available?
8   Making the decision.
9   Revisiting and reflecting on the decision.

(Kidder, 1995, pp. 180–187)

Kidder indicates that this model may be applied to a variety of dilemmas in any number of professions, including journalism. The journalism example he suggests is an editor deciding whether to print a story written by a reporter gathering information while posing as a prostitute (p. 188). An advertising example could involve an advertising director for a university newspaper pondering whether or not to continue accepting lucrative ads for legal firearms and ammunition in the student paper in the wake of shootings on various campuses across the United States. According to Kidder (p. 189), applying this model illustrates that "when you strip away the specifics and penetrate to the core values underlying [any professional] dilemmas, the resulting ethical structures lend themselves to just the sort of analysis and resolution" you find in his model. Kidder (p. 100) argues that shared values "provide the best opportunity for creating consensus," even on such volatile issues as abortion (see pp. 102–104).

As to core values, Kidder's book lists them as love, truth, fairness, freedom, unity, tolerance, responsibility and respect for life (pp. 91–92). A somewhat different list, of core values across all human cultures, was found in early 2009 on the Web site of the institute that Kidder founded. Those values, intended to apply to all human actions, included honesty and truthfulness; responsibility and accountability; fairness and acting equitably; respect and awareness of each individual's dignity; and compassion and caring (Institute for Global Ethics, 2009). This listing seems to have evolved from the institute's worldwide research asking people about "the most important moral values" for them and their future (Institute for Global Ethics, 2008).

BOK'S MODEL

Sissela Bok (1983) presents a three-step framework in *Lying: Moral Choice in Public and Private Life*. Ethics issues, according to Bok, should be examined in three steps:

1   Consulting one's conscience, or feelings, to see if an action is correct.
2   Seeking expert advice for options, or an Aristotelian Golden Mean, to an action that creates an ethical problem.
3   Conducting a discussion or forum with those involved in a dispute.

In a number of respects, Bok's model tends to synthesize portions of a few of the other models discussed so far. For instance, the first step of her model, consulting your conscience, melds the truthtelling and minimizing of harm that are the first two steps of the SPJ code and also reflect the ninth step in the Poynter model. Bok's second step, asking whether there might be another way to achieve the same goal that will at the same time not raise ethical issues, is reminiscent of Kidder's seventh step (investigate the "trilemma" options). And Bok's third step melds SPJ's call for accountability with Poynter's points 5, 6, and 7 (including others and examining the motives of, and putting yourself in the shoes of, stakeholders).

As is the case with the other models we have discussed so far, it is important to use all points in a particular process or model. For instance, Bok's model will be of limited use if you don't have a discussion with those involved in a dispute, just as the Potter Box can have a hollow ring to it if you don't consider conflicting loyalties, and the Kidder model will become flawed if you don't explore right-versus-right paradigms. As Patterson and Wilkins (2005) point out, Bok's model encourages media practitioners—whether they be in public relations, advertising, journalism or elsewhere—to consider options, and it is in pursuit of these options that mass media technique improves.

THE "SAD" PROCESS

The SAD (Situation—Analysis—Decision) ethical decision-making method, presented by Louis A. Day in his excellent ethics text (Day, 2006), was recommended as a useful way to reach a *defensible* ethical position by Fred Brown, a past president of SPJ and co-chair of its Ethics Committee. The highlights of Brown's (2008) summary were as follows:

1   Don't try to reach a decision by yourself. A meeting, even a small one, can provide the necessary consultation and feedback.
2   Describe the situation, especially "who's ultimately responsible for deciding a course of action" (the *moral agent*, who can be an individual or an institution). At this stage, the key principles and values need to be identified, whether those are truth-telling, minimizing harm, selling a product, protecting a client's reputation or any number of others (some of which may conflict with each other).
3   Decide which one or more of these principles is essential. (If this sounds to you somewhat like the "Values" section of the Potter Box, you obviously were paying attention to that material.) Finally, at this stage, "phrase the moral dilemma in the form of a question. It gives focus" (Brown, 2008).
4   In the analysis phase, you need to balance the principles and values you've identified, and weigh them against each other: for example, for the public relations practitioner, does truth-telling outweigh your obligation to keep private some details about your client's business? Bring into the mix here both "stakeholders" (who could range from "the public" to a news source whose privacy might be violated, or an advertiser who needs to increase sales dramatically to avoid going out of business) and various external factors (e.g., a policy or code of ethics within your PR agency or newsroom; or an impending opportunity to get your ad in front of a huge audience—the Oscars' ceremony or the Super Bowl, for example). "Analyze how your decision might affect each of them, and all of them," and then talk it out within the group you have assembled.

Brown, drawing on Day, suggests seeking an Aristotelian approach: "Look for a thoughtful balance, a middle ground that satisfies your basic instincts of doing the right thing." But you could just as well look for an answer that employs a utilitarian approach (finding the greatest good for the greatest number) or John Rawls's concern for protecting the weakest party or parties in the equation.

Finally, make your decision:

> Describe the best course of action for the decision-maker to take. Put it into a statement, a sentence, so you can be sure it has some logic to it. Defend that decision to the people who have been part of the discussion that brought you to this point. That will prepare you to defend it to your critics—and you can be sure that, in any ethically murky or controversial decision, there will be critics.
>
> (Brown, 2008)

BLACK's "5 Ws AND AN H" MODEL

Finally, this brief and simplified approach to "doing ethics" was put together and then refined in mid-2008 by Jay Black, long a leader in the media ethics field. This six-step approach (Black and Roberts, 2011)—which has echoes of several steps in the Poynter (Steele, 2002) model for ethics decision-making—is more comprehensive than it may appear to be at first. It requires the decision-maker to articulate the ethical problem clearly and then to ask and answer five more questions:

1   What's your problem?
2   Why not follow the rules?
3   Who wins, who loses?
4   What's it worth?
5   Who's whispering in your ear?
6   How's your decision going to look to others?

(Black and Roberts, 2011)

The first two questions, taken as a pair, are intended to determine if the problem is one of *ethics* and, if not, whether the decision-maker is willing to challenge authority and turn it into one. For the first one, Black asks you to specify in detail "what makes this situation a moral dilemma" and to make sure that you wind up with a clear question which requires an answer. The second question asks whether the issue could be dealt with simply by following institutional policies or the usual operating procedures, or by referring to such external sources of authority as laws, codes or other guidelines. If that's the case, the problem falls short of being a moral dilemma *unless* the decision-maker sees the situation as one where ethics *should* transcend the "usual" approach and is willing to go there. Only then do the remaining four questions become relevant.

In elaborating briefly on his third question, Black asks that you identify the stakeholders, the moral claims they each can advance, and the likely impact your decision will have "on each of them in the short term and in the long term." His fourth question is simply an exhortation to prioritize your (moral and other) values "and decide which one(s) you won't compromise." His fifth question asks which philosopher(s) or moral principle(s) "provides you with a moral compass" in general but particularly in the specific situation you're confronting. Finally, the last question is a shorthand way of asking you to imagine what your friends and people you respect will think about your decision-making, or how you'd feel if this showed up on Facebook (Black and Roberts, 2011)—whether this particular decision could stand what Black and others have referred to as the "test of publicity."

SIMPLIFIED NORMATIVE STANDARDS

It's not all that hard to get lost among the various decision-making techniques included in this chapter. Or, to lack the time to apply a complicated system when inflexible deadline pressures are squeezing. At such times, one often needs simple guidelines or norms. (It is partly for this reason that journalists and other communicators tend to "talk shop" and conduct post-mortems on stories and programs so extensively when relaxing after a hard day of making ethical and other decisions.)

What are some of these guidelines? The first, of course, is "truth," which is discussed at length in Chapter 3. Although "the truth, the whole truth, and nothing but the truth" is often hard to achieve, it also is hard to go very far wrong when keeping that concept in the forefront of one's mind when writing a story, a news release or an ad.

Another is "transparency." This "buzz word" refers to making sure that your audience is aware of how you go about whatever your media activities may be. This normally requires a reporter to identify him- or herself, and renders "hidden camera" or "ambush" journalism problematic, to say the least.

A third is "accountability," which implies the willingness to admit errors or short-comings, in some detail. It also precludes stonewalling, failing to apologize or explain errors, and the like.

The principles of *transparency* and *accountability* as starting points for ethical analysis were stressed in 2008 by Fred Brown, the SPJ past president and Ethics Committee co-chair. To restore their diminished credibility, news media

> need to pay more attention to being accountable. They need to tell their readers why they do what they do. They should be able to defend their decisions and be as open as possible about the process they use to make those decisions.
>
> (Brown, 2008)

He could just as well have mentioned public relations and advertising practitioners, who have the same need to tell their audiences (and clients) why they make the decisions they do, and be able to defend those decisions when necessary. This *transparency* concept fits the ethical decision-making process very well. Whatever model(s) you decide to use, you still must be able to explain and defend *how* and *why* you reached your decision—to others, but also to yourself.

A recently developed normative model, combining much of the above, is the "TAO of journalism" invented by John Hamer, president of the Washington News Council. TAO, in addition to being translated as "the way" in a religion bearing the same name, stands here for the criteria of "transparency, accountability, openness". This model was created when Hamer, a professional journalist for many years, noticed that journalists demanded that those they cover be transparent, accountable and open, but there was no reciprocal obligation.

The "TAO Pledge" would require individual or organizational agreement to be:

- *Transparent:* to disclose fully who they are, their journalistic mission and their guiding principles. This includes making information available on the background of the editorial staff, expertise and experience, and listing advertisers, donors and any other support received. Any other potential conflicts of interest will also be disclosed.
- *Accountable:* factual errors will be admitted and corrected (or at least clarified) promptly and publicly, and what caused the error will be explained fully. If appropriate, a follow-up story will be written to put the original material in better context. In short, a little humility will be shown.
- *Open:* opportunities to engage in public dialogue will be given to the other side(s) of the issue when there are credible differences of opinion or challenges to the organization's point of view, and opposing views will be sought out. It will be made clear when opinion and commentary, rather than news reporting, are being put forth, and comment and feedback will be invited.

Hamer, who runs one of the few news councils in the United States, thought that journalism would be more trusted if it followed these rules. So, something like the *Good Housekeeping* magazine seal of approval—used by generations of home-makers in making their purchasing decisions—was designed and publicized in 2010. Use of these standards and adoption of the Seal of Journalism was to be voluntary and unenforced by any outside organization. This would not require adherence to any particular code (see Chapter 5) but if one was being followed, that should be stated; if not, that also should be declared. If the seal users consistently violate their public pledge, they would be asked by the other users to stop using it—the reason why it is a registered trademark. (For further information, go to www.taoofjournalism.org). Whether this seal will be adopted by the media, and used by the public, is still unknown, but it is a unique kind of media accountability system (M*A*S) and was well received, particularly by those connected with newer media, at a "Journalism That Matters" conference in early 2010.

CONCLUSION

In applying these, or any other decision-making models or processes, to a pertinent media issue or case study, it is best to assess the philosophy or theory or guideline you believe is most logically applicable to that situation. It may be something as philosophical as Kantian absolute rules, or as pragmatic and universal as "Don't use the excuse 'Everybody was doing it'" and "Don't rely on 'But we used the money for good purposes' either" (Franke and Eisenberg, 2007).

The decision-making model you choose ultimately will be not only a reflection on the issue at hand, but also a reflection on you. One's leanings—whether they be, for example, inherently communitarian or individually focused—will be reflected in the models or processes one favors. And as an individual matures and gets more comfortable with his or her own moral philosophy, that person likely will merge aspects of the preceding process models with lessons learned elsewhere to create an individualized ethics problem-solving approach.

As you become more adept at dealing with ethics issues and case studies, two things likely will occur. First, you will tend to use some of the preceding models, and at the same time disregard others. You might also combine aspects of more than one of them. As you become more familiar with particular models, however, be sure that you are not disregarding others that might be especially well suited to a particular case!

Second, you may well come up with your own model—or at least a model that addresses certain aspects of ethics issues you find to be particularly important—and be able to articulate it when discussing an ethical problem with colleagues or family. As an example, William Babcock uses the following steps:

1   Define the ethics issue.
2   Articulate your "gut" reaction.
3   Balance the right to tell the truth with the responsibility to minimize harm.
4   Examine your loyalties.
5   Include other people in the decision-making process.
6   Analyze how you would feel were the roles reversed and you were in the shoes of one of the stakeholders.
7   Make a decision, and revisit the decision (before applying it, if possible).

As you can see, this approach borrows flagrantly from steps of other particularly useful models. Regardless of whether you prefer to use an established model or devise your own problem-solving process, it's important that you be *consistent*. Inconsistency will lead to applying different criteria in similar circumstances and thus will likely keep you from coming up with a process that can be easily replicated. Without replicability, not only will you be inconsistent, but also you will be spending an inordinate amount of time analyzing a case—a luxury that few mass media professionals will ever have.

Finally, regardless of which model you use—an established model or one of your own—you constantly need to pay attention to being balanced (Aristotle), to your duty to be responsible (Kant), to the benefits of empathy (Rawls), to the greater good of the community at large (Mill), and so on. Infusing your decision-making process with the theories of such philosophers will both enrich your thinking and help safeguard you from making trivial ethical decisions that are merely situational or relativistic.

REFERENCES AND RELATED READINGS

Bertrand, Claude-Jean. (2000). *Media Ethics and Accountability Systems*. New Brunswick, NJ: Transaction.
——. (2003). *Accountability Systems*. Cresskill, NJ: Hampton.

Black, Jay, Bob Steele, and Ralph Barney. (1999). *Doing Ethics in Journalism: A Handbook with Case Studies*, 3rd ed. Boston, MA: Allyn & Bacon.

Black, Jay and Chris Roberts. (2011). *Doing Ethics in Media: Theories and Practical Applications*. New York: Routledge.

Bok, Sissela. (1983). *Lying: Moral Choice in Public and Private Life*. New York: Vintage.

Brown, Fred. (2008). "SAD formula can turn happy ethical results." Retrieved from www.spj.org/rrr. asp?ref=4&t=ethics (June 19, 2008).

Christians, Clifford G., Mark Fackler, Kathy Brittain McKee, Peggy J. Kreshel, and Robert H. Woods, Jr. (2009). *Media Ethics: Cases and Moral Reasoning*, 8th ed. Boston, MA: Pearson/Allyn & Bacon.

Day, Louis A. (2006). *Ethics in Media Communications: Cases and Controversies*, 5th ed. Belmont, CA: Thomson, Wadsworth.

Franke, Ann H., and Meyer Eisenberg. (2007). "10 rules for avoiding conflicts of interest." *The Chronicle of Higher Education*, October 12, p. B-20.

Institute for Global Ethics. (2008). "Frequently asked questions (FAQs)." Retrieved from www.global ethics.org/about/faq.htm (August 2, 2008).

——. (2009). "Values." Retrieved from www.globalethics.org/mission-and-values.php (February 17, 2009).

Kidder, Rushworth. (1995). *How Good People Make Tough Choices*. New York: William Morrow.

Kittross, John M. (1979). *Television Frequency Allocation Policy in the United States*. New York: Arno Press. (Doctoral dissertation, University of Illinois, 1960.)

Kohlberg, Lawrence. (1981). *The Philosophy of Moral Development: Moral Stages and the Idea of Justice*. New York: Harper & Row.

Krasnow, Erwin G., Lawrence D. Longley, and Herbert A. Terry (1982). *The Politics of Broadcast Regulation*, 3rd ed. New York: St. Martin's Press.

Lambeth, Edmund B. (1992). *Committed Journalism: An Ethic for the Profession*, 2nd ed. Bloomington and Indianapolis, IN: Indiana University Press.

Land, Mitchell, and Bill Hornaday, eds. (2006). *Contemporary Media Ethics: A Practical Guide for Students, Scholars and Professionals*. Spokane, WA: Marquette.

McDonald, John. (1950). *Strategy in Poker, Business and War*. New York: Norton.

Morgenstern, Oskar, and John Von Neumann. (1953). *Theory of Games and Economic Behavior*. Princeton, NJ: Princeton University Press.

Patterson, Philip, and Lee Wilkins. (2005). *Media Ethics: Issues and Cases*, 5th ed. New York: McGraw Hill.

Potter, Ralph B. (1972). "The logic of moral argument" in *Toward a Discipline of Social Ethics* (ed. Paul Deats). Boston: Boston University Press, pp. 93–114.

Radio-Television News Directors Association. (2008). "Guidelines for avoiding conflict of interest." Retrieved from www.rtdna.org. Reprinted in *Media Ethics* 2009, 20(2), pp. 8–9.

Radio Television Digital News Association. (2010). "Social media and blogging guidelines." Retrieved from www.rtdna.org. Reprinted in *Media Ethics* 2010, 21(2), pp. 12–13.

Rest, James, Darcia Narvaez, Muriel Bebeau, and Stephen Thoma. (1999). *Postconventional Moral Thinking: A Neo-Kohlbergian Approach*. Mahwah, NJ: Lawrence Erlbaum Associates.

Shubik, Martin. (1954). *Readings in Game Theory and Political Behavior*. Garden City, NY: Doubleday.

Society of Professional Journalists. (no date) *SPJ Code of Ethics*. Retrieved from www.spj.org/ethicscode.asp (March 21, 2010).

Steele, Bob. (2002). "Ask these 10 questions to make good ethical decisions." Poynteronline. Retrieved from www.poynter.org/column.asp?id=36&aid=4346 (August 13, 2002).

Sternberg. Robert. (2009). "A new model for teaching ethical behavior." *The Chronicle of Higher Education*, April 14, pp. B14–15.

Williams, J. D. (1954). *The Compleat Strategyst*. New York: McGraw-Hill.

Part Three

Overarching Problems

Chapter 6

New Technologies and Techniques: New Ethics?

THE difficult tasks of adapting novel technologies and techniques to communication—and vice versa—are hardly new. Writing itself was a dramatic technological innovation thousands of years ago for people who previously could communicate only as far as their voices could carry. The printing press—enabling the rapid reproduction of written words and, later, images—spread around the world a little more than 500 years ago. Electrical technology first was used for (virtually) instant messaging, in the form of the telegraph, in the mid-1800s. Mass popular media such as radio and motion pictures are entering just their second century; your grandparents may well remember when television first entered their homes.

In the 21st century, we find ourselves needing to adjust to an entire family of new devices and ways to use them. As we move away from analog media and begin to harness the interconnectivity and ubiquity of digital technology, we are continually adapting our communication products and processes, not least in the way we think about them. Buying and mastering new gadgets is only a small part of this ongoing story of human ingenuity in finding new ways to create, exchange, and store messages.

However, there are continuities, as well. The broad purposes of mediated communication—surveillance of the environment, persuasion, and entertainment, among others—remain much the same. So do many of the more everyday uses of new communication technologies for the people who adopt them, including journalists. For instance, social media such as Twitter and Facebook, or mobile devices such as smartphones or portable tablets—or a host of other continually evolving systems, networks, devices, and programs—are used in much the same way, and for the same basic purposes, as traditional or "legacy" media. Twitter, for example, may seem to have more in common with interpersonal communication than with the mass media, yet the "micro blog" format is now widely used by traditional media outlets to obtain, create, and promote their content. The Associated Press recently created the position of "manager of social networks and news engagement" to oversee the wire service's efforts to locate social media sources as well as to use the platforms to promote AP stories.

But if the uses and purposes are recognizable, what about the core ethical principles of communication? Do they change as ever-newer technologies emerge and capture the imagination of both journalists and the public? We suggest that as these new communication forms compete for our attention and our support and squabble between themselves and older broadcast media over bandwidth, they require us to take fresh looks at ethical standards that may—or may not—draw on more traditional ones.

Indeed, all technological changes through the centuries have presented ethical choices and decisions about what and how to communicate. And every technological innovation has adopted not only some of the content but also at least part of the ethic of its predecessors.

When the oral tradition gave way to writing, the new medium's permanency required a revised ethic, even though some ethical principles of good story-telling (such as getting names right) remained important. When printing took over from one-copy-at-a-time scribes, the ethics of correction and attention to detail took on new meaning and significance, even though the basic purposes of narrative and information dissemination remained the same.

More recently, an emphasis on the accurate depiction of facts was brought to the fore by the speed of the transcontinental telegraph when it replaced the slower postal services, which could take weeks or even months to deliver a message that had to be physically carried from place to place. But the need for accuracy in communication did not originate with the telegraph, nor has it become obsolete today. Digital recording, whether of images or sounds, differs in many technical respects from analog recording processes, but the need for honesty in representing what was seen or heard remains unchanged.

As the Internet grows, spurring the feverish invention of additional services and devices designed to generate profits from this vast information reservoir, we may still refer to "new" media. But we have already seen that the *purposes* of communication remain much the same and so does the *content* itself, including its formats and styles. It can be argued that the difference between Twitter and spam is only in the intent of the message sender. The content of plays performed in a theater—a technique itself "borrowed" from story-telling in person, in pageantry, and later, in print—became the subject of motion pictures, radio, and then television broadcasting; such content now appears in video games and can be accessed on such personal devices as iPods. And of course, the news provided by newspapers or magazines appears online as well as in print, just as gossip among your friends can be shared through a computer screen or a cell phone—or over a cup of coffee at your favorite table. Similarly, editing is editing—whether done by pen on paper or by cursor on computer, whether of words or pictures or sounds or magnetic pulses—and the same basic ethical standards should apply.

Possibly the greatest effect of our newer, cheaper, and faster devices—from personal printers to portable phones—is that an ever-greater proportion of the public now participates in the online distribution of information and, arguably, should share the ethical standards that professionals previously saw as their special province. However, this spread of *capability* and (we hope) *responsibility* reflects the past, as well. A few centuries ago, just a tiny minority could read or write; before the telephone, only those who knew Morse Code could directly use electrical communication.

As we evaluate the ethics of today's emerging technologies and techniques, it is crucial to remember how much they have absorbed from the past. Individuals with "new" ideas for content, products, or services on the Web don't have to start from scratch; they can see if earlier ideas can be transferred or transformed. It would take a change as drastic as contact with a civilization from another planet or direct mind-to-mind communication to require something completely different in human-to-human communication.

What ethical principles should be applied to these "newer-in-form-but-not-in-concept" communication technologies? What past formulations of communication ethics are most applicable in this environment? And what new ethical formulations might be developed, after learning some of the (perhaps unintended) consequences of the emerging technologies and returning to the philosophical bases of communication ethics found in John Merrill's Overview?

We'll discuss ethical concerns about online advertising and persuasion in Chapter 12; here, we focus primarily on ethical uncertainties that have emerged as news and information move into new channels of dissemination. Neither Jane B. Singer nor Michael Dorsher thinks the ethical standards that have permeated media forms for hundreds of years should be thrown out just because we have labeled something as "new." However, they have drawn the line at different places. While the specifics of ethical behavior in this digital environment are open to debate, there may be less controversy over online ethics than there is over some of the other topics in this book. Or perhaps the controversies simply have not yet become apparent. After all, it is the readers of this book—not its writers—who will, over their careers, be the ones shaping and refining the digital revolution's ethical standards.

In this chapter, Singer details her belief that the basic ethical charges placed on journalism (and the purposes of most ethical systems) should and do apply to the new media—honesty, respect for others, independence, and accountability. But these "old" goals must be rethought and revised to apply effectively to networked media forms and users who lack a journalism background. She suggests that as the networked "audience" increasingly becomes part of the content-generating process, such additional requirements as transparency become more important. Dorsher maintains that the ethical principles or guidelines long in use can be applied with minimal revision, but must become more widespread to keep up with the spread of content generators. He stresses the need for ethics training of "amateur" journalists and touches briefly on whether hegemony (the concept that the people in power always win in negotiations about power) is increased in an online media environment. Like Singer, he also notes the great need for openness, transparency, and disclosure for both individuals and institutions using the new communication channels. Neither author applies the guidelines to every specific ethics dilemma; those applications are purposely left for you to work out.

Clearly, the "final" version of this chapter's discussion is a work in progress—work you will be the ones to continue. Act wisely!

SINGER: An interactive network, to which anyone can contribute and in which information is exchanged rather than simply delivered, creates ethical issues that go beyond those faced by professionals working in traditional media environments.

It is comforting, and therefore tempting, to say that "journalism is journalism" and so the ethics that guide journalists and inform their work in one medium should also be just fine for all the rest. Similarly, one might suggest that advertisers, public relations practitioners, or people in the entertainment industries all create messages that serve particular needs in our society—and those needs don't change just because technology does.

Yet I think the differences in media do matter, not because they change human needs or human nature but because they change how we humans interact. And ethics is essentially all about interactions: the ways in which we deal with one another. Social life in a network involves new types of relationships and connections, including some that pose challenges for media professionals.

CONSISTENCY . . . AND CHANGE

The list of principles and guidelines for, say, broadcast journalists (as put forward by the Radio Television Digital News Association) contain pretty much the same key points as those for newspaper journalists (from the American Society of News Editors) and the umbrella Society of Professional Journalists (SPJ) that encompasses both. The core ideas that journalists use to highlight their special way of serving the public—telling the truth, safeguarding independence, striving for fairness, and so on—are the same. Many of those principles, notably a commitment to truth-telling, can be found in codes of journalism ethics all over the world (Cooper, 1990; see also the national codes of ethics and rules of conduct for journalists, collected at http://ethicnet.uta.fi/codes_by_country).

Many of the same principles guide the work of other media professionals, as well. The Public Relations Society of America code of ethics, for example, stresses fairness and independence; it also pledges adherence to "the highest standards of accuracy and truth in advancing the interests of those we represent and in communicating with the public." The American Marketing Association code states its members "will tell the truth in all situations and at all times," while at the top of the American Advertising Federation's list of principles is the statement that "advertising shall tell the truth and shall reveal significant facts, the omission of which would mislead the public." (See Chapter 5 for a full discussion of ethics codes.)

These concepts are no less valuable now. In fact, they may even be *more* valuable. Here's why: When the ability to disseminate information was limited to those who owned the printing press or the broadcast transmitter, making information available to the public was one of the communication professional's main functions. Today, the availability of information isn't an issue in our society. Virtually anyone can be a publisher, and information is in overwhelmingly abundant supply—along with what seems to be equally abundant misinformation and disinformation.

That means people need some way to judge which is which and to figure out whom, among all these information providers, they can trust. Being an ethical communicator in this world comes to rest more solidly than ever on the decisions that are made as information is gathered, assessed, and converted into media messages—a news story, a press release, an advertisement, and so on—and, importantly, how easy it is to see what went into those decisions. Ethics, one might say, is what distinguishes trustworthy communicators from the millions of other "publishers" in today's vast media network, and transparency is what allows us to make these distinctions.

But it's not quite so simple, is it? Journalists may have a commitment to truth-telling, but that does not mean they have a monopoly on the truth—or that they always meet that commitment. They may try to be fair and accurate in their stories, but there is never enough space to include the voices of everyone involved or affected. Even with the best of intentions—and the moral strength to follow them amid the pressures created by deadlines, downsizing, and doctors of spin—21st-century journalists can and do face a great many ethical challenges.

Here is another way to put it: Commitments to truth-telling, independence, and other ethical precepts are indisputably necessary in a networked environment. But, at least as currently understood and interpreted by most media workers, they may not be sufficient. That is, they may not be enough to guide us as we move into new territory—"new," I would suggest, not only as in "uncharted" but also as in "different." For that is the heart of our debate: Are relatively unfamiliar digital media essentially the same as what we now call "traditional" media, such as newspapers and pre-digital television, or are there fundamental differences? If the latter, what might such differences be? How might they affect the ways that media workers do their jobs and think about their roles in society?

Again, I think the biggest difference lies in the fact that the digital media such as the Internet constitute a *network*. Unlike all the other forms, what networks contain at any point in time is neither finite nor concrete nor discrete. Instead, all content in a network is fluid; it can be continually changed, expanded, and combined with other material. Everything and everyone are inextricably connected. Your news story includes my comment about it. My advertisement is connected to your consumer evaluation of the product I am advertising. Your YouTube video of the rally downtown is linked to my news release about the event—and shows a very different view of what happened.

To explore the effects of those differences, let's look at several key ethical principles shared by journalists, advertisers, and public relations professionals. I am not going to deal directly here with entertainment media, social networking sites, or personal media technologies such as iPhones; however, you might think about whether (or how) the ideas apply to those forms of communication as well. Each principle is vital regardless of the medium in which communication takes place. But, I will argue, each also needs to be thought of in new—different—ways.

Today, the availability of information isn't an issue. . . . Virtually anyone can be a publisher, and information is in overwhelmingly abundant supply—along with what seems to be equally abundant misinformation and disinformation.

HONESTY

For journalists all over the world, truth gets pride of place as an ethical principle. Advertisers and public relations practitioners also view honesty as central to their professions, as we saw above. Indeed, truth-telling is basic to all forms of human communication; without it, others cannot trust the information they receive and therefore cannot confidently base their own ideas or actions on that information (Bok, 1999). The special type of information called "news" is (at least in the eyes of the people who provide it) central to democracy itself, so the stakes are high indeed. A journalist who makes things up or otherwise deliberately misrepresents reality is not a journalist for long.

Most journalists try to reflect the world as they see and understand it as faithfully as possible in their stories. Indeed, this desire to discover truth, regardless of whether absolute "Truth-with-a-Capital-T" can actually be attained or described, lies at the heart of journalistic ethics (Merrill, 1997). However, even 100% accuracy, difficult as it is to reach, does not necessarily add up to truth. For one thing, the truth is always too complex to be contained within the confines of a news story or even a series of stories, which must fit within logistical limits of time, space, and media format. (A photograph, for instance, may capture a scene with admirable fidelity, but it cannot reveal what led up to that scene, or the thoughts of the people in the picture, or much about what was happening outside the camera's frame.) For another, we can only look at the world through our own eyes, not through anyone else's. We will never see all there is to be seen, and what we do see will be filtered through our own interpretive lens. Moreover, as history painfully teaches us, journalists are perpetually vulnerable to being misled by sources who claim with great authority to speak the truth even when they do not. Quoting them accurately produces fidelity but not truth.

The journalist seeking to be truthful in a networked environment can and should continue striving faithfully to record and reflect the world he or she sees. But the nature of the network demands that the journalist not stop there.

It is not feasible, logistically or economically, to give every television viewer time on the air or every reader of a newspaper access to newsprint and the printing press. But it is both feasible and ethically desirable to give all users both opportunity and encouragement to contribute to an online story. The result may include some bits that are ungrammatical and potentially even inaccurate. But the combined overall result may well turn out to be closer to the truth than the journalist's story alone.

There are several reasons why this is so, of which two are of particular interest in our discussion of whether ethics are, or should be, different in networked environments. The first is somewhat hypothetical, though it offers an insight into how traditional notions of "truth" are changing. The concept of a "marketplace of ideas" suggests that truth is what prevails among various competing ideas. It is the idea that withstands and ultimately triumphs over all challenges. "Let her and Falsehood grapple: Who ever knew Truth put to the worse in a free and open encounter?" John Milton wrote in 1644 in *Areopagitica*.

In Milton's world, that idea could never be put to the test. In ours, it might, using the open, wholly participatory medium of the Internet. In this networked world, news is not a lecture but rather a conversation, as journalist, blogger, and media observer Dan Gillmor (2004) likes to say. And our audience, the people engaged in that conversation, know more

it is both feasible and ethically desirable to give all users both opportunity and encouragement to contribute to an online story

than we do, collectively and, often, individually. That is, truth potentially is revealed not only from the top down, as in traditional mass communications, but also from the bottom up. Instead of relying solely on the journalist to tell us what he or she believes to be true, this premise suggests that a more multifaceted and therefore "truer" version of reality is created when lots of people contribute and defend (or fail to defend adequately) their ideas. A similar idea holds for other public communicators, as the Public Relations Society of America highlights in its Statement of Professional Values: "We provide a voice in the marketplace of ideas, facts, and viewpoints to aid informed public debate."

In parts of the online world, information may not be tested for truthfulness at all before it is published. Some bloggers, for example, post preliminary thoughts or observations and rely on the resulting conversation to sharpen the focus and correct any errors. Whether they are right or wrong to take that approach remains a matter of debate.

But we are concerned here primarily with journalists, and I am not suggesting that journalists skip their fact-checking and start uploading any old thing onto the Internet to see if it survives the test of rough-and-tumble discourse. I am, however, suggesting that journalists necessarily relinquish a substantial degree of control over what is included in, and connected to, their stories when those stories go online—and that doing so produces something closer to truth than the original story alone. When more people contribute their ideas, insights, and, yes, even rebuttals and corrections of what the journalist wrote, the story becomes a richer, more complete rendition of always-complex reality. To date, those contributions have mostly come in the form of comments appended to items provided by the professionals, but many other options exist for integration and cross-referencing.

This brings me to the second, less hypothetical, reason why the notion of truth changes online: not necessarily because of the clash of ideas but on the contrary, because of their synergy.

Let me offer as an example a look at how this can and does happen through something called "crowdsourcing." In 2006, readers of *The News-Press* in Fort Myers, Florida, began calling the paper to complain about outrageously high charges for connecting newly built homes to water and sewer lines. "Rather than start a long investigation and come out months later in the paper with our findings, we asked our readers to help us find out why the cost was so exorbitant," Kate Marymont, then *The News-Press* editor in chief, told *Wired* magazine. The response was overwhelming. Newspaper readers, joined by other people who followed the story online, organized their own investigations. Retired engineers analyzed blueprints, accountants pored over balance sheets, an inside whistleblower leaked evidence that bids were rigged. And ultimately, the city cut utility fees by more than 30% (Howe, 2006).

This illustration shows how people with diverse areas of expertise can provide the details and conduct the analyses that are beyond the abilities of most journalists. That has always been true, and such people have always served as sources for diligent journalists. What is different is that their knowledge no longer needs to be channeled through the journalist to reach the public. Instead, the story becomes a cooperative effort. In my example, the newspaper instigated the process of turning news tips into a story, but it need not work that way; any contributor might have been the initial publisher who alerted the rest of us to an issue or idea. The pursuit of truth becomes a partnership that does not need a middleman to get the word out.

So what is the role of that middleman—the journalist—in this world of multiple paths to multifaceted truths? I think that although the role continues to be one of information gatherer, it also entails a greater emphasis on "sense-making." Lots more people can and will contribute pieces of the story, but the individual pieces may not look like much until someone fits them together into a coherent whole. And some may not fit the overall picture at all; they may turn out to be wrong or misleading or irrelevant. So journalism in this participatory world is a process of synthesis and verification, both checking the facts and helping us understand what those facts add up to (Kovach and Rosenstiel, 2001).

That sounds a lot like journalism in the "old" world, doesn't it? It is. The important difference is that the journalist no longer is alone in carrying out this process of determining what is true and meaningful, or in disseminating the results of that process. The role of truth-telling, of striving for honesty, is far more broadly shared at every stage of a story. The ethical principle of truthfulness, then, is stretched in different directions in this networked world—directions that encompass many seekers of truth and incorporate many voices in reporting and relaying it.

RESPECT FOR OTHERS

The American Marketing Association urges members to "acknowledge the basic human dignity of all stakeholders." The Society of Professional Journalists urges journalists to "minimize harm" by treating "sources, subjects and colleagues as human beings deserving of respect." The principle underlies the Golden Rule of Judeo-Christian thinking: "Do unto others as you would have them do unto you." Philosophers as well as practitioners have drawn on it over the centuries, from Kant (1998, p. 38) and his "categorical imperative" to Rawls (2005, p. 12) and his "veil of ignorance." Respect for others remains crucial to ethical behavior regardless of the medium, the message, or the messengers.

That said, a globally networked world does create a few new wrinkles. The "harm" that those in mass communications are most likely to cause generally is not physical. Rather it involves a disruption of the psychological space that people need to live their lives. Perhaps the most pertinent such disruption involves invasion of personal privacy (discussed in more detail in Chapter 10), and it is in this area that many of the new challenges arise. Let's look at a couple.

To start with the obvious: The amount of information available online is incomprehensibly vast and still growing exponentially. And none of us has control over what someone else might decide to publish—about their political views, their pet goldfish, or you or me. Just ask John Seigenthaler, a retired newspaper executive and former president of the American Society of Newspaper Editors. In May 2005, as a bit of a lark, someone whom he had never met posted a "biography" on Wikipedia that stated Seigenthaler was "thought to have been directly involved" in the assassinations of both John and Robert Kennedy, "though nothing was ever proven"; the item also stated that the journalist lived in the Soviet Union for 13 years in the 1970s and early 1980s, a period when he in fact was serving as publisher and then chairman of *The Tennessean* in Nashville and as founding editorial director of *USA Today*. The item remained on Wikipedia for more than four months before the site's editors, alerted by Seigenthaler, removed it. By that time, it had been picked up by Answers.com and Reference.com, where it remained for another three weeks before finally being deleted (Seigenthaler, 2005).

The point, of course, is that there are no safeguards around what is published and freely available on the Internet. Some of that information may be embarrassing; much of it may be downright wrong (and, in the Seigenthaler example, libelous as well). How to respond is a relatively easy ethical call for journalists. The openness of the digital network is, as suggested above, one of its strengths, but it also drives home my point about the importance of verifying information before putting it in a story—and the difficulty of doing so in a world with no barriers to publication. Being an ethical journalist—professional or otherwise—requires being very savvy about recognizing potential truth and very diligent about exposing potential untruth. And it increasingly requires a strong sense of *personal* responsibility (and some healthy skepticism), as technology combines with shrinking resources to create situations where fewer people see and perhaps question material before it is broadcast, published, or (especially) made available online.

But here's a tougher question: What about information, including harmful information, that people publish about *themselves*? Who would do such a thing? You would, quite likely. Think about your Facebook page, for instance. Does it contain material you would rather your mother not see? A potential employer? A journalist? Many people think of such pages as private, something between a personal diary and a journal shared among friends. But they're more. Virtually all of the information they contain is published in a space open to so many people that it is "public" by just about any definition. Legally, that makes it fair game for anyone who comes across it, including journalists.

So it is probably legal for journalists to use or refer to information from your Facebook profile in a story. But is it ethical? Here is where the principle of respect comes in handy—along with some serious soul-searching about news values and what the public really needs to know. Are you the president of your university? If so, a Facebook photo of a very inebriated you and your beer bong is probably something the community, in which your university likely plays a significant economic and social role, has a stake in knowing about. Are you the president of your fraternity? The editor of your school newspaper? The head of the campus branch of a major political party? How about if you're just an average 19-year-old who is majoring in social work and has an internship with the local chapter of Alcoholics Anonymous?

The point is that journalists need to ask themselves tough questions about the degree to which a story that will make someone look bad serves the public's need (not mere desire) to know. Using you and your alcohol-guzzling paraphernalia to indicate that some underage college students drink lots of beer may harm you—the personnel officer at that PR firm with which you're desperate to get a job may decide you're not the best choice to "interface" with its corporate clients—but it isn't much of a public service to anyone. (It's not news, either, is it?) Letting people know the university president thinks it appropriate to post a Facebook portrait of himself with a bong perhaps says something important about this community leader's judgment, not to mention his taste in beverages.

(Think this is all hypothetical? At the university in England where I worked in the late 2000s, the head of the campus chapter of a national political party posted highly offensive comments about gays on his Facebook profile; he also was listed as head of a group called "Homos burn in hell." The campus newspaper reported this, prominently. He said it was all just a private communication among friends. Nonetheless, the campus party lost no time in removing him as their leader. In fact, within short order, he was no longer a member of the party at all.)

One more, somewhat broader point about respecting others may be helpful in thinking about whether the networked environment raises different ethical concerns. Some aspects of what constitutes both respect and harm rest on cultural norms that are not universal, particularly as we are generally not talking about physical harm. In a world of concrete media forms, it was relatively easy to weigh how a particular message would affect one's own community—the audience for that message. News or advertising images of a female student wearing shorts and a T-shirt, for example, would not raise many eyebrows in the West. But they could be quite problematic if that student were a member of a religiously conservative Muslim community. When media content is part of an interconnected network, an item produced anywhere can be seen everywhere. So the medium demands especially close attention to a broad range of cultural sensitivities. Again, this need to walk in another's shoes (Rawls, 2005) is true for professionals working in traditional media, as well, but online, there are a whole lot more shoes to consider.

INDEPENDENCE

Journalists, particularly in the United States, have made independence part of the fiber of their being and have fiercely fought any attempts, real or perceived, to curtail it. "Journalists," the SPJ code says, "should be free of obligation to any interest other than the public's right to know." Practitioners have staked their claim to independence on the obligation to inform the citizenry without interference from, influence by, or obligations to the government or other external forces—and what might constitute an external force has been broadly defined. For instance, widespread professional resistance to the public journalism movement of the 1990s was based largely on suggestions that it would undermine journalists' ability to make their own independent news judgments and report accordingly (McDevitt, 2003).

The principle, like those we already have discussed, remains valuable in a networked environment—as long as it is interpreted fairly narrowly to mean independence from potential conflicts of interest that can compromise integrity. Indeed, when everyone can and seemingly does publish an opinion with a few quick clicks on a keypad or mouse, the value of an even-handed and impartial observer and analyst is heightened. The problem is that "independence" seems too often to go beyond the intention to safeguard fairness and to translate to "a kind of self-imposed solitary confinement from society at large" (Kovach and Rosenstiel, 2001, p. 101). In a traditional media environment, that stance can quickly turn to arrogance. In a network, it's an even quicker route to irrelevance.

Historically, journalists have literally walled themselves off from the world outside the newsroom each day in order to produce a self-contained media product such as a newspaper or a TV news program. But digital networks such as the Internet, as we already have seen, are all about connections, among products and among people. This means a virtually unbounded number of participants simultaneously serve as sources, audiences, and information providers for one another. All communicators and all communication become interrelated parts of a whole, neither finite nor free-standing. The roles of message producers and consumers are interchangeable—you can be reading a news item one minute, writing and publishing your own the next—and inextricably linked. And, again, we all lose some control over our message as soon as we upload it into an environment in which it can be freely copied, exchanged, extended, and challenged by anyone and everyone. So in this world, journalists find their precious independence challenged not so much by government—the threat they have guarded against for centuries—but by the very citizens whom they ostensibly serve (Singer, 2007a).

To illustrate the ways in which the ethical principle of independence is challenged in a digital media world, let's look more closely at a staple of American journalism: the notion of objectivity. What follows comes largely from an article I wrote for *Media Ethics* magazine in 2007 (Singer, 2007b). See what you think.

Objectivity is closely connected to independence because it provides a rationale for journalists to maintain their distance from both sources and readers, and thus presumably from any direct influence they might wield. An objective journalist stands apart from the world on which he or she reports, observing but not observed, attending (both in the sense of being physically present and the sense of paying attention) but not participating.

But in a digital network, all distances collapse. Boundaries of all sorts—among products, among ideas, among people, among social roles—are difficult to sustain. Just as physical distance is erased by the immediacy with which any message can span the globe, professional distance is erased by the interconnections among all manner of information producers. Standing apart from this world in order to observe it may no longer be as desirable as in the past. Such detachment is deeply isolating, and in a networked world, the one thing that has virtually no value is isolation.

Certainly, we still need journalists to be observers and to refrain from participating in the events they observe. We still need people who are willing and able to serve as trustworthy eyes and ears in places we cannot be. We still need people who can convey what they saw and heard from a perspective that bears in mind the interests of the public as a whole rather than the interests of a few of its members.

But journalists within a network do need to rethink what they mean by both "objectivity" and "independence." The terms do not mean obsessive detachment. They do not mean erecting walls around the journalistic product, process, or person. They do not mean a determination not to care about an event or its effects. They cannot mean those things if journalism is to retain any relevance in a world in which we are all so thoroughly intertwined.

Instead, objectivity and independence in a networked environment mean a re-commitment to the professed rationale behind making them ethical principles or goals in the first place. They help safeguard the credibility of what journalists produce, ostensibly free from outside pressures that might shape information toward ends that serve only vested interests (Hayes et al., 2007). As we have seen, the public no longer occupies a distinct space or role apart from the journalist's, within the media environment. We *all* are citizens of the

In a networked world, there no longer is the "journalist," the "audience" and the "source". . . . All those roles are intertwined; together, they form the network.

network, and we all contribute to it. As the discussion of truth-telling suggested, serving today's public means conveying not only the "news" itself but also as much as possible about the people, process, and products that shaped it—including us as journalists. In a networked world, there no longer is the "journalist," the "audience" and the "source" (Singer, 2007b). All those roles are intertwined; together, they form the network.

ACCOUNTABILITY

That last point brings us to ways in which people within a network are accountable to one another. Like truth, accountability is a controversial and multifaceted concept, incorporating such notions as responsibility, responsiveness, and transparency. From the 19th-century utilitarians and their emphasis on maximizing positive consequences (Mill, 1863) to present-day communitarians (Christians et al., 1993; Lambeth, 1986), ethicists have stressed the social nature and effects of actions, including those of media practitioners. Aside from a few dictatorships, most nations around the world have a least one code of press ethics that delineates the nature of accountability to peers, sources, subjects, and audience members (Bertrand, 2000).

We started our consideration of digital ethics with a look at the matter of trust. In a traditional environment, journalists simply tend to ask readers or viewers to trust them—to trust that they are being truthful, that they have been both diligent and open-minded in gathering information, that they have captured the most important part of a story in the ten inches or two minutes allocated to it. It is a lot to ask. Perhaps, as the declining reputation of the news media suggests, it is too much (Hayes et al., 2007).

The online environment, though, offers unlimited space and thus the opportunity to foster trust actively, not just demand it. Journalists, along with advertisers and public relations practitioners, can do this in at least two important ways. One involves personal disclosure, and the other involves the provision of supporting evidence for what they create.

The second way is easier for journalists to get their heads around, although many have been slow to take advantage of available opportunities (Paul, 2005). When everything is connected to everything else, media practitioners can show where their information comes from, and, obviously, provide links to it. They can offer background about their sources, expand the depth and breadth of any story, and solicit and accommodate additional input and feedback from users. Users can, ideally, ascertain who provided the information, check out those sources for themselves, and figure out what sorts of standards a provider believes are important (Hayes et al., 2007).

Personal disclosure is tougher for journalists; people committed to maintaining at least a veneer of objectivity tend to be uncomfortable talking about who they are or what they think, largely because of a not-irrational fear that such information could provide ammunition for those looking for bias behind every byline. But other members of the vast Internet community have given this element of transparency a central place in their ideas of how life in a network should work. Bloggers, in particular, have turned the idea of disclosure about the blogger's actions, motives, and financial considerations into their own "golden rule" (Lasica, 2005). In doing so, they have offered journalists and other media professionals a route to transparency: through their own blogs.

Blogs have become commonplace among the online offerings of major media outlets; public relations firms are making increased use of them, as well. For example, industry giant Hill & Knowlton has a large assortment of blogs on the "Collective Conversation" section of its Web site; over at competitor Edelman PR, bloggers include president and CEO Richard Edelman. In general, corporate communicators are finding that because of their informal conversational tone, blogs can help companies convey "some sense of human attributes existing behind an organizational façade" (Kelleher and Miller, 2006).

Journalists are finding that the inclusion of blogs on media Web sites contributes to accountability in at least two ways. First, journalists are using them to explain the rationale behind the news, particularly the reasons for making controversial editorial decisions—putting a disturbing photo on the front page of the newspaper, for instance, or including the name of a minor in a crime story. Second, blogs offer a way to humanize the reporting process. For example, Anderson Cooper's "360 Blog" for CNN and Brian Williams' "Daily Nightly" blog for NBC (both of which draw extensively on contributions of behind-the-scenes journalists) have been used to offer "how we got the story" information. Blogs enable the journalist to talk about the experience of covering a particular story or about personal reactions to news events (Hayes et al., 2007). And of course, blogs offer additional opportunities to solicit contributions from users, as well.

Speaking of blogs, they raise a final point about the ways in which notions of account-ability are shifting in a digital environment. Being accountable entails opening oneself up to criticism. And oh my, is there plenty of that to go around! In the networked environment, oversight of media workers' behavior has become a team sport, and once again, the professionals no longer control who gets to play. Journalists as a group are notorious for relishing the role of dishing out criticism but being far less happy when they are on the receiving end. In recent years, they have perhaps been startled by the scrutiny under which they have suddenly come, and by the fact that most of those doing the scrutinizing see them not as nobly independent and scrupulously objective but rather as active, and not necessarily altruistic, participants in the construction of news (Hayes et al., 2007).

Scary though it is for practitioners, this often-pointed criticism is essentially a healthy thing. Again, a network necessarily means connections, and connections necessarily mean relationships among whatever—or whoever—is connected. Those relationships cannot flourish and grow without partners being accountable to one another; communicating openly about their concerns, and working together to resolve them. Media workers had far less impetus to do that when they controlled information than now, when they must share it.

This kind of fluid interconnection is illustrated by an old issue lurking in new technology: determining what standards should be applied to reader comments posted in response to online news stories or opinion pieces. These are analogous to the familiar letters to the editor that newspapers have run for decades, but there are far, far more of them. And the interactive and instantaneous nature of the Internet requires a fresh look at how to deal with inflammatory or insulting posts and at what ethical standards should apply.

In another *Media Ethics* magazine article discussing whether journalists or people selected by them should moderate these comments, I listed some issues that moderators would need to deal with in this changing environment. Each issue clearly has a substantial ethical component relevant to the network environment:

- Addressing the journalist's responsibility to audiences, employers, and colleagues not to let the online conversation get out of hand;
- Keeping users from wandering off on tangents;
- Maintaining long-standing norms of fairness and impartiality;
- Establishing consistency in the way power is wielded; and
- Identifying users' roles in moderating one another.

(Singer, 2009)

SO . . . IS ETHICS DIFFERENT IN A DIGITAL ENVIRONMENT?

Does all this add up to a new animal or simply an old one with its nose pointed in a new direction? I have not offered any radically new ethical standards here for journalists or other professional media communicators. Nor have I suggested that existing commitments to truth-telling, respect for others, independence, or accountability be jettisoned; on the contrary, I have urged that those commitments be strengthened. The underlying values are not only sound but perhaps more important than ever; I am not alone in hoping they endure.

But in order to endure, the way that media professionals think about and enact those underlying values needs to change to suit the new relationship with the people who once were the "audience" but now share a common communication space. The task of the professional communicator used to entail controlling the flow and content of information disseminated to the public. But no longer. The nature of the network forces such control to be relinquished and replaced with the give-and-take of a far more collaborative arrangement.

The ethical principles guiding this communications partnership put significantly more emphasis on openness and cooperation, while norms designed to erect and maintain boundaries of various kinds become distinctly less useful. Serving the public becomes less about telling people what information exists than about sharing in its discovery, verification, and interpretation, as well as providing help with its synthesis into meaningful knowledge.

A case could be made that these all are differences of degree, not of kind. But how many degrees of difference does it take before they add up to real change? At what moment in the change process does a caterpillar become a butterfly? Social change is almost always a cumulative process; each step along the way may not seem to take us to a place that is all that different from the one before, but eventually, we end up with something that can take wing and fly rather than only crawl along inch by inch. I think the networked nature of the Internet adds up to changes that are similarly dramatic and significant.

Where can this ethical metamorphosis take us? The sky's the limit.

Serving the public becomes less about telling people what information exists than about sharing in its discovery, verification, and interpretation

---

KEY POINTS

■ The ethical values underlying the mass media are not only sound but also perhaps more important than ever in a networked environment where the role of the journalist becomes one of "sense-maker" as well as information gatherer.

■ Even in the participatory Internet world, journalism remains a process of checking and presenting facts and helping people understand what those facts mean—but those responsibilities are now shared with the online audience.

■ Accountability takes on increased importance in a networked environment. The network also offers new ways to enhance accountability. For instance, journalists' blogs offer a way to humanize the reporting process and provide a look behind the façade of any media organization.

DORSHER: Ethics transcends media technologies and methods, so developments such as convergence journalism, citizen journalism, blogs, and multimedia mobile phones require little if any rethinking of long-standing ethical principles or guidelines.

I agree with Jane Singer that new media yield new complications, but I believe that classical ethics are up to these new challenges. I argue that solid foundations are even more important when surfaces are shifting. All of us—professional and citizen journalists, new media users and sources alike—would operate better and rest easier if everyone in the network practiced the categorical imperative to balance truth-seeking with dignity or sought the win-win Golden Mean or sincerely tried to minimize harm while weighing the utilitarian pros and cons. As the digital divide disappears, so must the ethical divides among all involved. The answer to new media dilemmas is not new ethics but more widespread ethics.

> The answer to new media dilemmas is not new ethics but more widespread ethics.

Take, for example, the following case study involving citizen journalism. Citizens who actually feel and see the events around them (and their effects) now use new media to report and publish stories that supplement, supplant or scrutinize the ones that professional journalists present in established media. Citizen journalists, however, face the same challenges and criticisms as "amateurs" in all fields—that they lack the training, judgment, and skills to produce results that decision makers can rely upon. One self-described citizen journalist, Centennial, Colorado, mother-of-three Debbie Brown, posted nine stories from late 2005 to early 2007 on yourhub.com, an open-membership Web site created by Denver's (now defunct) *Rocky Mountain News*. Of those nine stories, seven were about Spenser Swalm, a Republican who was then running an ultimately successful campaign for a seat in the Colorado House of Representatives (Brown, 2007). Those stories tell of Swalm's "key" endorsements, his "grass-roots style," his diligence in knocking on 8,000 doors during his campaign, and his "refreshing" experience in business rather than politics. Suffice to say they are not paragons of hard-hitting, investigative journalism. They don't even mention Swalm's opponents. Nor do these stories—which Brown wrote in hard-news style with concise lead paragraphs, headlines and direct quotes—mention that Debbie Brown was a volunteer for Swalm's campaign.

ANALYSIS OF THE CASE STUDY

Brown's bias came to light for at least some readers long before the election, when Howard Rothman wrote about her in his February, 2006, blog for a professional Web site, *New West* (Rothman, 2006). Even if Brown's stories fooled some other readers into thinking she was giving an objective assessment of Swalm's qualifications to be a legislator, my point is that what she did is *obviously* unethical. It takes no special code of ethics nor any arcane analysis of new media to understand that.

Rawls's concept of the veil of ignorance teaches us it is unethical to prey upon the vulnerability of those who lack crucial pieces of knowledge, such as the biased connection between a seeming journalist and her source. Alternatively, we could analyze this case with Kant's categorical imperative, which mandates pursuit of The Truth. That makes Brown's lies of omission about her connection to Swalm every bit as culpable as lies of commission. And *agape* ethics would question how loving it is to mislead her neighbors about her motives— even if they are Democrats. Conflicts of interest have been unethical since before the founders of U.S. democracy wrote the First Amendment, and such conflicts will continue to be the enemy of information—which theorists have concisely defined as the reduction of uncertainty (Shannon and Weaver, 1949)—no matter the medium of communication.

Furthermore, citizen journalism and other forms of new media already contain the remedies for such attempts at furtive persuasion. After all, it was another new media outlet, not the *Rocky Mountain News* or *Denver Post*, that exposed Brown's bias (and I found both Brown's and Rothman's stories on yet another new media source, the "everyday ethics" section of the Poynter Institute's Web site) (McBride, 2006). Moreover, the *New West* site where Rothman's blog appeared and the yourhub.com site that hosted Brown's stories allow readers to comment on such stories and publish the comments right below the original stories. This lets readers expose the original's shortcomings in a way never before possible with traditional newspapers and newscasts.

Also, yourhub.com did include a byline link to an autobiography of Brown, and in it, she acknowledged that she does "volunteer for some Republican campaigns and at church." These, however, are the buyer-beware type of *caveats* we usually resort to with advertising and public relations, not journalism. Were Brown an ethical public relations practitioner, let alone a journalist, she would have acknowledged her connection to the Swalm campaign early within the text of each of her "stories" about him. Moreover, the *Rocky Mountain News* would not have posted any of her stories on yourhub.com before one of its staffers vetted her independence—or at least prominently acknowledged her bias. Such "gatekeeping," of course, could devolve into censorship in some cases, as citizen journalism advocates might complain. But rather than such complaints, what's most likely to preclude such vetting is the prodigious staff time and costs it would require.

Instead, it's up to the citizens in the audience to police citizen journalists, just as has always been true for the policing of professional journalists. In the past, audience members voted with their change purses which newspaper to buy, with their remotes which newscast to watch, and with their clicks which news Web sites to read. Now, they can do more than just silently turn away from the journalists they don't believe; they can use the Internet to find refuting evidence, to compare notes with other doubters across the world, and to publish their findings or opinions in blogs or comments they append to the original stories. They need no extra or special set of ethics for this, but if they are no longer going to rely on professional journalists, who have professional canons, the citizen journalists should be as ethically trained and perhaps even as diligent as the professionals. In other words, they cannot be amateurish. They must know how to assess the validity and reliability not only of numerical data but also of the disconnected pieces of factual data or propaganda that sources give them. Ignorance is no excuse for irresponsibility.

There are several bloggers' codes of ethics, just as there are several ethics codes for journalists, and they all have their strengths and weaknesses in application. They all demand transparency—the up-front disclosure of conflicts of interest, for instance, in contrast to the covertness that Brown exercised in her Swalm campaign stories. But none of the bloggers' codes of ethics offers any means of enforcement other than exposure by their cyberspace competitors or colleagues and citizen readers. In other words, with the advent of the Internet, where reputedly no one knows if you're a dog, journalists remain the traditional watchdogs of the government but they, too, have watchdogs eyeing them—the bloggers, who in turn have watchdogs in competing bloggers. The long-term quality of government depends on the quality of its watchdogs, and now the long-term quality of journalism and of blogging may well depend on the quality of *their* respective watchdogs. Complicated? Yes, but the interactive world is more complex than the few-to-many mass media world, and the quality of the various watchdogs remains both the curse—and secret to success—for journalism and democracy alike.

CONVERGENCE JOURNALISM

One of the most far-reaching of the many offspring of the digital media is "convergence journalism." For now, its practice is primarily the province of professionals, not citizen journalists, because it has greater barriers to entry, that is, it takes more money, training, talent and staff to combine video, audio, photography, graphics and print into nonlinear stories. But with the ubiquity of digital cameras in mobile phones, the advent of palm-size video recorders and the popularity of YouTube, the technology for convergence journalism is within reach of any average citizen in the developed world. The ethical concern, of course, is that their reach might exceed their grasp, even more so for citizen journalists than the pros.

The more videography there is, the less privacy; with the average New Yorker passing under the gaze of literally hundreds of security cameras a day, it gives new meaning to "The Naked City." London has many times that number and other cities will follow. The more microphones there are and the greater their sensitivity, the less likely a verbal gaffe goes unrecorded. The easier it is to update news on the Web continuously, the more pressure there is to rush to publication, even if the content constitutes no more than "unchecked facts," "incomplete information," "instant analysis," or other such oxymorons.

None of these problems, however, whether they confront the most versatile professional "mojo" (i.e., mobile journalist) or the most ambitious or overzealous multimedia blogger, presents a challenge too great for classical ethics. Kant tells us that every person has inviolate worth, whether we quote them in writing or capture them on satellite-transmitted video as, for instance, their house fills with flood water. Utilitarianism teaches us that getting a story first is no substitute for getting it right. Even Machiavellian ethics calls into question the means of hidden cameras and televised sting operations when the end—no matter how unintended—is a suicide, as happened after an episode of *Dateline NBC*'s "To Catch a Predator" exposé on Internet pedophiles (Eaton, 2006).

In 2007, *The Seattle Times* launched a convergence journalism initiative aimed at getting more news more quickly to its readers via the Web, then fleshing out stories for them to see in its next-morning newspapers (Fancher, 2007). At the same time, it pledged no relaxation of its accuracy or ethics. As one of its columnists put it a few months later, the journalists there were not about to devolve into point-and-shoot pundits:

> The hallowed halls of journalism that I was privileged to enter more than 20 years ago are looking more and more like the New York subway. The walls covered in bloggers' scrawl, the platform crowded with any yahoo with a camera and an open mike. All are headed to your computer screen or television for the 15 seconds you'll give them before moving on to the next hot spot.
>
> That's not how we do things at this newspaper.
>
> (Brodeur, 2007)

Supporters of convergence journalism call it an essential revolution in the way we gather, distribute, and consume news, but critics call it a fad that's likely to further erode the credibility and health of journalism, and, perhaps, democracy. What I believe is that the same ethical precepts that applied to 20th-century journalism can and must be applied to 21st-century journalism. It may well be that the public increasingly will create as well as consume mass media content, but that should be no excuse for an "anything goes" or "everyone's doing it" set of standards. As the authors of *Good Work* put it, "Adherence to the First Amendment does not entail reflexive support for work that undermines the values of journalism" (Gardner et al., 2001, p. 221).

MULTIMEDIA MOBILE PHONES

Online journalism has no monopoly on new media ethical dilemmas. The iPhone and its competitors, by the sheer multiplicity of their media capabilities, raise the potential for new dilemmas. If we were *Amusing Ourselves to Death* (Postman, 2005) with mere television, what must be the dangers of watching TV or streaming movies on an iPhone (or even texting or talking) while driving down a freeway, of shooting video at drunken bashes and transmitting it anywhere instantly, or of recording live concerts and converting them to infinitely exchangeable mp3 files?

Users of multimedia mobile phones might eventually be just as likely to become victims of new dilemmas as purveyors of new information. As these devices diffuse through the population, they will become more valuable to marketers, mappers and trackers. Advertisers will embed commercials and product placements within entertainment videos, music files and ring tones that they offer to mobile phone users at little or no cost. Parents and police are able to track the location of mobile phone users by triangulating the phone's signal among cell towers, and tracking becomes even more precise when the phones include GPS satellite devices, as they increasingly do.

When an area reaches some critical mass of high-tech multimedia mobile phone users, marketers will probably marry the phones' tracking and advertising capabilities. Thus, when mobile phone users drive near a mall or map a route to get there, a customized list of sale items at some of the stores will pop up on their phone. When a "mobile" user walks near a downtown restaurant, the phone will beep with the message that his or her favorite pie is on special that day. Convenient or creepy? You decide, but to avoid the latter, the question again is not whether new media communicators have new ethics but whether they have *enough* ethics. The push for short-term profits must not trample Kant's concern for individuals' dignity and privacy, nor would Rawls tolerate such an imbalance of information that vulnerable consumers must face temptation around every corner.

THE BEAUTY AND CHALLENGE OF NEW MEDIA: CYBERNETICS

Along with being digital, what makes new media different is that they are more cybernetic. "Cybernetics" is a concept that MIT researcher Norbert Wiener (1961) developed: the use of continuous potentially corrective ("negative") feedback to improve progressively the efficiency of any system. Multimedia mobile phones, the World Wide Web, and digital video recorders such as TiVo, or cable programming "on demand" are all examples of new media that provide continuous feedback to owners of media (and their advertisers) on how people use their outlet. They can then use these data to refine their offerings, making them more enticing to us and more useful to their clients' advertising or other persuasive objectives.

Older, one-way mass media such as newspapers and broadcast television never had these cybernetic capabilities, but new media do if they're digital and, especially, if they are part of a network. Communication networks not only complete the feedback loop, but also multiply the value of cybernetics by yielding data trails that show the relationships among media users and their content preferences and predilections. In this way, Amazon.com determines which books to feature for each shopper, ads for moving companies pop up on the screens of people selling their house, and bloggers unmask political campaign operatives masquerading as objective citizen journalists. New media users, however, still must seek out the news and information they want. What comes to them cybernetically *might* reduce their uncertainty, but it is just as likely to be a commercial come-on, or propaganda.

A corollary of cybernetics is that new media users consent to letting others in the network use them in some ways, so the new users themselves can get benefit from the network. A full discussion of this phenomenon, called hegemony (Gramsci, 1971), is beyond the limits of this book, but readers would do well to lift their veil of ignorance of it. Whether they know it by name or not, advertisers are using hegemony when they convince consumers it's just common sense to "save money, live better." PR practitioners are using hegemony when they return journalists' calls in exchange for getting a chance to shape the story's outcome. Online journalists are using hegemony when they offer readers a chance to question and criticize their stories but they selectively choose which ones to publish and respond to. It might be thought of as the coin of power. Hegemony always involves cultural give-and-take negotiations between the message senders and receivers, but the ultimate outcome is always the same: the people in power wind up with even more power than they started with, because the crumbs they've given away further pacify those without power. Online media have more potential for furthering hegemony than any previous media, because they are more cybernetic and facilitate more interactivity and forms of negotiation (Dorsher, 1999).

So is hegemony online essentially unethical? Inevitable perhaps, but not necessarily unethical, I'd say. Coercing—covertly forcing or manipulating new media users, or distorting their feedback—is unethical. But trading information with them transparently (i.e., with prominent disclosures and tangible benefits) and treating them as you'd want them to treat you would be ethical, according to both Kant's and Rawls's formulations.

The same also might define an appropriate relationship between blogs and professional news media. Both news and entertainment media could work with bloggers and non-professionals producing entertainment content, and trade some type of access to mainstream outlets for use of either the content or the concepts it contains.

CONCLUSION

Singer and I agree that new media really are different from analog, one-way ancestor media. We agree, also, that new media networks cannot operate ethically without greater emphasis on openness, transparency, and cooperation among members. We both were journalists, so we start our discussion there, but I want to stress that it is just as crucial for public relations practitioners, advertising professionals, and entertainers to use new media within the bounds of classical ethics as it is for journalists of all stripes.

New media, to my way of thinking, put even more pressure on non-professionals (and perhaps on beginning professionals) in the network to beware the content they access and to consider the consequences of their information exchanges. "There is no inevitability where there is willingness to pay attention," pioneer media philosopher Marshall McLuhan said (McLuhan and McLuhan, 1988, p. 128). And were he alive today, I think the evocative McLuhan would not mind being mentioned in the same sentence with the comic strip character "Pogo," whose comment on a 1970 Earth Day poster applies aptly to new media and their ethics: "We have met the enemy, and he is us" (Kelly, 1972).

KEY POINTS

- Citizen journalists, who have no widely accepted code of ethics, need to be as well versed in traditional ethical principles as are the professionals; they cannot be ethics amateurs.
- The quality of the various watchdogs in the complex interactive world remains both the curse—and the secret of success—for journalism and democracy alike.
- Hegemony always involves cultural negotiations between message senders and receivers, but the outcome is always the same. People in power wind up with even more power because the crumbs they've given away further pacify those without power.

MERRILL: Commentary

Ethics changes with time and technology? That is the question Jane Singer and Michael Dorsher skillfully traverse as they spar lightly here and there before retreating largely to the safe havens of classical ethical theory. Singer provides a more controversial vision, one that would see technology as increasing ethical problems and calling for different ethical solutions. Dorsher's view is more in line with ethical tradition: ethics is ethics, no matter if you are talking about traditional journalism, PR, advertising, broadcasting, cybermessaging or whatever.

Singer makes a good case that digital media are different from traditional media, but never quite declares that the *ethical principles* are different. Even within traditional forms of communication (e.g., advertising and journalism) she seems a little ill at ease when dealing with their ethical differences. Accuracy and truth, she mentions, are indeed all-important. The American Advertising Federation supports telling the truth and not misleading. This skirts a fundamental problem based on the ethical question: can advertising, for instance, whether in cyberspace or traditional media, really believe it has an ethical responsibility to lay out the truth and avoid misleading statements and images?

Singer may be right when we are talking about *mini-ethics* (or specific, rather narrow legalisms of a particular area), but Dorsher is taking a broader, more traditional *major ethical* perspective. For some reason Singer did not delineate the specific ethical changes that would accompany advanced technology. This is unfortunate because it would be interesting to see how the basic principles of honesty, integrity, balance, fairness, etc. would actually be applied differently (if they were) with the new communication technologies.

It would seem that as one goes from old-style journalism to the new pluralistic technological messaging, one moves in the direction of Machiavellianism. New ethical dictums are not so much needed and invented as old ones are ignored or modified to justify the pragmatic purposes of the communicator. Singer mentions that the new technology increases the need for audiences to be more trusting. Trusting a communicator has little to do with the communicator's ethics. The ethical responsibility is always on the formulator-sender of the message.

Dorsher, while certainly not opposed to the new technology in general, believes that "citizen journalists" increase the chance of unethical practices, and that they "lack the training, judgment and skills" to produce reliable results. Singer, on the other hand, contends that the growing multiplicity of perspectives and news-facts will get us closer to the truth. Noting that no communicator can give all of the truth, she sides with a multi-infusion of fact and opinion to give us the Big Truth. She maintains that increased citizen participation in communication will at least give truth an advantage as it contends with falsehood. The marketplace of ideas leading to the truth: that is the idea, but one that has not been proved.

Dorsher mentions balancing truth-seeking with dignity, a fascinating idea for class discussion. Both terms are full of semantic noise, and "dignity" is especially problematic. Such concepts as objectivity and independence (terms used by Singer) are particularly difficult to define when brought into a discussion of ethics. These two concepts are not only problematic semantically but also empirically impossible to prove. When we talk of objectivity, we should keep in mind that reality (to a journalist, at least) is no more than the product of observations strained through the journalist's own subjectivity. I may try to be fair or even balanced in a story, but I cannot be "objective" (see Chapter 15-A). I choose what to put in and what to leave out, what to emphasize or de-emphasize. My biases cannot help but influence my decisions, although I may not even be aware of them. As to independence, innumerable factors—even a desire to be ethical itself—impinge on my decisions.

Both Dorsher and Singer touch on the point that all the new technological channels and devices of personal communication are threats to privacy. This is certainly true. There is no way that one's activities cannot splinter in a million ways through cyberspace, never even to be seen by the principals involved. This, of course, is a new problem in ethics brought about by the new technology. But it is a "new" ethical problem only in the sense of scope or scale; we have always had the issue of privacy with us—even prior to the era of mass communication.

These two writers have produced excellent essays on the new technological expansionism of communication. They bring up a variety of controversial topics in this area, but not all they could have discussed. For example, most full-time editorial employees of *The New York Times* are "citizens" as well as "journalists." Other related questions could have been dealt with here: how does the concept of professionalism exist in this technological world of the "citizen journalist"? Or the "citizen PR practitioner"? As technology opens the field of journalism to everyone, just what meaning is left for traditional journalists and schools of journalism?

The introduction to this chapter was indeed correct in concluding that this topic is a work in progress and that you will be the people to put it into final form.

REFERENCES AND RELATED READINGS

Bertrand, Claude-Jean. (2000). *Media Ethics and Accountability Systems*. New Brunswick, NJ: Transaction.

Bok, Sissela. (1999). *Lying: Moral Choice in Public and Private Life*, 3rd ed. New York: Vintage.

Brodeur, Nicole. (2007). "Lessons in newsroom decorum." *The Seattle Times*, August 17, p. B1.

Brown, Debbie. (2007). "Stories posted by Debbie Brown." yourhub.com-Centennial, March 6. Retrieved from http://denver.yourhub.com/Centennial/Stories?userid=12507) (October 23, 2007).

Christians, Clifford G., John P. Ferré, and P. Mark Fackler. (1993). *Good News: Social Ethics and the Press*. New York: Oxford University Press.

Cooper, Tom. (1990). "Comparative international media ethics." *Journal of Mass Media Ethics* 5(1), pp. 3–14.

Dorsher, Michael. (1999). "Hegemony online: The quiet convergence of power, culture and computers." Unpublished dissertation. Retrieved from www.uwec.edu/mdorsher/ica2001/hegemony_online.htm (January 17, 2008).

Eaton, Tim. (2006). "Prosecutor kills himself in Texas sting over child sex." *The New York Times*, November 7, p. A10.

Fancher, Michael R. (2007). "Readers come first as we map our future." *The Seattle Times*, February 4, p. A21.

Gardner, Howard, Mihaly Csikszentmihalyi, and William Damon. (2001). *Good Work: When Excellence and Ethics Meet*. New York: Basic Books.

Gillmor, Dan. (2004). *We the Media: Grassroots Journalism by the People, for the People*. Sebastopol, CA: O'Reilly Media.

Gramsci, Antonio. (1971). *Selections from the Prison Notebooks*, trans. Q. Hoare and G. N. Smith. New York: International Publishers.

Hayes, Arthur S., Jane B. Singer, and Jerry Ceppos. (2007). "Shifting roles, enduring values: The credible journalist in a digital age." *Journal of Mass Media Ethics* 22(4), pp. 262–279.

Howe, Jeff. (2006). "Gannett to crowdsource news." *Wired*, November 3. Retrieved from: www.wired.com/software/webservices/news/2006/11/72067 (January 14, 2008).

Kant, Immanuel. (1998). *Groundwork of the Metaphysics of Morals*, trans. Mary J. Gregor. Cambridge, UK: Cambridge University Press (original work published in German, 1785).

Kelleher, Tom, and Barbara M. Miller. (2006). "Organizational blogs and the human voice: Relational strategies and relational outcomes." *Journal of Computer-Mediated Communication* 11(2), pp. 395–414. Retrieved from http://jcmc.indiana.edu/vol11/issue2/kelleher.html (January 14, 2008).

Kelly, Walt. (1972). *We Have Met the Enemy and He is Us*. New York: Simon & Schuster.

Kovach, Bill, and Tom Rosenstiel. (2001). *The Elements of Journalism: What Newspeople Should Know and the Public Should Expect*. New York: Crown.

Lambeth, Edmund B. (1986). *Committed Journalism*. Bloomington and Indianapolis, IN: Indiana University Press.

Lasica, J. D. (2005). "The cost of ethics: Influence peddling in the blogosphere." *Online Journalism Review*, February 17. Retrieved from www.ojr.org/ojr/stories/050217lasica/index.cfm (October 19, 2007).

McBride, Kelly. (2006). "The problem with citizen journalism." *PoynterOnline*, February 24. Retrieved from www.poynter.org/column.asp?id=67&aid=97418 (October 23, 2007).

McDevitt, Michael. (2003). "In defense of autonomy: A critique of the public journalism critique." *Journal of Communication* 53(1), pp. 155-164.

McLuhan, Marshall, and Eric McLuhan. (1988). *Laws of Media: The New Science*. Toronto: University of Toronto Press.

Merrill, John C. (1997). *Journalism Ethics: Philosophical Foundations for News Media*. New York: St. Martin's Press.

Mill, John Stuart. (1863). *Utilitarianism*. London: Parker, Son & Bourn.

Paul, Nora. (2005). "'New news' retrospective: Is online news reaching its potential?" *Online Journalism Review*, March 24. Retrieved from www.ojr.org/ojr/stories/050324paul (October 19, 2007).

Postman, Neil. (2005). *Amusing Ourselves to Death: Public Discourse in the Age Of Show Business*. New York: Penguin.

Rawls, John. (2005). *A Theory of Justice*. Cambridge, MA: Harvard University Press (reissue of first edition, originally published 1971).

Rothman, Howard. (2006). "Denver media offering politicos free PR outlet." *New West*, February 24. Retrieved from www.newwest.net/index.php/topic/article/6537/C37/L37 (October 23, 2007).

Seigenthaler, John. (2005). "A false Wikipedia 'biography.' " *USA Today*, November 29. Retrieved from www.usatoday.com/news/opinion/editorials/2005-11-29-wikipedia-edit_x.htm (October 18, 2007).

Shannon, Claude, and Warren Weaver. (1949). *The Mathematical Theory of Communication*. Urbana, IL: University of Illinois Press.

Singer, Jane B. (2007a). "Contested autonomy: Professional and popular claims on journalistic norms." *Journalism Studies* 8(1), pp. 79–95.

——. (2007b). "Objectivity in an interconnected world." *Media Ethics* 18(2), pp. 1, 15–16.

——. (2009). "Moderation in moderating commentary." *Media Ethics* 20(2), pp. 1, 10–12.

Wiener, Norbert. (1961). *Cybernetics, or Control and Communication in the Animal and the Machine*, 2nd ed. Cambridge, MA: MIT Press.

Codes of Ethics and Principles

American Advertising Federation. (1984). *Advertising Ethics and Principles*. Retrieved from www.aaf.org/default.asp?id=37 (November 6, 2007).

American Marketing Association. (2004). *AMA Statement of Ethics*. Retrieved from www.marketing power.com/content435.php (November 6, 2007).

Online News Association. (2003). *A Bloggers' Code of Ethics*. Retrieved from www.cyberjournalist. net/news/000215.php (March 10, 2010).

Public Relations Society of America. (2000). *Member Code of Ethics*. Retrieved from www.prsa.org/aboutUs/ethics/preamble_en.html (November 6, 2007).

Radio Television Digital News Association (formerly Radio-Television News Directors Association) (2000). *Code of Ethics and Professional Conduct*. See also various "guidelines" issued from time to time, e.g., "Avoiding conflict of interest" (October 2008), "Social media and blogging" (February 2010). Retrieved from www.rtdna.org (March 10, 2010).

Society of Professional Journalists. (1996). *SPJ Code of Ethics*. Retrieved from http://spj.org/ethicscode.asp (October 19, 2007).

Chapter 7

Digitally Manipulated Content

WE are still coming to grips with the technological communications revolution that we call "digital." With older analog media forms, it was possible to manipulate and change words, sounds and images, even though it wasn't easy. Photographic experts might work their magic in darkrooms and laboratories, artists could mimic or modify reality, printers could disseminate untruths as easily as truths, and once magnetic recording was available anyone with the right tools could rearrange the contents in ways that were hard to detect.

Each of these manipulative methods took time, expertise, and hence, money. Usually they could be detected by other experts who were looking or listening for modifications in an original item. The detection methods grew out of a long tradition of literary and artistic content analysis, tracing the provenance of antiques, and forgery detection.

So far, it is impossible to use many of these detection methods on *digital* media, because it is impossible to tell, from a long string of zeros and ones, the source, age and other attributes of an image, sound, or message. It is so easy to cut-and-paste words and modify images without detection that it is clear the digital revolution has already occurred, and we are merely trying to come to terms with its aftermath. Every photo shop and drug store is happy to provide the means to modify almost any kind of content.

Such "alterations"—including lip-synching—can arise on a larger stage, as well. When famous classical musicians performed at President Obama's inauguration, could the public really tell that they were listening to a performance that was pre-recorded because the day's frigid temperature in Washington could have led to broken strings and cracked instruments? Regardless, the lack of foolproof detection methods doesn't absolve those who make use of digitally altered materials from exercising ethical caution and warning their audiences—however imperfect current detection methods may be. More to the point, we *all* bear some responsibility, in dealing with digital materials, to exert caution and vigilance and pay constant attention to the age-old question of "what is reality?"

But there's another issue here. Electronic content can be easily and quickly transmitted, and thus is readily available to news operations, many of which believe they have a "deadline every minute." (That term goes back to the days of wire service battles to be "first with breaking news," between and among Associated Press, United Press and the International News Service.) If an Internet newsroom, or a cable or radio 24/7 news operation, wants to beat the competition by getting a story out first, the ideal of verifying the origin and accuracy of material sent by unknown individuals from cell phone cameras, or texted via Twitter or some other application, may go by the board. Some of these concerns were raised in Chapter 6, but they are very relevant to this discussion, as well.

None of the three authors of this chapter approves of anonymous manipulation of content, no matter how easy it is and who does it. Nor do they have an easy answer for how we identify content that has been digitally manipulated, whether for political, egocentric, or aesthetic reasons. But the two sides diverge on how serious the problem is, how it might be dealt with, and how much verification or "vetting" is ethically required before a newsroom makes digitally transmitted images or content available to the public. John Michael Kittross proposes the draconian approach that *nothing* that has been digitized can or should be trusted, and provides some thoughts as to how we can assure the validity of the pictures, sounds and even words that we use in portraying our environment. In a jointly authored approach William Babcock and David Gordon suggest that the authentication of digital material is *not* a serious ethics issue in mass media *except* in regard to how newsrooms should handle these materials under deadline pressure.

BABCOCK and GORDON: There is no ethical mandate to authenticate digital material, especially in the persuasive and entertainment realms, and news operations can rely on corrections if they find they have disseminated erroneous material.

John Michael Kittross makes the point in his half of this chapter that there is no present way to authenticate digitized visual images. The best we can do, he suggests, is to educate the public to this fact of technological life, so no one expects that photos will be totally accurate depictions of "reality" (whatever that term means). We don't think his position goes anywhere near far enough.

For reasons to be spelled out below there is nothing wrong (and much right) with altering digital images in the entertainment area of mass communication. On the persuasion side of the field, and even in the news area, some digital alteration is ethically permissible as long as the overall impression conveyed to the audience is not distorted.

It's important to remember that photographers must choose how to frame a photo and the angle from which it is taken, and those unavoidable decisions often eliminate unwanted or unsightly images from the finished product *before* taking the picture—just as airbrushing has often done after the photo is taken.

Let's consider a striking example of why manipulation of images (digital, or in this case, using older technologies) is beneficial. In May 1970, little concern was expressed (or merited) over the editing of a widely circulated and very dramatic photo from the Kent State University campus which depicted a young woman kneeling over a body and bewailing the deaths of four students shot during an anti-Vietnam War demonstration. From the photographer's perspective, the woman seemed to have a fence post rising out of her head. Some published versions of the photo had edited out the post. Without that image manipulation, the viewers' eyes would likely have followed the post upward, rather than staying on the young woman's face—the focal point of the picture—and the photo's impact would have been greatly diminished. With this editing, no important element of the photo (or of the situation being depicted) was altered, and the photo retained all the emotion inherent in the scene.

This was a news photo, and it illustrates why digital alteration of such photos (or videos) is in principle very little different from the selectivity that any gatekeeper in the news field has to exercise. Journalists have never been able to portray 100% of any situation they're describing—of "reality," if you will. There are always details that are omitted, quotations that are shortened or paraphrased or even omitted entirely when a story runs too long. The idea is to keep the reader, listener or viewer focused on the news story, in the same way that editing the Kent State photo was intended to keep the viewers focused on the key aspect of the picture.

As long as proper respect is given to the portrayal of overall "reality," we see no more of a problem with digital manipulation of images than we do with gatekeepers' "manipulation" of details to be included or excluded.

TWO FURTHER EXAMPLES

In 2003, the *Los Angeles Times* unknowingly published a digitally manipulated wartime photo from Iraq. The photo focused on a British soldier on the outskirts of Basra, directing Iraqi civilians to take cover. After the photo was published on March 31, it was noticed that several civilians in the background appeared twice. The photographer, Brian Walski, acknowledged he had used his computer to combine elements of two photographs to provide a more striking image. He was fired almost as soon as the manipulation was discovered, for violating the paper's photographic ethics policy. The paper in essence took a Kantian stance against *any* kind of digital manipulation, under *any* circumstances. (The two photos involved, together with the published composite version and the editor's note describing the digital manipulation, can be found at www.sree.net/teaching/lateditors.html.)

Was Walski wrong to provide a composite version of the scene he recorded with his camera? Did this distort the *overall* reality in any way? Was the greater good perhaps served better by a photo that portrayed what was going on near Basra at the same time that it used digital enhancement to do a better job of attracting the attention of readers? Was the real problem here that Walski failed to tell his editors what he had done, in advance? It could be useful to ponder how different classical ethicists might have answered these questions.

Is the *Los Angeles Times* situation really very different from the long-standing practice of *The Orange County Register*, a photographic Pulitzer Prize winner, in manipulating digitally all sky areas of its photos to what is referred to as "*Register* sky blue"? The *Register* is simply making photographs more attractive and user-friendly for the audience (and the region more attractive to tourists). Machiavellian, to be sure, but also utilitarian in benefiting both the audience and the local economy. Rawls might even approve of the time the *Register* used electronic imaging to zip a boy's fly and save him from embarrassment.

The Iraq photo situation described above really wasn't much more than another case of making the image more dramatic, and, in the process, trying to tell the story better than either image could have done separately. It's likely that most utilitarians would agree with this approach. Walski certainly might have told his editors about the digital manipulation before the photo was published, and they might then have decided it was acceptable to run the altered photo with a caption indicating that it contained some digital alterations which did not change the basic story it told. Or they might have decided to label it as a "photo illustration." While this latter approach appears to be a valid middle ground, as Aristotle and Confucius might have suggested, a "photo illustration" label can be confusing and this compromise can be less than perfect.

ADVERTISING AND PUBLIC RELATIONS

Is it okay to enhance the colors of the hamburger and the cheese in a fast food ad, to make them look brighter and more appealing (the advertising equivalent of that *Orange County "Register* sky blue" alteration noted earlier)? Would moving one of the Great Pyramids be acceptable in an *ad*, on the grounds that readers would simply assume that the image might have been manipulated? What about the ethics of digitally making female fashion models look thinner (see Reaves et al., 2004)? Is it appropriate—or even possible—to make the audience figure out whether there are digital alterations in ads?

Are the ethical guidelines the same for public relations agencies as they are for newsrooms? What if it were a PR agency that was creating the "*Register* sky blue" image instead of a newspaper? Is there an ethical obligation on the part of the agency to label that image as "visually enhanced"? (Incidentally, should the *Register* do that every time it runs a photo where the sky is digitally made bluer?) If the *Register* knew that the PR firm or the Chamber of Commerce habitually made these changes, should the paper alert its readers?

public relations practitioners are under the same ethical obligations as are newsrooms, in regard to digital manipulation

We believe that public relations practitioners are under the same ethical obligations as are newsrooms, in regard to digital manipulation. There's nothing wrong with it, as long as it doesn't distort the overall impression. However, PR operations have at least as much of an obligation to identify digital enhancements as news operations do.

Digital enhancements of products in ads is simply a continuation of what advertising has done for decades. In the 1960s, various display techniques were adapted for television ads: plain glass marbles placed in soup so that the advertised contents floated at the top; an open window used to demonstrate the clarity of automobile glass, and so on. Although the most blatant deceptions were later banned by the Federal Trade Commission as being unfair (both to consumers and to competing companies), others—especially those dealing with food products that could not stand up to photographers' lights—remain. Digital manipulation of advertising images differs from the banned techniques only because it is so hard to detect.

Aside from the legal controls on deceptive advertising imposed by the FTC and some other agencies, there remains the key question of what advertisers and their agents *should* do digitally within the areas that are not regulated. Those areas still offer opportunities (or temptations) to people working in advertising, perhaps especially to the creative types who see opportunities to make an ad more attention-getting with only minor changes on the computer. And there, we believe the standard should be that anything that's *legal* should also be regarded as ethically acceptable.

That's essentially a "buyer beware" (*caveat emptor*) standard, but most consumers are familiar enough with advertising to know that some of what appears in ads represents an ideal rather than depicting absolute "reality." This obviously is a Machiavellian approach, but it has echoes of a Kantian rule as well. To paraphrase the approach that Kittross will take in the second part of this chapter, consumers who see ads should *always* assume that the images in those ads *may* have been digitally altered, within the limits of what is legally permitted, and they should look at the products being advertised in that light. In this regard, as with Gordon's Chapter 11 argument, advertising should be given enough license to function as "commercial poetry."

ENTERTAINMENT AND DOCUMENTARIES

Entertainment often requires the "suspension of disbelief" and digitally altered images are nothing more than a contributing factor to that approach. They are commonly in use in films and television programming; images are routinely enhanced, now by computer but formerly through makeup and camera angle, and distractions are routinely removed digitally from the scene. Since the material is just *depicting* "reality" (or, in some cases, unreality) and since audiences in most cases are aware of that, we see no serious ethical problems inherent in the digital alteration of most entertainment content. Docudramas are somewhat different, and are discussed from a different perspective in Chapter 3 (pp. 105–106).

Documentaries would normally be an exception to that last paragraph, since the general rule about them is that they should portray exactly what was taking place, with no attempt at manipulating the images. But even there, the universally accepted Kantian "no tampering" rule might not hold in 100% of the cases. For example, one documentary maker found it necessary to substitute a 4.5 second clip from one of his own films on a TV screen that—by chance—was displaying an episode of *The Simpsons* as part of a scene crucial to the production. When faced with cutting the brief (and out-of-focus) interlude from the TV program, or paying a $10,000 fee to retain it, the filmmaker decided that the only viable alternative was to break the Kantian rule and, ever so slightly, digitally alter what actually took place (Netanel, 2008, pp. 16–17).

We see nothing wrong with this utilitarian approach. Without it, there wouldn't have been money to finish the documentary, and nothing essential to the situation was altered. If a "higher," more accurate truth is possible by altering an image so that it shows truth in a more holistic fashion, isn't that in the end more ethical than never digitally changing any aspect of images?

ETHICAL RULES FOR PHOTOGRAPHERS

Keep in mind that alteration of photos is not a new phenomenon. In the pre-digital era, Ansell Adams was a darkroom wizard, and retrospectives of his work provide examples of how he expertly dodged, burned and cropped the same image differently over a number of decades. Photographers have long used various filters to change the intensity of both color and black and white compositions. They always were able to crop or airbrush unwanted items from prints, and easily remove undesirable scratches, dust, telephone lines, birds, soda cans—and people—in the darkroom.

But *photojournalism* guidelines aren't simple. What about the difficulty of getting close-up shots (and sounds) for wildlife films? Does it really change "reality" to manipulate animal images digitally to provide what the audience would see if only the camera could safely have been brought closer? Or to add sounds that are too far away to be captured when using a telephoto lens (e.g., chewing a celery stick to simulate the sound of a lion biting into a wildebeest) (see Palmer, 2010)? We see nothing wrong with this type of enhancement in wildlife films as long as the underlying reality isn't distorted.

The Associated Press (AP) says that it does "not alter or manipulate the content of a photograph in any way," including "in PhotoShop or by any other means." But that isn't the whole story. AP's posted policy makes it clear that digital elements should not be added or subtracted from a photo. But "minor" Photoshop adjustments are permitted.

> These include cropping, dodging and burning, conversion into grayscale, and normal toning and color adjustments . . . minimally necessary for clear and accurate reproduction (analogous to [the techniques] often used in darkroom processing of images) and that restore the authentic nature of the photograph.
>
> (Associated Press, 2006)

Retouching to eliminate dust or scratches is acceptable, but digital blurring or elimination of backgrounds is (usually) not. Also not acceptable: "changes in density, contrast, color and saturation levels that substantially alter the original scene"—a provision that certainly would have ruled out *Time*'s darkening of O. J. Simpson's face on its cover, which Kittross refers to on p. 247.

In regard to video, the AP says it's okay to use "subtle, standard methods of improving technical quality, such as adjusting video and audio levels, color correcting due to white balance or other technical faults, and equalization of audio to make the sound clearer," as long as this doesn't alter the image's content in any way—an approach that may well be in conflict with itself. For both TV and online images, it *is* okay to edit the background to make it neutral, in order to feature a head shot of a newsmaker, provided the result is labeled as a graphic rather than a photo (AP, 2006).

For audio material, pauses or stumbles by AP correspondents can be edited out, but material from a newsmaker can't be altered in any way, except to use "the subtle, standard audio processing methods of normalization of levels, general volume adjustments, equalization to make the sound clearer," reducing extraneous noise and making smooth transitions in and out of sound bites. As with visual images, the wire service specifies that these methods cannot alter the audio content in any way (AP, 2006).

Even the NPPA ethics code, revamped in 2004 to take new technologies into account while maintaining the highest photojournalism standards, doesn't rule out digital manipulation provided "the integrity of the photographic images' content and context" is maintained. Image manipulation or sound alteration is forbidden only if "that can mislead viewers or misrepresent subjects" (National Press Photographers Association, 2004)—a stance that appears to allow the same kind of "traditional darkroom" image manipulation that is also okay with the Associated Press.

The NPPA, though, was quite unhappy when *Newsweek* magazine featured Martha Stewart's head on the body of a slimmer model on its March 7, 2005 cover. The organization criticized this as "a total breach of ethics and completely misleading to the public." *Newsweek*'s editor wrote that the digital alteration was intended as a "humorous photo illustration of Stewart coming back looking better than ever" as her prison term ended that week and that he thought—mistakenly—that it would be clear this was "playful visual commentary, not a real picture of Stewart" (National Press Photographers Association, 2005). This same "we thought it was obvious" explanation was used by *Time* magazine editors who had darkened Simpson's face.

It's clear that with all of those exceptions in the AP and NPPA statements, it comes down to judgment calls and how various terms are defined, which rules out any absolute Kantian prohibition against digital alterations. And that's appropriate, as discussed earlier. It may be a bit Machiavellian to say that, but also utilitarian. We contend that this approach is simpler and more understandable and therefore more useful to society than any convoluted efforts to implement electronic watermarks or schemes for certifying a photo's authenticity.

Instead, just put the information and images out there (altered or not), do your best to insure that the public is aware that neither text nor images represent "reality" 100% faithfully, and try to insure that whatever changes have been made don't distort the overall reality that you are portraying in words or images.

MESSAGES AND IMAGES FROM CYBERSPACE

What about the situation where you become the media gatekeeper for images or information transmitted digitally—and almost instantaneously—by people who are unknown to you but who have access to very newsworthy events occurring elsewhere? One recent example: the unrest in Iran in 2009, when major aspects of coverage came from cell phone photos and text messages ostensibly originated by protesters in the streets. Similar quandaries follow almost any newsworthy disaster or upheaval: recent examples are legion and you can come up with several of your own by following the news during the next week or two. This raises again the age-old question in news: is it better to be first, or to be right? Ideally, the answer is "both," but what if both can't be guaranteed as a ubiquitous 24/7 deadline is looming?

We would urge that newsroom gatekeepers make every effort to verify that photos depict actual events and that written accounts reflect those events as accurately as possible. If the people transmitting that material have axes to grind, that should certainly be noted. But if those verification efforts fail, and the information is useful for the public to know, our advice would be to get it posted or broadcast or (if a newspaper deadline is upon you) printed and distributed, but with appropriate cautionary notes.

This, too, is Machiavellian, but it also follows a rule utilitarian approach, namely, that it will produce a greater good for the audience you serve if the information is made available, rather than being held indefinitely for verification. *If* you identify the uncertain provenance of such information, your audience—particularly the Twitter or Facebook users among them—should understand that the information or images may have some shortcomings, and treat it accordingly. And, if and when you can ascertain that there were errors, those can be corrected.

A FINAL ILLUSTRATION

Video images, as noted above, are subject to manipulation, and this can be beneficial. For example, the telecast of the opening ceremonies at the 2008 Beijing Olympics contained 55 seconds of digitally re-created fireworks, because the Chinese were concerned that TV cameras couldn't capture the sequential explosions intended to represent "footprints" of the 29 prior modern Olympiads "marching" toward the stadium from Tiananmen Square. A Chinese visual effects team spent nearly a year re-creating all but the last explosion in an animation studio and inserted the three-dimensional animated clip—which even included a re-creation of Beijing's evening haze—into the live broadcast while the stadium audience watched the real thing (Magnier, 2008).

We see no harm whatever in this approach, and neither did an overwhelming part of the TV audience. This lack of reaction was summed up very well by Julia Keller, the culture critic of the *Chicago Tribune*, who noted that the digital enhancement wasn't really that unusual, because "we live in the Age of Fake. Wait, there's more: We live in the Age of Fake. (And, Like, Your Point Is?)" She added that fake photos, memoirs, blogs, bios on Internet dating services, résumés, home run records, and "fake—make that 'computer-generated'—stunts in summer blockbusters" have produced a "sense of unreality" that tolerates digital and other fakery (Keller, 2008, pp. 1 and 16).

It's worth noting that, in contrast to the United States, Internet postings in China—mostly anonymous—did raise concerns about what kind of a lesson this represented for Chinese children. The criticism related both to the fireworks animation and to the lip-synching of "Ode to the Motherland" that a photogenic 9-year-old "soloist" did on camera as the Chinese flag entered the stadium, with the voice supplied by a 7-year-old whose looks were thought to be less suitable for international display. The music director for the opening ceremonies was quoted as saying that the change was made "in the national interest. . . . The child on camera should be flawless in image" (Magnier, 2008).

It's doubtful that anyone in the viewing audience was damaged in any way by the digitized fireworks during the opening ceremonies, even if they became aware of the "fakery." So, what's the fuss about? Like Kittross, we think that undetectable digital alterations are here to stay. Unlike him, we're not wringing our hands over this. But we do agree with him that, *if* mass communicators, individually and collectively, can be guided toward acting appropriately as individual moral agents, that's all to the good.

However, since not everyone will be so guided, let us stress again the need to educate the public about what is reasonable to expect and what is unreasonable, and to accept these effects of digital technology.

KEY POINTS

- Some digital alteration is ethically permissible in news, persuasive communication and especially in entertainment, as long as the overall impression is not distorted.
- There is no more of a problem with digital manipulation of images than there is with print media gatekeepers' "manipulation" of details to be included or excluded.
- Information and photos sent digitally to newsrooms by members of the public should be verified if at all possible but if those efforts fail, they should be posted, broadcast or printed with appropriate cautionary notes.

KITTROSS: The ability to "doctor" visual images and audio content digitally and undetectably will not go away so we must live with it, and newsrooms should try to verify digital materials even at the risk of not being "first."

"Pictures don't lie." If you believe the preceding sentence, I've got a Brooklyn Bridge I'd like to sell you. Of course pictures lie, and always have! And we've learned how to live with that fact, although the situation may be changing.

THE HISTORICAL RECORD

Since the first artist or sculptor picked up a primitive brush or chisel, artists have been in control of the appearance of their subjects. Photographers may keep (or airbrush out) anachronisms, defects or embarrassing contradictions. For example, in his famous documentary *Man of Aran* (1934), Robert Flaherty carefully selected camera angles to make sure that no electric power lines showed in "primitive village" scenes. Is this honest? Clothing and makeup have covered flaws and emphasized good points for centuries. Is this deceitful? Press photographers always have been on the alert for an opportunity to snap a subject showing a compromising or misleading facial expression or gesture, regardless of whether the picture will be an accurate reflection of the event or person. Is this fair—to both subject and viewer? File footage might be broadcast or printed without attribution or with a dishonest provenance. For example, during the Vietnam War, a New York television station pretended to be airing daily pictorial coverage but was merely using stock footage. Is this in the public interest?

These "tricks of the trade" used by artists and photographers for centuries were often thought of as part of their hard-won set of skills. Nowadays, however, anybody with a computer can do the same things, and nobody will be the wiser. Here are some examples.

In the 1920s, the *New York Graphic* achieved notoriety by cutting out pictures of the faces of people in the news and pasting them over posed bodies or scenes that were believed to reflect more accurately or more entertainingly the underlying story (Mallen, 1954). More seriously, during wartime many pictures were doctored for propaganda purposes by all sides; and domestically, in 1950, the successful campaign against the re-election of Maryland Senator Millard Tydings carefully cropped two pictures to produce a composite that showed him "listening" to a communist.

The use of traditional cinematographic technologies for "faking" has been demonstrated in feature films such as *Forrest Gump* (1994) and Woody Allen's *Zelig* (1983), where the leading characters were inserted into a variety of historical newsreels through the use of optical mattes. In television, the use of an electronic traveling matte technique (such as chroma key), which allows an actor or reporter to be inserted into another location, is an everyday practice. (However, among television news directors, this is considered an unfair practice when used to pretend that an in-studio presenter is actually an on-the-scene reporter.) In countries where former leaders can become "nonpersons" overnight, it is now as easy for pictures to be modified to eliminate a person as it was for writings to be manipulated in the same way and for the same political purposes in George Orwell's *Nineteen Eighty-Four* (1949).

Closer to home, one can find in many shopping malls a growing business in electronically removing former spouses from family pictures, which can also be accomplished on a home computer. While many photojournalists of today (and yesterday) have been concerned about the ethics of their field, the instant availability of technology may be even more tempting to them than to other media practitioners.

Advertising . . . has long used artistic license to make the product or service being advertised look better.

Advertising, as was pointed out in the first half of this chapter, has long used artistic license to make the product or service being advertised look better. Within its first decade, radio acquired a corps of talented individuals who could copy almost any sound, from the animal noises in a jungle to nearly perfect imitations of world leaders. Surprisingly, radio was able to harness listeners' imaginations even more than film or television. Although early audio recordings, with grooves cut into discs, made it difficult to modify audio in the myriad ways that moving and still pictures could be modified, when magnetic audio tape recording came into use in the late 1940s, skilled hands using a razor blade or scissors could make sound do what the editor wanted it to do. But then it required a lot of skill. Today, of course, it can all be more easily accomplished with specialized multitrack recording and mixing equipment—or on any computer.

THE NEW PROBLEM: DIGITALIZATION WITHOUT DETECTION

Why does this "easier" manipulation create a "new" ethical dilemma? Today, once a picture has been reduced to digitized electronic form—whether by video, scanning, or direct computer generation—it can easily be modified. The results go far beyond the crude forgeries, editing, or composites of earlier times. Most importantly, *it can be changed without detection*, which is what makes this a "new" dilemma.

Until the 1980s or so, a faked or modified picture could be detected by careful analysis of each generation of negative, and one might try to warn or inform viewers of the deception. But nowadays it is possible for almost anyone to alter a picture digitally so that the change is impossible to detect (Phelan, 1992; Wheeler, 2002). This is a new, and disturbing, situation.

Let's repeat that. Today, anyone with the ability to digitize a picture and insert it into a computer can adjust the picture at will, and turn out a changed "original," with nobody realizing it. With digitization, the picture (original or modified) is merely a string of zeros and ones in a computer's memory or a magnetic recording medium, which means that there is no surefire way to tell what is original or what has been changed. Essentially, the same can be and is done with digital audio.

Such techniques are used in most media: film, television, newspapers, radio, and recordings. And magazines. The cover of the then-largest-circulation magazine in the United States, *TV Guide*, once published on its cover the face of Oprah Winfrey attached to the body of Ann-Margret. *National Geographic* once "moved" one of the Egyptian pyramids in order to compose a better-looking cover, and *Time*'s cover photograph of murder suspect O. J. Simpson in June, 1994 was darkened, possibly as visual commentary, to make him appear more threatening. It is unlikely that many would have noticed the *Time* cover, except that *Newsweek* ran the same picture on its cover that week—unretouched.

In each of these cases, it so happened that there were enough people who were familiar with how the picture *should* have looked to object loudly. But how often will there be people as familiar with a run-of-the-mill scene or person? Not very often! How many who see a doctored picture will also be exposed to a correction? Not very many! How many pictures that we see in the media have been altered without warning? Who knows? An estimate might be made from the accounts of digital manipulation by a Toledo *Blade* photographer, who had 21 doctored photos appear in print, 31 more online and 27 both in print and online in just over three months in 2007 (Royhab, 2007).

Hence, although it might be difficult to revise a scene or individual face familiar to millions without someone noticing, it is probable that all but a tiny handful of news photos could be modified without anyone being the wiser. All it takes is a few thousand dollars worth of equipment and a computer program, and somebody—anybody who has some access to the media—who wants to do so.

This prospect is dismaying. The possibility of doing harm to individuals and to society is large, yet the public may benefit from pictures that have been modified to clarify a situation or to prevent individuals from being shocked or unjustly portrayed. But more than any other ethical controversy I've written about in this book, digital manipulation of pictures shows fewest opportunities for an ethical solution that is, at the same time, practical.

Digital technology exists, and we will have to find ways to live with it. We've done so before, with technologies such as firearms or automobiles, both of which could be used for either good or evil. We can't stuff it back into Pandora's Box.

SOME LARGER QUESTIONS

The idea that manipulation and falsification takes place only when photographs, audio tapes, and similar processes are employed is a pernicious one. Most of our information, knowledge and wisdom originally is in the form of words, and words are even easier to manipulate using digital techniques than pictures.

Sometimes we don't even ask all of the questions (or the right ones). Babcock and Gordon described a problem faced by a documentary-maker who inadvertently incorporated a few seconds of *The Simpsons* in the background of a scene. When he discovered that the rights to those few seconds would cost him $10,000, he manipulated the picture so the background television screen showed a snippet from a film he had made and controlled. As Gordon and Babcock noted, the general rule about documentaries is that they should portray exactly what was taking place, with no attempt at manipulating the images. But they acknowledged that the universally accepted Kantian "no tampering" rule "might not hold in 100% of the cases" and noted that, here, "the only viable alternative was to break the Kantian rule and, *ever so slightly* digitally alter what actually took place" (emphasis added).

This documentary, however, focused on the contrast between the on-stage and backstage worlds during the production of one of Richard Wagner's *Ring* cycle operas. The scene in question was an important one: it showed a pair of stagehands playing checkers backstage, while the operatic gods were battling things out onstage. The television set was another character in the scene, one that would lose its importance if the 4.5 seconds of *The Simpsons* was replaced by just another film. As a result, this budget-driven decision eliminated

> a shot poignantly showing Homer Simpson, perhaps the quintessential popular culture foil to Wagnerian high art, as part of the stagehands' background to an opera about Teutonic gods. And, no less to [the filmmaker's] dismay, a film that is supposed to be a documentary contains a bit of calculated untruth.
>
> (Netanel, 2008, pp. 16–17)

One problem that has received short shrift here is the *un*likelihood that any correction of an error in the media—no matter what the source of the error or its importance—will ever catch up to the original publication. This makes it even more necessary for responsible writers, editors and producers who determine media content to do their job properly and in advance, because relying on corrections is unlikely to create a fair marketplace of ideas, words or images.

And let there be no mistake, the advent of digital media often makes things worse rather than better. It is now very easy and inexpensive to produce or modify publications, videos, audio recordings and social media using new technologies rather than the nearly 500-year-old technology of printing. But the task of perfecting or polishing a work hasn't caught up. For example, there were fewer typographic errors in a scholarly magazine I edited many years ago B.D. (before digital) than there are in the magazine I now edit, using all of the latest computerized gadgetry. Spellcheck is not a proper substitute for copy editors, as any careful editor or reader will testify. True, some aspects of writing are easier (no need to install new typewriter ribbons at the moments when one's creative juices are flowing, for example), but the reliance on the Internet to do one's research is misplaced. Personal experience has shown me that for every ten URLs, citations, or other Internet-based bits of content that are present when writing an article, at least one (or two) will have disappeared into cyberspace by the time the article is published.

The basic questions remain: how does the audience member find out whether something is true or false? And suppose that she or he then makes decisions on the basis of a falsehood? Doesn't the creator and distributor of the information being relied upon have some responsibility for this outcome, even though it may have been unintentional?

There are other interwoven factors here. The idea that an important duty of the media is to produce the "first draft of history" is something to think about more intensely as we stroke the keys and otherwise prepare the day's material for printing or airing. After all, if a documentary, or a news story or feature, or even a docudrama creates the context for our knowledge and interpretation of the world, then its content and preparation are very important, both at that time and later. Scholars and others in later years use newspaper accounts and similar ephemeral sources to construct major historical analyses that enable us to learn from others' actions and inactions, and warped accounts of what actually went on could distort those analyses.

THE IMPERFECT SOLUTIONS

Modifying copyright laws to give the creator of an image permanent control over that image *and* the responsibility for certifying its authenticity is (perhaps) the only possible practical fix that has been seriously proposed. It would require a change in the U.S. copyright law to give permanent artistic control over an image to its photographic or artistic creator (but leaving its economic ownership in the hands of those who happen to own the copyright). In exchange, this creator must be willing to certify the authenticity of the picture. This sort of separate, artistic right may be found in the copyright laws of numerous countries. An already-developed form of "electronic watermark" used primarily to certify the copyright status of still photographs might further identify the image as "original"—until someone finds a way to circumvent this technology.

However, digital video and film cameras are now ubiquitous. Few, if any, Americans are without a non-professional photographic life record such as family pictures. Computer programs such as Photoshop are available to all, and have many legitimate uses as well as fraudulent ones. Fortunately, very little of this non-professional photographic record will ever need to have its authenticity certified, although, as posters on Facebook can testify, it isn't all that hard to have one's "photos" modified, and sometimes show up in print or other mass public forum.

There may be practical problems, as well. For instance, photographers may not even be aware precisely of what they have shot because many of them now shoot dozens of pictures in a few seconds with a motorized still camera, or are involved in a half dozen video assignments a day. One photographer who took a picture of himself with a self-timer in front of the Berlin Wall was shocked to find, when the picture was developed, an unnoticed East German border guard a few feet away with an automatic rifle aimed in his direction.

Sometimes, a picture contains elements that should not be seen, and it is deemed necessary to black out the element in question rather than to change it. For example, one of the photos taken after the Zeppelin *Hindenburg* (a huge airship) caught fire and burned within seconds while landing at Lakehurst, New Jersey in 1937, showed a survivor staggering from the airship's cabin with his clothing burned off and his genitals showing. This photo was widely distributed, but a rectangle was pasted on the negative to cover the genitals, making it obvious that this part of the image had been censored and protecting those who might be shocked or offended over and above the basic horror of the scene. A similar technique might have been used as an alternative to removing a few seconds of *The Simpsons* television program playing in the background of the documentary mentioned earlier. The filmmaker could simply have obscured what was on the TV screen in such a way as to show that *something* was playing, and, if necessary, mentioning this in the voice-over narration.

We can also rely on the personal moral and professional ethical standards of the creators, and those who process and publish the pictures, to forego voluntarily the use of any manipulative techniques. But because communicators have used whatever technology was available to manipulate pictures for so many years—"dodging" and cropping photos were accepted practices for more than a century—it hasn't been thought of as wrong by most people in the field. Indeed, such enhancements were considered artistic and communicative. The difference with digital manipulation is that it is inherently undetectable.

From a practical standpoint, the best solution to unethical revision of the pictorial and audio record might be to provide universal fair warning to the public. One magazine reminds the reader in each issue that "Photographs often are digitally altered." Many newspapers identify such material as "photo montages" or "photo illustrations." The fact that the public and, indeed, some people in the industries involved, do not understand these identifications is beside the point: identification of pictorial modification would still be a useful means of warning the public.

The public should not trust pictures. They should look at all pictures through a veil of suspicion,

The last potential solution is to make it possible to use these techniques without harm to the public. Here I join Gordon, who proposed education of the public as the solution for another problem in Chapter 8. *The public should not trust pictures.* They should look at all pictures through a veil of suspicion, without any presumption that they are truthful. That is the bottom line. If no picture is trusted, then the public shouldn't easily be harmed by a doctored one. True, this would reduce the communication value of pictures to the public and lower the photographer, artist, or editor in terms of public esteem, but it may be the price we have to pay (Wheeler, 1995).

I'm forced to advocate that we take that Kantian, possibly draconian, position. The public should categorically never, *never*, NEVER trust a picture. By treating the problem in this way, while advocating the teaching of ethical as well as perceptual standards of "visual literacy," we may defuse digital technology's potential for harm.

Of course, such a Kantian solution may lead to a utilitarian nightmare. If we can't trust any digitized media—and almost everything now comes in a digital format—then the bonds of trust that hold a society together may also dissolve through this mistrust. At this time, I don't see any possibility of a technological "fix." To paraphrase a sentence in the preamble to the UNESCO constitution, if the human mind can cause us to mistrust one another, causing wars, then it is probably in the human mind that we will have to re-erect a societal structure in which trust—open-eyed, not blind—must be established (UNESCO, 1945).

But this is only part of the problem. Pictures taken by amateurs on cell phones and other devices are a growing part of the pictorial record and an increasing part of the potential news coverage of disasters or other chaotic situations. This is particularly true, for understaffed American media, if those events are taking place abroad.

This raises a very pertinent ethics question: what kind of authentication (or "vetting") is needed before photos of uncertain origin and unknown authenticity are aired, published or displayed on Web sites? The technology that allows those images to be digitized and transmitted instantaneously brings with it a crucial series of questions, all with important ethics overtones. The same questions apply to texted, written, or voice-mailed accounts of events, when they come from members of the public, and frequently members of the public who are unknown to you.

My incompletely formed position is that the "media literacy" classes frequently advocated in this book need to include discussion of the ethical requirements that should be followed by *all* who capture images. If it becomes possible to reliably distinguish unethically taken and manipulated pictures from those that are a more valid pictorial record of events, people, places and things, that also would be a good thing for the public to learn, even though I question its probability.

Although the individual communicator still has a utilitarian obligation to be as truthful as possible with pictorial matter, it would be sticking one's head in the sand to believe that an ethical approach is likely to be universal. The temptation, combined with the rapidly falling prices of the equipment that makes manipulation possible, may be too much for many otherwise-moral photographers or picture editors.

But any recording—a painted portrait, a photograph (whether on film or a magnetic medium such as tape or disc), a sound recording—is more than a record; it is also art. To deny the artist the possibilities provided by technology—stripping out background noise in a sound recording, changing contrast and composition by the twist of a knob or tapping on a keyboard, editing the content, or making a sponsor (advertising or product placement) happy by making a product look "good"—is probably asking too much.

At the same time, unfortunately, because most of the public has accepted the "pictures don't lie" aphorism as truth, these practices have a definite value for advertisers and propagandists. Here is a golden opportunity for formal or informal education.

CONCLUSION

One half of the ethical problem is very simple: anything that is in digital form can be altered, for aesthetic, political or any other reason, without the possibility of detection. The ethical solution may be equally simple: each of us working in or studying the visual mass media needs to make sure that our fellow citizens know that pictures *do* lie, and that every picture should be looked at with the same suspicion and caution that we've learned to employ when reading or hearing words that may be self-serving, wrong, or manipulative. In other words, don't trust anyone—including me—without first independently checking the truth of our verbal, aural, written and visual assertions.

The other half is equally simple: being first is nowhere near as important or as ethical as getting it right. So the Kantian rule has to be that, short of saving lives or preventing disasters, photos and text that come to a newsroom from sources outside its staff *must* have the accuracy of their content (words or images) established before they are passed on to the public. If a news outlet establishes this kind of reputation for credibility, its standing with the public will remain constant regardless of whether or not it is faster than the competition.

Writing early in the 21st century about the credibility of photos, Tom Wheeler said that the key question has become how (and whether) it is possible to "demonstrate that at least some photos can still be believed" in the face of the public's "well-founded skepticism of . . . published imagery." His answer, quoting writer and editor Randall Rothenberg, is applicable to text from uncertain origins, as well as to images. He wrote that credibility will have to come "from the organization and its personnel, not from the medium" (Rothenberg, quoted by Wheeler, 2002, pp. 206 and 207).

KEY POINTS

- A Kantian rule is the best approach here: never trust that a visual image is unaltered.
- Similarly, *all* photos and texts originating outside a newsroom's staff must have their accuracy established before being passed on to the public, unless delay would lead to loss of life or would fail to prevent a disaster.
- All who provide media content must do their jobs well and in advance, because it's very unlikely that corrections will ever catch up with errors.

MERRILL: Commentary

Here we go again. One author (Kittross) posits a pure Kantian position and the other two (Babcock and Gordon) a moderate partly utilitarian position. Like most of the ethical controversies dealt with in this book, this one dealing with digital manipulation of content boils down to this: *the presentation of truth*.

Should we stay as close to truth as possible? Or, should we deviate from it when we feel we need to for various reasons? Kittross provides a sterling recap of historical instances of technological manipulation of content, but does not condone them. He admits them, discusses some of them, and judges that they are unethical. Babcock and Gordon, on the other hand, are rather cavalier about them, noting that they have always been with us and there are no serious ethical problems with content alterations that don't distort the overall "impression." This is somewhat strange, it seems to me, since this is a book about ethics, not about justifying unethical behavior. "It has always been so; therefore it is not unethical." Please!

Babcock and Gordon give some interesting examples of digital (and other) manipulation, and imply that these are simply normal, commonplace practices in journalism. This is certainly true, but such things as cropping pictures and voice imitations on radio, when considered in the context of ethics, need to be approached from more than "it's a common practice" perspective. Truth should be the ethical journalist's objective. And I stress *journalist* here; one would, at least in our culture, assume that truth is the bedrock concept of a journalist. Truth will also be a key principle for the ethical public relations practitioner, and it certainly has to be in the mix for ethical advertising professionals, as well.

Of course, journalism will never provide the truth, the whole truth, and nothing but the truth. We all know that. But when a journalist knowingly abandons the basic goal of providing the most truthful picture of reality, it is at that moment that ethics rears its head. And unfortunately, as Kittross says, there are few opportunities with modern technology for an ethical solution. But there is (as Kittross also says) reliance on personal moral standards. If it distorts the truth, just don't do it. Period. A good Kantian imperative.

But, the Babcocks and Gordons of the journalistic world (and perhaps of the PR and advertising worlds, as well) might well say: the people know they will not get the truth, that they don't really need the truth, and ethics must take a back seat to the realities of society and communication. Not only that, but often it is more ethical *not* to be truthful. Utilitarianism, playing to the people's happiness or satisfaction, comes into play here. Truth becomes simply an instrument, not a goal; play with it, use it, discard it, manipulate it in order to bring about desired results. Truth, when it is needed, becomes simply an instrument and not a goal.

Babcock and Gordon, of course, are right when saying that *all news is manipulated in some way*. Reality cannot be passed on without changing it in some way. But does that mean that a journalist should not *try to keep distortions out*? In most cases, it is true, cropping one person out of picture does little or no real harm, if the intent is to show what the remaining person looks like. But it is another thing if by digital manipulation one person is changed and distorted.

I can hear retorts already: all right, then *all* journalism is unethical because no story is without some falsification. And to a degree they are right. But the key concept is *purposeful or willful falsification*. Journalists are somewhat like map-makers; they cannot present *all* the territory, but they can provide as reliable a picture of it as possible.

If the map-maker intentionally misrepresents a contested piece of land—for example, Palestinian maps that omit any indication that Israel exists, or Israeli maps that incorporate the West Bank into Israel by referring to it as "Samaria and Judea"—that's unethical because it is willful manipulation.

So perhaps the real question here is not whether manipulation is unethical, but whether willful manipulation with the intent to deceive is unethical. We don't really know how Babcock and Gordon would face such a question phrased in this way, but because of its obviously dishonest and deceptive nature, we can assume that they would deem it unethical. As for Kittross, he would naturally find it unethical. But there's one basic problem: how do we know when a manipulation is *intended* to deceive, or simply natural? How can the public—not endowed with psychic powers—know the intentions of the communicator? For that matter, how can the public (except on occasion) know that something is even being manipulated in the media?

As to the question of how to handle photos and written material that come unsolicited to a newsroom from unknown members of the public, the question to me isn't really "is it better to be right or to be first?" I've never been an advocate of "citizen journalism" and it would be much better, I think, to reject all such offerings. Let journalists with the proper training and experience report, edit and provide to the public all important and useful information, no matter where it originates. That, of course, isn't possible in these days of major news staff reductions, but it would be the ethical way to proceed. On this point, neither Kittross nor Gordon and Babcock have it right.

This is an interesting controversy and well worth the time to discuss it. Like so many other controversies in mass media ethics, the key problem is with honesty, with truth, with good intentions, and with acting within the parameters of the profession. The authors touch on this in regard to the entertainment media, in referring to the issue of truth in documentaries. But there, as more generally, there is no simple answer. We are left with the thorny question: as truth is always less than perfect in journalism (or in advertising, public relations or the entertainment media), how should journalists and others see their responsibility—if they have any—to depict it for the public?

REFERENCES AND RELATED READINGS

Associated Press. (2006). "The Associated Press Statement of News Values and Principles"—"Audio" and "Images" sections, February 16. Retrieved from www.ap.org:80/newsvalues/index.html (August 19, 2008).

Bok, Sissela. (1978). *Lying: Moral Choice in Public and Private Life*. New York: Pantheon.

Fosdick, Scott, and Shahira Fahmy. (2007). "Epistemic honesty and the default assumption that photos are true." *SIMILE: Studies in Media and Information Literacy Education* 7(1), pp. 1–10.

Harris, Christopher R. (1991). "Digitization and manipulation of news photographs." *Journal of Mass Media Ethics* 6(3), pp. 164–174.

"It's tough typecasting ethics: Technology gives newspapers a whole new crop of dilemmas." (1991). *Orange County Register*, March 24, p. A30.

Keller, Julia. (2008). "Oh well, whatever, never mind." *Chicago Tribune*, August 13, pp. 1 and 16.

King, David. (1997). *The Commissar Vanishes: The Falsification of Photographs and Art in Stalin's Russia*. New York: Metropolitan.

Lester, Paul Martin. (1991). *Photojournalism: An Ethical Approach*. Mahwah, NJ: Lawrence Erlbaum Associates.

Magnier, Mark. (2008). "China abuzz over lip-syncing singer in Olympics opening ceremony." *Los Angeles Times*, August 13. Retrieved from www.latimes.com/sports/la-fg-lipsync13-2008aug13,0,3009926.story (August 19, 2008).

Mallen, Frank. (1954). *Sauce for the Gander*. White Plains, NY: Baldwin.

National Press Photographers Association. (2004). "NPPA Board adopts new 'modernized' code of ethics." July 10. Retrieved from www.nppa.org/news_and_events/news/2004/07/nppa_adopts_new_ethics_code.html (August 19, 2008).

——. (2005). "NPPA calls Newsweek's Martha Stewart cover 'A major ethical breach'." March 9. Retrieved from www.nppa.org/news_and_events/news/2005/03/newsweek.html (August 21, 2008).

Netanel, Neil W. (2008). *Copyright's Paradox*. Oxford, UK: Oxford University Press.

Palmer, Chris. (2010). *Shooting in the Wild: An Insider's Account of Making Movies in the Animal Kingdom*. San Francisco, CA: Sierra Club Books.

Phelan, John M. (1992). "The pseudo context of the processed image." *Media Ethics* 4(2), pp. 9–10.

Reaves, Shiela. (1991). "Digital alteration of photographs in consumer magazines." *Journal of Mass Media Ethics* 6(3), pp. 175–181.

Reaves, Shiela, Jacqueline Bush Hitchon, Sung-Yeon Park, and Gi Woong Yun. (2004). "If looks could kill: Digital manipulation of fashion models." *Journal of Mass Media Ethics* 19(1), pp. 56–71.

Royhab, Ron. (2007). "A basic rule: Newspaper photos must tell the truth." *toledoBlade.com*, April 15. Retrieved from http://toledoblade.com/apps/pbcs.dll/article?AID=/20070415/NEWS08/704150316&SearchID=73278129833947 (August 18, 2008).

Sterling, Christopher H., and John Michael Kittross (2002). *Stay Tuned: A History of American Broadcasting*, 3rd ed. Mahwah, NJ: Lawrence Erlbaum Associates.

UNESCO (1945). Preamble to the constitution of the United Nations Educational Scientific and Cultural Organization. http://portal.unesco.org/en/ev.php-URL_ID=15244&URL_DO=DO_TOPIC&URL_SECTION=201.html

Wheeler, Tom. (1995). "Public perceptions of photographic credibility in the age of digital manipulation." Paper presented at a meeting of the Association for Education in Journalism and Mass Communication, Washington, DC, August.

——. (2002). *Phototruth or Photofiction: Ethics and Media Imagery in the Digital Age*. Mahwah, NJ: Lawrence Erlbaum Associates.

Chapter 8

Media Ethics and the Economic Marketplace

W HAT is the place of ethics in a business that depends on financial profit for its survival? That's the problem facing mass media practitioners who are concerned about ethics but who literally can't afford to ignore the economics of their calling. As long as most media are supported primarily by advertising, they will need to attract audiences they can deliver to advertisers, and that need can clash seriously with the desire to "do the ethical thing." Hence, this chapter necessarily deals heavily with economics, one of the practical *preconditions* for the environment in which ethical decisions are made, thus allowing the reader to explore in that context the ethical questions about media economics that arise daily.

This chapter assumes that all decision-making, including economic decision-making, requires *individual human beings* to weigh the alternatives, goals and responsibilities, including their own personal goals and those of the societies in which they live. Professions such as religion, teaching, and the military face the same kinds of alternatives, goals and responsibilities as do quasi-professions such as the mass media.

The typical company or other organization wants to grow, either vertically (controlling the entire process from raw materials or content through distribution and sales), or horizontally (expanding either through internal growth or by acquiring other firms in a given industry or function to reduce the competition). But there is a third model of growth, the conglomerate, which can have strong negative ethical effects, partly because its only business is money, rather than widgets, automobiles, or television programming.

The growth of conglomerate-owned mass media outlets has brought into top decision-making positions people who sometimes have little or no experience with the media channels they control, and minimal understanding of the ethical concerns that have arisen in a particular medium over the years. For example, might a publisher or owner unfamiliar with the nuts-and-bolts of journalism be more willing to remove a commentary that offends an advertiser than one who has a journalism background? Might an advertising agency manager with a background in sales be unwilling to take economic risks that may accompany new approaches to creativity? Might an accountant who heads the parent company of a TV production firm be negative about proposed programming that breaks new ground, and prefer to rely instead on tried and true formulas? Would a venture capitalist who buys into a media company solely to make a short-term profit really care about journalistic—or other—values?

There is a way out of this conundrum. In addition to individuals pondering specific ethical questions, it is possible for corporations to consider ethics as part of the corporate culture, as more than just a way to persuade employees not to pilfer paper clips or use the telephone for personal matters. CBS at one time hired a consultant on ethics, a former priest who knew the broadcasting industry well. The content of the *Mary Tyler Moore Show* and *Lou Grant* often dealt with journalistic ethical questions, without harming their popularity. To be successful, CEOs have to think about the consequences of their actions (and inactions). Unfortunately, most of them leave it to individuals lower on the corporate ladder to make decisions on ethics while playing their parts in the purely economic "game" that has the attention of so many.

In this context, we believe that owners, entrepreneurs, and managers should be held to the same ethical standards as other employees. They need to be at least as responsible as everyone else, although they have the advantage of being able to call on subordinates and consultants for specialized advice. Every person working in the media has a similar responsibility (to their audience, among others) to act ethically in an effort to preserve the functions as well as the good name of their industry, profession, colleagues and themselves.

Although economics is referred to above as a "precondition," this label does not diminish the practical importance of ownership, particularly when he who pays the piper decides what tunes should be played. A. J. Liebling put it well in the early 1960s: "Freedom of the press is guaranteed only to those who own one" (Liebling, 1961, p. 30).

One perspective on this controversy is the contention that economic realities make concerns for ethics more difficult, if not impossible, or perhaps superfluous. This is the position argued here by John Michael Kittross. If pressed, he will acknowledge that he sometimes denies both the value and the importance of profits in a world full of nonprofit associations, cooperatives, and barter economies. Another approach (though certainly not the only alternative) holds that economic considerations can have some positive effects on the ethical climate in which the mass media operate and has faith that new economic models can lead to ethical benefits. The public—the consumers—also can become more familiar with, and demanding of, their media. David Gordon espouses this position in the material that follows, and agrees that the nonprofit sector might take a larger role.

The important questions here might well be: Does the drive to maximize profits affect ethical behavior? If so, what results from that impact? And further, if there is an imbalance toward profit, what might be done to give ethics a stronger voice in decision-making?

KITTROSS: The economic marketplace is at best irrelevant and at worst counterproductive to media ethics and the marketplace of ideas.

Every field of knowledge has its shibboleths. Every era has its aphorisms. Every political or social movement has its slogans. Sometimes, they are inappropriately applied to other fields, such as media ethics. My thesis for this chapter is simple: The magic word of applied economics, "marketplace," has no useful function with respect to media ethics, either as an abstraction or as a euphemism for the quest for monetary gain. An exception to this asserted rule is that there probably *is* a "marketplace" where ideas are exchanged rather than money, and whose rules are analogous to the rules of economics, but are not identical to them.

There is no need to bring in formal economic theory or to ask "What would be the alternative to a market?" Pragmatically, I presume that both media ethics and economic marketplaces will continue to exist, but should be thought of as separate concepts, with separate criteria for evaluation. The purpose of the economic marketplace is generally to maximize profits of individuals and firms, nowadays usually in the short term. (To many in business, the 2008 worldwide economic recession might suggest substituting "survival" for "profits," but the principle is the same.) The purpose of media ethics is to enhance the lives of media practitioners, and through them the lives of the general public, in the long (as well as short) term. Although most mass media organizations are businesses, I maintain that they have social, psychological, economic, cultural, and even spiritual (in the broadest sense) functions that can benefit audiences, employees, and the society. An analogy would be the doctor, who collects large economic fees, yet has as her or his primary societal function the maintenance and improvement of the public's physical and mental health.

If we look at the traditional ethicists—Aristotle, Kant, Rawls, utilitarians such as Bentham and Mill—we find that their principles are either irrelevant to the economic marketplace (or vice versa), or in opposition to the very concept. However, to the extent that the goals of most Western societies (if not of all of their members) are based on economic principles, utilitarianism will be used to justify these goals. However, Kant, as well as the Judeo-Christian ethic, presumably would place the needs of the public (you and your neighbors) above both fiduciary responsibility to stockholders and the greed of the market.

Such a conflation of Kant's "rule-based" ethic and the utilitarian "consequence-based" ethic will show up in David Gordon's half of this chapter. While he speaks there of utilitarian "benefit to the most," I believe he actually is expressing a Kantian "monopoly and oligopoly are good" deontological rule, even though he treats this assertion as an axiom and doesn't justify his conclusion in terms of the public welfare.

In virtually all religions, and with few exceptions among philosophers, "greed" is a sin. A more-or-less neutral phrase like "economic realities" is, I believe, merely a way of making the sin of greed acceptable or, at least, semantically palatable.

CONTROVERSIES IN MEDIA ECONOMICS

So, what are the controversies in this chapter? Gordon and I take substantially different positions in this chapter, but in reality we agree much more than we disagree about the crucially important factor of media economics. Perhaps our greatest difference is over the *extent* to which media workers have even more responsibility to the society and their colleagues than they do to stockholders or employers. Another important area of controversy is whether the existing economic structure is the best—much less the only—possible way of utilizing money in what I consider its proper role: as only one of several measuring sticks rather than as a goal in itself.

In a nutshell, I hold that economics and media ethics generally are independent and often in opposition, unless one merely wants to find out one's price, or one's employer's price. Many sins have been committed by those who did evil while using the excuse, "Unless my business is profitable, I can't do any good." In the political arena, a similar approach is often taken by politicians: "Unless I do whatever it takes to get re-elected, I won't be in a position that empowers me to do good things for my constituents." I take a different position. It is often possible to "do well by doing good," and taking an ethical stand may often, serendipitously, bring the accolades and income that a weaker person hopes for—but rarely achieves—by selling his or her soul. To reverse this injunction—to do good by doing well— is, except to the spiritual descendants of the robber barons and some religious denominations of a century ago (and today's economic disciples of novelist and philosopher Ayn Rand), a logical impossibility.

It is often possible to "do well by doing good,"

Almost every facet of the mass media is influenced by economics. Most daily news-papers today rely on economic missions and goals, primarily their own but those of their advertisers and community as well. The same holds true for radio and television broad-casting, although economic power is shared with the power of a governmental agency trying to meet a legislatively imposed goal to serve the public interest, convenience, and/or necessity. Even nonprofit entities are concerned with questions of competition, monopoly, and income-gathering.

One sometimes can deduce the importance of economics in a particular industry by the language or form or location it adopts. Symbolically, in the newspaper industry, that part of the paper in which news is published is called "the news hole" (i.e., the space left over after the advertisements have been placed), while broadcasting stations refer to "commercial interruptions"—reflecting also the physical reality that, while additional pages *could* be printed in a newspaper, on a given channel the broadcast day cannot be stretched beyond 24 hours. The underlying reality here is economic. The feature motion picture industry and the television networks have long been headquartered in New York City (because that's where the banking industry that makes production loans is), even though actual production of most feature films and network television programs is located in Los Angeles.

In another example of how economics and performance interact, both newspaper and broadcast news operations, when the budget runs out, often are unable to respond to unanticipated disasters (and good news as well). Sometimes chains or conglomerates have a greater ability to shift funds around, and sometimes family-run media also have greater flexibility than the typical stockholder-owned firm, but almost every media outlet is fiscally conservative, because of its perceived need to make a profit. Sheer size, absentee—rather than community-based—ownership and a "one-size-fits-all" mentality, particularly in large conglomerates, tend to result in inflexibility and attention to economic gain rather than consideration of the public interest.

No matter how important news may be to the public; with few exceptions, if the annual budget has been spent or if income projections are lower than expected, news content is one of the first items to be produced "on the cheap," using such approaches as "rip-and-read" wire service reports, stock footage, "pools" of reporters, simple "stand up" or anchor-read news rather than expensive "packages" produced in the field or with major amounts of research, or just plain ignored. And increasingly, even in better worldwide economic times, newsgathering budgets got smaller, and news organizations closed their bureaus in foreign countries and state and national capitals, and provided less—or no—coverage of events that used to be considered important. Perhaps most noticeable is the axing of investigative reporting teams, mostly for budgetary reasons, but also possibly because the small (i.e., as compared to scandal, gossip, sport and entertainment) amount of real investigative reporting might occasionally tread on the toes of advertisers or political leaders.

This isn't to say that the news media universally make a habit of ignoring important stories. The annual lists of candidates for Pulitzer Prizes and SPJ Awards in these categories show that there are many significant, courageous and impressive stories that are covered by the news media every year. Yet, the overall amount of media time, space, and expense devoted to such matters is relatively tiny and there are many important stories that are *not* adequately covered. (For lists of the top overlooked and underreported stories, see the annual reports by Peter Phillips and Project Censored at Sonoma State University, published by Seven Stories Press, New York.)

IN A TIME OF FINANCIAL CRISIS

Figures gathered by the Radio-Television News Directors Association show what can happen in a time of declining revenues. Many stations no longer have newsrooms or reporters; some cut their reportorial staffs and hope that they can muddle through; some combine certain operations. For example, in November 2008, NBC and Fox, in cities where both networks have stations (New York, Los Angeles, Chicago, Dallas, and Washington) agreed to turn some of their camera crews over to a jointly run assignment desk. It remains to be seen whether the resultant saving in personnel costs will add to or subtract from the amount and quality of news available to the viewers (*USA Today*, 2008). The same holds true for newspapers—only more so. News holes have shrunk, the number of papers is down somewhat, and the number of newsroom employees dropped roughly 20% between 2000 and 2009 (Pickard et al., 2009).

This sort of "cut costs first" strategy, when combined with the more general approach of many news media to "convergence" (using the same personnel to provide content for several media platforms, from blogging to combinations of traditional media), ignores one unintended consequence: "Convergence" can lead to "contraction"—because there are only so many stories that a reporter can cover in a day. If a newspaper and a television station use the same people to report the news, it is likely that the benefits of different approaches will not be realized and the total number of stories (and depth of their coverage) available to the audience will dwindle. (This may explain some of "Project Censored" entries.)

It isn't only the journalistic function of the media that suffers in a time of "the sky is falling" panic. Certainly, most decisions to cut news staffs are economically based, but so are decisions to air cheap-to-produce game and reality shows. The quiz show scandals of the late 1950s show how flimsy the basis of these inexpensive programs can be, and a network that rests its future on low quality is taking a great risk.

ECONOMICS AND PUBLIC POLICY

In our era, some of the more consequential articles of faith—belief without objectively verifiable proof—are in the fields of theoretical and applied economics. Theoretical economics has justifiably been called the "dismal science," and is noted for its inability to predict either the fat years or the lean. Applied economists' income levels reflect the same patterns as those of their less-knowledgeable fellow citizens. Yet, the financial world has evolved to being almost as important as sports and weather on the 6 o'clock news—and, conceptually, we have come a long and tortuous way from the condemnation of money lending in many major religions (including Christianity and Islam) to the present glorification of Wall Street (and Las Vegas, which fulfills some of the same economic functions). Stories published or aired by the media have the power to affect prices—a power well known to the global financial community.

But when economics and politics join, very strong forces may be unleashed, as writers—from John Stuart Mill to the greenest pundit who yesterday reinvented the opinion that "people vote their pocketbooks"—have pointed out. Today, it would be silly to assume that government should have no role in the United States' economy, no matter what the slogans say. Our financial markets hang on every word spoken in public by the chairman of the Federal Reserve Bank, and the media cover them as if they were the utterances of a powerful oracle, which they are, because Main Street follows Wall Street which follows "the Fed."

Tax laws often have greater influence on policy than specific laws like the Communications Act of 1934. In the late 1970s and during the Reagan and George H. W. Bush administrations, government remained in the picture even amid the sudden popularity of "deregulation," "marketplace solutions," and similar manifestations that the pendulum had swung to the laissez-faire side of economics. This was so, even when it became fashionable to argue that government itself was the problem and should be reduced to an ever-smaller fraction of its present size—during the same administrations in which three-quarters of the subsequent national debt was being amassed.

A costly practice adopted from the start by the George W. Bush administration was to use governmental regulation and money in ways that would benefit private enterprise, improving the bottom line of large corporations, even before "bailouts." For example, many functions previously performed by the government are now conducted by contractors. In Iraq and Afghanistan, in 2008, there were slightly more civilian contractors paid by the U.S. government than members of the U.S. Armed Forces (Schwartz, 2009). These quiet connections between business and government are creating a very different world from when we considered our governmental structure to be one of independent checks and balances with the media serving as an independent watchdog.

Many conservatives, especially those in business and even if benefiting from government contracts, say that they desire less government. Government, however, has always had several useful functions in addition to being a tax collector and regulator. It also is a customer. Frequently, it is a facilitator, a source of research and development funding, such as that necessary to innovate technologies as old as the telegraph and as new as satellites and information displays. And its regulatory function may be aimed at one's competitors.

Although those arguing against regulation can be derided for having selfish motives, there are also a substantial number of those who might be called "right libertarians" who are philosophically and intellectually opposed to most or all current functions of government regardless of personal economic consequences. A former Speaker of the House of Representatives, "Uncle Joe" Cannon, maintained in the 45th Congress more than a century ago that "the function of the Federal government is to afford protection to life, liberty, and property. When that is done, then let every tub stand on its own bottom, let every citizen 'root hog or die'" (Weinberg and Weinberg, 1961, p. 96). ("Root hog or die" is an old phrase meaning self-reliance, fending for oneself.) Election campaign rhetoric reflects that many current members of Congress hold similar views today.

Gordon is dead set against governmental censorship of political content, and sometimes his rhetoric extends that idea into animosity toward any governmental activity that can affect content. My own position is that the enemy is not governmental regulation as such, but that the enemy is *any* form of bureaucracy acting for its own sake. To use a health care example, big insurance company bureaucracies certainly are just as inefficient and uncaring as big government bureaucracies. They also want to make a profit and, where employers select insurance carriers on the basis of price and the employee cannot make a free choice, there is no equivalent of the ballot box as a feedback or control mechanism.

> the enemy is not governmental regulation as such, but . . . *any* form of bureaucracy acting for its own sake.

Even while some still argued that the free marketplace or privatization would solve all problems of economic incentive and equitable (however defined) distribution of wealth, and while the myth of trickle-down economics held brief sway, ironically, it was expected that government itself could be used to achieve the ideological goal of small government that would leave "free enterprise" alone. Some have even imagined that the free market concept was enshrined in the U.S. Constitution, which, of course, it *never* has been.

Although one can hardly be called un-American for supporting some economic principle other than free enterprise, this false accusation was used in the United States during both the 1994 and the 2009 national debates over the funding of healthcare. Another example was the less visible debate, during periods when Republicans controlled Congress, over whether public broadcasting should continue to receive roughly 10% of its income— mostly for facilities—from the federal government (the rest comes from individual contributions and some "corporate underwriting").

Market economics is only one view among many of how to make the world operate efficiently, but it is a very popular one. Now that state socialism, as practiced in the former Soviet Union, is no longer a goal or an exemplar, particularly in less developed countries, free enterprise may indeed be the only economic *Weltanschauung*, or world outlook, for the 21st century.

ALTERNATIVES

And even today the "free enterprise" view isn't universal. In developing countries, micro-lending (small loans by nonprofit organizations to local entrepreneurs), and in economically developed countries the growth in number and size of nonprofit institutions, have given rise to calls to adopt a nonprofit model for journalism and mass communication. This idea isn't altogether new: the Associated Press is a cooperative, and the nonprofit/non-commercial National Public Radio is the major source of news in this decade for some 30 million Americans (up from only 2 million in 1983).

Most larger companies are run by non-family corporations that must satisfy all manner of institutional and individual stockholders who have little loyalty beyond the health of their own portfolios. Some media outlets are owned or controlled by families (occasionally through use of a two-tier stock ownership plan maintaining family control, as illustrated by the families operating the *The New York Times, The Seattle Times* and *The Washington Post*). A family's goals may include tradition or family and community loyalty as well as short-term profit. Others are owned—and sometimes operated—by foundations, organizations or family trusts that do not have to worry about what Wall Street thinks. Tax-supported (or tax-exempt) universities have published books, frequently provided a home for relevant organizations such as news councils or magazines, and many operate nonprofit radio and sometimes television stations. It has even been proposed that universities purchase and operate major newspapers in the public interest, now that the newspaper industry is faltering. As one writer put it, "What if the Sulzbergers [owners of *The New York Times*] could sell their shares to a trustworthy investor, one that was interested in maximizing *intellectual* value rather than *financial* value?" (L. Smith, 2008).

The activist public interest group, Free Press, proposed in mid-2009 that the way toward "saving the news" was for the United States to adopt policies that encouraged such new ownership structures as new nonprofit 501(c) (3), or low-profit limited liability (L3C) and cooperative media organizations. Additionally, Free Press suggested tax incentives and revised bankruptcy laws to encourage "local, diverse, nonprofit, low-profit and employee ownership"; a journalism jobs program; an R&D fund for journalistic innovation; and the establishment of "new public media"—a transformation of "public broadcasting into a world-class noncommercial news operation utilizing new technology and focused on community service" (Pickard et al., 2009). What may be most important about this set of proposals is that they were made in the first place, starting from scratch, and without funding from commercial firms.

One of the first signs that these ideas could and should be considered by the general public and the mainstream media was a lengthy, favorable op-ed column in *The Seattle Times* partially authored by one of the report writers (Pickard and Torres, 2009). The number of general-audience books and magazine articles analyzing the current media ownership and control situation and suggesting improvements has grown greatly in recent years, even though there is no consensus on which changes would best serve the public interest.

On the content side, a great deal of the investigative reporting in this country is done by (or in collaboration with) organizations such as the Center for Public Integrity, the Center for Investigative Reporting, and the like. Sadly, all of these proposals, publications and strategies together aren't yet enough to offset problems of "absentee owners, harvested investments, hollowed-out newsrooms [and budgets], and thus a diminished capacity to adequately find and tell the stories" (C. Lewis, 2007, p. 32).

THE MARKETPLACES—FREE AND OTHERWISE

Today's "free market" isn't quite the same as the laissez-faire approach of the robber barons of the 19th century. Neither does it show much resemblance to the populist and socialist economic views common (but certainly not universal) early in the 20th century, or the "keep government's hands off our economy" libertarian views expressed later. Now, it often uses the government's powers to support the strategies and profits of "private" business, even if public resources—such as the national forests or even the planetary ecology—are thereby harmed. It has even been argued that the live hand of government is a necessary backstop to the "dead hand" of classical economics in regulating markets. (In the interest of full disclosure, I personally believe in Goethe's more balanced view: that government is best that governs best, not the one that governs least.)

In this context, it is comforting to realize that the electromagnetic spectrum is infinitely and instantly renewable. If all stations (and sources of artificial electromagnetic interference) were shut down, the spectrum would be as large and pristine as it was before Marconi was born. If a nation is willing to exercise political power (on an international level, since any source of electromagnetic energy can create interference further than it can give service) it needn't take long to make changes in use of the electromagnetic spectrum, since no such change is permanent. But there are finite amounts of other resources, including money, diplomacy and talent.

We are constantly faced with making choices. Some choices will be better than others, and some will depend on which hat we are wearing (media person, family member, taxpayer, etc.). Which alternative(s) we choose are important—and that applies to all of us in all areas of life. For example, I have values and an agenda that go beyond the subject of media ethics; for example, to protect that which is good, and to leave the world a better place. I follow this agenda as an individual citizen, and as a teacher, family member, and author or editor.

Everybody makes choices all the time. And some of these are ethical choices that we *should* make, even if we avoid making them by using the excuse that any single individual's decisions may have limited effects. I believe that the allocation of resources (including money) is almost *always* a question of ethics—whether it is a congressional appropriation, the decision to spend millions making a movie, or plunking down some cash to see it. Abraham Joshua Heschel is quoted as saying, "In a free society, some are guilty but all are responsible." In other words, we can't legitimately shed our own responsibility and place it (or blame) on other players in the market of asset allocation.

There isn't only one marketplace, either. In addition to the marketplace of ideas, there are many economic, quasi-economic, and analogous markets in which communications in the United States operate. A sampling would include markets in which individual media organizations and groups compete for advertiser dollars; ideologies and political views compete for hearts, minds and votes; purveyors of goods and services compete for customers; creators search for patrons; performers and publicity-seekers compete for attention and "face time" with their rivals; program producers and syndication services compete for selection by media distributors; employees of the media compete for jobs, pay, and perks; communication schools try to attract students; nonprofit entities beg for contributions;

elective office seekers compete for votes; suppliers of equipment compete for its adoption by buyers; news reporters and producers compete for air time and "scoops"; promoters of new telecommunications services scrabble to secure a niche in whatever markets they choose to enter; providers of electromagnetic spectrum bandwidth—wired or wireless—on which information travels compete for paying users; box offices, coin boxes, and games of chance compete for our "disposable" income; and the "leisure time" attention of each person's 168 hours in the week is fought over by those who wish to claim it. And more!

Even though there is no *single* free market for communication, there are strong political tendencies to act as if one existed, and many new gadgets—and the software for them—are sold as if they were necessities.

Personal communication devices—cell phones, BlackBerrys, iPhones—have been introduced (and sometimes rendered obsolete) at a bewildering rate. Many of our appliances and other devices (including automobiles) have more computer power than the first spacecraft. They interconnect and communicate and store information to an extent probably exceeded only by the capacity of the human brain. It seems that the technical competence, financial resources, and entrepreneurial zeal we wondered about a very few years ago have all come together. But will these innovations really lead to either media business or media content competition, diversity and variety? And, if so, would such competition be merely "more of the same"—inherently wasteful, in a world where the burgeoning population, which has grown more than threefold in less than 80 years, doesn't know where its next source of energy is to come from?

When one looks at the limited amount of original programming produced by cable nowadays, the promises of nearly unlimited diversity in the future become illusory, regardless of advertising by manufacturers, retailers, and content distributors (cable and satellite) that tout as many as 500 digital channels. If the same movie is shown each week on a dozen cable channels, or if there are dozens of home shopping channels selling much the same merchandise—analogous to a shopping center with all the stores carrying the same brands of the same products—do those 500 channels really give the viewers more choice? Since TiVo or other video recorders allow each viewer to be her or his own programmer, why are we spending so much bandwidth (and money) on duplicative channels?

Some more questions: Should cable systems have competition in their franchise areas, or are they natural monopolies? Once the telephone and cable industries have fought to the death or have disappeared through mergers, what real competition will we have in the choice of channels or services, particularly access to the Internet? Although the electromagnetic spectrum is infinitely renewable (as mentioned above) it is still finite at any particular moment (as are the number of geosynchronous orbital slots for satellites) and vulnerable to disruptions. If *any* one entity is able to decide the menu from which we may select, what real choice have we? And, finally, is it an accident that the magazine, arguably the mass medium that most meets the multiple specialized needs (not just wants) of the American public, also—usually—is the one most removed from direct advertising sponsorship of specific content?

In addition to the marketplace of ideas, there are many economic, quasi-economic, and analogous markets in which communications in the United States operate.

DEREGULATION

"Deregulation," in the 1981 words of former FCC chairman Mark Fowler, was intended "to create, to the maximum extent possible, an unregulated, competitive marketplace environment for the development of telecommunications" (Kittross, 1989, p. 207). The evolution of technologies and the entrepreneurial urges of the 1990s have led to an even more fervent adoption of this principle, supported by the Reagan and both Bush administrations. Today many accept it—without much thought—as an immovable guidepost.

So, why do I look at it suspiciously? Simply, there is little evidence that deregulation of this marketplace of communication is the best economic regulatory mechanism, or that deregulation truly has provided any net benefit to the public interest over time. Even in industries that apparently had early success with deregulation—for example, the airline industry—the public has become aware of deregulatory drawbacks. The elimination of many of the regulatory safeguards in banking, originally established as a result of the Great Depression, certainly contributed to the 2008 subprime mortgage debacle.

When deregulation of mass communications is discussed, it would be ethical to consider the long-term consequences and potential downside as well as the hypothetical benefits predicted by our favorite economic and political ideological principles. For example, the use of wireless rather than wired communications often is at the expense of reliability; or, even though very profitable and convenient, satellite communications are highly vulnerable to solar flares during the high point of the 11-year sunspot cycle, or to human disruption or political interference. (As I have written frequently, when it comes to wireless telecommunication, Mother Nature has always been an important player.) I also worry about Gordon's lack of concern over the fact that the financial and managerial market is urging us to "unite (our) computers, telephones and cable channels" and wonder if he has forgotten the common sense warning against placing all of one's eggs in the same basket.

Indeed, the FCC's 2009 elimination of high-power analog television transmissions in favor of digital television transmissions is an example of the use of governmental power to enhance economic opportunity for private companies, and is not an impartial approach to invention and innovation. Instead of allowing the new technologies to "prove themselves" against the old in the marketplace, those in favor of DTV—such as the manufacturers and vendors of TV receivers and transmitters, or promoters of new personal communication devices seeking television's pre-2009 portion of the electromagnetic spectrum—have persuaded the FCC (and the FCC's masters, the Congress) to issue a fiat, decided with what I believe was inadequate public input. Although it took a number of years for the FCC to issue and implement its ruling, it actually was accomplished relatively quickly when compared to other examples of standards and frequency band changes over the years.

One implication of the analog-to-digital television broadcasting change is that most people with analog TV sets using over-the-air signals rather than cable or satellite distribution, who can't afford a (government-subsidized, to be sure) converter or get decent reception with one, will become second-class citizens, particularly those living in rural areas. Specialized content would become even more unavailable for those unable to afford the cost of cable or satellite, since "free" (formerly analog) television now will have additional costs. Further splintering of potential audiences or overall drop in number of viewers, in turn, could affect the economics of local advertiser-supported stations, and that, in turn, might have a detrimental effect on the collection and presentation of local news and public affairs, which, in further turn, might well have a deleterious effect on the practice of democracy.

MEDIA REFORM

In many countries, some of the media are either fully supported by governmentally collected fees or taxes, or otherwise subsidized by government, often *without* the specter of governmental control of content hanging over them. As indicated above, there are even some examples of this occurring in the United States (Nordenson, 2007).

A growing movement for media reform, if successful, will change the structure of the U.S. media in ways that are hard to predict. Organizations such as Free Press have produced the National Conferences for Media Reform, held every couple of years. The 2008 conference attracted approximately 3,500 participants of all sorts and political persuasions, and sent them home to spread the word about ways in which the public can have a larger voice in the ongoing national media debate. Much of the recent impetus for the public's interest in communication policy, particularly the concept of "net neutrality" (keeping the Internet open to messages of all ideological—or commercial—stripes rather than letting Internet providers restrict, charge more or otherwise discriminate against those they dislike, for whatever reason), has come from Free Press, which now has a half-million members, and a staff of 40.

Free Press is establishing itself as a focus for what previously had been isolated individuals and groups looking for a solution to the problem posed by one of its co-founders, Robert McChesney: "The [nation's] founders never held the view that if the rich guys can't make money off journalism, then we just won't have journalism." McChesney himself believes that the solution to questions of journalistic ethics should be on the macro, not the micro level; for example, suggesting that "before asking whether a journalist should reveal a source, we needed to know who was considered a legitimate source, why they were, and with what effect" (McChesney, 2007b, p. 34).

COMPETITION

(Note: *Some of the statistical data in the following section was provided by S. Derek Turner and Adan Lynn of Free Press, and some may be found in McChesney and Nichols, 2010.*)

The basic problem is that, according to both history and theory, uncontrolled economic competition generally leads, in the long run, to uncontrolled monopoly. The company that excels, with a differentiated product, will get the most customers. Weaker firms will go under until, eventually, only one (or an oligopolistic cartel) remains. In the media, it already is cheaper and easier for advertisers to deal with networks or the largest or group-owned stations, magazines, and newspapers than haggle with many smaller or local outlets.

In the 1980s, mergers of media companies, including advertising agencies, into giants became the rule. As long as advertisers want large numbers of people paying attention, the money will go with the numbers—and few managers will get into trouble with their boards if they go to the larger firms for such services. The fear shown by smaller players or even industries—the entire cable and broadcasting industries are very small compared to the computer industry or even the regional telephone companies—is quite justified.

Although we are discussing industries and institutions, we should note that from a content point of view—the marketplace of ideas, as discussed by Mill and Milton, not of economics—competition can be valuable. Ideas are inexhaustible, unlike most economic factors. Unfortunately, some of the best examples of content competition in specific media operations—such as ABC Radio's two-hour block of news and commentary in the 1950s, providing commentary from both the right and the left—have been eliminated in order to substitute more profitable programming. Such programming might well consist of oatmeal rather than raw meat in order to avoid offending potential listeners or advertisers. Or, on the other hand, those preaching to the choir—conservative talk shows (and an occasional liberal one), evangelical teleministries—are quite content to restrict their audiences to those who believe the same way and are glad to supply raw meat to their believers. During the runup to the 2008 presidential election, one could sometimes wonder if MSNBC and Fox News were discussing the same political developments on the same planet. Of course, the same could be said of political party or pro- and anti-president newspapers in the past.

There are both moral and economic reasons for and against such partisanship in the media. Those who believe in the sanctity of private property claim that media owners have the right to control its content, even though there are other stakeholders, possibly with equally strong rights. On the other side of the ledger, although competing newspapers in the 19th century were glad to carry the banner of a particular political party or faction, today there are only a handful of cities with competing newspapers and this level of political partisanship in most truly mass media—print or broadcast—may be detrimental to the body politic.

Not all of the major players or competitors in these interlocking economic markets or arenas think of them as zero-sum games. And the selection of strategies often is more art than science. Should one risk all one's eggs in one basket, no matter how carefully watched? Or should one adopt the strategy of John Malone, who built what was once the largest cable television firm in the United States, of "wanting a piece of everyone's business"?

Fortunately for the public interest, it is still possible to have a win-win non-zero-sum game, to "do well by doing good." An example would be the immensely popular and usually profitable Ben & Jerry's ice cream company, which embraced social responsibility in its original business operations. Not only did the company make a good product (if one wasn't on a diet), provide excellent working conditions, benefits, and support Vermont family farms and environmental protection, but also it spent a significant proportion of its profits on other worthy causes. Ben Cohen and Jerry Greenfield even restricted their own income to seven times the salary of their lowest paid employee—a policy and example they had to change in 1995 when selecting a new chief executive because few "outside" candidates would accept such a limit. But Ben & Jerry's was unusual, almost unique, and now is owned by others, perhaps with other values.

To show the difference, at the same time that Ben and Jerry were restricting their own salaries, on average the CEOs of 11 media companies were paid an average of *48 times* the

$50,000 salary of a top print reporter. Newer data show ratios that are even more startling: Although CEO salaries in leading news media firms were 23 times the average salaries of editors and reporters in the 1980s, they jumped to 54:1 in 1986–90, and then to an astounding 538:1 in 1996–2000. In 2005–09, in a time of financial strain on the entire economy to which the U.S. media belong, the ratio went down, but only to 232:1 (McChesney & Nichols, 2010, pp. 259–261). This certainly brings up the age-old question of whether managers and owners really are so much more important to the success of their companies than those who actually produce the goods and services.

The notion that being ethical can pay off, and some ethical companies are very successful, is not a contradiction of my generally pessimistic position because so few firms follow any ethic except that of improving payouts to managers and stockholders. These payments uphold one narrow ethic in the "free enterprise" scheme: fiduciary responsibility, which considers a profitable bottom line the sole responsibility to stockholders and doesn't need to do much (or anything) for customers, staff, suppliers or the public at large, although managers rarely ignore their own salaries and bonuses.

One of the staunchest proponents of "bottom-line journalism," Mark H. Willes, at the time publisher of the *Los Angeles Times* and chairman of the Times Mirror Company, maintained that the stockholder obligation is not optional, that it is "not a nice-to-do, it is a must-do." This was in response to being accused of being a person who "killed a great newspaper, but . . . raised the stock price," by a former employee of the closed-down New York City edition of *Newsday* (Peterson, 1998). In today's business climate and philosophy, it is unfortunate that one cannot draw the conclusion that being ethical leads to business success. I wish it did, because then this chapter would not be needed.

IS BIGGER BETTER?

Folklore (or marketplace ideologues) may say otherwise, but we should be aware that as time passes there are fewer and fewer real players in any economic field, from automobile manufacturers to airlines, from banks to broadcasters. Economies of scale are valuable to the larger players, but thereby we lose the very real values of, for example, local or demographically specialized media or even competition in general.

This is particularly true when it comes to the newspaper and broadcast mass media, which had their genesis in local communities rather than the United States as a whole, as might still be the case in smaller nations. These community resources and outlets claim to be locally oriented, even of "Mom-&-Pop" size, but most are really controlled by relatively few large (and growing larger) corporations.

The practice of licensing broadcasters to serve specific cities has led to the establishment of some 1,700 on-the-air television stations in the United States. But by 2006, FCC data showed that 87% of the 110 million U.S. "TV households" received their programs through multichannel video programming distribution (MVPD) services such as cable or satellite rather than directly from locally programmed stations. True, local stations are usually carried on cable, and more recently are available via satellite, but it is unfortunately also true that nowadays few local stations are noted for their original local programming.

Other factors—such as the importance of over-the-air network affiliates' willingness to take risks in the interests of their communities—do, of course, afford opportunities for decision-making at the station, regardless of the MVPDs' role.

The sometimes-disputed 2006 FCC figures indicate that the proportion of MVPD homes served by cable appears to have dropped slightly over the previous year and the proportion of homes served by satellite has risen slightly. Whether this trend continues is worth further analysis, since both ethical standards and ethical practices are often determined by an industry's structure. Regardless of the competition between MVPDs, the important point is that *this handful of cable and satellite (and miscellaneous other) MVPD systems actually controls the home supply of television programs—not the more than 1,700 stations on the air*—restricting the number of places where ethical decision-making can be done and where public pressure can be brought to bear.

As another example, there are more than 7,000 franchised cable systems in the United States, but the top 10 multiple-system operators (MSOs) control the "boxes" in an ever-increasing majority of homes. According to *Television Digest*, in 1998 the top 50 cable operators served roughly 97% of all U.S. basic cable subscribers and just the top five served 63.3%.

More recent (June 2008) data, using somewhat different definitions provided by the National Cable and Telecommunications Association, show that the two largest cable MSOs, Comcast and TimeWarner, served almost one-third of U.S. homes (nearly 38 million) with television. The largest satellite distributors, DirecTV and EchoStar, accounted for another 28%. In other words, nearly two-thirds of the American public receives television programs through the facilities of only four corporations. The switch to digital television may lead to even greater concentration, regardless of its out-of-pocket monthly cost to the consumer (U.S. Federal Communications Commission, 2009). As mentioned above, none of these MVTD services are anything like "Mom-&-Pop" local industries, although they do a good job of persuading Congress and the public that they are, and thereby discourage much regulation of the type applied to "big business."

In an earlier mass communication industry, the number of general-circulation daily newspapers covering all of New York City has shrunk more than two-thirds since World War II, and the number of dailies in the United States generally shows a slight decline each decade during the past century. For example, between 1970 and 2011 (projected), the number of daily newspapers will have dwindled from 1,748 to 1,422. Even more significant is the drop in daily circulation—from roughly 62 million to roughly 51 million over the same years (much of this loss occurred since 1995). When the overall growth in population during this period is taken into account, we have gone from one newspaper being distributed for every three Americans in 1991 to one paper for every six in 2006 (U.S. Census Bureau, 2009).

Over a longer period of time, the picture is even worse: In 1910 there were 689 cities or towns with competing daily newspapers; but by 2002 there were only 14 (C.E. Baker, 2002) and the newspaper competition in several of them (such as Seattle) has disappeared since 2002. Newspapers or stations controlled by individuals or families are an endangered species. Although there are still several thousand book publishers, they too merge—as has the publisher of this book—and also are at the mercy of the ever-fewer giant bookstore chains and Internet vendors.

both ethical standards and ethical practices are often determined by an industry's structure.

Conglomerates are not as popular on Wall Street as they were in the 1980s and 1990s. But the concept of ever-larger organizations in a single industry, such as the broadly defined entertainment industry—built through buyouts, mergers, and forcing weaker competitors to the wall—remains the goal of many business leaders, even in the face of a recession. A case in point is Comcast's successful effort to buy NBC Universal, and its many cable channels and programs, from General Electric—a strategy to enhance its vertical control within the industry. NBC's broadcast network and owned-and-operated stations were (to Comcast) a less desirable part of the package. Unfortunately, as Gordon points out, since many buyouts and mergers are "leveraged," with resulting huge loads of debt that must be paid off, it is not surprising that often too little money remains to support the quantity and quality of the staffs and operations that were the original reason for the acquisition.

Several 1990s megamergers, notably Warner Communications and Time, Inc., the purchase of CBS by Westinghouse (which later sold its industrial businesses and adopted the CBS name) and the $19 billion buyout of Capital Cities/ABC by the Walt Disney Co., are older illustrations of this trend. Other acquisitions, often in the field of "intellectual property," such as the 2006 merger between YouTube and Google, may have even more effect on content than sales and profit figures would predict. On a smaller scale, removal of restrictions on how many radio stations one firm may own enabled Clear Channel to build its stable to more than 1,200. It has since sold stations in many smaller markets to venture capital firms, while attempting to tighten its grip further by specializing in cities where, under the current FCC ownership rules, one company could control a half-dozen or more. Other group owners, such as CBS Radio and Entercom, employ a similar strategy on a smaller scale. The older values of "localism" and "dispersal of ownership" disappeared within months of the leash being loosened.

How does this sort of economic strategy affect media ethics? "Localism" is both a policy to be found in the Communications Act of 1934 and an ethical principle in a federal governmental system in which the states originally had sovereign power. I believe that content designed to give each community both a voice of its own and the information it needs to function (including local advertising) is vitally important to self-government at the local level. This can be looked at on two levels.

First, while television channels programmed from some larger community are fine for delivering entertainment, they are unlikely to deal adequately with social, political and other matters directly affecting the "satellite" community. Local radio stations are no longer required to be able to produce locally oriented programming from local studios—a result of the corporate desire for profit, and the FCC's removal of ownership restrictions. These have made a mockery of the concept of local broadcasting that was the key "public interest" principle spelled out in the Communications Act of 1934.

Of more immediate importance in many communities is the need for regular weather reports. In most places, daily weather reports are among the most truly significant local information needs, although farm crop prices in rural areas and traffic reports in urban ones come right behind, followed by political news. In an emergency, radio broadcasts can be received—while batteries last or generators can be cranked—when power failures have cut off access to both television and the Internet. Tornadoes in the Midwest, hurricanes in the South—whenever there are weather-related or other local emergencies, both speed and reliability are essential. For example, in Minot, North Dakota, when a freight train derailed in January 2002 and discharged a cloud of poisonous ammonia, there was no emergency warning on the cluster of "local" radio stations owned by Clear Channel. It was not because programming for this cluster was coming from a location several states away—even though when one owner controls several stations in a market or region, it is tempting to ignore the localism policies called for in the Communications Act and use identical programming on each. While the general rule is valid, in the Minot case local law enforcement hadn't paid sufficient attention to its own responsibilities to activate the Emergency Broadcast System (a task done frequently without a glitch by the Weather Service) and tried in vain to reach the stations by ordinary telephone. But without local personnel on duty, these stations—and the publics they served—had no backup system in place, and it was the public that was placed at risk. Plenty of blame to go around (Lee, 2003).

It isn't only small towns that are affected by media consolidation. For example, when I grew up in New York City, I could chose from more than a dozen daily newspapers, but would have fewer than half that number to choose from today. This, of course, further cuts back on the range of local news and features (or as in the previous paragraph, radio programming) available in that market. The amount of available local news in most cities, of every size, is severely limited, and getting more so, as layoffs continue and music is cheap.

THE NATIONAL PICTURE

On the national scene, there were six powerful communications companies in 1997—Microsoft, Disney/ABC, Time Warner, GE/NBC, Tele-Communication Inc. (TCI), and Rupert Murdoch's News Corp./Fox. Less than a decade later TCI was off the list and there were five. As mergers and takeovers continue, tomorrow's number may be even smaller. Ken Auletta (1997) pointed out that these firms didn't actually compete directly but, like the Japanese *keiretsu*, formed an interlocked web of agreements, activities and joint ventures. All six engaged in most or all of the following: cable, television and film production, Internet technology and content, and home video/games/interactive programs, with several having invested in sports teams and venues, satellite transmission, newspapers, magazines and books, telephone and wireless communications, TV broadcasting and stations, music and records, and theme parks and stores (Auletta, 1997).

Bagdikian (2004, pp. 27–54) listed the "big five" of that year as Time-Warner, Disney-ABC, Murdoch-Fox, Viacom (which owned CBS at the time) and German book publisher Bertelsmann, arguably the largest publisher of books in English. Clearly, the "players" can change at a moment's notice (insofar as the public is concerned), and ownership and control aren't always the same.

Comcast, which joined the list of largest conglomerates when its bid for NBC-Universal received federal approval in 2011, has become much more than a multichannel distributor of video programming: it also is the largest Internet service provider (ISP) and one of the largest providers of voice telephone service. Yahoo! and Google (and others) have extensive plans for converging content and services, and have grown tremendously in terms of public attention, but as economic entities, they aren't really all that huge—yet. Microsoft is an important player in any field it enters (Auletta, 2009). New lists of "major players" are almost inevitable, and they come and go quickly. It is likely that ownership and control will continue to concentrate, as is the case globally and affecting virtually all industries.

While *keiretsu*-like activities have many of the advantages of sheer size, such as economies of scale, they can lead just as easily to less attention being paid to customers, employees, the public interest, communities in which they operate, and ethical standards. Obviously, such joint ventures and cooperation among the leaders in an industry make it very hard for newcomers to enter a market, and certainly are not examples of truly "free" economic competition.

In the time since Auletta's (1994) analysis, not only have most of these corporations been merged but also the generation of their founders and early leaders has largely passed from the scene. Fortunate enough to be on the scene at the right time, with backgrounds that meshed with their abilities, most of them built their large corporations from small companies (see Gladwell, 2008). William Paley and his CBS "candy store," John Malone of cable giant Tele-Communications, Inc., David Sarnoff of RCA/NBC, Sumner Redstone, who moved from motion picture exhibition to broadcasting, Rupert Murdoch, who is a major force in newspapers and television around the world, Walt Disney and others were true industry leaders, with entrepreneurial vision. Many of the pioneers among them also had strong (but different) moral visions (Auletta, 1994). Because these captains of communications set the tone and the standards for their corporations, their longevity had ethical as well as ownership implications.

It is different today. As in other fields, most media organizations are run by professional "managers" and boards of directors and committees rather than by individuals with vision or ethical standards (whether high or low). Not being human, corporations are both immortal (in the sense that they don't necessarily grow old and die, although other corporations can kill or merge with them) and amoral, lacking any innate conscience or sense of ethics, which leaves a corporation's "culture" up to its leadership—and sometimes to those employees who are primarily loyal to the corporation's mission and not to its official chain of command. These mortal (and moral) individuals still retain some power to affect the operations of even the largest corporations.

THE PUBLIC INTEREST

As "Deep Throat" told Bob Woodward in *All the President's Men*, "Follow the money!" Without legal, enforceable requirements to operate in the public interest, most entrepreneurs have no commitment to anything other than a profit. Descriptions of the *actual* economic system of the 20th and early 21st centuries need to go beyond elementary textbook definitions. For example, separation of ownership from "professional" management has become virtually complete in larger firms. These professional managers, typically (but not always) the product of a few major business schools and fiscal organizations, rarely dare to "think big," or feel that ethics and morals transcend short-range economic goals.

Although management has a fiduciary responsibility to stockholders (if not to employees, customers, or the public), I believe that the typical M.B.A. logically desires to maximize her or his own income, and looks forward to retirement rather than public fame or adulation. Because managers often are given raises, stock options or cash bonuses on the basis of short-term (one-year or less) profits, rather than long-term profitability, it is rare that their horizon is for a longer period. This mindset, and short-sighted tax laws, have also led to reduced investment in research and development and production facilities, as well as praise and higher stock values on Wall Street when companies "downsize" or "outsource," abandon product lines (regardless of whether they are needed or desired by the public) or move production to areas with cheaper labor.

This ethic is not in the best interests of society. A free enterprise system generally is lively (until it evolves into a monopolistic or oligopolistic system), but there is a major cost—inefficiency due to duplication and loss of economies of scale, leading to higher than necessary cost and lack of real choice—for society to pay. Furthermore, in an open, competitive, system there are more opportunities for new ideas—including the benefits of acting ethically rather than blindly following a procedures list—and older ones, which can become a case of "doing well by doing good." On the debit side, errors of judgment can lead to a failed or bankrupt company, which moves an industry further along the line toward monopoly.

However, in an oligopolistic or concentrated economic system, such as the one that we seem to have now in the communications industries, the potential penalties for society are even greater. Reading corporate annual reports reinforces the idea that short-range salary or other personal goals of most high-level executives have become more important than societal goals in the planning done by communication media. Although cable television viewers have a growing number of TV channels from which to choose, real choice in content isn't growing much, if at all. Being a copycat is the easiest way to "succeed," except for a handful of creative programmers in the past such as Pat Weaver, Ted Turner, Gordon McLendon, Brandon Tartikoff, and the like. As Bruce Springsteen wrote, one can find lots of channels and nothing on. In other words, the "marketplace of ideas" may be adversely affected by lack of real competition in the "marketplace of business." As I've said before, the push for governmental deregulation is not matched by any efforts at self-regulation within industry and, therefore:

> we may find ourselves at the tender mercies of (monopoly) business. Since the loved and the rich don't really need much protection, only government can enable the minority and the mass publics to mobilize against economic power. While government doesn't always recognize or act for the "common good," who else is equipped or willing to even try on this role? Deregulation will be beneficial to some—but probably not to thee and me.
>
> (Kittross, 1989, p. 207)

OTHER FACTORS

Taxes affect most economic marketplaces and are a much truer reflection of public policy than the grand words of the First Amendment, the Communications Act of 1934, or the Telecommunications Act of 1996—and the federal income taxation framework has always looked more kindly on property than it does on creativity, since income is taxed at a higher rate than wealth. The many recent extensions of the exclusive time periods enjoyed by owners of copyrights and patents, usually the employers of creators rather than those who do the creating and inventing, do little to stimulate the goals found in Article I, Section 8 of the U.S. Constitution. When people who have accumulated wealth die, their heirs enjoy considerable protection from estate taxes, but it does not protect any institutions they built from being sold in order to pay the taxes that remain in place. This part of the tax code— which, although under attack, draws something of a line in the sand upon death—ignores the value to the public of, for example, family ownership of media. Laws can be very blunt instruments and often overlook differences. A translated quote from Nobel Prize winner Anatole France reminds us that "the law, in its majestic equality, forbids rich and poor alike from sleeping under the bridges of the Seine, to beg in the streets, and to steal their bread" (Le Lys Rouge [The Red Lily], 1894, ch. 7).

True, government can protect people and may even ensure honesty or a level playing field in the marketplace. The Securities and Exchange Commission (SEC) was established after the 1929 stock market crash to try to make it harder for those with predatory instincts and power to use them, although the Bernard Madoff "Ponzi scheme" that caused investors to lose billions of dollars in 2009 probably wouldn't have occurred if the SEC and similar agencies had been doing their jobs of protecting investors from the wolves of Wall Street.

Sometimes a society's restrictions (proscriptive laws) or mandated requirements (prescriptive laws) are extremely explicit, which may not always be good for society in the long run. Some legislators favoring political campaign financing reform propose (somewhat selfishly) that candidates be given free time on broadcast stations (not print media or cable). This would ignore how much this might adversely affect the station's performance in marketplaces where they compete with print media, and the need to make a profit with a limited inventory of "commercial minutes." As a further example, the urge to protect children has led to content restrictions that may also limit what adults can see, read, or do.

Let's go back to basics as we consider the relationship between economics and ethics. Ethics tend to arise from the internal needs of a specific group and aren't imposed from outside as are the laws and regulations applied equally to all of us. But, when "competition" and "free enterprise" constitute a deontological holy grail, no group—however well intentioned—has much of a chance to institute a code of ethics. In fact, if "competitors" (or even professional associations) *did* get together for this purpose, and were willing to expel or otherwise punish those who violated the code, might they be laying themselves open for an anti-trust suit? That throws responsibility back on the individual, because morality, arising from individual training, education, and experience within a culture, can still direct individuals toward making this a better world in which to live.

How does the marketplace concept apply to this dimension? As I see it, the only advantage of the marketplace concept in the field of media ethics is that it promotes a form of cowardice: do nothing that will make advertisers and the public (in that order) mad at you. Well-thought-out minority or extreme political or social views are rare in any truly mass medium run by corporations with an eye on Wall Street—unless the numbers of the attention-paying audience are large enough. News has been cheapened to gossip, political commentary to scandal-mongering. Newspapers justify astrology columns in the name of the First Amendment. Programming on national television is at best intended for the lowest common denominator of taste and appeal. Also, the media usually act timid and intimidated with respect to attacking any corporation, institution or politician with real political strength who is willing to fight. This was best demonstrated during the Nixon administration in the early 1970s (Lashner, 1984). There are exceptions to this behavior, however. Conservative media attacked Franklin Roosevelt, at least until the United States' entrance into World War II, and some media organizations (e.g., Fox News) nowadays believe that they have enough support from the right to have attacked President Obama from the very start of the 2008 campaign. Also, sometimes, an individual or a program shows a degree of independence and concern for society that attracts an audience—for example, Bill Moyers on PBS, until his retirement in the spring of 2010—but this merely proves the rule. Unfortunately, most public affairs programs that aren't timid are merely the kind of entertainment that belongs in the sports arena rather than in the realm of public discourse.

> Our ethical obligations will not be satisfied by relying on the "dead hand" of economic competition: they require active, not passive, behavior by individuals in the communication industries.

Unless one takes the simplistic or greedy path and maintains that profit—or success in meeting fiduciary responsibilities—is sufficient evidence of ethical media behavior, blind faith in the beneficial effects of the economic marketplace on media ethics is misplaced and superfluous. True, some religions, long the fount of ethical standards, interpret the accumulation of wealth as being proof that God approves of such a goal. However, this may be circular reasoning, and we need to examine the behavior, more than the bank accounts, of those being praised as exemplars in our society. Our ethical obligations will not be satisfied by relying on the "dead hand" of economic competition: they require active, not passive, behavior by individuals in the communication industries.

THE INFORMATION (SUPER)HIGHWAY

The Internet has given rise to a chance to start over. The Electronic Frontier Foundation and others have popularized the slogan, "Information wants to be free." Yet, it costs money to create and gather information, and to transmit it. For decades (until "pay-per-view" became common) advertising revenues paid for the majority of broadcast programs in the United States. Recent economic ideas, such as pricing content at zero but making money along the edges—e.g., "tie-ins" encouraging the sale of DVDs or even children's toys, subscriptions to entire series, "live" concerts, and the like—can provide a large part of the content income stream.

It isn't a foregone conclusion that new media will be supported by advertising, but no matter what business model is in fashion, good content requires expense and talent, so the multiple-marketplace economic-ethical model expressed in this chapter probably remains valid at some level, and the two concepts remain intertwined. There probably will always be someone paying the piper and calling the tune, no matter how many other tunes may be in demand (Anderson, 2009; Gladwell, 2009).

An information superhighway exists today, just not as tidy as the original projections and plans for it, and laden with entertainment, information, sales pitches, nonsense, and computer-generated bits and pictures on its hundreds of digital channels. While some of this highway—the Internet—carries the passive one-way traffic of television, it is now largely broadband and interactive, and also provides voice, data, graphics, sound, two-way and multi-way interaction by piggybacking on cable, telephone lines, and wireless systems. Even after the collapse of the "dot.com" industry in the late 1990s, these new channels and services continued to attract business entrepreneurs as though this superhighway was the only road from here to success. Despite political assurances that all Americans will have access to this highway, in the prevailing economic climate it certainly will build out as a toll road. This isn't "wrong" per se: it costs a great deal to build, and as Ayn Rand and Robert Heinlein have reminded us, TANSTAAFL—There Ain't No Such Thing As A Free Lunch.

But, as is discussed in Chapter 9, how many citizens will be able to afford access to it? Will countries be divided permanently into the information "haves" and "have nots"? Will those who manage the funding control the content? What is the meaning of "the public interest"? After all, the very concept of "the public interest" can change in the face of physical, economic or political disaster, or as population growth in the past century has made the allocation of scarce resources—including communications resources—a matter of life and death. Can the United States survive, to paraphrase the debate over slavery before the Civil War, half with and half without necessary or even merely desired information? Gordon quotes H. L. Mencken's description of democracy as making sure that the people get what they think is best for them as well as the consequences that follow. I'd like to counterbalance this by paraphrasing Winston Churchill: democracy is the recurring suspicion that more than half the people are right more than half the time.

THE BIG BATTLES

So it is no wonder that I consider the two most important economic conflicts in the communication field also to have political and social implications: the largely domestic conflict between "access" and "fairness" (Barron, 1973) and the New World Information and Communication Order (NWICO) debated in UNESCO (MacBride, 1980; A. Smith, 1980).

The first argues that there is a choice: Either professional communicators are scrupulous about being fair in allocation of resources (including time and newsprint), or each group or person, no matter how obscure, should be entitled to unfettered (and possibly unlimited) access to transmission and reception channels. I leave it to the reader as to which approach— "access" or "fairness" (or neither)—best describes the current U.S. communication system.

The second debate is over the New World Information and Communication Order, further discussed in Chapter 9. Under NWICO, even the smallest and most impoverished nation has the right to control information imported into and exported from their country, and access to the worldwide networks. Including the Internet. Again, I leave it to the reader to decide the extent to which the NWICO is in place and—because Western tradition embraces concepts such as free press and freedom of information without control or censorship of information flow—the extent to which it *should* be.

CONCLUSION

The easiest way to convert these industry-wide economic concepts to the ethical concepts that an individual can do something about is to remember that corporations, organizations, government bureaus and departments, and even industries are run by human beings; and the decisions made by these individual beings are important, no matter at what level they make them. Isn't it the individual or the industry (which is operated by individuals), and not some group of conspirators or super-powerful institutions such as the government (or "Wall Street"), that has decided (for example) that sex and violence "sell"? (Actually, a report by Weaver and Wilson (2009) indicates that such content may not appeal to many viewers, but that's beside the point.)

In the newsroom, since the early 1990s or so, the wall that theoretically existed between the business and the editorial sides of a newspaper often has been torn down (Jurkowitz, 1998), and it is a rare media organization that will purposely antagonize its advertisers. Some advertisers have been known to demand pre-publication access to magazine content, which leads to further editorial timidity in a medium that used to be relatively independent (R. Baker, 1997). In daily newspapers alone, because of the costs of printing and distribution, the amount of money that can be spent for all editorial functions is rarely more than 10% of revenues, but—until the recent economic turndown—often profit margins of two to three times that amount might be reported to stockholders every year; many broadcast stations and cable systems have similar ratios. This reflects the short-term profit-driven goal of the free enterprise system. Gordon mentions some of the many ways of paying for the media—at the box office, as a hobby, as ancillary enterprises, with donations, using tax revenues, license fees, etc.—but, as might be expected, generally falls back on the status quo of today's heavy reliance on advertising. True, public broadcasting shows that it is possible to operate media as nonprofit entities (even though "enhanced underwriting" is really advertising under another label), and a number of countries have successfully used license fees or taxes on receiving sets as a means of paying for broadcasting, but both of these approaches are, at best, a long way from permeating U.S. media. Yet the actual or theoretical existence of other ways of paying for the media may offer some guideposts to a new or revised system that need not always program for the lowest common denominator.

On the other hand, annual reports in *Journalism & Mass Communication Educator* show how the growing number of new graduates, all eager for jobs in the media, may allow the media to keep starting salaries depressed to the point where many of the best and brightest graduates switch to other industries—reducing the number of individuals who have thought about the purposes of the industry they plan to join.

The newspaper industry has largely destroyed its most articulate labor union, the Newspaper Guild, the remnants of which—joined to the former International Typographical Union—are now part of the Communication Workers of America. These last-ditch labor union mergers are analogous to some of the mergers in the communications industries themselves, which were discussed earlier. In fact, there now seems little to distinguish union leadership from business leadership; both have narrowly focused, self-interested, "I want mine, Jack" goals.

Media now are being bought and sold as commodities, and the antitrust laws and some provisions of the Communications Act of 1934 have recently been weakened to permit even more rapid turnover. Most sales tend to shake out the more expensive and experienced senior members of a creative or production staff. (Because many of these jobs are never refilled, such "downsizing" does not really help those trying to get their foot on the bottom rung of the ladder.)

This too is a function of making the marketplace a goal or end in itself, rather than merely a process: if someone will work more cheaply, hire them. If someone rocks the boat and adversely affects short-term income (even if doing the "right thing"), fire them. Only the public will lose, because your competition will act according to the same economic principles. For years, it was obvious that the National Association of Broadcasters favored emphases in American broadcast education that would provide them with a surfeit of candidates for entry-level jobs as technicians or disk jockeys, keeping—through competition!—wages low. Whenever communications faculty showed an independent turn of mind, trade organizations in the media often found ways to show their displeasure. Communications faculties and university administrators are aware of how much scholarship and other funding and how many internships come from the industries they study and teach about. Again, using otherwise charitable gifts to silence potential internal critics is an obvious strategy, but hardly one that would provide either stimulus or incentive to improve the mass media content that we all need in order to make better and more rational decisions in a democracy. In the long run, using the power of money for short-term selfish benefits may well prove counterproductive. I believe, along with former FCC member and Minnesota Supreme Court justice Lee Loevinger (1964, pp. 120–121), that providing this content is the *only* indispensable purpose and function of U.S. mass media.

If one considers the nitty-gritty aspects of media economics—profit, loss, wages—then I believe that the often-touted hypothetical free market rarely exists. If it does, it obviously isn't completely free. Certainly, it doesn't exist in media ethics, which are considered irrelevant by those who believe only in the innate greed of the strictly economic marketplace or who consider the free market to be a God-given goal rather than merely one of many economic concepts to be considered and questioned.

It is fairly easy to bring both Kant and the utilitarians into support of my separatist position on the economic marketplace and media ethics. I'll even throw in some political philosophies that are no longer in common use, such as Marxism, politically "left" libertarianism, and what I call true (i.e., conserving resources for future generations) conservatism. After many years in the academy, I support wholeheartedly, but no longer quite have Gordon's faith in, his proposals for increased and improved education.

The many relationships of economics to media content are, of course, uncertain. There is no guarantee that any particular economic model will prevail or survive. To act as though how we now operate in the stock market, boardroom, or accounting office will continue in linear fashion is both shortsighted and potentially unethical with respect to our responsibilities to future generations. As Loevinger (1964) pointed out earlier, the mass media both reflect the larger society and project their own view of the institutions of that society.

And this is where some of the difficulty faced by those who try to understand economic structures and situations comes from: it is caused by the media themselves. Most media that report on the financial markets and other economic matters do so in a narrow way. Today, for example, we find that business news primarily is used for investment information. Less commonly, it is reported for company- or ego-building purposes, or as merely another sporting event, gossip opportunity, or crime story in a somewhat less familiar setting. Only once in a great while is it used to educate those who need to understand the economic factors that affect their lives. If, instead, economic news was *focused* on the more altruistic goals of education or optimizing the U.S. (or world) economy, perhaps it might be more useful.

Unfortunately, I continue to believe that, in the few instances where a truly free marketplace exists, with goals that go beyond a simple grubbing for profits, it also tends to work to the detriment of both those who work in the media and the publics they serve. Economics, like Mother Nature, really doesn't care about human beings. After all, as one astronaut said to another as they looked at the spacecraft they were about to board, "Just think—all of that was built by the lowest bidder."

KEY POINTS

- Economics and media ethics generally are independent and often in opposition, but the allocation of resources (including money) is almost always a question of ethics.
- There is little evidence that deregulating the communication marketplace is the best mechanism to control the economic marketplace—or that it has created a net benefit to the public interest.
- The supply of TV programming is largely controlled by a small number of cable and satellite systems, not the 1,700-plus TV stations. A similar situation exists in the newspaper industry as it shrinks. This means there are fewer places where ethics decisions can be made and where public pressure can be brought to bear.

GORDON: The evolving economic marketplace can still help to hold the media responsible for their actions, with help from nonprofit organizations, knowledgeable media consumers, and farsighted privately owned media companies.

When I argued this side of the media ethics and economic marketplace debate for the first two editions of this book, I was more optimistic than I am now about the impacts of the American economic system on media ethics. It's not that John Michael Kittross persuaded me to change my mind, but rather that news media economics have changed for the worse since 1999.

Although the economic marketplace affects every facet of the mass media, my focus here will be on journalism economics. Public relations and advertising (and the integrated marketing field that increasingly is absorbing both), of course, have their own ethics-tinged marketplace concerns to deal with, including how to take full advantage of the opportunities offered by interactive media. Similar concerns abound in the entertainment field, which increasingly has to wrestle with the economic opportunities and threats of the Internet.

But journalism is the area of greatest crisis, and is also of vital importance because if news outlets fail—or fail to act ethically in providing adequate information to the public—the results would devastate a democratic society that relies heavily on information to conduct its business properly. Several groups have recently begun to explore alternative models for disseminating the information that a democracy needs, and other possibilities may eventually be considered.

I still believe that journalism can function effectively as a "fourth estate" in contemporary society. But that won't happen if the news media are prisoners of Wall Street, which might well be regarded these days as a "fifth estate" (and a controlling one, at that). Since 1999 we have seen the effects of numerous media mergers, purchases and other changes, as well as the impact of new technologies and the splintering of mass media audiences and advertising—not to mention major changes in the overall economy.

What follows here is a change in degree: I have no intention of withdrawing from the field in favor of Kittross's position. As numerous conversations and exchanges of correspondence have shown us, we are still far apart. Kittross has always been willing to go beyond the position he takes in this chapter, and ask critical questions about the ("so-called") free enterprise system itself. I still have some faith in the possibilities of a modified free enterprise marketplace system, despite some serious short-term dangers for both our current media systems and the society it serves.

In brief, I believe that the economic marketplace has produced mixed results in regard to media ethics but it still retains the potential to produce positive outcomes. Perhaps the strongest example of this is the ongoing cooperative effort by Google and a wide range of news organizations, to explore various possibilities for creating

> a reinvented business model to sustain professional news-gathering. . . . Google teams are working with hundreds of news organizations, which range in scale from the Associated Press, the Public Broadcasting System, and *The New York Times* to local TV stations and papers.
>
> (Fallows, 2010, pp. 48 and 50)

Google initiated these time-consuming and expensive efforts because it realized its own need to have interesting, professionally produced content available for its users to link to. It is much too soon to predict how successful these efforts will be, but just the fact that Google realized the need to undertake them exemplifies how the economic marketplace can exert a positive influence.

There is no requirement that communications systems be run by profit-making businesses, and there have been a number of recent efforts to establish nonprofit news organizations, often online. There has also been renewed discussion about whether government also might provide financial support—beyond its present minor share of the funding for public radio and TV, and the purchase of advertising for such things as military recruiting—for news operations without taking away their ability to operate independently. (See Downie and Schudson, 2009b and McChesney and Nichols, 2010. On overall government support of news media, see Cowan and Westphal, 2010.)

Regardless of what new models eventually emerge, there will still be questions of ethics in regard to the sources of financial support. One such question—ethics issues in nonprofit investigative journalism newsrooms—was explored in a 2010 report from the Center for Journalism Ethics at the University of Wisconsin-Madison (Ward, 2010). Some of the report's conclusions, especially in regard to funding, are discussed below.

One final point before plunging into the meat of this discussion—it may be tempting or even "fashionable" to blame *all* of the ills of the media field (particularly concerning newspapers) on the faltering economy or on the general economic structure of the American media. But we need to exercise care about jumping to such easy conclusions, and about speculating idly. For example, Kittross maintains in his portion of this chapter that investigative reporting teams have been axed "mostly for budgetary reasons, but also possibly because the small . . . amount of real investigative reporting might occasionally tread on the toes of advertisers or political leaders." The reference to "budgetary reasons" strikes me as a jump to an easy conclusion, and the lack of any valid or reliable data to support his speculation about offending advertisers or political leaders does a disservice to logical discussion. But it does serve as a useful reminder of the need to base our conclusions on something other than conjecture or ideological predispositions.

NEGATIVE MARKETPLACE EFFECTS ON ETHICS

I admit that the economic marketplace has exerted negative effects on the media and media ethics. From my perspective, that marketplace poses two primary dangers in regard to ethical media conduct: the increasing *centralization of media ownership*; and, much more important, the *public trading of the stock* of mass media companies and the resulting overemphasis on the price of that stock

The latter concern is not new. It was spelled out well in the early 1990s by former *Chicago Tribune* editor James Squires, who lamented that public (as contrasted to family or other private) ownership of media companies would lead to unacceptable pressures from stockholders concerned only with the price of their stock and, therefore, the bottom line—not with the quality of the information provided by the media outlets (Squires, 1993). Or, he might have added, with the ethics that go into providing that news and information.

Several years before Squires wrote, another well-known observer of the media—Everette Dennis (1990)—voiced a similar concern about the potential negative impact of general economic forces, including the growth of conglomerates, on the news media:

> News organizations that are a part of big business are governed by market forces, and market research is said to determine what America (and the rest of the world) reads, hears and watches. . . .
>
> [W]e are confronted by economic movements on Wall Street and in boardrooms around the world that think of the media mostly as machines producing widgets. We are told by some critics that the media more than ever are driven by the greed of a market that values short-run profits over long-term investments. The results . . . are shrinking staffs and depleted resources. The audience numbers that generate advertising revenues

drive news organizations and, in a circular fashion, cause them to court audiences to whom their advertisers can sell their products and services.

(Dennis, 1990, pp. 6–7)

Talk about foresight! In the years since Dennis and Squires wrote, the situation has only worsened. Exhibit A is the slide of the venerable Knight Ridder newspaper chain into a forced sale. First, it slashed its papers' newsroom resources, in an effort to satisfy stockholders by preserving its bottom-line profits regardless of the damage done to news coverage (i.e., viewing news content as Dennis's "widgets"). Those corporate demands for budget reductions led Jay Harris, publisher of the *Mercury News* in San Jose, CA, to resign, very publicly, in an effort "to make corporate executives take notice." Speaking shortly after his resignation in 2001, Harris said that Knight Ridder officials paid little or no attention to the *consequences* of the mandated budget reductions. He noted the lack of "discussion of the damage that would be done to the quality and aspirations of the *Mercury News*" and said that continuing to negotiate and seek compromises would have been "little more than slow and silent surrender" (Lewis, 2001). Five years later, and despite its Machiavellian efforts to survive, the publicly traded Knight Ridder chain was gone. It fell victim to institutional stockholders dissatisfied with the chain's earnings and united by their desire to maximize profits with little or no regard for the "news product." When it was liquidated, Knight Ridder's profit margins were in the 16–19% range—like most media companies, *higher* than many Fortune 500 companies but slightly below the newspaper industry average. Profits had fallen some 22% in 2004 and didn't rebound even after major staff cuts at individual papers and in the national and foreign staffs, and the sale of the financially troubled *Detroit Free Press*.

> When it was liquidated, Knight Ridder's profit margins were . . . *higher* than many Fortune 500 companies

Some 90% of the chain's stock was owned by large financial institutions, and Private Capital Management (PCM)—the largest single shareholder, with 19%—led the pressure for the company to put itself up for sale. In late 2005 the company—with 84 Pulitzer Prizes in its history—was sold to the McClatchy newspaper chain, which turned around and (as it had announced in advance) resold 12 of the 32 papers it had just purchased to offset some of the additional debt resulting from the purchase (Folkenflik, 2005; "Newspaper Chains . . .," 2006; Seelye, 2006; Vise, 2005).

New ownership was no panacea. In 2008, for example, MediaNews Group—keeping a close eye on profits—cut staff heavily at its 29 San Francisco Bay Area papers (including the *Mercury News* in San Jose). This led the regional Society of Professional Journalists chapter to voice "serious doubts about the newspaper chain's ability to cover local and regional news responsibly"—an implied utilitarian position undoubtedly combined with concern over lost jobs for its members ("Northern California chapter . . .," 2008).

One observer, a veteran of 18 years with Knight Ridder, faulted the company's leadership for lacking the ethical backbone to resist the marketplace pressures and noted that this "underscored the precarious position of publicly held news organizations" (Guzzo, 2006). That's especially dangerous if the investors know little, and care less, about the role that high-quality news media need to play in U.S. society.

Both Kittross and I agree that it's highly *un*ethical for news media investors to feel entitled to—almost as a God-given economic right—annual profit margins of 20% or more from their companies. Those expectations, which hold in few if any other industries, are particularly inappropriate because the media are the United States' only constitutionally protected businesses. No ethical theory, except *perhaps* something we might call "ethical egoism," could be construed as lending support to such a focus on profits to the exclusion of fulfilling the societal role that the First Amendment confers on the media. (See, among others, Glasser, 1986.)

This is really fuel for a different discussion, but it's worth noting that the financial expectations of investors in U.S. papers aren't necessarily shared elsewhere. In Sweden, for example, the average newspaper profit margin is 8%, which allows Swedish papers "to put more reporters on the street; invest more in technology and grow their franchise" (Suburban Newspapers of America Foundation, 2008, p. 24). I'd suggest that this much more utilitarian perspective deserves the attention of every newspaper owner and publisher in the United States!

In a similar vein, recent data regarding profit margins indicates that a lot of newspapers still are profitable despite the recession that started in 2008 and all the gloom-and-doom talk. Even in a recession economy, publicly (e.g., shareholder)-owned newspapers averaged a *10.8% operating profit* in the first three-quarters of 2008. It was debt service, resulting from the owners' relentless drive to expand their holdings—either the result of poor business judgment or of egoism—that was at the root of many papers' financial woes. The owners were simultaneously posting huge losses, at least on paper, and were "struggling to make payments on debt they took on under projections that didn't pan out" (Ives, 2009, p. 3). These newspapers remained not only profitable, but also able to attract increasing numbers of readers—to their Web sites.

How to "monetize" those eyeballs is a problem that the newspaper industry must solve if there's to be much hope of the marketplace exerting a positive influence on ethics concerns. This is what the Google-led experiments are all about. Downie and Schudson (2009a) provide half a dozen recommendations for possible new business models for journalism (in particular, nonprofit and low-profit corporations) and for ways that journalism's focus on local news might be financed. Some of these options will be discussed below.

ANOTHER NEGATIVE FACTOR

AT&T's 2007 campaign to persuade the Wisconsin Legislature to regulate cable TV franchises at the state rather than the local level was an example of perfectly legal but ethically questionable corporate behavior. To me, it was reminiscent of the "robber barons" who also were concerned only with profit, not with how their actions hurt the public. To be considered an ethical corporate citizen, corporations must think beyond the good of their stockholders and, in this situation, AT&T failed to do that.

AT&T proposed and lobbied heavily for legislation allowing it to use a single statewide application to compete with cable-delivered video in the 438 communities where AT&T already provided other services. This bill, which drew widespread opposition, greatly reduced government oversight; for example, it included no provision that would allow the state to deny an application (Gores, 2007).

Corporations legally may lobby and make campaign contributions, but AT&T's methods here went beyond ethical behavior: Legislation was drafted by AT&T personnel, the company employed at least 15 lobbyists (including, at one point, the *incumbent* chairman of the Wisconsin Democratic Party!) to work on the measure, and it made hefty campaign contributions to sitting legislators in the 18 months before the legislation was finally passed ("Senate OKs . . .," 2007).

The bill's content—ostensibly aimed at promoting competition that would lower prices for consumers—was also very disturbing. As happened in a number of other states, the bill not only freed cable providers from almost any kind of regulation, but also gutted public funding for public access channels throughout the state and opened the door for the telecommunication giants to move into only the most profitable local markets if they chose, a practice often called "cherry-picking."

These negative—for the public—consequences didn't matter to AT&T, which, like the Knight Ridder stockholders, was interested only in the potential for profits and showed no concern for the other stakeholders in the situation. Fortunately, and unlike Ohio and a number of other states, some of the legislation's worst provisions were removed or amended via line-item vetoes by the governor (Walters and Forster, 2007), who was lobbied heavily to use his veto powers by consumer groups and local government associations. But that didn't stop AT&T from returning in 2010 with an attempt to persuade the legislature to end all state regulation of telephone landlines—a bill that easily passed the lower house but died when the Senate session ended.

AT&T's lobbying of the legislature to "fast-track" the 2007 bill—and similar battles in other states, which produced some final products even worse than the one in Wisconsin ("Telecom-cable battle . . .," 2007; Laitman and Phillips, 2007)—illustrates out-and-out abuse of how the political and economic marketplaces should operate. These and similar developments leave me much less sanguine than I used to be about whether economics can be a positive force for ethical behavior.

But enough of sounding much like Kittross. Before going further, we should look at several ways in which the economic marketplace has over the years been *beneficial* to ethics and responsibility.

POSITIVE STRUCTURAL MARKETPLACE FACTORS

We sometimes overlook too easily the positive impact the marketplace can have—and has had—on ethics. For example, the origins of the concept of objectivity in news reporting have been traced to the need of the emerging "penny press" in the 1830s to appeal to readers of *all* ideological stripes, in contrast to the partisan press of the previous decades (e.g., Turow, 1992, pp. 158–159). This objectivity concept was reinforced in the mid-19th century by the fledgling Associated Press, which needed to put its news reports into a format that would satisfy clients at all points along the ideological and political spectrum. Those are clearly market-driven bases for objectivity which, hard as it is to define, has remained central to journalistic ethics over subsequent decades. (See Chapters 3 and 15-A for further discussions of objectivity.)

Much more recently, economic forces and technology have led to cooperation between cable systems, TV stations, and newspapers. This could provide additional (and more quickly available) news and information for the public, if such synergy continues to make economic sense to the firms involved. So far, the results have been mixed, and the jury is still out. Similar economic forces have led to an increasing number of cooperative efforts among newspapers that used to compete heavily with each other—at times to the point of sending their own reporters and photographers to cover events in their rivals' home territory. The need to use shrinking newsroom budgets more efficiently has led to more cooperation between papers that previously competed strongly (see the description of three major cooperative projects in Chapter 15-H).

The economic marketplace is increasingly encouraging consumers to unite their computers, telephones, and cable channels to send as well as receive increased amounts of information and entertainment, and to use their cell phones and various other devices for the same purposes. Many consumers have taken up that "invitation" in whole or part. Readers far younger than I am are able to list many more examples of how the convergence of formerly separate media industries and the exploding use of new technologies are producing greater benefits for an increasing number of media consumers. This may be viewed as a utilitarian outgrowth of economic forces affecting the mass media (even though some of us remain holdouts to 100% technological convergence).

If editors and news directors (and, by extension, creative people in the entertainment media) "learn to express their journalistic needs in counting-house language" (i.e., if they are able to argue persuasively that a high-quality product will boost revenues: Fink, 1988, p. 110), they *might* be able to get some of the resources needed to produce a product that serves the needs of the public *and* the corporate bean counters. This would provide the greatest amount of good or happiness (or satisfaction, or corporate income) to the greatest number of people and validate the perspective that views "newsroom and corporate imperatives as synergistic—not conflicting—forces" (Fink, 1988, p. 113). The emergence of new economic models for journalism could help this process.

IS THERE AN ECONOMIC ALTERNATIVE?

Before we condemn the existing economic marketplace as antithetical to ethical concerns—or as irrelevant, as Kittross does—let's recall that there are essentially only four outside sources for the operating funds necessary to keep mass media systems in business: advertisers, consumers, the government, and funders of nonprofit operations. This focus leaves for other discussions the private entrepreneurial investors who often provide start-up funding for media ventures, as well as the conglomerate owners who could opt to use operating revenues from non-media sources to finance the conglomerate's media operations.

Unless one or more of these four sources provides an adequate revenue stream to cover operating costs and (except for nonprofit operations) allow at least a small profit, even a well-capitalized commercial media venture will sooner or later fail. Relying on advertisers as the revenue sources, as most American mass media do, has its own sets of problems. But relying on consumers or on the government for funding would raise more serious concerns.

Government funding creates at least the possibility of political or ideological control of media content, and runs the danger of creating a much more repressive ethical climate than currently exists. One need only recall the vendetta against the National Endowment for the Arts, carried on from the late 1980s into the late 1990s by such political figures as the late Senator Jesse Helms (R-NC), to be aware that when the government pays the piper, it retains the power to call the tune.

Reliance on consumer fees to produce operating revenues runs the risk of creating economic barriers between the media and less-affluent segments of the public, a topic that is discussed in more detail in Chapter 9. Although some portions of American mass media do use consumer payments to cover part of their operating expenses (e.g., newspaper sales and subscription revenues to a degree, and premium cable channels—or books and movies at a much higher level), the vast majority of American media are financed mainly by revenues from advertising sales. Even such nonprofit information and entertainment channels as public radio and TV benefit from "commercial underwriting"—another term for advertising. And relying on advertising revenues and the economic marketplace strikes me as much more likely than the other two alternatives to produce—in the long run—media that have a concern for ethics.

The market-driven nature of most American media means that what the public wants must be taken into account; success often depends on how well the advertiser or programmer "reads" the public's desires. That's all to the good, unless one prefers to assume an elitist stance and determine media content (and practices) on the basis of what she or he thinks the public *should* want or need. Indeed, the idea of the media providing content that the public wants certainly is appropriate to a democratic society in which ultimate power is vested in the people. That won't always result in choices that "the experts" believe to be in society's best interests, but that's one of the risks you run in a free society, with regard to entertainment or news no less than to political choices.

Kittross's contention that marketplace economics requires the media to do nothing to anger advertisers or the public isn't realistic because it takes much too monolithic a view of both groups, particularly the public. There are, in fact, widely varying interests, values, levels of taste, and concerns for what's "right" among both groups, and offending no one is an impossible goal.

THE NEED FOR MEDIA "CONSUMER EDUCATION"

A number of emerging possibilities offer hope that the economic marketplace can encourage—or at least not subvert—a sense of ethics in the media. Foremost among these is the media literacy movement, whose goal is to produce individuals with "the ability to apply critical thinking skills to the mass media, thereby becoming a more aware and responsible citizen . . . in our media-driven society" (Turow, 2009, p. 29). Success along these lines would develop a reservoir of concerned media consumers who are knowledgeable about how the media operate, willing to exert pressure for higher standards, and able to do so effectively.

There are indications that the numbers of such people are gradually increasing—for example, the success of activist organizations in bringing pressure on the FCC on issues ranging from net neutrality to proposed mergers of media companies. The ranks of knowledgeable and critical media consumers could be increased steadily if more "consumer education" were provided for members of the potential media audience, something both the U.S. educational system and the media themselves have failed to do. Surveys have shown that the public *does* have concerns for ethical news media behavior. But a sizable portion of the public doesn't fully understand how the media operate, and therefore lacks guidance on how to pressure for improvement.

Education for 21st-century living should include required instruction—from grade school through college—in how the various mass media function and how citizens can influence those functions. Having a more media-savvy public might even reduce the temptation to pander to the lower elements of the public's tastes—in both news and entertainment content—in pursuit of larger audiences and more advertising dollars. Rather than merely decrying the possibility that marketplace pressures will dilute media quality, we need to move proactively to use the audiences' influence (actual and potential) to encourage ethical rather than unethical media practices. And a media-literate audience would make that approach much more feasible.

James Carey (1978) wrote eloquently of the need for informed and continuing public analysis and criticism of newspapers (and, by extension, the mass media more generally), which would "scrutinize the values upon which the institution is based." This would require a knowledgeable group of experts *and* ordinary citizens who would help "reconnect the newspaper to the community it serves" (pp. 363 and 364).

> The basic critical act in journalism is public scrutiny of the methods by which journalists define and get what we call news and the conventions by which they deliver it to the public.
>
> (p. 367)

Which, once again, argues for transparency in media operations.

Neil Postman and Steve Powers have written a guide "on how people should prepare themselves to interpret a television news show" and they argue that "anyone who is not an avid reader of newspapers, magazines, and books is by definition unprepared to watch television news shows" (Postman and Powers, 2008, p. x). On a simpler level, they suggest eight steps viewers can take to improve their understanding of television news (pp. 154–161). These include remembering that news programs are generally called "shows" and that commercials "are a serious form of popular literature" and "tell as much about our society as 'straight' news does, probably more." The authors also argue that it is essential "that TV news be made into an object of study" in elementary and secondary schools (pp. 156 and 161).

The idea of starting to educate media consumers in elementary school is one that I can't emphasize strongly enough! To me, media literacy is an ethical imperative for American society as a whole, if we expect the media's economic marketplace—and the marketplace of ideas—to function properly. Various organizations and programs dedicated to producing educated media users have been around for two decades or more—to note only a few, Elizabeth Thoman's Center for Media Literacy; Rushworth Kidder's Institute for Global

media literacy is an ethical imperative for American society as a whole, if we expect the media's economic marketplace—and the marketplace of ideas—to function properly.

Ethics; and Sut Jhally's Media Education Foundation. Others are much more recent, for example, the Center for News Literacy at Stony Brook University in New York and the News Literacy Project, which uses journalists to provide students in middle and high schools with the tools to recognize, understand and appreciate the value of high-quality news coverage and credible information.

A novel approach to help the public better understand how the news media function was suggested by Everette Dennis in 1990. His transparency prescription calls for news organizations to instruct their audiences

> about (a) the operative theory of journalism with which any given news organization guides itself; (b) the resources it has devoted to newsgathering; (c) the ways in which the public ought to assess and evaluate the results; and finally, (d) how individual readers and viewers might "talk back" to or interact with editors and producers of the news.
>
> (Dennis, 1990, p. 8)

An even more innovative option was proposed in 2008 by Mark Kiyak, who suggested that broadcast news organizations list daily on their Web sites every story *considered* for broadcast. Print and online media could follow the same approach, to promote transparency and stimulate discussion (and perhaps greater understanding) with their audiences. Opportunities for such interaction are increasing steadily as more and more newspapers and broadcast outlets provide and publicize ways for audience members to interact with their staffers through social media or by e-mail. McChesney (2007a) implied that media-literate citizens must be concerned about, and understand, media policy and its evolution, in addition to having insights into the media's operations and content. Such audiences could exert pressure through the economic marketplace and demonstrate through their choices that social responsibility, idealism, and ethical behavior can produce economic rewards. That would be a middle-ground approach derived from both utilitarianism and Aristotle's Golden Mean. The results would almost certainly fall well short of some utopian ideal, but on balance they could improve the ethical fallout from our dependence on the economic marketplace.

WAYS THE MARKETPLACE CAN HELP

If nothing else, informed and active media consumers would help prevent a situation analogous to H. L. Mencken's somewhat cynical definition of democracy as "the theory that the common people know what they want, and deserve to get it good and hard" (Mencken, 1955, p. 232). Democracy has somehow survived. And ethics in the marketplace could, too, with the help of such developments as citizen pressure groups, nonprofit journalism ventures, carefully crafted public financing of news media, and moves to online-only publication. None of these are panaceas, but together—and within the existing economic marketplace—they can help make that marketplace hospitable for media ethics.

Citizen Pressure Groups

The rise of citizen pressure groups demanding media responsibility and accountability could help reverse the recent negative impact of economics upon media ethics issues. McChesney (2007b) has questioned whether the media system's basic structure allows individuals working within it to make ethical decisions. He concluded that it "is structured in such a way as to make it rational, even 'ethical,' to produce dubious content" (McChesney, 2007b, p. 34). As Kittross noted, the Free Press organization reflects the belief that the system needs to be greatly revamped, and is working to organize citizen involvement in the economic and political policy decisions that will determine what that new structure looks like. (Incidentally, if you're interested in trying to move the current media environment in a more open direction, check out this group, at www.freepress.net)

McChesney's recent work, especially his book *Communication Revolution* (2007a), provides an approach that offers some hope, *provided* media consumers become more knowledgeable about their media *and* more involved in trying to influence media policy decisions. He notes the huge changes occurring in the media landscape as the digital revolution affects corporate organization, business models, and content, and argues that these changes must be planned carefully to maximize their benefits. McChesney insists that policy decisions about the future structure of the media marketplace should involve concerned and informed citizens, rather than being made behind closed doors by media owners and politicians. Unless the public is involved, he warns, consumers' interests will get short shrift and commercialization could well overtake every aspect of U.S. culture that is influenced by the media.

Among McChesney's goals are policies that would encourage more competitive media markets (including a milieu where individuals might be able to start their own outlets) and "support a viable, heterogeneous tier of noncommercial and nonprofit media, especially at the local level" (McChesney, 2007a, p. xiv), an approach that Kittross would undoubtedly welcome for the sake of both competition and localism. The underlying premise is that with the "right" policy decisions, many additional communication channels will become available for many more participants in the media marketplace. With smaller target audiences and niche marketing encouraging those participants, we may yet see economic as well as content competition where ethical concerns are valued.

The Free Press organization and others like it (e.g., Reclaim the Media) have had growing success in bringing pressure on Congress and the FCC on such issues as "net neutrality" and keeping as many independent media voices as possible—an approach that draws on utilitarianism and Rawls with a touch of the Judeo-Christian ethic.

Nonprofit Journalism

- "A greater role for nonprofits . . . could help lift all media" (Overholser, 2006, p. 3).
- "newspapers are so central to the public interest that they deserve to be recreated as nonprofits and operated for the public good"—like art museums, symphony orchestras and hospitals. (Kidder, 2009, pp. 1, 14).
- "the nonprofit model . . . answers to a different bottom line, so it fits neatly into a world where journalism is a public good" (Barnett, 2009).

Many examples of how nonprofit (by design, not involuntary!) journalism might improve the marketplace mix are showing up and are summarized concisely by Downie and Schudson (2009b, especially at pp. 36–39 and p. 42). One such approach led, by 2009, to six online daily political news sites (in Colorado, Iowa, New Mexico, Michigan, and Minnesota along with an umbrella news site in Washington, DC), funded by the nonprofit Center for Independent Media (CIM) and characterized by Downie and Schudson (2009b, p. 38) as "liberal-leaning." CIM bills itself as an "independent online news network in the public interest" whose journalists adhere to the SPJ code of ethics and also follow the "New Journalist Code of Ethics," which is posted on the CIM Web site (Center for Independent Media, 2009). CIM was founded in 2006 by David Bennahum, a former venture capitalist, advertising executive and a founding writer for *Wired* magazine, who saw a need for "more diverse sources of news" in order to sustain a democratic society (quoted in Perry, 2008, p. 13).

In the wake of retrenchments that left some 100 Minneapolis and St. Paul journalists out of jobs in 2007, Joel Kramer, editor of the Minneapolis *Star Tribune* from 1983 to 1991 and its publisher from 1992 to 1998, raised more than $1 million (including $250,000 from the Knight Foundation) to hire some of these journalists for a nonprofit news site. Operating five days a week, the site aims to "provide high-quality journalism for news-intense people who care about Minnesota." MinnPost.com promised not to "get distracted by trying to be all things or serve all people" and to "encourage broad-ranging, civil discussion from many points of view" ("About Us," 2008). By early 2008, Kramer was spending some $10,000 a week for experienced freelancers, and was hoping that a combination of donors and ad revenues would allow the site to break even within four years (Hartmann, 2008).

There are other models as well. One example is the "Voice of San Diego," a daily online news site established in 2005, emphasizing investigative reporting and funded in part—using the public radio model—by audience members (Downie and Schudson, 2009b, p. 42). It is one of at least three nonprofit news operations in San Diego. Other nonprofit efforts have been started in places ranging from Montana to St. Louis to New Haven to Austin, Texas (Downie and Schudson, 2009b, p. 38), and networks of nonprofit investigative organizations are growing, as well (Houston, 2010). So are instances of "ultra-local" reporting on neighborhoods, in blogs that are frequently nonprofit (and occasionally—as in Seattle—provide the local paper with coverage that was lost through staff cutbacks).

Joel Kramer's Web site "reflects a growing interest among philanthropists in finding ways to help rescue journalism—or in loftier terms, a pillar of democracy—from the brutalities of the market" (Perry, 2008, p. 12). One study estimated that "national and local foundations provided $128 million to news nonprofits from 2005 to 2009" (Downie and Schudson, 2009b, p. 42) but much of that went for start-up costs and more may be needed to sustain some of these operations.

The need to finance nonprofit journalism organizations raises new ethical questions as well as some older ones. A 2010 conference focused on a number of these—acceptable donors, transparency in regard to funders, and editorial independence, among others. Recommended "best practices" to protect nonprofit journalism included: Aim for the highest possible level of transparency; consider how taking funds from any donor could affect the organization's integrity; develop clear policies on conflicts of interest; and collaborate with other institutions as appropriate, "but be aware of the variety of editorial and fundraising standards of your partners" (Ward, 2010, p. 21).

One sign that the nonprofit approach is coming of age was the cooperation of ProPublica with *The New York Times* on an investigative series that won the 2010 Pulitzer Prize, and its collaboration with *The Washington Post* on three front-page stories within a week's time the previous year (Barnett, 2009). ProPublica, a nonprofit investigative reporting operation headed by the former managing editor of *The Wall Street Journal*, was perhaps the best funded nonprofit, with a $10 million start (see also Drew, 2010).

Another such sign was the mid-2009 gathering of more than two dozen nonprofit news organizations at the Pocantico conference center in New York, where they agreed to collaborate on editorial, administrative and financial concerns as well as working to establish "basic shared goals and news values" (Pocantico Declaration, 2009). As one observer noted:

> Nonprofits measure success not by the revenues and profits they generate, but by yardsticks such as how many people read their work, the educational value of that work and the impact it has on decision-makers.
>
> [The nonprofit approach] allows journalists to build islands of credibility in a[n] online sea of misinformation, disinformation and too much information. I've heard it said many times that in the online world, transparency is the new objectivity. The tax laws require nonprofits to disclose their major donors, and the good ones are taking disclosure to greater levels than that required by law.
>
> (Barnett, 2009)

Funding to specific media for specialized reporting—from health coverage and child development to education and foreign affairs—is available from a variety of nonprofit sources (Doughton and Heim, 2011; Guensberg, 2008; C. Lewis, 2007). And it's worth remembering that nonprofit news organizations include such venerable ones as the Associated Press and *The Christian Science Monitor*, plus more recent ones like the *Union Leader* in Manchester, New Hampshire and *The Day* in New London, Connecticut. And then there are the nonprofit magazines, ranging from *Consumer Reports*, *Foreign Affairs* and *Harpers* to *Mother Jones*, *The Progressive* and *National Review*. It's not a new concept, and it may well be worth asking whether a nonprofit model might be possible in the advertising or public relations fields, if it can succeed in the economic marketplace for news and opinion.

Remember, though, that nonprofit status didn't keep economic pressures from driving *The Christian Science Monitor* to drop its daily print edition in favor of online publication, starting in the spring of 2009. The move was expected to allow the paper's owner, the First Church of Christ Scientist, to reduce its annual operating subsidy from $12 million to $4 million over a five-year period—and to allow the paper to keep open its eight foreign bureaus, a commitment that runs totally counter to what has been happening among for-profit newspapers and chains (Clifford, 2008).

Operating as a nonprofit can eliminate many marketplace pressures, but the need to attract and satisfy an audience will remain, as will many ethics issues based in the economic marketplace.

Operating as a nonprofit can eliminate many marketplace pressures, but the need to attract and satisfy an audience will remain, as will many ethics issues based in the economic marketplace. And there are two other potential problems for nonprofits. One, surprisingly, could be reduced editorial independence compared to what can exist in an advertising-supported publication. Edward Wasserman (2008), a journalism ethics professor and formerly executive business editor of *The Miami Herald*, noted that

> advertisers could be sublimely indifferent to editorial content as long as it was drawing a crowd they could sell to (and wasn't about them). But foundations and public-minded plutocrats are less bashful about their preferences and convictions, and some philanthropies may even be obligated to ensure their money advances certain policy goals.
> (Wasserman, 2008)

Other restrictions on editorial independence could come, via the Internal Revenue Service (IRS), from a federal government interested in silencing opposition voices. Victor Navasky, former editor of *The Nation*, noted that while some opinion magazines have successfully gone the nonprofit route, his journal chose not to despite the clear financial advantages—especially lower postal rates—this change would have provided. That decision, he wrote, was made to safeguard the freedom to criticize any and all aspects of the government, endorse political candidates, and lobby for legislation. All of those might run afoul of a narrow reading of Section 501(c)(3) of the Internal Revenue code, which governs most activities of nonprofit and tax-exempt organizations and prohibits them from lobbying (Navasky, 2005, p. 200).

Navasky said he "worried about the potential for abuse of IRS discretion by selective harassment of political critics." And he quoted the 1985 remark by the editor of *Mother Jones*, which seems to sum up the confluence of ethics and economics where nonprofit status is concerned: "You could say that for a magazine like *Mother Jones*, if you are in the for-profit world you will be censored by corporations, and if you work in the nonprofit world you'll be censored by government" (quoted in Navasky, 2005, p. 201).

Public Financing of Media

Overholser (2006, p. 16) and others have raised this option, in the face of almost knee-jerk reactions that such an approach would fly in the face of the First Amendment. But "government has *always* played a role in American journalism. Major government subsidies include reduced postal rates, copyright protection, state sales-tax exemptions, government advertising, and the Newspaper Preservation Act" (Nordenson, 2007, p. 38), as well as decreasing subsidies to public broadcast media.

Wasserman expanded on this theme in early 2008:

> Public financing, too, long banished from polite conversation, is getting a new airing . . . in other countries, stand-alone systems of automatic funding have kept dying newspapers alive and made the press even feistier—more, not less, inclined to watchdog governments.
>
> The knee-jerk notion that the First Amendment forbids public support rests on a misreading of our own history of media subsidies, from creation of the postal system to invention of the Internet. Mechanisms could be devised to make funding automatic—fees tacked onto Internet hookup charges, for instance, like the license fees on TV sets

that British viewers pay to support their BBC—and insulate news producers from political meddling.

(Wasserman, 2008)

Considered in this light, getting government involved in this way would not be all that radical. Remember that Kittross, in discussing the free enterprise marketplace, noted that even in the deregulated business climate of the Reagan and Bush I and II years, government was considerably involved. And it remains involved in such other ways as the impact of federal estate tax laws on media ownership—particularly with regard to family-owned newspapers.

SOME FINAL CONSIDERATIONS

Jay Harris, the former San Jose publisher, put part of the blame for newsroom and other budget cutbacks on the high salaries paid to many newspaper executives. He described them as "golden handcuffs" which have become blindfolds and gags too much of the time. Harris stressed that the stockholders should not be regarded as the only "owners" of a newspaper. "All people with a stake in the newspaper need to be heard, he said, not just the shareholders, but also the journalists and readers" (J. Lewis, 2001).

Wasserman (2008) has suggested a radical approach to alter the media's economic marketplace—that journalism should use computer capabilities "to track and calculate" a charge for news on a piecemeal, on-demand basis.

Imagine a vast menu of news and commentary offered to you ad-free for pennies per item, the charges micro-billed, added up and presented like a utility bill at month's end. The money that journalism providers got would depend on their audience.

Plus, if you uploaded comment or video in response, to the degree it was downloaded by others you'd get credited for it—compensated like any other provider.

Illogical and impractical? Maybe. Or maybe it would free journalism from an advertising dependency that's in its death throes anyway, move us beyond the obsolescent distinction between producer and consumer and create new opportunities for independence and enterprise.

(Wasserman, 2008)

However, this could also have the negative result of causing people to consider each individual "news purchase" carefully, and might reduce the amount of news they consume.

One answer to economic pressures is to publish only online, following the examples of *The Christian Science Monitor* and *The Capital Times* in Madison, Wisconsin. The Madison paper dropped its print edition in early 2008 in favor of an online operation that utilizes a much smaller newsroom. The afternoon paper, part of a joint operating agreement (JOA), had lost money for decades but survived because it was subsidized by its morning partner in the JOA. It remains to be seen whether converting to an exclusive online publishing arrangement will reduce bottom-line constraints on acting ethically.

When the only local paper is chain-owned, and it goes to online publication, some additional questions arise. Utilitarians might argue that closing the print edition and reallocating resources elsewhere would in fact benefit the greater number of people in the chain's other markets. Rawls, of course, would disagree, perhaps with special regard for the employees who lost their jobs in the process.

Even decreased competition, with all the ethical alarm bells that raises, may have *some* benefits for the ethical climate. For instance, partnerships between cable and telephone companies might yet provide them improved technological and financial resources that would allow the companies to supply better service to a greater number of people—an approach that would warm the hearts of utilitarians. (Of course, Machiavelli might also triumph, if this led to less diverse programming.)

An increasingly common marketplace scenario is the end of newspaper competition within a given market, as occurred recently in Seattle. There, the *Seattle Post-Intelligencer* (owned by Hearst), which had survived for many years under a joint operating agreement with *The Seattle Times* (locally owned), dropped its print edition and faded away to a much-reduced online basis in the spring of 2009. This could strengthen *The Seattle Times'* profit margin, which in turn might reduce pressures to cut ethical corners. But it could also produce the negative effect of eliminating competition in the marketplace of ideas as well as the economic marketplace—always a danger in a monopoly situation. In Seattle, though, a surge of ultra-local news coverage fortunately helped to maintain some competition.

ARE ECONOMIC FORCES SUFFICIENT?

The short answer is that they are probably *not* sufficient to *ensure* accountability and ethical results, much less profit, in a marketplace that's already very different from the model that prevailed at the end of the 20th century. We need, among other things, more imaginative leadership in the newspaper industry, to find ways to boost profits without cutting back on staff and content. As noted earlier, the industry (now, perhaps with some help from Google) continues to wrestle with how to convert consumer visits to Web sites into advertising revenue—a major challenge that, so far, hasn't been met in the United States. In Sweden, by contrast, the audience has been trained to go to newspaper Web sites (for streaming video, among other attractions), and one paper with a daily circulation of 80,000 expected to sell approximately $100,000 in video advertising in 2009, with the anticipation that this amount would grow steadily (Suburban Newspapers of America Foundation, 2008, p. 13). With estimates like that from abroad, one wonders even more about newspaper industry leadership in the United States. Even an economic marketplace supportive of ethics could be trumped by poor leadership.

There is a need—for the economy in general, not just the media portion of it—for something similar to the social responsibility formula proposed for the media after World War II by the Commission on Freedom of the Press (1947). In essence, if business is not at least somewhat socially responsible, the government must be ready to step in to ensure responsibility, and has done so in a number of areas; minimum wage requirements and antitrust regulations are just two ongoing examples. In regard to the media's economic marketplace, government should be a court of last resort if such relatively new forces as nonprofit media ownership and organized citizen pressures can't do the job. For now, the impact of the economic marketplace on ethics in particular and on responsibility more generally may depend as much on whether the media entity is owned by stockholders or, for example, by a partnership or a family—or on whether it is a for-profit or a nonprofit operation—as on the moral concerns and codes of the media decision-makers.

Note, for example, the relationship between business and ethical concerns demonstrated by *The New York Times* (publicly traded but family controlled), in regard to advertising acceptability. The long-time head of its Advertising Acceptability Department, noting that a newspaper's credibility can be damaged by misleading or offensive advertising as well as by its editorial content, suggested that

> concern for the welfare of the reader and sound business practice are [not] mutually exclusive. On the contrary, self-regulation and discipline with regard to the acceptance of advertising is about as good an example as you will find to illustrate the profitability of principle.

> (R. P. Smith, 1984, p. 11)

We dare not ignore the ethical as well as economic (and legal) issues lurking in early-21st-century media ownership patterns, and in many aspects of new media technologies. So far, the results are mixed in regard to Joseph Turow's (2009) prediction that the future of the mass media industries will be linked to the concept of synergy. He defines that term as "the ability of mass media organizations to channel content into a wide variety of mass media on a global scale through control over production, distribution, and exhibition in as many of those media as possible," so that the whole is *greater* than the sum of its various parts (Turow, 2009, p. 235).

Of course, the results of such synergy can be both good and bad, economically *and* ethically—one need only look at Bagdikian's synergy scenario for a potentially *un*ethical example (Bagdikian, 1989). The economic benefits weren't a sure thing, either. As the Tribune Company learned after its purchase of Times Mirror in 2000, even the combined company's ownership of newspapers and TV stations in the United States' top three markets failed to "reap [the] editorial, promotional and advertising windfalls" that had been envisioned; the synergistic strategy failed to produce the anticipated "major, national footprint" (Smolkin, 2006–07, pp. 22 and 24). The end result was the sale of the Tribune Company (for $8.2 billion—slightly *below* the $8.3 billion purchase price of Times Mirror less than eight years earlier!) to a Chicago real estate mogul with no previous experience in journalism. He took the company private while continuing to reduce staff numbers across its different properties and, eventually, selling off both *Newsday* (to Cablevision Systems) and the Chicago Cubs. By 2009, the Tribune Company had filed for bankruptcy protection—but nonetheless was showing a 5.4% operating profit for the first nine months of 2008 (Ives, 2009)—another example of the dangers of buying with borrowed funds.

The *Tribune*'s problems arose from both the marketplace and the people making economic and other decisions. Once again, cutting costs didn't solve the problems (but it did, as usual, weaken the quality of the product). The problems plaguing the Tribune Company even after it was taken private are a jarring reminder that public stock ownership is not the only reason why media companies often emphasize the bottom line to the detriment of quality or ethics.

Two final thoughts: First, in view of the heavy newsroom staff cutbacks in the first decade of the 21st century, it's worth asking whether more ethical ways might be found for media companies to pursue a downsizing strategy—an issue still lacking definitive answers. Second, given the proliferation of discussions about how news media might survive— especially those originating within academia—it would be helpful if there were a bit more cross-fertilization between them in place of the separate tangents that seem to be the prevailing style.

CONCLUSION

So, are there reasons for optimism amid the cutbacks, layoffs, newsroom downsizing, bankruptcy filings and newspaper and magazine closings that marked the end of the first decade of the 21st century? Patrick Plaisance, guest editing a "Media Economics and Ethics" issue of the *Journal of Mass Media Ethics*, seemed to think so. He noted "the imperative of getting the business of journalism right, both economically and ethically" and added:

> Economic viability must come with the clear-eyed dedication to key principles and a steady acknowledgement that it all won't mean much if we compromise the pillar of journalistic credibility.
>
> (Plaisance, 2009, pp. 88–89)

It may well be that ethics (and high-quality performance) survive in part *because of* the pressures of the economic marketplace. Some research into newspaper ownership has found that "chain and monopoly newspapers place greater emphasis on product quality [than on profits] and can improve the quality of the product" (Demers, 1994, p. 2) though there are also data to the contrary. Alvah Chapman, then chair of (now defunct) Knight Ridder, noted back in the late 1980s that:

> good journalism is good business. As an information company, our success depends on the excellence, reputation and usefulness of that information which is our product. We want our readers and viewers to have the highest possible confidence in what we produce. This is essential to maintaining our credibility and consequently the loyalty and following of our readers and viewers.
>
> (quoted in Fink, 1988, p. 105)

Such concerns are certainly part of what Edmund Lambeth (1992) calls the *stewardship principle* of media ethics—the need to "manage [the] resources of communication with due regard for the rights of others, the rights of the public, and the moral health" of the mass communication industries (Lambeth, 1992, p. 32). But when media organizations fail to recognize the need for such stewardship, ethics and high quality will survive (despite the pressures of the economic marketplace) only to the extent that citizen groups and other consumers keep pointing out that stewardship can also be good business—and put their patronage where their ideals are.

The economic goals and concerns will always be there, of course—as they must for media that are run for profit. But even nonprofit organizations—to note just one alternative model—must have enough income to pay their bills and remain in existence. Over the years, I've found very few students who carry their idealism so far as to say that they're willing to work for a highly ethical mass medium that has too little revenue to pay them a salary.

If boardrooms and CEOs continue to regard the media as widget-producers even after media-literate consumers flex their economic muscle, it is even more up to media practitioners themselves to be continually aware of ethics and other non-widgetary aspects of their calling. Dennis (1990) was referring mostly to the news media in his descriptions, but these concerns, and the need to maintain a focus on ethics and on quality because (or in spite) of the bean counters, are equally applicable to those working in the entertainment media, public relations, and advertising. It's easy these days to become extremely skeptical that the economic marketplace could exert a good influence on *any*thing, much less media ethics. Owners have gone far too heavily into debt to finance acquisitions that have proved to be of dubious value. Stockholders, buyers and capital lenders have been totally unrealistic (and, I'd say, unethical in their desire to maximize profits with little regard for the quality of their products) in demanding double-digit returns even in a declining economy—especially in businesses protected by the First Amendment, whose owners should have voluntarily accepted the obligation to serve the public interest as well as their stockholders. And many in the news industry have hesitated to embrace the Internet in anything but a defensive posture. All of these have not exactly inspired confidence in the positive effects of the marketplace.

Nonetheless—and this is certainly not an original thought—I believe that the news business will survive simply because American democracy cannot survive without it. Self-governing citizens need information . . . a thought that goes back at least to James Madison and Thomas Jefferson. Downie and Schudson (2009b, p. 31) stress the need for "independent, original, credible reporting whether or not it is popular or profitable, and regardless of the medium in which it appears," and put a strong emphasis on "[a]ccountability journalism, particularly local accountability journalism."

New economic models for journalism are certainly going to emerge in the coming decades. Among the funding sources that might support essential journalism functions are foundations. The Bill and Melinda Gates Foundation has done this for nearly a decade to stimulate coverage of global health issues, although this raises some ethics questions about undue influence and conflict of interest (see Doughton and Heim, 2011). Other options include non-governmental organizations such as Human Rights Watch which, in 2009, was beginning to create news reports based on its worldwide fact-gathering network (Westphal, 2009). Downie and Schudson (2009b) list other potential sources for new models of independent news reporting, including efforts on college and university campuses and by activist groups, and suggest that digital content will be crucial to the eventual mix and that the marketplace will determine whether any of the many experiments will ultimately be successful" (2009b, p. 44).

While I can't begin to predict what platforms will be used to deliver the information that a democratic society needs, I'm hopeful that the news industry—perhaps with some help from academia—will develop them, either in flashes of brilliant insight or blundering, defensive luck, or perhaps both. I am certain, as James Batten said more than two decades ago, that the skills required to gather, package, and present significant information about our society will be needed regardless of what platform is used. As new platforms—and the funding to support them—emerge, it's first up to the people in the industry to fulfill Plaisance's exhortation that ethical principles must evolve along with new business models. And, I would argue that this dual evolution can—indeed, *must*—be driven by audiences who have both knowledge of how the media operate and concern that those operations be ethical.

McChesney, Downie, and Schudson, and others were absolutely correct in identifying the current media landscape as one where the convergence of new technology and economic pressures present an opportunity to bring about major and beneficial changes. If this is indeed possible, on even a relatively small scale, it could enable the economic marketplace —broadly defined, to include philanthropic support—to continue functioning as the basic source of media operating revenues while also contributing to an appropriate concern for ethical and societal responsibilities. If that can also be coupled with a more knowledgeable universe of media consumers and activist pressures aiming to preserve a multitude of voices, sufficient accountability will follow.

But it's not going to happen unless you and your peers in the media industries—news, persuasion and entertainment—*along with* your audiences, become the ones to make it happen.

KEY POINTS

- The economic marketplace has the potential to produce journalism with a concern for ethical standards, through nonprofit or government-assisted media outlets or such developments as Google's efforts to help find a viable economic model for good reporting.
- Nonprofit journalism organizations will still have to face ethics issues: for example, who is an acceptable donor, how much transparency is needed in regard to funders, and how can editorial independence best be protected?
- Publicly traded newspaper stocks have exerted a negative influence on quality and ethics because of pressure—especially by institutional investors—to maximize the price of such stock.

MERRILL: Commentary

Gordon and Kittross have, in essence, turned this chapter from a debate into a rush toward the center of moderation—with both critical of a laissez-faire economic media system.

Gordon has retreated from his earlier marketplace support of ethical media and now seems to see the necessity of a more governmental or populist or philanthropic determination of media action. Kittross retains his earlier belief that the economic marketplace serves no useful function with respect to media ethics.

Both writers provide the reader with a plethora of discussion about economics and government as they discuss the kind of media support most useful in bringing about media morality. Gordon is less optimistic than earlier about the ethical benefits of a marketplace media system, and his remarks basically agree with those of Kittross in many respects.

While both writers provide a wealth of information about this ongoing and complex controversy, neither one (in my view) gives us answers as to what would be a different and better solution. Both seem willing to take some editorial decision powers away from the managers and editors (or, certainly, the owners) of the media and put them somehow in the hands of some governmental or non-governmental agent. Both, in short, seem to have gotten on board a postmodern train inhabited by communitarians on one hand and governmental authoritarians on the other. Both seem to have little or no confidence in traditional "editorial self-determination" by the media themselves.

It is understandable why they have lost faith in media-determined ethics. News media have tended to perpetuate stereotypes, deal in gossip and entertainment, provide political bias in their reports, accentuate the negative, minimize their news content, exaggerate crime and sex stories, and indulge in questionable ethical practices. But the question still confronts us: What other system would assure ethical media practice?

If "the people" had more say in editorial decisions, would they be any more ethical? If government controlled the media, would that lead to greater media morality? (In the latter case, we might evaluate government's morality by looking at the political scene.) In the former case, a more populist media system, how would it be administered? Although both Gordon and Kittross seem to endorse the socialistically inclined views of Robert McChesney of the University of Illinois and his Free Press organization, there is no evidence that such nebulous ideas bring about higher ethical standards.

Gordon says he has become less optimistic about the marketplace system bringing higher ethical standards. One can understand this. It is probably a commonly held view in the general public. Kittross obviously agrees. But one wonders what the ideal situation would be? One extreme is a socialistic system and the other is a libertarian system. The libertarian system seemingly hasn't worked. And the socialistic media system has not really been tried—yet—at least in the United States. So it could be that both writers are headed in the right direction, wanting a leftward swing. A new and better system to develop more ethical media is surely badly needed. But the question is: what kind of system?

Gordon suggests that more media-literate audiences would help—seeing this as leading to citizen pressure groups. Citizens, he says, could then "demand media responsibility and accountability." Sounds good, but how would it be done? One would think that the marketplace would "demand" that media be ethical, but it has not. But there may be other ways of pressuring the media, although Gordon and Kittross have not made these clear. Maybe in time the Free Press organization, which seeks to get more citizen involvement (a goal praised so highly by these authors), can shed light on this important problem.

Kittross's contention that the economic marketplace is irrelevant and counterproductive to media ethics is, it seems to me, at least half true. I agree with him that it is irrelevant in that ethics is individual and personal (and not dependent on the marketplace). However, I can't see that it is "counterproductive" to ethics. How can it be both irrelevant and counterproductive at the same time? If it is counterproductive, it is certainly not irrelevant. What Kittross is saying, I think, is that the marketplace puts its emphasis on *quantity* and not on *quality*. This is a good point, but one that applies to the marketplace and journalism as a whole, not just to ethics.

It seems that Kittross has some hope that a government-controlled press *might* bring about a higher ethics. He agrees with the great German writer Goethe's claim that the best government is one "that governs best, not one that governs least," as the Enlightenment thinkers believed. What's interesting is that "best" is not necessarily the opposite of "least."

Gordon has not completely given up on the marketplace doing some good for media ethics. He says that the marketplace "can *still* help to hold the media responsible (italics added)." Private ownership, although losing much influence for Gordon, is still in the ethics picture. Citizen groups, nonprofit organizations like the Associated Press and newer models, and government subsidies, for both Gordon and Kittross, could lead to a more ethical media system. Both writers also note the recent emergence of nonprofit news media operations, and Gordon suggests that private foundation funding might be one means of support for them— an interesting idea but one that is totally unproven at this writing.

In conclusion, the two authors (and I) agree that the market system has not led, and probably will not lead, to an ethical media system. But if we are not willing to live with it, we must opt for some type of anti-market theory that will limit freedom. It may be best to have more ethics and less freedom. But as I see it, neither side of this argument really has anything to do with ethics but only with economic support or pragmatics. Economic systems do not determine ethics. Ethics has to do with individual virtue, with meanings of virtue tied up with specific cultures and traditions. Economics has to do with structure, whereas ethics has to do with humane visions and metaphysical insights that lead to right or good actions.

REFERENCES AND RELATED READINGS

"About Us." (2008). *MinnPost.com*. Retrieved from www.minnpost.com/about/ (May 24, 2008).

Anderson, Chris. (2009). *Free: The Future of a Radical Price*. New York: Hyperion.

Auletta, Ken. (1994). "John Malone: Flying solo (Annals of Communications)." *The New Yorker*, February 7, pp. 52–67.

——. (1997). "American keiretsu." *The New Yorker*, October 20, pp. 225–227.

——. (2009). *Googled: The End of the World as We Know It*. New York: Penguin.

Bagdikian, Ben H. (1989). "The lords of the global village." *The Nation*, June 12, pp. 805–820.

——. (2004). *The New Media Monopoly*. Boston, MA: Beacon.

Baker, C. Edwin. (2002). "Media concentration: Giving up on democracy." 54 *Florida Law Review*, 839.

Baker, Russ. (1997). "The squeeze." *Columbia Journalism Review*, September–October, pp. 30–34, 36.

Barnett, Jim. (2009). "Nonprofit journalism: The journey from anomaly to a new paradigm." *Nieman Journalism Lab*, August 11. Retrieved from www.niemanlab.org/2009/08/nonprofit-journalism-the-journey-from-anomaly-to-a-new-paradigm/ (October 7, 2009).

Barron, Jerome A. (1973). *Freedom of the Press for Whom?* Bloomington, IN: Indiana University Press.

Blethen, Ryan. (2009). "Journalism's identity crisis: The emerging hybrid media." *The Seattle Times*, September 20, p. B9.

Carey, James. (1978). "But who will criticize the critics?" In Everette E. Dennis, Arnold H. Ismach, and Donald M. Gillmor, eds., *Enduring Issues in Mass Communication*. St. Paul, MN: West, pp. 362–368. (Excerpted from James Carey. (1974). "Journalism and criticism: The case of an undeveloped profession." *Review of Politics*, April, pp. 227–249.)

Cathcart, Thomas, and Daniel Klein. (2006). *Plato and a Platypus Walk into a Bar . . .* New York: Abrams Image.

Center for Independent Media. (2009). Web site at http://newjournalist.org. See also http://new journalist.org/ethics.

Clifford, Stephanie. (2008). "Christian Science paper to end daily print edition." *The New York Times*, October 29, p. B8. Also available at www.nytimes.com/2008/10/29/business/media/29paper.html?_r=1&ei=5 070&emc=eta1&oref=slogin.

Commission on Freedom of the Press. (1947). *A Free and Responsible Press*. Chicago, IL: University of Chicago Press.

Cowan, Geoffrey and David Westphal. (2010). *Public Policy and Funding the News*. Los Angeles, CA: Center on Communication Leadership and Policy, Annenberg School for Communication and Journalism, University of Southern California. Also available online at http://communicationleadership.usc.edu/pubs/Funding%20the%20News.pdf.

Crystal, Graef. (1993). "Salary survey: The C.E.O. factor." *Columbia Journalism Review*, November–December, pp. 49–50.

Demers, David Pearce. (1994). "Structural pluralism, intermedia competition, and the growth of the corporate newspaper in the United States." *Journalism Monographs* 145 (June).

Dennis, Everette E. (1990). "In allegiance to the truth: News, ethics and split-personality journalism." Gannett Center for Media Studies, New York, speech delivered March 6, Honolulu.

Dotinga, Randy. (2008). "Nonprofit journalism on the rise." *The Christian Science Monitor*, February 12. Retrieved from www.csmonitor.com/2008/0212/p03s01-usgn.html.

Doughton, Sandi, and Kristi Heim. (2011). "Does Gates funding of media taint objectivity?" *The Seattle Times*, February 20, pp. A-1 and A-19.

Downie, Leonard, Jr., and Michael Schudson. (2009a). *The Reconstruction of American Journalism*. New York: Graduate School of Journalism, Columbia University. Retrieved from www.journalism.columbia.edu/cs/ContentServer? pagename=JRN/Render/DocURL&binaryid=12126 (November 2, 2009). (Available more easily through a link at www.columbiajournalismreport.org.)

——. (2009b). "The reconstruction of American journalism." *Columbia Journalism Review*, November–December, pp. 28–51. (This is a shorter version of the report listed immediately above.)

Drew, Jill. (2010). "The new investigators: Nonprofits are breaking new ground. Can they sustain themselves?" *Columbia Journalism Review*, May–June, pp. 22–27.

Fallows, James. (2010). "How to save the news: Google search—I'm feeling lucky." *The Atlantic*, June, pp. 44–52 and 54–56.

Fink, Conrad C. (1988). *Media Ethics: In the Newsroom and Beyond*. New York: McGraw-Hill.

Folkenflik, David. (2005). "Possible Knight Ridder sale brings unlikely suitors." NPR *All Things Considered*, December 29. Retrieved from www.npr.org/templates/story/story.php?storyId=5074829.

Gladwell, Malcolm. (2008). *Outliers: The Story of Success.* New York: Little, Brown.

——. (2009). "The critics/books/priced to sell: Is free the future?" *The New Yorker,* July 6 and 13, pp. 80–84.

Glasser, Theodore L. (1986). "Press responsibility and First Amendment values." In Deni Elliott, ed., *Responsible Journalism.* Beverly Hills, CA: Sage, pp. 81–98

Gores, Paul. (2007). "Concerns aired on Wisconsin cable bill." *Milwaukee Journal Sentinel,* March 27. Retrieved from www.freepress.net/news/22053.

Guensberg, Carol. (2008). "Nonprofit news." *American Journalism Review,* February–March, pp. 26–31, 33.

Guzzo, Glenn. (2006). "The Knight Ridder sale and the outlook for newspapers." Project for Excellence in Journalism, April 4. Retrieved from www.journalism.org/node/137.

Hartmann, Anath. (2008). "A thinking person's Web site." *American Journalism Review,* February–March, pp. 14–15.

Houston, Brant. (2010). "New networks, new challenges." In Stephen J. A. Ward, ed., *Ethics for the New Investigative Newsroom: A Roundtable Report on Best Practices for Non-Profit Journalism.* Madison, WI: Center for Journalism Ethics, School of Journalism and Mass Communication, University of Wisconsin-Madison, pp. 17–20.

Information Infrastructure Task Force. (1993). *The National Information Infrastructure: Agenda for Action.* Washington, DC: U.S. Department of Commerce.

Ives, Nat. (2009). "It's not newspapers in peril, it's their owners." *Advertising Age,* February 23, pp. 3 and 19.

Jurkowitz, Mark. (1998). "Move by L. A. Times sparks industry debate." *The Boston Globe,* May 23, p. F1.

Kidder, Rushworth W. (2009). "Read all about it—In nonprofit newspapers?" *Media Ethics* 21(1), pp. 1, 14.

Kittross, John Michael. (1979). *Television Frequency Allocation Policy in the United States.* New York: Arno Press. (Reprint of University of Illinois dissertation, 1960. Contains new "Afterthoughts and Second Guesses" section.)

——. (1989). Commentary on "Deregulation." In Frederick Williams, ed., *The New Communications,* 2nd ed. Belmont, CA: Wadsworth, pp. 206–207.

Kiyak, Mark G. (2008). "No American citizen left behind." Research paper presented at the Academic Research for Media Reform conference, Minneapolis, MN, June 5.

Laitman, Cynthia J., and Katy Phillips. (2007). "Cable bill a sellout to telecom giants." Op-ed article in the Eau Claire, WI *Leader-Telegram,* November 8, p. 4A.

Lambeth, Edmund B. (1992). *Committed Journalism: An Ethic for the Profession,* 2nd ed. Bloomington and Indianapolis, IN: Indiana University Press.

Lashner, Marilyn A. (1984). *The Chilling Effect in TV News: Intimidation by the Nixon White House.* New York: Praeger.

Lee, Jennifer. (2003). "In Minot N. D. Radio, a single corporate voice." *The New York Times,* March 29.

Lerner, Edward M. (2009). "Rock! Bye-Bye Baby." *Analog* 129(11), pp. 43–52.

Lewis, Charles. (2007). "The nonprofit road." *Columbia Journalism Review,* September–October, pp. 32–36.

Lewis, Johnny. (2001). "Jay Harris emphasizes newspapers' need to balance public trust with bottom line." *asne reporter 2001,* April 6. American Society of Newspaper Editors. Retrieved from www.asne.org/2001reporter/friday/harrisspeech6.html.

Liebling, A. J. (1961). *The Press.* New York: Ballantine. (Chapter originally published as "Do you belong in journalism?" *The New Yorker* 1960, May 14.)

Loevinger, Lee. (1964). "The role of law in broadcasting." *Journal of Broadcasting* 8(2), pp. 113–126.

MacBride, Sean. (1980). *Many Voices, One World.* London: Kogan Page; New York: Unipub; Paris: UNESCO.

Martin, Hugh J., and Lawrence Souder. (2009). "Interdependence in media economics: Ethical implications of the economic characteristics of news." *Journal of Mass Media Ethics,* 24(2–3), pp. 127–145.

Marty, Robin. (2006). "About." *Minnesota Monitor*, August 21. Retrieved from www.minnesotamonitor.com/showDiary.do?diaryId=23 (May 24, 2008).

McChesney, Robert W. (2007a). *Communication Revolution: Critical Junctures and the Future of Media*. New York: New Press.

———. (2007b). "Ethical implications of the National Conference for Media Reform." *Media Ethics* 18(2), pp. 34–35.

McChesney, Robert W., and John Nichols. (2010). *The Death and Life of American Journalism: The Media Revolution that Will Begin the World Again*. New York: Nation Books.

McDonald, John. (1950). *Strategy in Poker, Business and War*. New York: Norton.

Mencken, H. L. (1955). *The Vintage Mencken*. New York: Vintage.

Morgenstern, Oskar, and John Von Neumann. (1953). *Theory of Games and Economic Behavior*. Princeton, NJ: Princeton University Press.

Mutter, Alan. (2007). "PCM dumps publishers." *Reflections of a Newsosaur* blog, July 18. Retrieved from newsosaur.blogspot.com/2007/07/pcm-dumps-publishers.html.

Navasky, Victor S. (2005). *A Matter of Opinion*. New York: Farrar, Straus & Giroux.

"Newspaper chains face tough financial challenges." (2006). PBS *NewsHour* Media Unit Report, March 9. Retrieved from www.pbs.org/newshour/bb/media/jan-june06/paper_3-9.html.

Nordenson, Bree. (2007). "The Uncle Sam solution." *Columbia Journalism Review*, September–October, pp. 37–41.

"Northern California chapter concerned over cutbacks." (2008). *Quill*, May, p. 6.

Overholser, Geneva. (2006). "On behalf of journalism: A manifesto for change." Philadelphia, PA: Annenberg Public Policy Center of the University of Pennsylvania.

Perry, Suzanne. (2008). "Nonprofit newshounds." *Quill*, January–February, pp. 10–13. Reprinted with permission from *The Chronicle of Philanthropy*.

Peterson, Ivor. (1998). "Media." *The New York Times*, March 9, p. D7.

Pickard, Victor, Josh Stearns, and Craig Aarons. (2009). *Saving the News: Toward a National Journalism Strategy*. New York: Free Press. Available for download from www.freepress.net/files/saving_the_news.pdf.

Pickard, Victor, and Joseph Torres (2009). "Saving America's democracy—sustaining journalism." *The Seattle Times*, July 5, p. B9.

Plaisance, Patrick. (2009). "Guest editor's introduction." *Journal of Mass Media Ethics* 24(2–3), pp. 88–89.

"The Pocantico Declaration: Creating a nonprofit investigative news network." (2009). Retrieved from http://watchdogsatpocantico.com (October 7, 2009).

Postman, Neil, and Steve Powers. (1992). *How to Watch TV News*. New York: Penguin.

Schwartz, Moshe. (2009). *Department of Defense Contractors in Iraq and Afghanistan: Background and Analysis*. Washington, DC: Congressional Research Service. Retrieved from www.fas.org/sgp/crs/natsec/R40764.pdf (September 26, 2009).

Seelye, Katharine Q. (2006). "What-ifs of a media eclipse." *The New York Times*, August 27. Retrieved from www.nytimes.com/2006/08/27/business/yourmoney/27knight.html?pagewanted=1&_r=1.

"Senate OKs cable deregulation plan." (2007). Associated Press/Leader-Telegram Staff story in the Eau Claire, WI *Leader-Telegram*, November 9, p. 2B.

Shanahan, Edward K. (1994). " 'Read all about it!' But read about it where?: No news is not good news." *The Boston Globe Magazine*, November 6, pp. 20–34.

Shubik, Martin. (1954). *Readings in Game Theory and Political Behavior*. Garden City, NY: Doubleday.

Sinclair, Upton (2003). *The Brass Check: A Study of American Journalism*. Urbana, IL: University of Illinois Press. (Reprint of 9th ed., published in Long Beach, CA, by the author, 1928.)

Smith, Anthony. (1980). *The Geopolitics of Information*. New York: Oxford University Press.

Smith, Lee. (2008). "Point of view: The wealthiest colleges should acquire 'The New York Times.' " *The Chronicle of Higher Education*, May 9, p. A32.

Smith, Robert P. (1984). "Advertising acceptability policies protect newspaper's credibility." *INAME News*, June, p. 11; quoted in Fink, 1988, p. 127.

Smolkin, Rachel. (2006–07). "Tribune tribulations." *American Journalism Review*, December–January, pp. 22–31.

Squires, James D. (1993). *Read All About It!: The Corporate Takeover of America's Newspapers*. New York: Times Books.

Suburban Newspapers of America Foundation. (October, 2008). *Developing the Local Media House: Lessons Learned from Norway and Sweden*. Traverse City, MI: Suburban Newspapers of America.

"Telecom-cable battle hits states." (2007). McClatchy-Tribune story in the Eau Claire, WI *Leader-Telegram*, May 17, p. 5B.

Television Digest. (1998). *Television Digest* 38(18), pp. 2–3.

Turow, Joseph. (1992). *Media Systems in Society*. New York: Longman.

——. (2009). *Media Today: An Introduction to Mass Communication*. New York: Routledge.

U.S. Census Bureau. (2009). *Statistical Abstract of the United States: 2009*, 128th ed. Washington, DC: U.S. Census Bureau (CD edition).

U.S. Federal Communications Commission. (2009). *13th Annual Report in the Matter of Annual Assessment of the Status of Competition in the Market for the Delivery of Video Programming*. (Required to be provided to Congress by Sec. 19 of the 1992 Cable Act). FCC 07–206, adopted November 27, 2007, released January 16, 2009.

USA Today (2008). "NBC, Fox stations to share resources." November 14. Retrieved from NAB365 news service.

Vaillancourt, Meg. (1991). "Labor chief blasts quick stock gains." *The Boston Globe*, June 15, p. 91.

Vanacker, Bastiaan, and Genelle Belmas. (2009). "Trust and the economics of news." *Journal of Mass Media Ethics* 24(2–3), 110–126.

Vise, David A. (2005). "Shareholder pressure leads Knight Ridder to announce sale." *The Washington Post*, November 15, p. D03. Also available at www.washingtonpost.com/wp-dyn/content/article/2005/11/14/AR2005111401363.html.

Walters, Steven, and Stacy Forster. (2007). "Doyle toughens, then signs cable bill." *Milwaukee Journal Sentinel*, December 22. Retrieved from www.jsonline.com/story/index.aspx?id=699450.

Ward, Stephen J. A., editor-in-chief. (2010). *Ethics for the New Investigative Newsroom: A Roundtable Report on Best Practices for Non-Profit Journalism*. Madison, WI: Center for Journalism Ethics, School of Journalism and Mass Communication, University of Wisconsin-Madison. Retrieved from www.journalismethics.info/2010_roundtable_report.pdf.

Wasserman, Edward. (2008). "Can journalism live without ads?" *The Miami Herald*, February 18, p. 21A. Retrieved from www.miamiherald.com/430/story/422975.html.

Weaver, Andrew J., and Barbara J. Wilson. (2009). "The role of graphic and sanitized violence in the enjoyment of television dramas." *Human Communication Research* 35(3), pp. 442–463.

Weinberg, Arthur, and Lila Weinberg (1961). *The Muckrakers*. New York: Putnam.

Westphal, David. (2009). *Philanthropic Foundations: Growing Funders of the News*. Los Angeles, CA: Annenberg School for Communication, University of Southern California.

Williams, J. D. (1954). *The Compleat Strategyst*. New York: McGraw-Hill.

Chapter 9

Access to Media

Equity in Receiving and Disseminating Information

CONCEPTS such as "communication inequality" and "information apartheid" are difficult to pin down. In this chapter, William A. Babcock and A. David Gordon wrestle with these important concepts, and look for the controversies enmeshed with them.

In our increasingly information-based society, some equality of access is crucial unless we are willing to settle for a society where some people or groups are disadvantaged. The risk is that society could become stratified on the basis of information available for people to use, as well as along economic, educational, racial, or other lines.

A number of observers of the media–society relationship raised this issue in the early 1990s. Their concerns ranged from general warnings about a possible "informational underclass" (McQuail, 1993) or "information apartheid" (Representative Edward Markey, in a 1992 commencement address) to newspaper subscription drives that deliberately ignored low-income rural and city neighborhoods where the delivery risks and costs outweigh the possible subscriber and advertiser cash flow (Ghiglione, 1992). We have come a long way from the days when television was considered an unessential luxury for those on welfare. Today, many consider it a necessity for everyone in society to have access to information through one or more of the mass media.

There are two basic kinds of access discussed here:

- Access of audiences to the content disseminated by the media.
- Access of groups to media in order to spread their messages.

But are these really media ethics issues? After all, why should the purveyors of media products have any greater responsibility than the producers of other goods and services to ensure access to those products? The answer is that the media industries have First Amendment protection precisely *because* they fulfill a societal role that is different from that of other businesses. The inherent questions of ethics and responsibility are similar regardless of whether new or traditional channels are used for access to mass-mediated content, so our discussion here will focus on both older and emerging forms of mass communication.

THE MACBRIDE COMMISSION REPORT

One of the few major attempts to deal broadly with the need for equity in the use of modern communication technologies was the MacBride Commission Report, produced for the United Nations Educational, Scientific, and Cultural Organization (UNESCO) in 1980. Its conclusions and recommendations called for many changes that followed from its

> firm conviction that communication is a basic individual right, as well as a collective one required by all communities and nations. Freedom of information—and, more specifically the right to seek, receive and impart information—is a fundamental human right; indeed a prerequisite for many others.
>
> (MacBride, 1980, p. 253)

Among the recommendations made by the MacBride Commission Report were those that later became known collectively as the New World Information and Communication Order (NWICO), intended primarily to solve a number of concerns of developing nations. These included support for communications training, access to the worldwide telecommunications network (including satellites, most of which orbit over equatorial countries), control over information that leaves a nation (including a proposal for licensing reporters and other governmental oversight of media, and a willingness to punish one's own reporters who offend another country), and control over what information comes into a country's territory. These recommendations weren't universally applauded; indeed, the United States found many of them unacceptable, and eventually withdrew from UNESCO. But most of the principles (if not all of the recommended practices) largely remain valid today, except possibly those that might be classified as "censorship" by Americans used to the First Amendment—even though the United States has been quietly adhering to a number of these "control of information" recommendations for its own purposes for years (starting well before 9/11/01). For instance, export and finance regulations are used to dry up most reporting from Cuba, foreign individuals whose views offend an administration may find themselves banned by the immigration service and at least one anti-Vietnam War film was prevented by U.S. customs officials from entering the United States from Canada during that conflict.

New technologies developed since 1980 have changed the details of some areas of disagreement between nations over NWICO, but not the basic human right quoted earlier. But the factors that limit access to information are no longer technological. They are primarily economic. The media need money to produce and distribute content, and much of that money comes from those who want access to the content—they buy television sets (which distribute content, even as they are part of the manufacturing industry), subscribe to an ISP or to a publication, pay for admissions, and indirectly pay for content through purchase of media advertisers' goods and services.

Everette Dennis put the issue succinctly in 1991 when he noted the "reasons to be concerned about information-rich people versus information-poor people. Information is power and some information will no doubt be priced so high that it will be out of the reach of many people" (Dennis and Merrill, 1991, p. 75). To approach this from another perspective, the United States has always stood for access—to education, politics, and libraries as was noted at roughly the same time by Eric Elbot, then the director of communications for the National Center for Accessible Media. With the advent of the information age, he suggested, this concern must also include access to information and entertainment available through new as well as older media channels.

Babcock and Gordon agree on a number of points, such as the opinion that the essential inequity of some people's access to communications is unethical. They disagree on others, even on the definition of access. Gordon concentrates on access of the public to the media, while Babcock is broader in his approach. Neither devotes much attention here to other forms of access—what the news media need to acquire from others (such as government and business) to produce content, or information that may interest their audiences about people's lives (see Chapter 10).

The key issue seems to be not what must be accomplished but whose responsibility it is and how far this responsibility extends. Gordon maintains that the mass media must make some special efforts to ensure that they continue to reach a truly mass audience and, in the process, bring the information age to all strata of the society. Babcock rejects this solution on the grounds that market forces and competition sufficiently provide whatever access is needed. He shows some concern over the desire of groups—social, political, religious, other—to have their messages spread through the media; Gordon ignores this aspect of "access."

This is a rapidly changing area and the discussion that follows affords the reader an opportunity to identify the relevant ethical issues. Those issues center around conditions of inequality—whether deliberate or accidental—in accessing and disseminating information in mass media channels—what the McBride Report referred to as the fundamental "right to seek, receive and impart information."

GORDON: Mass media must guard against practices that isolate some groups in society from access to information they need.

Helping to insure "information equity" throughout the society is not just an ethical obligation for the mass media, nor is it strictly a public policy concern. There are also some very practical reasons—and benefits—for the media to follow this course.

As society becomes more aware of the importance of access to diverse sources of information, pressure could well build for government action to ensure this if the media themselves don't take steps to make sure it happens. Such a move would put the governmental nose inside the communications tent. This has already begun to happen in regard to "net neutrality," a topic discussed elsewhere. Those practical reasons are also grounded in economics: if groups in society are deprived of access to information, the media lose potential customers and, therefore, potential targets for advertisers.

However, the most important reason for media concern about information equity is the utilitarian viewpoint that it is *right* for both the society *and* the media. The ethical consequences of what some have rather dramatically called "information apartheid" are simply too serious to be tolerated either by the media or by the publics they serve.

For me, the key issue is how to provide equitable opportunities for access to information that has passed the scrutiny of various professional media gatekeepers and has been made available to the public. (News media access to the information needed to report fully on society is a related but separate concern.) It is not enough to say, as William Babcock does, that the proliferation of bloggers provides ample opportunity both to speak and for access to such communication. That's fine as far as it goes, but we also need to insure access to news and information gathered and processed by people and media institutions grounded in journalism, with a commitment to accuracy and—I hope—ethics.

We're now in an age of increasing dependence on information as the currency of everyday living, and this has created crucial ethical concerns. Babcock notes that alternative media can be one very good source of information for certain segments of the population, and can be even more useful if the mainstream media pick up material from them. I agree on those points. As mainstream media outlets shrank in number or cut back on staff and content, starting even before the 2008 economic downturn, the alternative media became even more important in giving the public more options for access to useful—in some cases, essential—information increasingly ignored by "mainstream" media (e.g., a neighborhood association meeting in a large metropolitan area).

Certainly, that's key to the role that Bruce Brugmann has seen for the alternative media since founding *The San Francisco Bay Guardian* with his wife, back in 1966. They viewed the *Guardian* "not as a substitute for the daily press, but as a supplement that can do much that the San Francisco and suburban dailies . . . cannot and will not do" and, in the process, "offer an alternative voice for an urban community" (Brugmann, 2006). As his weekly paper reached its 40th anniversary in 2006, Brugmann noted that there were some 126 alternative papers in 42 states nationwide with a total circulation of some 7.5 million, "competing effectively with their local chains" (Brugmann, 2006). But that's all taking place within the newspaper genre, and doesn't begin to address the desire for widespread access to broadcast, cable and online sources of content.

The long-standing concern for diverse voices was summarized nicely in 1997 by Eli Noam and Robert Freeman, who recalled the days when three networks—"all within ten blocks of each other in Manhattan"—controlled the television scene and

> the fear of control over hearts, minds, pocketbooks, and voting booths was amplified from the left and right. And today, with electronic media becoming smart, powerful, and persuasive, and with media mergers reported every week, the same fear is around more than ever, that in the end there will be only four media companies left in the world, and running the world, half of them owned by a guy named Rupert [Murdoch].
>
> (Noam and Freeman, 1997, p. 18)

It remains to be seen whether new information sources—available via the Internet, mobile phones and their newer cousins and, potentially, the additional channels that digital TV can offer—will in fact develop in ways that make them accessible to all strata of society,

It is not enough to say . . . that the proliferation of bloggers provides ample opportunity both to speak and for access to [professional media] communication.

especially those low on the income scale. I don't think it will happen without a commitment to that goal—ideally, by the media themselves but, if not, then perhaps by government. U.S. mass media of all stripes have First Amendment protection precisely so they can help create an informed citizenry that is capable of governing itself. But we can't expect a fully participatory democracy unless we aim for the ideal of providing all citizens the opportunity to acquire meaningful information on a relatively equal footing. As information becomes more and more important in society, it becomes ever more crucial to ensure access to whatever sources people want (or need) to use.

It is also worth noting that even if the almost impossible goal of an "abundance of channels" is equally available to everyone, many of these channels will be providing duplicate or overlapping content. Look no further than the cable services carrying the same films, competing newspapers getting most of their non-local news from AP, or the newscasts that carry much the same information on each station. Thus, Babcock or others should not argue that merely increasing the number of stations—or bloggers—will provide real diversity in the marketplace of ideas. It is worth mentioning, as well, that Babcock relies heavily for support on Adam Thierer of the Progress & Freedom Foundation, a Washington, DC organization whose Web site describes it as a "market-oriented think tank . . . based on a philosophy of limited government, free markets, and individual sovereignty" (Progress & Freedom Foundation, 2009). Thierer's book makes it very clear that he is marshalling his arguments against "regulatory mandates that essentially seek to control the size of the soapbox an individual or corporation uses to speak to the American people" (Thierer, 2005, p. 17). In other words, he is in opposition to almost any kind of government regulation of the media. Those certainly are valid positions to espouse, but he definitely has an ideological axe to grind.

Perhaps oversimplifying, an essential question emerges: will our mass media remain *mass*? Or will we see a combination of economics, new media technologies, and even new niche marketing techniques reduce greatly—or even eliminate—the media's ability to serve society as a whole? Might those same factors curtail seriously the ability of many different people and groups—especially people at the lower end of the socioeconomic spectrum but also non-economic groups (e.g., the more than 30 million Americans with vision or hearing impairments)—to use media of their choice in obtaining ideas and other information and content? At stake is the ability of citizens to participate fully in the American democracy and to obtain information or entertainment that will increase both their satisfaction with such participation and their general quality of life.

What's really at issue here is the 21st-century version of the frequently ignored second sentence in Thomas Jefferson's well-known comment about newspapers and government, the part that is almost never included when newspaper folk quote him on the importance of their calling:

> The basis of our government being the opinion of the people, the very first object should be to keep that right; and were it left to me to decide whether we should have a government without newspapers or newspapers without a government, I should not hesitate a moment to prefer the latter. *But I should mean that every man should receive those papers & be capable of reading them.*
>
> (Jefferson, [1787] 1984, p. 880; italics added)

Jefferson's second sentence is the crux of a key issue the mass media face today in a democratic society: the need to ensure that everyone who is capable (or potentially capable) of understanding the information has an opportunity to connect to media distribution systems and receive that information. And, unfortunately, Babcock's easy dismissal of the so-called "digital divide" as an outdated 20th-century artifact is little more than wishful thinking.

Although it may seem as if Internet access has become ubiquitous, that's certainly not quite the case for home access and even less so for broadband (high-speed) access from home. According to an April, 2009 survey, 63% of American adults had home broadband access, up from 54% at the end of 2007. But that meant that more than one-third of the U.S. population still lacked such access. And about one-fifth of American adults had no home Internet service at all, for reasons ranging from cost to availability to lack of interest. Internet service, though, was considerably less affected by the recent economic recession than were such media as premium-tier cable TV and cell phones, where more than twice as many users said they had cut back or cancelled their service because of the economic conditions. Some groups within the overall population had much lower percentages of home broadband access—for rural households and African Americans, the figure was 46% and in households with annual incomes below $20,000, it was 35% (Pew Internet & American Life Project, 2009).

The survey also found that the average monthly cost of broadband service increased from $34.50 to $39 from 2008 to 2009, and was significantly higher ($44.70) in areas where there was no competition among service providers. People without broadband service (or Internet service at all), cited the cost as a prominent reason for not having it (Pew Internet & American Life Project, 2009). All of this indicates that while it's shrinking, there's still a "digital divide"—as a reality, not an artifact. As noted earlier, it is thus an ethical necessity to expand the marketplace of ideas into a digital marketplace of both ideas and information, with assurances that everyone—those over 65, people with a physical disability and those low on the economic scale—will have the opportunity to participate in that marketplace and to share in the benefits of access to information services of all kinds.

THE PROBLEM OF LESS AFFLUENT AUDIENCES

Magazines, newspapers, radio, and television (cable, satellite and over-the-air broadcasters) have all aimed at least some of their content at specialized audiences, often at more affluent segments of the mass audience because that's what appeals to advertisers. This is just good business sense. With the dependence of most of the U.S. media system on advertising revenues, the media have little choice but to sell the audiences that advertisers want to buy.

But this approach can also leave less affluent members of society cut off from considerable amounts of entertainment, news, and advertising that would interest or be useful to them. This can lead to "media redlining," a term derived from the practice by some lending institutions (before subprime lending became so widespread) of drawing a red line around low income areas on a map—most often occupied predominantly by minority group members—and refusing to make mortgage loans there.

Similar practices have shown up across the media landscape. In 1991, *The Courier-Journal* in Louisville, Kentucky, allowed home sellers to purchase their real estate ads *only* in editions going to more affluent circulation zones, without the cost of serving the poorer and predominantly minority circulation areas (Barr, 1991). This kept residents of these areas from knowing about homes for sale in other parts of the newspaper's circulation area where they might aspire to live, unless they made special efforts to obtain a copy of the paper zoned for areas with higher average income than their own. This situation was eventually resolved by the paper's offer to dump press overruns of two-zoned inserts at convenience stores in the less affluent neighborhoods. The paper dealt with the ethical issue—by providing the inserts—in part because of its commitment to its community, although legally it was not required to do so.

Related problems involving the mass media include the pricing of various tiers of cable TV service beyond the means of some economic groups, the dropping of magazine subscriptions and promotions in lightly populated rural areas, or the removal of newspaper sales racks from areas where they are repeatedly vandalized—or have few customers. Newspapers sell fewer copies in high-crime areas, and that's in part out of concern for the safety of newspaper carriers, but it's also because readers in those less affluent areas are far less important to most advertisers than are more upscale readers.

Local cable TV system operators were long criticized for rushing to wire more affluent neighborhoods while dragging their feet in providing service to lower-income areas, where they were less likely to sell their add-on packages. Similar issues have arisen in regard to the Internet, where concerns about "digital redlining" have been raised in regard to efforts by telecommunications companies to make high-speed Internet and cable TV services available only to affluent customers. Those efforts most often have taken the form of heavy lobbying for national or statewide cable franchising procedures, removing control of those franchises from local municipalities and usually eliminating any requirements to serve an entire area regardless of income levels (Dixon, 2007). State-level franchising also tends to reduce or eliminate requirements for cable companies to support public access channels on their systems. (For an account of how this scenario played out in Wisconsin, see Chapter 8.) By 2008, about half the states had some form of state-level franchising, which lessened the push by the telecommunications giants for a federal franchising statute.

Some magazines have adopted the strategy of selectivity in soliciting subscriptions, preferring to exclude lower-income ZIP codes from their mailings in order to concentrate on areas where family income levels appeal more to their advertisers. *Life* magazine, in its last throes as a weekly, publicly decided not to accept subscriptions from counties with low average income. These market-driven forces are all perfectly logical from an economic perspective, but they pose serious ethical questions about the willingness of media to cut off certain segments of society from access to various *supposedly mass* media channels. (Many people, of course, are unwilling to pay attention to the media, or restrict their attention to tabloids, comics, extremist politics or sports, but that's a different concern.)

Among the new information technology issues is one posed by the increasing use of the Internet—and of computer-generated telephone dialing—by political candidates or parties to reach potential voters, without the need to go through traditional (and expensive) media gatekeepers or to use paid advertising. Citizens without access are foreclosed from unsolicited advertising on the Internet, of course, and while some people may be happy to be ignored, ethical concerns about information equity (particularly in the political process) should not be overlooked. As the chief architect of one of the earliest uses of this technique reminded us, this "is an issue of information rights. . . . The rich and powerful are going to have this stuff. The question is whether the average person is going to get it, and, if so, how?" (Radin, 1992, p. 26).

INTERNET ACCESS ISSUES

As noted above, Internet access (especially the use of broadband technology) for everyone is still not universal and these concerns about inequality remain alive. As of mid-2010, the FCC seemed to be moving toward making broadband service more available to the whole population but that still left unanswered the question of how to provide broad access to those at the lower ends of the socioeconomic scale or those with disabilities? More important, whose responsibility is it to see that "information apartheid" doesn't subvert the democratic goal of an informed citizenry? The key practical issue, as usual, is "who should pay" for the added costs of producing greater social benefits (i.e., spreading those benefits to the greatest number of people) by preventing or at least reducing inequities of informational access.

> whose responsibility is it to see that "information apartheid" doesn't subvert the democratic goal of an informed citizenry?

I believe that only five possible institutions can take separate or combined responsibility for continually ensuring information equity in the information society—media consumers, the nonprofit sector, the government, advertisers, and the media themselves. Because income (economic capability) varies widely among media consumers, it is highly unlikely that the economic marketplace can cure inequities stemming originally from this economic disparity, regardless of whether technology manufacturers make content available as a spur to sales.

Relying more heavily on government financing to expand the mass media system's infrastructure—and thereby increase access to it—carries with it risks of increased government control, not to mention even more unbalanced budgets. Although governments have often provided seed money and sometimes protection from competition for new technologies, government operational support of media has been rare under the U.S. constitutional and economic systems, with the exception of some support to public broadcasting, postal and legal advertising subsidies, and the government's own publications, films and electronic output.

An approach that once seemed to promise widespread free access to citywide wireless networks had come almost to a standstill before 2009. This attempt originally involved a number of cities—including Philadelphia, Minneapolis, Milwaukee, Portland, Oregon, and San Francisco—setting up free city-wide Wi-Fi systems that would broaden greatly the opportunities for residents to access the Internet. The main problem, as usual: who would foot the bill?

Portland's system, which covered some 30% of the city and was considered successful to that point, foundered because the private service provider couldn't attract enough advertising to keep the operation going in the absence of city funding. Milwaukee, which also had a successful pilot project, announced in mid-2008 that the demonstration area would not be expanded, since no one (including both the city and the private service provider) was willing to come up with the $20 million it would take to go citywide. Service providers had also pulled out of Philadelphia, San Francisco, and New Orleans because, they claimed, they couldn't make a profit (Barrett, 2008). And in Oakland County, Michigan, a partnership between this suburban Detroit county and a private service provider was shut down—after an expenditure of $5 to $6 million—because there was no advertising support and investors were unwilling to put up some $70 million needed to complete the project (Witsil, 2008). There have been several new efforts to establish more limited Wi-Fi networks with *paid* access (see LaVallee, 2008; Newman, 2010) but free Wi-Fi efforts are largely dormant.

It seems to me that—on ethical if not financial grounds—providing Internet availability to all citizens is as important a governmental goal as some of the bailouts of financial institutions and others that we saw in 2008–09. As an analogy, considering that providing public education has been a policy of U.S. governments since early in the 19th century, isn't providing the Internet—and instruction in its use—merely an extension of roughly two centuries of governmental aid to citizen communication since the Republic was founded?

"'Minneapolis is about the only big city where Wi-Fi is apparently working,' said Glenn Fleishman, editor of Wi-Fi Networking News" (Barrett, 2008, p. 7A). And that came at a cost of more than $1 million to the city, plus some 10,000 subscribers who were paying nearly $250 a year for wireless access throughout most (but not all) of the city. The Minneapolis system turned out to be highly valuable to rescue workers responding to the I-35W bridge collapse in the summer of 2007 (Barrett, 2008), but that benefit goes beyond an ethics-based discussion of Internet access.

Key questions regarding the ethics of access are whether traditionally underserved parts of the population will benefit fully, and how these new systems can be paid for. Advertising is one option for providing support without draining municipal budgets, but so far it has failed to yield enough revenue to support new systems that could increase free access. And skeptics wonder if such systems could really remain free, or whether public or private operators would succumb to the temptation of trying to turn them into revenue streams (Griffith), or emulate the example of cable TV in charging all customers for access—and thereby once again make second-class "information citizens" of the people at the low end of the economic scale.

If advertisers and cities are unwilling or unable to insure widespread public access to wireless—or wired—networks, state governments could, if they chose to do so, follow the lead of states such as Vermont and Rhode Island in trying to extend high-speed telephone and computer access throughout the state. At least a half dozen other states have begun to expand broadband access, but with less ambitious coverage goals (Sneyd, 2007). These efforts may help expand Internet access but they are no panacea: they will require some government funding and even that—whether it comes from federal economic stimulus package funds or elsewhere—may not be enough to overcome all of the obstacles posed by problems such as Vermont's rugged terrain. Even if those goals are reached, consumers will still have to pay for access from their homes (or find some free access point, such as the local public library) and that leaves us once again pondering how best to insure that economics don't prohibit access to basic information on the Internet (or elsewhere, for that matter).

Government can also help assure public access to information through regulation as well as through economic support. The regulation possibility arose regarding the concept of "Net neutrality," which is basically shorthand for the idea that Internet service providers (ISPs)—particularly the large broadband carriers—should not set up categories of service, or of access, that selectively deny access to the Internet to ideas or individuals. In particular, advocates of Internet neutrality argue that access should not depend either on content or on the ability to pay ISPs for "preferred" (so-called "fast lane") status. Nor should ISPs block users' access to some Web sites or discriminate against content providers who compete with the ISP's own content (Noam, 2006).

Verizon, AT&T and Comcast all ran foul of these principles in one way or another in 2006 and 2007, attempting to favor certain types of content in regard to access or speed of transmission, or to prohibit certain types of messages or the use of their systems by competitors or spectrum-gobbling video or film downloads that might slow service to other Internet users. The Verizon action—reversed only after considerable negative publicity—was strikingly ideological: the company originally "refused to allow NARAL Pro-Choice America to send text messages over its network" (*The New York Times*, 2008).

Such actions violate the principle that Internet channels should not play favorites, but rather should serve everyone in a non-discriminatory manner by treating all content, platforms and sites equally and transmitting material on a first-come, first-served basis.

This quasi-"common carrier" concept, supported by organizations such as the Electronic Frontier Foundation, harks back to the early regulation of railroads as well as such early electrical communication channels as the telegraph or the telephone, when those channels simply transmitted the words entered into them, at a published rate and without discrimination. In 2005, the FCC adopted a similar policy pertaining to the Internet, requiring that broadband networks be accessible to all customers as well as being open and affordable. Three years later, the Commission applied that policy to Comcast (23 FCC Rcd 13028, 2008) and ordered the ISP to stop its selective blocking of some types of peer-to-peer transfers of large data files (e.g., TV shows and movies). Comcast agreed to modify its network management practices but asked a federal appeals court to decide whether the FCC actually had the power to issue that order. In April, 2010, the court ruled (Pelofsky, 2010; see also *Comcast* v. *FCC*) that the agency lacked such authority, leaving the FCC the option of reclassifying broadband networks as telecommunication services, which would unequivocally give it the authority to implement policies promoting universal access. In a related action, the FCC in December, 2010, issued Internet neutrality rules that charted a middle course, and which drew immediate fire from Free Press, Senator Al Franken of Minnesota, and others who were upset that the rules failed to protect net neutrality for *mobile* broadband services. These interrelated issues will continue to play out well after this book's publication.

Returning to the question of who might pay for the costs of insuring access, advertisers might well support media channels that help them reach targeted consumers, but they are not likely to contribute voluntarily to any approach that locks them into a system where their messages go to people they don't really care about reaching. In the absence of some sort of "carrot" for the advertisers, extracting such financial support may be both politically and constitutionally difficult.

The remaining option for achieving information equity is to make the media themselves responsible for it, perhaps as part of what Theodore Glasser (1986) has called the affirmative responsibilities imposed (as a matter of ethics if not law) by the First Amendment. Here, too, constitutional issues must be dealt with, unless the mass media—or those operating a given medium—agree that they have a responsibility to their community—or to society—to provide information access more equally across the board. This isn't as simple as it might appear.

MASS MEDIA RESPONSIBILITIES

Given both the ethical requirement for equity of access and a dearth of acceptable alternatives, I believe that the primary responsibility for meeting this need must fall squarely on the media themselves, to whatever degree is necessary. Such an ethical obligation clearly stems from both the utilitarian concern for providing the greatest benefit for the greatest number of people and John Rawls's emphasis on protecting the most vulnerable members of the community. It can also be argued cogently that if social responsibility means anything at all, it means finding a way to avoid creating a clearly defined group of second-class citizens in what is increasingly an information society.

Working out access in practice remains a difficult question, but many possibilities exist. Newspapers might, for example, *give* merchants advertising that runs in all editions, charge them only for zoned ads (if that's what they want), and write off the lost revenue and expense to the paper's social responsibility to make information available to all readers regardless of their ability to pay. Alternatively, the Louisville approach regarding real estate ad sections might be expanded to include some or all advertising inserts. As long as advertisers weren't charged for these (to them) marginal buying prospects, they could only benefit from this.

Cable TV and satellite distribution operators might agree (or be persuaded by government) to provide a free public affairs service (whose content extends beyond C-SPAN's) to anyone who subscribes to at least the least expensive tier of program service. But truly low-cost universal access to a multitude of basic information sources isn't likely to happen unless the franchising authority—whether that eventually winds up at the local, state or national level—provides some sort of trade-off benefits for the franchise holders. And even these plans would not reach citizens without TV sets, or those who stick with over-the-air reception rather than cable or satellite.

New information technologies and media may provide better opportunities than do traditional mass media operations for new practices and—more important—public policies that foster rather than discourage information equity. Overcoming economic barriers to user access could give the public increased control over dissemination procedures (for information, persuasion or entertainment) while reducing the power of media gatekeepers to direct messages according to their vision of who *should* receive them.

Such shared control—between audience and message originators—would combat the increasing selectivity by information sources in targeting their desired audience and thus democratize the mass media. For example, audience members—regardless of economic status—would have the *opportunity* for access to content that *they* were interested in regardless of whether the "conventional wisdom" would have included them in that audience.

One pioneering attempt to provide such equality of informational opportunity was suggested two decades ago by an Alabama state task force report that zeroed in on specific Internet access problems and suggested a rationale of equity as the basis for dealing with them:

> [A] philosophy of social equity and social responsibility should guide planning for the network. Special efforts should be made to guarantee extended universal information service . . . to the poor, the disabled, and minorities.
>
> (Alabama Information Age Task Force, 1991, pp. 5–6)

The report also made some specific recommendations for implementing that philosophy, which in essence embrace the utilitarian approach. These include the possibility of rate structures that take ability to pay into account, free public access points in libraries and shopping malls, and subsidized network access for people with a disability, to be funded by the state and federal governments, private industry, and the disabled community. Although this approach has not been broadly implemented, access through public libraries has grown steadily. In addition, the educational system—from elementary school on up—is insuring that computer literacy is increasingly widespread. If some of the major players in the information industries come to realize that they must play a role in this process (and perhaps that taking on such a role would increase their profits in the long run), the door will remain open to further exploration of these concerns.

Google's efforts to digitize the holdings of more than a dozen major research libraries, and make them freely available online, are one step in the direction of Internet information equity. The Google project began slowly, in part because of copyright objections by some publishers, but once other Internet players (including, until 2008, Microsoft) joined forces to explore a similar approach, the possibility of more openly available online material began to take shape. It was helped considerably by a 2008 settlement between Google and the publishing industry and by late 2010, Google had scanned more than 15 million books from more than 100 countries in over 400 languages (Crawford, 2010).

This approach could also be adapted to more traditional mass media, in such ways as newspapers making their electronic news libraries accessible to the general public at little or no cost. Making that access free would reduce a potential source of added income for the papers, but would add little or nothing to existing costs of operation. In light of newspapers' continuing explorations of new ways to relate to and serve their communities—efforts that are tied fundamentally to the need to stem, if not reverse, the persistent decline in newspaper readership—the opportunity seems well worth seizing.

The alternative—a multi-tier information economy, with the information-rich media costing considerably more than those in the lower tiers—is something that should frighten us both practically and ethically. As a society, and as media practitioners, we must be concerned that economics could deprive some citizens of the opportunity to obtain information of their choosing. (The question of equality of access to entertainment is a related issue, but one that falls outside the bounds of this discussion.)

To let
government
shoulder this
burden alone
would raise the
possibility for
further
intrusion into
areas where
the media
should have
the choice of
responsible
actions.

These issues should be addressed by the media themselves with some assistance from government, particularly regarding the formation of policies to regulate new technologies. The government might also help by creating economic incentives for the existing, traditional mass media to address this problem of differential access to media.

But the basic responsibility should remain with the media. To let government shoulder this burden alone would raise the possibility for further intrusion into areas where the media should have the choice of responsible actions. Failing to deal at all with the information equity gap would be an ethical abdication, and equally unacceptable. And, beyond the ethical obligation, reducing the information gap could well lead to the long-run development of more consumers for the mass media and the advertisers supporting them.

In regard to making communication network services available and affordable to the state's citizens with disabilities, the Alabama task force summed up the crux of the larger issue for society. Such availability, the task force said, would allow all citizens to play more active and independent roles in both the social and commercial aspects of the information age society (Alabama Information Age Task Force, 1991, pp. 8–9). This goal is one that the mass media—as one of the key players in and beneficiaries from an information age society—must work actively to implement.

KEY POINTS

- Although it's shrinking, there still is a "digital divide" in the United States, according to a 2009 Pew survey.
- Making sure that access to information is widespread is both an appropriate application of the utilitarian approach (with a touch of Rawls's philosophy) and good business for the media.
- "Internet neutrality" means that ISPs—particularly large broadband carriers—should not selectively deny or restrict Internet access for ideas, individuals or types of groups. A late 2010 FCC ruling on this topic fell far short of what Net neutrality activists had hoped for.

BABCOCK: Market forces are sufficient safeguards against any groups in society being deprived of access to necessary information, or of expressing themselves.

Everybody agrees that communication is essential to every society. In a complex, modern, heterogeneous society, the complex and varied mass media are particularly important participants. According to the analogy of Hiebert et al. (1991, p. 565), they are "the central nervous system of the United States, the critical information chain that vibrates without pause." The media help to keep people informed and entertained, help shape opinions about all sorts of issues, survey the environment, transmit culture, and help the economy by promoting goods and services. They help educate and socialize diverse populations. But the mass media must reach a meaningful audience—in terms of both composition and size—and be accessible to most (ideally, all) members of their society, to be fully effective.

Further, virtually all complex developed nations have some form of market economy, with some more attuned to competition than others. Henry Ford supposedly once said that the consumer could buy a Ford automobile in any desired color—so long as it was black. The mass media usually reflect the market economy in the countries where they operate, certainly with respect to the belief that growth of individual companies is a good thing, and—while giving lip service to competition (cars now do come in many different colors)—understand that the logical end result of competition might be a very profitable monopoly.

But is "lip service" enough? Just as the automobile provides transportation as its primary task, regardless of how ego-satisfying or attractive it may be, the media have functions that—for the benefit of society—must be satisfied. I believe that the free market system can provide these functions—and that such services are moral and ethical imperatives. One such paramount function is access.

ACCESS

Please recall that there are two different kinds of media access, as noted in the introduction to this chapter. One is the ability of any individual or group to receive the media. The second is the ability of any individual or group to have its story told, or its position reported, by or through the mass media. Those people who propose that both of these kinds of access to the media are moral rights, and that any limit on access is unethical, give media far more credit than they can possibly deserve, and more responsibilities than they can possibly fulfill. It may be unwise for a news or entertainment medium to disregard an individual's or a group's desire for both media content and media attention, but I believe it is not unethical, and will discuss this position later. (A third form of access, the desire of news media for access to sources of the information they spread, is of primary interest to news-gathering organizations. Nevertheless it is important to the people who ultimately receive and act upon that information, although it is not this chapter's main thrust.)

ACCESS OF THE PUBLIC TO THE MEDIA

Paradoxical as it may seem in view of the increasing concentration of media ownership, consumers probably have more choices than ever as the 21st century unfolds. Although there are fewer media companies today, the ones that remain are growing in size and variety of titles or channels provided. So, even though there are only a handful of conglomerates (Bagdikian, 2004, pp. 27–29) that are major players across media, there are many more choices of content. Some independently programmed and edited media outlets remain, including some that are also financially independent. Increasing numbers of truly alternative media voices are available—or potentially available—to the public. David Gordon makes this point for me in his discussion of the role filled by alternative media such as *The San Francisco Bay Guardian*.

Although the number of mainstream media competitors may be in decline, and the number of separate news-gathering services has shrunk precipitously, there still has been an increase in the amount of diverse content provided through a myriad of technologically based channels. In broadcasting, there used to be only three or four commercial networks (plus PBS in television and NPR in radio). Few communities (or geographically defined markets) had more than that number of television outlets. Then the number of TV networks (national programming sources) rose to six while most radio networks disappeared. But except in a small number of markets, TV channels were not available for more outlets because of the need to avoid interference with stations in nearby markets on the same or adjacent frequency (since interference can extend much further than can service from any transmitter). That may perhaps change, as a result of the move to digital television transmission, replacing a less efficient system adopted in the 1930s.

Today, the average household can view sports, Western movies, old sitcoms, or political commentators (from the right or from the left) most of the day over literally dozens of channels provided by cable or satellite distribution firms. Often this permits what used to be a network with one outlet per city to attract profitable audiences spread over several channels—a reduced number of people watching each channel, but attractive to advertisers in the aggregate. For example, NBC executives have programming responsibility for not only NBC, but for MSNBC and CNBC as well. CBS programs the CW network (which itself is an amalgam of two earlier networks, WB and UPN) as well as CBS. But some networks are more focused: Univision is aimed at the Hispanic population, and Fox strives to cater to entertainment-lovers and right-wing conservatives. For the information-hungry, there are at least five full-time cable channels (CNN, HLN, Fox, MSNBC, CNBC) as well as two or even three C-SPAN networks and, in some areas, a local or regional news channel and the news departments of local stations as well.

And let's not forget the other media—notably radio—that have adopted similar multiple-channel approaches. Newspapers and magazines often have geographically zoned editions, and almost universally are distributing content over the Internet; low-power FM is becoming more and more common; and some full-power FM stations may use digital "HD" channels or satellite radio to provide repeats, high audio quality, and full-time service and alternative channels that AM radio cannot supply. The "streaming" of such content on the Internet is almost limitless in concept.

Adam Thierer, then a senior fellow and director of the Center for Digital Media Freedom at the Progress and Freedom Foundation, wrote in 2005 that:

> most households had six or fewer local television stations to choose from 25 years ago, [only] three of which were affiliated with a major broadcast network. But thanks to the rise of cable and satellite competition, the average home now receives seven broadcast television networks and an average of 102 channels.

(p. 26)

He might have added that the number of radio stations had almost doubled since 1970 and the United States had reached new highs in the number of published magazines and other periodicals. Compared to the media landscape of 20–30 years earlier,

> today's world is characterized by information abundance, not information scarcity . . . . some psychologists and social scientists fear that citizens now suffer from "information overload" because of all the choices at their disposal.
>
> (Thierer, p. 35)

Add to that the Internet, and it is clear that market forces combined with new technologies are making more rather than fewer media outlets available to us. Thierer (p. 146) noted a 2003 estimate by information systems researchers at the University of California-Berkeley that there were about 170 terabytes of information available on the Internet, which is "17 times the size of the Library of Congress print collections." That reservoir of information (and entertainment and persuasion) has certainly increased since then. Looking from a somewhat different perspective, Thierer (p. 35) quotes Richard Wurman (1989) in suggesting that there is more information in a weekday edition of *The New York Times* than an average 17th-century resident of England was likely to encounter in a lifetime. In brief, he wrote:

> There has never been a time in our nation's history when the citizens had access to more media outlets, more news and information, or more entertainment. Abundance, not scarcity, is the defining fact of our current media age.
>
> (Thierer, p. 161)

Eli Noam, director of the Columbia (University) Institute for Tele-Information (a research institute focused on strategy, management and policy issues), argued in 1997 that—despite conventional wisdom to the contrary—U.S. media had not become more concentrated at the national level. He and his co-author wrote that:

> while the fish in the pond have grown in size, the pond did grow, too, and faster. The growth of the information industry has been 8% faster than inflation since 1987. Second, all these separate ponds are becoming more of a large lake, as the technological and regulatory dikes between them fall.
>
> (Noam and Freeman, 1997, p. 19)

The real weak link in regard to media concentration, they argued, was at the local level, where—among other concerns—very few American cities have more than one daily newspaper and "98% of American homes have no choice in their cable provider" (p. 22). This is where alternative local communication services, regardless of medium, can and do enrich and diversify the mix, even though the cost of news-gathering may pose obstacles to providing local news and similar information—a particular problem for broadcast stations licensed to serve a specific community but budgetarily constrained in their mission of local service.

Even so, considered on a national level, all this reflects an ever broader pool of information and opinion upon which citizens might draw, thereby enhancing the likelihood of an ever richer civic discourse that every democracy needs. The current increasing array of diverse mass communication channels, supporting a marketplace for goods and services, thus provides a setting for the successful functioning of a diverse and multifaceted marketplace of ideas.

Some critics of media concentration support regulation in the name of maintaining media diversity, local news, or democracy itself. Gordon seems to be taking that path. Such concerns make little sense in today's vast marketplace of ideas, where citizens are better off now than ever before. As I've said, present-day citizens—or media audiences—are exposed to more choices of news, information and entertainment than at any time in the nation's history. Indeed, consumers in the news and information audience suffer from information overload, if anything.

Thierer made the point in a similar fashion, but from a worldwide perspective. He quoted an analyst from McKinsey & Company, a global management consulting firm, who noted that "entertainment and media are still fragmented compared with other industries such as pharmaceuticals and aerospace," even if the number of major media companies worldwide is little more than 100 (Thierer, 2005, p. 58)—a figure that may be high, when compared to other industries. Or, to look at it from a different perspective, Clear Channel Communications owned slightly more than 1,200 U.S. radio stations in 2000, all playing popular music and with small staffs, at the height of its radio acquisition activities (Ahrens, 2006), constituting only about 11% of the total number of commercial radio broadcasting stations in the United States, and a somewhat smaller proportion of all such stations worldwide.

Even though we might not know precisely how much local fare citizens demand, members of the public still get a wealth of news and information about developments in their communities from the tremendous number of sources to which they have access. (Note that the FCC, since 2007, has indicated an interest in determining local information needs. See FCC, 2010.) While citizens are increasingly opting for more (and more convenient) sources of entertainment and national news, local programming and information still are popular and likely will not disappear even if a truly competitive media marketplace were established by the Obama administration (reversing many years of laissez-faire treatment of large corporations intent on becoming larger). True, the citizen may have to hunt a little, but the variety of mass media available to the public helps guard against what Gordon fears: "information apartheid" or a "digital divide" turning some people into second-class citizens.

Rather than rushing headlong into a media monopoly, today's media marketplace of ideas remains incredibly competitive and, indeed, not significantly more concentrated than was the case in past decades. Or, put another way, competition and concentration are not mutually exclusive, so that even if ownership were to become more concentrated, citizens would often be able to have more choices. The challenges are to find ways to entice the public to pay attention to more than one information source and to more than sensational topics, and to think about using new media channels in creative ways

One striking example of how ordinary citizens can gain access *to* the media to disseminate their news or commentary was a video posted on YouTube in the spring of 2008, showing deplorable barracks conditions at Fort Bragg, North Carolina. The video, posted by the father of a soldier who was housed in one of those barracks, drew more than 300,000 hits on YouTube and received major attention in the national media, including stories on CNN and the major networks. It also prompted the Army to launch a worldwide inspection of its troop housing facilities (Powers, 2008). The man who posted the video said that all he was trying to do was "to get the attention of a few people to contact their congressmen" and was pleased and proud to see "how many people got outraged by this," which transcended whether "people are for or against the war" (Powers, 2008).

In this 21st-century environment of greater media availability, Americans have an ever-greater opportunity to debate and learn more about democracy. Thierer (2005, p. 126) has argued that government regulation of media ownership can have negative impacts on the quality as well as the quantity of media content and that democracy will be healthier without such restrictions.

> If we as a society care about freedom, and freedom of information in particular, we must end all media ownership controls before technological and market convergence create regulatory convergence as well.
>
> (Thierer, 2005, p. 162)

I believe he is correct that unfettered (except for some requirements in the Communications Act of 1934) private entry into media operations has served the American people well. It would appear obvious that new media outlets or technologies—including the Internet—will play an important role in this debate, thus calling into question the need for ownership restrictions on traditional media, especially in countries where most of the population is able to access the Internet. (As Gordon noted earlier, nearly 80% of the U.S. population had such access by 2009.)

People often substitute one form of medium or one distribution system for another. Nearly 90% of American households with television currently subscribe to satellite or cable television even though they still have over-the-air (free) TV available. The advent of digital television and the cessation of analog over-the-air service may well increase this proportion. Healthy competition of another kind clearly is alive and well when papers such as *The New York Times*, *The Wall Street Journal* and *USA Today* circulate nationally.

Let me repeat: American citizens now have available more news, information and entertainment—through access to more media outlets and technologies—than at any other time in the nation's history. The availability of the Internet, the evolution of such local media as low-power FM and television, and the ability of anyone with a computer and printer to become a publisher have created possibilities for a new golden age of localism. Whether such an age will actually occur, and whether it could equal the decades when local coverage and local service were the lodestones of both print and broadcast journalism, remain to be seen. But it seems clear to me that, with just our current conspicuous media overabundance, any question of who owns what, or how much they own, is of little importance, even if the "who" is Rupert Murdoch and the "what" is the nationally distributed *Wall Street Journal*.

American media have grown almost unbelievably from the middle of the 19th century when the telegraph was a novelty, the telephone and motion pictures and broadcasting didn't yet exist, and the only mass medium was the newspaper. Any printer with a shirt-tail full of type and a press could become a publisher—and quickly turn out multiple copies of accounts of events, trends, and people. And, of course, advertisements, which became the financial

with just our current conspicuous media over-abundance, any question of who owns what, or how much they own, is of little importance, even if the "who" is Rupert Murdoch and the "what" is the nationally distributed Wall Street Journal.

mainstay of most mass media. Today, these early printers and publishers have been replaced in part by large corporations—but, even more importantly for a democracy, in part also by tens of thousands of 21st-century bloggers of all ages and widely divergent intentions.

Consequently, the current market forces—both for ideas and for goods and services—have enabled a richness and diversity of outlets that is unique in the United States' history, and, indeed, in the history of virtually all nations around the globe. Accordingly, I believe that having fewer media regulations allows a profitable news and information media industry to be financially viable and, as a result, better able to serve the needs of an ever larger, more diverse citizenry.

Bloggers, regardless of whether or not one would consider them journalists, have in just a few years become a part of many nations' media fabric. As most daily newspapers are cutting their staffs, more and more individuals are blogging, giving citizens more channels of communication both to express themselves and to receive information (and opinion) from others. Public libraries and Internet cafes make it possible to use a computer even if one can't afford to buy one. Such access for every computer user in many respects provides the potential for the greatest good for the greatest number in a way that Mill never could have imagined in his wildest dreams. As the price for computers continues to plunge and many communities and schools from kindergarten through university provide computer access, the so-called "digital divide" has become a memory of the 20th century, rather than a real issue in the current era.

So in the end, it seems that nearly everyone, with the exception of a rapidly shrinking small legion of aging newspaper journalists, enjoys and is well served by the vast array of media—much of it available with the touch of a thumbs-driven smart phone or the aid of eight additional digits racing over an inexpensive laptop keyboard. Is the capitalistic marketplace not adequately feeding the marketplace of ideas? Hardly! The audience—we!—simply need to take responsibility to access this cornucopia of omnipresent information. If we seek to be well informed, it can happen. It simply is a matter of intent.

KEY POINTS

■ Despite increasing concentration of media ownership, U.S. citizens have never had greater access to news, information and entertainment than they do now in an age of media abundance, not scarcity.

■ The Internet, the evolution of low-power FM and TV, and the ability of anyone with a computer and printer to publish have created possibilities for a golden age of localism.

■ Having fewer media regulations allows the news and information media to be financially viable and therefore better able to serve the needs of an ever larger, more diverse citizenry.

MERRILL: Commentary

The contending authors have pitched into what is certainly an interesting and important topic: inequalities among various audience segments. Most of us, I think, would agree—at least at first glance—with David Gordon's contention that the mass media have the ethical responsibility of providing a more equitable distribution of news, opinion, and entertainment as well as access to it. William Babcock deprecates this position and thinks that the marketplace provides adequate safeguards.

Strangely, however, he does seem to agree with Gordon that the inequity of some people's access to communication is unethical. How so, he does not say. But he, and I think correctly, places most of the responsibility on audience members, most of whom ignore the wealth of information already provided by the great variety of media and select entertainment rather than serious political news.

Gordon seems to see this inequity in information presentation as an ethical problem for the media, whereas Babcock in a sense wipes away ethics from the whole situation. The information market forces, for Babcock, are sufficient safeguards in this controversial area. Not so for Gordon, who thinks that media must think of ways to reach all social segments with their offerings.

This, of course, brings up the economic factor, and poses this question: how can the non-affluent citizens get access to the same quality and quantity of media as the affluent? This must be done, according to Gordon, or the media will continue being unethical. Maybe wealthy donors could help. Maybe putting unsold newspapers in strategic places for the taking. Maybe government subsidies to the media. Maybe even government providing tax monies to make available media free for all. This might be a possible Gordon solution, but it would find stiff opposition from "market-supporter" Babcock.

One other problem here is that neither author pays much attention to the news media's need for access to government and other sources, to obtain the information they process and disseminate, although Babcock makes a pass at it. But perhaps that's for a different book.

Information equity is a fine-sounding term. Gordon says the mass media have an ethical obligation to help ensure information equity. But in addition to being semantically fuzzy, it perhaps is an impossible goal. Media have enough trouble just trying to be thorough, accurate, and meaningful in the information they distribute. Gordon would have them also worry about making sure that this information reaches everyone. Should all people be equal in their access to information (all information? some information? which information?) or does it mean that various types of information shall get equal exposure to audiences (some audiences? all audiences?)?

> Information equity is a fine-sounding term . . . [but] it perhaps is an impossible goal. Media have enough trouble just trying to be thorough, accurate, and meaningful in the information they distribute.

What we seem to have in the United States is the fact that many (actually most) of the American people process very little of what some would consider essential information for intelligent popular governance. Provided with, yes. Is this clear? But such "exposure" does not mean that the citizens actually ingest it. Media provision of information is not the same as what citizens actually receive or pay attention to.

Perhaps Gordon is too hard on the media for being "unethical" in this respect. But even if we shift responsibility to the people (the audiences), it may not be an ethical matter on their part to ingest serious information; it may simply be a matter of information preference.

If I read a story about a horse falling into a ditch, am I being less ethical than if I read about a politician giving a speech?

Even if all Americans had access to all broadcast programming and to all newspapers and magazines, at least three-fourths of them probably would not avail themselves of even the obviously important information they contain. They either could not read the print media (due to some state of illiteracy, or of eyesight deficiency) or could not find or appreciate high-quality programs. And, if they did get the "appropriate" information, would they be more likely to vote or otherwise participate in government? Or to do so thoughtfully rather than emotionally?

The disputants in this chapter do not pay enough attention to audience responsibility. Actually, I am not trying to place any kind of obligation on the public. I am simply saying that if portions of this public desire more access, they need to get busy trying to get it. If they don't want it, then let them be ignorant; that is their natural right. It is not enough to sit back and expect the media, government, or somebody else to see that they are supplied with information. Babcock may well be right: the marketplace in the communications sphere provides adequate information for the public.

The First Amendment to the U.S. Constitution won't help with this problem. In fact it gives the mass media a safe haven if they decide to give unbalanced information or provide an inequity of news for different social segments. And as Gordon correctly notes, an increase in the number of media units (e.g., bloggers or radio stations) will not provide assurance of equitable access to these media. So what is the answer? Perhaps there is no answer. Even a strong turn toward socialism will not help the access problem. If every family were given every communications device available, there would be a disparity among families as to usage. Some people are just going to be better informed than others; it is a law of nature.

Gordon would modify the foregoing somewhat, I'm sure. Believing that having media is important and that reading (using) them is essential, he mentions Jefferson's famous saying that newspapers are preferable to government, and that "every man should receive those papers." Utopian socialism, that. Every person would receive newspapers only if provided them by the government. Gordon does add that Jefferson did go further and say that everyone must "be capable of reading" these papers. Sounds good, but even if every person were to read the copy he or she received, much would be skipped or slighted in the reading. And not only that, but no family would be likely to receive and read *all of the newspapers*.

Gordon correctly notes that the market system doesn't prevent the cutting off of certain social segments from the media. Or for that matter, that such a system fails to influence or direct what messages the audiences will prefer. It may make a plethora of information available (somewhere in the public's purview), as Babcock says, but it doesn't have much to do with qualitative information choice in specific cases.

Gordon comes close to the truth when he says that responsibility for media access actually could rest with everybody. He mentions consumers, the nonprofit sector, the government, advertisers, and the media. It is interesting that he mentions the media last, although his main point has been that the media are responsible for the inequity situation and, in fact, are unethical if they fail to remedy it. The idea of us all being responsible for the access-inequity is rather disquieting to me. If we audience members and all the institutions he mentions are responsible and unethical, then this would seem to wipe out any ethical dimension altogether. If we all are guilty, then maybe there is no guilt. As for Babcock's argument confirming the capacity of the market to assure access, there is little evidential support that this is true. For we know that there are such inequities existing all around us. Why hasn't the market eliminated them?

This whole topic being argued here implies a right of the people to have equal access to information. I certainly won't try to answer the question as to the source of such a questionable "right," but it might be well for media students to consider it. The U.S. Constitution provides the press with freedom from Congressional control, but gives it no instructions as to what kind of information it should provide or to whom it should be provided.

It seems that perhaps we are worrying too much about the quantity of information that gets to the American citizen and about the availability of the technology that gets the information there. Perhaps we need to put more emphasis on the *quality* and *kind* of information that media supply—on the social benefits of such information for those who receive it. Maybe it counts more to get the right kind of information to interested people (the opinion leaders and educated disseminators) than to try to spoon-feed everybody with a plethora mainly of entertainment. Neil Postman (1985), in his excellent *Amusing Ourselves to Death*, provides insights into the increasing proclivity of the media to titillate and entertain us. Certainly the media come in for their share of blame for this situation, but audience members confound the situation by their growing and enthusiastic attention to such stories and programming.

After all, in a representative democracy the people are, by and large, satisfied to be passive and let their representatives make the decisions. Basically, they form a community of passivity and relative unconcern. Great masses of citizens show this by the low voter turnout in most every election. A case might be made for the proposition that the uninterested masses, for the sake of an ongoing society, should not have information equity with interested, educated, and politically active citizens. William Henry III (1994), formerly of *Time* magazine, develops this theme in his book *In Defense of Elitism*. There is no doubt that the American public generally is not obsessed by serious news and interpretation. The mass media, except possibly for television, touch the masses of the population very peripherally—and even TV impacts mainly on the emotions, not on the mind.

It is impossible for market forces to ensure all groups in society information equity; the market was never set up to do that. But market forces are not alone in being incapable of providing total access to various kinds of information. The government is also incapable, as are the media themselves. Community consciousness and a social concern on the part of the media will not get the job done. Certainly, as Babcock notes (but not enough), audience members themselves bear responsibility for getting information that will make them better citizens. A personal desire to be informed, an educational system that prepares citizens for the complexities of the modern world, and an insatiable hunger for diverse perspectives—these are vitally important factors in the whole discussion of information equity and media access.

Let's face it. The bottom line is that there will never be information equity. It is an unrealistic, albeit worthy, expectation. Certain groups in society had best resign themselves to "information apartheid," to being isolated from information of various kinds. Most of them probably won't care very much, although their spokespersons may moan and groan about the inequities of the world, including those related to information.

REFERENCES AND RELATED READINGS

Ahrens, Frank. (2006). "Clear channel sale to end era." *The Washington Post*, November 17, p. D01. Retrieved from www.washingtonpost.com/wp-dyn/content/article/2006/11/16/AR200611600537.html.

Alabama Information Age Task Force. (1991). *Founding a First World Alabama: A Summary of the Information Age Task Force Report*. Alabama Information Age Task Force.

Bagdikian, Ben H. (2004). *The New Media Monopoly*. Boston, MA: Beacon.

Barr, Stephen. (1991). "Careless zoning can look a lot like redlining." *NewsInc.*, December, pp. 37 ff.

Barrett, Rick. (2008). "Wi-Fi is a no-go for now: Without cash infusion, Milwaukee's pilot project is unlikely to be expanded." *Journal Sentinel* (Milwaukee, WI), June 23, pp. 1A and 7A.

Brugmann, Bruce B. (2006). "The first 40: 40th anniversary special. How we made it against all odds—and why we'll be here for the duration." *The San Francisco Bay Guardian*, October 17. Retrieved from www.sfbg.com/blogs/bruce/ or at www.sfbg.com/entry.php?entry_id=1870.

Bryant, Jennings. (1993). "Will traditional media research paradigms be obsolete in the era of intelligent communication networks?" In Philip Gaunt, ed., *Beyond Agendas: New Directions in Communication Research*. Westport, CT: Greenwood, pp. 149–167.

Champlin, Dell, and Janet Knoedler. (2002). "Operating in the public interest or in the pursuit of private profits? News in the age of media consolidation." *Journal of Economic Issues* 36(2), pp. 459–468.

Comcast v. FCC, 600 F. 2d 642 (DC Circuit, April 6, 2010).

Compaine, Benjamin M., and Douglas Gomery, eds. (2000). *Who Owns the Media? Competition and Concentration in the Mass Media Industry*, 3rd ed. Mahwah, NJ: Lawrence Erlbaum Associates.

Crawford, James. (2010). "On the future of books." Posted on *Inside Google Books*. Retrieved January 5, 2011 from http://booksearch.blogspot.com/2010/10/on-future-of-books.html.

Dennis, Everette, and John Merrill. (1991). *Media Debates*. New York: Longman.

Dixon, Bruce. (2007). "Black lawmakers digitally redline African-Americans." *CounterPunch*, March 14. Retrieved from www.counterpunch.org/dixon03142007.html.

FCC. (2010). "Public Notice: FCC launches examination of the future of media and information needs of communities in a digital age." GN Docket No. 10–15, January 21, 2010. Retrieved from www.scribd .com/doc/25745220/FCC-Future-of-Media-Questions.

"FCC threatens to lift ban on cross-ownership, consolidation." (2006). *St. Louis Journalism Review* 36(291), p. 26.

Ghiglione, Loren. (1992). "Are marketplace values overwhelming the news media?" *Social Responsibility: Business, Journalism, Law, Medicine* 18, pp. 21–30.

Glasser, Theodore L. (1986). "Press responsibility and First Amendment values." In Deni Elliott, ed., *Responsible Journalism*. Beverly Hills, CA: Sage, pp. 81–98.

Griffith, Eric. (2006). "The problems with citywide wireless." *Wi-fi Planet*, April 14. Retrieved from www. wi-fiplanet.com/news/article.php/3599176.

Henry, William A. III. (1994). *In Defense of Elitism*. New York: Doubleday.

Hiebert, Ray Eldon, Donald F. Ungurait, and Thomas W. Bohn. (1991). *Mass Media VI: An Introduction to Modern Communication*. New York: Longman.

Jackson, Pamela Taylor, and James Ronald Stanfield. (2004). "The role of the press in a democracy: Heterodox economics and the propaganda model." *Journal of Economic Issues* 38(2), pp. 475–482.

Jefferson, Thomas. ([1787] 1984). "The people are the only censors." Letter to Edward Carrington, Paris, January 16. In Thomas Jefferson, *Writings, Selected and with Notes by Merrill D. Peterson*. New York: Library of America, and Literary Classics of the United States, p. 880.

LaVallee, Andrew. (2008). "A second look at citywide wi-fi." *The Wall Street Journal*, December 8. Retrieved from http://online.wsj.com/article/SB122840941903779747.html (May 16, 2010).

Liptak, Adam. (2007). "Verizon reverses itself on abortion messages." *The New York Times*, September 27. Retrieved from http://nytimes.com/2007/09/28/business/28verizon.html?r=1&scp=1&sq=Verizon%20Reverses%20Itself%20on%20Abortion%20Messages&st=-cse (April 9, 2008).

MacBride, Sean. (1980). *Many Voices, One World: Towards a New More Just and More Efficient World Information and Communication Order*. Paris: UNESCO.

McChesney, Robert W., and John Nichols. (2004) *Our Media, Not Theirs: The Democratic Struggle Against Corporate Media*. New York: Seven Stories Press.

McQuail, Denis. (1993). "Informing the Information Society: The task for communication science." In Philip Gaunt, ed., *Beyond Agendas: New Directions in Communication Research*. Westport, CT: Greenwood, pp. 185–198.

Morehead, Joe. (2000). "Service for Whom? Information haves and have nots: Small thoughts on large themes." *The Reference Librarian* 34(71), pp. 131–143.

Negroponte, Nicholas. (1995) *Being Digital*. New York: Knopf.

Newman, Jared. (2010). "Time Warner gives free wi-fi to NYC customers." *PC World*: "Blogs," March 26. Retrieved from www.pcworld.com/article/192564/time_warner_gives_free_wifi_to_nyc_customers.html (May 16, 2010).

New York Times, The. (2008). "Democracy and the Web." *The New York Times*, May 19. Available online at www.nytimes.com/2008/05/19/opinion/19mon2.html.

Noam, Eli. (2006). "A third way for net neutrality." *Financial Times*, August 29. Available online at www.ft.com/cms/s/2/acf14410-3776-11db-bc01-0000779e2340.html.

Noam, Eli, and Robert N. Freeman. (1997). "The media monopoly and other myths." *Television Quarterly* 29(1), pp. 18–23.

Pelofsky, Jerome. (2010). "Comcast wins Web traffic fight against FCC." Reuters article, April 6. Retrieved from www.reuters.com/article/id_USTRE6352YW20100406 (December 30, 2010).

Pew Internet & American Life Project. (2009). *Home Broadband Adoption 2009*. Available online at www.pewinternet.org/Reports/2009/10-Home-Broadband-Adoption-2009.aspx?r=1.

Postman, Neil. (1985). *Amusing Ourselves to Death*. New York: Viking.

Powers, Pamela. (2008). "Veterans' advocates." Eau Claire (WI) *Leader-Telegram*, May 3, pp. 1A and 2A.

Progress & Freedom Foundation, The. (2009) Web site at www.pff.org/about, accessed on September 5, 2009.

Radin, Charles A. (1992). "MIT plugs citizens into President race." *The Boston Globe*, November 2, pp. 23, 26.

Sneyd, Rose. (2007). "Douglas praises telecommunications bill." Associated Press story in *The Burlington* (VT) *Free Press*, May 30, pp. 1B and 3B.

Thierer, Adam D. (2005). *Media Myths: Making Sense of the Debate over Media Ownership*. Washington, DC: The Progress & Freedom Foundation.

U.S. Government Accountability Office. (2006). *TELECOMMUNICATIONS: Broadband Deployment is Extensive throughout the United States, but It Is Difficult to Assess the Extent of Deployment Gaps in Rural Areas*. Washington, DC: GAO-06-426, A report to Congressional Committees. Available online at www.gao.gov/new.items/d06426.pdf.

Witsil, Frank. (2008). "Oakland's plan to be a hotspot cools off: Wi-Fi project off-line until more cash found." *Detroit Free Press*, June 27, pp. 1B and 5B.

Wurman, Richard Saul. (1989). *Information Anxiety*. New York: Doubleday.

Part Four

Hot Topics in Media Ethics

Chapter 10

Private Lives, Public Interests in a Digital World

W HEN *The Washington Post* was working on its 2007 story revealing deplorable conditions encountered by wounded Iraq War veterans at Walter Reed Army Medical Center, its guidelines for respecting individual privacy included showing and identifying only those who gave the paper specific (and informed) permission. One highly newsworthy photo, which was said to capture particularly well the almost surreal situation at the hospital, was never run—because of concerns that some of the veterans in the photo could be identified without their permission (Priest, 2008).

For decades, many people have questioned how (and whether) news media should avoid excesses in reporting on individuals who unexpectedly find themselves in the limelight. The Walter Reed coverage (which won a Pulitzer Prize for *The Washington Post*) illustrates a situation where the news media recognized that privacy concerns existed, and proceeded with caution. But there have been other instances where such concerns have been ignored, and that mixed history—privacy is one of those "I know it when I see it" concepts—provides the context for this chapter's debate.

Because of idle curiosity or voyeuristic desire, whole industries have grown up that must deal with privacy every day. The 1997 deaths of Diana, Princess of Wales and her companion as her automobile was being chased in Paris by freelance photographers—"paparazzi"— led many to blame her death on media that were willing, even eager, to purchase and publish almost any photos of the rich, famous or notorious (what is sometimes called "being famous for being famous"). Although the media have often argued that the public has a *right* to know almost anything, after Diana's death, there were some guilty glances exchanged among journalists. Like obscenity and other controversial content, privacy stands on the line between "the public interest" and "what the public is interested in." And, like obscenity, privacy has evolved into a legal as well as an ethical concept.

At one time, we thought that the growth of databases in public and private hands warranted a separate chapter on "data privacy"—but after further consideration we concluded that the concepts of privacy were the same, whether using the techniques common today or 400 years earlier.

It may come as a surprise to realize that both the development of large databases and the technology for mining and manipulating them efficiently dates back to 1890, when machines first were used for tabulating census data. That is the same year in which Warren and Brandeis published their seminal article on privacy in the *Harvard Law Review*, arguing for legal recognition of a protected zone around what they called "the sacred precincts of private and domestic life" (Warren and Brandeis, 1890, p. 195). But the crude mechanical sorting and counting devices used for the 1890 Census moved to a new plane of efficiency nearly half a century ago, with the development and widespread governmental and business adoption of the electronic computer. As recently as the early 1960s, many business and government agencies still kept most records by hand and people hadn't yet started to blame all their errors (and troubles) on the computer.

Privacy, according to legal texts, is divided into four parts: unreasonable intrusion, appropriation of someone's name or likeness (usually for commercial purposes), being placed in a "false light" (akin to defamation), and public disclosure of facts that (even if true) offend the community's sense of what should remain private. We will focus primarily on the fourth of these categories because it is the one where ethics has the biggest overlap with the law. Many, however, would argue that *any* use of a database from which the names of individuals might be teased—even without public disclosure of the results—is an intrusion into an area that one might reasonably expect to remain private (Ernst and Schwartz, 1962).

In its most elemental form, privacy can be defined as an individual's right to be let alone. It has also been defined as the right to peace of mind, in contrast to defamation (libel and slander), which is an attack on one's reputation. Once articulated, it was relatively easy to associate privacy with the Fourth Amendment "right of the people to be secure in their persons, houses, papers, and effects, against unreasonable searches and seizures." But it took decades for this right to become established to the point where courts were consistently willing to entertain such arguments and render decisions based on them, particularly where private (rather than government) breaches of privacy were involved.

However, each state has its own law of privacy—and these are only a start toward the difficult task of pinning down privacy as a concept. One individual may not be bothered by the revelation of personal information that would drive the next person to despair. There can be honest and principled disagreement about the degree to which "newsworthy" people must give up some of their right to be left alone in the interest of providing information that the public either needs or wants. Resolving this conflict of individual, public, and media rights and needs would call for the application of ethical principles even if there were no legal ones.

One reason for this is that decisions in several First Amendment cases have scaled back traditional privacy protections for individuals to the point where the law sometimes allows *more* than media standards—and, equally important, public expectations of "good taste"—permit. Thus, ethics must take over in the gray area between what the law says the media *can* do (i.e., what they can "get away with" and still be protected under privacy law) and what they *should* do.

Nowadays, the general run of television news (and infotainment) and publications such as those devoted to show biz gossip, raise serious concerns about how far the media should pursue and transmit details of individuals' private lives, and under what circumstances this is justifiable. Confronting these issues often can leave media people in a quandary—wondering how they would feel if their own privacy were targeted.

Although the privacy issue dates back more than a century in the United States, the collection of personal data by both the government and private parties raises new questions. Such data, stored in various kinds of databases, often have important and beneficial purposes, but are sometimes used later in ways not intended when they were collected or were unanticipated by the individual who supplied the data in the first place.

For example, in 2008, a federal judge ordered YouTube (and its parent, Google) to turn over the log-on names and Internet addresses of each of the tens of millions of persons who had viewed material on YouTube's site. This came in the course of a copyright infringement suit brought by Viacom (which owned numerous popular programs often viewed over YouTube). As Mark Rotenberg, executive director of the Electronic Privacy Information Center remarked, "[rulings like this] will remind folks that companies like Google are sitting on top of a lot of personal information that they can't always control" (Menn and Guynn, 2008, pp. D1 and D2).

The potential problems are far more serious when supposedly secure data—through carelessness or malevolence—are made public. There have been many examples of how easily hackers can get into supposedly secure government or corporate databases ("ChoicePoint sifting . . .," 2005; "Credit problems . . .," 2006). In addition, laptops have been stolen along with the data they contain, or disks have gone missing, and it took only one erroneous command to put private data such as Social Security numbers on an address label ("Tighter security . . .," 2008).

Arthur R. Miller, a farsighted law professor, listed in the early 1970s some of the problems that could arise from "the computer, with its insatiable appetite for information, its image of infallibility, and its inability to forget anything that has been stored in it" (Miller, 1971, p. 3). As he sadly put it:

> not enough is being done to insure that computerized data, either in their stored form or while in transit, are any more immune from the intrusive activities of snoopers than private telephone conversations have been protected against the machinations of wire-tappers.
>
> (p. 20)

The computer's ability to store data, and the inability of government and business to do without such data (or safeguard it from others), have provided opportunities and temptations for the media themselves. Sometimes media use of such data—in news, advertising or public relations—can involve the inappropriate dissemination of personal data. For example, a magazine publisher might sell subscription lists for use in a mass mailing of marketing materials for some totally unrelated product, or even for spam. The numerous instances of such "data mining" by communications and many other companies has raised serious ethical questions both about how databases should be used, and who should have access to them.

So, we will look here at whether these technological innovations—and their impact on data storage, retrieval, and distribution of electronic messages—pose new questions about the ethical responsibilities of the mass media (and various other societal institutions), or whether they merely call for an updating of some of the older and more familiar concerns about privacy in mass communication. Among these various questions: should the media be subject to the kind of protective "human subject" rules that social scientists must follow? How should we deal with the insatiable desire for ways to correlate data in more than one database in relation to the problem of identity theft? These questions remain far from resolution, but are important to pose to a generation that grew up with computers and accepts them uncritically.

In the discussion that follows, John Michael Kittross and David Gordon wrestle with many traditional aspects of privacy, while leaving much of the heightened "data privacy" concerns for separate consideration by Julianne Newton. Gordon argues that leaving such decisions solely to the media hasn't worked well enough in the past, and other controls may be needed. Kittross maintains a "First Amendment absolutist" position, holding that the media themselves should have both the power and the responsibility to make decisions concerning boundaries between newsworthiness and individual rights of privacy.

In regard to data privacy, Kittross thinks that the technology itself has gotten beyond us, and that trying to control its abuses—whether by the government and business or by the mass media—is merely spitting into the wind. Newton, on the other hand, maintains that while there is a right of informational privacy that must be respected, there are circumstances in which both government and the media *should* have the ability to obtain private information from databases, and argues that new guidelines are needed to balance an individual right to privacy with a community right to know.

GORDON: News and entertainment media cannot be the sole judges of the privacy boundary between appropriate and excessive coverage, even for public figures.

Beyond the broad right to be let alone, privacy is an important concept for anyone who respects the dignity and autonomy of fellow human beings. To avoid inflicting needless emotional distress or embarrassment, or the possibility that people could gain power over us if they "manage to obtain sensitive personal knowledge about us" (Parent, 1992, p. 97), there is general agreement that *some* things about almost *any* person should remain private. The debate arises over when the media (or anyone else) can justifiably breach those bounds of privacy, who makes those decisions, and what criteria should be used.

I agree completely with what John Michael Kittross says in his part of the chapter, that in an ideal world, the mass media could and should be allowed to be the sole judges of where to draw the line between appropriate and excessive coverage of individuals' private lives. However, we operate in a less than ideal world, and not everyone is as responsible as *The Washington Post*. In fact, too many media people over the years have made poor and sometimes indefensible decisions on such issues. Therefore, there seems to be little alternative but to rely on more than just the good judgment of media practitioners, by backstopping those judgments as needed with some forms of outside guidance or pressure (a position that Julianne Newton also espouses).

This argument is much easier to make when the subject matter involves privacy for people who have *not* opted to enter the public sphere, but who have inadvertently become newsworthy through circumstances such as becoming an accident or crime victim or a battle casualty. Too often, the media have gone overboard in exploring aspects of those people's lives that have little or no relationship to what made them momentarily newsworthy. But even for people who have voluntarily entered some aspect of public life (politics, sports, entertainment, etc.), the mass media have proven time and again that they—and society—would benefit from some external checks on their sense of what is fair game and what should remain private. Kittross's repeated emphasis on what media people really *should* do in safeguarding privacy only reinforces my argument, since they are too often failing to do it on their own.

Perhaps, for someone as powerful and important as the President of the United States, it can be argued that there are few if any areas where privacy concerns outweigh the public's right and need to know. For instance, presidential medical conditions and concerns should be public knowledge, even if they would remain private for other individuals. Woodrow Wilson's debilitating stroke in 1919 was kept from the public, who didn't know until much later that Wilson's wife was acting as the *de facto* president for much of the rest of his term. Similar issues were portrayed in a fictional setting when, in 2000, *The West Wing* took up the impact of "President Jed Bartlett's" multiple sclerosis—not only whether it would affect his ability to function as president, but also whether the public should know about it. Franklin D. Roosevelt—arguably the most important president of the 20th century—benefited (as Kittross will note) from the press's reticence about stories or photos showing the effects of his bout with polio and about his relationship with Lucy Mercer, who was with him when he died.

Questions surrounding President George W. Bush's service in the Air National Guard during the Vietnam War got quite personal at times, and deservedly so, although a private individual in a similar situation might well have been entitled to keep those concerns private. In regard to Bush's predecessor, even Paula Jones's allegations about President Clinton's genital markings and the detailed allegations about the president's involvement with Monica Lewinsky have been considered appropriate matters for discussion by the mainstream media. (See, among many useful sources, Witcover, 1998.) I believe that such questions *are* appropriate to ask about a U.S. president or presidential candidate. The president's power is so wide-ranging that *almost* any aspect of the incumbent's life has some relationship to the way official duties are—or are not—carried out.

Similar reasoning was expressed back in 1979 by Richard Stolley, then the editor of *People* magazine, regarding its detailed coverage of speculation that former Vice President Nelson Rockefeller died while engaged in sex with his mistress. Stolley argued that members of the Rockefeller family simply have *no* right to privacy:

> They've had such a profound effect on this country, its society, its politics, and its image of itself, that any inquiry into the circumstances of a Rockefeller's life or death, particularly one who lived in the public arena as Nelson did, is important.
> (quoted in Anderson, 1979, p. 2)

It might be argued to the contrary that even people at the level of the Rockefellers ought to have some privacy in regard to activities that don't involve the public. (See the standard proposed, below, by Lee Wilkins.) But men and women who enter the various public arenas even at lower levels, in efforts to exercise leadership or make money or achieve fame, also must realize that they cannot fully shield other areas of their lives that the media may deem appropriate for coverage. Even people thrust into the public arena only by the force of circumstances, who have far less power or importance than more willing participants, cannot entirely avoid media attention to those aspects of their lives that are often deemed relevant or newsworthy.

Sometimes, the line is hard to draw even when the media are trying to be sensitive. One particularly difficult example of this was the 2006 school shooting rampage in Pennsylvania that left five Amish girls dead. The undisputed newsworthiness of the story conflicted with the natural human reaction of wanting to be left alone in grief, which was further complicated by complex Amish feelings about being photographed. *The Washington Post*'s ombudsman, in assessing the coverage—and the balancing act it required—some two weeks later, said it "presented a situation of great sensitivity" to the paper's editors and photographers. Most of the paper's photos were taken from public places, often using telephoto lenses so as not to intrude, and using angles from the back or side. Nonetheless, the paper's coverage was criticized by some readers and even one of the photographers had reservations:

> Personally, it bothered me to take photos of the Amish. . . . But as unpleasant as it is to be on either end of the camera, this was a story of historical magnitude that does warrant coverage, tasteful and sensitive coverage and photo documentation.
>
> (Howell, 2006)

If this degree of sensitivity were more prevalent in the news media, I could happily agree with Kittross. But, unfortunately, the media have too often ignored what I see as their ethical obligation to use discretion in deciding how far to go in covering private portions of individuals' lives. And there simply is no basis for believing that they can always be trusted to exercise good judgment in the future. Even in this case, the question might have been asked as to *why* the public needed to see these photos. Relying on a "newsworthiness" standard unfortunately opens the door to abuses.

Edmund Lambeth (1992, pp. 57–58) criticized utilitarianism as one reason for the media's failures. He argued that the utilitarian approach can lead media people to define the maximization of *good* in terms that enhance the media organization's interest rather than from an independent or societal ethics perspective. Too often, he wrote, the organizational good translates into sensational material designed to increase audience size, sometimes justified as the public's "right" to know anything that the media learn about.

It would be well for media people—and the public—to keep firmly in mind that the knee-jerk invocation of that *right to know* doesn't always justify printing or broadcasting intimate personal details. This so-called right is not always the same as the public's *need* to know. Both of those certainly differ from the public's *desire* to know. If the latter is used as the only standard for invading individual privacy, the media stand guilty of simple pandering to the audience, and that has happened more often than is comfortable—sometimes spurred by excessive media competition. It is not enough for us as a society just to hope that the media will exercise both good news judgment and good taste in deciding how far to go in

the knee-jerk invocation of [the] *right to know* doesn't always justify printing or broadcasting intimate personal details.

revealing personal information. Some outside catalyst clearly is needed to help the media maintain appropriate standards here. If nothing else, the pendulum of acceptable privacy standards may well need to swing back somewhat so as not to discourage the best people from entering public life.

UNDERCOVER REPORTING AND HIDDEN CAMERAS

The privacy issue affects not only what news the media print or broadcast, but also how that information is gathered. For example, should news reporters (print or broadcast) go undercover and use that fairly mild form of deception to further their newsgathering? Should they lie to gain access? Or use hidden cameras or recorders? A North Carolina jury emphatically said "No!" to a combination of these techniques in 1997, when it awarded $5.5 million (later vacated) to the Food Lion supermarket chain because two ABC producers had used fraud to obtain jobs where they could use hidden cameras to document a story about tainted meat. (For more detail on the *Food Lion* case, and on the use of deception in reporting, see Chapter 15-G.)

Ethicist Deni Elliott (1997) argues even more broadly that

trickery, sleight of hand, and misrepresentation are tools for the magician, not for the journalist. From the passive practice of a journalist allowing a source to erroneously believe that the intended story will be a flattering one to the elaborate illusion of the journalistic mole in corporations and convalescent homes, deceptive gathering techniques cause more harm than good to the profession of journalism and to society . . .

(Elliott, 1997, p. 3)

A set of criteria for weighing the ethical soundness of methods to obtain private information is here paraphrased from a very useful source (Parent, 1992), which listed six questions:

1   What is the purpose for which the information will be used?
2   Is the purpose legitimate and important?
3   Is the desired information relevant to this purpose? [And I would also ask whether it is *necessary* to the purpose.]
4   Is invading an individual's privacy the only—or the least offensive—way to obtain the information?
5   Does the technique to be used to obtain the information have some sort of restrictive safeguards built into it, or will it likely result in indiscriminate invasions of the individual's privacy?
6   What safeguards will exist to insure that the information will be used only for appropriate purposes once it is obtained?

(Parent, 1992, p. 100)

Some critics insist that any misrepresentation, such as undercover reporting, is a form of lying and is not appropriate. Ethicist Sissela Bok, while not ruling it out in cases of extreme importance, called such deception "morally questionable" (Bok, 1982, p. 263) and noted that it may well lead to reduced media credibility. She found some irony in the news media's often unquestioning acceptance of the need for undercover reporting, which she called "a stance that challenges every collective rationale for secrecy save the media's own" (p. 264).

Bob Steele of the Poynter Institute and DePauw University has also compared the use of hidden cameras to lying, and has argued that they should be used only if other concerns— for example, a need to protect vulnerable members of society by reporting consumer fraud as it happens—clearly outweigh reservations about such deception. This situational ethics approach meshes well with the criteria suggested by Parent (1992), and both demand thought before action. In essence, such approaches weigh the importance and benefits of the story—and the relevance of the information—against the degree of deception or invasion required. Some journalists argued that the Food Lion story failed on all counts, especially since ABC delayed airing it until sweeps month (see Glossary) (*Media Ethics*, 1997).

Whereas the ethical issues involved in undercover reporting usually focus on deception by the reporter and touch only tangentially on privacy concerns, the ethics of using hidden cameras in TV newsgathering focuses directly on privacy. As longtime Supreme Court reporter Lyle Denniston (1994, p. 54) pointed out, the use of hidden cameras "is, by definition, an intrusion that raises ethical questions." The practice can easily lead to such specific invasions of privacy as displaying hospital patients on screen as part of an investigative report of the hospital. Although some such reports may be worthwhile, others might well be using footage taken by hidden cameras when other means could have been used to tell the story just as effectively, or where the topic may not really matter.

At such times, using hidden cameras seems more a technique to boost ratings than one required to obtain important but otherwise unavailable information. For this reason, among others, the media cannot be allowed to be the sole judges of when to use hidden cameras.

ENTERTAINMENT AND PRIVACY

Visual communication in general often threatens to invade privacy and raises questions of taste. This is true whether one is talking about still photos, motion pictures, or video. All have captured images of victims or grieving survivors and have relayed pictures of other situations which many readers, viewers, and critics felt might better have been left private. The fact that these scenes were photographed or taped in public places was important only because the public locale meant that no legal action for privacy was likely to succeed. But the raw emotion that was put on public display for a wide audience to see (and, often, to view repeatedly) still raises valid ethical concerns about the news media's conduct as it affects individuals' right to be let alone.

Privacy issues, and the closely related question of good taste, can also arise for the entertainment media. Producers of documentaries, TV dramas or movies that focus on the lives of private individuals must either use materials entirely from the public record or get the individuals' permission to feature them this way. Producers of "reality" programming also must obtain the participants' permission to safeguard themselves legally. (Think of the problems that could arise if "ordinary" people participating in programs such as *Big Brother*, *The Biggest Loser* or *Cheaters* had second thoughts about the portrayal of previously private portions of their lives.) Even when participants have given their permission to be displayed on TV, the question of taste, particularly regarding how much voyeurism is appropriate, arises here as an ethical even if not as a legal concern.

"Reality programming," using non-professionals and unfailingly less expensive than writing scripts and hiring actors, can trace its roots back to Allen Funt's *Candid Camera* series in the late 1940s. Those programs raised ethical issues at the time, mostly in regard to whether it was appropriate to show ordinary people in embarrassing reactions to pranks which were sprung on them. The genre received a shot in the arm from the 1988 Writers Guild of America strike, as producers realized that writers weren't needed if they could fill the on-air gaps with this type of programming. And the 2007 Writers Guild strike (this one stemming from a dispute over residual payments to writers when their films and TV programs were shown on the Internet) gave reality programming a renewed vigor, with *Big Brother* being revived from the summer scrap-heap, and programs such as *Wife Swap* suddenly finding themselves as prime-time centerpieces (de Moraes, 2008).

The fact that ratings for these programs were about as high as for as many scripted series must not be allowed to obscure the ethical question of how far into people's private lives these shows *should* go. The participants may desire this exposure at the moment, but friends and relatives could well feel uncomfortable with the public voyeurism. An impartial observer could reasonably conclude that many such programs crossed the line separating good entertainment or useful information from out-and-out sensationalism, but good ratings (or at least the avoidance of disastrous ratings) and low costs trumped any possibility of media self-control.

POLITICAL CANDIDATES AND PUBLIC FIGURES

Kittross is correct in saying that news media scrutiny of political candidates' backgrounds has become more important with the demise of the "political boss" system where candidates were screened and selected behind the scenes. Few people would argue that the "smoke-filled back rooms" were better than the more open political system that now exists, so today's news media have a role to play in helping to weed out candidates with problems in their background. But that media responsibility has arguably been abused at times in recent decades, and has occasionally been exercised with a zeal that has sometimes drawn valid public criticism and concern.

With specific reference to those facets of private life that may illuminate politicians' character, Lee Wilkins (1994) has suggested that such private facts must "be linked to public, political behaviors before publication or broadcast becomes ethically justifiable." She added that revealing private information without establishing that link "is a form of tabloid journalism that casts doubt on journalistic motives and credibility" (pp. 160 and 162).

Political candidates must accept that they give up much of their right to claim private areas within their lives. But, at the same time, they should retain the right to keep *some* aspects of their lives private, especially those that have no direct bearing on their public actions—and perhaps even some that do if the motivation to reveal details is based only on a desire to improve ratings or circulations or just to titillate the public.

The news media gatekeepers help determine not only what information about candidates—or others seeking attention—should be made available to the public, but also which candidates should be taken seriously. That role in the political process does allow the media, to a considerable degree, to be the sole judges of how far to go in reporting on erstwhile private matters, especially in regard to candidates and others who have consciously chosen to enter the public sphere. But while the news media have a responsibility to provide all information that's necessary for citizens to make informed choices and decisions, there have been problems (including poor judgment) over the years in defining *necessary*.

People who choose to become active in politics and government (or in business, education, or any other aspects of life in the public sphere) must therefore live with public scrutiny. But they do have a valid point when they insist that the media gatekeeping role be exercised responsibly and that private aspects of character or behavior must, as Wilkins (1994) suggested, be connected to public actions to justify their disclosure. Once again, on the basis of the overall media track record, defining *responsible* or *appropriate connections* should not be left entirely to the news media. Some mechanisms are needed to check their excesses, or at least to call enough attention to them to make repetition difficult.

As mentioned earlier, media attention may be even harder to bear for those who become newsworthy through no conscious decision of their own, such as the survivors of people who have died in ways that make them newsworthy. For example—in the context of visual communication and privacy—consider the feelings of the family of a boy whose drowning death was documented in a front page photo of his family anguishing over his body shortly after its recovery. Was the family's grief—displayed as it was in a public location—really fair game for the newspaper photographer who snapped the picture (and for the editors who decided to run it)? Was it worth the impact on the victim's survivors to present a very dramatic picture and (as editors from two papers argued in this instance) to promote water safety in general and to warn the general public to be more careful when children are swimming (Christians et al., 2009, pp. 118–121, with the photo itself appearing on p. 121)?

In such circumstances, it seems highly appropriate for the media to consider more than just their own definitions of *news* (or even of *entertainment*), no matter what ethical theory is used for guidance. John Rawls's concern for protecting the weakest party in a situation would certainly give priority to the privacy needs of accident victims and their families. But even stopping short of Rawls's approach, the reaction of the people involved and questions of public sensibilities should certainly be relevant factors. Concern for them might prevent such complaints as one expressed in a letter to advice columnist Ann Landers by a mother whose teenage son was killed in a traffic accident. She called media coverage of the tragedy "absolutely heartless" and noted that the boy's grandmother got the news of the accident from TV before the mother could notify her. "Is 'news' that important?," the mother asked. "Do people really enjoy tragedy that much? Where has compassion gone?" (Landers, 1994).

The media need to ponder such questions and discuss them with people who have differing and detached viewpoints, in order to develop some reasonable and thoughtful guidelines. The media also should be proactive, and develop mechanisms through which they can be held accountable when serious privacy concerns are at stake. Waiting to do this until deadline pressures loom, with no input from media critics or the public, is not a sensible approach.

SOME PRINCIPLES FOR DEALING WITH PRIVACY

In considering such issues, Clifford Christians and his co-authors enunciated three moral principles to serve as guidelines for the use or nonuse of material that may invade privacy. The first of these "promotes decency and basic fairness as nonnegotiable" and bans such things as innuendo and exaggeration. The second principle posits "redeeming social value"—specifically as opposed to "prurient interests"—as the basis for deciding what (private) information should be disclosed. The third principle holds that "the dignity of persons ought not be maligned in the name of press privilege. Whatever serves ordinary people best must take priority over some cause or slogan" (Christians et al., 2009, p. 110).

As Bok has noted, even the First Amendment's "*legal* right to free expression cannot do away with the need for *moral* scruples in choosing what to publish" (Bok, 1982, p. 255, italics in the original). The need to pay "special attention to individual privacy" is especially important, she said, when the media provide material that satisfies the public's curiosity rather than content that affects the public welfare (p. 258).

Parent's (1992) first four questions might also be used in determining whether or not information of a private nature should be revealed, even if its acquisition was ethical. For instance, consider whether a rape victim's identity should ever be revealed by the media, an issue that becomes even more complex if the trial is televised. One might argue that the media should help society overcome the stigma that has traditionally adhered to rape victims by publishing or broadcasting their names just as if they were victims of other crimes. But that argument is flawed by its failure to ask what the victim prefers and by the fact that identifying the rape victim against her will usually results in *additional* pain and trauma for her, and discourages other victims from reporting rapes. Moreover, it appears to have little or no impact on reducing rape's societal stigma. Thus, printing rape victims' names fails Parent's (1992) third test of relevance to the larger purpose, and probably the fourth test as well, because there have to be less harmful ways of pursuing the elimination of rape's stigma. Printing the victim's name also fails to meet Christians' criteria of decency, fairness, and preservation of personal dignity.

The same argument might be used with respect to the publication of any *accused*'s name until the trial (as is the case in some countries) or even until the verdict has been delivered. For example, the rape charges leveled at Duke University lacrosse players in 2006 (and dropped over the course of the following year) raised the question of whether the alleged perpetrators should have been identified prior to any trial, even though they were formally (and, as it turned out, wrongly) charged with the crime. This case eventually led the Raleigh (NC) *News & Observer* to identify the accuser despite its well-established policy of *not* naming rape victims, to review that policy, and to invite readers to take part in the discussion but to do so civilly (Sill, 2007). (This case is discussed further in Chapter 5.)

Kant would require that rape victims be treated as individuals worthy of consideration rather than as vehicles to educate society that rape is not a stigma. He would probably agree with a guideline that victims' names could be made public only if they were willing—a middle position that Aristotle would undoubtedly support, as would many situational ethicists. Utilitarians would argue for the greatest overall good, which might allow identification even of victims who object, if that *truly* could lead to beneficial changes in societal attitudes and behavior. Rawls would support the protection of the weakest party in each situation, and that would almost certainly be a rape victim who desired anonymity.

The Supreme Court has held (*Cox Broadcasting Corp.*, 1975) that, in the case of rape victims, no invasion of privacy suit is permitted if the name or other information is obtained by the news media from a public record or proceeding. Nonetheless, most media outlets still refrain from identifying living rape victims, even though they are legally protected if they do.

Questions have also arisen over the broader issue of reporting the victims' names in crimes other than rape. Although some countries do it differently, the U.S. media have routinely reported such names as part of their "watchdog" role. But this practice may well need further consideration and perhaps some guidelines developed by more than just the media gatekeepers. Some newspapers that used to print routine "police log" reports of crimes have modified or eliminated the practice after complaints that running names and addresses of burglary victims has set up the likelihood of repeated attempts. Similarly, printing names of those arrested may be prejudicial when cases come to trial. Other papers apparently take the utilitarian position that the overall benefits of running such details outweigh any harm that might come to individuals.

This issue gets even more complicated when news media make available personal details that can pose a serious risk of bodily harm or death to an individual, and in this area the courts have on occasion stepped in to provide some guidance. In one such case, a woman escaped from an abductor who briefly kidnapped her off the street, but became a further victim when the abductor began stalking her and terrorizing her with phone calls—after a local paper had printed her name and address!

The woman sued the city and the paper for releasing and using that information negligently and a state court held that, regardless of the state's open records law, there were valid grounds for her suit. Such a "foreseeable risk" of future harm should have led the paper to omit the woman's identity even if it was obtained from public records. (See *Hyde* v. *City of Columbia*, 1982, as discussed in Scott, 1993.) Although this precedent has not taken hold, it illustrates how outside forces have at times limited the media's ability to act as the sole judges of what privacy limits are appropriate.

It is worth noting that, over the years, courts appear to get involved in mass media issues more often when they perceive that media excesses require remedies. Thus, Kittross is correct in saying that if the media want to retain their control over such things as determining appropriate boundaries for privacy, they would be very well advised to exercise more self-control. But they have repeatedly failed to do so! And as long as that remains the case, the public—and the judiciary—may well start to clamor about media excesses and begin to protect individuals by imposing monetary damages for such practices, or by threatening the First Amendment's existence.

OTHER POSSIBLE SOURCES OF GUIDANCE

In addition to the courts—which are *not* my preferred remedy—what other sources might provide outside guidance? News councils and ombudsmen (a combination of inside and outside sources of guidance) or journalism reviews (e.g., the "Darts and Laurels" column in the *Columbia Journalism Review*) and outside media critics might serve this function. At the risk of being called slightly heretical, I'd also suggest that such criticism and guidance is something academics could do better than they have, especially if some of them (or their students who rely on scholarships and internships) were less dependent for support on some of the media companies that such critiques would target. Various other non-governmental media accountability systems have been suggested by Claude-Jean Bertrand and others (Bertrand, 1993, 2000).

Classes in media criticism—or other efforts to educate media users about what they should and should not expect from their media—might be another step in this direction. A *Columbia Journalism Review* editorial ("Supply and demand," 2008) suggested that a cooperative effort in this direction, involving major media companies as well as the education establishment, would "give students the skills to judge the reliability and credibility of news." In the process, students would become better able to judge media performance in such areas as respect for individuals' privacy. Another step in this direction could come from increased media efforts to promote feedback from their audiences, through such options as advisory boards or town meetings, or via comment boards for online stories.

Exploring whether the media need outside help in setting boundaries for respecting individual privacy raises many other questions. Among them are naming juveniles accused of violent crime, naming "johns" arrested for patronizing prostitutes, identifying HIV victims, and many other situations where the media have to make daily decisions about privacy.

A CONCLUDING EXAMPLE

Here is an example—a difficult one—of decision-making about the privacy of an individual and a family. Some years ago, the local paper learned that a very promising and talented young woman from Missoula, Montana, who had gone east to college, had been found dead on a Washington, DC, street after turning to prostitution. The emotion-laden decision about whether to print the information was made more agonizing by the fact that the story was being distributed in the Missoula area by a regional paper using a very complete account distributed by *The Washington Post* news service. The *Missoulian* decided to publish much of the story, despite insistent requests from the victim's family not to do so. The decision brought down a firestorm of local criticism, as well as strong criticism from its own editorial page editor—*on its own editorial page* (Hart and Johnson, 1979; see also Christians et al., 2009, pp. 115–118).

The Missoula decision could well be argued either way, but at least it was made after considerable internal discussion and debate. Less responsible news and entertainment media are also faced with similar decisions on a regular basis, and they have all too often shown too little concern for the individuals whose privacy was at stake, and have done so *without* the careful internal discussion that preceded the Missoula decision. It therefore would seem, on balance, that concerns about individual privacy are too important to be left solely to the discretion—or lack of it—of the news and entertainment media.

KEY POINTS

- Decency and basic fairness, "redeeming social value," and individual dignity are suggested by Clifford Christians as guidelines for determining where to draw the boundaries of privacy.
- Such outside entities as news councils, ombudsmen, and journalism reviews could help the media determine what kinds of information should remain private.
- Private aspects of the character or behavior of public figures must be connected to public actions in order to make their disclosure justifiable.

KITTROSS: News and entertainment media should be the sole judges of how their activities impinge on individuals' privacy rights. Furthermore, the mass media need not be concerned about using personal information from private or government databases, but we all should be concerned about its collection and abuse by others.

The most important word in the above assertion is "should" in the first sentence. I am not arguing that nobody is able to make decisions on privacy, or that privacy isn't worthwhile for the media to worry about—only that many of the cures suggested by David Gordon and others are worse than the disease. In five words, my mantra is "don't let the lawyers decide." I believe that the men and women who staff the mass media are capable of taking responsibility, assessing what the public needs to know, and accepting criticism, rebukes and even legal action when they are wrong.

Sometimes, it isn't easy. And sometimes media staffers do things that they wish they hadn't done. On the public radio program *This American Life* (December 1, 2007), a lengthy story explored the nuances of the following privacy situation. A television station in Boise, Idaho, wanted to pull up its ratings and become a real competitor in the local news game. Accordingly, when they received a tip that a registered sex offender was working with young people at an ice rink, the station pulled out all the stops.

Even after it learned details of the offender's transgression with a willing 15-year-old more than a dozen years earlier, that he had a spotless record thereafter, and was a hockey referee (not a coach) with essentially no non-public contact with any minors, the TV station for many days emphasized that the story was exclusive and milked it as hard as possible. (In this instance, "exclusivity" might have meant that the other news media in town didn't think it was a worthwhile story.) A graphic showing the offender's mug shot and very young children skating on the rink—children with whom the offender had no contact—was frequently used.

The one thing the station *didn't* do was contact the offender for his side of the story, which included the additional facts that he had registered, that the judge had dismissed his case, that he hadn't offended again, was a productive member of the community with a family (his wife knew what had happened) and that a governmental board had decided that he was not a predator after he had told the hockey league about his record.

The TV station clearly didn't care about what it was doing to the man and his family; it had decided that someone who had to register for the rest of his life deserved no privacy (and neither did his wife, 9-year-old child, and the rest of his family), and kept on the story for weeks. (On the public radio documentary, the TV reporter—who left the station soon after-wards—told how she tried to get out of reporting the story day-in and day-out. Her super-visors and station management, though, told her to "get over it" and do her job.) At the end of the day, the offender's life was in ruins, the reporter had left the market, and the station's ratings had gone up. Legally, the TV station was on solid ground: the offender's record was a public document. Station management was happy, even though many staffers felt that it wasn't much of a story. But what about the ethics of this kind of targeting of someone who had made one mistake many years before and wasn't a public figure? (And, in fairness, should we have offered the TV station a chance to defend itself in this account?)

The issue of privacy is a partially charted minefield, and nobody is guaranteed safe passage through it. It is arguably the most sensitive, most controversial, matter faced by the mass media—and it might arise every day in almost every newsroom that sends out reporters to cover news. The fact that journalists *can* find out things that subjects might not want publicized doesn't mean that they *should* seek or publicize anything and everything.

Today, much "reality" entertainment programming is voyeuristic. A few individuals—Paris Hilton, Anna Nicole Smith (both before and after her death), Britney Spears and others—have a virtually symbiotic relationship with the media. They both need each other—for reasons of ego satisfaction (the individuals) and audiences (the media). It is a rare member of the audience who doesn't like to hear gossip, and the media cater to that desire.

But how far should the media go? My position is that they shouldn't go any further than the average person would go in collecting rumor, gossip and scandal. Journalists must scrutinize their own motives as well as the motives of their sources and the people and organizations they are reporting on. They must validate facts and contexts and they have the responsibility to judge the possible consequences of their work. These consequences could fall on them and their organization—in terms of reputation as well as money—as well as on the people they decide are without rights to privacy. Larry Flynt, the publisher of *Hustler* magazine, said of his $1 million offer for first-hand information or documentation about anyone who "had a sexual encounter with a current member of the U.S. Congress or a high-ranking government official" that "The last thing I could ever do is publish something that wasn't true, because it'd kill me. And I know that. So I function at a higher standard than mainstream media (Richards and Calvert, 2007).

This is a teleological (consequence based) view of the ethical issues involved. There are no deontological rules, although some would argue that serving information to the public should have no boundaries except, possibly, "truth."

PRIVACY AND POLITICS

Although advocates of privacy repeat the traditional "right to be let alone" mantra, even the most ardent realize that most people are inquisitive—even nosey—and want news and gossip about other people, particularly other people whose actions may affect them. They also want sordid or scandalous details about celebrities for no other reason than salacious curiosity and the media are surrogates for those who are unable to collect "dirt" for themselves. The public enjoys this material even when it doesn't tell them more than they already knew or merely suggests or invents new possibilities—and immediacy is one of the few things that media outlets can use to get people's attention.

Most "celebrities" are created as the result of self-advertising (or hired publicists), which renders moot the privacy claims of many sports figures, popular movie or television "stars" and pop music performers. Finding out hidden facts about the lives of politicians is often considered to be as legitimate as "show biz gossip" because most politicians use their "character" as a selling point when seeking votes or other approval. Accordingly, I believe it is a rare reporter or editor who doesn't think at times that *everything* in a candidate's past or present life is fair game, deserving of overwhelming coverage.

Yes, I agree that prior events involving the candidate's character are appropriate fodder for the press—but what an elected official actually does *while in office* should be far more important to all of us than previous activities of the official or his or her family. It is beside the point that some candidates want their private lives disclosed, others are able to shrug it off, and still others—such as former presidential candidate Gary Hart, early in his 1988 campaign—take the risk of daring the press to uncover verifiable proof of their peccadilloes, and suffer the consequences.

The unwillingness of news media to be "scooped" on a political figure's life has been aided by the growth of computerized databases available to collectors of news or gossip.

The unwillingness of news media to be "scooped" on a political figure's life has been aided by the growth of computerized databases available to collectors of news or gossip. The ubiquitous presence of portable and miniature video and still cameras and audio recorders, in the hands of amateurs or "citizen journalists" as well as professionals, provides even more resources for media to pursue the private sides of politicians' lives.

Years ago, the qualifications of aspiring political candidates were scrutinized in smoke-filled rooms. The fraternal assessments made there usually screened out truly unacceptable candidates, concentrated on electability, and often concluded with unspoken agreements to overlook or remain silent about anything that would handicap the favored candidate. This system, one that worked in the past, has been greatly changed. Reporters have become more skillful, perhaps bolder, and they use portable electronic equipment to record words and images verbatim and to access data about candidates that once was hard to find in paper files. And there is considerable competition among media to report details about political figures to a public that has more education and more opportunities to use the mass media than ever before.

To capitalize on this media attention, national election campaigns now start in public nearly two years before the election, with the media continually emphasizing the "horse race" aspects of electoral politics. Primaries and caucuses come ever earlier in the calendar, and the "open hunting season" on candidates stretches out in the same fashion.

No one knows for sure whether mass media scrutiny gives the public better government, but it is becoming evident that anyone even considering running for office has to be ready to affirm or defend virtually every minute of his or her past. Previously, rumors and facts about candidates or officials that didn't directly bear on their governmental actions were often ignored by the press. It was widely known—but rarely reported—that President Kennedy had a strong libido. That President Franklin D. Roosevelt was with a long-time woman friend when he died at Warm Springs, Georgia early in his fourth term was even more unlikely to appear in the press; in fact, it was rarely mentioned and almost never shown that he was largely wheelchair-bound because of the effects of polio.

Illegitimate children, serious illnesses, sexual dalliances—all were once considered "private." In recent years, though, such matters have become public. Perhaps the most salient recent case would be the sexual contacts in the White House between President Bill Clinton and intern Monica Lewinsky, which led to highly publicized impeachment proceedings, although not conviction, for the president. A decade or so later, the big "political" stories were about former Senator John Edwards, Senator John Ensign, Governor Mark Sanford (and others in similar and lesser offices) admitting to extra-marital affairs.

This is a serious matter for potential candidates and the public. Candidates must be able to respond clearly and quickly to questions about their "character" as it is reflected in their past activities and associations. Few subjects involving political figures are taboo, but the media can err egregiously when they blithely accept and use information about private lives, supplied by candidates or by any other source, without seeking verification and considering relevance. The media have the responsibility to consider information carefully rather than acting merely as conduits for the "spin doctors" and "political operatives" who are trying to frame the political agenda at all times.

> the media can err egregiously when they blithely accept and use information about private lives, . . . without seeking verification and considering relevance.

IN THE PUBLIC EYE . . . AND THE UNEXPECTED SPOTLIGHT

The public arena is not limited to government and politics. Any person who finds him- or herself in the public eye can expect media scrutiny. This is true whether (as in the case of performers on the screen or the playing field) this is a voluntary act, or is merely the result of being in the wrong place at the wrong time or doing the wrong (or sometimes, right) thing (as in the case of victims and perpetrators of violent crimes).

Sometimes the person focused upon is already well known (such as former football player and sometime actor and advertising spokesman O. J. Simpson when accused of his wife's murder). At other times, people become well known only as a result of what they did or are suspected of doing. I'm confident that any reader of this book who peruses the news for the previous month will find plenty of examples. It doesn't matter to the media: this is what the public is interested in. The definition of "newsworthiness" is usually in the hands of the media, although there have been some attempts to override this power by the courts.

Hence, it is necessary for the media to accept the responsibility of making these determinations wisely.

As the plethora of inexpensively produced "reality" shows proves, the public is fascinated by violence and crime and people watch, listen and read about a given case until bored or distracted by the next such event. We remain uninformed about many other political, social, technological or economic issues that may be much more important to us in the long run. In other words, the audience prefers—whether through free will or as the result of conditioning—titillation and other short-term rewards rather than making the effort to deal with longer-range matters. And that preference frequently translates into coverage that fails to respect the privacy of its subjects, whether they are central to the story or not. Some with only tenuous connections convince the media that they have little to offer, while others seek the limelight and still others find it thrust upon them.

Some people move quickly from private person to public figure because of the momentum and scope of the situation. Regardless of how or whether they participated publicly in formal proceedings, some of them will have to guard their own privacy in the future if they wish to maintain it. The media make few distinctions between these categories and thus must assume responsibility for the decisions made about every privacy situation—and the reasons for those decisions—regardless of the legal distinctions between voluntary and involuntary public figures.

Media people, too, are subject to the same consequences of being public as the subjects they cover, whether they like it or not. The bigger their reputations, the greater the scrutiny paid to their activities. Some grumble about it and others are diligent in trying to avoid any association or activity that brings unwanted public attention. But some become savory fare for the media's piranha-like feeding frenzy.

So, what happens to the "right" to privacy when people are thrust into the public spotlight by circumstances over which they have little control? These people may be living quietly, not seeking attention, when an event or situation intrudes and thrusts them into the news. The starting point may be an innocuous article based on a police report about victims of alleged crimes. It may even involve someone who by chance has the same name. Before such people know it, reporters are on the phone or at the door, asking questions of neighbors, co-workers, anyone even remotely connected with them. Sometimes opinions and speculations expressed by these "sources" overshadow any facts that are available and sometimes even reporters begin to believe that opinions repeated often enough spare them from checking with the individuals involved or otherwise verifying them as facts. Ethical questions of propriety—or its lack—on the part of information seekers and tellers alike, abound in such situations.

David Gordon later discusses criteria to evaluate methods for obtaining private information. If media people or organizations apply these criteria, they can judge whether they are invading an individual's privacy. Media can control how information is gathered, especially when hidden cameras, false identifications, and disguises are used to uncover important information that the public needs to know—or unimportant information that gets dredged up—and can determine whether or not these methods are ethical.

Let's not forget that media mailboxes, phone lines, and e-mail are often filled with offers from people—or their representatives—who want even the most sordid details of their own lives told for a variety of reasons. The mass media market is big and enticing to them, and they want what Andy Warhol called their "15 minutes of fame." These people display their ethics selectively, and so do the media that use such material, and few steps are made without legal consultations and firm contracts. Personal fame and financial gain don't always equate well with public well-being, standards of taste, and ethics.

THE TASK BEFORE US

The media people who make decisions about who and what is public or private have serious obligations to the individuals involved *and to the public*—as well as to themselves and the media they represent. They must regularly ask themselves whether the invigorating highs they get when they publish something that beats the competition and virtually demands public attention are in accord with the real significance of the story. After all, not only is the subject (no matter how much he or she wants publicity) often harmed, but also the reputation of the media—and all who work there—as serious suppliers of needed information is damaged, and the entire concept of "news" is debased.

Media scrutiny of public persons has been defended by the courts as a "greater good" that results when the public has as complete information as possible about a person who works or offers to work in the public arena. Political candidates and public officials are voluntarily public people. So are performers and other individuals who seek and achieve public attention. As Gordon explains, even aspects of their lives and activities that they prefer not to be subject to public scrutiny often are deemed appropriate for media coverage.

A few "name" people are able to remove themselves from media attention even though the media and their audiences would prefer that they don't. Jacqueline Kennedy Onassis lived an extraordinary public life as First Lady. After President Kennedy's assassination in 1963, she remained on public view until shortly after his funeral. As a beautiful, young, brave widow, the media felt she still was news. She determined, though, that she and her children deserved privacy and she was persistent in protecting it. She developed what one reporter called "a passion for privacy" and defended it for years with every means at her disposal, including lawsuits. Major media commentators and reporters, many of whom had covered the White House, began to respect her wishes. Reporters often knew about her activities but didn't report them. They continued that reserve in their coverage of her final illness and death, even though millions of people probably wanted to know as many details as possible. Her legacy is that privacy is possible in a very public media world.

Crime and accident victims are involuntarily public people. In big cities, there are so many of them that only the most dramatic or gruesome usually make it into the media. Big city or small town, the media decide who and what will be published or broadcast and they must be able to justify their decisions both to those who want more and those who want less coverage of such violence and its aftermath.

Nothing is really simple, and distinguishing between "good" and "bad" (or "right" and "wrong") is harder than a simplistic formula might imply. For example, many believe there is no reason why databases tend to have birth dates as well as all sorts of other data. Almost every reader of this chapter is known by a Social Security number, various other ID or credit card numbers (typically, with enough digits to make them hard to remember and allowing for more unique numbers than the population the planet will support), an address, and who knows what else. Why also have a birth date listed on each of these databases? Isn't that an invasion of privacy—both for those who don't want others to know how young they are and for those who don't want others to know how old they are?

The typical response to the above question is that it is possible that many people have the same name—and often the full name is omitted. For an example of the difficulty this can cause, the current American Psychological Association citation style, which uses only initials rather than given names, has made life very difficult for those trying to trace the intellectual and career development of any scholar with a common name like "Smith."

Reporters and others who process crime and accident stories should also be sensitive to injured people or grieving families. The media have no special right to information from or about them, nor do their audiences. Often, however, media people assume they have the right to invade a family's privacy simply because one of its members was victimized. Helen Benedict (1992), in her excellent study of media coverage of sex crimes, suggests that reporters wait at least until after the first shock of the crime, and then tell families that they can choose to be interviewed or not and that they can ask not to be identified. Reporters would do well to take to heart the still-famous parody of reporter insensitivity after the assassination of President Lincoln: "Apart from that, Mrs. Lincoln, how did you like the play?"

ordinary people need protection in moments of crisis.

Media people should identify themselves to every person they interview, and they should remind distressed or traumatized individuals that they do not have to reply to any question. And, as Gordon explains, reporters should not include any information in their reports that could further endanger a crime victim. If all this sounds like a *Miranda* warning, it stems from the same goal: ordinary people need protection in moments of crisis.

With few exceptions, journalists are not "hired" by their audiences to serve strictly as voyeurs. They, like the police, are expected to protect as well as serve—and if they allow others (the subjects of their scrutiny, the courts, politicians, even public clamor) to do the deciding, they lose the greater share of their power to make a difference in how their society evolves. They cannot escape their responsibility to draw the line between privacy and appropriate disclosure by deferring to the perhaps conflicting desires of their story's subjects in deciding what to publish. Nor should they assume it is their right, and even their duty, to make their pages and screens the place to see, hear, or read about ordinary neighbors and leaders alike in embarrassing situations.

This has nothing to do with why the press has the protection of the First Amendment. The media need to balance carefully the public value of disclosure against the private harm to individuals, an Aristotelian Golden Mean approach. They should never forget the utilitarian notion that media's client is the public (Bates, 1994). When it comes to personal information and personal attacks, fairness and the public interest are the criteria that should be employed. Only the media are in the position to deal with both of these criteria.

Media sometimes pay a price for being ethical—such as reduced audiences and revenues, nitty-gritty harassment, and lack of governmental cooperation. Media people also may pay a personal price for being ethical. When they reveal private information that the public needs but that public officials or candidates for office would prefer not be discussed publicly, they may have doors closed to them, and sources cut off. When they are compassionate, they may be criticized for not being aggressive or for being "soft."

When they don't heed the public's cry for details about the private lives of people, they may lose audiences. But they can live with themselves. They can enjoy the confidence and support of people who understand and respect individual rights of privacy. And they strengthen the argument that they alone *should* be the sole decision-makers in matters of individual privacy.

DATABASES AND INDIVIDUAL PRIVACY

Here I'm taking a pragmatic and perhaps paradoxical position. In a nutshell, I believe that far too many data about each of us are being collected by government and business, and they are often used in ways that harm rather than help us. But, *once the information has been collected, there is no particular reason that it shouldn't be used by the mass media.*

Ethically, I find myself in an ambiguous position on this question. It is analogous to using what lawyers call the "fruit of the poisoned tree" or answering affirmatively the question "is it ethical, in order to save lives or for other worthwhile purposes, to use data (such as medical data generated by the inhuman Nazi experiments) that were collected by someone else in shameful or inappropriate ways?"

Indeed, it may be that resentment over the *publication* of personal information will lead the public to protest its *collection*—if so, great! If this is sophistry, let's make the best of it.

Other than the government, the largest collectors of individual data probably are credit reporting firms. Their original purpose was to disseminate valid and reliable data received from merchants so that other merchants wouldn't be cheated and pass those costs on to all of us. Such firms have occasionally abused their responsibility by being careless and sloppy, and public outcry has led to remedial legislation: copies of records must now be made available to the citizen being examined, corrections must be made promptly, and limitations have been placed on the number of years that negative data may be used. The mass media are more like credit reporting bureaus than we may care to admit, often guilty of indiscriminate collection of data, sloppiness in reporting and editing, and unwillingness to admit error.

WHY THE MEDIA NEED DATABASE ACCESS

I discussed earlier the gathering (and publication) of birth dates. Here is an example of why they can be important to journalists: in December 2007, *The Seattle Times* published a multi-part series on how vulnerable people are exploited by financial service companies and others familiar with how "the system" works. A particular case in point was a 96-year-old woman who lost her home, approximately $2 million and nearly all her possessions. The reporter working on the story, Susan Kelleher, was bothered by what she called "a dissonant picture." Was there a pattern here, or was this an isolated case? Why would an older, established, even wealthy person take out subprime loans, and eventually lose her property? And she wasn't alone: testimony before Congress on the subprime loan debacle showed that there were many others in the same boat. These "weren't first-time buyers seeking the American Dream; they had refinanced their way out of it" (Fancher, 2007).

Although the federal government tracks mortgages by categories such as race, there was no single database that tracked them by age. So, the newspaper (with the aid of a specialist in database reporting) found a way to obtain such data. It focused on one lender (a major "player" in the subprime loan field) and went to the County Recorder's Office. It downloaded all 4,000 deeds of trust involving this lender over a five-year period, but that provided only each borrower's name, filing date, recording number and legal description. Then the researchers obtained addresses by linking the property parcel number to the property database. Finally, with names and addresses, they searched voter registration and driver's license databases to find birth dates from which to calculate age. As Cheryl Phillips, the editor who oversaw the data analysis, said, "There is no way that this story could be told without the dates of birth" (Fancher, 2007).

In other words, having dates of birth on records required for identification, even if they also have photographs or fingerprints, served the public interest in this case. The argument that age data are meaningless is pretty clearly refuted in this instance—even though the data might have been redundant for their original purpose of identification. But, as Fancher (2007) said in his column, "Efforts are under way in the courts and Legislature to exempt birth dates from public disclosure. Proponents of exemption argue that they are trying to prevent identity theft."

This story illustrates two valid public purposes, with conflicting views of what is in the public interest. Bearing in mind the "law of unintended consequences," on the one hand, there is a general public benefit in preserving personal privacy. On the other hand, there is a public interest in protecting a vulnerable subgroup: in this instance, those whose age makes it unlikely that they could recover from a home loan foreclosure caused by being cajoled—even swindled—into repeatedly refinancing with high-interest subprime loans.

Bearing in mind the history of journalistic oversight of government, and almost every government's oversight of its citizenry, it seems unlikely the ethic and the law of privacy will ever lend themselves to easy construction and reconciliation, with regard to databases as well as more generally.

PERSONAL DATA, THE GOVERNMENT, AND IMPERSONAL USES AND MISUSES

I'm certainly not arguing against the collection of personal data that normally are used only in *impersonal* ways. Most of these data are used only in the aggregate. A telephone company needs to know usage patterns, to staff and plan for new capacity. The decennial census and its supplements supply the United States with quantitative data that allow valid planning to take place, ameliorate problems, and tell Americans where we, as a nation, stand.

Even though these data are collected from individuals, until very recently strict procedural safeguards have prevented a pattern of misuse. We allow them to be collected because—as a collection—such data are extremely valuable to us. As Sir Francis Bacon said more than 400 years ago in his meditations on heresies, "knowledge is power." So, I support the collection and use of such data, from whence may come knowledge, and I hope that wisdom may evolve from that knowledge. However, there are dangers in collecting these data, particularly after their conversion from paper to digital form. Even though the data are aggregated, they often can be examined to determine individual behavior and characteristics.

Some "databases" have a long history. Every reporter or public relations practitioner has a file of telephone numbers of potential sources. Does putting them on a computer and sorting them somehow change their intent or effect and create an ethical dilemma? I don't think it does. If aggregated public data are used for public purposes, it doesn't matter whether or not we call them a "database." To a great extent, I follow the teleological approach—looking at consequences rather than duty—in deciding whether or not using a database is ethical.

If aggregated public data are used for public purposes, it doesn't matter whether or not we call them a "database."

But what about records of *individual* drug prescriptions, adoptions, video rentals, cashed checks or telephone calls—information that the individuals who are reflected in these data almost certainly have no intention of making widely public? The Web sites an individual has accessed may be even more sensitive. Such information obviously exists in databanks or in the sales records of various stores or service companies. Can we justify media (or government and business) access to them for any reason other than direct benefit to the customer, or is their very existence an unreasonable intrusion into the individual's privacy?

I believe we should try to keep such aggregated types of information private, even though I'm aware that, because these data exist and businesses have legitimate uses for them, it is likely that a hacker or an unscrupulous person with access would find it relatively easy to tease out knowledge of individuals status and habits. In 2008, some employees of (and contractors working for) the U.S. State Department were fired because, out of curiosity, they accessed the passport records of political, sports and show business personalities. That same year, a Los Angeles hospital clerk allowed her curiosity to get the better of her, and accessed the medical records of a number of celebrities. As one might expect, that information quickly appeared in the media. It is common to hear of the theft of laptop computers —some of which contain information that can be used for identity theft.

Individuals whose records appear in some databases have received a little protection. For example, a 1984 amendment to the Communications Act of 1934 (47 U.S.C. 551) now makes it necessary for cable companies to secure subscriber approval before distributing most personally identifiable data. A similar law affects information about the video movie rental habits of individuals. I'm sorry to have to say that both laws were passed because of fear that the media could not forgo the deliciousness of reporting such material.

On the other hand, the media are pikers compared to the government itself. Since 9/11, the mantra of "national security" has allowed the government to examine both the flow (from whom and to whom) and the content of any telecommunicated messages, with senders and receivers of these messages being none the wiser.

A major ethical concern is that the administration doesn't do all of this by itself. Although the National Security Agency (NSA), with its tremendous computer capacity, almost certainly is able to listen to or read all messages (telephone, text, data, e-mail) that enter the United States (even if their intended destinations are elsewhere in the world) some of this eavesdropping requires the quiet cooperation of software and telecommunications firms. Because of this, Canada, for instance, won't use carriers whose circuits pass through the United States to carry sensitive economic information. Microsoft has been supplying law enforcement agencies in the United States and other countries with free "thumb drive" devices (known as Computer Online Forensic Evidence Extractors) that, by merely being plugged into a USB port, can dramatically cut the time to gather digital evidence, decrypt passwords, and obtain data on Internet usage activity as well as other information (Romano, 2008).

Such technology—currently unavailable elsewhere—allows governmental agencies to learn what they want to learn from any computer, without seizing it physically. This, of course, makes their jobs tremendously easier. At the same time, millions of dollars worth of firewalls, anti-spyware, encryption and similar programs are being sold to individuals who value their privacy. Both the government and the software companies have well-rehearsed rationales to use whenever the public becomes aware of these windows into their electronic lives.

In addition, a number of telecommunications firms apparently have given governmental agencies trolling for data full access to everything that passes through their hands or servers—e-mails, telephone (including cell phone) records, and the like, without anyone telling the consumer. With its massive computer capabilities, NSA can pluck pertinent messages out of the telecommunicated data streams using key words, phrases or numbers, and can automatically extend this search to those in contact with their targets. "Full access" goes as far as physically connecting cables to National Security Agency computers or servers located in special rooms in telephone company technical centers.

After 9/11 and the passage of the USA PATRIOT Act of 2001, the Bush Administration apparently believed it had authority to eavesdrop without needing a judicial warrant. The FBI, in particular, has used (so far) hundreds of thousands of "National Security Letters" requiring third parties to provide access to all sorts of documents, such as hotel, airline, credit card, and other records including many involving individuals or organizations having little or nothing to do with national security.

The public became aware of these actions in 2007, and they were an issue in the 2008 election campaign. One problem with this sort of governmental activity, unlike the normal subpoena or judicial warrant process called for in the Constitution, was that the subject of an investigation wouldn't be told about it by the government. Moreover, the telephone company (or bank, under the misnamed "Bank Secrecy Act") weren't permitted to inform the person whose accounts were being reviewed, even though access to these records might have been successfully contested in court if the subject had known about the government's desire. Another, perhaps larger, problem is that the government has issued "general" warrants or National Security Letters affecting the lives—specifically, the privacy—of many people. For example, a quarter million visitors to Las Vegas on New Year's Eve a few years ago were affected when it was feared that some of them might be planning a disturbance or terrorist act—a fear raised by using "data mining" techniques rather than directing attention to individual suspects ("Spying on the home front," 2007).

It is particularly disturbing to note that privacy laws passed some years ago were aimed at preventing a governmentally controlled national database, but that technology and normal usage have passed them by. Such a database isn't needed, because business has conveniently made a tremendous amount of information on individuals available to government: the government merely taps into the data collected in the normal course of business by credit card companies, hotel chains, telecommunications companies and the like. Accordingly, the restraints on government use of databases adopted in the 1990s do not apply and a "national databank" is no longer hypothetical. In theory, it could remove our last vestiges of freedom from government supervision of our lives, finances, education, communications, travel, and health, but the data are being collected by compliant commercial firms and only the analysis and correlation of data are in government hands. That seems to be plenty.

Another often-overlooked aspect of this situation is that sometimes the records are incorrect or misleading. Because his name was similar to one on a government travel "watch list," even so well known a person as Senator Edward Kennedy found himself delayed and questioned at airports.

True, somewhere in the middle of the continuum of available data on individuals are records for which there may be narrow but justified public purposes: arrest records, tax returns, records of psychiatric interventions, license plate assignments, and the like. The police would be hard-pressed to do their jobs without such data. It can be argued that vital statistics, such as individual records of marriages, divorces, births, and deaths should be available to all—but here the question is whether they should be available only as summary statistics or as records pertaining to individuals. For example, for public health reasons, we may need to know how many people died of AIDS in our community last year, but it probably isn't necessary to know the cause of John Doe's death.

CURRENT PRACTICES

Today, almost every bit of information anyone could ask for (as long as it was generated in the past 40 years or so) is on a computer somewhere. Older records are being processed so that they, too, can be computerized. The networks or linkages between computers—the "information superhighway"—on a worldwide basis are so many that for most practical purposes they approach infinity. An endless array of data—financial, health, production and sales, school records, scientific information, news, real estate sales and valuations, personnel, pet licenses, utilities and thousands of other categories—are aggregated into accessible databases.

Some are restricted; it is unlikely that a utility, manufacturing, or service company will release its customer list to a potential competitor. Others are open to anyone with a few dollars or even just an Internet connection, including commercial services such as Lexis/Nexis and Google. Yet others, such as the catalog of a university library, and certain kinds of "directory data" beloved by direct mail marketers, often require special arrangements for access. Government data, once available only in rigid formats published by the U.S. Government Printing Office, are now often available in "raw" form online through the Internet, with politicians of both parties seeking acclaim for instituting this practice (Shribman, 1995) and a legion of analysts avid to see what might be teased from these data.

Data can show up online in more informal guises, as well, and often without any means of validating them. Are unedited and un-vouched-for data, such as that provided by

Wikipedia's volunteer contributors, valid and reliable? Might the electronic "morgue" of a newspaper be manipulated for political reasons somewhere along the road to becoming history? While the Internet has made all sorts of data available all the time, are there *any* ethical standards or practices that make it possible to have confidence in the information that threatens to overwhelm us?

Another new information-laden technology with negative implications for privacy is the almost ubiquitous surveillance camera. Cameras outside one's home or place of business preserve privacy for a few—but deny it to many. Police departments and others find it relatively easy to add thousands of private security cameras to their own surveillance networks because of the ease and cost efficiency with which they can use the Internet for this purpose, but this fails to provide security for the signal. In a rural, or even a suburban, area an individual's privacy can (possibly) be secured if one stays indoors and away from windows, from telephoto lenses, even those on aircraft and satellites. In a metropolis, instead of true privacy, we tend to accept anonymity as a substitute.

In other words, we can become almost invisible among the crowds of fellow workers and residents, until the ubiquitous surveillance cameras and facial-recognition software are brought into play. While it may not be thought of as "data," real-time information about our appearance, location, and behavior is a form of data that, when thought about, deserves privacy. Doesn't it?

Web sites are different only in degree, not in kind, from most other electronic communication, which all may be transmitting private information or misinformation—or may be using false identifications. All of them, for many years, have frequently been used by news gatherers, even though totalitarian states try to prevent listening to transmissions from other countries and there is a Federal Communications Commission regulation against using "ham" radio for news reporting in the United States, since it is intended only for experimentation and for communication between individuals. As is noted elsewhere (see Chapter 6), it is crucial to remember that *nothing* remains private once it's posted on the Internet—a point that is especially important in regard to social media or reporters' stories being sent back to the newsroom. The social media danger was illustrated all too well in 2010 by Facebook's unintentionally sending hundreds of private messages to the wrong recipients, due to a programming bug, and its conscious decision (later modified) to make much of its users' information broadly available online even if the users had previously asked that it be kept private. (In regard to Facebook and privacy in general, see Swartz, 2010.)

We are familiar with local and international broadcasting, intended to be heard or seen by everyone. But even signals intended only for a specific receiver—such as a cell phone, or aviation or police transmissions—may be heard by anyone with the readily available (although sometimes illegal) proper equipment. It is possible to intercept *any* radio transmission, even if it is those intended to be point-to-point rather than broadcast—for example, embarrassing cellular calls from or to politicians, errant spouses, business executives and even members of the British royal family. Any of these transmissions may include private information (or misinformation) and may be using false identification.

Encryption offers only minimal protection (the government wants to be able to intercept anything it hankers to intercept, so "back doors" are inserted in many encryption programs). Many companies and organizations have found to their sorrow that e-mail circuits are neither

It is possible to intercept *any* radio transmission

secure from tapping nor ephemeral: messages might be stored on any server that the e-mail packets pass through. The fact that a computer's output enters a telephone cable doesn't mean that part of the circuit won't be carried on radio—usually microwave or space satellite relays. Web sites are no different, which is why they are so easily "hacked."

Regardless of whether wire or radio is used, the ability of hackers to enter databases has been demonstrated many times. Such talents are made to order for reporters who believe that nothing should stand between them and the information they wish to acquire. This may not have been realized by the general public until the highly publicized pilfering of Tonya Harding's e-mail inbox during the 1994 Olympics, or Wikileaks' publication of State Department and other sensitive messages in 2010. The fallout from these unofficial leaks and even from televised crime entertainment programs—such as *Law & Order* or *NCIS*—have raised our awareness. So do the highly publicized instances of hackers breaking into databases, such as the mid-2009 breach that provided access to 130 million credit card records.

Every high school—and probably every newsroom—has a resident "technoid" or six capable of simple technical miracles with a pocket screwdriver and some non-commercial computer programs. Unless information is given a high level of encryption or physical protection, there is no circuit free from the possibility of someone looking into it. Unfortunately, this abridgement of privacy is not limited to online bulletin boards and databases. The unscrupulous reporter (or police officer, FBI agent, private detective, voyeur, or hobbyist) with a satellite dish and the proper receiving (and decryption) equipment may get sound and pictures as well as data from almost any location at any time.

Privacy laws are unlikely to stop privacy abridgements, just as they haven't stopped the use of radar detectors on the highway. Appropriate lines can be drawn—for example, a photographer cannot legally trespass on private property but can take a picture of private property from the public street. Similarly, a reporter can ethically make use of a computerized database that's available to the public, but should not hack past firewalls, encryption, and password protections to break into the files to isolate an individual's record amid the aggregated public data.

Obviously, advertisers and others wish to sell legal goods, services, and causes and, in our economic system, there should be few time-place-manner impediments to this. And if marketers are able to use databases to focus their sales efforts more narrowly, wouldn't those of us tired of too many poorly targeted sales messages actually benefit? Recorded sales messages tying up our telephones (too often, right at dinner time), the direct marketing advertising of goods and services by junk mail or, in recent decades, online (Musgrove, 2008), or many kinds of fundraising by political, social and environmental causes are only a few examples of what we might avoid, if we add the Web to the limitations of the "do not call" lists maintained by state and federal governmental agencies.

DATA PRIVACY: PAST, PRESENT, AND FUTURE

Are our new abilities to store, manipulate, and use data really so different from old ways of dealing with data? I don't think so. The public, and business, apparently have insatiable appetites for information under control and at one's fingertips. The biggest, most used, and most usable database is the ubiquitous telephone directory. Human society has watched the government's insatiable demand for data grow for thousands of years: the only reason Joseph and Mary were in Bethlehem when Jesus was born was because Caesar Augustus decreed that all the Roman world should be counted, listed, and taxed. Present-day governments also count and tax, but with more efficiency—and perhaps greater concern for their "security"—than formerly. For example, passports used to be little more than a letter from one country asking that another country be nice to the first's citizens, but have evolved into an exit permit as well as high-tech identification.

As economic interactions become global, there have been continuous increments in the collection of data by both governments and businesses. The modern computer merely has made things technologically easier for both to collect and process data.

During several administrations, government collected most of these data, relying on and fomenting fear to encourage the passage of bills such as the USA PATRIOT Act of 2001. In addition to such laws which, in an open legislative system, at least give fair warning, there also are less known executive branch tools, such as Presidential Orders, Department of Justice Opinions, and National Security Letters that often remove the few remaining legal safeguards against governmental misuse of data. The cozy relationship between some officials and some media reporters, which has always existed, tends to provide easier media access to such data. If the data are there, they will be used.

How they will be used by the media should be up to these users, rather than having a "one-size-fits-all" set of regulations that usually will be interpreted for political purposes. The arcane methods used by the legislative and executive branches to protect their own workings rarely if ever lead to ethical standards and practices that others (including the media) might employ to prevent abuse.

As late as the 1930s, it was possible for an individual in the United States to change his or her name and disappear. Today, a change of identity is almost impossible for a person without extraordinary and extra-legal resources. And yet we are more afraid of "identity theft" than ever before. Social Security numbers, originally restricted to Social Security and unemployment insurance purposes, soon were used everywhere from military serial numbers to drivers' licenses and student ID numbers. More recently, because of the dangers of "identity theft," different identification numbers, sometimes amplified by PINs or passwords, often have been employed in place of Social Security numbers. This practice leads to inconvenience and—if a given ID or password is used for several purposes—no improvement in "security."

Barely a quarter of a century after the setting for George Orwell's *1984*, paying with cash is suspect and credit card use may be traced anywhere in the world. Bank records are almost wide open to police or other government agencies. "Free citizens" in the United States must show a government-issued "photo ID" when taking a plane ride, even if paying with cash. U.S. citizens' pride in the "undefended" borders with their neighbors of Canada and Mexico surely has taken a hit with the requirement—in the name (if not the reality) of increased security—that even day trips, which used to be essentially "undocumented," now require a passport or other government-issued, presumably tamper-resistant, ID such as special "smart" drivers' licenses issued by border states that are packed with personal data.

The dogged rearguard fight in the UK against "smart card" IDs, packed with information the state might want to know ("Identity crisis," 1994) finally succeeded, at least temporarily, when the coalition government in power during 2010 scrapped the scheme and computers holding such data were literally smashed. This resistance was aided by the uproar in Parliament over a mid-2007 loss in intra-government mail of CDs containing millions of citizens' financial and other data. In the United States, the federal government recently passed a law requiring the "sovereign" states to issue driving licenses that are, in all but name, national identity documents of such a level that the fake IDs used for decades by underage drinkers to obtain alcohol may well become a relic of the past. With these and many other violations of the more than 200-year-old U.S. concepts of freedom, largely made economically practical through the development of computerized data collection and processing, it is no wonder that to the government—any government —the idea of privacy for its citizens is a joke.

If the government leads, and business is right up there with government, what reason do the media have for restraint—other than the ethics of its individual practitioners?

I'm in favor of making information available to the citizens who provide it, and who need it to make rational decisions about their own government, finances, and lives, but I'm not so naive as to think that government and business will feel like sharing data they have collected from the citizenry or have generated within the bureaucracy. For example, although almost all unclassified government data obtained through the expenditure of taxpayer dollars is public property, it has been turned over to private firms in the guise of privatization (a business subsidy that actually forces taxpayers to pay for the information twice!).

Many police departments jealously guard their exclusive access to rap sheets—records of individuals' previous arrests—and point to abuses in the use of addresses on driver's license records by both benign advertisers and predatory sexual stalkers. One of the most egregious abuses was Procter & Gamble's 1991 use of the courts to secure telephone records of some two million people in the Cincinnati area in an attempt to discover which of their employees had been leaking information to the press ("P&G Calls in the law to trace leaks," 1991). (We mentioned in Chapter 2 that there is no inherent right of the reporter to obtain and publish them.) A similar abuse occurred in 2007, when federal prosecutors attempted to make Amazon.com identify thousands of customers of an online used-book dealer who used Amazon Marketplace for his business, to enable prosecutors to use some of those customers as witnesses in a tax and fraud case. After a federal magistrate ruled that customers had a First Amendment right to keep their reading habits from the government, the government found another way to locate potential witnesses—merely have Amazon.com send letters to the customers directly, asking for volunteer witnesses (Foley, 2007).

JOURNALISM AND DATA PRIVACY

If a news organization or a bookseller were to use public access to a database, such as a list of library users, as a means for marketing itself, it might be considered mildly wrong both by library users and by commercial competitors, such as book vendors or magazine dealers. But one merely has to go online to see that similar acts are committed by all sorts of

most magazines consider their subscription lists to be little more than another commodity to sell.

organizations. There is no universal legal or ethical standard applied to online persuasion although most ISPs don't want to lose customers. Some people still are horrified to find that most magazines consider their subscription lists to be little more than another commodity to sell. Whether we like it or not, this is normal practice.

Examine the postal meter imprints and minor address or addressee variations on the direct mail you receive, and it becomes obvious that much of it originated in a database entry that was initiated by your order for some product, publication, or service. Sometimes these lists become very specialized—your name can be sold on the basis of geography (including the average income level of those living in your census tract or ZIP code area), industry in which you work, or college attended, and this barely scratches the surface of the ability of computers to sort data.

But what about use without abuse? Obviously, journalists and those in advertising and public relations should have normal (presumably, paid) access to all commercial databases—making it likely that reporters and persuasive communicators will have to add instruction in computerized information retrieval to their college or professional enrichment courses of study. If reporters Bernstein and Woodward, as recounted in their book *All the President's Men* (1974), could go through thousands of charge slips in the Library of Congress in their investigation of President Nixon's cover-up of the Watergate break-in, why shouldn't reporters use the computerized equivalent today? The media should continue their fight to have access to public records (or available commercial data) in convenient form, that is, direct access to the computerized database and the software to open and manipulate it, whether the database is online, on magnetic tape or preserved in some other electronic storage medium (Reporters Committee for Freedom of the Press).

Such access troubles some government agencies—those which claim that providing the data in convenient form (together with the often patented software that makes it possible to use the data) is too time-consuming, disruptive, expensive, or troublesome. So far, while there may be some truth to this side of the argument (although providing access to paper copies also may be time- consuming, disruptive, expensive, or troublesome, but of similar public value), it also seems to be driven by a disinclination to have anyone from outside rummaging in the files. "Data mining" is thus often restricted to government and those firms that collect the data. This is analogous to the prohibition against possession of pens and pencils when reviewing paper files—a fear that computer access might make it easy for an unscrupulous person to make changes in the files themselves. Passwords and "read only" restrictions are too easily circumvented; this fear is justified.

On a more mundane level, some agencies (or private holders of these kinds of data) might take financial advantage of the needs of journalists, scholars and other researchers, and supply access only at a very high monetary cost to the inquirer. Private firms also often consider information a commodity, and have it for sale. More than one such firm advertises that it can supply, for a fixed price, all sorts of financial and other information about almost any individual. Information available includes employer, salary, pension, stock options, bank accounts, telephones, credit card account numbers and limits, home ownership and mortgage details, and the like (McConnell, 1994).

For the merely curious, as well as for those who have a specific reason for obtaining such data, at least one online service has exhibited its services—personal demographics, past and present addresses, property, bankruptcies, liens and judgments, criminal histories, driving histories, phone numbers, neighbors, relatives, assets and more—at an RTNDA convention. Reporters should abjure such often unreliable (and even illegally obtained) data. They should also fight the greed shown by both commercial and governmental agencies (including the FBI). It is likely that the latter group uses its legal right to recoup costs for commercial use of their data as a means of circumventing the Freedom of Information Act (5 U.S.C. 552) by raising prices for access and copying so high as to discourage prospective users.

This leads to another series of questions: is it wrong for a reporter to tap into a non-public database? The answer depends on whether access to the database is or should be restricted. But who decides this? Hmmm. If one favors personal privacy and property rights as paramount, then the database *should* be restricted, and this might be considered a categorical imperative. On the other hand, a utilitarian approach would ask whether more people would benefit from seeing what is in the database. And using Rawls's impartial distributive justice principles (the "veil of ignorance") might require one to determine the weaker party in any given situation.

The news business is a business. But taking anything—including information—from another person is theft. There are laws restricting hacking into computerized memories, and reporters are subject to these laws. Just as it is possible to prosecute for theft a reporter who, when invited into a home to interview its residents, steals a photograph that might be used to illustrate the story, so might criminal or civil prosecution be initiated against a reporter who takes improper advantage of access to a computer databank. No special law is necessary.

A laudable and common—but alas, not universal—journalistic practice is to focus on a story of significance to the audience. This tends to reduce the likelihood of merely conducting a dragnet for gossip with which to libel unwitting subjects or titillate others. For example, in writing a story about a political campaigner, one shouldn't use journalistic access to computerized data as an excuse to drag out dirt that can be smeared over others who happen to be in the same database. Indeed, such a use may be tantamount to blackmail, and over the years unscrupulous columnists and reporters actually have demanded money to keep names out of the paper or off the air.

By the same token, medical records of illnesses that could have no effect on a political candidate's ability to serve in office are hardly appropriate to air or publish unless voluntarily released by the subject. In the United States, the onus caused by any knowledge of contact with the mental health system can destroy a candidate, but the willingness of a candidate to get professional mental health help in the past is unlikely to help us predict her or his future behavior. Is knowledge of a candidate's elementary school grades or family finances before entering public life going to help the electorate make its decisions?

For another example, the public needs to know how well its tax laws are working, and a newspaper's analysis of the proportion of income paid by the wealthiest individuals would be instructive. But is it necessary to know the names of the rich individuals in order to instruct our representatives to amend the tax law? What about corporate taxes? After all, corporations are "persons" only by virtue of a legal fiction, although the U.S. Supreme Court gave them "political speech" rights in 2010 in the *Citizens United* decision. Suppose the argument is made that publicizing such corporate data would adversely affect the business climate in your state, thus reducing economic growth? Your answer may well depend on whether you choose to follow a Kantian "tell the truth no matter what" rule, or take a utilitarian approach that says the greater number will benefit from a lack of openness—or follow one of the other ethicists available for guidance.

CONCLUSION

If the public interest—not merely "what the public is interested in"—is met by analyzing databases, then the practice is benign, at worst. If care is taken, as I argued in Chapter 3, to be fair to all—particularly the audience—then such practices are beneficial, and there is certainly no need for special efforts aimed at achieving informational privacy.

As an individual, I fight for my personal privacy whenever I can, to the annoyance of many telemarketers and bureaucrats. But I believe in the benefits of aggregated data such as the Census, and cooperate fully with it. I hope that others will do the same because, while individual privacy is an increasingly rare condition in a world that is doubling its population every few decades, we need to have an up-to-date picture of the entire population.

On the other hand, it is legitimate for media to distinguish between private and public lives. If I were voluntarily in the public eye as a candidate, business leader, or entertainer, I would legitimately be subject to scrutiny and should expect the media to examine the databases that contain information on my public persona, though perhaps not my private life. In an interdependent society, our desire for privacy probably should not extend to the point where nobody can reach us, nobody can know anything about us—whether the information is used for our benefit, or for theirs, or for both.

How can the media take warning from the discussion early in this chapter about what happened to the credit reporting companies with respect to data privacy? The answer is simple and obvious: the news media must maintain the same high ethical standards of truth, fairness, and accuracy in dealing with databanks that they should maintain elsewhere. I hold that this is (or should be) normal practice in the newsroom, the sales department, and the marketing office, not an extraordinary special effort, or one requiring a computer expert. And applying these criteria doesn't require a computer expert.

> Using data in ways that were unintended at their collection is not necessarily an ethical problem,

This is easy for me to say, but hard for the working journalist to resist temptation and accomplish. Yet if our collective reputation, credibility and freedom are to be preserved, it must be done. We can't turn back the clock. Databases are here to stay. Using data in ways that were unintended at their collection is not necessarily an ethical problem, although its effect on individuals may be. Although we can—and should—work to limit the seemingly insatiable informational appetites of government and business, as long as these databases exist I maintain that journalists should have both the ethical and the legal right to use data from them *for the public's benefit*. Few news media make use of existing data, such as that in census reports (an exception is *The New York Times*), to generate news stories that will serve the public interest. They should. This utilitarian approach is difficult to separate from merely satisfying the public's curiosity about its neighbors, but it is a much more defensible goal.

KEY POINTS

■ The news media should go no further than would the average person in obtaining information about rumor, gossip and scandal.

■ *Nothing* remains private once it's posted on the Internet, which is especially important in regard to social media or reporters' stories being sent back to the newsroom.

■ Government and business are collecting too much data about each of us and are using it in ways that often harm us. But once the information has been collected, there is no reason why the mass media shouldn't use it.

NEWTON: News, entertainment, and persuasion media, as well as other businesses and the government, must respect privacy concerns in collecting and using personal information in their databases.

In the film *Minority Report* (2002), lead character John Anderton enters a department store and is immediately greeted by voices calling his attention to products of particular interest to him. The implication is that marketers not only know Anderton's preferences but also are free to use that knowledge to encourage specific purchases.

Such marketing tactics are the least of Anderton's worries, however. In a complex exploration of free will versus determinism, psychics, called "pre-cogs," foresee a murder by Anderton. In this imagined world of 2054, pre-cogs sense future crimes, eye scanners confirm identities, and spider-like robots race through the cracks under doors to prop open the eyelids of those hiding from retinal identification scanning.

For better or worse—depending on whether one favors guarding private information for the sake of individual autonomy or using information to protect humans from one another—Anderton's world is not as futuristic as it may seem. Department stores such as Wal-Mart routinely use video surveillance cameras to track customer shopping patterns as well as to detect thievery. Biometric scanning of eyes, fingers and faces is moving toward replacing other, more easily faked, forms of identification. Harvard's Microrobotics Laboratory has developed a tiny fly-like robot its creator expects to "nimbly flit around obstacles and into places beyond human reach" for "rescue and reconnaissance operations" (Wood, 2008, para. 4).

MIT Media Lab's Sixth Sense device enables its wearer or user to search for, organize and display information about the user's environment in an instant. "An unrecognized person," for example, "might prompt the display to show their contact details" or other information (Eaton, 2009, para. 4). Furthermore, marketing spyware, which many of us unwittingly download while surfing the Internet, already compiles data about our interests and purchasing habits. Functional magnetic resonance imaging (fMRI) is starting to reveal how the inner workings of the brain—our most private space of all—respond to ads and other stimuli. In the hands of ethical individuals who respect privacy rights, these discoveries can improve human life. In the hands of the unethical, these discoveries can become harmful weapons.

The fact is that many of us willingly give information—totaling billions of bits—when using the Internet to purchase items or services: credit card numbers, home and work addresses and phone numbers, birth dates, numbers of various accounts, and sometimes, even Social Security numbers. And those are just the items that we—among the estimated 1.8 billion active (i.e., once a month or more) Internet users in 2010 (ClickZ, 2008)—knowingly convey.

In addition, public and private institutions, including governmental and health-related organizations, regularly gather information from us via paper forms, and then enter that information into computer databases. Although these institutions, as well as reliable Internet sites, assure us that our personal information is protected against misuse or inappropriate disclosure, reports of security breaches, warrantless searches and seizures, and stolen data are becoming alarmingly frequent. Cyber-thieves now can design e-mail spam that looks identical to trusted sites, thus luring unwary individuals into revealing personal account numbers. We know far too little about what some analysts call the Wild Wild West of cyberspace.

Legal scholar Daniel Solove puts it bluntly:

> Today we face new technological challenges. Many of the problems we currently encounter are created by the profound growth in the creation and use of digital dossiers . . . large organizations we know little about are producing digital dossiers about us. The dossiers capture a kind of digital person—a personality translated into digitized form, composed of records, data fragments, and bits of information. Our digital dossiers remain woefully insecure, at risk of being polluted by identity thieves or riddled with careless errors. And all the while, we are . . . constantly kept on the outside while important decisions about us are being made based on our dossiers.
>
> (Solove, 2004, p. 226)

I maintain a dual position on the collection and use of personal data by mass media and government. On the one hand, no form of media or government, or, for that matter, any other organization, is above using (or misusing) personal information as a means to any end it believes is justifiable—including convenience, or misplaced curiosity by individuals within those organizations. This means private individuals need protection to insure their personal information is indeed secure. On the other hand, media, government and other organizations at times need access to personal information in order to meet their social responsibilities. Thus, there are times when media and government rightfully *should* be able to obtain personal information about us.

The bottom line is that any entity—including the media and the government—that collects personal information about individuals is ethically bound and should be legally required to maintain the privacy of that information unless (1) directed by a court of law, because of the significance of the information to national security or to a criminal investigation, (2) the entity determines through careful examination of potential consequences that it is in the best interests of a person or community to use the information, perhaps even making it available to other entities, or (3) those individuals agree to release the information for specific uses.

That's a long way of saying, "It all depends . . ." It depends on a contradictory continuum of definitions and understandings about media, government, privacy and data. For starters, it depends on whether "mass media" are run by socially responsible professionals who respect individuals' right to privacy, or whether "mass media" are unscrupulous manipulators intent primarily on profiting from the use of personal information about individuals, or whether their motives fall somewhere in between. It depends on whether "government" refers to constitutionally defined powers that protect citizen rights or to totalitarian practices driven by fear and desire to control. It depends on whether "privacy" refers to an individual's right to lead a personal life known only to him or her so long as he or she doesn't cause harm to others, or to a concept that is so open to violation by pervasive electronic technologies that it is impossible to achieve in a 21st-century world. Finally, it depends on whether "data" are points on a scale that cannot be linked to individuals in ways that might bring them harm or embarrassment, or details of lives that only the individual who "owns" the data should know—like thoughts in one's own mind.

DEFINITIONS

I find definitions—shared meanings—helpful in clarifying basic points while keeping reasonably free of ideology. Some of the concepts in the topic sentence for this part of the chapter (e.g., media, mass media) are defined in the Glossary, while others are explained where they first appear.

Cyberspace includes the Internet and World Wide Web. In imagined form, cyberspace is an area our minds envision as a limitless expanse holding and exchanging information electronically. Another term, *infosphere*, is particularly useful. McDowell et al. (2008, p. 10), define it "as encompassing the overall universe of electronic communication and networking" and including "not only the actual connections that join diverse electronic media, but also the idea of a space 'out there' that one can enter" vicariously.

For the current discussion, I use the words *cyberspace* and *infosphere* interchangeably to refer to electronic information-friendly environments. We can access cyberspace with a variety of tools, ranging from desktop, laptop or notebook computers to iPods, cellular mobile phones, satellites and such relatively new devices as Amazon.com's (2008) Kindle, a portable, wireless reading device (and its competitors), which "lets you think of a book and get it in less than a minute."

It is important to define *government* broadly as a managing, political entity with the power to make, enforce and even disregard laws for a country or an area, because the Internet transcends political borders. It takes less than half a second to send a message to someone on the other side of the world (Internet Traffic Report, 2008), about as long as it takes the brain to perceive a stimulus and meaningfully organize the perception (Gazzaniga et al., 2002). Because 21st-century technologies make it easier for technically savvy global citizens to transcend the boundaries of material storage systems and even political states, devising globally binding policies that transcend borders becomes increasingly important to protecting both publics and individuals. Our discussion of data collection and use is so significant for exactly that reason: the ability to work as fast as one can think allows anyone, anywhere, with access to the Internet, to find information, much of which we do not even know is available electronically, about our personal lives.

Finally, I define *privacy* as being free from observation, intrusion or attention of others. Once again, however, this definition is but a starting point. An intrusion to one person— something as simple as a phone call—might be welcome to another. And privacy concerns shift with generations. As *New York Magazine* writer Emily Nussbaum (2007) writes, "As younger people reveal their private lives on the Internet, the older generation looks on with alarm and misapprehension not seen since the early days of rock and roll. The future belongs to the uninhibited."

> I define *privacy* as being free from observation, intrusion or attention of others. . . . however, this definition is but a starting point.

PRIVACY IN A DIGITAL AGE

From here, let's explore the proposition through a number of examples.

Personal Medical Information

A doctor, pharmacist or hospital needs to have access to up-to-date medical histories and records of individuals in order to provide appropriate health care. Is it ever appropriate for that information to be released without the individual's consent? Although medical practitioners routinely hand out forms detailing their care in handling your records, they also require you to sign forms giving them permission to release information to insurance companies and other health providers. That information goes from local files in your doctor's office to corporate databases in who-knows-where. Health providers at least should be legally required to encrypt private information, to strengthen security systems to prevent accidental disclosure and theft, and to maintain the privacy of personal information.

What happens if you have your DNA tested, and lab records contain information indicating you probably will die in your 50s of heart disease? Or that you have tested positive for a highly contagious disease? Should you have control over the information and the right to keep it known only to yourself? Or are these two cases different? Should the government have the right to know, if or when the condition might threaten others? Should a health insurance company or your employer have the right to know you are likely to develop an illness that will lead to long-term incapacitation?

In the past, such information was not available, so maintaining privacy through a policy like doctor–patient privilege worked fairly well. As the secrets of the body open to scientific reading, new policies must be developed, and our expectations regarding privacy shift dramatically. A utilitarian might argue that the good of society warrants revealing the illnesses of a few. In the realm of the body, however, the numbers reverse: the few are those whose health is excellent, leading to a long life free of illness; the many are most of us, who develop various maladies as we age. I favor Clifford Christians' (2005) universal ethic, which is grounded in the sacredness of human life. Basing medical privacy issues on that principle might focus new policies on protecting as many people as possible while also respecting the value of one person by providing appropriate care regardless of the kind of illness. In the case of the 2009 H1N1 "swine flu" scare, for example, individuals suspected of having the disease often were isolated and treated in order to protect the "many," but some media chose not to publicize the names of those individuals—thus protecting both the "many" and the "one."

Government Records

In order to run a country's agencies and institutions, even the most democratic government must maintain records to substantiate citizenship, birth, death, employment and taxes paid. When does the government cross the privacy line by collecting and using records of other information about private citizens? After the 9/11 attacks, the U.S. federal government increasingly sought easy access to personal information previously available only after court authorization, even while that same administration prohibited newspapers and television crews—in the name of privacy—from photographing or taping the coffins of U.S. military personnel killed in Iraq or Afghanistan.

In the first example, the government argued it was acting in the interest of national security to protect its citizens. Yet at the same time, its invasive policies violated the privacy rights of some U.S. citizens. Does protecting the many justify violating the rights of the few? A utilitarian would likely say "Yes." One who adheres to the categorical imperative would likely say "No."

In the second example, the government argued that publishing or broadcasting photographs of coffins of U.S. war dead threatened national security by lowering citizen and military morale, and furthermore, was disrespectful of the dead and their families' privacy. At the same time, prohibiting publication left U.S. citizens less aware of the human cost of the war and also made the deaths less visible to the public for whom the soldiers died. In this instance, the debate might well be between utilitarians and followers of John Rawls with their concern for protecting the weakest parties.

Does the second example relate to data privacy as well as to emotionally charged pictures? Yes. The names and "mug shot" photographs of military personnel killed in Iraq are made public, and then the names go into the gruesome total, or aggregated data, of those killed. In this example, *respect* becomes the pivotal concept. Is it more respectful to protect a family from the public eye or to acknowledge the death and invite shared mourning through public representation? If you favor the second alternative, consider what effects on the survivors would result from the actions of members of a fundamentalist church in Topeka, Kansas, who demonstrate outside the funerals of soldiers who had died in the Middle East—to protest U.S. tolerance of homosexuals. (The church members claim that the deaths are God's punishment.)

What should we do? In the *first* example, I believe that we should return to the practice of requiring court authorization based on evidence before invading a citizen's privacy. President Obama's administration balanced concerns in the *second* example by allowing the family to decide whether the return of their loved one's coffin should be open to media coverage. On the other hand, we might argue, as I do, that if someone dies in the act of fighting for the public good, that public not only has the *right* but also the *responsibility* to be aware of the death and to participate in acknowledging it. Here, an absolutist position might argue either way: always protect the family or always publish images documenting the death. Again, an Aristotelian and Confucian middle ground, as well as Christians' (2005) universal ethic, support the idea that both the family's private pain and the public's right to know can find respectful expression in ethically principled news media. A newspaper might adopt a policy against taking or publishing photographs that identify family members in the throes of grief on meeting the coffin of a son or daughter killed in battle. That same newspaper might also follow a policy that respecting the person who died, as well as the person's family, means publicly representing the death in some visual form, such as publishing a photograph of a funeral procession to the cemetery.

As for the third scenario, it was taken to court by a service member's family, angered by what it regarded as the Topeka church's disrespect to the individual involved. The legal conflict really boils down to Rawls's protection of the weakest party against the utilitarian interest in being able to protest a governmental policy. (The Supreme Court went even further in March, 2011, in a decision favoring the church. The Court used a rule-based approach in holding that the First Amendment protects even this kind of "hurtful" speech on public issues, but it also upheld the "time-place-manner" standards adopted by more than 40 states to limit protests at funerals in order to respect the grieving families—a dash of Rawls's philosophy to leaven the broader deontological approach.)

Individual Marketing and Other Personal Data

Keeping track of your purchases from an Internet supplier can help that supplier better serve you as a customer. Amazon.com, for example, regularly sends me e-mails, with my approval, about new publications related to books I have purchased from them in the past. The key is "my approval"; ethical companies maintain strict policies against selling information to other firms unless a customer or client has specifically indicated the company may do so.

Yet, without your awareness, Internet spyware can track your Internet surfing activities, and department store cameras can track your movements in order to discern buying patterns and plan marketing strategies accordingly. Even if you do not grant permission for a company to sell the data it has collected about your buying habits, the data still are considered an asset of the company.

In these cases, an ethical solution might be an absolutist stance: the marketer should always ask Internet users if information about them may be used in specific ways. Violators could be punished with significant monetary fines and denied access to Internet publication.

Social networking sites such as Facebook and Twitter are increasingly popular. Less concerned than previous generations about maintaining a particular public image, many young people reveal details about their personal lives that would have been embarrassing to previous generations: drinking at parties, relationship issues, intimate details of sex lives. Lulled into a false sense of security by the assumption that only their own friends access such personal sites, many have been surprised to learn that potential employers found ways to access the information as part of screening applicants.

Are the employers unethical for obtaining access to such sites? Or are those posting the information naive for thinking it does not become available beyond their peers? Should such sites be regulated to protect people from themselves? I would not go that far, but I do recommend increasing awareness through public education about the potential for information published on social network sites to get into the hands of entities beyond one's intended social group, sometimes with serious consequences.

More generally, Facebook itself in mid-2010 was trying to walk the challenging line between adequately safeguarding its members' privacy while also generating income from advertisers interested in using that wealth of personal data to reach specific types of potential customers (Swartz, 2010).

Aggregated versus Individual Data

John Michael Kittross has argued that data often are compiled into generalizable statistics and that using them is not only ethical but necessary for understanding our contemporary society. To an extent, I agree with him.

Here's where we go back to the fiction film *Minority Report*. This motion picture features characters with a talent for pre-cognition—the ability to witness crimes in their minds' eyes before the crimes actually occur. In teams of three, these "pre-cogs" communicate their visions to the authorities so potential perpetrators can be apprehended before the crimes take place. If one pre-cog's vision differs from the other two visions, the differing report becomes a "minority report" filed with the "majority report" but not acted upon. In this film, it is a hidden *minority* report that helps Anderton realize he has a choice about whether to commit a murder.

We don't (yet) have "pre-cogs," but the FBI and other agencies do have "profilers" who use data originally compiled for other reasons. So, what happens to the innocent person whose data fit a criminal "profile"? A person charged with a crime in the United States is "presumed innocent" until proven otherwise—yet publication of the charge alone can damage or even ruin a person's reputation. Might reputations also be damaged by publication of a profiler's report identifying an individual as someone who fits a negative or "dangerous" profile?

In social science and marketing research, people's lives often are translated into aggregates of data that in turn are used to support policy decisions. Yet people's lives are complex combinations of events, experiences, characteristics, feelings and thoughts—individualized data that are unique to each individual. In social science research it often is the individual whose characteristics do not "fit" the mainstream, or one characteristic that distinguishes a person or group from the mainstream, that truly informs scholars. Journalism, too, relies on unusual activities or people whose distinctiveness makes them newsworthy. For the purposes of our discussion, then, the aggregate can mask the truly significant—the uniqueness of one person, one group, one entity.

That's the problem with the utilitarian approach: who is looking out for the one who is in the minority or cannot voice his or her concern? Yet the aggregate also can protect or hide the one who dares to be different—or exclude him or her, making invisible the value of difference. My point is that aggregating data does not insure its ethical use. The individual can be lost within the aggregate—for good or bad. Christians' (2005) universal ethic, which respects both individual and collective rights, balances these concerns against the value of human life. As noted above, this ethic focuses on the sacredness of life, whether one or many,

Might reputations . . . be damaged by publication of a profiler's report identifying an individual as someone who fits a . . . "dangerous" profile?

which would argue for careful consideration of individual privacy, as well as careful concern for the "whole" that is made up of those individuals.

GUIDELINES FOR PROTECTING DATA PRIVACY

Public Awareness and Clear Policies

First, citizens should assume responsibility for knowing what laws do and do not prohibit or protect, and for thinking about ethics standards that go further. Although U.S. laws traditionally protect an individual's right to privacy, we have seen troublesome changes in those laws, particularly since September 11, 2001. Perhaps more troubling—yet less public an issue—is the paucity of regulations protecting the privacy of information in cyberspace. Individuals need to become aware of both situations in which their privacy is violated (often without their knowledge), and of the possibility for putting regulations in place where appropriate. Citizens should demand clear and open policies from government, health providers, technology providers, marketers, entertainment providers and journalists. A democracy can be only as effective as its citizens are responsible, aware and active.

Redefine Privacy

We need to define privacy in the context of the global information networks through which we now run society. This will be difficult and will require international cooperation. Idealistic? Yes. However, if we begin with one person, one network, one company, one government at a time, we can make progress. The alternative of continuing the status quo is not acceptable.

Here is a start on a redefinition. *Privacy is the right of an individual to keep thoughts and information to himself or herself.* An individual's right to privacy should be challenged only in those instances listed earlier: when (1) a court rules that it is pertinent to national security or a criminal investigation; (2) the individual and/or community interest in using the information outweighs any possible consequences; or (3) the individual agrees to the release. This policy needs to be vetted internationally with the goal of establishing global practices and systems for maintaining appropriate levels of privacy.

Design Protective Regulations

Entities dealing with private information must be encouraged or required to enact clear procedures for protecting that information and against its misuse. To be considered ethical, health-related organizations, as noted earlier, should encrypt all information, train data coders about privacy issues, and use firewalls to minimize potential for privacy violations and data theft by hackers. These procedures will not stop all violations, but just as locks, a burglar alarm, lights and security patrols can deter all but the most determined thieves, data protection procedures can make privacy violations more difficult. Giovannetti et al. (2008, p. 1) have developed a "cheat sensitive quantum protocol" that ensures "perfect data privacy" using quantum mechanics. As data management systems become more sophisticated, so must our fervor for developing privacy protections increase.

Develop Systems for Maintaining Accurate Information

Systems for correcting inaccurate data need to be developed and implemented as part of the social responsibility of communicating in a democracy. It is all too easy to spread false information that quickly becomes accepted as fact. Groups such as Snopes.com, which regularly checks on the accuracy of troubling stories distributed as e-mail spam, should become standard for all entities working with individuals' personal information. Just as we need to protect personal data from misuse, we also need to protect it from manipulation that can lead to misrepresentation. Perhaps a "quantum archive protocol" could be developed to track data and reconcile inaccuracies.

Strengthen Interrelationships and Oversight of Data Collecting Entities

We need to reinforce the democratic system of checks and balances among and between legislative bodies, the courts, the administration, the press, as well as other institutions such as the civil service, corporations, organizations and society in general. The not-for-profit sector, through such groundbreaking groups as the Electronic Frontier Foundation—an organization that seeks to protect civil liberties in the electronic sphere—should be regarded as essential to protecting the private and public spheres alike as a check on both government and corporate abuse of cyberspace.

The issues are more complex than protecting privacy; they also include protecting free speech and press. Balancing privacy rights against the right to free expression has never been easy. Consider the discussions in this chapter and elsewhere about publishing the name of a rape victim. In an environment that makes possible free, global expression, individual rights and responsibilities need to be balanced with community rights and responsibilities. When government and corporate entities have unfettered access to unfettered information, individual rights too often are violated.

ETHICS GUIDELINES

As we have discussed throughout this book, a number of principles from ethical theory can be helpful in sorting through these issues. In his seminal article about journalistic reporting and privacy, Louis Hodges succinctly summarizes issues:

> The moral right to privacy consists of the power to determine who may gain access to information about oneself. Individual human beings need some measure of privacy in order to develop a sense of self and to avoid manipulation by the state. Journalists who respect the privacy rights of those on whom they report should especially be careful not to intrude unduly when gathering information; in publishing they should be able to demonstrate a public need to know private information. Individual journalists should establish their own guidelines for reporting on the private lives of different categories of people in the news.
>
> (Hodges, 1994, p. 197)

"Individual human beings need some measure of privacy in order to develop a sense of self and to avoid manipulation"
—Louis W. Hodges

We can apply Hodges' conclusions more broadly to other forms of media publication and to government: Individuals need and deserve a degree of privacy; media and government should respect both privacy and "need to know" in terms of both gathering and using information; and all parties need to develop policies for protecting and using information in ways that are realistic for current and future electronic environments. Neither a utilitarian principle nor the categorical imperative suffice here. The wisdom of balancing the needs and rights of the "one" and the "many" was espoused by Aristotle and Confucius and beautifully articulated by Christians (2005):

> Media technologies are increasingly and dramatically global. Our work in media ethics should be commensurate with them. Individual autonomy has been the axis of classical theory. Universal human solidarity, its radical opposite, ought to be the centerpiece of ethics now.
>
> (Christians, 2005, p. 3)

We need not abandon concern for the individual person or local community in order to restructure our points of view and policies within the context of concern for humanity across the globe.

CONCLUSION

We live in a time in which many previous rules for ethical behavior regarding private information, and legal redress to insure the protection of private information, are inadequate. Are we going to accept an increasing tendency to operate as a collective at the expense of the individual? The often-contradictory continuum of legal, ethical, scholarly, commercial and personal understandings of the critical issues underscoring media, government, privacy and data deserves time, intelligent reflection and well-considered action.

Responsibility for protecting privacy correlates positively with protecting speech, press, religion, petition and assembly. There are times when the law, *in the name of ethics*, should specifically prevent unwarranted invasion of privacy or revelation of private information. There also are times when the law, *in the name of ethics*, should allow news media or the government to invade private domains and reveal private information. These issues have always been complicated. Now, in this critical era of shifting public concern about privacy, of ubiquitous technologies, and seemingly infinite storage and retrieval systems, the world needs carefully conceived and enacted regulations to balance effectively competing rights and responsibilities. As early as 1994, ethicist Jay Black wrote that "a sensitive balance must be struck between freedoms and responsibilities, and between unlimited and irresponsible access to and utilization of information" (1994, p. 134) in what he saw as an emerging electronic marketplace of both ideas and data. When Black wrote those words, few could conceive of the extent of 21st-century cyberspace. Similarly, few can now conceive of the extent to which the concept of privacy will change in this century.

Like so many issues in media ethics, it gets down to balancing an individual's right to privacy against the public's right to know. The problem now is that we no longer are talking about a relatively limited purview of the material world. We are talking about the seemingly boundless purview of cyberspace, an ephemeral universe into which we potentially reveal everything about everyone to everyone. Cyberspace environments such as Facebook and Second Life are more real than virtual to many individuals today. As Bivins and Newton assert, whatever we pursue in the virtual world (even if we think we're visiting it privately) inevitably affects us in the real world:

> By expanding our realities, we can move beyond who we are in the objective world, and we can use virtual experiences to inform the real in positive ways. With the careful reflection that leads to moral growth, as in a mythic hero quest, we can return from our virtual explorations to the real world more whole, unified, grounded in understanding gained through our journeys into a new state of consciousness, prepared to share our insights with others.
>
> (Bivins and Newton, 2003, p. 228)

Our "realities" now include the possibility for personal intrusion and revelation of a magnitude humans have never experienced. As we move seamlessly between the real worlds of our bodies and the electronic worlds of boundless data—both true and false, private and public—we need to pause and reflect on the effects of such travels on individual and collective identities and interactions.

We need new laws and policies such as the ones suggested in this chapter to help us move forward on solid ethical ground in this time of new media. We cannot allow the complexity of the challenges before us to deter us from working together as a global society—in the interests of individuals as well as communities—to develop workable systems to protect us from unwanted and unnecessary intrusions into our private lives. Meglena Kuneva, commissioner of consumer affairs for the European Union, recently convened a "consumer summit" to toughen policies protecting "privacy, transparency and control on the Internet." One result was that a number of online companies agreed "to cut the [length of] time they store personal data" (Euronews, 2009, para. 1 and 2).

At least it's a start.

KEY POINTS

- Media and government should respect both privacy and the "need to know" in gathering and using information in current and future electronic environments.
- When government or corporate entities have unfettered access to information, individual rights too often are violated in order to advance community rights.
- Clifford Christians' universal ethic, which respects both individual and collective rights, focuses on the sacredness of life, whether one or many; this argues for careful consideration of individual privacy as well as the needs of the "whole."

MERRILL: Commentary

John Michael Kittross and A. David Gordon present a lot of salient information and analysis in their controversial statements in this chapter. Julianne Newton has a separate perspective, focusing on individual and community concerns regarding data privacy. The mass communicator interested in this topic of privacy should be stimulated by their words, even if not convinced by a specific position. The main problem, of course, is that nobody really knows what *privacy* is. Especially for public figures (and what are they?). The person, "public" or not, who expects privacy is living in a fool's paradise.

If journalism would take privacy seriously, it would commit suicide.

Kittross maintains that the media themselves should determine the limits of privacy, whereas Gordon sees them as having failed in this—thereby needing more socially binding norms. Although our two authors have a thoughtful fling at this difficult topic, basic questions linger: What is privacy? Who has a right to it? What is the source of such a right? How would such a privacy right comport with the "people's right to know"? Is it in the public interest to know so much about other people's lives? Furthermore, when does a private person become a public figure, and why should it make any difference?

A basic question, largely unmentioned in discussions of this topic, is this: Do I really believe in a free press? Not really, and, of course, very few people do. Limiting a totally free press is at the very heart of media ethics, and if the media won't do it voluntarily, then some type of outside force must be brought to bear. So what we have here in this controversial duel is the simple, yet complex, question: who will manage media messages?

Clifford Christians (2005) is quoted as proposing that privacy rests on the assumption that media will be decent, fair, and will preserve personal dignity. So much for the concept of freedom. What Christians says sounds great, but a semantic hurricane is raging within it. And John Rawls is made to assert that the weakest party should be protected; that would be, of course, the private person and not the privacy-invading media. Just how this protection will be provided is still an open question. It's hard to protect weak parties when the press is free.

In general, media themselves determine when and how to focus attention on people, public and private. Broad and fuzzy guidelines do exist (such as not invading the sanctity of private homes), but such notions at best only moderate media behavior and at worst are completely ambiguous or meaningless (e.g., if you use a telephoto lens from a public road). The right of privacy immediately comes in conflict with the First Amendment's press freedom clause. And it also comes in conflict with the assumed right of the people to know. So as long as we honor a free press, the controversial topic of privacy will exist.

If broadcasters were to leave people alone, to generally ignore them, where would television be today? Television is, even more than the print media, a leech, sucking every possible drop of personal dignity from the principals in its stories. An exaggeration? Watch the talk shows, the Hollywood celebrities shows, the *Oprah* show and many of the lesser lights among the "people exposure" shows. People and all their human foibles are being held up for constant public gaze—warts and all, especially warts. Most of these people, by the way, are public figures only in the sense that they are presented *to the public* and—surprising as it may seem—a large proportion of participants *ask* to appear on these shows.

It is certainly true that most Americans today realize that they are fair game for the media if they, in any way, happen to get in the way of the sweeping media searchlight that constantly shifts around hoping to fall on someone caught in the unexpected grip of circumstance. Pity the poor mother who finds herself beside her wrecked car with her dead daughter lying beside her. Pity the parents of the soldier in Iraq whose body has been blown apart. Remember the pictures of the crumpled Mercedes in which Diana, Princess of Wales was killed? The frivolous, pitiful antics of Britney Spears? You can count on it. The cameras are there and they eagerly portray every detail. Do the people need to know such things? See such things? Will it help them be better citizens, more informed voters? Just what are the limits of the so-called right of privacy? Should there be limits on the so-called right to know?

I suppose a basic ethical question revolves around the degree of, and limits to, media exposure of people, and also the *need* for audience members to have access to such information. This may well be the "justification" for violations of this amorphous right of privacy: audience need. But it is doubtful that many mass communicators predicate their digging into people's lives on the question of *need to know*. Journalists, for example, see themselves as free agents in their determination of what is to be made public. After all, if you were to retain in the average daily newspaper only the news that the readers actually *need*, you could probably get it all on the front page.

The main question usually asked by mass communicators of themselves (if they ask themselves *any* questions) is: what do I want to present to the public? If *I* think it is proper, then it *is* appropriate. This is, indeed, an egocentric test, but it is generally used, and it is consistent with the whole theory of editorial self-determination—a basic and traditional American concept of press freedom or freedom of speech. But what about the *ethics* of such publishing or broadcasting? If this question is asked at all, it is easily rationalized away by the media person who is skilled at justifying any action taken. The *ethical question* is usually sacrificed in the hurry-and-scurry of everyday media work to the more immediate and tangible *pragmatic questions*. Will it work? Will it accomplish my goal? Or will it please some constituency, even a very callous one, a small one, or one with a need to have its prurient interest satisfied?

Goldfish may not mind being in a bowl, but people do. They do, on most occasions, desire privacy—and individually they seem to know what that means. The media, on the other hand, live off of depriving people of their privacy. The conflict is real, and it will continue to baffle the media and the courts. Perhaps it would be helpful for the media person to include in a kind of unstated footnote to every story *an explanation of the justifications for that story and the tactics used in getting it*. Actually, too many media people in the United States seem to see themselves as above the *moral law*, falling back on media rights and press freedom granted by the U.S. Constitution.

> Perhaps it would be helpful . . .to include in a kind of unstated footnote to every story *an explanation of the justifications for that story and the tactics used in getting it.*

Often the invasion of privacy is simply related to poor taste, especially in the use of pictures. Weeping parents, corpses beside the road, mutilated or starving children, suicidal people, couples involved in sexual intimacies. Recognizing full well that many will reply that "poor taste" is relative and therefore not an appropriate determinant for publishing or not publishing information, there is little doubt that most media people recognize poor taste when they see it. For economic or egoistic reasons, they simply desire to pass it on, to titillate, to entertain, to shock, to expose, to generate gossip, and to mock normal conventions. And their actions are contagious; other media follow suit, not to be outdone by their competitors.

As one of our contenders in this chapter noted, the revered journalistic tendency in the United States is for the media people themselves to determine when privacy is invaded. Certainly it is implied in press freedom. Both Gordon and Kittross, recognizing this freedom problem, take weak stabs at their favored position. Kittross is more forceful, perhaps, but Gordon gropes his way toward a more social ethics of public pressure on a too-often wayward press. But since ethics concerns freedom and voluntary decision-making, not coercive legalism, and media ethics pertains to the media voluntarily making these decisions, I would come down in a location nearer that of Kittross, although lurking in the back of my mind is a deep sympathy with Gordon's position.

As for the issues of data privacy engendered by computerized databases, this is a controversy that I don't feel strongly about one way or the other. Kittross and Julianne Newton have made their respective points and I am almost inclined to let it stand at that.

The reader may feel, as I do, that both of these authors submerge us with so much information and opinion that we are rather confused as to what is the central point. I see a lot of individual trees, but where is the forest?

Newton, to put it briefly, places the ethical imperative on both media and government (once the databases exist) and maintains that they must respect privacy concerns relative to the information. She does, however, note that in some situations, information from databases *should* be available to both media and government, to serve the common good. She also suggests the need for new laws to help clarify this troublesome topic in the postmodern information age. But in saying this, she is slipping away from ethics and over into the realm of law.

Kittross maintains that media (and, in particular, the government) need not be concerned about using personal data from databases, as long as it is used for public benefit, but that everyone should be concerned about data collection and abuse. Such a statement has a strong current of ethical challenge, but it is a general assertion that is short on semantic precision as to collection and abuse by others. As is so often the case with ethics issues, the devil is in the details.

I think that most people don't worry much about the use of personal information obtained by media from databases. Probably very few of them are concerned about preserving their informational privacy, a term that is alien to most people. What the term means, presumably, is keeping computer-held personal information under the control of the person who put it there, or restoring control to those to whom it pertains—perhaps especially if it was gathered without their knowledge. One position would respect the people's right to such informational privacy; the other sees little to be concerned about. I tend to side more with the latter view, although I admit that I am somewhat confused about basic definitional problems and, of course, the degree to which such privacy is invaded.

Undoubtedly Newton is correct in maintaining that electronic databases pose great temptations for mass communicators eager to obtain personal information for their stories. However, the question is just what data use constitutes an invasion of privacy; and, as we know, privacy is one of the most troublesome concepts facing the mass media worker. Kittross, taking a cautionary approach, bemoans the "misuse of data" by anyone or any

---

ethics concerns freedom and voluntary decision-making, not coercive legalism, and media ethics pertains to the media voluntarily making these decisions,

institution, and warns that the data amassed by business, and also used by government, have created a *de facto* national data bank despite laws intended to prevent one. An ominous Orwellian prospect!

Although Kittross finds himself in an ambiguous position on this issue, he makes a simple argument: "If the data are there," he says, "they will be used" by the media. But he also invokes a more utilitarian approach and supports the use of personal data when it is "in the public interest," believing that from it may come knowledge, with wisdom perhaps evolving from that knowledge.

After delving into many of the intricacies of databases and media temptations to use the data, both authors seem to have trouble coming to any firm conclusion as to the ethics of the matter. Newton is more legalistic and, indeed, pessimistic about media and data. Kittross is more sanguine in his approach to data privacy, saying that the answer is simple: news media must have high ethical standards of truth, fairness, and accuracy. But does this "simple answer" solve the problem? I doubt it. Cannot truth prove to be an invasion of privacy? Cannot accuracy? Now, as to fairness, there is the rub (as is discussed in Chapter 3). Perhaps this concept alone relates to the mass communicator's concern with ethics: Indeed, fairness may cancel out both truth and accuracy, both of which Kittross extols.

But it is doubtful that a concern for truth (and accuracy) will solve the problem of privacy invasion. Doesn't truth include the concept of thoroughness—of providing more than a partial story or one filled with gaps? Is a half-told story truthful even though it is accurate? Any reporter tapping into fact-filled databases is potentially filling in the gaps and adding to the truth of the story.

Kittross hedges his support of available databanks at the very end of his essay. He maintains that journalists should use them for the public's benefit, and not merely to satisfy the public's curiosity. This has a good, wholesome ring to it, but why should we not say this, then, about all journalistic reporting (as Kittross might well do)? Everyone knows that journalism supplies information that satisfies the public's curiosity all the time. Journalists have no qualms about using such material. So why should they feel differently about such information obtained from databases? Curiosity may feed the cat as well as killing him.

Here we have the difficult clash of professional (legalistic) reportorial integrity with a more teleologically based ethical position. One key issue here is whether there should be limits on how much access reporters (and marketers) should have to the vast contents of databases and, if so, who should set them? A second is whether there should be limits on the use of information from computerized databases and how those limits should be set. Finally, should mass communicators report truthfully and fully information available to them, or should they ignore or tamper with the facts available because of some consideration of possible consequences? Those are basically the questions we are left with.

REFERENCES AND RELATED READINGS

Amazon.com (2008). "Kindle: Amazon's revolutionary wireless reading device." Retrieved from www.amazon.com/ (May 18, 2008).

Anderson, Jon. (1979). "People's five big years of all the faces that are fit to print." *Chicago Tribune*, March 6, sec. 2, pp. 1–2.

Auletta, Ken. (1994). "Under the wire." *The New Yorker*, January 17, pp. 49–53.

Bates, Stephen. (1994). "Who is the journalist's client?" *Media Ethics* 7(1), p. 3.

Benedict, Helen. (1992). *Virgin or Vamp: How the Press Covers Sex Crimes*. New York: Oxford University Press.

Bernstein, Carl, and Bob Woodward. (1974). *All the President's Men*. New York: Simon & Schuster.

Bertrand, Claude-Jean. (1993). "Media ethics in Europe: Media accountability systems." *Media Ethics* 6(1), pp. 7–9.

——. (2000). *Media Ethics and Accountability Systems*. Edison, NJ: Transaction.

Bivins, Tom, and Julianne H. Newton. (2003). "The real, the virtual and the moral: Ethics at the intersection of consciousness." *Journal of Mass Media Ethics* 18(3–4), pp. 213–229.

Black, Jay. (1994). "Areopagitica in the Information Age." *Journal of Mass Media Ethics* 9(3), pp. 131–134.

Bok, Sissela. (1982). *Secrets: On the Ethics of Concealment and Revelation*. New York: Pantheon.

Branscomb, Anne Wells. (1994). *Who Owns Information? From Privacy to Public Access*. New York: Basic Books.

"ChoicePoint sifting through customers after security breach." (2005). Associated Press story in the Eau Claire, WI *Leader-Telegram*, February 22, p. 6C.

Christians, Clifford G. (2005). "Ethical theory in communications research." *Journalism Studies* 6(1), pp. 3–14.

Christians, Clifford G., Mark Fackler, Kathy Brittain McKee, Peggy J. Kreshel, and Robert H. Woods, Jr. (2009). *Media Ethics: Cases and Moral Reasoning*, 8th ed. Boston, MA: Allyn & Bacon.

ClickZ. (2008). "Stats – Web Worldwide." Retrieved from www.clickz.com/showPage.html?page=stats/web_worldwide (May 18, 2008).

Cox Broadcasting Corp. v. *Cohn*, 420 U.S. 469 (1975).

"Credit problems prompt stricter security measures." (2006). Associated Press story in the Eau Claire, WI *Leader-Telegram*, February 24, p. 3C.

de Moraes, Lisa. (2008). "As scripts run out, reality kicks in." *The Washington Post*, January 7, p. C01. Retrieved from www.washingtonpost.com/wp-dyn/content/article/2008/01/06AR2008010601163.html?sid+ST2008010700877&sub+AR.

Denniston, Lyle. (1994). "Going too far with the hidden camera?" *American Journalism Review*, April, p. 54.

Eaton, Kit. (2009). "MIT's sixth sense machine makes reality better." *Fast Company*, March 23. Retrieved from www.fastcompany.com/blog/kit-eaton/technomix/mits-sixth-sense-machine-makes-reality-better (April 6, 2009).

Electronic Frontier Foundation. (2008). Web site at www.eff.org/ (January 30, 2008).

Elliott, Deni. (1997). "Journalists' con games can backfire." *Montana Journalism Review* 26, pp. 3–6.

Ernst, Morris L., and Alan U. Schwartz. (1962). *Privacy: The Right to Be Let Alone*. New York: Macmillan.

Euronews (2009). "Internet companies warned over privacy." Euronews, March 31. Retrieved from www.euronews.net/2009/03/31/internet-companies-warned-over-privacy/ (April 7, 2009).

Fancher, Michael R. (2007). "Inside The Times: Investigation reveals exploitation of vulnerable." *The Seattle Times*, December 2, p. A-25.

Foley, Ryan J. (AP). (2007). "U.S. withdraws subpoena seeking Amazon identities." *The Seattle Times*, November 28, pp. C1-2.

Gardner, Howard, Mihaly Csikszentmihalyi, and William Damon. (2001). *Good Work: When Excellence and Ethics Meet* (with a new Afterword by the authors). New York: Basic Books.

Gazzaniga, Michael, Richard B. Ivry, and George R. Mangun. (2002). *Cognitive Neuroscience: The Biology of the Mind*, 2nd ed. New York: Norton.

Giovannetti, Vittorio, Seth Lloyd, and Lorenzo Maccone. (2008). "Quantum private queries." *Physical Review Letters* 100(23), pp. 230502, 1–4.

Hart, Jack, and Janis Johnson. (1979). "Fire storm in Missoula: A clash between the public's right to know and a family's need for privacy." *Quill*, May, pp. 19–24.

Hodges, Louis. (1994). "The journalist and privacy." *Journal of Mass Media Ethics*, 9(4), pp.197–212.

Howell, Deborah. (2006). "Was it unethical to take pictures of grieving Amish?" Eau Claire, WI *Leader-Telegram*, October 17, p. 7A (distributed by the L.A. Times-Washington Post News Service).

howstuffworks. (2009). "How much water is there on Earth?" howstuffworks.com. Retrieved from www.howstuffworks.com/question157.htm (July 17, 2009).

Hyde v. *City of Columbia*, 637 S.W.2d 251 (Mo., 1982), cert. den., 459 U.S. 1226 (1983).

"Identity crisis." (1994). Editorial. *The Times* (London), October 14, p. 21.

Internet Traffic Report. (2008). *Internet Traffic Report*. Retrieved from www.internettrafficreport.com/ (May 18, 2008).

Lambeth, Edmund B. (1992). *Committed Journalism: An Ethic for the Profession*, 2nd ed. Bloomington and Indianapolis, IN: Indiana University Press.

Landers, Ann. (1994). "Mourning mother resents TV news." *The Boston Globe*, October 17, p. 36.

McConnell, Sara. (1994). "No financial secrets are safe from prying eyes." *The Times* (London), October 15, p. 34.

McDowell, Stephen D., Phillip E. Steinberg, and Tami K. Tomasello. (2008). *Managing the Infosphere: Governance, Technology, and Cultural Practice in Motion*. Philadelphia, PA: Temple University Press.

Media Ethics. (1997). 8(2). Includes seven articles on the *Food Lion* case.

Menn, Joseph, and Jessica Guynn. (2008) "YouTube ordered to turn over records on users." *Los Angeles Times* story in *The Seattle Times*, July 4, pp. D1 and D2.

Miller, Arthur. (1971). *The Assault on Privacy: Computers, Data Banks, and Dossiers*. Ann Arbor, MI: University of Michigan Press.

Musgrove, Mike. (2008). "Internet spam turns 30: Few likely to celebrate." *The Seattle Times*, May 3, p. B2. (Originally published in *The Washington Post*.)

Newton, Julianne H. (2008). "Visual representation of people and information: Translating lives into numbers, words and images as research data." In Donna Mertens and Pauline Ginsberg, eds., *Handbook of Social Science Research Ethics*. Thousand Oaks, CA: Sage, pp. 353–372.

Nussbaum, Emily. (2007). "Say everything." *New York Magazine*, February 12. Retrieved from http://nymag.com/news/features/27341/ (April 6, 2009).

"P&G calls in the law to trace leaks." (1991). *The News Media and the Law* 15(4), pp. 2–3.

Parent, W. A. (1992). "Privacy, morality and the law." In Elliott D. Cohen, ed., *Philosophical Issues in Journalism*. New York: Oxford University Press, pp. 92–109.

Paul, Ellen Frankel, Fred D. Miller, Jr., and Jeffrey Paul, eds. (2000). *The Right to Privacy*. Cambridge, UK: Cambridge University Press.

Priest, Dana. (2008). "Secrecy and the media: A view from the trenches." Ann Devroy Memorial Forum lecture, University of Wisconsin-Eau Claire, April 24.

Reporters Committee for Freedom of the Press. (no date) "Access to Electronic records." A "guide to reporting on state and local government in the computer age," published periodically, sometimes as part of *The News Media and The Law*.

Richards, Robert D., and Clay Calvert. (2007). "The ethics of exposing sexual affairs: An inside look at the 'flynting' of politicians." *Media Ethics* 19(1), pp. 11, 25.

Romano, Benjamin J. (2008). "Microsoft helping at cyberscene of crime." *The Seattle Times*, April 29, pp. E1–2.

Schwartz, Rachael E. (1997). "Prior restraints and the First Amendment: From press licensing to software export licensing." *Media Ethics* 9(2), pp. 6, 16–19.

Scott, Sandra Davidson. (1993). "Blood money: When media expose others to risk of bodily harm." Paper presented at the annual convention of the Association for Education in Journalism and Mass Communication, Kansas City, MO, August 11–14.

Shribman, David M. (1995). "The odd trio: The Tofflers, Gingrich look to crest on the third wave." *The Boston Globe*, January 23, pp. 1, 4.

Sill, Melanie. (2007). "N&O's decision to identify accuser was made with care." *The News & Observer*, Raleigh, NC, April 12. Retrieved from www.newsobserver.com/1185/story/563049.html.

Smith, Jeffery A. (2008). "Moral guardians and the origins of the right to privacy." *Journalism and Communication Monographs* 10, Spring, pp. 63–110.

Solove, Daniel J. (2004). *The Digital Person: Technology and Privacy in the Information Age.* New York: New York University Press.

——. (2007). *The Future of Reputation: Gossip, Rumor, and Privacy on the Internet.* New Haven, CT: Yale University Press.

Solove, Daniel J., Marc Rotenberg, and Paul M. Schwartz. (2006). *Privacy, Information, and Technology.* New York: Aspen.

"Spying on the home front." (2007) *Frontline*, aired November 27 over PBS.

"Supply and demand." (2008). *Columbia Journalism Review*, January–February, p. 4.

Sutter, John D. (2009). "Governments trying to reel in 'ocean sprawl'." July 15. CNN.com/technology. Retrieved from www.cnn.com/2009/TECH/science/07/15/ocean.planning/index.html (July 17, 2009).

Swartz, Jon. (2010). "At Facebook, it's privacy vs. profit." *USA Today*, June 16, pp. 1B and 2B.

This American Life. (2007). Produced by WBEZ (Chicago) and Public Radio International. December 1.

"Tighter security urged after states' breaches." (2008). Associated Press story in the Eau Claire, WI *Leader-Telegram*, April 29, pp. 1A and 2A.

Warren, Samuel D., and Louis D. Brandeis. (1890). "The right to privacy." *Harvard Law Review* 4(5), pp. 193–220.

Wilkins, Lee. (1994). "Journalists and the character of public officials/figures." *Journal of Mass Media Ethics* 9(3), pp. 157–168.

Wise, J. (2007). "This is your brain . . . This is your brain on an fMRI scan." *Popular Mechanics*, November, pp. 64–70.

Witcover, Jules. (1998). "Where we went wrong." *Columbia Journalism Review*, March–April, pp. 18–25.

Wood, Robert. (2008). "Fly, robot, fly." *IEEE Spectrum Online*, March. Retrieved from http://spectrum.ieee.org/mar08/6017 (April 6, 2008).

Chapter 11

The Ethics of Persuasive Communication

THE mass media in contemporary capitalistic societies are supported mainly by commercial advertising. The major exceptions in the United States are film, much cable television, books, and some magazines. This is so common and so well accepted that the few exceptions, such as *Consumer Reports* magazine, are noteworthy. Even public broadcasting, with its commercial underwriting and on-air "begathons," often seems similar to commercial stations and their paid ads.

As advertising and public relations have begun to overlap increasingly under the "strategic communication" umbrella, concerns about ethics in both fields—particularly in regard to truth-telling—have been raised more frequently than in earlier decades. Some people would argue that advertising or public relations ethics are oxymorons. Others argue strongly that advertising and PR practitioners should have no problems adhering to "appropriate" ethical standards. But even in that camp, there is disagreement on how to spell out what is meant by "appropriate."

The key point here is that advertising's goals differ greatly from those of the media that aim to present news and information, or offer entertainment, to the public. And PR presents information only as part of its efforts to manipulate public opinion, which differentiates it from the news media. Answers to the question of whether advertising and PR operate ethically must be sought within the context of what they set out to do and the roles they play in the U.S. media and economic systems. And their standards of ethics must be evaluated in light of those factors.

This doesn't mean that persuasive communicators shouldn't be socially responsible in the messages they bring to the public, and in how they convey those messages. But definitions of "social responsibility" can vary widely, depending on one's perspective. In the advertising area, there is also a fine line between standards of advertising acceptability and outright censorship. Keep in mind, too, that although we are referring here mainly to persuasive communication about products or services, the advertising of ideas, or of political candidates, are areas that also raise many important ethical issues. So does the prominent placement of products in films and television programs. (This issue is discussed further in Chapter 12.)

In the discussion that follows, Peter Gade and David Gordon agree that there are some ethical standards that certainly should apply to persuasive communication. But they disagree as to what those standards should be. Gordon argues that truth is not an appropriate ethical norm to apply to advertising in particular, and Gade maintains that honesty and a lack of deception or duplicity should be important ethical concerns for advertisers and public relations practitioners.

GADE: Advertising and public relations, no less than news, should be held to standards of truthfulness, which is to say they should not be intentionally deceitful.

David Gordon and I agree that persuasive communication usually is an attempt to emphasize the appealing aspects of a product, an idea, an image or an organization, and for these reasons persuasive communication is often filled with "opinions" and puffery rather than facts. Suggesting these opinions must be the "truth" is problematic, as the Federal Trade Commission and Supreme Court have wrestled with this issue and determined the truth of an opinion cannot always be demonstrated. But this view seems to me to focus on issues of law (what *must* be done or not done) while neglecting issues of ethics (what *should* be done or not done). As the examples in this chapter will show, there is much room for ethical thinking in regard to persuasive communication, and telling the truth is more complex (and important) than it appears.

Ethicist Sissela Bok (1978), in her thoughtful and provocative book *Lying*, contends that telling the entire truth about anything is an unreasonable expectation (people don't know the "whole truth": the totality of facts, relevant information and background are beyond their grasp), but she emphasizes the ethical approach is to be "truthful." To Bok, being truthful means avoiding intentional deception, which is to mislead purposely and to make others believe what we ourselves know not be to true. She defines a lie as a statement that is an "intentionally deceptive message" (Bok, p. 13), and this deceit can have important consequences on those being deceived. "For them, to be given false information about important choices in their lives is to be rendered powerless. For them, their very autonomy may be at stake" (p. xvii).

Bok's method of defining lying by its motives (intentional deception) is very close to how scholars have distinguished propaganda from other forms of persuasive communication. At first glance, it appears a bit harsh to lump advertising, public relations and integrated marketing—all widely practiced and generally accepted forms of mass communication—with propaganda. However, the areas of overlap are probably more than most of us are aware, and the distinctions between persuasive communication and propaganda are key ethical considerations.

Using the mass media as a tool for propaganda has long held a negative connotation, and for good reason. Propaganda tries to manipulate the audience in a manner that benefits the source of the propaganda at the expense of the audience. Harold Lasswell, a social science pioneer who wrote his doctoral dissertation on the effects of propaganda in World War I, later defined propaganda as "the technique of influencing human action by the manipulation of representations. These representations may take the spoken, written, pictorial or musical form" (Lasswell, 1937, p. 521). Lasswell concluded that both advertising and publicity fall under the rubric of propaganda. Today, most professionals and scholars tend to differentiate persuasive communication from the negative connotation of propaganda, offering these distinctions (Merrill, 1997; Severin and Tankard, 2001):

- Persuasive communication provides *mutual benefit* for the source and receiver (public). Propaganda, by definition, is focused on creating a benefit for the source, but no apparent benefit for the receiver.
- Unlike other forms of persuasive communication, the propagandist is *manipulating the audience/public as a means for achieving the propagandist's ends* (goals).
- The propagandist is *deceitful*, attempting to conceal from the audience the nature of the propagandist's goals.

These distinctions are important in view of recent developments in strategic communication that make persuasive techniques more difficult for the public to identify. In the sea of information that media make available to the public, even the most discerning citizens have a hard time knowing when they are being subjected to mediated messages that attempt to get them to think and act in ways that probably aren't in their best interests.

An important development is that the forms of persuasive communication are merging, becoming more intertwined, and the lines that distinguish the practices are becoming less clear. Advertising has always been understood as an effort to sell something—products, ideas, lifestyles—and contribute to the revenue streams of private companies. Marketing is related to advertising, or it is more precise to say that advertising is a form of marketing. In the Internet Age, marketers are rediscovering the value of public relations as a marketing tool, with efforts targeted at positioning and branding products, as well as promoting images and ideas (Bush, 2006). Some of these efforts include attempts to influence news content, blurring further the distinctions between news that is determined by the norms of journalism and advocacy or persuasive content that is created, produced and packaged by private organizations, corporations, special interest groups, or government officials.

This intertwining of persuasive practices, and developments such as the additional media tools available to communicators, make apparent the need for a renewed debate about ethical practices and the impact of persuasive communication on the individual and society. One thing is certain: the debate would be much less contentious if persuasive communicators were more straightforward with the public, willing to disclose their attempts to influence and their motivations for doing so. In a word, to be *truthful.* Doing so not only would clarify the murky ethical waters associated with many contemporary persuasive practices, but also would assist the public to distinguish between ethical persuasive messages and pernicious propaganda.

ADVERTISING: ITS VALUE, IMPACT, STRATEGIES

Americans have long had a love-hate relationship with advertising. People admire its creativeness, originality and reflections of U.S. cultural values. Advertising informs us of the products and services that are in the marketplace, it humors us, and it constantly reminds us of the things we could have if we only had the money to afford them.

Advertising is also the primary source of income for media companies. It lowers the price of media for the public, and without it, many people could not afford the media they depend upon so heavily. By bringing sellers and buyers together and contributing to the relatively low cost of media to the public, there is little doubt that advertising can be useful to both the producers of products and the public who consume those products.

But must we have so much of it? Advertising is everywhere, and the amount of it continues to increase as the Internet and emerging electronic and digital media (e.g., cell phones, BlackBerrys, iPhones, and iPods) attract larger numbers of consumers. The trade journal *Advertising Age* reported that $149.6 billion was spent on mediated advertising in 2006 (Johnson and Brown, 2007). The British advertising firm ZenithOptimedia (2006) projected this figure would reach $197.4 billion in 2008, and that U.S. advertising represented more than 40% of the entire planet's advertising expenditures. According to the Federal Trade Commission (2007), children between ages 2 and 11 watched about 25,600 television ads in 2004, which ran a total of 178 hours, or about 3.5 hours per week.

Some people question the value of the constant barrage of ads on society. Leo Bogart (1995), a former ad agency executive, argues that advertising fuels consumerism, materialism, and a distinctly American "commercial culture." This culture is characterized by people placing high value on material possessions and assigning these possessions a prominent place in everyday life, a type of "whoever has the most toys wins" mentality. Bogart contends that advertising's hyperbole and bold claims create a distorted worldview that encourages Americans to focus on our individual wants and away from the problems and needs of the broader society. Media scholar Arthur Asa Berger (2004, p. 1) claims this awareness has led advertisers to "talk out of both sides of their mouths." Berger writes that advertisers find themselves trying to convince their clients that advertising is necessary and effective in generating sales, maintaining product loyalty and attracting new consumers, while at the same time trying to convince consumer groups and government regulators that advertising has little real impact on consumers and society.

Advertisers also deflect criticism by saying that they are simply providing information that the public wants. However, media sociologist Michael Schudson (1984) contends this claim, too, is misleading. Advertisers, he writes, do not actually seek to discover what consumers want; rather, they attempt to persuade audiences to purchase what producers have to sell. Perhaps, Schudson suggests, it is too much to expect advertisers to do anything else; after all, advertisers must help clients to sell their products to remain in business. However, trying to get people to purchase their clients' products is very different from saying "we always keep the customer in mind" or "we're just giving people what they want," phrases that advertisers and marketers like to use to deflect criticism.

Certainly the public doesn't always think that advertisers are trying to give them what they want. A 2004 national poll for the American Association of Advertising Agencies

(AAAA) found that a clear majority of Americans are increasingly annoyed by the "tidal wave" of advertising to which they are exposed. Among the key findings:

- 65% said they "are constantly bombarded with too much" advertising
- 61% said that the amount of advertising and marketing to which they are exposed "is out of control"
- 60% said that their opinion of advertising "is much more negative than just a few years ago"
- 54% said they "avoid buying products that overwhelm them with advertising and marketing"
- 69% said they "are interested in products and services that would help them skip or block marketing."

(Elliott, 2004)

Advertisers don't read these statistics to mean that they should do less advertising. Actually, they see the public's tiring of ads as a signal that they need to develop new, strategic, creative ways to reach consumers. "The great agencies don't say 'The 30-second commercial is dead, so we're dead.' They understand that, they embrace that, and will reinvent themselves and what they do to market brands and products," said Ron Berger, who was 2004–06 president of AAAA (Elliott, 2004).

Under the headings of "entrepreneurial marketing" and "integrated marketing," advertisers are reinventing themselves. Aware that audiences are moving away from traditional mass media, and that the Internet can be a valuable marketing tool, especially when used in conjunction with other forms of promotion, advertisers are embracing marketing practices—guerrilla, viral, stealth, disruptive, and buzz marketing, for example—that on the basis of their names alone, point to ethical questions.

Advertisers are putting people on the streets, in subways, in bars, even in public school classrooms to talk up products, often without divulging their purpose or affiliation. These campaigns tend to begin as an old concept—word of mouth advertising—and they use media to develop a "buzz" or spread the message like a virus (inconspicuously but effectively) through the use of Web pages, blogs or by purchasing "product placements" in movies and television programs. The goal is to be as "organic" as possible; that is, to fit in with the existing environment in a way that the ad is not perceived as a traditional attempt to persuade.

Consider two examples of viral marketing and product placement advertising. First, Coca-Cola attempted in 2006 to promote its new soft drink targeted at 20–29-year-old males, Coke Zero, by creating the Zero Movement. As part of an $18 million campaign in Australia, the company used unbranded advertisements—chalk on sidewalks and hand-written billboards—with catch phrases such as "Why not have a sick-of-work day" to attract attention to the Zero Movement and promote a Coke-created movement Web site. The site initially looked like a blog, without Coke branding. Soon, anonymous web users were popping up in chat rooms recommending visits to the Web site. However, after it became clear the Web site was a marketing effort, angry consumers claimed that Coca-Cola was misleading the very market it had aimed to capture (Mathewson, 2006).

Second, Revlon, in a multimillion-dollar deal with ABC, integrated the cosmetics company into a 12-week "story arc" plot on the soap opera *All My Children*. The plot included a fictional Revlon executive who appeared in 25 episodes, attempting to lure employees from a cosmetics company owned by one of the antagonist characters in the show. A senior vice president for ABC said that she sees this type of product placement as the "future of advertising," adding "the key was that the placement was 'organic' to the show's ongoing theme, because there is a danger that audiences may view poorly developed marketing schemes as an intrusion" (Werner, 2003, p. 264).

Beyond the stealth marketing techniques mentioned above, the Internet has become an integral tool for targeted marketing. Advertisers hire "behavioral targeting companies" that track the habits of their potential customers. These companies match the ads one sees on the Web with the consumer's Web use patterns. For example, if a consumer has clicked on an automobile-orientated Web site, and later goes to a different Web site, car ads are likely to show up on the second site. This type of targeted advertising is a way to get online ads in front of consumers most likely to respond, even though the consumer has now moved on to an unrelated site and is often unaware of how the technique works (Street, 2007).

targeted advertising is a way to get online ads in front of [the] consumers most likely to respond,

Industry officials say "innovative" marketing is a necessary response to the changing media environment, where the Internet and emerging electronic media have put the audience in control of the media it consumes. Online consumers actively choose their media and consequently expect more gratification from those media. Audiences are less likely to sit passively through television ads or even be exposed to ads in traditional mass media. However, online consumers find themselves targets of advertising that they have no way of avoiding or controlling, raising ethical questions of whether advertising media have an obligation to inform the audience members that their Internet habits are being monitored and used to target them for additional advertising, whether they seek the intrusions or not. (This concern is discussed further in Chapter 12.)

The stealth techniques speak to how new media technologies are redefining the practice of advertising. Gordon would like you to perceive advertising as a clever and innocuous art form, a kind of "commercial poetry." However, the examples above illustrate that when advertisers employ media technology to disguise their methods and deceive the audience, this is deceit even if it is art or poetry. As Gordon suggests, and I agree, the key ethical issues with the Internet and emerging media are not so much the content—or poetry—of the ads, but the lack of transparency. Put another way, if advertisers make the claim that they are providing a benefit to society by giving the public information it wants, then why are they working so hard to hide what they are doing?

Although the above examples make clear how the Internet creates new ethical quandaries for advertisers, this is not to say that long-standing concerns about advertising have gone away. As traditional mass media—newspapers, television, radio, magazines—lose segments of their audiences to the Internet, these traditional media are doing what they can to keep and please their advertisers, who are their primary sources of income. Media companies feel compelled to create a sort of "market-driven journalism," which media scholar John McManus (1994) defined as content created for audiences that advertisers are willing to pay to reach. One could argue that all journalism is created for its audience (or market), but McManus's point is that when the interests of the advertisers begin to infiltrate the news media, then the "objectivity" and "truth" of the news is tainted by the commercial interests of the media company and advertiser.

This very thing occurred several years ago when the *Los Angeles Times* devoted a special Sunday magazine to what was then the new Staples Center Sports Arena. The *Times* journalists wrote the articles as pieces of journalism, unaware that the paper had an agreement with the Staples Center to split the advertising revenue that the magazine produced. The reporters, who found out about the arrangement by reading about it in other media (a business journal and alternative paper), were so outraged that they pushed for an internal investigation into how the deal came about. Long-time *Times* media critic David Shaw was put in charge of the probe, which resulted in a 14-page special section, a front-page apology from publisher Kathryn Downing and editor Michael Parks, and the unveiling of new ethical principles and guidelines for future conduct (Risser, 2000). Those guidelines did not prevent the *Times* from using its entire front page a decade later for an ad for Disney's *Alice in Wonderland* movie, featuring Johnny Depp's face in costume and makeup, superimposed over old news copy and topped by the paper's masthead (*Los Angeles Times*, March 5, 2010, p. 1).

This discussion would not be complete without a few words about political advertising, which has become a multibillion-dollar business (Teinowitz, 2006)—even more so since the 2010 U.S. Supreme Court decision that removed limits on what businesses could contribute to political campaigns. For political ads to be effective, they need to persuade the audience that one candidate is superior to the other, or that one candidate is undeserving of office. This often leads to inflated claims on behalf of one candidate or exaggerated accusations that condemn the opponent. Because political advertising is a source of political information for many citizens, and evidence suggests that negative advertising generally works, the tendency for much political advertising is to be negative—often beyond the bounds of truth. Examples of such deception cut across party lines, as was shown in the 2004 presidential election. An ad for Democratic Party candidate John Kerry claimed that "President Bush says sending jobs overseas makes sense for America," while Bush supporters ran ads saying that Kerry supported a 50-cent-a-gallon tax increase on gasoline. Although neither candidate ever made these statements, polls showed that the ads were successful in shaping citizens' notions of where the candidates stood on these issues. A national poll of voters in 18 states where the ads ran on television indicated that 61% believed that Bush favored sending jobs overseas, while 46% responded that they believed that Kerry wanted to raise gasoline tax by 50 cents a gallon (Rutenberg, 2004).

These examples provide evidence of the potential impact of advertising on the democratic process. Citizens make voting and political decisions in part based on media content, and political advertising has become an important and pervasive method for candidates to get their messages into the public's mind. Political candidates have found that negative, deceptive and even untruthful ads about their opponents are effective and acceptable. Thus, it should be no surprise that candidates resort to this type of political advertising, even though these ads are intended to distort the truth and confuse the public.

PUBLIC RELATIONS: BEYOND PROMOTION AND PUBLICITY

As public relations has attracted an increasing number of students to journalism and mass communication departments and has developed into its own academic discipline, scholars in the field have attempted to move the practice from simple attempts at promotion and publicity into the realm of persuasive social science. Emerging norms and theories of public relations have stressed that excellent public relations involves "two-way" and "symmetrical" flows of information that serve as the basis of a dialogue between an organization and its stakeholders or publics (Grunig, 1992). Public relations practitioners remain committed to advancing the interests of their clients, but doing so can be ethically performed only when the practitioner weighs the client's goals within the broader interests of their stakeholders (internal and external publics) and society—a utilitarian approach if not quite one following John Rawls's "veil of ignorance" ethics.

Proponents of this conception of public relations tend to agree that for public relations to be perceived as a positive social force, it must be altruistic and socially responsible. From this perspective, an emphasis is put on the public (as opposed to special or private interests) and how public relations can be a tool for public communication. These tenets of "excellent" public relations are taught in many universities and reflect the importance of ethical thinking among public relations practitioners and scholars; however, these norms are only a part of the story. Examples of public relations practices that attempt cleverly to manipulate audiences are easily found, and these practices are seemingly accepted by some media—including news media—as a standard way of doing business.

Journalists have long relied on public relations practitioners to provide information for their stories and often for story ideas. Media scholars Sallot and Johnson (2006) studied the relationship between journalists and PR practitioners between 1991 and 2004, and found that journalists estimated that 44% of news content in the United States is influenced by public relations. Journalists interviewed during the later years of the study (2002–04) valued public relations more, and those who reported higher levels of PR influence also indicated that they have better relations with PR practitioners. These data suggest not only the extent to which public relations influences news content, but also the extent to which public relations practitioners and journalists rely on each other to execute their work. The ethical problems begin when attempts are made to disguise or cover up the nature of their interdependence, and often the news media are as much to blame for the deception as PR practitioners.

The widespread use of video news releases (VNRs) in the first decade of the 21st century has spurred much of this debate. VNRs are the video equivalent to a press release. They are intended to be newsworthy, yet advance the goals of the client, who hopes the tape is shown to the public as a "news" report. There is a wide range of VNR techniques, each capable of generating questions about ethics. Almost all appear to be showing a professional broadcast journalist covering a story. Some feature voice-overs. Others supply "B-roll," additional video without sound, that the station can edit, rewrite, and have sound—such as the voice of the station's own anchor or reporter—added. Typically, a script is provided for that purpose. The most sophisticated involve a tape where, after introducing the package, the local reporter reads questions from the script (on or off camera) and the VNR supplies the answers. To mimic an interview in this manner is very convincing, as the audience trust of the local reporter becomes part of the presentation's effect. In an era of limited resources for news gathering, many television stations use VNRs in their newscasts. Some make a practice of identifying the source of the VNR content, but many do not (Purushothaman, 2005; see also Aiello and Proffitt, 2008).

Many Americans watched a 2003 televised news report on changes in Medicare resulting from the Medicare Drug Improvement and Modernization Act of 2003 that established the Medicare Part D drug benefit. The narrator identified herself as Karen Ryan, and in a report that looked and sounded like news, reported that the new government policy would help seniors "stay healthy and have a better quality of life." What some stations did not disclose, however, was that the report was produced by U.S. Health and Human Services Department, and that Ryan works for a Washington, DC-based public relations firm that contracted with the government to produce a VNR promoting Medicare's new drug benefit. The government's use of a VNR to promote its policies is not new, but because Ryan did not identify her purpose or affiliation (an omission one would assume was intentional), the video appeared to attempt purposely to mislead viewers into believing that it was a news report, not a piece of promotion produced by the government (Chepesiuk, 2006).

This incident led to an investigation of federal use of VNRs by the Government Accountability Office, which found that 20 federal agencies had produced and distributed them. The GAO concluded that the Bush administration had violated rules prohibiting the government from engaging in "covert propaganda" (Pugh, 2004). The Federal Communications Commission took a broader stance, expanding a long-standing rule requiring program sponsors to be identified so that it also required disclosure of "sponsored programming," including the use of VNRs. Some broadcasters have been fined for violating those rules, which are intended to require transparency about the source of news program content."

Commercial media and public relations firms are now buying "guaranteed placements" for their VNRs, an agreement where the video producers buy spots on stations and networks the way an ad agency would. These deals allow for a new technique called "branded journalism," which is viewed as an effective way to advertise in a splintered media market. Instead of sending out VNRs in hopes that stations will air them, branded journalism involves public relations firms "actually creating the newscast" and then buying time for the spots, which usually run 30–90 seconds (Mandese, 2005). The spots are then placed in the newscasts, usually with the station's anchor or a reporter providing the lead-in so that the segments appear to be part of the newscast produced by the station. These paid spots don't fit the traditional distinctions between advertising (which is paid for) and public relations (which is free). In this way, branded journalism is an example of the blending of public relations and advertising into news. An article in *PRWeek* notes, "Public relations isn't always free. The paid-for model has earned a place in the industry, and guaranteed-placement VNRs are the most obvious examples of it" (Trickett, 2006, p. 11). And because these branded journalism videos are professionally produced to look like news, viewers could have trouble discerning between these mini-infomercials and news updates from segments produced by journalists.

Even more blatant efforts to (using John McManus' term) "infiltrate the news media" have been tried recently by the health care industry, where some hospitals have struck deals with TV stations to feature only that hospital and its health care providers, in their health-related stories. One such effort, involving the NBC affiliate in Eau Claire, Wisconsin, fell apart after Glen Mabie, the station's news director, resigned rather than carry out his general manager's order to convince the newsroom staff that the agreement was a good thing. The deal, which Mabie had opposed from the time he first heard about it, specified that, in exchange for payments from one of the local hospitals, the station was to run twice-weekly health-related stories featuring only employees of that hospital and its medical affiliates (Emerson, 2008). Even with Mabie's resignation, this exclusive agreement might have been implemented if the newsroom staff had not made it absolutely clear that there would be mass resignations unless it was scrapped (Mabie, 2008). Mabie was honored by the Society of Professional Journalists in September 2008 with its national Ethics in Journalism Award, but as of late-2010 had not found another job in journalism—a sad commentary on the price of ethics in some cases.

The WEAU-TV situation, unfortunately, was not an isolated incident. A 2007 article in the *Columbia Journalism Review* outlined a number of instances nationwide where hospitals were paying TV stations to have their medical staffs featured in what would be perceived as news stories. The common goal was to attract patients who could afford to pay for elective procedures, in order to boost the hospital's bottom line (Lieberman, 2007). These attempts to "buy news space" were blatant violations of such journalistic codes of ethics as those of the Society of Professional Journalists and the Radio Television Digital News Association, and they also transgress some key principles (e.g., operating truthfully and transparently, and avoiding deception) in the ethics code of the Public Relations Society of America.

The use of product experts, who are sent on "satellite tours" of local television stations, is yet another example of the blurring of the lines between public relations, advertising and news. These "experts" often show up at stations after the distribution of a promotional VNR, and make themselves available for interviews (Kurtz, 2005).

Corey Greenberg appeared on the NBC's *Today* show a couple of years ago to praise Apple's iPod as a "great portable musical player," adding it is the "coolest-looking one" and "this is the way to go." Greenberg, an NBC contributor who was the technology editor for the show at the time, decided it wasn't so important to tell his audience or his NBC employer that he was also receiving $15,000 from Apple to talk up its products on news shows. Reports in *The Wall Street Journal* also linked Greenberg to similar contractual agreements with Sony, Hewlett-Packard, Seiko Epson, Creative Technology and Energizer Holdings. After becoming aware of Greenberg's apparent conflict of interest, NBC updated its policies; however, it didn't sever its relationship with Greenberg, who subsequently appeared on CNBC, WNBC, and other network affiliates in major markets to promote products for the companies listed above. One NBC official was quoted as saying, "This is a way of doing business for these people. It's hard to find a contributor who doesn't have a connection to one of these things" (Kurtz, 2005, p. C1).

The growth of the Internet affords strategic communicators additional tools to spread their messages, while at the same time, providing an opportunity to be less than forthright about who is creating the message and why. A blog called "Wal-Marting Across America" first appeared in September of 2006. Two bloggers, Jim and Laura, posted messages about their cross-country travels in a recreational vehicle (RV) that they parked for free in Wal-

Mart parking lots. The blog identified its sponsor as the organization Working Families for Wal-Mart, and its postings related human-interest stories about Wal-Mart employees. One story told how a woman was able to advance from a cashier to a project manager, and how the woman was proud that Wal-Mart was working to protect the environment. Another entry discussed how a worker's son had a costly surgery and pacemaker, which were paid for by company insurance, and that the son had recovered and gone to work in the automotive department of a Wal-Mart store (Craig, 2007).

The blog had no apparent affiliation with Wal-Mart, but it was later discovered that Working Families for Wal-Mart was created by Edelman, Wal-Mart's public relations firm. The group was formed as a response to criticism from labor advocates and unions that Wal-Mart does not treat its employees well. Also uncovered was that Working Families for Wal-Mart is funded by Wal-Mart. It paid for Jim and Laura's travels, providing them an RV, paying for their gas, setting up the blog, and even paying Laura, a freelance writer, for her blog entries. Jim, whose photographs appeared on the blog, was discovered to be a staff photographer for *The Washington Post*.

Thus, once again, a public relations ethics case spilled over into journalism ethics as well. Gordon has asserted that the problem with these cases is that the news media are not vigilant enough, and we agree on this. But he also suggests that there are essentially two standards of public relations ethics: one for the marketing sphere (where the truthfulness of information is not important) and one for the public sphere (where public relations practitioners want the news media and public to view their messages as credible). As this Wal-Mart case illustrates, the line where marketing spills over into the public sphere is not apparent, and to suggest that public relations practitioners have the interest, ability and *will* to make these distinctions is not only impractical, but unrealistic.

CONCLUSION

So, is it accurate to assert that advertising, public relations and integrated marketing are forms of propaganda? Based on the examples in this chapter, sometimes the answer is "Yes."

Gordon claims that it is the *public's responsibility* to be aware that persuasive communication is not accurate or truthful. It seems to me that this line of thinking excuses advertisers, PR practitioners and marketers from any consideration of ethics. Gordon apparently thinks that some deceit is to be expected and is ethically acceptable, and the burden is on average citizens to determine when and how they are being deceived—even if these same citizens are not aware of the polished methods and tools that persuasive communicators have at their disposal. He seems to be saying it is fine to be a propagandist, as long as your propaganda falls within the law.

I've argued from a different perspective, one more in line with Bok's (1978) thoughts about being "truthful." Purposive deceit is not truthful; failing to disclose the sources of messages, and the motives or affiliations of the sources, is also not truthful. These notions of truthfulness fit well with other long-established strains of ethical thought. In the 19th century, Immanuel Kant argued that to use people as a means to achieve your goals was immoral. Certainly, being deceitful in an attempt to persuade others to think and act in ways

> is it accurate to assert that advertising, public relations and integrated marketing are forms of propaganda? . . . sometimes the answer is "Yes."

you'd like them to is using people as a means. The utilitarian principle, articulated by 19th century philosophers Jeremy Bentham, John Stuart Mill and others, suggests that for persuasive communication to be ethical it should result in the greatest good for the greatest number of people. It is hard to understand how the public benefits when persuasive communicators intentionally manipulate the public *without the public's knowledge*. More recently, media ethicist Edmund Lambeth (1992) asserted that a basic ethical principle is to be "humane," which is to say that the media should avoid exploitation and intentional harm. However, as the numerous examples in this chapter show, the deception used by persuasive communicators is often not only intentional, but also *meant* to exploit.

While these ideas are relatively simple, the examples in this chapter show how persuasive communicators often push the fuzzy ethical boundaries of persuasion into something akin to propaganda. What is clear is that the convergence of advertising, public relations and marketing, along with the Internet and emerging technologies, has provided persuasive communicators some new and effective tools to practice their crafts. These developments create the potential for unethical practices that disguise the persuasive communicator's motivations, interests and goals. The sad results of these practices are that it is becoming increasingly difficult for citizens to know when the media are deceiving them and how, and citizens are becoming increasingly tired of being targets of commercial and ideological marketing schemes.

KEY POINTS

- To ethicist Sissela Bok, being truthful means avoiding intentional deception; persuasive communicators too often fall short of this standard.
- The distinctions between persuasive communication and propaganda are key ethical considerations.
- Michael Schudson contends that advertisers don't seek to discover what consumers want, but instead attempt to persuade audiences to purchase what producers have to sell.

GORDON: Because the function of persuasive communication is to sell products, services, and ideas, there is no need for persuaders always to adhere to absolute standards of truth—but transparency is needed.

Arguing that advertising and other persuasive communication is creative rather than factual, and attempts to persuade as well as inform, does not automatically mean that those fields should or do have absolutely no concerns for ethics. Rather, this ought to lead one to consider carefully *which* ethical standards should apply to advertising and other forms of persuasive communication, and how any such standards should differ from the ones applied to the news, information, and entertainment media.

This is especially important for advertising and public relations students to ponder, because mass communication education too often fails to differentiate among its various subfields. Thus, when the talk turns to ethics, that discussion often is centered on what the standards should be for the news media—if for no other reason than that we are all news media consumers—with too little attention paid to the other parts of the wide-ranging mass communication field.

There are no True opinions.

ADVERTISING ETHICS STANDARDS

Turning first to advertising, let's consider carefully what ethical standards should *not* apply to advertising communication. I believe that chief among such inapplicable standards is any reference to absolute "truth"—an elusive enough concept when applied to the news media, but one that is both irrelevant and nearly impossible to define when applied to advertising. I'm not suggesting that ads and other persuasive communication should deliberately try to lie or deceive, but rather that rigid standards of truth are inappropriate in this area.

Supreme Court justices, among others, have written that although the truth of factual statements may be ascertained, one cannot prove the "truth" of an opinion. The same might be said for persuasive communication such as advertising, where the validity of many claims is subject to opinion rather than to factual proof. The Federal Trade Commission (FTC) has had a great deal to say about outright deception in ads. That is a legal issue as well as an ethical one, and we'll proceed here on the assumption that advertisements must adhere to the requirement not to make false statements in an effort to deceive, for legal if not for ethical reasons.

Beyond that minimum requirement, however, there is no need for ads to be "truthful" in the same sense that the news must be accurate or truthful. News reports are supposed to provide a fair, accurate, and complete account while ads need not do that. Advertising practitioners have a responsibility to do the best job they can to persuade potential customers of the value of a product (or an idea) while avoiding the kind of deception the FTC has banned. Such persuasion usually requires that the advertising communicator emphasize the strong or appealing points of the product and omit or conceal the weaknesses. A full, fair, balanced picture is not what is intended or, I'd suggest, expected.

Ads vs. News → Requirement

I believe that the public has a responsibility to be aware of this, to understand the conventions of advertising, and to use advertising as it is intended—as an attempt at persuasion that often can and does provide useful information. To help produce this increased public awareness and understanding, the advertising profession might well commit itself to do a better job of explaining to the public just how it works and what might fairly be expected (and not expected) from it. Such consumer education is also very much needed in regard to the news media, but that's a different argument, which I set forth in Chapter 8.

Starting in the early 1990s, television advertising spots moved for a while toward greater realism, particularly in regard to using "ordinary people" rather than actors in commercials.

A 1993 article in *The New York Times* noted that this "so-called real people school of casting eschews the glamour and glitz of actors and models for the genuineness and imperfections of ordinary consumers" (Elliott, 1993). By 2006, the pendulum had swung back to featuring celebrities in about 20% of U.S. ads, about double the total from a decade earlier (Story, 2006). Both approaches had their roots in the desire to persuade more effectively, rather than in any general concerns about ethics. They focus on the ways in which the purveyors of the persuasive messages are perceived, not with the truth or completeness of the message itself, and illustrate well that ads and advertisers shouldn't be held to the same absolute standards of truth that exist for news people.

The use of actors or models, celebrity endorsements and the "documercials" which came earlier all have bottom-line rather than ethical roots and, driven by market forces, will be used only as long as they are perceived to be effective. This gives the public the power—and the responsibility—to provide feedback that will determine whether any or all of these approaches should continue in advertising. Indeed, the public may also help "regulate" advertising that goes beyond acceptable ethical limits simply by conveying its displeasure to the sponsor or the ad agency involved (directly, or by refusing to buy the product).

"CREATIVE EMBELLISHMENT" AS ETHICAL ADVERTISING

Richard Johannesen and his co-authors have made an interesting argument for the application of "ethical standards rooted in truthfulness and rationality" to advertising's claims about "the actual nature or merit of a product." They suggest that "the evidence and reasoning supporting the claim [must be] clear, accurate, relevant, and sufficient in quantity," and that any emotional (or motivational) appeals must be directly relevant to the product being promoted (Johannesen et al., 2008, p. 110). But advertising, as Johannesen et al. note, is inherently not necessarily an exercise in rational communication. Rather, it is persuasive communication, and I'd suggest that it should be given free rein as long as it remains within the legal boundaries regulating blatant deception. Indeed, Johannesen himself questions whether the truthfulness/rationality standards should still apply when advertising is aimed not at product quality, but simply seeks to get the attention of the reader or viewer in order to create awareness of the particular product (pp. 112–113). This distinction between emphasis on product quality and "mere" attention-getting efforts seems to lack a clear dividing line, and strikes me as somewhat irrelevant when one considers the basic persuasive and pervasive nature of advertising.

Indeed, one observer argued in 1970 that advertising is a form of commercial poetry, and both advertisers and poets use "creative embellishment—a content which cannot be captured by literal description alone" (Levitt, 1970, p. 86). Accepting this approach would allow for some poetic license in the creation of advertising that, nonetheless, remained ethical.

Advertising (along with public relations) has also been described as having "the goal of creating metaphors that resonate in the minds of the target publics: 'The Good Hands People,' 'The Friendly Skies,' " and so forth (Blewett, 1994, p. 42). Creating metaphors is clearly an approach to which standards of truth cannot and should not be applied in the usual ways.

advertising is a form of commercial poetry, and both advertisers and poets use "creative embellishment"

The "commercial poetry" approach goes further, and sees advertisements as symbols of human aspirations that "are not the real things, nor are they intended to be, nor are they accepted as such by the public" (Levitt, 1970, p. 90). If, indeed, this perception about the audience is correct, there is clearly no need to hold advertising to the same standards of truth and accuracy that are required for the news media. Alternatively, if the audience does see ads as reality, the advertising industry—and perhaps the educational system as well—should take steps to ensure that the public comes to understand better the role, practices and "commercial poetry" of advertising.

Sissela Bok (1979), though holding that truth is clearly preferable to lies except under very special circumstances, nonetheless suggests that it is better to focus on being "truthful" rather than on always telling the exact truth (Bok, 1979)—perhaps similar to Stephen Colbert's concept of "truthiness." Applying this to advertising could well mean that literal truth is not required as long as outright deception is avoided, and it would seem to sanction the "poetry" concept of advertising copy.

Some people have seen political or ideological advertising as a special case, and therefore subject to a different set of ethical (and legal) expectations. Ads extolling or attacking political candidates serve a different purpose than do product ads, and may be more important to society. Critics in recent decades have often lamented the tendency of political ads to deal with images rather than substance, and at least one TV station (WGN-TV in Chicago) tried a short-lived experiment in which it refused to run political ads of less than five minutes. Although the goal of forcing political candidates to deal with serious issues rather than stressing only quick imagery and soundbites in their ads was a laudable one, opposition from both politicians and the public doomed the experiment.

And that's not necessarily bad. Political ads should no more be subject to standards of "truth" or "substance" than should the general rhetoric of political campaigns. It's a nice goal in the abstract, but difficult and dangerous to try to implement. It became more difficult to implement in Washington state in 2007, when the Supreme Court struck down a state statute that made it illegal for a political candidate to lie, with malicious intent, about an opponent, on the grounds that such a ban violated protected rights of free speech.

The goal of all advertising—perhaps especially political ads—is persuasion. If political ads sometimes stray from the truth, or concentrate on image rather than substance, then the best remedy is neither legal restrictions nor efforts to impose an ethical standard of truth. Rather, as in the Washington case, the remedy lies in further comment and discussion, either by opposing candidates or—as has been taking place since the 1980s—by news media analyses that look at the truthfulness, content, validity and perceived effectiveness of political ads. (*The Seattle Times* continued to run its "Truth Needle" analyses after the 2010 election—focused on public statements by newsmakers—because the public liked them.)

It seems to me that what it boiled down to in Washington state—and this could be applicable elsewhere, as well—is that it's too difficult to determine when a candidate is lying about an opponent (not to mention the difficulty of determining "malicious intent"), so government should avoid that thicket. Once again, as with product ads, the public will have to decide whether a political candidate is straying too far from "truth," whether that's in ads or in other campaign rhetoric. This responsibility may become even more important as advertising, political and otherwise, continues to grow and become more pervasive on the Internet.

In considering ideological ads, we can look at one of the most extreme cases imaginable in pondering whether such ads should be held to some standard of truth. Ads denying the existence of the Holocaust surfaced in many college and university newspapers in the late 1980s and have continued to appear through the 1990s and into the 21st century. Arguments have raged on every campus where this took place—and usually in the surrounding community as well—as to whether such ads should be accepted, or whether it was appropriate to reject them on the grounds that they were attempting to perpetrate a monstrous lie.

Some school newspapers wound up running these ads—often while attacking them editorially—and others refused them on various grounds, often including the fact that they distorted or perverted historical truths. I disagree strongly with the ideological position taken in these ads, and would much prefer that they never appeared. But I am uneasy with the position that they should be rejected because they fail to adhere to a standard of truth. If that stance is taken, we are opening ourselves up to an endless series of arguments as to just how "truthful" a political or ideological ad must be in order to be permitted to see the light of day. In these situations, as in so many others, I believe that we are better off worrying less about the truthfulness of an ad, and concentrating instead on making sure that those who disagree with the contents have an ample opportunity to respond. More speech, rather than regulation of content (including the truth or falsity of the ad), seems to be a remedy far better suited to an open, democratic society—and this should be as true for ideological and commercial ads as for other forms of communication in such a society. (For a thoughtful argument to the contrary, see the essay by Stephen Klaidman in Knowlton, 1997, pp. 167–169.)

ETHICAL STANDARDS FOR PUBLIC RELATIONS

Public relations practitioners who adhere to the code of ethics revised and approved in 2000 by the Public Relations Society of America (PRSA) should—on paper—have no difficulty determining how truthful they must be. The code says, clearly, that members should adhere to the highest standards of truth and accuracy, and that they should be honest and accurate in all communications. Moreover, they should quickly correct any erroneous material for which they are responsible and reveal all information needed for responsible public decision-making. Lying by omission is specifically noted as something that should not occur.

All of that seems straightforward enough. But there's another section of the code that perhaps casts things in a different light. That section discusses responsible advocacy, and says that PRSA members should provide "a voice in the marketplace of ideas, facts, and viewpoints to aid informed public debate." I noted above that news reporters are expected to provide a fair, accurate, and complete account in the stories they present. Public relations practitioners, on the other hand, deal with viewpoints and opinions as well as facts, and have a responsibility not only to the public but also to their clients. And, as Peter Gade notes, public relations is increasingly involved in various kinds of marketing activities.

I'd suggest that the standards of the PRSA code could well be followed in regard to factual statements released to the media or to the public. But I don't think they should be applied literally and rigidly to situations where public relations people are actively engaged in efforts to market a product or an idea. Under those circumstances, I believe that the same standards and arguments outlined above regarding advertising are also applicable to public relations.

I suggested earlier that it's up to the public to expect that advertising will of course resort to exaggeration or "puffery," and to be knowledgeable enough to sort out these approaches and make up their own minds about the value of the message. A similar argument applies to public relations and absolute truth, except that in this situation it's up to news media practitioners to be knowledgeable enough to sort out the message and make up their own minds about what to pass on, and how. Peter Gade made my point here quite well, that examples of PR attempts to manipulate audiences are easy to find, and are quite often *accepted by the news media* (my emphasis) as standard practice. *That's* where the problem lies!

Let's not criticize public relations practitioners for doing their job, which includes providing information that news media need and have come to rely on for nearly half of their news content (as Gade notes). As long as the public relations efforts are not intentionally deceptive, and don't try to buy their way into the news columns, I see no need for them to be held to absolute standards of truth unless they are claiming to provide factual information which they put forth as being correct, accurate, or whatever synonym for "truth" you prefer. Rather, it is up to the news media, as our societal gatekeepers, to avoid being manipulated— or letting their audiences be manipulated—by PR efforts. (That, of course, is one of the reasons why we need journalism training and standards in the blogosphere, but that's a different topic and one that's discussed in Chapters 5 and 6.)

TRANSPARENCY

What is more important than truth is *transparency*—that is, making absolutely clear the genesis of a statement or a claim, and whether it is intended to be factual or to present opinions or judgments (i.e., whether it is intended to persuade). I'll argue that the need for transparency is equally applicable to advertising and public relations, when both are involved in the marketing function.

As long as there is adequate transparency, I don't consider video news releases to be inherently deceptive or inappropriately manipulative, either. Again, the burden here should fall on the news media, not the public relations practitioners. I have no problem with a PR campaign that distributes video releases to TV stations, as long as the source is specified. I have a considerable problem with the ethics of a TV station that uses the VNR without identifying its source and making clear that it's a public relations tool, regardless of how accurate or inaccurate its information may be. I have the same problem with newspapers that run news releases (even if they're from nonprofit organizations) without indicating their source.

I keep going back to some early 1990s studies which indicated that, even in major metropolitan markets, the availability of video footage and how well it's packaged have a definite impact on news directors' and producers' decisions to air them. One of those studies examined nearly 400 items, such as news releases and meeting notices, and concluded in part that the ease and efficiency with which information could be gathered, along with a station's resource constraints, were among the strongest influences on whether a particular story would be considered for broadcast. Other important factors included a balancing of the story's visual impact with its importance (Berkowitz, 1990).

Such results—whether they stem from limited resources or just laziness—violate virtually every major perspective on ethical issues involving the news media. Both of Kant's categorical imperatives (acting on a maxim that you would like to see as a universal law, and not "using" people in order to achieve your ends) are ignored when media manipulators succeed in getting their self-serving messages to the public without appropriate scrutiny from the usual gatekeepers. The utilitarian ideal of the greatest good for the greatest number of people is in serious danger when the good of the manipulators is served at the expense of the public as a whole.

John Rawls's concern for protecting a situation's most vulnerable participants fares no better in such circumstances. Even Aristotle's Golden Mean approach is in danger if the manipulators become better at presenting their messages than media people are at screening and evaluating them, as—arguably—happens regularly in smaller (and some larger) news operations. One observer has even argued that the use of video news releases without clearly identifying their source breaches the unwritten "covenant between news producers and news audiences that the news will be independently gathered and produced" (Linn, 1992, p. 15).

I agree with Linn, and with concerns about VNRs that fail to disclose their source. Such a lack of transparency—whether by government or in the private sector—falls short of virtually every ethical principle we've dealt with except Machiavelli's. It would be a step in the right ethical direction if the FCC were to require more transparency from broadcasters not only regarding VNR sources and program sponsorships, but perhaps even on such matters as product placements.

As long as the "branded journalism" approach that Gade describes is transparent, this would not present serious ethical issues. These "guaranteed placement" VNRs are very little different from the print media "advertorials" that date back at least to the 1970s, when Mobil Oil (among others) published ads (often full-page ads) that were very similar in format to the editorial material in a variety of publications. The initial furor over what some people saw as attempts to deceive evaporated quickly when this material was labeled as paid advertising, so it could be distinguished from news copy.

The same rationale holds for all those late-night hour-long "infomercials" on many TV channels—or for blogs such as the one that Gade describes. Label them clearly, so people know what they are, and stop worrying about whether they shade or stretch the truth, provide only selected information, or otherwise fall short of news media standards of truth, objectivity and fairness.

However, I do take issue with Gade's overly simplistic description of my position on all this. I'm not suggesting that anything goes in regard to propaganda, as long as it doesn't transgress legal boundaries. I *am* arguing that, in the *marketing* sphere (as contrasted with the one where public relations or other communicators are providing what they say is accurate information), absolute truth is not necessary *but* transparency is required *in addition to* observing the legal requirements. The issue is not whether news releases meet standards of absolute truth. Rather, it's how thoroughly the news media vet the information they receive from public relations practitioners and whether they inform their audience of that information's source. When the media fail in this regard, it makes a travesty of the social responsibility ideal.

ADS FOR HARMFUL PRODUCTS

Observers over the years have articulated ethical concerns about advertising for products that might be harmful in some way to the users. Indeed, some legal restrictions on that score are already in place, such as the prohibition since 1971 of cigarette ads on television, and the 1998 multi-state settlements under which the tobacco companies agreed to major restrictions on their advertising and marketing activities. Advertising acceptability standards and practices of individual media—and retail—outlets can also sharply curtail the freedom to advertise, quite aside from any legal restrictions, and this opens up a different set of ethical issues.

The question comes down to whether it is proper, in the name of ethics and social responsibility, to restrict or prevent advertising about products that may be legally sold but that some people regard as harmful to society or to potential users (or as just plain embarrassing). Might it be better to make additional information about these products available to the public so people can make up their own minds? The late 1980s argument over whether radio and TV stations should run condom advertising illustrates both the acceptability issue and the impact that increasing public acceptance can have on such standards.

The acceptability problem is complicated immeasurably by the "commercial speech" doctrine under which the Supreme Court historically has excluded a considerable portion of advertising from First Amendment protection. In essence, what the Court has done under this doctrine is to equate the nonprotected parts of commercial communication with obscene communication, in that neither category is protected by the First Amendment. This seems to be unfair, unrealistic, and unwise because most if not all advertising conveys at least a kernel of potentially useful information (the "redeeming social value" of advertising, to carry the obscenity parallel just a small step further). Such restrictions also convey a very paternalistic view of an audience that is deemed to be incapable of making its own decisions or resisting advertising blandishments.

A much more pragmatic approach would hold that if a product is legal, it should be advertisable. That would appropriately shift the focus of any disagreements from the advertising sphere to the question of whether harmful products should be made illegal. As is, the opponents of particular products such as tobacco, alcohol, guns and X-rated movies don't necessarily have to face up to the underlying issue of whether the use of that product should be allowed. Instead, they can shift the concern to the backs of the mass media and their advertisers, in the hope that by restricting or eliminating the ads, they can reduce product usage.

The 1990s flap over the successful use of the "Joe Camel" figure by the R. J. Reynolds Tobacco Company illustrates the problem well. Attempts to ban Joe Camel, because of its reputed appeal to children, raised both legal and ethical issues. As *The Boston Globe* asked, "Are we to tell advertising firms that they can do their work as long as they are not too good or too successful?" The paper went on to note that this (laudable) attempt to protect children from being influenced to start smoking conceivably could be extended to some unlikely areas, such as banning the movie *Casablanca*:

> As John Banville wrote in *The New York Review of Books*, Humphrey Bogart, who died of throat cancer, was the "emblematic smoker" of his day. "No doubt many an adolescent boy bought his first pack of smokes after seeing a Bogart movie."
>
> ("Joe Camel's rights," 1994)

As it happened, Joe Camel was sent to pasture in 1997 as part of the legal settlement between the tobacco industry and many states that had sued the industry over the Medicaid costs of treating the consequences attributed to cigarette smoking. On balance, it seems to me, the issues of advertising acceptability and whether to advertise potentially harmful products pose far more serious ethical concerns for the advertising field than does the issue of adhering strictly to "truth."

ETHICAL FRAMEWORKS REGARDING ADVERTISING

Edmund Lambeth (1992) has set forth a framework of five principles that he recommends as the basis for news media ethics. One of these—humaneness—might be argued as a principle that should also apply to advertising communication. This seems to require that ads avoid exploitation, that they not degrade individuals or groups, and, in general, "do no direct, intentional harm to others" (p. 30). But as Lambeth points out, the idea of avoiding direct harm to others is more of a universal human ethical principle (a protonorm, if you will) than one that applies particularly to journalists or to advertisers. As for the balance of the humaneness principle, if advertising does not adhere to it, that's perhaps unfortunate, but (possibly with the single exception of ads that exploit young children) no more so—and no more preventable—than such occurrences are in the news and entertainment media.

It can be argued that it is up to parents rather than the advertising industry to control what their children watch. If children happen to be in the line of fire of ads aimed at different and more mature audiences, that's unfortunate but it's hardly the fault of the advertisers. The sponsors, in fact, would unquestionably prefer that their ads reach only the target audiences they're paying the media to reach, rather than being seen by children and others who are not immediate customers for the advertised products or services.

In addition to humaneness, and to truth—which has been discussed at length previously—Lambeth (1992) listed freedom, justice, and stewardship. These other three principles don't seem directly applicable to advertising, although Gade seems to like the idea of stewardship on the part of advertisers. There are also a number of other ethical standards that don't apply here. For instance, Aristotle's Golden Mean, by definition, is not going to be useful concerning goal-oriented persuasive communication.

Given the roles advertising plays in the media and society as a whole, a utilitarian argument for wide-open advertising might be mounted. This argument would posit that in terms of helping consumers to fill their needs and gratify their desires, the greatest good is achieved by giving considerable latitude to advertisements, particularly if the public is knowledgeable about the conventions of advertising. But this approach must also contend with the nagging question of how one judges what advertising practices or restraints produce the greatest good (or the most pleasure) for the largest portion of society, and that uncertainty seemingly defies a conclusive answer and therefore weakens the utilitarian approach to this topic.

If one were to view the issue in strictly economic terms, the argument could be made that advertising is clearly good for the economy and for the survival of the U.S. media system, and that Gade's insistence on absolute truthfulness would cripple the free media in the United States. Therefore from an economic standpoint, we need to settle for something less than an absolute position on this issue.

And that's where transparency comes in. Although it's not an ethical theory per se, let's reiterate how important an ethical guideline transparency has become in regard to persuasive communication, both for its own value and as a tool that could help educate media consumers about how persuasive communication should be understood.

Patrick Plaisance (2007) connected the concept of transparency to Kantian roots, and said that it should apply not only to journalism, where "it is an essential element of credibility" (p. 193), but also to persuasive communication. He suggested that transparency is implicit in the codes of ethics of the Public Relations Society of America and the American Marketing Association and that it is particularly important regarding "the pledge among public relations practitioners to make sure their service to clients also conforms with the broader 'public good.'" More generally, "[t]ransparency, or truthful forthrightness, is not just another vogue word, according to Kant; it defines much of what it means to live an ethical life." Because it is key to rational human communication, it "must inform every decision made by those in the media industries" (pp. 204 and 205).

Although I support unequivocally the idea of transparency, I stop well short of applying Kantian absolutes indiscriminately to advertising. Nor do I find it useful to argue for the total elimination of advertising, as former ad man Jerry Mander (1993) has done. Rawls's concern for the most vulnerable members of society also seems less useful as an approach—with the possible exception of ads aimed at young children, which he would likely regard as inherently unfair—than aiming for transparency (whether it stems from Kant or other sources). The goal should be an educated public, one that understands advertising and takes it for what it really is: an effort to make people aware of products and services and to persuade them to buy.

The special case of television advertising directed at young children is one where ethical concerns might well be held to be paramount. However, the Children's Television Act of 1990, as strengthened in 1996 by additional FCC rules, seems to have preempted the ethical perspective on this by establishing some minimum legal requirements aimed at preventing advertisers from exploiting young viewers. It therefore seems sensible to treat this area of concern similarly to the way the FTC dealt legally with deception in advertising and just accept those rules as a given, rather than arguing about their ethical dimensions.

The controversy over the appropriateness of exposing school children to ads beamed into their classrooms over Channel One raises some of the same ethical (and economic)

advertising is clearly good for the economy and for the survival of the U.S. media system, and . . . Gade's insistence on absolute truthfulness would cripple the free media

questions. This venture, launched in 1990 by Whittle Communications, provided 10 minutes of news and two minutes of product or public service ads daily. It may have reached as many as 40% of American high school students before running into serious financial problems originating largely in other parts of Whittle's holdings and resulting in its sale in 1994 (Stewart, 1994). In early 2006, the operation was still reaching some 350,000 classrooms daily, in more than one-quarter of the nation's schools, each of which received some $30,000 in audio-visual equipment in return for showing the program (Austin et al., 2006, p. e424). The network's Web site in early 2011 said that it had become a division of Alloy Media + Marketing. The network said it reached nearly six million middle and high school teens in 8,000 schools, that it provided "global and national headlines from a teen perspective with a fast-paced production style, youthful reporters and contemporary music" and that it has won numerous awards for its reporting (Channel One, 2010).

This approach has been criticized on the grounds that the students are a captive audience, that it is inappropriate to expose them to ads in a school setting and that a great deal of the programming is "soft" content that often promotes products and services. The counterarguments have been that the informational programming provided more exposure to news than the students would otherwise receive, and that Channel One's donation of TV sets, VCRs, and satellite dishes to the schools receiving its broadcasts enhanced the opportunities for improved educational experiences for all their students. A small 2004 field study of middle school students in Washington state reported that students recalled more of the advertising content of the program than of the news, and confirmed earlier studies that the ads had at least some impact on students' buying behavior (Austin et al., 2006).

I'd suggest that, for students living in a society where advertising is so prominent, exposure to ads in a school setting is not appreciably more of a problem than such exposure in the rest of their lives. It has also been argued that Channel One provided an excellent (but largely unused) opportunity for teachers to discuss advertising's role in the economy and to help educate their students to have an increased understanding of advertising. All in all, taking a utilitarian approach to this specific problem, one might conclude that on balance, Channel One produced greater benefits for more people than its absence would have done.

The same can be said for the general role played by advertising even if it is not held to ethical standards of truth. One can certainly argue cogently that it is better for the society as a whole if advertising adheres to ethical standards concerned primarily with the overall welfare of society. One can even argue for the benefits of advertising codes of ethics, bland and unenforceable as they often are.

Although I don't disagree with those arguments, I much prefer to let the audience determine whether the subjects of the ads are plausible. I find it totally unrealistic to think about requiring (or even advocating) an ethical stance that focuses solely on absolute truth, as long as advertising and the marketing aspects of public relations serve the purposes they do in our society—namely, as a provider of important commercial information and as the economic engine that drives (or "drive$") the media. That engine must be free to attempt to persuade and to serve the needs of the clients who are paying for that persuasion, subject to the basic legal standards acknowledged previously and to a healthy dose of transparency.

Any other approach runs the risk of making advertising less effective in the name of imposing such ethical standards as plausibility or literal truthfulness. Such results would diminish not only the effectiveness of the advertising-driven economy but also the economic viability and the independence of the U.S. mass media. Advertising, after all, is the major alternative to having the media financed (and perhaps controlled) by the government, or to placing the entire burden of paying for the media on the shoulders of media users. Although advertising should not be beyond the reach of some ethical principles, it certainly should not be saddled with such excess ethical baggage as concerns for truth, which are really not relevant to its function in society.

KEY POINTS

- Truth is less important in advertising than is transparency, which could help safeguard the public and educate media consumers about how persuasive communication works.
- "Creative embellishment"—rather than literal description—is appropriate in advertising copy as long as it avoids blatant deception.
- The PRSA code sets useful standards for factual statements released to the media or to the public, but these shouldn't apply literally and rigidly to the marketing of a product or idea.

MERRILL: Commentary

Here we have the ends–means problem. Because the purpose (end) of advertising and PR is to create images and sell products, there (is? is not?) a need for it to be truthful. The deontologist on this issue (Peter Gade) would say that there is a need for truth because truth is per se an ethical principle; David Gordon, taking the teleological position, contends that because advertising needs to create good images and make sales, and because people understand this, it can be excused from telling the truth.

This seems a rather strange "controversy" for an ethics book, but here it is and we must deal with it. One would think the teleological position is really pragmatics, not ethics, and that Machiavellian considerations dominate instead of more ethical ones. But, of course, there are other times in ethical discourse where truth is set aside because of possible consequences, so it could be that this is what we find here.

Sissela Bok (1978) is often cited as saying that telling the entire truth about anything is unreasonable. Of course it is, but if truthfulness is important to one's ethical theory, then at least an attempt should be made to tell the truth. And Gade is correct, I think, in his contention that this would apply to PR and advertising as well as to news.

What bothers me is the new term for this persuasive enterprise—"strategic communication." This implies some cunning or underhanded techniques that come close to being what is generally termed propaganda. Admitted, Gordon is right that PR/advertising is pragmatically (commercially) oriented and that conforming to absolute standards of truth is not effective. Would that mean that certain deception is warranted? "Creative embellishment" is a term that Gordon uses for advertising. And this is "ethical"? Perhaps so, in the sense (Gordon quoting Johannesen) that advertising is not inherently "an exercise in rational communication." Irrational communication, then, may also be ethical—in a different contextual linguistic world?

But don't advertisers give the people what they want? "No," says Gade; by and large, "Yes," say Gordon and the advertisers. But let's say they do. Does that make it ethical?

The contention is often that the truth needs to be used liberally in advertising, not only to sell ideas and products, but also for the benefit of the public. For example, it might be contended that people *need* to accept some advertising messages, such as the warnings that smoking is dangerous to one's health. Is it, then, not ethical to stretch the truth somewhat, or to hide certain peripheral facts, in order to accomplish your purpose? Such a case *can* be made, weak though I think it is. Does a beneficial end justify the means (even when the means may be unethical)? I agree with Immanuel Kant and Peter Gade that it does not. But this kind of rationalization is used in political advertising all the time. In order to keep "that scoundrel out of office" where he might be destructive to the people's best interest, it is justifiable to paint him as more villainous than he really is. If truth were the criterion for political advertising, there would be very little such advertising, which might not be all bad.

So we can see that, in a very broadly interpreted altruistic sense, advertising and public relations (the selling of products and images) that are less than truthful *can* be considered ethical if we are thinking pragmatically or teleologically. The purpose of advertising and PR is to sell, we are often told; therefore, if tampering with the truth helps us to sell, what is wrong with that? Of course, what is wrong is that it ignores the normal ethical consideration of truth-telling; it contributes to misrepresentation, to providing false images, to exaggerated expectations, to unwarranted expenditure of money, and often to getting something that does not live up to promises.

Again we hear the voice of Kant: *just tell the truth*. Be principled; feel a duty to truth-telling, without worrying about possible consequences. But then, from somewhere inside our rationality, comes the voice of the consequence-oriented ethicist, exemplified by Gordon: Think of the expectations of your employer. Think about the purpose of your work. Think about the good that selling this product (or this candidate) may do for others.

The perennial question arises: truth or consequences?

Advertising—at least certain kinds—can lead to obvious benefits to others and to society as a whole. But advertising can also result in overspending, conspicuous consumption, and the inculcation of unrealistic and frustrating expectations. Should truth play a key role in such advertising? Machiavelli would have said "Yes"—*if* your purposes can be secured by telling the truth. If not, then it would be permissible, even wise, to tamper with the truth to the extent necessary to achieve your ends.

It seems to be all right with Gordon that PR and advertising can play fast and loose with the truth; after all, he might say it is no more than a form of "commercial poetry" and that departing from the truth is simply creative embellishment. I believe that audiences of advertising *expect* and *desire* truth even though they may recognize that they seldom get it. It is regretful that Gade does not take a firmer position against untruthful advertising in his

> If truth were the criterion for political advertising, there would be very little such advertising,

arguments. But he does, I think quite effectively, point out other potential problem areas in advertising ethics, such as the misleading and inflated contentions of political advertising.

There is, throughout this debate, a thin mist of permissive deception. Is *some* deception at some times ethical? I would think that *all* deception any time is unethical. But, then, maybe not in today's permissive moral climate.

Gordon is taking the Machiavellian view, or at least a modified version of it. Gade does seem to try to keep truth at the core of his ethical posture, agreeing, although at times half-heartedly, with Kant that truth-telling is a categorical imperative. Just who is correct? Who has the right ethical perspective on this truth-in-strategic-communication question? I can't give an answer. Both perspectives may well be correct (ethical), depending on which mega-theory of ethics one accepts.

I prefer the Kantian view that *never* in PR and advertising should the communicator resort to untruths. Perhaps the reader will be able to cut his or her way through the thickets of ethical confusion and find a comfortable and satisfying clearing in which to find a moral resting place. But I doubt it. As with all the controversies in this book, there is simply no clear and completely satisfying answer. But that is no reason for us to discontinue the search.

REFERENCES AND RELATED READINGS

Aiello, Lauren, and Jennifer M. Proffitt. (2008). "VNR usage: A matter of regulation or ethics?" *Journal of Mass Media Ethics* 23(3), pp. 219–234.

Austin, Erica Weintraub, Yi-chin "Yvonnes" Chen, Bruce E. Pinkleton, and Jessie Quintero Johnson. (2006). "Benefits and costs of *Channel One* in a middle school setting and the role of media-literacy training." *Pediatrics* 117, pp. e423–e433. Retrieved from www.pediatrics.org/cgi/content/full/117/3/e423 (October 28, 2007).

Berger, Arthur. (2004). *Ads, Fads, and Consumer Culture: Advertising's Impact on American Character and Society.* New York: Rowan & Littlefield.

Berkowitz, Daniel A. (1990). "Refining the gatekeeping metaphor for local television news." *Journal of Broadcasting and Electronic Media* 34(1), pp. 55–68.

Blewett, Steve. (1994). "Poetry and public relations: Reality in a waterball of glass." *Journalism Educator* 48(4), pp. 39–46.

Bogart, Leo. (1995). *Commercial Culture: The Media System and the Public Interest.* New York: Oxford University Press.

Bok, Sissela. (1978). *Lying: Moral Choice in Public and Private Life.* New York: Random House.

Bush, Michael. (2006). "The agency business: Firms want to share in customer interaction." *PRWeek*, March 20, p. 9.

Channel One. (2011). "About Channel One news: Who are we?" Retrieved from www.channelone.com/about/ (February 4).

Chepesiuk, Ron. (2006). "Fake news or valuable resource: The controversy surrounding the VNR." *Quill* 94(1), January/February, pp. 10–13.

Craig, David. (2007). "Case and commentaries: Wal-Mart public relations in the blogosphere." *Journal of Mass Media Ethics* 22(2–3), pp. 215–218.

Elliott, Stuart. (1993). "Advertising: In creating a spot, many say there's nothing like the real thing." *The New York Times*, November 26, p. D15.

————. (2004). "The media business: Advertising—A survey of consumer attitudes reveals the depth and challenge that agencies face." *The New York Times*, April 14. Retrieved from http://query.nytimes.com/gst/fullpage.html?res+9C00E2DD163BF937A25757C0A9629C8B63&sec=&spon=&spon=&pagewanted=print (October 2, 2007).

Emerson, Julian. (2008). "Ethics dispute leads to resignation of WEAU news director." Eau Claire, WI *Leader-Telegram*, January 15, p. 1B. Retrieved from www.leadertelegram.com/story-news_local.asp?id=BFGHV2K19MM (March 8, 2009).

Federal Trade Commission. (2007). "Children not seeing more food ads on television." Retrieved from www.ftc.gov/opa/2007/06/childrenadstudy.shtm (October 2, 2007).

Fink, Conrad C. (1988). *Media Ethics: In the Newsroom and Beyond*. New York: McGraw-Hill.

Grunig, James, ed. (1992). *Excellence in Public Relations and Communication Management*. Hillsdale, NJ: Lawrence Erlbaum Associates.

"Joe Camel's Rights." (1994). Editorial. *The Boston Globe*, February 26, p. 16.

Johannesen, Richard L., Kathleen S. Valde, and Karen E. Whedbee. (2008). *Ethics in Human Communication*, 6th ed. Long Grove, IL: Waveland.

Johnson, Bradley, and Kevin Brown. (2007). "Data center." *Advertising Age* 78(12), March 19, p. 8.

Knowlton, Steven R. (1997). *Moral Reasoning for Journalists: Cases and Comments*. Westport, CT: Praeger.

Kurtz, Howard. (2005). "Firms paid TV's tech gurus to promote their products." *The Washington Post*, April 20, p. C1.

Lambeth, Edmund B. (1992). *Committed Journalism: An Ethic for the Profession*, 2nd ed. Bloomington and Indianapolis, IN: Indiana University Press.

Lasswell, Harold. (1937). "Propaganda." In E. Seligman and A. Johnson, eds., *Encyclopedia of Social Sciences* 12, pp. 521–528.

Levitt, Theodore. (1970). "The morality (?) of advertising." *Harvard Business Review*, July–August, pp. 84–92.

Lieberman, Trudy. (2007). "Epidemic." *Columbia Journalism Review* 45(6), March/April, pp. 38–43.

Linn, Travis. (1992). "Video news releases: Breaching the covenant with viewers." Paper presented at the annual convention of the Association for Education in Journalism and Mass Communication, Montreal, August 5–8.

Mabie, Glen. (2008). "Ethics in journalism." *The West Side*, broadcast on WHWC, Menomonie-Eau Claire, WI, January 22. Archived by Wisconsin Public Radio and available at www.wpr.org/regions/eau/twsarchive.cfm.

Mander, Jerry. (1993). "Four arguments for the elimination of advertising." In Edd Applegate, Sharon Brock, Joseph Pisani, and Eric Zanot, eds., *Advertising: Concepts, Strategies, and Issues*. Dubuque, IA: Kendall/Hunt.

Mandese, Joe. (2005). "The art of manufactured news." *Broadcasting & Cable* 135(13), March 24, p. 24.

Mathewson, Catriona. (2006). "Web stunt sends coke from hero to zero." *The Courier-Mail* (Brisbane, Australia), January 28, p. 13.

McManus, John. (1994). *Market-Driven Journalism: Let the Citizen Beware?* Thousand Oaks, CA: Sage.

Merrill, John C. (1997). *Journalism Ethics: Philosophical Foundations for News Media*. New York: St. Martin's Press.

Plaisance, Patrick L. (2007). "Transparency: An assessment of the Kantian roots of a key element in media ethics practice." *Journal of Mass Media Ethics* 22(2–3), pp. 187–207.

Preston, Ivan L. (1996). *The Great American Blowup: Puffery in Advertising and Selling*. Madison, WI: University of Wisconsin Press.

Pugh, Tony. (2004). "Medicare ads violate federal law, GAO concludes." *Knight Ridder Tribune Business News*, May 20, p. 1. Available at http://search.ebscohost.com/login.aspx?direct=true&db=nfh&AN=2W 60062907757&site=ehost-live.

Purushothaman, Shoba. (2005). "The truth about VNRs." *Broadcasting & Cable* 135(16), April 15, p. 62.

Risser, James. (2000). "The wall is heading back." *Columbia Journalism Review* 38(5), January/February, pp. 26–27.

Rutenberg, Jim. (2004). "Campaign ads under fire for inaccuracy." *The New York Times*, May 25, 1A, pp. 21A.

Sallot, Lynn, and Elizabeth Johnson. (2006). "Investigating relationships between journalists and public relations practitioners." *Public Relations Review* 32(2), pp. 151–159.

Schudson, Michael. (1984). *Advertising, the Uneasy Persuasion: Its Dubious Impact on American Society*. New York: Basic Books.

Severin, Werner, and James Tankard. (2001). *Communication Theories*, 5th ed. New York: Addison, Wesley, Longman.

Stewart, James B. (1994). "Grand illusion." *The New Yorker*, October 31, pp. 64–81.

Story, Louise. (2006). "Celebrities embrace advertising's limelight." *International Herald Tribune*, October 11. Retrieved from www.iht.com/articles/2006/10/11/business/adco.php (October 15, 2007).

Street, Emily. (2007). "Advertising's brave new world." *The Wall Street Journal*, May 25, p. B1.

Teinowitz, Ira. (2006). "Political ads shatter records on way to $2B." *Advertising Age* 77(45), pp. 1, 79.

Trickett, Eleanor. (2006). "Media/PR relationship crucial as paid-for model blurs lines." *PRweek* 9(24), June 12, p. 11.

Werner, Thomas. (2003). "A round 'PEG' in a round hole." *Federal Communications Law Journal* 56(1), pp. 239–268.

ZenithOptimedia. (2006). "World Cup to boost adspend growth in 2006; Internet to sustain momentum to 2008." Retrieved from www.zenithoptimedia.com/about/news/pdf/Adspend%20April%202006.pdf (March 16, 2010).

Chapter 12

The Ethics of New Advertising Technologies and Techniques

W HEN this subject was proposed for this new edition of *Controversies in Media Ethics*, it seemed like a no-brainer. There were new technologies and techniques showing up everywhere, and it seemed only logical that new ethical questions would be generated by the use of these new technologies for persuasion.

However, in writing this material, both Kim Sheehan and Michael Dorsher concluded that there were far fewer unique ethical conundrums than originally thought, in using new technologies for persuasive communication. But this conclusion didn't prevent both Sheehan and Dorsher from having strong differences of opinion about the fundamental ethical factors involved.

These factors are, to a great extent, economic rather than ethical. The rise of the Internet—and the negative effects of the recession that lasted for several years after its start in 2008—have greatly eroded the usual revenue sources for many traditional media and even caused some to predict the demise of the newspaper as a mass medium. Nicole Brodeur (2009), a Seattle newspaper columnist, put it this way: "To some extent, we did this to ourselves. All these smarts, all this warning, and we still can't figure out how to make money from the work we put online."

So, although the Internet's use for persuasion was the focus of this chapter, its authors are not concentrating on the particular technologies and business models of this year or, indeed, any particular year. There will be little mention of Twitter, smartphones or the other new communication devices and applications that show up every few months. Rather, both authors concentrated on the *use* of these devices and the ways in which the public relates to them. They looked to the history of previous "new" technologies and their *use* for advertising over the years—and, to a great extent, drew some conclusions that might be germane when the next generation(s) of new communication devices and techniques are adopted—whatever they may be or whenever we see them in the stores.

In other words, they found that the *use* of most communication "technology" isn't new, with respect to its functions, and what advertisers wanted to do with it. Printing is printing, whether it is done on a briefcase-sized printer attached to one's computer or on an enormous rotary newspaper press. How these recorded messages are distributed—by postal services or by data packets on the Internet—makes little or no difference. Different techniques (from dot matrix to letterpress, carbon paper, and many others since the development of writing) all have the same function: providing a record of words and making copies of them.

All content has evolved from earlier forms. As an analogy, the same rule applies to drama, whether on a stage, on a movie theater screen, or on a television or computer monitor. So, as discussed in this chapter, the communication of messages that are intended to persuade people to buy a product or service (advertising) or think well (or badly) of some person or organization or nation (public relations and propaganda) has always used the complete arsenal of available technologies.

Are there differences between spam and direct mail advertising? Yes, but the functions are almost identical. Similarly, telephone and radio broadcasting transmission and receiving technologies may differ, but there is very little difference between the messages themselves. The content of movies on the large screen and television programs on the small screen is much the same.

Such attention-gaining and persuasive techniques as "product placement"—using brand name products (or even just the name) unobtrusively in an entertainment program, movie, or publication—associates the brand with the stars of a production and the enjoyable content. Product placement is much the same (although less overt) as the neon signs with the logos of different brands of beer in the neighborhood bar or the billboards around a baseball field. Just a few figurative steps away is "plugola": When a respected news commentator, columnist or talk-show host mentions a brand, it shouldn't be surprising if a couple of cases of the product were delivered to their doorstep the next day. There are some performers who did this deliberately in the days before this procedure developed a bad reputation. One popular figure even carried it to the extreme of reading out over the air a list of products that one of the show's producers (about to get married) was yearning for.

Yet another aspect of product placement is the negative side of this practice. No advertiser wants their product shown being used for evil purposes. For example, in the film *Judgment at Nuremberg* (1961), the phrase "gas ovens" in dialog referring to the poison gas used by Nazis to murder Jews during the Holocaust was strongly (and successfully) objected to by companies supplying gas for cooking and heating in the United States. On a more banal note, in the 1930s and 1940s, the motion picture industry built generic automobiles in their scene shops both to avoid free advertising for automobile manufacturers or using another firm's copyrighted designs for which they might be asked to pay.

In summary, once the basics of a communication device or technique are understood in their historical relationship to other devices, techniques and uses, the ethical questions seem to be much the same as in the past. Their application may be different; for example, looking to the future, if (let's use a little science fiction here) we develop techniques for using mental telepathy, we certainly will have to be careful how it is used in order to deal ethically with all of the stakeholders involved. In particular, we must consider the effects of such messaging on those being reached by this technique (particularly those who aren't able, perhaps because of youth, to develop defenses), the advertisers who use it, and the creative persons who produce the messages—as well as the society at large. If we develop forms of hypnotism for the sale of goods and services or someone starts inserting habit-forming drugs into the coffee we drink at our morning break, there are ethical implications. But they aren't new; ordinary caffeine can be habit-forming, as can alcohol and tobacco.

One of the reasons that the use of media, old or new, for advertising is so controversial is because the public fears that mere exposure to a persuasive message will result in people responding to the message without thinking about it. Psychologists would think of this as an S→R (stimulus→response) reaction, and it is a counterforce to the concept of truly free will. Advertisers have their own goals, which may or may not be beneficial to consumers or congruent with their goals. It should come as no surprise that *Consumer Reports* magazine has much of its high reputation for honesty and fairness because it does not accept advertising in its pages.

In the late 1950s, the idea of subliminal advertising messages to modify attitudes frightened many people and led to an FCC edict against its use on television, even though advertising agencies soon realized that this technique was generally ineffective. Given half a chance, people are capable of thinking about the messages they receive, or ignoring them. Can you remember each product advertised on the billboards along the most recent route you drove? The commercials on the television program you just watched? The advertising inserts in the Sunday newspaper?

Notice the phrase "given half a chance" in the previous paragraph. Some of these techniques—such as hypnotism or subliminal persuasion or habit-forming drugs—are intended *not* to give the audience or consumer a chance to counter them. Although protective laws exist in some instances, it really is up to those constructing messages to prevent unethical uses—and up to consumers to realize that just because they've been exposed to a brand name, there is no necessity for them to buy it. There is no law that stops an advertiser from being honest, avoiding deception, or otherwise making sure that the viewer, listener, or reader has that "half chance." In other words, just because something is possible doesn't mean that it is ethical, wise, or even practical to do.

This is where the ethics of new media and techniques comes in, and both Sheehan and Dorsher have picked up the gauntlet. Sheehan accepts the idea that our economy rests on commerce and the advertising that feeds it. She essentially accepts the use for advertising and public relations of any *legal* technique or technology that makes efficient persuasion possible. Dorsher refuses to accept the idea that all new and legal techniques are valid, and asserts that traditional ethical principles apply no matter what technologies are employed.

SHEEHAN: Product placement, spam, "pop-ups," and similar techniques are ethical tools for advertisers and their clients to use, as long as they are legal and can sell a product.

Have you received any e-mails for penile implants recently? In 2007, before the collapse of the home mortgage industry triggered a recession, how many pop-up ads promoting low-interest mortgages did you see on your computer in an average week? Were you surprised by the number of product placements in your favorite TV show? Have you ever wondered why there is so much advertising surrounding us wherever we go?

Advertisers and marketers use a host of techniques to construct and send persuasive messages to consumers. These communicators act ethically when they provide messages and operate within systems where *both* consumers and advertisers have some degree of control over the message. Persuasive messages are part of our lives because we live in a market society, a society of relative abundance, where we have many choices for almost everything we do, vote for, or buy. Because of this, we often use persuasive messages to help us make decisions. We balance the trade-offs of the options and assess both the "upside" and the "downside" of choices.

Non-traditional messages, such as product placements, commercial e-mail, and all sorts of Internet advertisements appear in hitherto unfamiliar contexts. Unlike traditional messages during television programs and in magazines, where the context is fairly well established, non-traditional messages appear in contexts where advertisements may not be expected. At the same time, the context changes at the click of a mouse button, and consumers are more open to advertising messages at certain times than others.

Ethical examinations of persuasion communications (specifically, a model developed by Jaksa and Pritchard, 2004) use the idea *of information utility* to assess the ethicality of persuasive messages. Information utility evaluations are based on how well the information allows consumers to make decisions. Jaksa and Pritchard (2004) suggest that persuasive messages are ethical when:

- The information in the message is truthful and relevant.
- The information helps us make good decisions.
- The messages allow us time to reflect on the information before making decisions.
- The messages contain important benefits for consumers to consider.
- The messages treat consumers with respect.

We can use Jaksa and Pritchard's ideas to show that non-traditional messages are ethical because they not only provide information but also allow for consumers to make decisions by providing access to a range of information at appropriate times. Two ethical frameworks support this proposition. First, consumers consistently report that they find the information provided in non-traditional messages to be valuable in their decision-making about products and services. Therefore, persuasive messages give them the ability to be more in control of their decision-making. Second, evidence exists to suggest that consumers view marketing activities based on specific ideas of exchange; that is, consumers evaluate what they *get* from a communication in order to determine whether the exchange is fairly equal to what they are *giving up*. This speaks again to consumer control, in that consumers negotiate what they will give up in order to maintain control.

ADVERTISERS AND "NEW" TECHNOLOGY

Advertisers have always been eager to use new technologies for their advertising messages. More than 400 years ago, advertisers used the new technology of the printing press to produce multiple copies of the first flyers promoting services to the public (printed on paper left over from religious texts). In the 1920s, advertisers used the new technology of airplanes for aerial advertising by towing banners advertising products and local stores, and later used skywriting to create giant logos and slogans in the sky. Starting in the 1920s, the new technology of radio used popular entertainment and messages to associate brands with popular personalities. After World War II, the new technology of television helped advertisers create memorable characters that viewers associated with products (Geary, 1999).

It is not surprising that the growth of the Internet in the 1990s led advertisers to investigate how to use this new media channel for persuasive messages. All advertising messages, whether they are delivered through traditional or non-traditional methods, attempt to persuade consumers to learn something about a product or service, to develop an emotional attachment to a brand, and/or to prefer one brand over another, all with the ultimate goal of selling more products and services. Advertising is part of the grease that keeps the wheels of our economy moving forward.

The 21st century has seen all sorts of advertisers, from high-tech start-ups to Fortune 500 companies, investigating the use of new media to deliver advertising messages. Why have advertisers increased their spending in new media over the past few years? For one thing, the fragmentation of traditional (television and print) media audiences continues to increase. Because of fragmentation, it is difficult for advertisers and marketers to find the best audiences for their messages and to find them in large enough numbers to have an effect on their business. In addition, these already-fragmented media audiences now have access to technological innovations that provide them with more control over what content they watch and hear. Even if advertisers and marketers can find the audiences, the audiences now have the ability to use digital video recorders (DVRs) and devices such as TiVo to avoid traditional television ads completely, and it has always been possible to ignore ads scattered throughout newspapers and magazines.

Given these media realities, advertisers and marketers are continually searching for new techniques to find their elusive target audience and, when found, to provide that target audience with information about products and services that may be of interest to them. And consumers do pay attention to these messages. A phenomenon called the Van Restorff effect explains that any type of message that appears in an unlikely or unexpected place draws increased attention and generates higher recall (Balasubramanian, 1994).

Throughout history, advertisers' use of non-traditional techniques has raised eyebrows among critics, even though humans have engaged in persuasion since the dawn of time. At least since the first printed advertisement, critics questioned whether this or that form of persuasion is ethical. The act of delivering persuasive techniques with new technology may generate increased criticism specifically because of the Van Restorff effect: as consumers, we are not used to seeing messages in certain places and may thus have a heightened sensitivity to their appearance.

THE NATURE OF PERSUASION

Let us stop a moment and consider the nature of persuasive communication. Persuasion is a communication technique that seeks to "change, resolve, or formulate other people's opinions, feelings or actions through the deliberate use of argument, reasoning or entreaty" (Bendinger, 2001, p. 33). Persuasion is a process. In our society, audiences scrutinize and question the messages that they see and decide for themselves whether the message is appropriate for them. Said another way, consumers decide for themselves whether they will purchase the product the persuasive message is asking them to buy. You might be familiar with the phrase *caveat emptor*, which translates as "let the buyer beware." What this means is that audiences know—or should know—that advertisers will highlight the advantages of a product while hiding its flaws and disadvantages. In other words, advertisers expect audiences to be skeptical. All this allows audiences to use their own judgment to evaluate different messages. And the ethics of persuasion rests on the extent to which a persuasive message allows the audience to make free choices about the matter being presented.

> the ethics of persuasion rest on the extent to which a persuasive message allows the audience to make free choices

This idea of persuasion as a process focuses on audience members being active consumers of information. The idea of active consumers comes from information processing theory, which has its basis in psychology (Assael, 1995). Information processing theory states that our brains process information through the application of logical rules and strategies in terms of what to attend to, what to process and what to avoid (Sutherland, 1993). When exposed to messages, we initially decide whether we will pay attention to the message (also known as selective perception). If we choose to pay some degree of attention to the message, we then decide if we will retain any portions of the message in our short-term memory (selective attention). Finally, we decide what information in our short-term memory to save in our long-term memory for use at a future time, such as when we make a purchase decision (selective recall).

As our minds have a limited capacity for what we process, we active consumers are pragmatic participants in communication who critically decide which messages to evaluate, and what exactly we need to learn before we make decisions (Assael, 1995). Our minds are not foolproof, though. We may pay attention to a message initially (selective perception) because it is annoying or offensive. We may choose to remember it initially so we can *avoid* purchasing it, but over time the annoyance goes away and the product with the annoying ad becomes simply one more product we are familiar with. While often we are consciously thinking about the information in the advertisements, other times we may recognize familiar images or sounds that get us to pay some attention to the message merely because it reminds us of something else we have seen or heard before. We may not process the information in the ad directly, but the ad has made some type of impression on us that we will use in the future to make a purchase decision. Product familiarity can create the sort of positive emotional reaction that advertisers like.

When I worked in the advertising industry, the idea of consumer control led many advertising professionals to develop a pragmatic attitude toward their output. Advertising agencies and their clients are successful only if the ad "works" on some level. Advertisements are one of several persuasive techniques used to influence customers to select one brand over another (such as buying Coke instead of Pepsi) or one category over another (such as drinking milk instead of water). When advertising and other persuasive messages provide the best information in the best context for a specific target audience, they can create preferences that lead to consumers buying the advertised product when they are in the market to do so. There is an economic benefit for consumers since producers can become more efficient when they increase production, with the result that they are able to lower prices to consumers. Economically, then, advertising is a win-win situation for both consumers (who are able to buy products at lower costs) and companies (who can spread their costs over more units and improve their bottom-line profit).

If advertising does not work, the whole system is mucked up. Specifically, if consumers do not like the content of an advertising message, or where that message is placed, or something else about the persuasive process, they will communicate that dislike in a variety of ways. They may recommend that others not buy the product. They may seek alternative products. They may take the station's Web site off the "favorites" list on their computer or cancel their subscription to the newspaper. They may complain to the company whose name is on the product, or to the media outlet where the ad appeared, or to their local retailer, and they may complain to the government. But most of the time, they simply will not buy the product. Therefore, it is in advertisers' and marketers' best interest to make sure that consumers believe companies are acting ethically throughout the persuasion process.

As I look at the industry from an academic perspective, though, I see that there is a major flaw with this pragmatic perspective. Specifically, it suggests that market forces will identify and weed out the unethical practices. But there isn't anything stopping advertising from pushing the ethical envelope, just to see if the theoretical market forces really will have an effect. Because of this, today we have ads that are annoying to consumers but are also selling products. Does this mean that these advertisers are acting unethically?

Argument and evidence presented below suggest that consumers perceive non-traditional messages as providing benefits even beyond the information benefits, and this mitigates potentially problematic aspects of these messages. For example, that consumers find value in the messages is an example of a utilitarian ethical perspective. A second function of persuasion suggests a social contract perspective. Both of these will be discussed in detail below to support the stance that marketers and advertisers may well be acting ethically when they choose to use non-traditional messages and media to promote their brands.

THE UTILITARIAN PERSPECTIVE

Utilitarianism derives from the philosophy of John Stuart Mill, and suggests that "certain actions are right in proportion as they tend to promote happiness, wrong as they tend to produce the reverse of happiness" (Crisp, 1997, p. 95). Advertisers have interpreted that rule as meaning that advertising is ethical if it provides the greatest good for the greatest number (Rotzoll and Christians, 1980). Rotzoll and Christians further suggest that in situations where outcomes (such as information value and consumer attitudes) can be studied and/or predicted, utilitarian ethics should apply.

Let's look at what's shown by some of the studies of consumer reactions to non-traditional advertising. These studies conclude that, in case after case, consumers appear to appreciate the information they get from these ads and have fairly positive feelings toward such messages—showing that the messages are providing benefits that outweigh their negative aspects.

- A study by Schlosser et al. (1999) provided a benchmark for assessing attitudes toward advertising on the Internet. The study found that the majority of respondents found non-traditional ads online informative, and more than half agreed that they liked to look at the advertising on the Internet. Less than one-third reported that they were offended by online advertisements.
- A study by a firm called Dynamic Logic (2004) found that more than two-thirds of consumers had either positive or neutral opinions on Web site ads and opt-in e-mail; these opinions were similar to consumer opinions on television advertising.
- The same study investigated specific Internet formats and found that more than half of consumers had positive or neutral opinions about banner (horizontal) and skyscraper (vertical) ads (Dynamic Logic, 2004).
- The Newspaper Advertising Association (2006) examined the answers to similar questions. This study reported that consumers viewed the Internet as a valuable way to save time while shopping and to do comparison-shopping for products and services. Internet messages were second only to newspapers in their information value to consumers.
- In August, 2005, a study reported that half of consumers did not mind product placement in movies. Among those who did not mind, half of the respondents remembered the names of brands that the characters either used or spoke (Simmons Market Research Bureau, 2005). Another study showed that product placement can create a positive brand connection that encourages people to purchase products: when Tom Cruise wore Ray-Ban sunglasses in *Risky Business* (1983), sales immediately jumped by more than 50% (Sauer, 2005).
- The Pew Center for Internet Life found that online users in 2007 reported they received more unsolicited e-mail than they did in 2003 but were less bothered by it than they were in 2003 (Fallows, 2007). The same study found that only 18% of online users called spam a "big problem," compared to 25% in 2003. Such a finding is attributed to both a technological factor explanation and a psychological one (Fallows, 2007). Technologically, consumers have more access to spam-blocking software for their computers. Psychologically, consumers have become more accustomed to spam as a "cost of doing business" with e-mail. Or to say it more specifically, receiving un-solicited e-mail is the trade-off for having access to e-mail in the first place.

This last point moves the argument beyond simple information utility to other types of benefits that consumers assess when making choices about messages and ethics. As a next step, we can use the ethical framework of the *social contract*, which suggests that people evaluate both their own role and the communication role in exchanges in our society, in order to determine whether the marketing is being done in an ethical manner.

THE SOCIAL CONTRACT

The original idea of a social contract is based on the writings of John Locke, who expressed the view that citizens' moral and/or political obligations are dependent upon a contract or agreement between them to form society. This idea of a social contract complements definitions of marketing as exchange; that is, in marketing situations consumers implicitly agree to give up something in exchange for something else (Gordon and Lima-Turner, 1997).

The social contract, when referring to advertising, is about control over choices and assessing the benefits and detriments of our choices. Here is an example. Premium cable channels, such as HBO, provide commercial-free viewing opportunities. However, consumers pay a monthly fee to access the programming. Not all consumers subscribe to HBO, though, because they do not perceive the value of the programs to be worth the cost at that time in their lives or because they lack discretionary income to pay for it. However, if HBO announces a new program that is of interest to them and money is available, they may re-evaluate that decision.

Michael Dorsher's contention in his part of this chapter—that the social contract approach is really "social hegemony"—fails to credit consumers with the ability to make rational choices for themselves. With the social contract, consumers assess both the perceived benefits and perceived detriments when making choices. In the case of non-traditional advertising, consumers balance the benefits of what the non-traditional message supplies with the costs of the exchange.

What are some of these costs?

- *Annoyance Costs:* when ads are annoying, they disrupt the content that we wish to see and cause our online sessions to be less enjoyable or productive. Annoying, of course, means different things to different people. Some can find the content of a message annoying; others can find the frequency of messages annoying. Since we all have different tolerances for things that annoy us, it is hard to quantify the costs for these types of messages.
- *Time Costs:* ads can take up digital space, causing some Web sites to load more slowly, thus interrupting our online activities. Unsolicited commercial e-mails clutter our inboxes and make it time-consuming to find the messages we really want to read.
- *Privacy Costs:* advertisers and marketers can collect data about online consumers without their knowledge or permission (see Chapter 10).
- *Confusion Costs:* when advertisements are not labeled as advertisements (such as in product placement), they may cause consumers to mistake the paid nature of the message.

It is important to remember something I said earlier: These costs may vary given the particular context in which a consumer is viewing the message. When we are leisurely exploring sites or surfing on the Internet, we may have less concern with these costs than when we are searching for a quick answer to a pressing problem. Since the context of the Internet changes with the click of a mouse button, it is difficult to assess the real value of the costs. For example, I cannot argue that a particular number of annoying messages are worth free access to the CNN Web site and all the information it provides. It is clear, though, that consumers are willing to assess costs *and* benefits for the particular context that they are experiencing.

As said earlier, information value is one benefit. Other benefits include:

- Non-traditional advertising decreases the costs of consumer access to media channels and content.

In our mass-mediated society, the presence of advertisements allows consumers to access much media content for low or no fee. While many consumers pay some type of access fee for the Internet, once that access is fee is paid much online content is available free of charge (Sheehan, 2004). Today, selling space for online advertisements and product placement is the primary way that Web sites can provide free content. Whether or not a new model—perhaps a more complex one—will emerge isn't yet known.

In a similar way, product placements in media content can reduce the cost of production, helping shows to continue to be available on "free" television and reducing the net costs of motion picture production. Today, the movie ticket price accounts for less than 10% of the revenue received by the producing studio. Without other income, such as book tie-ins, toys using the film characters, video recordings (in various formats) for rent or sale, or product placement in films—including the assistance provided by some hungry-for-tourists locations shown in the film—it is likely that the ticket price would increase beyond acceptable levels for many consumers, or that production costs would be cut and quality suffer.

In terms of a social contract, there is a certain amount of advertising volume that consumers feel is a "fair trade." Hallerman (2002) found that 72% of online users are not opposed to receiving a limited number of ads, as long as they don't feel over-exposed to the commercial content. Results of this study showed that as many as two to six ads per hour are "appropriate" to support free content. Moreover, if they do see too many ads, consumers have access to technological fixes. The availability of spam filters and pop-up blockers provides technological ways for consumers to control their exposure to advertising on their computer screens—or, looked at from the other side, advertising's access to their ears, eyeballs, and wallets. Digital recorders can skip over televised commercials.

These types of technologies allow consumers to control what messages they will and will not watch, allowing advertisements to reach those consumers who are willing to view them. In fact, many consumers do seem willing to view them—data on usage of available technological fixes show that consumers, while aware of such fixes, are not hurrying to adopt them. The fact that only about 25% of consumers used pop-up blockers available to everyone in 2004 suggests that many people may not perceive the volume of such ads as inappropriately high (Hansell, 2004), and others may find the complexity of blocking too high.

- Non-traditional advertising supports the costs of providing content.

Consumers today experience a constant flow of new content. A new blog is created every minute, and more than 10,000 videos are uploaded to YouTube every hour. In fact, the Online

Publishers Association indicated in 2007 that the primary role of the Internet has shifted from "communications to content," as consumers indicate an interest in having more content about a variety of topics (Burns, 2007).

Television networks also need constantly to develop and produce programming with the hope that a show will become popular with audiences. Some shows, especially reality TV shows, receive significant funding from product placement. This funding allows a variety of new and different types of shows to be produced and different kinds of products to get a visual or verbal message to consumers. Finally, this income supplies new revenue streams that may allow new films, books and Web sites to be developed and supported (Sheehan, 2004).

- Non-traditional advertising enhances consumers' experience.

The presence of "real" brands of foodstuffs, automobiles, appliances, and the like (rather than "fake" brands constructed by the prop departments of the producing studios) makes the content of movies and television programs seem more real and believable (and hence improved) to viewers, enhancing the viewing experience with this verisimilitude. People use media to understand the world around them. If media did not contain brands, media credibility would be reduced as content would seem unrealistic to viewers. In fact, audiences enjoy the ability of product placement to mimic reality when this does not interrupt their chosen entertainment (Schmoll et al., 2006).

While the presence of brands might be acceptable, critics dislike it when the paid nature of the placements is disguised. Critics ask how we, as consumers, can assess trade-offs in a social contract framework if we do not even know that the placement is a paid commercial. The advocacy group Commercial Alert requested that the Federal Trade Commission (FTC) require that the word "advertisement" must appear on screen during each instance of a paid product placement during a television program or movie. Commercial Alert maintained that this was the best way to ensure that the paid nature of the placement was clear to consumers. The group feared consumers would be deceived into believing that the placements were not paid advertisements if no disclosure aired.

The FTC denied Commercial Alert's petition, stating that it had found no indication that product placements were either misleading or confusing to consumers. The FTC's letter went on to say that the Commission would investigate if "false or misleading objective, material claims" about a product's attributes were made during a program. The FTC said its practice of evaluating on a case-by-case basis whether an ad format is deceptive remains the best way to protect consumers, including children, from misrepresentation in persuasive messages (Engle, 2005). (The Federal Communications Commission has long had a rule about the identification of program sponsors, which was expanded to include announcement of major "promotional considerations"—but this requirement applied to a much narrower range of content than that proposed by Commercial Alert.)

- Non-traditional advertising can enhance the online user experience by providing information that appeals directly to specific targets.

As I previously mentioned, the context in which a non-traditional ad appears on the Internet can change at the click of a mouse button. This idea of context takes into account both how media are being used and who is using them. Advertisers and marketers learn about online users' habits and interests to decide what types of messages are most appropriate for each visitor. This increases the information value of the messages that online users see. Consumers report that they like receiving targeted ads based on click stream data (a history of Web sites visited) (Gordon and Lima-Turner, 1997).

These targeting methods can use data not directly linked to someone's personal information, thus avoiding all manner of privacy concerns that can be associated with targeting (see Chapter 10). Public opinion polls from a range of sources indicate that online users are most concerned about the collection and usage of information that removes their anonymity. This information, including names, addresses, and Social Security numbers, is very rarely part of the information used by data aggregating software for targeted marketing activities. Advertisers and marketers thus provide messages based not on a user's demographic profile but on the sites he or she chooses to visit online. While this type of targeting does not exist for product placement, the concept of verisimilitude suggests that the most realistic content will contain brands used by the viewers of the content. A television program or movie that is geared toward college students, for example, is unlikely to include product placement for Crayola Crayons or Barbie Dolls. Similarly, content aimed at children will avoid product placement for inappropriate products—a list that is smaller than one might think because children taken on shopping trips frequently specify (by grabbing for familiar or desired brands) at a very early age.

The social contract, then, allows consumers and communicators to negotiate relationships using these concepts of control. As stated earlier, if consumers do not believe that advertisers are holding up their part of the relationship, they can ignore the messages and stop buying the products or services advertised in the messages. This alone suggests that advertisers will pay attention to consumer wants and needs and find ways to balance consumer needs with their own in order to create ethical messages.

CONSIDERATIONS FOR THE FUTURE

As technology continues to evolve, it is likely that marketers and advertisers will continue to utilize non-traditional advertisements to provide messages to consumers. What these messages will look like, though, is hard to predict. Advertisers and marketers constantly track their online media portfolios and quickly drop those formats that consumers do not respond to—or that consumers respond to in a negative way.

Here is an example: In 2004, Columbia Pictures announced it would promote the movie *Spiderman 2* using a unique media channel: advertisements in baseball parks. Specifically, Columbia planned to place the logos for the film on all the bases in Major League Baseball parks. Immediately, both ESPN.com and AOL.com put up online polls to gauge market reaction to the idea. Tens of thousands voted *against* this intrusion and, within 48 hours, the studio cancelled the promotion, citing the polls. This illustrates the huge amount of control consumers may have over non-traditional messages.

Advertisers and marketers should always keep Jaksa and Pritchard's (2004) guidelines in mind when considering new techniques and non-traditional messages. Advertisers should distinguish between messages that provide actual information that consumers can use to make decisions and those messages that serve to trick someone into seeing the information. "Trick" banner ads (those that challenge one to click on a monkey or participate in a meaningless quiz to get a click through) and unsolicited e-mail with misleading subject lines and/or sender names should be considered unethical (as well as legally deceptive). To state it another way, any type of a non-traditional ad that takes away control from the consumer is unethical. Neither should ads that take over a computer screen, that limit the ability of consumers to continue with their online activities, be considered ethical.

> any type of a non-traditional ad that takes away control from the consumer is unethical.

Advertising provides consumers with information to make better decisions, and consumers have control over the messages that they see and hear. Any type of new technology throws a kink into established systems that advertisers and consumers have mutually developed, but history has shown that, given time, the social contract and market forces will address many of the ethical issues that arise.

KEY POINTS

- Advertisers and marketers are ethical when they operate within systems where *both* consumers and advertisers have some degree of control over the messages.
- Advertisers have interpreted utilitarianism to mean that advertising is ethical if it provides the greatest good for the greatest number of people.
- Viewing advertising as a social contract requires one to say that, in marketing situations, consumers implicitly agree to give up something in exchange for something else, while still maintaining control over choices and assessing the benefits and detriments of those choices.

DORSHER: The "anything goes" philosophy regarding the use of new advertising techniques is not only unethical but also counterproductive, and will destroy the credibility of the advertising industry.

As one of the founding editors of washingtonpost.com, I know full well how expensive it can be to run a high-quality online site, and how difficult it can be to generate advertising revenue online, even with millions of readers per month. So I'm not going to be so hypo-critical as to issue a blanket condemnation of pop-up ads. To the contrary, I sincerely believe it is *possible* for a pop-up ad to be ethical, as can a targeted banner ad, a product place-ment, and even a "spam" message. Unlike Kim Sheehan, however, I cannot give blanket approval to *all* product placements, pop-ups, and other forms of new media advertising—whether or not consumers voice objections to them. And I certainly will *not* concede that consumers' acquiescence to them constitutes a social contract that makes all those ads ethical.

When Sheehan says advertisers are continually in search of new techniques to tell audiences about products and services "of interest to them," I agree, but I think "them" is usually the advertisers, not the audiences. And I think the contract between "them" is between the advertising agencies or media, and their advertiser clients, not the audiences, and it's much more of an economic contract than a social contract or ethical compact. It is a bastardization of social contract theory to say that once consumers seek out free Internet content, free broadcasts or affordable cable TV and movies, they implicitly agree to accept all the spam, pop-ups and product placements that advertisers can throw at them.

Social contract theory is not about tit for tat. As John Locke conceived it in the 17th century, social contracts are about the sublimation of self interests to form self-government for the sake of families—and to forsake tyrants. For 20th-century philosopher John Rawls, social contract theory requires equality among parties and a commitment to remove others' vulnerabilities, not take-it-or-leave-it tactics aimed mainly at strengthening oneself.

What Sheehan describes as a social contract is actually more like social hegemony. In its least complex (and least lasting) form, hegemony simply refers to a system where the strength of one party (the hegemon) is so superior to the others that it controls them—at least until they're able to turn the tables. But social hegemony is much more subtle, and effective. Social hegemony is an ongoing process whereby the people in power increase their control by using culture, rather than brute force, to negotiate for the consent of those beneath them (Dorsher, 2002; Gramsci, 1971). Hegemony's beauty—or deviousness, depending on which side of it you stand on—is that it leads people to give up some of their power without a fight. In fact, they implicitly thank the power mongers for taking it off their hands, and soon ask if the hegemon would like more power!

This is the picture Sheehan paints of consumers who trade off free access to Web sites for cookies that track them and ads that pop up over the content, of moviegoers who "don't mind" more than a dozen product placements per film, and of e-mail users who say they're getting used to spam. But what other choice do they have? Their only choice is not to use the Web or e-mail, not to go to the movies, or not to watch them at home. The negotiations are never fair in hegemony; the hegemons always have the upper hand—until they push people too far. Then, as Sheehan suggests, the oppressed start fighting back by doing things such as downloading music and movies for free, text-messaging on phones instead of e-mail, disabling cookies, and deploying pop-up blockers. In turn, however, companies respond by buying out Napster and YouTube, extending spam to text messaging, and embedding crucial content in pop ups. "And so it goes," as iconoclastic newscaster Linda Ellerbee used to say, before the networks fired her for the final time.

So what makes the difference between an unethical new media ad and an ethical one? Sheehan concludes that unethical ads are the ones that break the social contract, the ones that wear out their welcome, in essence. But I'd say those are among the least problematic ads; they're the ones obviously wearing too much makeup. It's the sly seductive ones that worry me—the black widow spiders of the wired (or wireless) world. Sheehan identified four factors that affect the ethics of new media advertising: their trade-off for lower user fees; whether or not they are overwhelming; their transparency (i.e., obviousness); and their targeting or compatibility. I will respond to each of those factors, then delineate my own criteria for separating the unethical ads from the merely innovative ones.

MORE ADS = FEWER FEES

I don't hear many consumers demanding lower Internet fees these days. The digital divide is now based more on knowledge than income (Parayil, 2005). Most U.S. students get Internet access free on their campus, and many workers in the information economy use the Web at work. The cost of computers equipped for Internet access is a small fraction of what it used to be, and a number of locations and firms (Starbucks is a good example) provide free Wi-Fi or other Internet access, but benefit from the increased traffic in their stores. "Package deals" and price reductions are hard to compare, but obviously are weapons in the competitive search for online customers by telephone companies, cable companies and other Internet providers—each firm looking for the perfect profit-making formula. For example, Comcast, which may have found that formula, in 2009 not only used its broadband (cable) facilities for television to a quarter (24 million) of U.S. homes, but is the United States' largest Internet service provider, and third-largest telephone service provider (Blethen, 2009). Its success in acquiring a majority share of NBC Universal early in 2011 added control of considerable program content to that list.

The reason for trying to get more customers is Metcalfe's Law, which postulates that the value of any network increases proportionally as more people use it (Metcalfe, 2000). Advertisers want Web sites and movies and TV shows to have as large an audience as possible—not so those people can use and enjoy the media's content but so that more of them will see their ads and buy their products and services. In other words, advertisers don't subsidize consumers' media use, as Sheehan says; it's consumers who subsidize advertisers.

ADS ARE OK UNLESS THEY OVERWHELM

If consumers didn't feel that advertisers were giving them enough rent for their eyeballs, Sheehan supposes, they could revolt. They'd all start using pop-up blockers, they'd all get TiVo and excise the commercials, or they'd boycott "reality shows" and other big users of product placements. But that theory presumes that consumers could get all the entertainment they want from alternative media with low concentrations of advertising. Although there are some specialized outlets (notably sports) that are able to subsist on pay-per-view or similar schemes, most such media outlets (e.g., the BBC, the Public Broadcasting Service, National Public Radio, and Canadian Broadcasting Corp.) struggle to exist in countries with capitalistic economies unless they are associated with political power that, in turn, has the desire or incentive to control culture.

Instead, it is commercial media that have the capital to invest in the entertainment and news producers who best know how to draw a big audience, giving us the stories we can't wait to discuss around the office water bubbler or in the blog. The producers learn this as a matter of economic survival. The advertisers who ultimately make the producers' salaries possible want big audiences to see their products, and they want audiences that are loyal, meaning captive. Do any of us doubt that if consumers had affordable, ad-free alternatives for high-quality content, they would flock there? One piece of evidence: the burgeoning success of satellite radio, for which subscribers now pay $7–$13 per month to get ad-free music channels and dozens of entertainment, sports and news channels with reduced advertising.

TRANSPARENCY OF SPONSORSHIP

Transparency here means that consumers should be able to tell the advertising from the media's entertainment or informational content. That's not to say that advertising cannot or should not be entertaining or informative. It often is, sometimes more so than the programming around it. My mother loves to tell the story of how I, as a toddler, would buck back and forth on my spring-suspended rocking horse for 15 minutes nonstop—until a commercial came on our black-and-white television. Then I would halt and pay rapt attention for the two minutes of loud, all-smiles ads. As soon as the program returned, I'd resume my rocking racket. If the programs then would have had product placements instead of commercials, I would have rocked my way to a hernia even sooner than I did anyway.

Sheehan says consumers want product placements in TV and movies seamlessly folded into the storyline. Having a dozen or more product placements per film doesn't bother audiences or the Federal Trade Commission, she says, as long as the brands are believable in context with the content and enhance the entertainment. But not all content producers are so sanguine about product placements. "Bullshit," writer-director David Lynch replied when a 2007 film festival interviewer asked how he felt about product placements. "Total, fucking, bullshit" (Lynch, 2007). From his standpoint, the problem is that writers and directors sometimes must rewrite scenes in order to accommodate product placements (Wenner, 2004). When Ford Motor Co., for instance, bought product placements on the TV show *24*, it insisted that none of the terrorists drive its vehicles and that super-agent Jack Bauer cruise regularly in its SUVs (George, 2005). Maybe that's okay if the purpose of art is to imitate life in a military or industrial society, but if the purpose of art is to shed light on life, product placement shades the truth.

AD COMPATIBILITY AND TARGETING

Finally, Sheehan says new media advertising is ethical if the ad message complements the content around it and so long as any targeting of the ad does not violate the privacy of its recipient or target. I disagree that those criteria are sufficient, and in some ways, they raise more questions than they answer.

Some women's magazines are notorious for not only juxtaposing stories about, say, makeup with makeup ads but also for giving glowing reviews to makeup products that just happen to be in adjacent ads (Thompson, 2006). That's payola, pure and simple. It misleads the public and erodes the publication's credibility. A more sophisticated example of unethical complementary advertising occurred on the forbes.com business Web site in the summer of 2004, when it quietly introduced something it called "IntelliTXT" into its stories (Giuffo, 2005). IntelliTXT was a system that automatically made hyperlinks out of every word in forbes.com reporters' stories that related to one of the Web site's advertisers, and the link went directly to that advertiser's site or ad.

Not many readers complained about IntelliTXT during the five months that forbes.com used it, but the publication's reporters sure did. They resented having their words used as launching pads for ads, especially when they had no idea which words were safe and which would backfire on them. IntelliTXT amounted to product placements in online news stories, they said. Readers were free to bypass the links, Sheehan might argue, but discerning ones had to wonder whether forbes.com's word choices were based more on reportage or revenue.

Similarly, it's the *appearance* of impropriety, or at least the potential for it, that dogs online targeted advertising. Sheehan says online advertisers are targeting ads at consumers merely by passively tracking their Web surfing and aggregating those data with that from online users who showed similar interests. They then send pop-up ads suggesting we might like to buy the same products and services that those with similar interests may have bought.

Sheehan and the advertisers assure us that market researchers never tie our Web surfing tendencies to our personal information, such as the names, ages, addresses, credit card numbers, and even Social Security numbers we must sometimes enter to do business on the Web. But how do we *know* whether that's true, and if it is, why do we sometimes get targeted pop-up ads or spam e-mails addressed to us personally? Even if it is true, what if other family members or business associates share our computer? Might it violate our privacy for them to receive targeted ads meant for us, or vice versa? If ad targeting becomes an exact science, then we in the audience become little more than sites for surgical strikes, but if ad targeting remains an *in*exact science in order to maintain privacy rights, then we risk becoming collateral damage.

CRITERIA FOR ETHICAL NEW MEDIA ADVERTISING

I'll start to answer this challenge by repeating my argument to Jane Singer in Chapter 6: new media do not require new ethics; classical ethical philosophies are plenty robust enough to govern new media dilemmas. New media, like all their ancestor media, are extensions of humankind (McLuhan, 1964), and all the dilemmas they pose are extensions of the dilemmas that ethicists have analyzed for millennia. The details of new media dilemmas might be different from those of the past, but that does not make them—or their solutions—distinctive. Keeping that in mind, I would propose just three criteria for ethical new media advertising: truth, accountability, and responsibility, and I will briefly examine each of them separately.

TO TELL THE TRUTH

First and foremost, advertising—no less than journalism or any other form of mass communication content—must be completely truthful to be ethical, whether or not it uses new media or product placements. The American Advertising Federation (AAF) unequivocally says as much in its code of ethics: "Advertising shall tell the truth, and shall reveal significant facts, the omission of which would mislead the public" (AAF, 1984). Kant's categorical imperative, of course, would require the same standard of absolute truth. For pop-up ads, that would mean not only that their copy be completely true but also that their disclaimers would be. They could not redirect you to look-alike Web sites. They could not sell your personal information or click-through data to other companies, if they promise not to do so. They could not have any unspoken influence on the editorial content of the site.

For product placements, the burden not to deceive is just as great, if not greater. Telling the truth here means, at a minimum, that the video cannot show products operating beyond their capabilities. For example, it would be inaccurate and misleading to show a small partly electric hybrid car speeding after the bad guys at 100 m.p.h. or more. And while everyone knows that the person playing a doctor on a soap opera is an actor, not an M.D., she or he had better not prescribe a diet pill, no matter how much that product placement would pay. Moreover, the only really truthful and ethical product placements—from the perspective of the artists—would be those that fit in *after* they've completed the script and rehearsals.

To be considered ethical, these product placements could not change the script or action in any way, and they could only add to the scene's reality, or verisimilitude, as Sheehan calls it, not detract from it. A scene depicting life in modern-day Cuba, for example, could not include a product placement for Pepsi, because the only U.S. soft drinks in Cuba are Coca-Colas smuggled in from Mexico. Such self-restraints would, indeed, limit the number of product placements available to advertisers, but those that did qualify would have enhanced value for everyone involved: the artists, the audiences, and, therefore, the advertisers.

ACCOUNTABILITY

This goes hand-in-hand with truthfulness, and it's related to what Sheehan referred to as transparency. Advertising media should be accountable to consumers as well as to their clients. Under Kant's second categorical imperative, in addition to being truthful, advertisers should treat consumers with dignity, that is, I would say, treat them only as they themselves would like to be treated. Under Rawls's veil of ignorance, consumers are vulnerable to new forms of media advertising and therefore deserve protection. The public often lacks knowledge of the situation's details, such as who's tracking them online or when a product had a paid placement in a film as opposed to when it was a normal prop or backdrop.

> The public often lacks knowledge of . . . who's tracking them online or when a product had a paid placement in a film

To be accountable, online advertisers should make it crystal clear how consumers can unsubscribe to their spam and opt out of their pop-up ads. They should, in fact, ask consumers if they *want* to make an opt-in trade-off of receiving pop-up ads and letting advertisers track them online in exchange for receiving free content they desire. They certainly should make it clear—and not just in gobs of small-print legalese—if they intend to gather personal information on the consumer and/or sell their data to other companies.

Product placements could be more accountable and transparent, too. In the same way that some TV shows now list "promotional considerations," the closing *and* opening credits of television and film productions could include lists of all the products placed in the show.

To benefit advertisers as well as audiences, such lists could enhance product placements by including Web addresses for the products.

As TiVo and other digital video recorders diffuse through the population, fewer people probably will be watching commercials, resulting in product placements becoming commonplace, perhaps ubiquitous. Lists of product placements in the credits could get quite long, which means they'd scroll by fast, but consumers wishing to could offset that with their DVRs' slow motion, zoom and stop-action capabilities. Since DVRs marry cable television with computers and the Internet, it is conceivable that subscribers could use a wireless mouse to click on any URL in the product placements list and go directly to its Web page on their TV screen, then order the product right from there if it impressed them. Ultimately, the way to give consumers control over product placements on TV and in-home movies would be to make them all "clickable," that is, DVR subscribers could use their wireless mouse to click on any product they see in the show, and if it were a product placement, their screen (or perhaps just a window in it) would go to the product's Web site. If nothing happened when they clicked on a product, that would mean it wasn't a paid placement.

This system, however, would make it even more imperative that product placement salespeople didn't get access to the script and set until after the artists had finalized their work. Still, there would be extreme temptation for payola between advertisers and corrupt writers, directors, set designers and the like. At best, such a system would intensify social hegemony, because the most prevalent products would be most likely to be backdrops on screen, so they would get the most product placement opportunities, and that would deepen their market dominance.

RESPONSIBILITY

Ultimately, each new media advertiser must be responsible for being truthful and accountable, for not exploiting consumers. They cannot wait for the FTC or TiVo or their own industry associations to make them act responsibly and ethically. If they are deceptive, or if they inundate consumers with spam, pop-ups, or product placements, they will eventually reach a point of counterproductivity, where consumers will opt out and spend their media time elsewhere. If new media advertisers take an "anything goes" approach, two of the things to go will be their credibility and their audiences.

The unrelenting expression of power amounts to coercion, and Gramsci's theory says that inevitably leads to counterhegemony, which is not the opposite of hegemony; it is merely someone else's hegemony in the making. Rather than that, responsible new media advertisers should seek Gramsci's third way: *pluralism*, which is the sharing of knowledge and power, not necessarily with their competitors but with their consumers. This is Aristotle's mean, and it's not just the arithmetic compromise but the golden solution, the win-win synergy where all sides agree to move from their original position to common ground that's (on average) better for all (Covey, 1989).

If advertisers limited spam to messages that consumers confirmed they wanted, it could become their ham and eggs. If they parceled out pop-ups wisely, they'd hit more home runs. And if advertisers played their product placements right, they could turn them into works of art. After all, how much did Campbell's pay Andy Warhol for his pop art painting of its tomato soup cans? Nothing. How much was it worth to Campbell's? Priceless, as it was for Warhol. How much *would* it have been worth to Warhol or anyone else if it had been a product placement? Nothing. My point is simply this: advertising may not be an exact science, but it shouldn't be mistaken for art.

KEY POINTS

- Advertising—no less than journalism or any other mass communication content— must be completely truthful to be ethical, whether or not it uses new media or product placements.
- The *appearance* of impropriety, or at least the potential for it, is a major concern in regard to online targeted advertising.
- Responsible new media advertisers should use Gramsci's *pluralism* approach—the sharing of knowledge and power—with their consumers, as Aristotle would have suggested.

MERRILL: Commentary

The arguments in this chapter about ethics in advertising seem to me to throw us right into the middle of a Machiavellian world. And its nature stares us in the face. Do we do whatever is good for us or do we act from virtue and principle? Kim Sheehan is the Machiavellian here and Michael Dorsher is the traditional Aristotelian virtue ethicist. This is not to say that Sheehan is wrong in saying that e-mail spam and pop-up advertising are "valid." It is simply to say that it is Machiavellian, pragmatic, ego-centric, and ends-oriented. Presumably what is meant here by "valid" is that it is ethical. Dorsher takes strong exception so far as ethics is concerned.

But, of course, Sheehan is right: such advertising is "valid" in the sense of being effective and achieving the advertiser's purpose. However, I would agree with Dorsher that it is not valid in an ethical sense, and he gives some strong arguments to support his case. Sheehan, making the case for "anything goes-advertising," maintains that such advertising must be legal and "sell a product." And, as for selling products, this is justified by appealing to utilitarian ethical theory and to the notion of a social contract, in my view rather weak rationales. As to legality, this is obviously not the same as ethicality.

Dorsher takes a more moderate, middle-of-the-road position. He admits that some "pop ups" and other new technology ads may be ethical, but certainly not all of them, as he says Sheehan suggests. Many observers of the communication world would say that Dorsher is mired in the old media world and is not attuned to the new realities in advertising. I think he is simply applying old ethical principles to the new advertising reality and sees these principles as still appropriate. It is my position that what he is saying can be applied to advertising generally: It is mainly unethical due to its biased nature, its propagandistic tactics, and its premeditated intention to deceive the people—and this regardless of the utilitarian pragmatic benefits.

For Sheehan, the ethical status of any persuasion is valid if the audience is allowed to "make free choices about the matter being presented." So—if you tell me a lie and if I am free to believe it or ignore it, then the lie is ethical? Freedom and market forces count highly with Sheehan, as does social contract theory. I wish Immanuel Kant—and philosophers like Confucius and Aristotle—were considered more important.

Dorsher proposes three criteria for ethical advertising: telling the truth, being accountable, and being responsible. Great. Advertising, being largely one-sided, is far from truthful in a comprehensive sense. And so far as basic ethical practices are concerned, advertising is unaccountable—to anybody. Whereas accountability relates to consequences to the advertiser for unethical acts, responsibility relates to what should be done prior to the action. Only the advertiser can be responsible—a concept that has moral overtones, whereas accountability has legal overtones.

In spite of my basic agreement with Dorsher, evidencing my more Kantian (rather than utilitarian) sympathies, I can understand the basic appeal of Machiavelli, especially in the field of advertising. Being successful, achieving one's selfish ends, using tactics that bring about these ends—some ethical and some not. But, as I see it, advertising is mainly a business of pragmatics, not ethics. It is easy to take exception to this last statement, and I hope that as this important subject is discussed and debated, my opinion will be questioned and maybe even discounted.

REFERENCES AND RELATED READINGS

American Advertising Federation (AAF). (1984). "Advertising ethics and principles." March 2. Retrieved from www.aaf.org/default.asp?id=37 (October 26, 2007).

Assael, Henry. (1995). *Consumer Behavior and Marketing Action*, 5th ed. London: PWS-Kent.

Balasubramanian, Sira K. (1994). "Beyond advertising and publicity: Hybrid messages and public policy issues." *Journal of Advertising* 23(40), pp. 29–46.

Bendinger, Bruce. (2001). *Advertising and the Business of Brands*. Chicago, IL: The Copy Workshop.

Blethen, Ryan. (2009). "Protect consumer choice: Block NBC/Comcast deal." *The Seattle Times*, November 22, p. B-9.

Brodeur, Nicole. (2009). "Black, white and bleeding red all over." *The Seattle Times*, March 3, p. B-1.

Burns, Enid. (2007). "OPA analysis: Content dominates time spent online". Retrieved from www.clickz.com/3626731 (December 3, 2007).

Covey, Stephen R. (1989). *The Seven Habits of Highly Effective People: Restoring the Character Ethic*. New York: Simon & Schuster

Crisp, Roger. (1997). *Mill on Utilitarianism*. London: Routledge.

Dorsher, Michael. (2002). "Hegemony online: The quiet convergence of power, culture, and computers." Paper presented to the Association of Internet Researchers international conference, Minneapolis, MN, October.

Dynamic Logic. (2004). "Consumer perceptions of various advertising mediums." Retrieved from www.dynamiclogic.com/na/research/btc/beyond_the_click_mar2004_part2.html (December 3, 2007).

Engle, Mary. (2005). "Letter to Commercial Alert." Retrieved from www.commercialalert.org/FTCletter2.10.05.pdf (November 3, 2007).

Fallows, Deborah. (2007). "Spam 2007". Retrieved from www.pewInternet.org/PPF/r/214/report_display.asp (November 30, 2007).

Geary, Sean R. (1999). *Sell and Spin: A History of Advertising.* Video recording produced by Weller Grossman Productions for the History Channel.

George, Lianne. (2005). "Is Keifer Sutherland trying to sell you something?" *Maclean's* 118(8), February 21, pp. 30–35.

Giuffo, John. (2005). "Ad-monishment at forbes.com; a newsroom says no to a dodgy new ad scheme," *Columbia Journalism Review*, March–April, p. 9.

Gordon, Mary Ellen, and Kathleen D. Lima-Turner. (1997). "Consumer attitudes towards Internet advertising: A social contract perspective." *International Marketing Review* 14, pp. 5362–5375.

Gramsci, Antonio. (1971). *Selections from the Prison Notebooks*, trans. Q. Hoare and G. N. Smith. New York: International Publishers.

Hallerman, David. (2002). "Mindshare over matter: Interstitials, pop-ups and pop-unders." February 20. Retrieved from www.emarketers.com/analysis/marketings/20020220_mark.html (March 11, 2002).

Hansell, Saul. (2004). "As consumers revolt, a rush to block pop-up online ads." Retrieved from http://query.nytimes.com/gst/fullpage.html?res=9F06E4DB1439F93AA25752C0A9629C8B63 (December 3, 2007).

Jaksa, James, and Michael S. Pritchard. (2004). *Communication Ethics: Methods of Analysis.* Belmont, CA: Wadsworth.

Lynch, David (2007). "David Lynch on product placement." YouTube.com, March 25. Retrieved from www.youtube.com/watch?v=F4wh_mc8hRE (October 26, 2007).

McLuhan, Marshall. (1964). *Understanding Media: The Extensions of Man*, paperback ed. New York: McGraw-Hill.

Metcalfe, Bob. (2000). "Laying down the laws." *Forbes* 165(4), February 21, p. 96.

Newspaper Advertising Association. (2006): "Attitudes toward media advertising". Retrieved from www.naa.org/docs/Research/Attitudes%20Toward%20Media%202006.pdf (December 3, 2007).

Parayil, Govindan. (2005). "The digital divide and increasing returns: Contradictions of informational capitalism." *Information Society* 21(1), pp. 41–51.

Rotzoll, Kim, and Cliff Christians. (1980). "Advertising agency practitioners' perceptions of ethical decisions." *Journalism Quarterly* 57, pp. 425–431.

Sauer, Abram. (2005). "Product placement: Making the most of a close up." Retrieved from www.brandchannel.com/features_effect.asp?pf_id=282 (December 3, 2007).

Schlosser, Ann E., Sharon Shavitt, and Alaina Kanfer. (1999). "Survey of Internet users' attitudes toward Internet advertising." *Journal of Interactive Marketing* 13(3), pp. 34–53.

Schmoll, Nicole M., John Hafer, Michael Hilt, and Hugh Reilly. (2006). "Baby boomers' attitudes towards product placements." *Journal of Current Issues and Research in Advertising* 29(2), pp. 33–54.

Sheehan, Kim Bartel. (2004) *Controversies in Contemporary Advertising.* Thousand Oaks, CA: Sage.

Simmons Market Research Bureau. (2005). *2005 National Consumer Study.* New York: Simmons Market Research Bureau.

Sutherland, Max. (1993). *Advertising and the Mind of the Consumer.* St. Leonard's, Australia: Allen & Unwin.

Thompson, Bonnie. (2006). "Paying for content: That's a line you don't cross." *Advertising Age* 77(26), June 26, p.4.

Wenner, Lawrence. (2004). "On the ethics of product placement in media entertainment." *Journal of Promotion Management*, 10(1–2), pp. 101–132.

Word of Mouth Marketing Association. (2005). "Practical ethics toolkit". Retrieved from www.womma.org/ethics/ (December 3, 2007).

Chapter 13

Infotainment, Sensationalism, and "Reality"

FEW people pay attention to the mass media *only* to find out what is going on in the world around them—"surveillance of the environment." Many also pay attention to entertain themselves or occupy their time, to see what others are doing, and to learn the details of gossip or scandal. Even such significant events as election nights—when large numbers of people tune in—have entertainment elements consciously mixed in with the news, with some coverage more like that of a horse race than a report of the voters' choices.

For generations, individuals entertained by novels or the theater have used ideas in these forms of communication to stimulate their own serious thinking. (One of the authors of this book remembers staying up until breakfast with his wife, discussing crime and punishment as presented in the previous night's televised episode of the then-popular police drama, *Naked City*—a show not likely to be remembered as long as Dostoyevsky's classic novel on the subject, but able to stimulate thought in the same way.)

"Infotainment," the entertainment component in the mix of entertainment and information, may make the information component more appealing and therefore more available to audience members. Sometimes—whether making a political point on the *Tonight Show with Jay Leno*, recounting the latest escapade of a Hollywood or sports star, using a drama to "change" history, or informing (or scaring) the audience about a disaster—such content influences the public's agenda, or our own.

This chapter raises the following question: does such material distract us from important things that may affect our lives, or is it a useful technique for attracting us to significant content? The debate is over content, not the medium or news platform. If a comedy show can humorously make a point about a real political issue, it is at least potentially useful to the public. If *The New York Times* devotes major space to a sports or show business star's various mistresses, the fact that it appears in the *Times* does not mean it is legitimate news—it simply means the *Times* now reports tabloid news.

(Note: in this chapter, both authors use the word "tabloid" as a pejorative. However, it wasn't always a "dirty word." Originally, "tabloid" referred to newspapers cut and folded to roughly half the page size of a regular or broadsheet newspaper. These smaller-sized publications often found it profitable to appeal to audiences that were less interested in news than in sensationalism, titillating photographs and gossip—often to the exclusion of most "hard" news.)

INFOTAINMENT

Although usually referring to television programming that is disapproved of as being in poor taste, a more neutral recent definition of infotainment is "information-based media content or programming that also includes entertainment content in an effort to enhance popularity with audiences and consumers" (Demers, 2005, p. 143). In practice, regardless of medium, it is material that blends serious information with titillation, entertainment techniques or other types of lighter content. In this discussion, we will *not* apply the term to programs or publications that happen to provide small pieces of possibly useful information amid content that is clearly intended as entertainment or titillation. "Infotainment," here, will refer to conscious attempts to make information more "interesting" by including entertainment elements, *and* to purely entertainment content which nonetheless includes material on serious issues of public importance. That will exclude most "trash television" or "super-market tabloids" (such as the *National Enquirer*).

Although the word and its definition are new, infotainment itself isn't a new phenomenon. It can be traced back to the "morality plays" of the Middle Ages that were intended to provide memorable Bible lessons to a largely illiterate society. For centuries, speeches have been started with jokes and traveling peddlers provided entertainment along with their pitches. A politician running for office in a red vest with a Dixieland band in tow is showing his knowledge of public behavior, not his political leanings or strengths. A radio station that hires a singer-songwriter to comment on the day's news understands how to reach a larger audience. (Both of these examples, by the way, were the products of communications professors.)

However, the public seems to have an almost insatiable appetite for lighter, titillating material and the media claim to be merely responding to this demand by providing it in many guises. Some such programs also claim that they wedge occasional useful information into their contents. Some "reality TV" shows are examples of this, as are interview and discussion programs on "all news" cable channels that concentrate on crime, disaster, scandal and gossip. Many of these programs aim to attract the voyeur or are about "celebrities" who are only famous for being notorious, and most of them will not fit under Demers' definition of "infotainment."

An extreme example took place in late 2009 when a Hong Kong company began releasing daily more than 20 computer-generated, digitally animated videos "often depicting events that no journalist witnessed—and that may not even have occurred" (Cohen, 2009). These videos provided what the production staff "considers to be informed guesses about how events unfolded and [gave] a vividness and a sense of reality to what is basically conjecture." These proved popular, and despite a Chinese-only soundtrack, the animated "report" of Tiger Woods's SUV crash drew more than 1.7 million hits on YouTube alone in the week after it went online (Cohen, 2009).

Sensationalism can occur in any medium. It can be defined as "the use of strongly emotional subject matter, or wildly dramatic style, language, or artistic expression, that is intended to shock, startle, thrill, excite, etc." (retrieved from www.yourdictionary.com/sensationalism) or as the use of material that arouses or tends "to arouse (as by lurid details) a quick, intense, and usually superficial interest, curiosity or emotional reaction" (*Merriam Webster's Collegiate Dictionary*, 10th edition, 1993, p. 1066, using definitions of "sensational" and "sensationalism"). For our purposes, the key question about "sensationalism" is whether it is ethical to appeal to such a lowest common denominator in order to increase the audience—something that comes up in regard to infotainment but is also important in connection with other types of media content—news, advertising and entertainment.

Gossip, scandal and other varieties of infotainment programming may blur public awareness of some of the media's other functions, perhaps especially when they are presented in formats and styles that are easily confused with genuine news. And the picture is complicated even more by the growth of Web sites which provide a new platform for entertainment content that may—or may not—include at least occasional serious or useful information.

There is one other aspect of this issue that deserves consideration. By following the 1994–97 O. J. Simpson courtroom drama, the argument goes, the public learned far more about how the judicial system operates than was generally known before that exposure. The sensational nature of the trials, especially the first one (on murder charges) attracted a far larger audience than, for example, the much more routine court cases that failed to attract viewers (and, therefore, advertisers) to the Court TV cable channel. Whether the Simpson trial viewers actually took away an increased understanding of the court system remains an unanswered question.

Otherwise traditional coverage of events of questionable importance in the infinite scheme of things—the death of Diana, Princess of Wales in 1997, the coverage given to the 2009 "Jon and Kate" break-up and its aftermaths, almost anything involving Britney Spears or Paris Hilton—has often expanded into seemingly unending attention from mainstream news programs and publications. At that point, it becomes "sensationalism" as well as "infotainment." And if this sensationalized infotainment takes our attention away from news and other information that we *need* to learn and understand, then it is harmful to society.

Such programming can provide viewers with useful information. But the value of what we learn may not be worth the attention that is diverted from more important news and information.

That's the crux of the argument in this chapter. Are news and information "debased" by *any* addition of frivolity, froth or "fluff," intended to amuse as well as inform? This position is argued by William Babcock, who maintains that the entertainment and titillation aspects of these programs often confuse the public and drive out useful information that might benefit the audience more in their daily lives. Or, can infotainment programs serve a broader useful purpose in addition to their entertainment function? David Gordon takes the latter position in the following discussion.

GORDON: News and entertainment content are both valid avenues for delivering useful information and ideas to citizens of a democracy, thus helping them make informed choices.

I'm not going to suggest that reality programming such as *The Biggest Loser* or *Kitchen Nightmares* or *Cops* is even a mediocre source of the information needed by citizens of a democracy, despite the incidental useful information that they occasionally provide—for example, what *not* to do when stopped by the police or heeding the "biggest loser's" tips on exercise and nutrition during an era when obesity is a major health issue. And I'm very concerned about such phenomena as the animated accounts of news events like the Tiger Woods situation that were noted in the introduction to this chapter. Even if these Internet "reports" are presented as "illustrations," their heavy emphasis on stories infused with violence and sex seem to me to be nothing more than a Machiavellian attempt to attract viewers.

But there are *some* types of infotainment (or material intended as entertainment) that *are* helpful in providing useful and important information about the society and the world we live in. For example, almost all satire and parody can have valuable political and social implications and should be classified as informative (even if opinionated). Programs or print materials that deal with significant topics are justifiable on utilitarian grounds despite the fact that they often are less than ideal vehicles for informing the public.

It certainly would be wonderful if most people wanted to watch the *PBS NewsHour* (until its 2009 name change, *The NewsHour with Jim Lehrer*), digest the op-ed pieces in their local newspapers, or otherwise make an effort to inform themselves in depth about issues that "should" be important to them as citizens who make the ultimate decisions in a democracy. Such an abstract ideal is not realistic, however. Even if we could reach a consensus on the definition of what is "important," it's unlikely that we would agree on who should decide what fits that definition. (That "who decides" question could lead to a discussion of whether such decisions should be made by "average people" or by those who may appoint themselves— or are hired by media organizations—to determine what's important to the public. This goes beyond the scope of this topic, but merits much further thought.)

In fact, the vast majority of people don't, and won't, spend much time watching in-depth news on PBS, reading the op-ed pages, or attending to BBC news on radio, TV or the Internet. That doesn't mean the general public is uninterested in important issues like global warming, immigration, the economy, trade policies or war and peace. It's just that, with all the distractions bedeviling today's society, the public is selective about the time it devotes to what the news media deem important and is likely to pay at least some attention to complex topics which are presented in "entertaining" formats.

For example, some TV late night variety shows such as *The Tonight Show* and *The Late Show* began attracting presidential candidates in the 1990s (*Saturday Night Live* featured candidate walk-ons—and Richard Nixon's appearance on *Laugh-In* attracted an enormous audience—as early as the 1970s). By the early 21st century, they became almost required stop-offs for those candidates, who also started visiting such hosts as Jon Stewart (*The Daily Show*) and Stephen Colbert (*The Colbert Report*) who make no pretense of hiding their satirical approach to public affairs. But until the 2008 presidential campaign, there rarely was any serious intent to provide information to the public with these brief late night appearances, although they gave audiences a deliberately informal view of the candidates. Right up until election day in 2008, virtually all of these programs could boast of lengthy interviews and other appearances by candidates—with NBC able to draw huge audiences because *Saturday Night Live* writer- comedian Tina Fey could imitate Republican vice presidential candidate Sarah Palin so perfectly that both could appear on the same programs—and many audience members couldn't tell them apart.

President Obama's guest appearance on *The Tonight Show* with Leno some two months after his inauguration, in the midst of his administration's efforts to deal with the ongoing recession, was the first time a sitting president had appeared on a TV talk show. Leno's ability to mix humor with serious (if sardonic) commentary on news events and trends fit well with the president's desire to discuss his economic recovery goals through a new channel. The program combined humorous banter with serious discussion and made one wonder if, in the future, we might see presidents hiring joke-writers in addition to speech-writers, to help them use infotainment programming to explain complex policies and events to the public without going through the usual news gatekeepers.

Several of the late-night "variety" program hosts have brought the combination of information and entertainment to a very high level. *The Tonight Show*, which has been aired for decades with such brilliant hosts and commentators as Steve Allen, Johnny Carson and Leno, features a nightly topical monologue—often based on the day's news events—and has a steady stream of news-making guests from outside (as well as inside) the entertainment world. Such programs are usually very profitable, and all the networks try to play in this arena with much the same format. As early as 2000, a growing number of individuals reported that they "got their news" from such sources.

William Babcock makes that point for me in noting that many news events are reported with their own logos and theme music, in entertainment as well as news channels. The article he quoted also noted that the media have become "a virtual 'news saga' industry" and concluded that these "sensational news sagas may even provide conditions for enhancing certain forms of public engagement" (Lawrence and Bennett, 2000, p. 377). Using the coverage of President Clinton and Monica Lewinsky as an example, the authors added that its entertainment value "did not automatically rule out the possibility that serious issues were at stake for engaged publics" (although there is no evidence that this led to greater *discussion* of serious issues) and that those issues "can all be productively explored through engagement with comedy and dramatized narratives as well as traditional news" (p. 379).

Mainstream print news and information media make use of entertaining *non*-news content (e.g., astrology and bridge columns). But that entertainment content is pretty clearly separated from the news, information, and analysis that are the usual justifications offered for the social importance of those media.

By contrast, when the media (especially television, film and some genres of literary fiction) provide information along with entertainment content, the two types of material are often woven together tightly and will be processed together by the audience. I'd suggest, therefore, that information can—and should—be conveyed to citizens as infotainment which tries to meet people where they are, rather than where the idealists wish they were. Such an approach would embrace the so-called tabloid news programs and talk shows—especially the latter—as excellent vehicles for focusing public attention on what the media gatekeepers regard as important issues.

I am *not* arguing in favor of the "Space Alien Romances Angelina Jolie" approach of some of the supermarket tabloids or for the peepshow segments of some syndicated tabloid TV programs. Nor am I defending sensational television programs whose motto may well be "a scandal a day (or 'a freak of the week') keeps the real world away," or so-called "reality shows" which often treat their participants as means to better ratings rather than as human beings in their own right. An example of such uncaring Machiavellian behavior was the *Britain's Got Talent* (similar to *American Idol*) program which was widely criticized in 2009 after one contestant—arguably its most famous one, "an amateur singer with learning disabilities who lives alone with her cat"—wound up hospitalized for nervous exhaustion, and three children left the program's stage in tears (Katz, 2009). There's no useful information and little, if any, "redeeming social value" in such programs (although, to be fair, I must note that the hospitalized singer went on to become a best-selling recording artist after her recovery).

Online "social media" including Twitter, Facebook and much blogging can't consistently be relied on to inform people about topics of importance, amid the entertainment and chit-chat they provide. YouTube supplies pictures only (while also lowering standards with its "anyone can do it" approach). While they certainly contain *some* useful information about *some* important topics, these outlets often lack context or aim at "insiders" rather than a general audience. Additionally, their sources are not necessarily reliable and the sheer volume of that information makes it hard to process easily.

By contrast, talk and tabloid news shows aim at a broader audience and are more focused (sometimes along political lines), and people *do* tune in to them, to escape, have their own views supported, to be distracted or sometimes entertained. This is particularly true as the programs have multiplied to fill the 24/7 demand for content on an increasing number of both cable channels and those created when digital television took over from analog transmissions in 2009. I believe that many of these programs can and do provide some useful and even important informational wheat amid the chaff that often fills up air time.

Oprah Winfrey, for example, dealt with a wide range of important topics—both national and international—during the run of the TV show bearing her name. There may be more informative ways to consider these various issues, but I'm pretty sure *The Oprah Winfrey Show* drew a much larger audience, and greater public attention, to a topic than would any "more thoughtful" or less sensational alternative approach. Oprah's endorsement of Barack Obama early in his successful 2008 presidential campaign reinforces this point. (Among other characteristics, her format—able to devote an entire hour to a specific subject or issue—had much more flexibility than most other programs.)

The "NPR news quiz" *Wait, Wait, Don't Tell Me* manages to hit many topics of national importance each week, with high good humor, and it's not unique in its ability to be both informative or educational. Even supermarket tabloids occasionally provide information that helps the democratic decision-making process. And programs such as *Larry King Live* on CNN do this with some regularity. King's hosting of the 1993 debate between former independent presidential candidate Ross Perot and Vice President Al Gore on the North American Free Trade Agreement remains a milestone of national debate and discussion of a major legislative issue because it took place while final Congressional action was still pending. According to the A. C. Nielsen Company, it drew a very impressive audience—ratings of 18.1 for cable households and 11.9 nationally.

Radio talk shows have impacted the electoral process, beginning with their major role in some state elections toward the end of the 1980s. By the 1992 presidential campaign, they played an important role in conveying both images and information to potential voters. Some of these programs have served as forums for the exchange of information and opinion—and, sometimes, invective and humor—on various public issues since at least 1980 (Rehm, 1993). Their listenership—and resulting political power—has fluctuated since 1994, but no political figure can overlook them, and they can be a good way to increase public exposure for candidates who are running behind in the polls and/or in fund-raising. Some of the call-in talk shows (particularly those featuring right-wing hosts) have reveled in their new-found political power, though the 2008 election results raise some questions about just how effective that power is.

The more sensational publications, tabloid programs and talk shows can—despite their excesses—enlighten as well as entertain and titillate. And this kind of sensationalism has attracted audiences for many decades by appealing to viewers' " 'insatiable appetite' to hear horrors, crimes, disasters, sex scandals, etc." (Tannenbaum and Lynch, 1960, p. 382, quoting from an unpublished preliminary study by Wayne A. Danielson et al., "Sensationalism and the life history of magazines"). At the same time, sensationalism tends to evoke emotional responses in the audience, often at the expense of reason or understanding (Gorney, 1992, p. 458). Because sensational material "limits experience as a source of knowledge in favor of emotional or sensory stimulation" (Gorney, 1992, p. 455), supplying too much of it could be a barrier to disseminating useful information to the public through these infotainment channels.

sensational publications, tabloid programs and talk shows can . . . enlighten as well as entertain and titillate.

BLURRING LINES BETWEEN NEWS AND INFOTAINMENT MEDIA

When Jon Stewart of *The Daily Show* finishes in a fourth-place tie with NBC, CBS and CNN news anchors as the journalist Americans most admire, it's clear that infotainment programming has reached the news and information mainstream (Kakutani, 2008). A study comparing Stewart's satirical program to network newscasts, analyzing the coverage during the 2004 major party conventions and presidential debates, illustrates the blurring of boundaries between traditional news media and infotainment.

> The proportion of stories per half-hour program devoted to the election campaign was greater in "The Daily Show," and [the researcher] found no significant differences in substance.

"The networks were more hype than substance, and 'The Daily Show' was more humor than substance, but they were equally substantive," she said. "It's certainly no worse than the source people have relied on for decades."

(Neuman, 2006, p. 2 online)

The Web site for *The Daily Show* defined its approach very succinctly in 2010:

Tired of having your news spoon fed to you by big network suits and the smaller, chattier suits on cable news? Join Jon Stewart and the Best F#@king News Team Ever as they bring you the news like you've never seen it before—unburdened by objectivity, journalistic integrity or even accuracy.

The Daily Show . . . takes a reality-based look at news, trends, pop culture, current events, politics, sports and entertainment with an alternative point of view . . . employing actual news footage, taped field pieces, in-studio guests and on-the-spot coverage of important news events.

(*The Daily Show*, 2011)

Come to think of it, maybe that's not all that different from those animated "news illustrations" from Hong Kong that were noted earlier. Or perhaps *The Daily Show*'s deliberate satire *is* a different breed.

Keith Olbermann's *Countdown* program—before he left MSNBC in early 2011 to join Al Gore's Current TV network—and Bill O'Reilly's *The O'Reilly Factor* (and various imitators and competitors) provide other examples of news, information and commentary reaching the public from sources that differ vastly from what was once thought of as "traditional" news outlets (even though there always have been thundering editors, columnists and commentators). Some of these—laced heavily with opinion and sarcasm and coming from opposite ends of the political spectrum—appeal particularly to different demographic groups or to groups with differing political ideologies. Only a few attract a general audience.

A 2005 study of the impact of infotainment on politics noted that there are many different types of infotainment content, and not all have the same impact. In addition, not all people are affected the same way. This study concluded that late-night comedy programs in particular tend to energize "political sophisticates at a rate greater than those who are politically unsophisticated" (Moy et al., 2005, p. 125).

More traditional news media seem to have realized the appeal of some techniques used by infotainment media to attract audiences, and have begun to include them in more mainstream news coverage. One of *The Daily Show*'s "signature techniques—using video montages to show politicians contradicting themselves—has been widely imitated by 'real' news shows" (Kakutani, 2008). Content, too, has often been adapted from tabloid to traditional news outlets, including both an increase in feature stories and "soft" news on local and network news programs, and their use of stories that first surfaced on infotainment programs.

Media critic Barbara Ehrenreich noted in the mid-1990s how entertainment content and more serious material were beginning to come together even then:

[T]he TV news magazines everybody likes to criticize so much are actually putting on more serious pieces every week than we've ever had before. Every news magazine

has its tabloid piece, but also has its relatively serious piece that either relates to something people care about or goes out and does a foreign leader and watches its ratings
go down.

("Talking about the media circus," 1994, p. 54)

When Ted Koppel retired from ABC's *Nightline* in 2005, even that program switched
from its focus on a single topic to the pattern described by Ehrenreich, with at least one
"fluff" or sensational story almost every night along with one or two weightier pieces. This
is simply one more example of the marriage of information and entertainment.

Tabloid news shows concentrating on crime, sex, violence and/or scandal have also influenced some stations' local news programming, in some instances replacing it. Originally aired
in "fringe" time periods, such infotainment programs drifted into prime time, together with
"reality" and various other lowest-common-denominator programs.

For example, a Miami television station, which had been airing up to 10 hours a day of
such "news" programming for more than 20 years, argued that its approach retained the core
of sound journalistic practice in a community plagued by crime while adapting the
presentation to attract viewers who no longer were "wowed by this little picture coming
through the box" (Siegel, 1993, p. 52). Whether this sort of crime and violence coverage
creates rather than reflects a climate of fear is a serious concern.

Ethics concerns need to be wider-ranging than just that question, however, especially
if we're talking about news programs or publications that use some entertainment techniques
and/or content to liven things up, rather than entertainment programs (or magazines) that
provide only bits and pieces of serious content. *If* journalistic ethics and values (truth,
fairness and accuracy, to list three) continue to govern the way *news* programs present
information, then all is well. But I must draw the line at letting entertainment values take
over news outlets, a possibility that Babcock is justifiably concerned about.

While it is most obvious on television, it shouldn't be surprising that almost all news
media provide infotainment of some sort. As noted above, such features as crossword
puzzles, astrology columns, and the comic pages are popular staples of most newspapers.
Magazines and books (particularly around April Fool's Day) are known to present hoaxes
and satires. Even radio all-news stations are always looking for humorous or human interest
or show business (complete with music in some instances) "stories" to segue between hard
news and commercials.

Both Daniel Boorstin in the 1960s and Ken Auletta in the 1990s—and many others as
well—have noted that American audiences want excitement and drama in their news and
information programming. When the "real" world can't provide this, the news media have
turned to coverage of celebrities or "pseudo-events" (Boorstin, 1962) and to TV's shock
programming or "sock-em-in-the-nose novelty," which helped erode the dividing line
between news and entertainment while netting additional viewers and thereby boosting news
division revenues (Auletta, 1991, p. 459).

This narrowing of the gap between traditional and tabloid news programs shouldn't be
surprising. News, after all, has always been defined to include material that departs from
the expected or the norm, so we really need to focus on *how much* deviation is appropriate.
A utilitarian approach would seem appropriate here—attracting a larger audience *and*

getting them interested in absorbing important news/information is good for both the media outlet and the general public.

If *some* infotainment techniques and inclusion of some sensational content are indeed appropriate for the networks or magazines—or for local stations or newspapers, or on the Internet—then we cannot condemn this approach wholesale. Rather, the discussion must focus on where to draw the line in regard both to techniques and to content. We must also deal with how to distinguish between news and infotainment programming and the ethics appropriate to each, and how to make all this clear to the public. (The need for audiences to develop the ability to analyze media messages is discussed elsewhere in this book, usually as an aspect of "media literacy"—see, for example, the section of Chapter 8 dealing with "The need for media 'consumer education'." It would also improve media literacy if the education system could infuse students with a sense of excitement about finding and using information, including that found in the news media.)

A classic example of tabloid television providing highly useful information overlooked by the mainstream media came in the aftermath of the 1993 gang rape of a 14-year-old Minnesota girl and her father's fatal shooting of one of the assailants. Initial accounts of the situation, in the Bemidji and St. Paul papers, relied almost entirely on sources other than the rape victim and her family, and resulted in the young victim being "called a liar, a slut, and a murderer more times than she could count. She was spit upon at football games, received death threats . . . [and] finally dropped out of school" (Mengelkoch, 1994, p. 36).

With assistance from a local couple, the family eventually appeared on the *Sally Jessy Raphael* show, *Hard Copy*, and *Donahue*. This not only gave the family a chance to tell their side of the story, but also helped pay for a lawyer to defend the father. Perhaps more important, these appearances gave the family "a sense of authority in their own community and legitimized their concerns and complaints." They also directed intense local and statewide scrutiny at the case "ever since the national [tabloid] media paid attention."

> The tabloids' greatest virtue . . . is exactly [what] makes people sneer at them—they're often foolish and not very selective. As gatekeepers they're lousy, and that's often fortunate for those who need them most. They will listen to your story when nobody else will, if it has the elements and the angles they're looking for. If we truly believe in access, that journalists should be dedicated to comforting the afflicted and afflicting the comfortable, the tabloids must be recognized as sharing that mission.
>
> (Mengelkoch, 1994, p. 38)

One danger with this (paraphrasing Bob Steele of the Poynter Institute and DePauw University) is that a successful tabloid news approach can co-opt journalistic ethics into the service of sensationalism aimed almost solely at increasing audience size and/or improving its demographic makeup. This concern deserves attention, perhaps especially from the perspective of whether tabloid news adequately respects the human dignity of its subjects (a question that Kant might well have asked). But that's a very different question from whether infotainment content provides useful information in ways that in fact catch the public's attention beyond what "straight news" might accomplish.

Another perspective on the role of infotainment came from an Australian researcher who studied TV news content in his country and concluded that tabloid news helps get the average viewer more involved with significant content, rather than distracting them from it. It serves, then, "not to trivialize the serious news but instead to act as [a] . . . wedge into it" for the viewer (Langer, 1998, p. 30).

PRODUCING AND PACKAGING THE PRODUCT

We should focus not only on the content of infotainment TV shows, but also on their packaging and production values. One successful approach was the "Rock the Vote" campaign originated in 1990 by people in the recording industry and aired on MTV in an effort to get more young people to register and vote in presidential elections.

In mid-1998, this campaign was expanded to encourage not only voter registration but also activism in community affairs (Schultz, 1998). Prior to the 2008 election, this project's Web site (www.rockthevote.com/) had links to a voter registration process, Facebook, YouTube, Flickr and myspace.com, plus music from a variety of artists. A year later, Twitter and iTunes had been added, along with material on such topics as the health care debate, environmental protection and reining in the cost of higher education. All of this was aimed (as the 2009 Web site said) at its mission of engaging and empowering the 45 million young people in the United States, and increasing their "political power . . . in order to achieve progressive change." The organization said it "uses music, popular culture and new technologies to engage and incite young people to register and vote in every election." In 2008, MTV claimed to have registered more than 2.3 million individuals through its Web site and, with its get-out-the-vote effort, said it hoped to "forever change the perception of the youth vote."

But if one looks objectively at this MTV effort to increase political participation, any surprise at its goal is primarily due to our pre-existing opinion of MTV, and not to this particular content. Similarly, the *16 and Pregnant* program on MTV is a serious "scared straight" program designed to curb teen sex. This is contrary to the stereotype we hold of MTV—whose music videos may have introduced some new television production techniques but otherwise are largely without redeeming social importance, and which also airs programs that counterbalance any serious programming.

If the MTV approach can get across information or a concern with issues, then perhaps we need to re-examine the norms of how traditional news and information are presented. Techniques that have worked almost since the infancy of television and its news operations may no longer be the most appropriate approach for the 21st century. If news departments can learn from MTV's production techniques and from the packaging of infotainment programs, society may benefit from new and more successful ways to make all sorts of useful information and opinion available *and* to get it absorbed by the viewers. Audiences may pay closer attention to mainstream news and information presented with new production techniques that are more attention-getting, stimulating, and familiar.

There are parallels in the newspaper world, where the arrival of *USA Today* in the early 1980s was greeted by criticism of its format, which many dubbed superficial. It was

Techniques that have worked almost since the infancy of television and its news operations may no longer be the most appropriate approach for the 21st century.

fashionable then for more established papers to say that they were not being influenced by *USA Today*, at the same time they were changing their weather sections and their graphics and adding various quickly read roundups of short news items.

Earlier newspaper practices involved sensational papers whose origins go back to the 19th century. Though justifiably criticized for much of their content, those earlier papers—with their mixture of humor, satire, fiction and often sensational or scandalous news—still provided some useful news and information for audiences that otherwise might not have read newspapers. Some modern-day tabloids have followed a similar pattern. For example, the scantily clad (or unclad) women on page 3 of some British tabloids do not necessarily distract readers' attention from their more worthwhile news coverage and editorial opinions, and may even attract some readers to them. In the United States, the *New York Daily News*, starting early in the 20th century, placed the juicier sex scandals and divorce stories on its page 4.

Even such a publication as the old *Confidential* magazine—which author Tom Wolfe once called "the most scandalous scandal magazine in the history of the world"—claimed to provide some useful information along with its particular brand of sleaze. Wolfe quoted the magazine's publisher as saying that *Confidential* regularly ran stories exposing racketeering and other societal problems. "But we had to have the other stuff, the gossip, to sell the magazine, or we could never have run these stories at all" (quoted in Wolfe, 1965, pp. 180, 199). TV's tabloid news and infotainment shows thus have followed in some well-trodden paths blazed by the print media, and should be recognized both for what they are and for the information they do provide. As Van Gordon Sauter, former president of CBS News, noted in the late 1980s:

> What these people do is a form of journalism. Not the capital J variety, that's for sure. But it's a journalism that would have been recognized and appreciated by some of the great editors and publishers of the popular press that thrived in this country before journalism became hopelessly corporate, upper-middle-class, complacent and condescending.
>
> (Sauter, 1989, p. 4)

The important questions here are whether the public can and does distinguish one kind of content from the other, and whether the sensational material draws readers into the more serious news coverage. In addition it's worth noting that "trash TV" and sensational journalism—and bloggers—also get some subjects out in the open, where the more "responsible" or "respectable" media can provide fuller coverage from perspectives that go beyond titillation. We've seen this repeatedly as mainstream media report on coverage by the sensation-seeking media of stories that otherwise would not be made public: for example, the first mention of the Walter Reed Army Hospital scandal (noted in Chapter 10); some portions of the Clinton–Lewinsky scandal leading to President Clinton's impeachment; and the political demise of many lesser figures as a result of tabloid coverage of their sexual activities. It's happened, as well, in regard to some aspects of stories overlooked by the mainstream media, such as the Minnesota rape story noted above. This process can be carried to excess, of course, but it isn't necessarily a bad thing. Once again, a key question is *which ethical guidelines to use in drawing that line* between "appropriate" and "excess."

ATTRACTING AND HOLDING THE AUDIENCE

Kant's categorical imperative would probably dictate that we avoid the infotainment/MTV approach unless we're willing to make that the universal standard for news and information programming. But that absolutist standard simply won't work for the first two decades of the 21st century and their changing audiences. In fact, such an absolutist standard has never really worked in regard to the news. Both print and broadcast journalists have always been concerned with the need to attract and hold their audiences, and have used various techniques—going well beyond unadorned presentation of news and information—to reach that goal. Think for a moment about the bridge or advice columns, comics, and various "soft" news features one finds in almost every daily newspaper in the country, or the "fluff" that has become part of most TV news programs.

To be sure, like editorial cartoons, some comic strips have also served very well over the years as sources of commentary and ideas about current concerns in society, and have provided commentary on political and social issues. Walt Kelly's *Pogo* and its strong stand against McCarthyism in the 1950s will probably always be the benchmark for this genre. More recently, Garry Trudeau's *Doonesbury* has managed to work on some extremely short deadlines to remain topical on a variety of political subjects—or ahead of events, as he did with his decision before the 2008 election to run a strip the day after the election premised on an Obama victory. Trudeau's periodic Sunday comics pages roll-call of U.S. military deaths in Iraq and Afghanistan also ventured into previously uncharted waters. Some papers either furloughed the strip or put it on the editorial pages during election seasons, because of its pointed liberal outlook. Others run this strip—and, in some cases, *Mallard Fillmore* from the other end of the ideological spectrum—on the editorial pages at all times, viewing them more as social and political commentary than entertainment.

Another early comic strip that dealt from time-to-time with social issues—which today isn't uncommon—was *For Better or For Worse*. One lengthy 1993 story sequence dealt with an important character's homosexuality and provided both information and differing perspectives for readers who may well not have gotten that exposure through more traditional news and information channels. It also resulted in a staff revolt at *The* (Macon) *Telegraph* in Georgia "led in part by two lesbian staffers upset by the paper's decision" not to run the strip (Shumate, 1995, p. 14); the result of the discussions that followed that decision was a four-day, 17-story series titled "Gay in Macon" and the addition of a lesbian to the paper's diversity committee. But when this strip returned to the same theme in 1997, at least 20 newspapers used syndicate-supplied reruns with less pointed content instead ("Some newspapers . . .," 1997).

The reaction to homosexuality was more muted in 2005 when *The Simpsons* featured an episode in which one of Marge Simpson's sisters came out of the closet. This was in the context of Homer Simpson conducting many same-sex weddings after Springfield legalized them as a ploy to boost tourism. While *The Simpsons* is clearly entertainment rather than infotainment, it's worth noting that, like the movies, the stage and popular music, the program over the years has explored a number of issues that are important to our society, in its case ranging from the environment to education to religion.

On the subject of race, Robert Entman and Andrew Rojecki (2000, p. 217) noted that while entertainment media "have even less responsibility or ability [than news media] to clarify America's world of race, . . . some movies and television shows may occasionally do a better job at this than most news outlets." More generally, both movies and TV programs can provide important information and new points-of-view for their audiences, and grist for the public's agenda on major topics, in addition to their primary entertainment focus.

The West Wing TV series illustrated this well. And movies have done this in thousands of feature films, on wide-ranging subject matter, ever since the motion picture became popular entertainment a century ago. A quick glance at the topics included in Robert Hilliard's *Hollywood Speaks Out* (2009) will drive that point home. The book deals with films on subjects ranging from the prison and justice system and labor-management issues to politics, poverty, racism, anti-Semitism, sexism and homophobia—all matters of concern to citizens of a self-governing society, and presented as entertainment.

One striking example was the depiction of a number of AIDS-related issues in the fiction-based *Philadelphia* in 1993, the same year that *And the Band Played On* (a fact-based made-for-HBO production dealing with the same general topic) was released. I believe it was no coincidence that mainstream news media finally began paying attention to this disease after these films brought it to public consciousness, after more than a decade of sparse references to its growing presence in the United States (and a far longer period of ignoring it in Africa). Cinema was used in a similar way with the 2008 release of *Hope*—an independent film shot in India and the United States—which focused on the conflict over embryonic stem cell research and addressed that controversy "through one fictional family's struggles with the issue." The author of the book on which the film was based said the movie's aim was "to put the whole issue in a personal perspective. . . . All of these people saying no (to the research), what would they say if they need it some day?" (Associated Press, 2008).

Television news has always been concerned with production values as well as news content. In a visual medium, this is not inappropriate. The problem comes when visual values (or availability) completely overwhelm news judgment. For example, the use by NBC News of the Telemundo tape showing a Florida man shooting his ex-wife (discussed in more detail in Chapter 14) was criticized on the grounds that the tape's availability was the key factor in the decision to use it, and that news values and the need for context were ignored (Winslow, 1993). There are many other examples of news coverage being blown out of proportion because a broadcast outlet had compelling (or titillating) video that far exceeded the story's real news value—once again an indication that the gap between traditional and tabloid news is often not really that great.

But just because there have been excesses in using the infotainment approach, the media shouldn't overlook the value of such techniques (in moderation) in reaching a larger audience than would otherwise be interested. If that larger audience can be attracted to useful information by packaging it in new and innovative ways, the net results will be positive rather than negative. CBS's *60 Minutes* program over the years has provided much important information while at times packaging it in different ways; it was described by actor Alan Alda, in the program's 2009 tribute to Don Hewitt, its late guiding genius, as having "fed us hotdogs which somehow had the nourishing quality of broccoli" (*60 Minutes*, CBS Television, August 23, 2009).

Similarly, if infotainment programs can use human drama and emotion to unearth and present some worthwhile stories better than the conventional media can, that's good—on balance—for society. Such an approach draws on Aristotle and utilitarianism. Using some infotainment techniques while maintaining a concern for news and information seeks a middle ground that will make that material available to a wider audience, thus benefiting a larger portion of the public and entertaining the viewers or readers in the process. Rawls, of course, might well caution that this approach blurs the line between fact and fiction and thereby endangers people who can't tell the difference.

Talk shows have often exemplified this combining of news, information, and entertainment to produce very useful results. These programs—which range from very good to awful—are perhaps the late-20th-century/early-21st-century equivalent of the colonial tavern, the early-20th-century Main Street barber shop, the 1960s coffeehouse, or just the old backyard fence back when we were much more likely than now to talk to our neighbors and friends in such venues. Talk shows give us a chance to be heard and to talk (if somewhat indirectly and anonymously) with some of our fellow citizens, and can be a source of information on topics that are—or might be—of interest to us. Similarly, Internet chat rooms and postings in response to blogs—or news articles—offer some of the same opportunities and do provide occasional information amid the opinionated comments that often seem to dominate these interactive forums.

> Talk shows . . . are perhaps the late-20th-century/early-21st-century equivalent of the colonial tavern, the . . . Main Street barber shop, the 1960s coffeehouse

For people who want their news and information "unadulterated," the options are there. There are all-news radio channels, two CNN news channels, MSNBC and even FOX News spending some of their broadcast day providing more-or-less straight news, though entertainment aspects (and very often opinion) have increasingly crept into the programming. C-SPAN provides raw information such as proceedings in Congress (and elsewhere) with little concern for entertainment values, as do various specialized sources of information such as much of the Weather Channel's daytime programming or Bloomberg and CNBC's coverage of business. All-news radio stations and regional TV news operations ranging from New England Cable News to Northwest Cable News don't ignore entertainment values, but their main focus is on news and information, as it is in *The New York Times* or *The Washington Post*, to single out only two prime examples in print journalism. The emergence of newspaper and TV station Web sites and other online sources of news and information provides even more opportunities for most people to get as much straightforward information as they want, along with the softer, entertaining stories also available on almost all of these platforms.

But as noted at the start of this chapter, there are huge numbers of people for whom such news sources have only limited appeal. If the United States is to have an informed, *participatory* democracy, those people must be reached through other channels. It's much too easy to dismiss "tabloid news" programs and talk shows as exercises in excess or fluff, but this isn't true across the board. Even where it may be largely true, the programs' entertainment value does attract audiences, and this is a phenomenon and an opportunity that the elitists or purists among us shouldn't overlook.

Rather than just criticizing or ignoring these approaches, a more logical and beneficial idea would be a twofold Aristotelian approach. First, we might adapt more of the infotainment production techniques that would make serious news more appealing. Second, we could strive to improve the content of these infotainment channels, recognizing that they will continue to reach a significant percentage of the potential audience. Developing explicit ethical frameworks—perhaps aimed particularly at helping audiences to understand that these are *not* mainstream news channels—could provide guidance, or help set reasonable expectations, for programs such as talk shows or *The Daily Show.*

This might well accomplish more for our social fabric than condemning many of them out of hand. This truly is an area where the Golden Mean approach to media ethics could be valuable.

KEY POINTS

- The public is selective about the time it spends on what the news media say is important, and is likely to pay some attention to complex topics presented in "entertaining" formats.
- The key questions are whether the public can and does distinguish serious news coverage from material that sensationalizes news or merely titillates, and whether the more sensational material will entice readers to pay attention to the serious news coverage.
- News has always included material that departs from the norm, so a utilitarian approach is appropriate in striking a balance between traditional and tabloid news—attracting a larger audience *and* getting them interested in "important" news is good for both society and the media outlet.

BABCOCK: Tabloid news publications and programs, "reality" and talk shows, and other forms of infotainment confuse the public and offer "fluff" at the expense of more important content.

Whether he intended to or not, in setting up his argument that infotainment media exert a necessary and *positive* influence on the democratic process, David Gordon suggested many of the *negative* aspects of such media offerings. I will do the opposite. In other words, although I oppose infotainment, I must acknowledge that infotainment media can positively influence the democratic process—but I question "how much" or "how well." I believe that Gordon went too far—he gives the impression that he believes that "infotainment" contains *all* of the positive aspects of both entertainment and information.

My position is that "infotainment" has a negative aspect that far outweighs its potential for good and is inherently harmful to society. This includes "reality shows," which are an extreme extension of one of television's journalistic excesses. In addition, the staging of news conferences and other pseudo-events is so common as to be easily dismissed. Even then, many reputable journalists will turn their backs on this technique.

In other words, although one of the functions of all media is and always has been entertainment, I maintain that journalism is not, and should not, be considered merely a branch of "show biz."

The infotainment media often appeal to audiences that give little, if any, attention to more serious media. In that respect, I must agree with Gordon that those containing even minimal amounts of information can help such people make decisions—they can help make universal democracy work. But because infotainment media tend to overemphasize entertainment, to oversimplify, trivialize, and titillate, they often confuse their audiences about important issues and encourage amusements over important matters. It might well be argued that they epitomize a media form of Gresham's Law: in the limited time and space available for media content, popular—often simplistic—content prevails at the expense of more useful material.

SOME CONCERNS

At a bare minimum, we need to develop a recognized ethic for those areas where news and entertainment overlap, that is, what the minimum standards must be for infotainment content. I'd suggest that the "do no harm" (or "minimize harm") rule should be the threshold here, and that the Judeo-Christian Golden Rule approach also provides a solid guideline, particularly if considered through the lens of media consumers. Going further, we might take a Kantian approach and posit a general rule that infotainment must be based on truth, not half-truths, and that it must not sacrifice information for the sake of entertainment. Clearly, in the current media scene, infotainment content falls far short of that standard.

It isn't surprising that media owners follow Henry L. Mencken's dictum that "Nobody ever went broke underestimating the taste of the American public." This also is true in other countries. For example, following increasing popularity during the 1990s in Australia of talk shows, infotainment and reality television, producers in that country developed "the tabloid," an entertainment-based type of current affairs programs. These current affairs programs use hidden cameras, set-ups and checkbook journalism to generate stories. The resulting content contains spicy human-interest stories focusing on trivial aspects of everyday life. Such programming has been tremendously popular.

In the United States young people increasingly get their news from entertainment rather than from more traditional venues—and probably will keep these habits as they grow older. Unfortunately, such programs tend to debase and trivialize political culture, and the public thus becomes disengaged. I believe the democratic process is threatened when even a handful of viewers consider TV humorist Stephen Colbert to be a real, live, legitimate right-wing journalist (instead of a satirist with liberal leanings), and accept the monologues of late night variety show hosts as providing all the public affairs commentary they need.

Many journalists and those media executives who care about the need for news in our society have been concerned about the trend toward more sensational local news coverage, particularly in larger markets. They have criticized national tabloid—sex, scandal, crime, disaster—shows that first achieved prominence with *Hard Copy* and *A Current Affair*. Such shows, they say, fuel sensationalism, blur the line between entertainment and news, and hurt the credibility of television journalists. But when push comes to shove, "profit" is the determiner of most broadcast—as well as print and motion picture—content. If large audiences are desired by advertisers who are willing to pay to reach them, television will do what is necessary to create such audiences—because it pays.

Infotainment media too often stretch the truth and give false perceptions of reality. To entice audiences and to fit the constraints of media time and space, they rely heavily on stereotypes, exaggeration, half-truths and innuendo that impressionable audiences accept as reality. While news and information are not immune from such tactics, infotainment media capitalize on them. After a period of watching such material, few are able to determine what is true and what is false, since everything shown may be partly true and partly false. As Christopher Hanson commented in the early 1990s:

> When I started writing this column in 1981, it was easy to tell the difference between the *CBS Evening News* and, say, *Kojak. Hard Copy* had not yet been loosed upon the world. And rumor-sprinkled Hollywood-style coverage had not been transplanted wholesale here to Washington, where the presidential briefs-or-boxers question was still to be raised. Those were the days. Since then, we've been Top Cop-ed, Gennifered, and Bobbitted into a New World Infotainment Order that makes the tabloids of yore seem almost cerebral by comparison.
>
> (Hanson, 1994, p. 23)

If this is true, one might ask parenthetically, who is to blame for this situation: the infotainer who isn't expected to meet high standards, the mainstream media person who has shifted the focus of what's covered to a lower common denominator that will do better fiscally, or the audience which doesn't know (or perhaps care) about the difference?

Dramatic programs and articles about crime—real and alleged, actual or fictional, exaggerated or edited for dramatic effect—can generate powerful negative stereotypes and unintended, unnecessary fears among members of the public. Boisterous, poorly reasoned arguments and impertinent questions, the lifeblood of popular talk shows and call-in programs, can set the style for listeners and viewers and spoil their own interpersonal relationships as well as their ability to follow important national and international debates. A further problem is that opinionated talk show hosts and others who don't claim to be "reporters" can poison the well, and cause legitimate news sources to reject questions from everyone ("Tough calls," 2008, p. 34). Reality programs such as *Big Brother* or *Survivor* may also supply some lessons that the viewer can apply to an actual crisis—but so do dramatic programs as varied as soap operas and *MacIver*. The difference? "Reality" is less expensive to produce.

THE IMPACT ON NEWS

The familiar event-centered news story has evolved into new forms as tabloid media have increasingly influenced the content and agenda of mainstream media. Today's news consumers may also witness directly events such as natural disasters and the immediate aftermath of violent crime in real time because of new technologies such as the Internet, greater cable TV bandwidth, and mini-cams, including millions of cell phones in the hands of the public. With the cooperation of police departments and other first-responding agencies, such programming is often very inexpensive as well as visually arresting and psychologically desired. Thus, people today live in an era of big stories where the media's long-standing interest in turning dramatic news events into news serials has rapidly evolved into a virtual "news saga" industry, according to one observer (Cook, 1996, especially at pp. 474–475).

> tabloid media increasingly influence the agenda and the content of the mainstream media. . . . Breaking news events that promise dramatic story developments are quickly translated into stories of the day, week, or month, often complete with their own logo and theme music, and the public is exposed to big stories through both news and entertainment channels in both traditional and virtual formats.
>
> (Lawrence and Bennett, 2000, p. 377, and citing Cook, 1996)

It is possible to provide this kind of coverage well: the original ABC *Nightline*, with Ted Koppel, started in 1980 as a nightly hour-long recap of events during the time of "America Held Hostage" when Iranian militants imprisoned the staff of the U.S. embassy in Iran for 444 days. After the initial furor, it evolved from that to quickly—but professionally—assembled programs, concentrating on one story, usually of public importance rather than mere titillation, per night. But eventually its budget became too high and its audience too low, and it was dropped to a half-hour in length, Koppel (one of the finest interviewers in the United States) left, and today *Nightline* is a pale shadow of its former self, mixing scandal, crime and disaster with serious news and analysis.

The devolution of *Now*, on PBS, is a similar tale, although its original host, Bill Moyers, stayed on the air until 2010 with another program (*Bill Moyers' Journal*), using his interviewing skills to give us his insights into important events, trends and developments. Whether PBS will attempt to maintain the same high level of analysis was unknown at this writing.

The long-running, trend-setting *60 Minutes*—CBS's television magazine program which was the first news program to break into the "top ten" in program ratings and be a profit center—has a format that has been copied widely in the United States and abroad. Each major network has its own flagship program of this type, such as *20/20* (ABC) or *Dateline* (NBC), and for years many had more than one. Each *60 Minutes* program includes several (usually three) segments cast as news stories, each with a recognized reporter involved as interlocutor, interviewer, observer and interpreter of the situation or event under consideration.

Although some would maintain that the single-topic documentary program (rarely seen today except on PBS's *Frontline*) is the highest type of long-form broadcast journalism, the well-done magazine program runs a close second, except when many of the topics are selected mainly for their entertainment value, which seems to be the trend. While a range of staff assistance is credited, the impression is given that the reporter has investigated the situation under discussion and is giving the audience a balanced investigative report. The ever-increasing promotional hype for the program and for individual segments begins hours—even days—before air time, peaks at the introduction to each segment, and is recapped as the credits scroll at the end of the hour.

Although some of *60 Minutes'* early award-winning episodes, such as "Biography of a Bookie Joint," could be considered infotainment, somewhat similar to the "undercover" exploits of early newspaper woman Nellie Bly in hospitals and businesses, most of these topics have been of interest to the public. By bringing them into the open, so that the general public becomes both more interested and knowledgeable, it became possible for politicians and others to employ corrective measures. This can't be said of programs devoted to the life and death (and, often, trial) of "celebrities" who are only famous for being famous.

Mainstream news media also have become increasingly "infotainmentized" to the point where most science reporting focuses on the amazement factor, with entertaining music and graphics and an oversupply of high-tech computerized video. Because of time constraints, budgets, and lack of a constituency, more traditional television news programs are rarely as entertaining as their infotaining counterparts. As a result, news programs lacking an infotainment glitz are hard pressed to attract viewers willing to engage with them (and buy their sponsors' products and services), much less to learn and cultivate the kinds of discourse they offer.

American Morning, Today, Good Morning America and their counterparts on other channels have for some time been more infotainment than news-focused. It may be significant that CBS reached into the morning programs to select Katie Couric to succeed Dan Rather as anchor for its flagship evening news program.

"SHOW BIZ" POLITICIANS

Politicians, realizing that the public is more engaged with infotainment-rich programs than with the more traditional media, are responding accordingly. In 2003, body-builder and Hollywood action star Arnold Schwarzenegger announced he was running for governor of California—on *The Tonight Show*. A plurality of the state's voters appeared unconcerned that, at the time, Schwarzenegger avoided issues of public policy, since his supporters "knew" who he was, having seen him in theaters and on TV.

He won, and joined the ranks of show business personalities who have entered politics. Ironically, during a post-election press conference, Schwarzenegger thanked the assembled reporters, most of whom he had managed to avoid during the political campaign, by saying:

> I got a lot of publicity, and that helped me really to become the highest paid entertainer in the world. . . . It was really the press that has helped me to get to the place where I am today. . . . So I want to thank all of you for this great job.
>
> (Skelton, 2004)

At the election booth, California's voters knew very little of their governor-to-be's public plans, policies, or likely priorities, as he had effectively shielded himself from the press and usually "talked" to the people only through a variety of infotainment venues. The problem was that Schwarzenegger was running for office, not promoting an upcoming Hollywood action film. The state's media should have doggedly questioned him on his views and not accepted simplistic answers, investigating his past and treating him as a candidate, not a curiosity. This was an ethical responsibility on their part—which they muffed. As then *Los Angeles Times* media columnist Tim Rutten said:

> Schwarzenegger's gubernatorial campaign is dealing with the media in an entirely novel and unforeseen way, almost completely shutting out experienced political journalists, while making their man available only to friendly forums—right-wing talk radio and the congenial celebrity chat shows. Two questions arise: Will it work? And, if it does, can Arnold's happy ending become a school for other candidates?
>
> (Rutten, 2004)

With a "show biz" candidate such as Schwarzenegger—or Ronald Reagan, a few years earlier—much of the public neither sought nor appreciated it when journalists occasionally treated the actor as a gubernatorial (or presidential) candidate, clearly preferring the news about him to be entertaining. Steve Lopez, another *Los Angeles Times* journalist, commented:

> What we're witnessing is not a civic awakening, but a further descent into the hellfires of modern society. The worst elements of politics, media and pop culture have converged to deliver a lurid spectacle, rife with candidates who seem plausible only because our standards have sunk so low.
>
> (Lopez, 2003)

It can be argued that the 2008 appearances on *Saturday Night Live* by John McCain and Sarah Palin—while perhaps portraying them sympathetically to viewers—actually trivialized their campaigns. In this case, humor and entertainment were not adequate substitutes for substantive information about their positions, even though few if any national candidates would—or did—turn down a chance to appear before such a huge television audience.

THE IMPACT ON DEMOCRACY

In an era when many in the public think that tabloid news publications and programs, talk shows, and other forms of entertainment constitute or substitute for legitimate news and information, we are in danger of one day having few or no media interested in covering hard-news topics. What will happen to our democracy—and, indeed, to humanity in general—in such a world is very unlikely to be beneficial to the citizenry.

On the other hand, some topics require more time to explore than the formats of conventional news broadcasts permit. The solution to this is to find entertaining ways—through documentaries or other formats—to cover complex issues. A good example has been the hour-long radio programs on economics (e.g., the origins of the subprime mortgage debacle, the resulting effects on Wall Street, what a "bank balance sheet" is) that were aired on NPR's *This American Life* program in 2008 and 2009. These programs helped many thousands—possibly millions—of Americans better understand what was happening to their credit and investments, as well as other frightening financial developments during the meltdown and crash that started in 2008. And they did it *without* resorting to sensationalism or "dumbing down" or other techniques common to infotainment programming.

Admittedly, it's not easy to define what a "journalist" is or even what "news" is. What about an educator who writes an occasional op-ed piece for her local weekly newspaper. Is she a journalist? What about Oprah? Does she qualify? Or Stephen Colbert? Or a 14-year-old blogger? Or former political candidates such as Al Gore or Sarah Palin? Or Rush Limbaugh? (It's worth noting that in the wake of the 2008 election, arguments over the Republican Party's future direction raged very publicly between Limbaugh and the chairman of the Republican National Committee. In some people's eyes, Limbaugh—who was extremely popular with his conservative audience—became for a time almost the *de facto* head of the conservative movement, if not the Republican Party.) Is the gathering of right-wing "contributors" and "commentators" on Fox News a political or a journalistic redefinition?

If we have difficulty in defining a journalist, is it any wonder that there might be confusion between what constitutes entertainment or infotainment or news and information? Of course, it may be that younger individuals have a more expansive view of what constitutes a "journalist" or "news," while older members of the population tend to anchor their definitions in mainstream journalism.

Be that as it may, the effects of tabloid television programs, scandal-filled newspapers, and infotainment on other media are negative, regardless of the generation of those selecting such material. These infotainment media often tend to entertain and/or to roil with endless blather with the loudest participants "winning", and thus confuse individuals in search of a truthful and contextual account of the day's—or the era's—news.

SOME FINAL THOUGHTS

Reality television (and some hoaxes or other "make-believe" media content) are yet another problem. While many find them entertaining, and some are truly "real," many are not. True "reality" shows, such as those of chases taken by cameras in police cars, are relatively harmless, and—unless edited or narrated too freely—are easy to tell from fictional accounts of the same sort of events.

But many contests, programs dealing with families changing parents, or those featuring people engaged in physical or social challenges of an extreme kind, are usually scripted—or to use a nastier word, fixed. This isn't even a new phenomenon, if one recalls professional wrestling over the years and the quiz show scandals of the 1950s, when seemingly genuine contests were corrupted in order to make them more appealing to the audience: see Anderson (1978) or the movie *Quiz Show* (1994). It seems unlikely that what the viewer sees on the screen bears much resemblance to the actual situation the participants are in—with a camera crew, a director, hordes of onlookers carefully kept out of the picture and an editor waiting in the wings to change what the producer wants changed for dramatic effect. This kind of faux voyeurism makes it even harder to tell truth from fiction than does the "fake news" on *Saturday Night Live* or *The Daily Show*.

The issue raises more concerns because large numbers of children are left on their own with television, the "big babysitter," and many adults are alone with TV rather than interacting with other humans. For all of these, infotainment programs have the potential for setting new standards of social or antisocial behavior, and they can be personally and socially destructive: this should frighten those who believe in an engaged citizenry.

It might be argued that if infotainment media truly entertain, they offer pleasure and escape from our day-to-day obligations, and thus fulfill John Stuart Mill's concept of utilitarianism: offering happiness to the greatest number of people. In fact, the original definition of utilitarianism related not just to "happiness" but rather to "hedonism," and some would argue that our current media consumer model comes close to fulfilling that definition. Similarly, if infotainment content prompts audiences to consider the serious material presented there—including, sometimes, taboos that traditionally have been repressed—they also fulfill the "greatest good for the greatest number" approach, although the taboo perspective stretches Mill's philosophy a bit.

Infotainment is to be found in all media. Publications are not immune from the pitfalls of infotainment—the eagerness to entertain readers, even at the price of accuracy, truth and completeness. Television, though, has a much greater reach than any publication, and contemporary television is entertainment-based and has exceptional capability to attract audiences that get its messages inexpensively (or even, once a receiver has been purchased, for free).

Still, publication staff continually make value judgments about what is and is not included in their publications and how information is presented, based on information and opinions about the desires (if not the needs) of their readers. As is the case with their broadcast media counterparts, they can mislead their audience, intentionally and unintentionally, especially when they let the entertainment aspect of their efforts overrun the information. They can confuse the adrenaline flowing from their own work with readers' interest in a story. They can resort to clever words, phrases or examples that only they, who have been working full-time on a story, fully understand. Reporters, editors, designers, and others who create publications must be wary of the nuances of language and display. They must be sensitive to audience interests and level of maturity. While ethical standards or guidelines specific to infotainment aren't plentiful, media personnel have the responsibility to treat almost every decision as an ethical one in order to serve their audiences properly.

When infotainment confuses the public, when it misleads or promotes antisocial actions, the gatekeepers need to take responsibility. Thus, while it is unrealistic to condemn all combinations of information and entertainment, we should carefully discern what is entertainment and what is the information we and our neighbors need to function as citizens of an ever-more-complex media world.

It is difficult to assess definitively the ethics of the mass media, especially those that offer infotainment. The diversity of media, of potential subject matter, of sources and styles of presentation, the varied creative talent that produce the media, and even the diversity of the media audiences must be considered. Infotainment has a dual role: to offer information and entertainment. It can be useful to society, but—in addition to the ethical responsibilities of media workers—those who watch such programs have what might be termed an ethical obligation to retain a healthy skepticism for information laced heavily with entertainment, or vice versa.

KEY POINTS

- Infotainment media can positively influence the democratic process, but they often appeal to audiences that give little, if any, attention to more serious media.
- Infotainment epitomizes a media form of Gresham's Law: in the limited time and space available, popular—often simplistic—content prevails at the expense of more useful material.
- Infotainment media too often stretch the truth and give false perceptions of reality, by relying heavily on stereotypes, exaggeration, half-truths and innuendo that impressionable audiences accept as reality.

MERRILL: Commentary

As we get further into the 21st century it seems that "infotainment" is (or can be) pushed from the so-called mass (conventional) media into the hands of a multitude of cybermessage channels from which audience members may select. The programmers of these channels are always hoping to set up a situation where the material becomes overwhelmingly popular ("viral") quickly. It is my hope that both of the contenders in this chapter are largely wrong; that the traditional media purpose will remain: to provide citizens with serious, credible and extensive news and informed commentary. Entertainment is someone else's job, and can come through other channels. I would like to believe that infotainment has peaked in the traditional media and if one wants entertainment he or she will fish in the expanding cyberspace pool.

However, it is obvious that there will continue to be a fuzzy line between serious news and its entertainment component. The noteworthy and the notorious will continue to dart across our TV and computer screens and even catastrophes (valid news) will provide, for many, a sort of entertainment. Separating entertainment from news is impossible, but whereas today news rides on the coattails of entertainment, maybe soon this will be reversed.

Serious news consumers must hope that subjects like Britney Spears and Paris Hilton will be put in a more realistic perspective in the new informatics systems. And that the fluff, the slapstick, the gossipy and comedic news anchors on TV will, like old soldiers, fade away.

David Gordon is not so sure the demise of entertainment in the media is a good thing. He sees it, as well as news, as a valid avenue for providing useful information to citizens of a democracy. He may well be right, depending on how you understand "useful" information. I find that the infotainment portions of public communication are little more than distractions from the serious core issues, a kind of opiate for a depressed national psyche. Gordon says that most people spend little time with serious news and commentary and care little for complex issues. But he says that, when mixed with entertainment, they will at least manage to catch a few glimmers of important fact.

the infotainment portions of public communication are little more than distractions . . . a kind of opiate for a depressed national psyche.

Tabloidism and talk shows, according to Gordon, provide considerable amounts of news—an escape, he says, into a more personal, subjective world of postmodern entertainment. The "wheat" they provide is a useful thing compared to the "chaff that often fills up air time." It is true that even from a talk show like Rush Limbaugh one can get some news, but it would be a hard stretch to see it as "wheat" when it is often made up out of whole cloth wrapped around a series of conservative regurgitations and egocentric promotions. But, as Gordon says, there is some news here; one just has to work hard to separate it from the chaff of personal opinion.

Oprah Winfrey, entertainer or news communicator? Both, says Gordon, and he notes that her programs can draw more public attention to a newsworthy topic than would a program aimed at a "more thoughtful" audience. No doubt. But it is the "experts" she has on the program, not necessarily Oprah's views of the news, that gives the program some claim to importance beyond entertainment. Ditto for other interview or public affairs shows like Larry King, for all the years before he left his show. Infotainment is not just a television phenomenon. Other media, however, have found that even with more jazzy journalism, they cannot really compete with TV. And they are in real trouble. Every day we hear of more newspapers going out of business, reporters and editors being laid off, as a heavy financial malaise settles over print journalism. One can see what is happening by noting the thinning of magazines (*Newsweek*, and *Time*, for example) both in size and substance. So Jon Stewart is one of the journalists most Americans admire. This means, says Gordon, that infotainment programming "has reached the news and information mainstream." Stewart's bitterly humorous format may well have helped some of the audience understand more of the Wall Street actions that led to so much distress. Possibly, but maybe not. I'm not sure that the complex economic situation facing the United States from 2008 onward was understood by anyone.

Gordon notes that lines are being blurred between entertainment and news. True. Actually they have always been blurred; the music concert may be news to me and mainly entertainment to you. Actually, it is both. This blurring is similar to the blurring that is going on between "objective" and "subjective" news reporting. One might say that *all* news is subjective and *all* news is entertainment. But no news is totally subjective, just as no entertainment is totally entertaining. Anyway, the blurring goes on.

Now we come to William Babcock, who says that infotainment publications and programs "confuse the public" and offer entertainment at the expense of other, more important, content. He opposes infotainment, but acknowledges that such material can "positively influence the democratic process"—but he questions "how much" and "how well." In this stance, he provides himself safe footing on the slippery slope. He faults Gordon for going too far in believing that infotainment "contains *all* of the positive aspects of both entertainment and information." Babcock says that infotainment's negative aspect "far outweighs its potential for good and is inherently harmful to society."

I'm not sure that infotainment "confuses" the public, as Babcock says, but there is little doubt that it contributes little or nothing to public awareness and concern about serious national and world issues. Exactly what he means by infotainment influencing the "democratic process" is unknown. How does entertainment, chit-chat and humor mixed into the news have any effect on democracy? At any rate, I must agree with Babcock that the often simplistic and truncated content of news messages tends to dissipate the core substance of the news event and reduce its importance.

Babcock notes that in the United States young people get most of their news from entertainment rather than from traditional news media. Not very encouraging—especially if one is concerned about a meaningful democracy. Negative stereotypes, Babcock says, are caused by dramatic programs and articles. This is, of course, true, but such stereotypes can be caused by non-entertainment programs as well. And, besides, negative stereotypes may be as valid as positive stereotypes. Both kinds will always be with us.

Opinionated talk show hosts and other non-reporters can "poison the well," Babcock says. True, but the well can be (and is) poisoned by all kinds of communicators. And this is increasingly so as bloggers with unrestricted freedom dump their narcissistic offerings into the public arena. While I am sympathetic with Babcock's concern about well-poisoning, I think we must expect this in a communication system that is relatively free. If free people were all wise and moral, our communication would be better, but that is not the case. Who would keep people from poisoning the well? Who would extract "entertainment" from the news media?

Babcock presents some impressive cases where entertainment tends to take over from serious substance in the mainstream media. Such events as CBS's substitution of Katie Couric for Dan Rather, the live banter of such shows as *Good Morning America*, the "show biz" candidacy of Arnold Schwarzenegger, the civic-mindedness of Oprah Winfrey—these all are evidence of the impact of entertainment's integration into the public media. The position taken by Babcock that such a trend is bad for the public, however, lacks evidence. At least it is not presented in this debate, though Babcock would probably argue that a dumbed-down audience is inherently undesirable. But, he asserts, the "gatekeepers" need to take responsibility for the damage to the public caused by infotainment. Just how this will be done we don't know.

Ethics, says Babcock, is a main player here. Media executives must think of ethics, not pragmatics—the bottom line—in determining the kind of entertainment, and how much, will be fed to the public. Obviously the public wants to be entertained, wants to retreat from the realities and worries of the world, wants to be happy. So, Babcock says, John Stuart Mill's utilitarianism should not be discounted by media managers. Bringing happiness is important. How to balance this happiness with enlightenment is the question. The mainstream media (and they will certainly continue to exist in restricted form) need to make such balance a priority in the coming years. And they can, for now they can surrender most of their entertainment function to the bloggers and other non-news functionaries.

Both Gordon and Babcock are tentative in their positions in this chapter. Each recognizes the value of *both* entertainment and straight news. They both pay their respects to each position's contribution to democracy. Gordon puts his emphasis on serious news programs, such as the *PBS NewsHour* with Jim Lehrer and others. Even so, he believes that both entertainment and news are needed for an informed public. Babcock is more negative in his assessment of entertainment, believing it "confusing" and limiting the impact of serious information.

The reader might be wondering just what the two discussants would do to solve this problem—if it is one. Would they separate news from entertainment? Or would they change the integration mix in some way? For Babcock the mix has too much entertainment, causing the programs and stories to be "confusing" to the public. Just how far (if at all) Gordon would go in integrating the two positions in programming is vague. Both positions are important, he says—but separately or mixed? We really can't tell. Ditto for Babcock: he recognizes, as he must, that both exist and are often indistinguishable. But he sees far too much entertainment in public communication and not nearly enough serious substance.

Just who in today's media are entertainers? Who are propagandists? Information purveyors? What about Larry King, Oprah Winfrey, Chris Matthews, Jim Lehrer, Bill Moyers, Rush Limbaugh? They are all *news purveyors*, *propagandists*, *AND entertainers*. Certainly I realize that there is a big difference between a Jim Lehrer and a Rush Limbaugh, and between a Bill Moyers and an Oprah Winfrey. But they all do, in fact, provide entertainment and news—and they manage to work in some degree of propaganda. In short, they are biased; they are subjective and egocentric. Even with these characteristics, many in the public are both entertained and informed by them.

Both Gordon and Babcock would probably insist that it is the *ethical* issue they are concerned about. And what might that be? Well, it would seem that the citizens (readers, listeners, and viewers) are having their media content *misrepresented* to them. They think they are getting the news when, in effect, they are getting somebody's propaganda or somebody's version of entertainment. This, many would say, is unethical. Evidently news should always be clearly identified as news and entertainment as entertainment. However, this is impossible. Although news and entertainment merge and diverge constantly; they will not separate. And infotainment, of course, is intended to *divert*.

I recommend that the reader of this chapter take a good course in general semantics, a Korzybskian perspective that stresses a multivalued orientation rather than a two-valued (either/or) one. Another main emphasis of general semantics is likewise relevant to this "controversy": the basic concept of flux or change, that each of us is in a state of *becoming* a later version of ourselves. As the concept of news changes, it might be that it could evolve into something completely different—e.g., news to entertainment, entertainment to news. This constant process philosophy of change, in which our labels are inadequate to keep up with reality, is an extremely important one for the person interested in communication. I recommend it heartily.

REFERENCES AND RELATED READINGS

Anderson, Kent. (1978). *Television Fraud: The History and Implications of the Quiz Show Scandals.* Westport, CT: Greenwood.

Associated Press. (2008). "Stem cell research novel hits the silver screen." Eau Claire, WI *Leader-Telegram*, September 14, p. 12A.

Auletta, Ken. (1991). *Three Blind Mice: How the TV Networks Lost Their Way.* New York: Random House.

Babcock, William, and Virginia Whitehouse. (2005). "Celebrity as a postmodern phenomenon, ethical crisis for democracy, and media nightmare." *Journal of Mass Media Ethics* 20(2–3), pp. 176–191.

Boorstin, Daniel. (1962). *The Image: A Guide to Pseudo-Events in America.* New York: Athenaeum.

"CNN in the A.M.—Get serious." (2007). Editorial. *Broadcasting & Cable* 137(15), April 9, p. 54.

Cohen, Noam. (2009). "Animated video of Tiger Woods crash draws a crowd." *The New York Times*, reprinted in *The Seattle Times*, December 6, p. A4. Retrieved from http://seattletimes.nwsource.com/html/nationworld/2010435912_animatednews06.html.

Cook, Timothy E. (1996). "Afterword: Political values and production values." *Political Communication* 13, pp. 469–481.

Demers, David. (2005). *Dictionary of Mass Communication and Media Research: A Guide for Students, Scholars and Professionals*. Spokane, WA: Marquette. (Other dictionaries provide variations on the definition of "infotainment." See, e.g., Wikipedia.)

Entman, Robert M. and Andrew Rojecki. (2000). *The Black Image in the White Mind: Media and Race in America*. Chicago, IL: University of Chicago Press.

Gorney, Carole. (1992). "Numbers versus pictures: Did network television sensationalize Chernobyl coverage?" *Journalism Quarterly* 69(2), pp. 455–465.

Hanson, Christopher. (1994) "The triumph of fuzz and wuzz." *Columbia Journalism Review*, November–December, p. 23.

Hilliard, Robert. (2009). *Hollywood Speaks Out: Pictures that Dared to Protest Real World Issues*. Chichester, UK: Wiley-Blackwell.

Kakutani, Michiko. (2008). "Is Jon Stewart the most trusted man in America?" *The New York Times*, August 17. Retrieved from www.nytimes.com/2008/08/17/arts/television/17kaku.html?_r=2&em=&oref=slogin&pagewanted=print&oref=slogin (September 15, 2008).

Katz, Gregory. (2009). "'Talent's' Boyle fairy tale sours as singer enters clinic." Associated Press story printed in *The Burlington* (VT) *Free Press*, June 2, p. 10A.

Korzybski, Alfred. (1933). *Science and Sanity: An Introduction to Non-Aristotelian Systems and General Semantics*. Lancaster, PA: Science Press.

Langer, John. (1998). *Tabloid Television: Popular Journalism and the 'Other News'*. London: Routledge.

Lawrence, Regina G., and W. Lance Bennett. (2000). "Civic engagement in the era of big stories." *Political Communication* 17(4), pp. 377–382.

Lopez, Steve. (2003). "Pitching the recall: California politics meets 'Survivor.'" *Los Angeles Times*, August 8, p. B1.

Mengelkoch, Louise. (1994). "When checkbook journalism does God's work." *Columbia Journalism Review*, November–December, pp. 35–38.

Moy, Patricia, Michael A. Xenos, and Verena K. Hess. (2005). "Communication and citizenship: Mapping the political effects of infotainment." *Mass Communication and Society* 8(2), pp. 111–131.

Neuman, Steven R. (2006). "No laughing matter." *Oregon Daily Emerald*, October 17. Retrieved from http://media.www.dailyemerald.com/media/storage/paper859/news/2006/10/17/News/No.Laughing.Matter-2370755.shtml (September 16, 2008).

Raschke, Jessica. (2006). "Tabloid current affairs programs and the production of meaning." *Screen Education* 42, pp. 94–96.

Rehm, Diane. (1993). "Talking over America's electronic backyard fence." *Media Studies Journal* 7(3), pp. 63–69.

Rutten, Tim. (2004). "Regarding media: Arnold plays hardball on a softball circuit." *Los Angeles Times*, September 20, p. E1.

Sauter, Van Gordon. (1989). "In defense of tabloid TV." *TV Guide*, August 5, pp. 2–4.

Schultz, Tom. (1998). "Campaign promotes youthful activism." *Lansing* (MI) *State Journal*, May 26, p. 6A.

Shumate, Richard. (1995). "Discovering central Georgia's gay community." *American Journalism Review*, January–February, p. 14.

Siegel, Ed. (1993). "What Cheatwood brings to Ch. 7: Miami-style glitz or just good TV?" *The Boston Globe*, August 21, pp. 41, 52.

Skelton, George. (2004). "Press corps can't assume role as Governor's flacks." *Los Angeles Times*, January 29, p. B6.

"Some newspapers won't run comic strip's series on gays." (1997). Eau Claire, WI *Leader-Telegram*, August 14, p. 3A.

"Talking about the media circus." (1994). *The New York Times Magazine*, June 26, pp. 26 ff.

Tannenbaum, Percy, and Mervin Lynch. (1960). "Sensationalism: The content and its measurement." *Journalism Quarterly* 37(2), pp. 381–92.

The Daily Show (2011). Web site at www.thedailyshow.com/about.

"Tough Calls." (2008). RTNDA *Communicator*, September–October, p. 34.

Viles, Peter. (1993). "News execs grumble about tabloid TV." *Broadcasting & Cable* 123(39), September 27, p. 42.

Winslow, C. Katherine. (1993). "Is it news?" RTNDA *Communicator*, March, pp. 8–9.

Wolfe, Tom. (1965). "Purveyor of the public life." In Tom Wolfe, *The Kandy-Kolored Tangerine-Flake Streamline Baby*. New York: Farrar, Straus & Giroux, pp. 180–203.

Chapter 14

Violence and Sexuality

VIOLENT content in the mass media is a hot topic today. And in the 1990s. And in the 1980s. And the 1970s. And the 1960s, and back about as far as there have been mass media. The dime novels of a century ago were criticized for portraying excessive violence in print. Since then, films, popular music recordings of various kinds, and television have each been blamed for fostering additional violence in society, including "copycat" violence. There were even U.S. Senate hearings in the mid-1950s on the dangers posed by violent comic books (see Twitchell, 1989).

Media portrayals of violence have been given renewed and heightened scrutiny since the late 1990s, perhaps reflecting concerns over violence in society at large. That's the crux of this issue: does media violence for example, contribute to societal violence, or merely reflect it? Or both? And what role should the media play in regard to this problem? Such questions can occur in many guises—suspects accused of crimes who blame their antisocial actions on conditioning by media content; or blaming the use of torture in U.S. military prisons (in Iraq and elsewhere) on the popular program *24*, which frequently shows torture. The media's role might well be examined from both an *ethical* perspective—which is the one taken in the material that follows—and from a *political* point of view, which might well conclude that the media have already been found guilty of contributing to violence in society and we therefore need only to ask what should be done about it.

Sexual content in print media and, more recently, in broadcast, cable, and cyberspace, has been of concern to some segments of society for longer than the controversy over violence.

Obscenity laws, regulation of "indecency" on the airwaves, the ill-considered Communications Decency Act of 1996, movie ratings, outright censorship, and various types of pressure group tactics have all been used in efforts to regulate the portrayal of sex in the mass media. This can be carried to extremes: a student of photography who took artistic pictures of her nude child for a class assignment was arrested after a commercial photo lab called the police upon seeing the photo.

But from the legal perspective, there have been relatively few efforts to regulate violent content. Several attempts to impose limits on alleged media incitement to violence through the award of monetary damages have failed, as the courts quite uniformly held that the First Amendment bars such restrictive penalties. That leaves it up to consumer and political pressure groups—and to the ethical standards of both media practitioners and media consumers—to serve as checks on media violence.

When we discuss violent media content here, we are referring mainly to television (both entertainment and news), film and videogames. Newspapers, magazines, books, and some records (particularly rap music, which has been a target of concerned parents and others) also figure into this discussion, but to a lesser degree. Related topics, going back many decades, such as concerns over guns and other violent toys, although posing important ethical issues for society as a whole, lie largely outside the scope of this discussion.

The authors are very far apart in the positions they take in this chapter. John Michael Kittross argues that outside efforts to control media violence would be a solution that is worse than the problem. David Gordon maintains that violent content must somehow be controlled if the media refuse to do it themselves.

KITTROSS: Violence and sexual pornography in the media, however regrettable, are merely reflections of the world, and government or group measures to control them would create a "cure" that is worse than the disease.

Let's ask some simple questions of those who blame most of the evils of the world on the mass media. Were there murders before television? Was there child abuse before the daily newspaper? Were sexual deviations known before the movies? The answers, obviously, are "Yes." As is the answer to the questions: do violence and illicit sexual relations exist in the world today—and are they portrayed in today's media?

But does this latter, absolute *yes* answer the implied questions about the *relationship* between these practices and the media, particularly the implication of causality: that the media (in their entertainment, persuasion, and informational functions) *cause* violence; and that hard- and softcore pornography in the same media content *cause* sexual violence? And, are all these of equal importance? I think not.

Lee Loevinger, former associate justice of the Minnesota Supreme Court and former member of the Federal Communications Commission, wrote in 1968:

> [M]ass communications are best understood as mirrors of society that reflect an ambiguous image in which each observer projects or sees his own vision of himself and society . . . . However, broadcasting is . . . an electronic mirror that reflects a vague and ambiguous image of what is behind it, as well as of what is in front of it. While the mirror can pick out points and aspects of society, it cannot create a culture or project an image that does not reflect something already existing in some form in society.
>
> (Loevinger, 1968)

Hence, as Loevinger goes on to say:

> A substantial element of violence in American television reflects a tolerance and taste for violence in American society. This is somewhat offensive to Europeans, who have

a different attitude toward violence and there is less of violence in European broadcast programming. On the other hand, European television has fewer sex and religious taboos than American television and this corresponds to European attitudes, which are looser in these fields than American attitudes.

(Loevinger, 1968)

In this connection, a British visitor to the 1994 U.S. National Association of Broadcasters convention, when asked from the dais whether television content was a problem in the UK, responded that "We enjoy rather more sex and rather less violence" than people in the United States.

Loevinger added that "all mass media are censored by the public since they lose [their audience] if they become too offensive or uninteresting." He also noted that individual members of the audience "project or see in the media their own visions or images" (Loevinger, 1968, pp. 108–109).

APPORTIONING BLAME

Let's also not forget that the media are a very convenient whipping boy. Because most media generally depend on the good will of as many people as possible, in order to attract advertising or subscribers, it is very difficult for the media to fight back, even with the First Amendment on their side. This has given rise to a virtual cottage industry of criticism against the media. When a member of Congress needs something to attack in order to raise his or her reputation with the voters, the media are there. When psychologist Fredric Wertham needed to provide reasons for the apparent causes of juvenile dysfunction, he wrote accusatorily first about the movies, in the early 1950s about comic books, and later about television, blaming each medium in turn for the various faults identified in children.

the media are a very convenient whipping boy.

When a child does something antisocial or an adult perpetrator blames his or her childhood upbringing for a crime, much of the public is glad to take the easy road and blame TV, the big universal babysitter and tutor.

But complaining about juvenile delinquency has been a practice for as long as there have been children. Juliet was only 14 when she and Romeo started their relationship, and then committed suicide; *Oliver Twist* featured a subculture of young thieves; and for millennia there have been both tales and treatises on how children—including Beavis and Butthead—have acted immaturely. Both the ancient Greeks and the Romans complained about those who harmed children by their teachings, and Socrates was condemned to die as a result.

The saving grace is that very few children turn "bad," in the sense of being acute dangers to society. Most children—in all eras—grow into mature adults who are a functional part of society. The fact that more people are jailed in the United States than in any other nation is more likely the result of draconian anti-drug laws and other "mandatory sentencing" legislation than it is of exposure to the mass media. Although the number of gunshot deaths (including accidents) is nearly three-quarters of the number of motor vehicle deaths, the absolute number for *both* of these causes of violent death *combined* only approximated 3%

of all deaths in 2004. Were there homicides by gunshot in that year? Yes, but there were fewer than 12,000 in a population of nearly 300 million, in spite of what is seen on the screen. And neither law enforcement nor medical professionals can explain fully the drop-off in those with a heroin addiction after age 45. "Maturity" has many facets!

VIOLENCE

Even if someone is looking for simple solutions to dysfunctional behaviors, from road rage to drive-by shootings, the arguments by the Surgeon General and other governmental and private bodies about a cause-and-effect relationship between violence on television and violence in the home or on the street have something of a fallacious *post hoc, ergo propter hoc* (that which went before caused that which followed—regardless of any other possible relationship) ring to them.

This is akin to saying that "all children were given milk as infants, all murderers were once infants, therefore milk caused all murderers." Simple logic should reject this kind of argument, regardless of how many people assert it.

For an analogy, the fact that a large proportion of those occupying prison cells are dyslexic doesn't mean that their criminal behavior is caused by dyslexia, but rather may reflect that some often intelligent, motivated, and above all frustrated and misunderstood dyslexics may feel that they have nowhere to turn except to crime in order to make a living.

Television isn't the only medium blamed for violence. Numerous police forces object to "gangsta rap" lyrics on records and the radio that seem to be advocating violence, particularly when directed toward police officers. Almost since its origination, the motion picture industry has been blamed for antisocial actions of its viewers. Indeed, the conflict between self-expression and the potential for harm that might result from artistic expression has been going on for millennia.

The causal hypothesis found so useful by politicians and others seeking publicity isn't the only flawed argument about violence and the media. The commercial media, as far back as the (televised!) Senate hearings on juvenile delinquency in the 1950s, developed an even more simplistic—and less testable—position that "television's fictional violence is a catharsis that defuses and prevents real-life violence."

HOW DO WE KNOW WHAT WE THINK WE KNOW?

Nobody is denying that the media have *some* effects—unspecified but almost certainly interactive with other causes—on individuals and even on society. In fact, there is an old saying in media psychology that "some kinds of media content have some kinds of effect on some kinds of people—sometimes." But it is going too far to claim that *this* causes *that*, whatever there may be.

Obviously, *any* media effects join many other factors—current economic conditions, social changes and conditions (e.g., the role of the family, career-limiting effects of converting the U.S. economy from production to service, easier travel, greater longevity), genetics, education, mental health, war, a burgeoning population whose members feel they can't control their own lives, climate change, etc.—when identifying the influences on individual behavior. But these factors are complex and interactive, and don't make easy targets for those looking for simple solutions. It also is possible that some contributing factors, such as parental abdication of responsibility, *can* be blamed on media performance as "big babysitters."

David Gordon's claim that I am dismissing "the extensive and increasing research on TV violence" as "irrelevant" because it "doesn't conclusively prove a cause–effect relationship" is flawed. First, I'm sorry to have to say that far too many of the hundreds—perhaps thousands—of papers on this topic I've evaluated for publication and other reasons are not very good. Hypotheses are often fuzzy, methodology (including samples, independent variables, and data collection) is often flawed or unexamined, and conclusions—like many of Gordon's exhortations—often are based on neither data nor logic. Some so-called studies are really sermons consisting of thin veneers of jargon superimposed on "don't confuse me with facts, my mind's made up" jumps from hypothesis to inference without going through other steps in the scientific process. Bad research (even that whose conclusions are socially desirable) leads to bad decision-making.

Second, what standard of proof should be applied? Gordon apparently believes that whatever supports his argument is satisfactory, often because, on its face, it appears reasonable or even logical to him; this is at best a very weak "face validity" argument. "Face validity" is *not* a good basis on which to judge any research and, particularly, not a good basis on which to make policy decisions.

Third, the causal relationship he implies is circular. Think about this possibility: *people who are jailed for violent crimes might have a personality type that is attracted to **both** violent criminal acts and violence on TV*. This alternate interpretation—correlation rather than causality—also might explain everything from non-criminal or pre-mass media violent behavior to contact sports. Which comes first, the chicken or the egg?

Further, claiming causality on the basis of "copycat" crimes is questionable. For example, the person who shot at residents of a Midwestern town during the showing of a made-for-TV movie about the 'Texas Tower' sniper turned out not to have known that the film was on television that night. As we've all experienced, peer pressures in high school generally are much more important than the mass media. Research on persuasive communication, including psychological warfare and advertising, illustrates the weakness in *any* simple cause→effect (stimulus–response) media effects model. There is inferential evidence that some automobile crashes are really suicides by people affected by the news of the death of a movie star or political leader (Phillips, 1977). But this does not mean that everyone will run out and mimic what is shown on television or reported in the paper.

Even something as basic as a definition of violence is difficult to nail down. Some would include virtually any physical (or mental) interaction, because each person has the right to be left alone. Some would include child-against-child aggressiveness; some wouldn't. A surgeon would have a different view from a patient. A child has a different opinion of a spanking than a parent. Verbal attacks can be as harmful as physical ones. A football player would take in stride what an ordinary observer would think of as unconscionably violent. One study I've seen tabulated a parent's "good night kiss" as an assault on the child.

The periodic surveys by George Gerbner and others, while "suggestive" (to repeat Gordon's opinion) still have unanswered questions about their methodology. Some information about the sample was withheld, and alternative explanations—for example, even small children can distinguish cartoons from reality (Comstock et al., 1978, pp. 64–70), or news from drama—often were ignored. In other words, how can we know that there wasn't an alternative conclusion?

The best research is peer-reviewed and appears in reputable scholarly journals. Gordon's reliance on secondary sources searching for an audience is disappointing—that is, what *Newsweek* thinks is adequate research or how it interprets the findings of research, rather than on the original properly conducted scientific studies that are completely described with precision in scientific journals, rather than in journalistic reports—is disappointing.

Of course, no matter how valid and reliable the methodology and reasoning, it is silly to expect that the results of all research on any important social question will agree 100%. I never said it would, or that we should be paralyzed until it does. As in a civil court, all we need is the preponderance of the evidence on our side or, if life or liberty are at stake, the criterion for decision usually is the stricter criterion of evidence "beyond a reasonable doubt." Both parents and media may feel justified to opt for this stricter criterion with regard to televised violence. But not everyone is the parent of impressionable children—yet many of the existing and proposed programming restrictions are promulgated to "protect" children who, at some later point, would be exposed to "adult" programming without any preparation.

We also need to be very careful as to how we interpret findings. For instance, although content analyses that compared the incidence of well-defined nonverbal violent behavior shown on television (e.g., a deliberate shooting or stabbing) with the incidence of such behavior in the nation's crime and death statistics show that American television is unquestionably violent, it *doesn't* prove a cause-and-effect relationship, in either direction. Correlation does *not* equal causality. Again: it is quite possible that people prone to violence watch violent programs because they are there—not because they trigger violent acts.

This is particularly true when we realize that bodily collisions in football and hockey are clearly violent, or when the evening news is full of war, murder, mayhem, and accidental death. News coverage of hurricanes, fires, traffic accidents and earthquakes also belongs in this litany. It is up to individuals (and, in the case of children, their parents) to decide whether to watch such images: whether to view the "Puppy Bowl" or the "Super Bowl" is a choice that can be made by each of the 100+ million television households looking for something to do on "Super Bowl Sunday."

Researchers aren't the only ones jumping to conclusions. Legislators and officials can spend millions of dollars of taxpayers' money to sponsor research or require program restrictions that are supposed to protect children. All of this—surprise!—tends to support the climate of fear that brings them votes, and may itself cause harm to children. (This practice can be found elsewhere; in many respects, the color-coded "threat level" of the "war on terror" apparently was originally intended to create fear and insecurity and support for the administration's plans rather than a sense of security.)

WHAT WE ARE DOING ABOUT IT—AND SHOULDN'T

A 1996 federal law required the installation of a "violence chip" (V-chip) in new television sets. On receipt of a warning signal from the station, the V-chip will prevent suitably equipped and programmed sets from displaying violent programs. Even assuming that parents can or will bother to learn the way to activate the V-chip, what level of violence should trigger such a device? Should it be aimed at 5-year-olds or teenagers if both are in the household? The latter question can be answered, "that depends on the parents who are empowered to adjust the V-chip settings." But the entire system overlooks some difficulties. For example, both the station (or network) and the parents must have a practical degree of agreement in the definition of violence. Is there time to rate breaking news and public affairs programming—and differences in what is acceptable on each of them? Further, many children are very capable of adjusting almost any piece of electronic equipment, without parental awareness. And no such system can be so complex that adults find it frustratingly difficult to program. Also, how do children learn how to handle adult fare as they grow up? Do all children of a given age think and react the same way? Suppose there are adults who will miss significant information as a result of an arbitrary label, much as there are people who miss important films just because they carry an "R" rating? Finally, shouldn't parents take the responsibility to regulate individual programs in a manner suited to their own children's psychological health rather than rely on a somewhat arbitrary rating system and then assume that the V-chip will do their thinking?

This device—sometimes called a "C-chip" by both its advocates ("Choice!") and opponents ("Censorship!")—is a real can of worms. Obviously, I reject Gordon's belief that the handful of letters and numbers of each program "rating" (assigned how, and by whom?) is enough of a guide to prevent harm to all children at all times. I believe these ratings are unable to provide sufficient valid and reliable information that parents could block all undesirable programs from their children—while not inadvertently barring the entire family.

Remember also that almost every culture has had "scary" and often violent bedtime stories, fairy tales and the like. They are part of passing along cultural wisdom—warning children of dangers—and have been part of this ritual for many generations. We tend not to look at how violent or frightening they are, because we were exposed to them when we were young. These stories and myths undergird most of our literature—including new examples such as *Lord of the Rings*, the Harry Potter books, and the television programs that Gordon decries—and form a huge part of the value systems of most people. This is neither new nor necessarily bad.

After all, when one is an adult, one may have the opportunity to think through any situation anew, which is why some Quakers become soldiers and some children of military officers become pacifists and conscientious objectors to wartime demands.

Violence is a very shifty concept. To ban all violence in the media would remove the media from their role as a reflection of life. Any medical doctor will admit that procedures such as setting a broken bone or giving a "shot" does violence to the human body, and patriots will tell you that it is necessary to be willing to give up their lives for their country if they believe that preservation of their nation is a good thing. True, one person's "martyr" is another person's "suicide bomber," and violence isn't necessarily an *effective* tool—but both Mother Nature and history show us that violence is an integral part of life. Preparation for violence has survival value for the individual, the family, the nation, and for the human race.

I'm afraid that, by jumping to the conclusion that violent media are the primary *cause* of violent behavior and ignoring other factors, Gordon has presented several syllogisms that I think are untenable. They start with the conclusion, and never go further in either direction. To take just one of his assertions, "violence in U.S. society seems to be an epidemic that is increasing": even if we ignore the frightening implications of the word "epidemic" (or "plague," used earlier), there are far too many unsupported-by-data premises to this argument to allow it to be accepted without question. Yes, some places are more dangerous than others and some people are more prone to violence than others, but that is a long way from being an "epidemic."

Furthermore, even if this relationship is proven—should it be the government or individuals who decide whether something should be aired, printed or shown? Considering the potential for mischief in the "government" choice, I have no hesitation in saying that individuals—in the audience or in the media—should be the ones to make these decisions.

Some experimental studies and some field studies on the topic of media violence, and its possible effects, are useful in the policy-making process. But all research needs to be both valid and reliable. My mother used to decide what her children should wear on the basis of the calendar, not the thermometer—certainly an invalid approach, particularly in spring and autumn.

Let's take another tack: is all violence "bad" and its presentation similarly unethical? I think not. Lessons can be learned from violence, and I consider those who reject any and all forms of violence, without regard to other lessons that can be learned to be short-sighted. To eliminate violence would eliminate Shakespeare, and a large proportion of all fiction, good and bad.

AND WHAT SHOULD BE DONE ABOUT IT?

Almost from the start in his portion of this chapter, Gordon asks that the government be given the power to censor television with respect to violence and pornography. He apparently believes that the First Amendment (and the "public interest, convenience and necessity" standard for the issuance of broadcast licenses) are somehow a social contract that applies to the media in the same way as it does to the government. This sort of mistaken emphasis will inevitably affect other media—the fiction that there is a difference between programs received over broadcast television and those received via cable, satellite or DVD player makes little practical sense—and probably, in the future, other kinds of content.

Absolute reliance on the government, in a democracy, is a dangerous trend. It is akin to citizens not bothering to prepare individually for an emergency—a hurricane, for example, or a sudden storm while out sailing—just because it is the stated task of FEMA or the Coast Guard or some other agency to be prepared to make rescues. During one major widespread power failure, a hospital tried to absolve itself of the need to have an emergency generator for its operating room because it was the job of the power company to supply electricity—

I'm sure this reasoning wouldn't have been appreciated by anyone needing emergency surgery that night.

I believe in individual responsibility to the extent practicable. This means that it is up to media programmers, and to parents (rather than officialdom) to do what can be done to prevent harm to children from television. And this responsibility is not misplaced—as any parent probably can tell you. When they became aware that certain cartoons might trigger epileptic fits, the media immediately reacted—and took these programs off the air until changes in them could be made. There is an ethical interaction here: the public (and the researchers) must make sure that the media are aware of potential problems.

Absolute reliance on the government, in a democracy, is a dangerous trend.

Although eventually most people find themselves enjoying the thrills of a horror movie or a frightening amusement park ride, it takes careful preparation on the part of everyone involved to avoid emotional trauma the *first* time such content is experienced. Motion picture exhibitors are part of the system that labels films and in which an "R" rating supposedly prevents minors unaccompanied by adults from entering the theater. This industry-wide self-regulation resulted from society's reaction to a perceived problem—and the industry's reaction to a public relations crisis.

It is much easier to regulate the attendance of children to a theater, with limited entrances and exits, than to achieve unanimity among parents with respect to controlling television viewing in the home. Also, if parents go to the movies with their children, they provide security and comfort, and often can warn the child of what to beware of—and children need little encouragement to hide their eyes (or "need" to go to the restroom) if they feel in danger of being emotionally overwhelmed.

And in the home, while watching television, there is always an "off" switch or other channels to select. Yes, there is desensitizing of individuals to mediated horror, but *it is a normal part of growing up*. The world contains both bad and good things, and children need to learn how to deal with them. An adult can place a violent or horrifying event or image in context and, if children are viewing with them, use it as a lesson in "what to avoid," much as driving instructors spend time on "defensive driving" techniques that include mental preparation for emergency maneuvers—for example, what would I do if a delivery truck suddenly came out of that side street? A child needs to learn the defensive maneuvers for many threats.

Gordon has frequently implied that television causes violent behavior, apparently hoping that repetition is a convincing persuasive technique. He says that where there's smoke there's fire—ignoring smokescreens designed to conceal rather than burn, or dust, fog and clouds, which mimic smoke. He calls the risk of stepping on First Amendment toes "theoretical"—but it isn't theoretical at all. Carol Gilligan's (1982) argument that women are more nurturing than men may or may not be valid; but what would Gordon say if, in an attempt to reduce violence, it were mandated that all governmental posts had to be filled by women?

Gordon says that it is possible for parents (and children) to avoid disturbing *sexual* content by merely turning off the set, but he believes that it will require the government to regulate the amount of *violence* illustrated or described in the mass media. I'm not sure why, because this would open the door to all sorts of governmental content control—of the news, as well as entertainment—that might stand in the way of the citizens being able to perform their civic duty. News coverage of the violence and casualties of war can cause the public to think more about what is being done in their name (think about the abuses at Abu Ghraib prison or the Vietnamese hamlet of My Lai), and the consequences that follow. In a democracy, this is an essential ethical function of the media.

Arbitrary rules are the enemy of reason. Following the Watts riots in Los Angeles after the assassination of Martin Luther King, Jr., the media in some communities decided to follow a rule of "don't report a disturbance until after the police have controlled it." This seemed like a good idea, until, some time later in Chicago, hundreds of commuters found themselves being the target of bricks thrown from roofs as they drove through an affected area, unwarned by their favorite traffic-and-news-reporting radio stations that a violent disturbance was occurring. How does one decide that it is okay to warn of an oncoming tornado—but not okay to warn of a drunken brawl or a violent demonstration downtown? Put that way, it seems obvious that the media must avoid arbitrary rules and, instead, use their brains to decide what will do the most good for the most people. If this sounds like we need to be utilitarian and not Kantian, so be it.

Does this section mean that I am completely oblivious to the possibility that violent media content might have deleterious effects on some members of the audience? Hardly! In many respects, Gordon and I agree—gratuitous violence probably has little if any redeeming social importance. (My arguments against bad research—and the use of that research—involve the standards and ethics of research, not the ethics of the subject of the research.) Accordingly, reducing the amount of violence and improving the quality of programs may reduce the effects of this possibly harmful content.

The problem is thus thrown back into the hands of those who control what is seen on the screen: network or station programming executives, program creators and producers, and the millions of parents who can and should decide what their children are allowed to see during their most formative years. Like practical politics, all media ethics is local—and one can't rely either on "the research" or "common sense." The research isn't close to definitive, and there are many alternative hypotheses that may explain more than doctrinaire "common sense" can.

PORNOGRAPHY

Pornography, however, is even harder to define than violence. Satirical songwriter Tom Lehrer claimed that "When correctly viewed, everything is lewd." To many feminists, pornography is the precursor to violent acts directed against women, and thus should be considered a form of violence. Some Islamic fundamentalists maintain that *any* depiction of contact between male and female is obscene. Some fundamentalist Protestants have similar opinions about sexual practices outside of marriage and outside of conventional heterosexual behavior. There are many who are made uncomfortable by advertisements for condoms (even considering the AIDS epidemic), underwear, or menstrual products. Obscenity, indecency, profanity—all have their varied definitions. The weakest, of course, is Justice Potter Stewart's "I know it when I see it."

BLASPHEMY, OBSCENITY, AND PROFANITY

Blasphemy charges can lead to assassination and threats of assassination, as in the case of Salman Rushdie, a British author whose book, *Satanic Verses* (1988), made him the worldwide target of Islamic extremists who claim that the book is blasphemous. The publication of some cartoons depicting the Prophet Mohammed in a Danish publication caused the same reaction, since many Muslims believe that any depiction of the Prophet is forbidden. Profanity is a punishable crime in some U.S. jurisdictions—particularly when children can hear it. Obscenity and indecency on the airwaves now can lead to hundreds of thousands of dollars in FCC fines. But blasphemy, obscenity, and profanity are really outside the scope of this chapter. Two aphorisms reflect my feelings: "Sticks and stones may break my bones, but words will never hurt me" and, to sum up Heywood Broun's (1927) superb chapter on censorship, "Who ever heard of a woman ruined by a book?"

CENSORSHIP WAITING IN THE WINGS

But if—as has happened in many times and places before—religious or "moral" groups succeed in securing political power, formal or informal, then the media will have to concern themselves with such matters or accept any censorship that will result. The pendulum has been swinging in this more restrictive direction in recent years—but governmental removal of cable and satellite television content ("cable isn't *broadcasting*") from the jurisdiction of the Communications Act (and the Criminal Code prohibitions against depictions of sex) has obscured this trend.

Make no bones about it: censorship *is* about to step into the limelight, in spite of the popularity of *Jersey Shore* or even *South Park* and similar TV content. Perhaps its entrance will be blatant, much as the 18th Amendment established Prohibition against manufacture, sale and use of alcohol after World War I. Perhaps it will be the result of a national consensus, much as public smoking of cigarettes became increasingly unacceptable in the 1990s. Perhaps it will be the result of fear of the effect of either legislation or consensus, and will take the form of self-censorship, as seen in the motion picture and television "codes of good practice" of bygone years and in today's rating systems. Perhaps it will be by government edict, as in 1997 when CompuServe (then a major Internet content service provider) had to pull the plug—worldwide, as it turned out—on any Web site that might violate German content laws relating to the former Nazi regime. And all content providers must walk a tightrope when dealing with totalitarian countries, such as China.

Sometimes "voluntary" restrictions are the most pernicious, as when members of Congress called upon the FCC to chastise NBC for not adhering strictly to a *voluntary* content rating code, and they might also have unintended consequences. For example, these content labels, which are industry approved and awarded, may be used in an unintended manner. Since young people in their teens and twenties—prime audiences for movies—wouldn't be caught dead at a "G" rated film showing, some filmmakers will insert gratuitous sex, violence, or strong dialogue in a film in order to get an "R" rating, which makes the desired audience more likely to attend. Already, Internet service to libraries and schools (as well private homes) has restrictions that have led to unintended consequences. For example, the prohibitions by networks, schools, textbook publishers, libraries and others against depictions of nudity, genitalia and breasts has hampered awareness of the war against breast cancer. Similar restrictions sometimes are in place against written and visual materials on the Internet.

And we shouldn't make the mistake of assuming that all of the above is limited to the visual media. Media other than television and film have their own problems with both violence and pornography. Radio is a "theater of the mind," with the ability to be both startling and frightening, particularly for children to whom euphemisms can be terribly frightening ("the dog was put to sleep" can make "go to sleep, dear" an awful injunction to a young child). The recording of Archibald Macleish's epic poem, "The Fall of the City," contains a 13-second scream that, in context, provides a message of horror that can't be forgotten. The growth of 900-number "verbal sex" services shows other powers of aural media. And the textual abilities of the written word—and the resulting print media—are virtually unlimited with respect to sexual arousal.

In any case, with or without legislative or executive mandates, it is more likely that there will be a tendency toward "the wholly inoffensive, the bland" (FCC, 1964, p. 179) on the part of advertising-supported media. If this tendency wins with respect to something like "violence," it is unlikely to be too long before many religious or political dogmas become equally unacceptable.

The First Amendment refers to Congress passing "no law" abridging freedom of speech and the press. The media should demand no less, no matter how much of a fight it takes, and how unpopular the causes that will benefit. Fairness to the citizens of the United States is at stake.

CONCLUSIONS AND SUGGESTIONS

The media may not be the *cause* of violence, but there is considerable evidence that real-life violence is more acceptable to more people as the result of violence in the media. Yet, as I wrote after President Kennedy's assassination:

> [H]ave the American people become inured to violence as a way of life through a constant diet of dramatic programs that seem to look at one type of personality warped by life and solving all his problems through violent action? Thankfully, the reaction of almost all of us to the senseless slaughter in Dallas gives the lie to this line of reasoning. Violence has not yet lost its power to horrify. . . [H]ave we lost the capacity to feel deep emotion after a generation of viewing human lives summed up or torn apart in the [very short] framework of a dramatic program? No. Even though we felt, at the end of four days, that we were drained of all emotion, we were not.
>
> (Kittross, 1963, p. 284)

So, *can we*, as media practitioners, reduce the destructive cycle of violence in the United States, prevent the Oswalds (and the Rubys and those who walk into a school or a store with firearms and kill their classmates and neighbors) from developing as they did? Perhaps.

Should we? Do we have an ethical duty to try? I believe that the answer is "Of course!" Both the utilitarians and Kant demand no less. Although the sales department may argue that such a course of action would put the size of a media audience at risk, or an advertiser may want maximum shock value, if all media adopt the same moral standards, then nobody has an unfair advantage. True, the *National Enquirer* and its broadcast and cable equivalents seem to be with us always. But although occasional "good news" news services have shown little success, the most important argument in favor of trying to reduce violence is a personal one for media practitioners: do we want our own children to be exposed to it? Are we personally comfortable with it—and why? Dare we have the arrogance to say that different standards should be applied to the masses than we apply to our own families? Far too many major figures in the communication industry restrict their own offspring's viewing for the rest of us to be complacent about the content of the media. If we want to sleep well, we need to do what we can to benefit humanity.

Must we? Aye, there's the rub. Morally and ethically, I believe that we should do what we can, as individuals. But the First Amendment is under enough stress in the current political climate to prompt me to answer "No" to this question. I don't think it inconsistent with the preceding paragraph to argue that the mass media should fight against allowing any "outsiders" to determine what we broadcast and print. The end is commendable; the means unacceptable. If, as Gordon maintains, "at this point in our history . . . violent content should be no more protected under the First Amendment than is libelous content," then we are a long way down the slippery slope to determining content on the basis of what the U.S. Congress says it should be.

> we are a long way down the slippery slope to determining content on the basis of what the U.S. Congress says it should be.

Would pictures of Americans fighting leading to American dead during the Vietnam "living room war" or the more sanitized pictures from Iraq and Afghanistan have been allowed under Gordon's formulation? These pictures were surely violent, but they also had a significant and, many would argue, beneficial political impact. It is arguable that the Vietnam War—and its casualty lists—would have been longer if television hadn't shown this true violence.

The quick fix to this argument might be to allow journalistic, but not fictional, coverage of such violence. Another quick fix would be to have (as we do) special rules that apply to materials available to (or, in some cases, directed to) children. I discussed this above, asking such questions as at what age does one stop being a child? Can we really help children to grow by swaddling them in bubblewrap? And, in protecting the most vulnerable in a Rawlsian manner, do we take away the liberty of everyone else? Would I, like Gordon, throw the First Amendment baby out with the bathwater? Obviously not. I look at the positive, rather than the negative potential of the media. In a world with violence, any news broadcast would still be supplying violent images to everyone, including those who might be harmed by shocking graphic images. And to prevent dramatic coverage, in the form of documentaries or drama, of human activities that include violence such as war, crime, imprisonment, torture (let's not forget sport and medicine), would be a frightening political act of the greatest significance. Of course, if such censorship were carried out, there soon might not be enough of the non-brainwashed around to realize how significant such a decision had been.

KEY POINTS

- No causal relationship has been proven between TV violence and violence in real life.
- It is appropriate for the mass media to reflect the violence that occurs in society, in both entertainment and news content.

GORDON: There is far more violence in today's mass media than is good for society, and that violent content must somehow be controlled.

The key concerns in this argument are where the line should be drawn regarding how much violence is too much, and who should draw it. John Michael Kittross argues that wherever the line is drawn, it must be purely an internal decision within the media. And he seems to be saying that, because there is no absolute proof available in this dilemma—and new questions can always be raised—we must leave any palliative efforts to the same voluntary self-regulation that has underwhelmed the problem to this point.

I disagree! I start from the premise that this is an increasingly crucial issue for U.S. society, as the current plague of violence seems to escalate into all corners of the society (including, unfortunately, college campuses and supermarket parking lots). I am not going to deal here with pornography as an issue separate from sexual content or from violence in the media, although pornography is certainly degrading to women. However, I can't buy the argument of feminists Andrea Dworkin (1985) and Catharine MacKinnon (1985) that a clear link has been established between it and violence directed toward women. (Others also have problems with the Dworkin-MacKinnon desire to define pornography sweepingly and deal with it legally as a violation of women's civil rights: see, e.g., Strossen, 2000.) Should such a link be established, it would be easy for me to argue that pornography ought to be regulated because of the violence it could provoke. In the meantime, because some legal controls are already in place regarding pornography and obscenity, I prefer to focus mainly on the ethical aspects of violent mass media content.

I believe that the concern in many European countries over violent media content, combined with a much more laissez-faire attitude about sex, is an approach that would benefit U.S. society (although it would run into all sorts of opposition from the deeply ingrained streak of American Puritanism that persists regarding sex). I don't believe there is any need to control television's sexual content in any way other than by turning off a program if one is offended by it. But violence is far more dangerous to society than sex is, and experience has shown—unfortunately—that media decision-makers have too often failed to confront the problem of excessive violent content.

As of 2010, violent content was still considerably less regulated than was sexual content, either by the media themselves or externally by parents or others. Even the existence of a system to rate TV program content—implemented in 1997 at the urging of Congress—and the inclusion since 2000 of the so-called V-chip in all TV sets 13 inches and larger (manufactured for the U.S. market) haven't made much of an impact.

In 2007, a Kaiser Family Foundation study reported that among parents who had purchased a new TV set containing a V-chip, 57% were unaware of the chip and only one in six parents overall had ever used it to block content. The foundation also reported that about 70% of parents with children between 2 and 6 years of age were unable to identify what *any* of the content ratings meant and some 10% thought that a "fantasy violence" (FV) rating really stood for "family viewing" (Eggerton, 2007). With this lack of parental concern and knowledge, it's no wonder the media decision-makers saw no mandate to *alter* content rather than merely labeling it.

Protesters are perfectly within their rights to oppose both sexual and violent content on TV, to organize boycotts, and to urge viewers to turn off the offending programs. One might argue that such efforts to influence TV content are enough, and that the television industry should be left to deal with these concerns guided only by viewer and pressure group reactions. In regard to sexual content, I agree. But I believe violence poses greater threats and, because it is still such a prominent part of the TV and film landscapes, some limits on it must be established, with assistance from outside the media—if industry self-regulation continues to prove inadequate. Either utilitarianism's concern for the greater good, or Rawls's emphasis on protecting the weakest parties (here, children) demands no less.

Since Kittross is adamant that much of the data from studies of TV violence and its impact on young viewers are the result of shoddy research, there's little point in going into detail about them here. If I were to pursue this in detail, I believe he would continue to object to virtually any assertion that violence is a problem and demand more detail than is possible to provide in this format. And, since the studies do not prove beyond any possible doubt that violence is harmful to young viewers, he would dismiss that contention as heresy and the data as meaningless. So, to simplify matters, I'll raise a number of important issues, provide citations to some of the studies (or to summaries of them) in the References, and let you make up your own minds.

Studies

There are an increasing number of longitudinal studies that follow children for 20 years or more to see if there are behavioral differences between children who watched a lot of violent TV and those who watched less. As in most media violence studies, the research shows correlations rather than clear cause-and-effect relationships. But the number of studies showing such correlations is too large to dismiss out of hand. Let me be absolutely clear that I am *not* arguing that violent media are the *primary* cause of violent behavior (contrary to Kittross' assertion on p. 468). I agree with Kittross that we don't yet (and may never) have *definitive* proof of a causal relationship between the viewing of media violence and violent individual behavior. I *am* asserting that media violence does have effects on *some* kinds of people in some circumstances, and I believe the scientific evidence clearly supports that position and demands action.

SOME PRIMARY ISSUES

First Amendment Concerns

Rather than an absolutist approach to the concept of freedom for the media, I'd suggest a utilitarian perspective that concerns itself with the greatest good for the greatest number of people, or perhaps the "ethics of care" embraced by ethicists such as Nel Noddings (1984, 2002). The First Amendment can't be overlooked in this discussion, but First Amendment rights have never been widely regarded as absolute. A reasonable argument can be made, at this point in our history, that violent content should be no more protected under the First Amendment than is libelous content. Libelous material is allowed when it deals with matters relating to public life, and such an approach might work very well as a guideline for government regulation of violence in the media. Certainly, it seems no harder to define violence than it has been to define obscenity over the decades, and the definitional difficulties haven't kept the courts from regulating the latter.

> violent content should be no more protected under the First Amendment than is libelous content.

The V-Chip

The V-chip "reads information encoded in the rated TV programs and blocks programs from the set based upon the rating *selected by the parent*" (FCC, 2008, italics added) or any other responsible adult. Let's be clear about this—the programming is blocked only on the set controlled by that V-chip and the level of blockage is determined by the adult who controls the chip, and can easily be tailored to "their own children's psychological health," as Kittross suggests. Such technology, together with more precise classification of each program's violence—and with viewers who gain a better understanding of the choices—would be a self-regulating step in the right direction.

Desensitizing Viewers

Violence in U.S. society seems to be a growing epidemic, perhaps fueled in part by the apparent growth in its acceptability or "normality." Portrayals of violent incidents in both news and entertainment programming seem ever more prevalent, often shown as an acceptable solution to problems and too often failing to show any real *consequences* resulting from the violent acts. All of this tends to desensitize viewers, which may be as great a danger as the possibility of violent content promoting either short-run or long-term violent behavior.

GRATUITOUS VIOLENCE

It would be helpful if entertainment programs—and news, as well—would reduce *gratuitous* violence. When violence is necessary to the plot—and particularly when it simply reflects the violence in society—it is arguably more appropriate than when it is used for shock value. The late Meg Greenfield (1993) noted that Shakespeare's works, among others, contain violent episodes that are "every bit as shaking and horrible" as anything on TV. But she cited crucial differences in the classic literature:

> the violence in the story meant something; it was singular; it was committed by a particularly cruel character; it had some purpose beyond its mere power to titillate, frighten and repel. Nor do I think any age has seen anything comparable to our own unending, daily inundation of the home by filmed, superrealistic close-up portrayals of human violence, of maiming and mutilation and slaughter.
>
> (Greenfield, 1993, p. 72)

A similar perspective would be useful with regard to violence on the news. Where violent footage is needed to illustrate violent news—or sports—events, it is far more justifiable than when the story can be told just as well without what one news director called "the graphic blood" (quoted in Simmons, 1994). When news accounts include violent footage gratuitously—or when violent stories are hyped simply to promote interest in an upcoming newscast segment—there are ethical concerns that cry out for responsible behavior.

This approach obviously leaves itself open for the criticism that one person's gratuitous violence is a necessary illustration for another person. It's easy to criticize efforts to eliminate "unnecessary" violence by arguing that it would require "value judgments" affecting the content of the news or entertainment program, and would give the "judges" inappropriate power over media content.

With all due respect, I suggest that this is no more of a problem in regard to violent content than it is in regard to any other aspect of media content. Media gatekeepers make value judgments all the time regarding the inclusion or exclusion of certain materials in their communications. What, after all, is "news judgment" if not a kind of value judgment? The Communications Act of 1934 requires broadcasters to serve the "public interest, convenience and necessity," and that's a phrase that clearly requires some value judgments to be made. And ethics, by definition, is a series of judgments about values. There is no reason to be afraid of applying value judgments—from outside the media, if no one will do it internally—to reduce the gratuitous violence appearing in both the news and the entertainment media.

EVIDENCE

I don't think it works to argue, as Kittross has done, that because the extensive and increasing research on TV violence doesn't conclusively prove a cause–effect relationship, it should be dismissed as irrelevant. It's easy to allege that much research on televised violence "does not meet generally accepted scientific standards for validity and reliability" and, without doubt, some studies illustrate that charge. But recent studies, and the increasing willingness of the medical and scientific communities to oppose TV violence on the basis of those studies, make them impossible to ignore, and raise questions about Kittross's blanket condemnation of such evidence.

It is hard to argue (though Kittross has tried) against the proposition that televised (and video game) violence—*in combination with other factors*—affects some people in ways that lead to antisocial behavior in the long run as well as the short term. Even correlational evidence can't be dismissed out of hand. As one researcher put it, "correlational studies are routinely used in modern science to test theories that are inherently causal. Whole scientific fields are based on correlational data (e.g., astronomy)" (Anderson, 2003). And it's certainly not logical to dismiss the many studies indicating that TV violence may be harmful by saying, as Kittross does, that many must be flawed because he saw a lot of shoddy research, on this and other topics, in his dozen years as editor of a scholarly journal.

A 2007 study reported in the journal *Pediatrics* concludes that "(p)re-school boys who watch violent television become markedly more aggressive and anti-social as they grow older," although pre-school "girls appear impervious to the effects of television violence." The study "didn't establish that TV violence causes such subsequent behavior problems," but the researchers "weeded out variables such as spanking to isolate TV's effects."

> The study, which focused on years of data for 330 children around the nation, found that each hour of violent shows viewed per day by boys ages 2 to 4 increased their aggression threefold, as reported by their parents five years later. It adds to a large body of evidence that kids learn from what they watch, the study's lead author said.

And that author added: "Speaking broadly, the link between on-screen violence and subsequent violent behavior is as strong as evidence that smoking causes lung cancer" (Song, 2007).

No single study proves a cause–effect relationship, but the growing number of studies with similar results demonstrates that the impact of TV violence on violent behavior can't easily be dismissed as merely *post hoc, ergo propter hoc*.

There is also considerable anecdotal evidence. One of the more striking stories concerns a 4-year-old girl who asked "Who killed him?" when told by her parents that a playmate's father had just died:

> The parents were prepared to discuss the many concerns that a child might have about the death of a parent, but not the question that she asked. After explaining that her playmate's father had died of a disease, they asked why she thought someone had killed him. "Isn't that the way people die?" the girl asked. "That's the way people die on TV."

> (Slaby, 1994, p. B1)

Increasingly, though, there is more than just anecdotal evidence to link televised violence with violence in society. The 2007 *Pediatrics* study is only one of many since the early 1990s that demonstrate a connection. A 1992 article in the *Journal of the American Medical Association* noted that some 20 long-term field studies in recent years have shown a positive correlation between watching violence on TV and violent or aggressive behavior (Centerwall, 1992). More recently, six prominent and reputable medical groups warned that media violence will affect children in a number of unfavorable ways: increases in antisocial and aggressive behavior; less sensitivity to violence and the victims of violence; viewing the world as mean and violent, with increased fears of becoming a victim; a desire to see more

Increasingly . . . there is more than just anecdotal evidence to link televised violence with violence in society.

violence in both entertainment and real life; and a belief that violence is an acceptable way to settle conflicts (Congressional Public Health Summit, 2000—the six groups included the American Academy of Pediatrics, the American Medical Association and the American Psychiatric Association).

MORE EVIDENCE

Since the 1950s, there have been more than 1,000 studies that have examined the effects of TV and movie violence. (Postman and Powers (2008, p. 143) put the total at more than 3,000.) Kittross is right that not all of these are methodologically sound, but many of them have passed muster with medical and other scientific journals. The "majority of these studies reach the same conclusion: television and film violence leads to real-world violence" (Senate Committee on the Judiciary, 1999). The Congressional Public Health Summit (2000) put the case even more strongly:

> At this time, well over 1000 studies – including reports from the Surgeon General's office, the National Institute of Mental Health, and numerous studies conducted by leading figures within our medical and public health organizations . . . point overwhelmingly to a causal connection between media violence and aggressive behavior in some children. The conclusion of the public health community, based on over 30 years of research, is that viewing entertainment violence can lead to increases in aggressive attitudes, values and behavior, particularly in children.
>
> Its effects are measurable and long-lasting. Moreover, prolonged viewing of media violence can lead to emotional desensitization toward violence in real life.
>
> (Congressional Public Health Summit)

It is noteworthy that, as long ago as the early 1990s, the *Journal of the American Medical Association* and *TV Guide*—leagues apart in audiences they target—both called TV violence a public health problem. In addition, according to Postman and Powers (2008, p. 143), "the American Academy of Pediatrics concluded that TV violence 'promotes a proclivity to violence and a passive response to its practice.'" If there is *any* validity to such widespread and recurring concerns, our society is facing—or is already in the midst of—a crisis that requires *some* entity to act almost regardless of whether such steps raise First Amendment concerns.

Although the evidence is not unequivocal and the data are not *totally* conclusive in regard to cause and effect, there is enough smoke coming from the myriad of TV violence studies to weaken greatly the claim that no fire has been scientifically proven. To paraphrase an old saw, if it looks like a fire, smells like a fire, and if it smokes like a fire, it probably is a fire.

PORTRAYALS OF VIOLENCE

Some of the problems may stem from the way in which violence is shown on American television. George Gerbner, a research pioneer on the impact of televised violence, noted that a study comparing Japanese and American television "found that Japanese violence, unlike ours, is not happy violence. It's painful, it's awful, it teaches a very different lesson" ("The experts speak out . . .," 1992, p. 15).

A similar observation about violence on American TV (and in films) was offered nearly two decades earlier by author Tom Wolfe (1976), who noted that it is usually shown from the perspective of the perpetrator (or from a third-person perspective). Rarely if ever is violence seen from the perspective of the victim, which would convey the consequences much more graphically and help to deglamorize it. Wolfe (1976) called the usual approach "porno-violence" because

> in almost every case the camera angle, therefore the viewer, is with the gun, the fist, the rock. The pornography of violence has no point of view in the old sense that novels do. . . . You live with the aggressor, whoever he may be. One moment you are the hero. The next you are the villain. No matter whose side you may be on consciously, you are in fact with the muscle and it is you who disintegrates all comers, villains, lawmen, women, anybody.
>
> (Wolfe, 1976, pp. 183–184)

A major part of the TV problem is the sheer volume of violent acts shown on regular entertainment programming, especially in children's programs. A study of the 1991–92 TV season showed that children's programs (including cartoons) have far higher rates of violence than do prime-time programs—an average of 32 violent acts per hour in children's programs compared to four in prime time (Waters et al., 1993).

A study commissioned by *TV Guide* analyzed 18 hours (6 a.m. to midnight) of programming on April 2, 1992, on each of 10 channels (including 4 cable channels—HBO, WTBS, USA, and MTV) in Washington, DC. The 180 hours of programming included no exceptionally violent movies or news events that day, but the study still identified 1,846 individual acts of violence; 175 scenes where violence resulted in at least one fatality; 389 scenes showing serious assaults without guns and 362 involving gunplay; and so on (Hickey, 1992, p. 10).

OTHER ISSUES

The exact number of people affected negatively by TV violence is certainly debatable. I would suggest, however, that even if we can prevent—or discourage—"only" a few killings or a relative handful of assaults each month, or if we can alleviate that sense of insecurity for even a few people, it is well worth trying to do so even if, theoretically, this risks stepping on some First Amendment toes.

Another concern—one noted by the medical groups mentioned above—focuses not on viewers whose aggressive actions might be stimulated by televised violence, but rather on the reactions of those who constantly see a violent video world portrayed. To quote Gerbner again:

> [T]elevision trains us to be victims. Our studies, as confirmed by many independent investigators, show that the most pervasive, long-term consequence of growing up in a media cult of violence is a sense of pervasive insecurity, what we call "the mean-world syndrome." It's a sense of feeling vulnerable, of dependence, of needing protection.
>
> ("The experts speak out . . .," 1992, pp. 12–13)

Programming such as music videos and reality shows have also been blamed for increasing significantly the amount of TV violence, as have commercials for violent theatrical movies and TV series. So have cartoons, which were found by a *TV Guide* study to be "the most violent program form, with 471 scenes," which may be particularly inadvisable for very young children (ages 2 to 5 years), "who may not distinguish between animated violence and the real thing" (Hickey, 1992, p. 10). In all, critics have concluded, the average U.S. child sees a huge amount of televised violence while growing up—by one estimate, "roughly 13,000 killings [and] about 200,000 violent episodes" by age 18 (Postman and Powers, 2008, p. 142). Others have placed those estimates as high as 40,000 murders and the same 200,000 violent acts (Huston et al., 1992—a study by the Taskforce on Television and Society of the American Psychological Association).

Films have also come in for their share of criticism regarding violent content, even though many of the top box office hits since 1980 have been relatively nonviolent (often family-oriented) movies rather than "R" titles (see Medved, 1992, especially pp. 287–289). But one study showed that "among all major releases in 1991—including PG- and G-rated 'family films'—62 percent featured violent fight scenes, and 39% showed 'graphic deaths' " (Medved, 1992, p. 187).

One critic has also lamented the increasing violence in televised sports events, creating an audience that "has, because of TV, become accustomed to seeing [violent] displays. . . . Almost all technological advances in the [sports] broadcasting industry [e.g., super slow-motion] have been concerned with transporting violent images more effectively" (Twitchell, 1989, p. 12).

VIDEO GAMES

Violent video games also have been criticized as one possible incubator for violent behavior. A former CBS vice president for program practices told the story of an erstwhile West Point psychology professor, paratrooper, ranger and Vietnam veteran who "has been particularly troubled by the coexistence of increasingly violent films and video games and the considerable rise in criminal assault." The ex-soldier drew a parallel to the training given to U.S. infantry to increase their willingness to fire their weapons in battle—training that helped raise the rate from 15 to 20% in World War II to 95% in Vietnam—and the ways in which American children are influenced by violent cartoons and by what he calls the reflex training in violent video games. The former CBS executive suggested that—no matter how unlikely the connection might seem (and he added violent feature films to the mix)—we ignore the possibility at our societal peril (Dessart, 1996, pp. 39–40).

Similar concerns cropped up in the 1999 report by the Senate Judiciary Committee, which cautioned that some researchers believe "that the violent actions performed in playing video games are more conducive [than violent TV or films] to children's aggression. As one expert concludes, 'We're not just teaching kids to kill. We're teaching them to like it' " (Senate Committee on the Judiciary, 1999; see also Anderson and Bushman, 2001).

More recently, one of the leading researchers on the effects of violent video games suggested that such games "may be even more hazardous than violent television or cinema." He noted that video games, especially the new generation starting in the early 1990s, "reward players for killing innocent bystanders, police, and prostitutes, using a wide range of weapons including guns, knives, flame throwers, swords, baseball bats" (Anderson, 2003):

> when one combines all relevant empirical studies . . . five separate effects emerge with considerable consistency. Violent video games are significantly associated with: increased aggressive behavior, thoughts, and affect; increased physiological arousal; and decreased prosocial (helping) behavior.
>
> (Anderson, 2003; see also Anderson et al., 2007, which includes some longitudinal study results)

NEWS MEDIA

Television news has also come in for criticism and these concerns cannot be dismissed merely by pleading First Amendment protection for the news media. Some of the problem is very clearly in the ethics realm, such as the decision by NBC to show the actual 1993 murder of a Florida woman by her ex-husband on its *Nightly News* program. The shooting occurred during an interview of the ex-husband by a tabloid Spanish-language news program (*Ocurio Asi*—"The way it happened"), after he asked the program to investigate whether his ex-wife was involved in their pregnant teenage daughter's suicide. He was being interviewed at the cemetery where his daughter was buried when his ex-wife showed up unexpectedly. The camera continued to roll while he pulled a gun and shot her.

The tape was offered to the major networks by Telemundo, the Spanish-language network that produced the original program. Only NBC used it. Some news directors at NBC affiliates questioned whether this incident had enough news value to warrant its use, or whether (as one of them said) it "was thoughtless, irresponsible and shouldn't have been done" (quoted in Winslow, 1993, p. 8). As another affiliate news director put it, in criticizing the use of this material, "It was real, not the movies, not entertainment" (quoted in Winslow, 1993, p. 9).

There are other major ethical questions here as well—for instance, whether the whole shooting sequence should have been shown, if it were used at all, and whether the audience should have been cautioned much more fully about what was coming. Although NBC claimed that showing the video illustrated the horrors of domestic violence, which the network is committed to cover, one critic noted that the story was run without any references to that larger context (Winslow, 1993, p. 9). This after-the-fact, self-serving justification by the network serves as a pointed and forceful argument that some type of outside influence can be not only helpful but also necessary in setting limits on violent content. I am not suggesting direct censorship in regard to such portrayals of violence on the news, but it might well be appropriate to consider—as part of the FCC's license renewal process for individual stations—whether this kind of material truly serves the "public interest, convenience and necessity."

Another concern regarding violence in news programming is the so-called copycat syndrome in civil disturbances, where viewers see live televised violence occurring and take to the streets themselves. Ted Koppel, among others, blamed such "live, unedited telecasting of the [1992] Los Angeles riots [for spreading] the virus from one part of the city to another" ("The experts speak out . . .," 1992, p. 18). Kittross may be right, though, in questioning any direct relationship where "copycat" crimes or suicides are concerned, though there is anecdotal evidence that this may have happened.

ENTERTAINMENT MEDIA

The social responsibility theory put forth by the Hutchins Commission in 1947 included the media goal of helping to raise social conflict from the level of violence to the level of discussion (Commission on Freedom of the Press, 1947). This would seem to mandate that the media cooperate in limiting the amount and types of violent content they provide. As Greenfield noted in 1993:

> Most of this stuff has long since abandoned any pretense to what the Supreme Court once called, in the context of an obscenity ruling, "redeeming social value." It is gore for gore's sake, drama based on violence as a first and only resort in conflict.
>
> (Greenfield, 1993, p. 72)

Greenfield added her concern that TV's fictional violence "will dull our reactions to the kind that is filmed not on a set but from Bosnia or Liberia or places in this country." Or, to update her references, from Iraq or Afghanistan.

One key ethical question is whether the entertainment media—ranging from TV and movies to the music industry—should be putting forth material that demonstrates different methods of violence, romanticizes teenage suicide or focuses on the murder of police officers. Should there be restrictions placed on television gatekeepers in order to keep some of the mindless violence off the airwaves—especially if those gatekeepers lack the responsibility or the good sense to excise it on their own? Should there be restrictions on films that provide models of violence even if only a few people may copy-cat? When at least 14 accused murderers may be said to have emulated the film *Natural Born Killers* (1994) (Gibeaut, 1997, pp. 63–64), are such restrictions overdue? Is this perhaps a public health issue—or, as novelist and lawyer John Grisham has suggested, a product liability issue—rather than a First Amendment issue (pp. 64, 66)?

Because the media have failed to exercise much self-restraint, some outside forces must be brought into play to help reduce the levels of violent media content. Pressure groups—such as the Parents Music Resource Center, organized by Tipper Gore to twist the recording industry's arm to label records with violent content—are one possibility, with economic marketplace forces lurking in the background. But with violence continuing as a societal problem, it may become necessary for the government to intervene indirectly or even directly, despite the very valid concerns this would raise about First Amendment rights.

GOVERNMENT OPTIONS

One possible avenue for that intervention was suggested by the Federal Communications Commission in 2007, in a report stemming from a request by 39 members of the House of Representatives to look into the issue of TV violence. The FCC suggested that Congress could establish time parameters (the so-called "safe harbor" late night approach that has been used, albeit with mixed results, in regard to "indecent" material on the airwaves) within which violent material could be broadcast on TV. If this "indecency" approach were followed, violent material could be broadcast only between 10 p.m. and 6 a.m., a time slot when (it is assumed—perhaps erroneously) most young children would not be watching. The report suggested that First Amendment concerns would not be endangered: "properly defined, excessively violent programming, like indecent programming, occupies a relatively low position in the hierarchy of First Amendment values because it is of 'slight social value as a step to truth'" (FCC 2007, p. 12, quoting *FCC* v. *Pacifica* at p. 476, which in turn was quoting *Chaplinsky* v. *New Hampshire* at p. 572).

A second suggestion—this one giving consumers more control to avoid violent content—calls for Congress to require cable companies to offer channels to subscribers on an *à la carte* basis. This would allow the customers to pick and choose among the available channels they want to receive rather than being required to take all or none of the channels in specific service tiers. The *à la carte* proposal is a highly controversial one, though, and isn't likely to be implemented any time soon as a means of combating the availability of TV violence. And it certainly won't be a panacea—an informal scan of cable channels one evening in the fall of 2009 showed violent programming airing simultaneously on a dozen channels, ranging from TBS to Bravo and even the Discovery Channel.

One thing appears increasingly clear: the media need to follow the Hutchins Commission directive and become part of the solution to the societal violence plague, rather than contributing to it. It would be best if the media would do this themselves. But, lacking that, society should not shirk the responsibility of pressuring or compelling the media to take on this responsibility, at least with regard to the long-term effects of violent TV and its desensitizing aspects.

KEY POINTS

- Most media violence studies show correlations, rather than clear cause-and-effect relationships, between viewing violent TV content and violence in later life. But the number of studies showing such correlations is too large to dismiss out of hand.
- TV and video game violence is often shown as an acceptable solution to problems but the *consequences* resulting from violent acts are ignored, creating a situation where viewers may become desensitized to violence.

MERRILL: Commentary

On this perennial controversy of the impact of public communication on violence and sexual pornography we have strong arguments on each side by David Gordon and John Michael Kittross. One (Gordon) is for extra-media control, and the other (Kittross) takes the internal or media responsibility position.

At least the two antagonists are not reductionists or logical positivists, believing that moral statements like "it is wrong to publish violence and sex-explicit material" are ethically meaningless. The combatants here at least see validity in moral pronouncements, whether coming from the media, from society or from government sources.

A basic question is, of course, is freedom absolute or constrained by law? Or, as Kittross would modify it: do the media themselves restrain their own freedom? The libertarian in me causes me to side with Kittross; the Platonist in me pushes me in Gordon's direction. Common sense tells me that social stability and moral order take precedence over personal freedom. As Gordon points out, the media seem incapable (or unwilling) to control violent content or sex voluntarily.

Kittross does not deny that violent and sexual content is rampant in the media. He insists, though, that no conclusive evidence exists that violent media content *causes* violent social action. The media, says Kittross, are like a mirror held up to society. If the society is violent, the media will give great play to violent acts. Gordon believes that media attention to violence stimulates social violence. Although Kittross is right in that no *single* cause is attributed to violence, various studies show that violent content does indicate a "contagion" or at least a correlational factor.

Let the parents and other audience members control (or censor) their own material, says Kittross. A good point in a free and open society. But, says Gordon, they won't do it. Neither will the media gatekeepers. So, concludes Gordon, an outside moderator or controller must enter the picture. And maybe—suggests Gordon—women might be the best gatekeepers, presumably having less tolerance for violence and sex than do men. Of course, that opens up a new can of controversy and cries out for evidence.

Kittross argues that there was violence before television. True. But there were vacations and medicines also prior to TV, so the question might become: have the media stimulated more vacations and an increased use of medications since TV? Perhaps Kittross's most potent point is really a legal one: the First Amendment to the U.S. Constitution gives the media the right to determine their own content. This would mean that outside forces should avoid meddling in media content.

This controversy is a real brain-teaser, an ethical conundrum of the first order. It reflects the age-old clash between freedom and responsibility, between power and impotence, between leadership and followership and between social growth and social decay. It shows that when ethics comes into the picture, freedom is forced to retreat at least a few steps backward. If we were sure—and many researchers insist that we are—that violence and sex in the media adversely affect society, then I think that any person concerned with media ethics should want to see such violent emphasis modified or even eliminated. But the jury is still out, at least on the extent of the danger of violent messages in the media.

In this chapter, Gordon is taking the more communitarian or absolute (legalistic) ethical position, whereas Kittross is defending the liberal or libertarian—some would call it permissive—position. I tend to agree with Kittross, although as I read, hear, and view the plethora of rubbish that assails us from the media every day, I am sorely tempted to slide over into a more absolutist legalist position. Perhaps, as Gordon intimates, the government should go further than it does in protecting us from invasions that damage our minds and souls as well from those that endanger our property and lives.

REFERENCES AND RELATED READINGS

Anderson, Craig A. (October, 2003). "Violent video games: Myths, facts, and unanswered questions." *Psychological Science Agenda* 16(5), pp. 1–3. Available at www.apa.org/science/psa/sb-anderson.html.

Anderson, Craig A., and Brad J. Bushman. (2001). "Effects of violent video games on aggressive behavior, aggressive cognition, aggressive affect, physiological arousal, and prosocial behavior: A meta-analytic of the scientific literature." *Psychological Science* 12(5), pp. 353–359.

Anderson, Craig A., Douglas A. Gentile, and Katherine E. Buckley. (2007). *Violent Video Game Effects on Children and Adolescents: Theory, Research and Public Policy*. Oxford, UK: Oxford University Press.

Broun, Heywood. (1927). "Censorship." In Heywood Broun and Margaret Leach, *Anthony Comstock: Roundsman of the Lord*. New York: Boni & Liveright.

Centerwall, Brandon. (1992). "Television and violence: The scale of the problem and where to go from here." *Journal of the American Medical Association* 267(22), pp. 3059–3063.

Chaplinsky v. *New Hampshire* (1942). 315 U.S. 568.

Commission on Freedom of the Press. (1947). *A Free and Responsible Press*. Chicago, IL: University of Chicago Press.

Comstock, George, Steven Chaffee, Natan Katzman, Maxwell McCombs, and Donald Roberts. (1978). *Television and Human Behavior*. New York: Columbia University Press.

Congressional Public Health Summit. (2000). "Joint statement on the impact of entertainment violence on children." July 26. Retrieved from www.aap.org/advocacy/releases/jstmtevc.htm.

Dessart, George. (1996). "Reflections on the V-chip." *Television Quarterly* 28(3), pp. 37–40.

Dworkin, Andrea. (1985). "Against the male flood: Censorship, pornography and equality." 8 *Harvard Women's Law Journal* 1, pp. 1–29.

Dworkin, Andrea, and Catharine A. MacKinnon. (1988). *Pornography and Civil Rights: A New Day for Women's Equality*. Minneapolis, MN: Organizing Against Pornography.

Eggerton, John. (2007). "New Kaiser study sends mixed message." *Broadcasting & Cable*, June 19. Retrieved from www.broadcastingcable.com/article/109288-New_Kaiser_Study_Sends_Mixed_Message.php (September 26, 2010).

FCC v. Pacifica Foundation. (1978). 452 U.S. 726.

Federal Communications Commission (FCC). (1964). "Memorandum opinion and order In re application of Pacifica Foundation for renewal of licenses KPFA–FM, . . . et al." Jan 2. Reprinted (1965) "The 'Pacifica' Decision: Broadcasting and free expression." *Journal of Broadcasting* 9(2), pp. 177–182.

——. (2007). *In the Matter of: Violent Television Programming and its Impact on Children*. MB Docket 04-261, April 25. Washington, DC: Federal Communications Commission.

——. (2008). "V-chip: Viewing television responsibly." Retrieved from www.fcc.gov/vchip/ (March 10, 2008).

Gibeaut, John. (1997). "Deadly inspiration." *ABA Journal*, June, pp. 62–67.

Gilligan, Carol. (1982). *In a Different Voice*. Cambridge, MA: Harvard University Press.

Gladwell, Malcolm. (2000). *The Tipping Point: How Little Things Can Make a Big Difference*. Boston, MA: Little, Brown. (pp. 222–223 contains a brief popularization of the original report in *Science* magazine. See "Philips, David P." below).

Gordon, David. (1996). "A response to Beechner." *Media Ethics* 8(1), pp. 12–13.

Greenfield, Meg. (1993). "TV's true violence." *Newsweek*, June 21, p. 72.

Hardie, Mary. (1996). "KVUE-TV takes a bite out of crime coverage." *Gannetteer*, May–June, p. 15.

Hickey, Neil. (1992). "How much violence." *TV Guide*, August 22, pp. 10–11.

Huston, Aletha C., Ed Donnerstein, Halford Fairchild, Norma D. Feshbach, Phyllis A. Katz, John P. Murray, Eli A. Rubinstein, Brian L. Wilcox, and Diana Zuckerman. (1992). *Big World, Small Screen: The Role of Television in American Society*. Lincoln, NE: University of Nebraska Press.

Kittross, John M. (1963). Editorial: "Four days." *Journal of Broadcasting* 7(4), pp. 283–284.

Lehrer, Tom. (1981). "Smut." In Tom Lehrer, *Too Many Songs by Tom Lehrer*. New York: Pantheon, pp. 100–105.

Linz, David, Edward Donnerstein, and Steven Penrod. (1984). "The effects of multiple exposures to filmed violence against women." *Journal of Communication* 34(3), pp. 130–147.

Loevinger, Lee. (1968). "The ambiguous mirror: The reflective-projective theory of broadcasting and mass communications." *Journal of Broadcasting* 12(2), pp. 97–116.

MacKinnon, Catharine A. (1985). "Pornography, civil rights, and speech." 20 *Harvard Civil Rights-Civil Liberties Law Review* 1.

Medved, Michael. (1992). *Hollywood vs. America*. New York: HarperCollins.

Noddings, Nel. (1984). *Caring, a Feminine Approach to Ethics and Moral Education*. Berkeley, CA: University of California Press.

——. (2002). *Educating Moral People: A Caring Alternative to Character Education*. New York: Teachers College Press.

Phillips, David P. (1977). "Motor vehicle fatalities increase just after a publicized suicide story." *Science* 196, pp. 1464–1465.

Plagens, Peter, Mark Miller, Donna Foote, and Emily Yoffe. (1991). "Violence in our culture." *Newsweek*, April 1, pp. 46–52.

Postman, Neil, and Steve Powers. (2008) *How to Watch TV News*, rev. ed. New York: Penguin.

Senate Committee on the Judiciary. (1999). "Children, violence, and the media: A report for parents and policy makers." September 14. Retrieved from http://judiciary.senate.gov/oldsite/mediavio.htm.

Signorielli, Nancy, George Gerbner, and Michael Morgan. (1995). "Violence on television: The Cultural Indicators Project." *Journal of Broadcasting and Electronic Media* 39(2), pp. 278–283.

Simmons, Bob. (1994). "Violence in the air." *Columbia Journalism Review*, July–August, p. 12.

Slaby, Ronald G. (1994). "Combating television violence." *The Chronicle of Higher Education*, January 5, pp. B1–2.

Song, Kyung M. (2007). "Research links TV violence to aggression—but not in girls." *The Seattle Times*, November 5. Retrieved from http://seattletimes.nwsource.com/html/localnews/2003994412 _violent tv05m.html.

Strossen, Nadine. (2000). *Defending Pornography: Free Speech, Sex, and the Fight for Women's Rights*. New York: New York University Press.

Surgeon General's Scientific Advisory Committee on Television and Social Behavior. (1972). *Television and Growing Up: The Impact of Televised Violence*. Washington, DC: U.S. Government Printing Office.

"The experts speak out: *TV Guide*'s panel: 'The new face of violence on TV.'" (1992). *TV Guide*, August 22, pp. 12–22.

Twitchell, James B. (1989). *Preposterous Violence: Fables of Aggression in Modern Culture*. New York: Oxford University Press.

Waters, Harry F., Daniel Glick, Caroline Friday, and Jeanne Gordon. (1993). "Networks under the gun." *Newsweek*, July 12, pp. 64–66.

Wertham, Fredric. (1954). *Seduction of the Innocent*. New York: Rinehart. (This book—focused on comics—is the best known of his many writings.)

Winslow, C. Catherine. (1993). "Is it news?" RTNDA *Communicator*, March, pp. 8–9.

Wolfe, Tom. (1976). *Mauve Gloves and Madmen, Clutter and Vine: And Other Stories, Sketches and Essays*. New York: Farrar, Straus, & Giroux.

Zoglin, Richard. (1994). "All the news that's fit." *Time*, June 20, p. 55.

Chapter 15

More Topics in the Ethical Debate

Even minimal attention paid to current news of the mass communication media shows the number, variety, and complexity of ethical controversies facing all media practitioners today. They include many topics that we couldn't tackle in the preceding 14 chapters.

To write this book, we chose the areas of controversy we deemed most important at the time. None of us was satisfied that all of our pet concerns had been covered, and other matters have risen to prominence since we started, and will continue to do so: As this book was going to press, the Wikileaks controversy continued, the Comcast/NBC Universal merger was approved, and the FCC was promulgating often-controversial rules and making decisions—and new and old questions of ethics were being dealt with throughout the mass media.

To deal with this formidable and foreseeable problem, we reserved this chapter for the presentation—if not the full two-sided argument—of some other ethical controversies facing the media. We call the following sections "mini-chapters." Some of them are presented here but are developed at greater length on the Web site associated with this volume (www.routledge.com/textbooks/9780415963329). Some are two-sided arguments. But some of them merely present one point of view, allowing you to look at the problem for yourself—with an argumentative eye.

We hope you will!

CONTENTS

- Another Point of View (A. David Gordon): News *is* a commodity, and journalism is surviving very well, thank you.
- Your Point of View:

15-C. Citizen Journalism

- One Point of View (Gordon): Citizen journalism is an innovative way of bringing media closer to their communities and potential audiences.
- Another Point of View (Kittross): Citizen journalism is nothing more than a cleverly disguised way of saving money by cutting news staffs and replacing them with volunteers.
- Your Point of View:

15-D. Source Confidentiality

- One Point of View (Gordon): Journalists frequently use confidential sources unnecessarily, thereby weakening their credibility and setting up avoidable legal confrontations.
- Another Point of View (Michael Dorsher): Journalists must be more careful about promising confidentiality to sources, but once made, that promise must be kept regardless of consequences and even if it turns out the source lied.
- Your Point of View:

15-E. Arrogance

- One Point of View (Kittross): The arrogance of journalists who accept speaking fees and "freebies," while holding news subjects to higher standards than they themselves are willing to meet, is unethical.
- Your Point of View:

15-F. Civility, "Dirty" Language, and Religion

- One Point of View (Kittross): The right to swing one's fist ends where someone else's nose begins.
- Another Point of View (Gordon): If "civility" is the concern, why are we ignoring the lack of it in cyberspace?
- Your Point of View:

15-G. Honesty in Reporting

- One Point of View (Kittross): To lie to get access to the news may be justified, especially if it is the only way the public can get the information it needs.
- Another Point of View (Gordon): I'm sorry, Mr. Machiavelli, but lying to get access to the news is a lazy excuse for not wanting to work very hard at the task, and is both unethical and unwise.
- Your Point of View:

15-H. Pack Journalism p. 522

- ■ One Point of View (Kittross): The news media's current practice of "pack journalism" is both inefficient and unethical.
- ■ Another Point of View (Gordon): "Pack journalism" will largely disappear from the news media landscape within a decade, so why are we worrying about it?
- ■ Your Point of View:

15-I. Interviews p. 527

- ■ One Point of View (Kittross): The interview is an unreliable, often invalid, and even harmful way of obtaining information for the media.
- ■ Your Point of View:

15-J. Co-option p. 529

- ■ One Point of View (Kittross): The media not only can be bought, but also are.
- ■ Another Point of View (Gordon): The media do a better job of remaining independent than almost any other institution in society.
- ■ Your Point of View:

15-A: OBJECTIVITY?

MERRILL: It is ethical to be non-objective, and giving an incomplete or unrealistic picture of events is unavoidable.

Let us take a close look at the question of whether it is ethical for a reporter to be non-objective when reporting a story—to falsify or invent "reality," or give an unrealistic or incomplete picture. This is obviously a question of extreme importance to the journalist and to the audience. An answer is likely to be very complex, because the word "objectivity" has become a shortcut for expressing a paramount goal of journalism.

I maintain that it is *impossible* for any human being to be truly and fully objective. If this is so, one can be ethical by being non-objective, or else one is always unethical! If one wants to be ethical, one *must* put aside the idea of objectivity. It is really the only realistic stance. One's ethics, in all cases, is formed within the shadow-world of non-objectivity. Therefore complete truth and ethics are not mutually dependent. One can be ethical without being truthful. And one can be truthful without being ethical.

A news story never provides the full reality it purports to report. A moment's thought will explain why this is true. For one thing, details are always left out, and the selection of those details is a subjective choice. The reporter's perceptions are *always* biased in some way.

But beyond this, there is an epistemological barrier to objective reporting. The person being presented in a story is a constantly changing "process person." The person (or subject or anything else) always is changing, ever "becoming." He or she never "is." The "is of identity," as the general semanticists tell us, is no more than a myth. This reality of change, of flux, actually makes the person *unreportable*, since that person is always becoming another person. And, of course, at the same time the reporter is constantly becoming a different reporter.

This may seem esoteric and unimportant in the everyday world of journalism, but it is important to the concept of objectivity. Language can never capture the substance of reality—and certainly it is impossible to describe a person in the "process of becoming" and make it mean anything.

So, in regard to objectivity, what is the ethical thing for the reporter to do? Try to be objective or forget the concept since it is an impossibility?

If the reporter is concerned with giving the reader or viewer as close a version of "truth" as is possible, the answer is simple. *Recognize the impossibility of full disclosure and do what you can to capture the essential or important aspects of the person or thing or event being reported.* No bias, no interpretation, no spin. Do not worry about consequences. Just tell the story —replicate the reality—the best you can. That is the ethical thing to do.

Such behavior would please Immanuel Kant, a *deontologist* who believed in rules, but might not find favor with J. S. Mill, a *teleologist* who saw consequences as more important than the closest approximation to unreachable truth. Mill's (and other utilitarians') duty or allegiance here is to "fairness" and good consequences, not to objectivity.

If I want to do the right thing, I may well decide to leave out certain facts that might affect negatively the person being described. Kantians, on the other hand, would see such a pragmatic (or Rawlsian) stance as not being ethical at all. If one may borrow from an old radio and television game show, what we have here is an ethics conflict between truth and consequences. So, let's recognize a semantic problem and say that, in common parlance, the "ethical" and the "right" are used interchangeably. Two people both can be ethical even when they take opposite actions.

Suppose that I steal a letter from a senator's desk; it brings me happiness and provides the public with needed information—good consequences (Mill). So, I am being ethical. But stealing is wrong, period (Kant), and if I steal for any reason, then I am being unethical. Looking at it from a different angle, the reporter can test whether actions are ethical by holding them up to predetermined rational maxims, or by considering the consequences. Either way, he or she is ethical.

But something is wrong here! It seems that I am trying to justify contradictory ethics, or untangle a contradiction. The only way I see out of this quandary is by revising Kant's theory of the Categorical Imperative (see Overview, pp. 22–23) to read something like this: *What is ethical is doing what you would like to see universalized, by following predetermined maxims that stem from actions that have brought the best consequences in the past.*

In other words, consider utility or consequence theory as an absolute or duty-bound theory of ethics. No, I don't believe that this merger is contradictory. One's duty, therefore, means following maxims that have had, and will likely have, the best consequences. So we might argue that Kant's theory of rational maxims was based originally on something akin to the theory of good consequences that Mill developed later on. The basic maxim "don't steal" did not appear to Kant to be devoid of the context of consequences. It is a rational maxim resulting from a consideration of consequences.

So here we have a new duty-bound theory linked with a consequence theory. Maybe we could call it, as I suggested years ago (Merrill, 1989), the *deontelic theory*—combining the deontological and the teleological theories of ethics.

References and Related Readings

Merrill, John C. (1989). "Deontelic ethics: A synthesis." In John C. Merrill, *The Dialectic in Journalism*, Chapter 9, especially pp. 199–201. Baton Rouge, LA: Louisiana State University Press.

Ward, Stephen J. A. (2004) *The Invention of Journalism Ethics: The Path to Objectivity and Beyond*. Montreal: McGill-Queens' University Press.

15-B: CHECKBOOK JOURNALISM: THE FINAL MARKETPLACE

KITTROSS: Treating news as a commodity eventually will destroy journalism as a public benefit.

The theory is very simple. The reporter digs out news (sometimes against the wishes of those who prefer to keep it hidden) and it gets edited and transmitted to the audience. Never mind that the public's interests seem tipped toward titillation rather than edification, or that there are sometimes legitimate privacy interests (which we discuss in Chapter 10)—journalistic theory and traditional standards say that there is nothing other than dogged legwork and luck (or serendipity) for the reporter to be concerned about.

In practice, there is something else: *greed*. And that which feeds it: checkbook journalism.

We seem to be converting newsgathering into a buy-and-sell business, and members of the public who have information (eyewitnesses, record keepers, people with cameras at the right time and right place) now think that they have something to sell that the media want to buy. If the media keep pandering to this commodification of the news, there will be precious little remaining for the reporter to find or dig out.

It is easy to claim blandly that checkbook journalism—the buying for cash of information that one can print or air—is the province only of yellow journalism, supermarket checkout-stand scandal sheets, gossip gazettes, and "flying saucers stole my Pomeranian" periodicals. But, unfortunately, it isn't true. Today, it almost seems as though the only media organizations that do not engage in checkbook journalism are those that don't have enough money to enter the bidding.

The amount of money one must now ante up is impressive. When O. J. Simpson was arrested on charges of murdering his ex-wife and Ron Goldman, it was reported that one of

Simpson's friends was offered up to $1 million (which he turned down) for his story. The owners and a salesman at a cutlery store where Simpson bought a knife shared $12,500 ("Simpson case . . .," 1994). Prices have continued to rise. Checkbook journalism also can lead to disruption of the legal process: a friend of the woman who claimed to have been raped by William Kennedy Smith (a next generation member of the Kennedy political family) reportedly invented testimony, in part to earn $40,000 from television's *A Current Affair*.

One might ask why anyone should raise an objection over a "willing buyer/willing seller" transaction, even if the checkbook journalists engage in ruinous bidding wars for gossip, scandal, and the like. How can this affect "real" news, hard news, important news—what the public needs in order to make rational decisions in a democracy? There are two simple answers.

First, the person who sells a story may lose credibility. In the Simpson case, the Los Angeles district attorney's office decided to drop a witness after she was interviewed on *Hard Copy*. In the Michael Jackson child molestation case, two witnesses reportedly sold stories to tabloid television shows that contradicted (and were more sensational than) what they said in sworn depositions, which may have played a part in keeping them off the stand before an eventual out-of-court settlement. Of course, nobody thought twice about paying for interviews with members of Michael Jackson's family after his 2009 death.

More importantly, checkbook journalism destroys the credibility of *all* journalism. Sure, there are precedents for checkbook journalism. All reporters are familiar with the long-standing practice of providing sources with a cup of coffee, a beer, a meal, $10 or $20 or $100 to those who need it or who need to feel that the reporter is a fellow human being. Even the prestige press often buys not the news (or so it claims), but a picture, diary or some other commodity for $1,000 or more—but both parties obviously are well aware that there is a *quid pro quo* when sums that high are involved.

> checkbook journalism destroys the credibility of *all* journalism.

The visual media issue large checks for photographs and videotape, ranging from pictures as significant as the Zapruder film of President Kennedy's assassination to the wedding picture of a run-of-the-mill murder victim. Such payments also are made for life stories or first-person accounts; the first astronauts, government employees all, made particularly advantageous "exclusive" deals with *Life* magazine. Are such payments different in any significant way from the cup of coffee or meal? Yes, because the cup of coffee would never be thought of as conveying *exclusive* rights to the part of the story that the source is telling the reporter between refills.

But in exchange for hundreds or thousands of dollars, the bean-counters in media management insist on written contracts and exclusivity—the ability to prevent other media organizations and, consequently, the public, from using the story. How can there be a marketplace of ideas when there are early and preemptive purchases in the marketplace of news-as-a-commodity?

There is nothing illegal about selling news and information, nor is it illegal to buy news and information. But the buyers—the media—have the power to refuse to buy, in order to protect their most essential attribute, their stock-in-trade: their credibility.

Most of the news media are profit-making, and many of the rest would like to make a profit. If media organizations really want to spend money for news, they can always hire more reporters, pay them better, and give them more newsgathering resources.

If the current trend leads to the condition where all important news (not just scandal) is bought from greedy sources or (conversely but with similar effect) "given" to the news media by self-serving PR practitioners or advertisers—a case where the source's checkbook buys the news medium!—bias will be more likely and we will all lose. "All" doesn't refer merely to media organizations that lose in the bidding and become roadkill on the information superhighway. It also refers to the "winners" in the checkbook journalism bidding wars, who become ever-larger and ever more monopolistic—and less able or willing to compete in traditional journalistic digging. Most important is the loss suffered by the public, which will get its news on the basis of price, not quality.

If media professionals don't show restraint in using checkbook journalism, then they (we) lose credibility—hardly a utilitarian approach. If the news media have lost credibility, not only are they dead in the water, but their practitioners don't sleep well. Checkbook journalism isn't merely economic. It is also both an ethical (with respect to the professional group and its clients, the body politic) and a moral matter.

Regardless of David Gordon's interpretation, a clear Kantian or "universal law" view would also reject checkbook journalism. After all, if we believe that information is only a commodity to be bought and sold, how long will it be before we, ourselves, also are on the block? What will be our price? Who will pimp for us?

GORDON: News *is* a commodity, and journalism is surviving very well, thank you.

This argument is really an offshoot of our economic marketplace discussion in Chapter 8. News has always been an economic commodity, at least since the advent of newspapers. Paying sources for information may well be somewhat different from the ways in which various news items were gathered in prior decades, but it isn't automatically any less ethical.

This issue must be considered within the context of news that concerns private areas of individuals' lives. If one refers to material that is (or should be) in the public realm, freedom of information laws should make unnecessary the purchase of information. Certainly, no one can argue that a public official has any right to demand payment for releasing information over which she or he has jurisdiction—although friendships, as well as the coffee, beer, or dinner noted by John Michael Kittross, clearly have influenced decisions about which media are favored with the initial release of such information.

But with private individuals or the private portions of the lives of public parties (perhaps especially people who are thrust unwillingly or unwittingly into the public spotlight), it's a very different situation. It shows more respect for privacy, or for individual dignity, to pay for a picture that the media want to run than it would to palm the picture from the home of its owner. This practice of stealing pictures (especially of disaster victims) was not unheard of through the early decades of the 20th century (and, perhaps, even more recently than that). Such actions were nothing more or less than theft, justified by citing the "public's right to know" (and perhaps the newspaper's need to attract circulation by any means). In offering to pay for such pictures or videotapes, the media are at least giving the owners both an option to refuse to release them and an opportunity to be compensated if they agree to their use.

Kittross is correct when he says that paying for information will reduce the amount of material that reporters will need to dig out on their own. But that digging has too often resulted in considerable incursions on individuals' privacy, with no opportunity for those individuals to influence what becomes public and no compensation for it.

Potential news sources who are offered money for such material can always say "No," as Al Cowlings did in the O. J. Simpson case—a point that Kittross noted but then ignored. I also think Kittross is far too alarmist in his concern for what happens when information is purchased (or the words copyrighted) for exclusive use by one media outlet. Although this certainly might keep some specific presentations of this material from other outlets, there's simply no way that it will keep the public from learning about the story.

Competition between news and infotainment outlets will ensure that at least one version of the material reaches the public. It's absurd to say that exclusivity diminishes the availability of that information to the audience at large. The actual live interview may well be the property of the outlet that paid for it, but the information (or the titillation) contained in it can freely be picked up by any and all other outlets and thereby spread as widely through the marketplace as is warranted.

It's not inconceivable that there may be some impact on the media's credibility from widespread use of checkbook journalism. But that's speculative, at best, and not really worth worrying about at this point, in view of all the more likely problems that also might diminish the media's credibility.

Before we condemn checkbook journalism out of hand, let's refer back to my Chapter 13 example, where the tabloid checkbook journalism route was the only one available for a gang rape victim's family to tell its side of the story (Mengelkoch, 1994). In sum, one might argue that checkbook journalism is a utilitarian approach: it provides benefits to most people in the society (i.e., information for the public, and both control and cash for the people selling the information). One might also argue that it follows the Kantian ideal of treating private individuals who have become newsworthy as ends in themselves rather than merely as means to be exploited toward the end of providing information or titillation for the public. And this combination of Kant and utilitarianism—rather rare in our survey of ethical concerns in the media—should be fostered rather than condemned.

References and Related Readings

Boynton, Robert. (2008). "Learning curve: Checkbook journalism revisited: Sometimes we owe our sources everything." *Columbia Journalism Review*, January–February, pp. 12–14.

Mengelkoch, Louise. (1994). "When checkbook journalism does God's work." *Columbia Journalism Review*, November–December, pp. 35–38.

"Simpson case puts checkbook journalism on trial." (1994). *The Boston Sunday Globe*, July 3, p. 4.

15-C: CITIZEN JOURNALISM

GORDON: Citizen journalism is an innovative way of bringing media closer to their communities and potential audiences.

Done properly, citizen journalism can be beneficial both in strengthening the connection between mainstream news media and their publics, and by enlarging the reservoir of material from which those media can draw their reports. Done improperly, of course, it can sink to being only an excuse for cutting staffs and thereby reducing costs—as seemed to be the case in early 2007 when a small TV station in Santa Rosa, CA, cancelled its nightly newscasts and fired most of its editorial staff. The station said it would replace the professionally produced news product with stories generated by members of the public; a station executive acknowledged that this would mean a loss in local coverage, but added that "there are a lot of other places to get most of that information" (Associated Press, 2007). (While this station acted before the economic meltdown of 2008, since then most newsrooms have been looking for various ways to cut expenses.)

John Michael Kittross, as usual, assumes the worst case scenario in regard to citizen journalism. A more balanced—though still cautious—approach was expressed in 2006 by Philip Meyer, a distinguished veteran of both newspapers and academia. Meyer, noting the serious problems of the newspaper industry, was quoted as saying that he was "inclined to root for all sorts of radical experiments that I would have opposed before" and added: "The industry has been too cautious in the past and needs to increase its rate of risk-taking. Citizen journalism might not work out, but it is worth trying" (quoted in Snedeker, 2006).

Kittross ignores the fact that it is advances in broadcast technology (e.g., much lighter cameras, allowing one-person crews) at least as much as management wanting to cut costs that has resulted in fewer TV journalists being sent out to cover live news stories. Citizen journalism certainly *could* be used as an excuse to cut costs but, done properly, that wouldn't necessarily be the case. Among other factors, reductions in the number of print or broadcast reporters would need to be countered by an increase in editors to handle the material submitted by citizen journalists.

As Kittross notes, advances in technology have enabled citizens with consumer-level camcorders and cell phones to capture audio or visual images of breaking news events and make them available to the mainstream media or to alternatives such as YouTube. Other types of citizen journalism, such as blogs and other independent Web sites created to display citizen-generated content, are fueled by some of the same new technology plus increasingly easy procedures for individuals to establish their own Web sites. These sites can still serve as sources for traditional media, whether in traditional or cyberspace formats, even if they were set up with the goal of bypassing the mainstream gatekeepers. Such sites raise many of the same ethical concerns that apply to online media material (see Chapter 6), plus two additional ones that are crucial: how concerns for media ethics can be learned by information purveyors who have no journalism training and no exposure to media ethics; and how the public might acquire the insights that can help weigh the credibility of those news sites.

For mainstream media, a key ethical question here is how to balance having additional citizen-generated material available against the risks of poor quality (visual and/or text) and the heightened possibility of unknown amounts of bias and/or incompleteness in the report. That question requires an answer whether this additional content is picked up from Web sites or comes from citizens who intend it for the mainstream.

Citizen journalism already has a history (see Gillmor, 2004), and it's going to be around in some form as long as the technology continues to make it possible. Some citizens—many of them untrained—are going to use this technology to capture and make news-related material available and some news media are going to wind up using at least portions of it. And if, somehow, all mainstream media were to refuse this material, citizen journalists have the easy recourse of posting it online themselves in a blog or through such vehicles as YouTube, even though such material may require the average audience member to search a little harder. I believe it is far better to develop a true collaboration between citizens and professional journalists, and to run the citizens' material through the vetting (reviewing its validity and reliability) and editing processes that mainstream media can—and should— provide as part of getting citizen-generated material to the public.

Thus, the questions we should ponder are how to hone the skills of citizen journalists so they provide high-quality images and written information, and how to improve the ability of professional journalists to weed out or modify citizens' material that is inaccurate, incomplete or biased. In other words, how can we best train citizen journalists (actual or potential) to be better reporters? And how can we ensure that when their material is supplied to the news media, it is vetted properly by trained journalists working for those outlets?

Improving the skills of citizen journalists shouldn't be all that difficult. By 2006, some newspapers were "hosting Saturday morning workshops to teach readers how to be reporters, a sort of journalistic boot camp" (Snedeker, 2006). This approach could easily be broadened and perhaps made a requirement for citizen journalists who furnish materials to mainstream media outlets. Schools, from elementary level onward, are another venue for training in visual communication, as they have done for newspapers for many decades. In addition to the basics of reporting, that training should also include an introduction to media ethics issues. (After all, why should you and the others in your ethics class be the only ones to have this kind of fun?)

Weeding out bias in visual images shouldn't be any more of a problem when dealing with citizen journalists than it is when dealing with professional photographers or videographers. For written materials, it could be trickier, but—as has been demonstrated too many times—there aren't any ironclad guarantees that stories written by professional reporters will be bias free.

The Gannett chain was one of the early users of citizen-created journalism, including at *The News-Press* in Fort Myers, FL, which reported some immediate successes (which Jane Singer also noted, in her portion of Chapter 6, as an example of "crowdsourcing").

Undertaking a story investigating the high cost of a local sewer expansion program, it called on its readers to help on the leg work. Within just half a day nearly 70 volunteered. One reader led the paper to a damning city-commissioned audit of contractors. That in turn provided data that led to one local official's resignation and a slashing of utility bills for taxpayers.

(Snedeker, 2006)

Or, consider the approach suggested in 2006 by the associate director of the Knight Center for Environmental Journalism at Michigan State University, who argued that

the environment is the biggest, yet most underreported story that's out there. . . . Simply put, the story is too big and too important to leave only to professional journalists. As a reporter, I often interviewed highly informed citizens who lived an issue for years—the same issue that I spent mere days, or perhaps hours, reporting. So why not let them directly report what they know?

(Poulson, 2006)

Kittross seems to assume that in citizen journalism, there will be no control exercised by newsrooms. On the contrary, I believe that for citizen journalism to be successful in the mainstream media, the newsrooms *must* have the final say on whether something is printed or broadcast, with how much editing, and in what format. Anything less would be both irresponsible to the audience, and potentially damaging to the media outlet's credibility. But if that control is exercised—judiciously—then citizen journalism can enrich the flow of information to the public. It *might* even save the media some money, but that should have a lower priority than providing the public with good information if citizen journalism is to realize its potential.

With proper supervision and control from news professionals, citizen journalism is no less likely than "professional journalism" to be complete, honest and unbiased. In fact, because citizen journalists are in a unique position to add perspectives and (as noted above) depth that sometimes are missing from stories, the result is likely to be richer and certainly less superficial than much of what has traditionally been provided to news consumers—definitely a utilitarian outcome.

Since individual citizen journalists will each be providing material on only a few topics, there will still be plenty of people out there in the audience for each different news story, so Kittross's alarm on that score is simply crying "wolf." Having people tell their story in their own voices—or adding their voices to the mix of material prepared by regular newsrooms staffers—is a good thing, not a negative one as Kittross seems to be saying. (Singer makes a similar point in her discussion of online ethics in Chapter 6, but she is referring there only to unsolicited comments and rebuttals from readers, rather than to any organized "citizen journalism approach.")

The benefits of citizen journalism, in addition to the potential to re-engage the audience with news media outlets, really come down to added perspectives, insights and voices that can be included in any particular story, or which can bring to media attention stories that might otherwise be missed by "traditional" newsroom operations.

Like it or not, we need to come to terms with citizen journalism, because it's not going to go away. As just one example, the MSNBC TV Web site has, since 2005, invited the public to submit coverage of "stories that touch our lives," for publication on MSNBC.com—though, to be fair to Kittross, I must note that MSNBC makes it clear that there will be no payment for such submissions. The invitation continues: "Be part of the dialogue of the issues affecting everyone. Tell us YOUR story by being a Citizen Journalist." (MSNBC, 2011)

The challenge, then, is to do more than just wail and gnash our teeth over the potential problems that citizen journalism poses. Rather, we need to prod the media to deal affirmatively with these risks and opportunities.

KITTROSS: Citizen journalism is nothing more than a cleverly disguised way of saving money by cutting news staffs and replacing them with volunteers.

In one of his last columns, Michael Fancher (2007), *The Seattle Times* editor at large, wrote about how journalism has historically served the public trust:

> journalism was mostly a one-way relationship. The [*Journalist's Creed*, by Walter Williams] was written at a time when information was scarce and access to it was limited. Journalists were called upon to be high-minded, because they were the trustees who would decide what served the public best. They were the gatekeepers.
>
> The Internet has flung the gates open. People are increasingly serving as reporters and editors for themselves and others. exercising their own news judgment, telling their own stories in their own voices.
>
> (Fancher, 2007)

"Citizen journalism" and "civic journalism" aren't exactly the same, although they have a lot in common, and both were facilitated by the Internet. Supporters of "civic" or "public journalism" think of themselves as returning to the early functions of newspapers and other news media. As Harold Lasswell (1948) listed them, these functions include surveillance of the environment, correlation or helping society make policy, and cultural transmission and socialization, to which we might add advertising and entertainment. In civic and public journalism, the intent is to serve the local community, at the same time drawing upon it for ideas, criticism and focus. It also promotes other means (e.g., surveys, lectures, public meetings) of media working with citizens on solutions to public problems. "Citizen journalism" certainly can have much of the content of civic journalism, but its means—and its purpose—is to use volunteer members of the public as reporters, bringing in the news and saving money for the station or paper at the same time (see Paterson, 1977 and Gade, 1997).

Citizen journalism gathers its strength from the fact that many members of the public find themselves in positions to report events—and are encouraged to believe that they know how. Technological advances have aided in this; within the professional lifetime of many reporters and photographers, they have rushed to the scene of an event only to find that members of the lay public who happened to be on the scene have been taking still pictures with their digital cameras and cell phones, recording events and uploading them to the newsrooms of their local (or not so local) media. Motion and sound are now captured and transmitted the same way. Some citizen journalists will even interview others at the scene.

With these volunteers avidly seeking out what used to be the territory of the professional reporter and photographer, it is no wonder that the owners of media outlets think that this is, at least for them, a "win-win" situation. Not only does it give people who normally would only be part of the audience a chance to show themselves or what they have experienced to the public as a whole and establish a strong bond with a particular media outlet, but also they do it for free. Consequently, the desire of almost every business for increased profit—which every business executive knows can be secured by either increasing income or by reducing costs—is being met, with almost no investment on the part of the media. Suddenly, into their laps has dropped a great way to reduce costs—the number of newsroom employees has been steadily dropping for the past few decades—and gain some public appreciation at the same time. Who—aside from those trained potential staff members who now can't get a job— could ask for more!

At this point, ethics raises its head. The news media are essentially utilitarian: the most good for the most people. Does the mass audience benefit from having their news provided by untrained individuals who are under no obligation to prevent their biases from shaping the story and who are unaware of story-telling conventions, legal prohibitions and ethical constraints? (There are also serious technological drawbacks to the use of non-professional equipment—as any online visit to YouTube will show.) These individuals have benefit to their egos, of course, but it is a rare "average citizen" who is in a position to provide the context and the other connections to a story's past and potential future. As a result, I believe that the benefits of citizen journalism to the body politic cannot overbalance the drawbacks. Not only is it likely that presentation of the news won't be as expert as it should be, but also the very selection of news will be warped.

David Gordon's expectations that citizen journalism is inherently helpful to the media as well as the public require something more than his hopes or prayers. He opines that there will be more editors; instead, we now appear to have fewer editors and more uses of spell-check programs in their place. It is becoming harder to determine who should get the credit—or blame—for any given story. When he says that "there will still be plenty of people out there in the audience for each different news story," he overlooks that there will be fewer reporters available in the newsroom to assign to each story if citizen journalism is relied upon to do more than be "on the scene" when dramatic events occur. There isn't really a large supply of "news junkies"—in the audience or behind the camera.

There is an aphorism used in television journalism, "when it bleeds, it leads." Although it shouldn't be ignored, and is of great consequence to those directly affected, immediate-reward news of accidents, crime, and weather disasters is really of less importance (not necessarily of less interest, however) to most people than is the delayed-reward news of economics, politics, science and the like. A snowstorm—the kind that comes almost every year in a given place—will receive tremendously more attention in every local news medium than its happening or its consequences deserve—and a lot of that coverage today comes from citizens who unlimber their cell phones, aim, shoot, and upload.

In the meantime, professional news operations hire and retain fewer and fewer staff members—until about the 1980s, a television station field "crew" would consist of three, and sometimes as many as four or five members; today many stations require the one-person "crew" (often called a "one-man band") to drive the van, set up the camera, and ask the questions—increase workloads, and cut budgets to the bone. When the evening newscast is being put together, professional content will be mixed with amateur content—and nobody will be in a position to certify that "the news" that night is complete or honest or, in another borrowed-but-useful phrase, the truth, the whole truth, and nothing but the truth. Fancher (2007) may want readers "to come along for the ride, get behind the wheel and do some of the driving," but they may regret it in the long run. Like "public access" to a radio microphone—if everyone is talking, who is available to listen?

References and Related Readings

Associated Press. (2007). "Santa Rosa TV station tries citizen journalism." *Napa Valley Register*, February 12.

Fancher, Michael R. (2007). "Inside the Times: Exploring a new path as journalism evolves." *The Seattle Times*, December 19, p. A23.

Gade, Peter, J. (1997). "A response to Patterson." *Media Ethics* 9, pp. 5, 14–16.

Gillmor, Dan. (2004). *We the Media: Grassroots Journalism by the People, for the People.* Sebastopol, CA: O'Reilly Media. (The Open Book content is available at www.oreilly.com/catalog/wemedia/book/index.csp.)

Lasswell, Harold D. (1948). "The structure and function of communication in society." In Lyman Bryson, ed., *The Communication of Ideas: A Series of Addresses.* New York: Harper.

Merrill, John C., Peter J. Gade, and Frederick P. Blevins (2001). *Twilight of Press Freedom: The Rise of People's Journalism.* Mahwah, NJ: Lawrence Erlbaum Associates.

MSNBC. (2011). "Send in your photos, video and text, share your stories at CJ@MSNBC.com." Retrieved from www.msnbc.msn.com/id/6348977/ (January 19, 2011).

Patterson, Maggie. (1997). "An open letter to a concerned colleague." *Media Ethics* 9, pp. 4, 13–14.

Poulson, Dave. (2006). Presentation on luncheon panel, "Citizen Media: J-School Entrepreneurial Ventures," Association for Education in Journalism and Mass Communication convention, San Francisco, CA, August 4. Available online via J-Lab: the Institute for Interactive Journalism, at www.j-lab.org/aejmc06 poulson.shtml.

Snedeker, Lisa. (2006). "A most noble idea, citizen journalism." *Media Life*, November 22. Retrieved from www.medialifemagazine.com/cgi-bin/artman/exec/view.cgi?archive=501&num=8701.

15-D: SOURCE CONFIDENTIALITY

GORDON: Journalists frequently use confidential sources unnecessarily, thereby weakening their credibility and setting up avoidable legal confrontations.

First, we need to define two key terms. "Confidential sources" are those who provide information on the understanding that they will not be identified as the source of the information, and who have been promised by the reporter that—come what may, including legal proceedings—their identity will not be revealed. "Anonymous sources" provide information with the understanding that they will not be identified, but there is no specific agreement that their identity will be safeguarded if the reporter is pressed to reveal it. There obviously is overlap between the two categories, in that all confidential sources are also anonymous sources, and the reporter is asking the audience to "trust me." But, in theory, at least, some anonymous sources don't have the guarantee that their anonymity will be protected by the reporter at almost any cost.

Michael Dorsher appears to use these terms almost interchangeably and, in practice, that's probably pretty accurate. I prefer to make more of a distinction between the terms, in part because the legal concept of "confidentiality" has become a recognizable subdivision of First Amendment law. Thus, I'll be focusing specifically on "confidential sources" and the ethical (and legal) challenges they pose for journalists in general, with particular emphasis on those journalists who want to act ethically with regard to their confidential sources. The crux of my argument is that confidentiality should be promised rarely, if ever, given the current legal climate and the need to rebuild journalists' credibility with their publics.

From the 1970s until the early years of the current millennium, courts and journalists seemed to have reached an uneasy accommodation on the topic of protecting confidential sources. Except in cases involving law enforcement, the courts generally followed the three-part test set forth by Justice Potter Stewart in his dissent in *Branzburg* v. *Hayes*. That dissent would have allowed claims of confidentiality to stand unless the opposing party (whether that was the government or a private individual) could establish that the source's identity was critical and necessary to the resolution of a significant legal issue, that this information could not be obtained by any alternative means, and there was "a compelling and overriding interest in the information" (*Branzburg* v. *Hayes*, 408 U.S. at p. 743).

However, a series of high-profile confidentiality cases—several of them centered on the "outing" of Valerie Plame as a CIA agent—and a number of court decisions adverse to confidentiality claims have changed the pitch of the playing surface. These developments have made it seem the better part of valor to avoid legal confrontations over confidentiality, so as not to risk further adverse rulings, and have led to renewed and serious efforts to pass a federal "shield law" that would supposedly safeguard journalists' rights to protect confidential sources in federal court proceedings. I don't intend to debate the merits of shield legislation here—or of how the 2010 Wikileaks developments might influence that debate— except to note that 20th-century history has shown repeatedly that courts can too easily interpret these laws in ways that negate the protection legislatures thought they were providing. In fact, at one point in the 1970s, more journalists had gone to jail for refusing to name their confidential sources in states *with* shield laws than had been jailed in states *without* them. That was due in large part to the repeated tendency of New Jersey courts to interpret that state's shield law—and its various revisions—extremely narrowly in ruling that its protective provisions didn't apply in several cases where courts demanded that reporters reveal their confidential source's identity (Gordon, 1971).

It's not surprising that a new, large-scale study of the use and impact of subpoenas issued to daily newspapers and local TV newsrooms indicates that they are being issued increasingly frequently, especially for confidential material. The study suggested that the financial burden of fighting subpoenas has led to a decrease in the use of confidential sources and a willingness on the part of the news media—especially small operations—to comply without a fight. Compounding the problem, according to the study, is the finding that more than 20% of the newsroom supervisors who responded didn't know if their state had a shield law, and some 60% of the respondents in non-shield law states thought that they *were* protected by state statute (Jones, 2009).

All of this indicates, at least to me, that even a federal shield law is unlikely to be a panacea for journalists. And beyond the question of whether shield laws actually work, it's well worth discussing whether journalists have a responsibility to use confidential sources much less often than they have done and to make sure that, if they do, it is (1) as a last resort rather than as a lazy way to avoid hard-nosed reporting efforts; and (2) in regard to topics that are seriously important to the public. I believe strongly that journalists must improve in these areas—as a matter of ethics; to protect their credibility with the public and to avoid creating situations where courts can too easily rule against them and against their colleagues who may need to rely on confidential sources in the future.

Judith Miller, formerly of *The New York Times*, seems to me to be the poster girl for the irresponsible and in many ways unethical use of confidential sources. Unless she was looking for either publicity or sympathy, it's hard to understand her willingness to spend 85 days in jail before she finally identified Lewis "Scooter" Libby as the source who told her that Plame was a CIA agent, especially since Miller never wrote a story using that information and since Libby eventually said he had no objection to Miller's testifying about him.

Miller's earlier articles in the spring of 2003, supporting the Bush administration's case for war in Iraq, led some at *The Times* to feel uncomfortable with her approach early on and others to look back ruefully, after Miller's jailing, at the way the paper had handled the whole Libby situation (Van Natta et al., 2005). In retrospect, it appears that Miller's claim of journalistic privilege to keep Libby's name confidential may well have been needless at best. At worst, it was made to protect some of her sources in the White House or their political agendas. There certainly doesn't appear to have been a valid journalistic purpose behind Miller's claim of confidentiality nor an ethical underpinning for her refusal to obey the court order to identify her source. The upshot of the whole situation was unquestionably a weakening of confidential relationships for future reporters who may need to use them in far more positive and effective ways, on stories of greater importance to the public. It also almost inevitably reduced journalism's credibility with the public.

All that said, how might journalists best approach this issue from an ethical perspective? First, they need to look for an Aristotelian "middle ground" between the extremes of never using confidential sources and overusing them to save on effort—or perhaps just to make themselves (and their stories) look important. Applying a modification of Justice Stewart's three-part test seems quite useful here as at least a threshold *ethical* guideline to reporters (*and* their editors) as to when they should use confidential sources. I would suggest that— regardless of legal protections or their absence—a sense of ethics requires that they do so *only* when the information available from the source is critical and necessary to their reporting of a significant societal issue, when this information cannot be obtained by any alternative means, *and* when there is "an overriding public interest" in having the information made available.

To make this approach work beneficially for both journalists and the society they are serving, there must be careful scrutiny of whether the information is available to the judicial process through some alternative means—*and* a willingness on the part of editors to reject the recounting of even an important story if in fact it could be documented using alternative sources for whom confidentiality is not a concern. It would also be worthwhile for reporters who must make use of confidential sources to explain to their audience *why* there was a need to follow that approach. Such transparency can only increase the confidence with which the public regards the particular story involved and—more generally—how and why journalists sometimes need to use confidential sources.

I believe that if this approach were followed, there would be a whole lot fewer stories that rely on confidential sources. If that happens, the chances would be considerably reduced for clashes between journalists protecting confidential sources and the legal system trying to extract the identity of those sources. In addition, I believe that the public's confidence in journalists would be increased, thus enhancing the credibility of the entire field.

This in essence would be a utilitarian approach, with a smidgen of Rawls added to protect confidential sources who might well be vulnerable to some form of retaliation. The ultimate beneficiaries would be not the journalists or their sources, but U.S. society overall. And that's a good ethical goal to have in mind in approaching this topic.

DORSHER: Journalists must be more careful about promising confidentiality to sources, but once made, that promise must be kept regardless of consequences and even if it turns out the source lied.

First, I don't believe anyone can successfully argue against David Gordon's contention that too many U.S. journalists too frequently and too needlessly use anonymous sources—and in turn get used by them. As far back as 1862, President Abraham Lincoln leaked an early copy of his State of the Union address to the *New York Herald*, because that paper was sympathetic to him and he knew the leak would distract readers from criticism by his detractors at the *New York World* (Kennan, 1993). Moreover, Gordon is right about weakening the credibility of those journalists and of journalism overall. But none of that is the same as saying that there's never a need for journalists to use anonymous sources, that it's never ethical to use them, or that it never benefits the public. Bill Moyers, a onetime Baptist minister who became one of the most ethical and best broadcast journalists of our time, says that news is whatever someone else doesn't want us to find out. The rest is all public relations and propaganda, he says, and he ought to know—he also served as White House press secretary under President Lyndon Johnson in the mid-1960s.

On rare occasions, there is no other way for journalists to obtain closely held information without promising confidentiality to the source who is sticking his or her neck out to provide the key to the puzzle. The most famous example, of course, is the Watergate reporting that led to the resignation of Johnson's successor, President Richard Nixon, in 1974. *Washington Post* reporters Bob Woodward and Carl Bernstein have acknowledged they could not have cracked that story without help from, among many others, their anonymous source dubbed "Deep Throat." And they maintained that source's confidentiality for more than 30 years, even to the point where Woodward watched helplessly in 2005 as *Vanity Fair* magazine scooped him and *The Washington Post* in running W. Mark Felt's revelation that he had been "Deep Throat" back when he was the No. 2 man at the FBI.

At the time, the demise of a corrupt presidency seemed reason enough for practicing underground journalism, but ends-justifying-the-means Machiavellian ethics is not the only rationale for maintaining sources' confidentiality. Under *agape* and Rawlsian ethics, journalists are justified in refusing all demands to identify vulnerable sources like Felt, who surely would have lost his livelihood, or like covert agents whose lives might then be in danger.

Most times these days, I believe, serious journalists go beyond Machiavellian ethics and informally think in utilitarian principles when deciding whether to use and maintain confidential sources. They roughly calculate the potential benefits to their audience, the public, the source (and yes, their own careers), minus the potential erosion of their credibility, the source's accountability (and yes, their own freedom and bottom line if they have to go to court or jail to protect the source's confidentiality). They often try to reduce the harm by describing sources as fully as they can without identifying the person (e.g., "a high-ranking State Department official"). Good journalists also corroborate whatever information they get from anonymous sources, even if the verification only comes from other anonymous sources. The use of anonymous sources can even approach Aristotle's Golden Mean if it leads journalists to public documents and on-the-record sources that can verify and expand upon the anonymous sources' information, thereby advancing the story while negating the need to cite those anonymous sources.

Supporting a source's claim to anonymity is looked on more favorably than trying to pin responsibility on someone else in an effort to avoid blame or preserve reputation. The 1996 best-selling satirical political novel about Bill Clinton's run for president, *Primary Colors*, was written by "Anonymous"—and the real author (Joe Klein, of *Newsweek*) took a major hit to his reputation after he denied his authorship when asked point blank if he had produced the book.

Gordon says one of the reasons journalists should avoid using anonymous sources is to stay out of legal confrontations, but I don't see that as an ethical issue at all. Often, prosecutors have in mind nothing more than their own win–loss record or expediency when they demand that journalists identify their confidential sources, whereas journalists are often pursuing the public good—or at least the enlightenment of their audience. The First Amendment makes journalism the unofficial "fourth estate" of the U.S. government, not the right hand of law enforcement and the courts. Journalists, judges, lawyers and law enforcement officers share a common pursuit of truth and justice, but if they team up together, who will be left to scrutinize the judiciary? Bloggers? Then who will scrutinize the journalists? And when should judges compel bloggers to reveal *their* sources—if they even have sources? The answers to some of these questions lie outside the bounds of this brief analysis, but my point is that what's ethical for journalists is not always what's legal and vice versa. In fact, sometimes the only ethical thing for a mass communicator to do is to break the law, such as when a judge orders a journalist to reveal a confidential source.

When a journalist reveals a confidential source, it has a "chilling effect" not only on that source but also on all of that journalist's sources, all of the sources of all of the reporters within that newsroom and, indeed, all sources of all journalists. In 2005, for example, when Norman Pearlstine, editor in chief of Time Inc., ordered *Time* reporter Matthew Cooper to turn over his notes and testify to a grand jury investigating the White House leak of CIA agent Valerie Plame's name, a watchdog group called the Project on Government Oversight informed *Time* reporters that it could no longer put them in touch with whistleblowers.

"It was a bombshell for us when we saw what *Time* had done," said Danielle Brian, the Project's executive director. "We had always worried about a sloppy reporter, but I never thought there'd be a concerted decision made to turn over names." In an e-mail to a trusted *Time* reporter, she wrote:

> In the future, I will, of course, do everything I can to assist you with your stories, but because of your editor's actions, I simply will not be able to give you access to people whose identity needs to be protected.
>
> (quoted in Smolkin, 2005, p. 32)

To be sure, not all confidential sources have clammed up, but *Time* is not the only news organization feeling the effects of its acquiescence to authority. Soon afterward, Cox Newspapers' Washington reporter Rebecca Carr lost a key FBI source in a terrorism investigation she had been conducting, much to her chagrin. As she told *American Journalism Review*:

> It's about telling stories that matter, and those stories often require anonymous sources to confirm records or the direction of a story. If those sources start drying up, then the future Watergates won't be told. The loser in all of this is the public, because they won't know what is really going on in the government they pay for.
>
> (quoted in Smolkin, 2005, p. 35)

Beyond its utilitarian benefits, journalists who maintain their crucial sources' confidentiality at all costs are supporting the Kantian quest for truth and dignity. The consequences need not be life or death, either for the sources or the story's subjects, to justify maintaining sources' confidentiality. Back in 1982, Minnesota Republican Party public relations executive Dan Cohen lost his job and his dignity when editors at the two newspapers in Minneapolis and St. Paul separately decided to overrule their reporters' confidentiality promise to Cohen and name him as the source for a story revealing the Democratic candidate for lieutenant governor had an expunged conviction for shoplifting. Cohen, however, gained a measure of satisfaction by suing both newspapers for breach of oral contract and winning a $1 million verdict. The papers appealed all the way to the U.S. Supreme Court and won a reduced judgment, but the high court upheld Cohen (*Cohen* v. *Cowles Media Co.*, 1991).

"In journalism, maltreatment of sources seems to be part and parcel of the job," said one researcher (Awad, 2006, p. 2) who wondered why anthropologists and every other type of social scientists guard their subjects' confidentiality as a matter of course while journalists say it is their duty to name their sources, whenever possible. Kant would not justify journalists trampling dignity in pursuit of The Truth. Not all the stories that confidants reveal actually add to the truth; for example, Cohen's and the White House officials who leaked Plame's name. So those stories need not be told. The truth must be told in other cases, such as *The Washington Post*'s Watergate stories and *The New York Times*' 2005 stories on warrantless wiretapping, even when they hinge on anonymous sources. To protect those sources' dignity and privacy, and often their jobs, their confidentiality must be maintained.

Finally, what if anonymous sources lie to journalists—or worse, lie in court about what they told journalists? Are the journalists justified in "outing" them and their lies, then? Legally, perhaps, but ethically John Stuart Mill and I would still argue "No" most times. The benefit of "burning" a source, even one who deserves it, will seldom outweigh the cons of showing all other sources they can't trust journalists to maintain their confidentiality, of showing prosecutors and judges that journalists will cave in to them, and of showing audiences that you're trying to make a right out of two wrongs (Wolper, 2006). Ultimately, many observers believe, it will take a federal "shield law"—granting protection like that provided by statute or the courts in 49 states—to protect journalists bound and determined to protect their sources' confidentiality in federal cases (Alter, 2005). Such a law could contain a balancing test, whereby judges could make the utilitarian decisions as to when national interests are truly at stake versus when prosecutors or sources are being ingenuous or lazy. That would at least give sources and journalists some expectations and guidance on when their confidentiality bets might be off. Meanwhile, however, Congress may well refuse to pass a federal shield law and the courts might well strike one down if Congress does act, leaving vulnerable sources unprotected—at least in part because journalists like Judith Miller keep trying to protect unscrupulous sources like "Scooter" Libby, and media owners appear to be more interested in shielding their dwindling profits than fighting to protect confidential sources.

References and Related Readings

Alter, Jonathan. (2005). "You shield us, we'll shield you." *Newsweek* 146, July 11, p. 55.

Awad, Isabel. (2006). *"Journalists and their sources: Lessons from anthropology."* Paper presented at the annual meeting of the International Communication Association, New York, October 5.

Branzburg v. Hayes. (1972). 408 U.S. 665.

Cohen v. Cowles Media Co. (1991). 501 U.S. 663.

Gordon, A. David. (1971). "Protection of news sources: The history and legal status of the newsman's privilege. Unpublished Ph.D. dissertation, University of Wisconsin. Available from University Microfilms, Ann Arbor, MI.

Jones, RonNell Andersen. (2009). "Media subpoenas: Impact, perception, and legal protection in the changing world of American journalism." 84 *Washington Law Review* 317. Abstract available at: http://ssrn.com/abstract=1407105.

Keenan, James F. (1993). "Confidentiality, disclosure, and fiduciary responsibility." *Theological Studies* 54(1), pp. 142–159.

Smolkin, Rachel. (2005). "Uncharted terrain." *American Journalism Review* 27(5), October/November, pp. 32–41.

Van Natta Jr., Don, Adam Liptak, and Clifford J. Levy. (2005). "The Miller case: A notebook, a cause, a jail cell and a deal." *The New York Times*, October 16. Retrieved from www.nytimes.com/2005/10/16/national/16leak.html (September 2, 2009).

Wolper, Allan. (2006). "Ethics corner: Should we protect sources who lie?" *Editor & Publisher*, 139: 20.

15-E: ARROGANCE

KITTROSS: The arrogance of journalists who accept speaking fees and "freebies," while holding news subjects to higher standards than they themselves are willing to meet, is unethical.

In 1994, ABC's *PrimeTime Live*, co-anchored by correspondent Sam Donaldson, attacked a junket that some congressional staff members had taken at the expense of the Independent Insurance Agents of America. Only a few months earlier, the same insurance group had paid Donaldson a large lecture fee (Auletta, 1994).

Arrogant.

Journalists often demand that their sources have perfect memories—"Where were you on the night of January 14th?"—even though the questioners would be equally unable to recall such chronological details were they so queried without access to their diaries, datebooks, Palm Pilots or BlackBerrys.

Arrogant.

That is the best description of news people who keep an eagle eye on politicians and others while ignoring how they look themselves, or would look if subject to the same degree of scrutiny.

It is unfortunately true that, except at the top, few journalists are paid well. But those at the top, particularly in television, are also invited to give well-paid speeches to groups that might have good reason to want journalists to be on their side.

Does he who pays the piper call the tune? Maybe not, but if the public believes such a cause–effect relationship exists, the independence of the piper certainly can be questioned.

Of course, most journalists are honest—it may be that the insurance group realized too late that Donaldson apparently hadn't understood the unspoken definition of being honest in business (and some areas of politics): someone who will stay bought.

Donaldson himself argued that he was being paid more for his celebrity status than for his journalistic reputation—which may be true (Knowlton, 1997, pp. 172–175). Yet this situation still would puzzle an objective observer: here is someone who accepts money to speak on a controversial topic, however dispassionately, and yet refuses to admit that there might be a reduction of his objectivity when reporting on this topic, or a loss of credibility and reputation in the eyes of those who find out about these payments. Even worse, the same journalist attacks those in other professions—expert witnesses, researchers funded by drug or tobacco firms, government officials, and so on—who also claim that they can maintain objective standards while taking the Queen's shilling.

It doesn't take actual dishonesty for such an arrogant exercise of conflict of interest to be harmful to journalism, to those who need to rely on journalism, and to the public at large. When someone says, "Trust me," then—like Caesar's wife—he or she must appear to be above suspicion. Journalists, even more than most other professionals, *must* retain their credibility.

I'm against the practice of journalists who make tens—possibly hundreds—of thousands of dollars giving frequent paid lectures or allowing themselves to be part of the window dressing of large business gatherings. Even worse are regular paid appearances on televised entertainment programs or service as an advertising shill or spokesperson for goods and services. My opposition isn't just jealousy, fueled by the fact that I've never received more than a token fee and expenses. Many journalists refuse all "outside" or freelance work on principle, may speak rarely, and then accept only token fees or expenses. Those who speak to journalism associations or in communications classrooms may do so for free, but some charge the school, student government, or association a great deal of money. About all that can be proven about such work is that those no longer regularly on the air can no longer command such large fees.

Since U.S. universities also need to lobby for funding, wouldn't the support of major news figures be useful in their lobbying? Isn't the thought of a university job attractive to a burnt-out journalist? Isn't there a potential conflict of interest on both sides? Yet, at the same time, aren't there benefits to journalism if students in communications schools "hear it like it is" from recently practicing journalists?

I think we need to find some solution to the problem of what Auletta (1994) calls "fee speech," other than strict abstinence.

The obvious solution is to be found in the basic principle of informative journalism: shedding enough light on situations and events that the public may learn enough to make their own rational decisions. I propose that the following practices be mandated in every newsroom, and that the public be educated to be very wary of any journalist who doesn't follow them:

■ All news personnel must get approval from a high-level supervisor before accepting any money—fees or expenses—for giving a talk or appearance of any sort.

- All news personnel must periodically provide their supervisors with a list of any nonpaid talks or other participation in activities in any way connected with present or future news stories.
- These lists and approvals should be a matter of public record.

Will such practices reduce the take-home income of top-ranking journalists? Unfortunately, yes—which may lead to a salutary examination of the pay scales in all media. Will these practices infringe on the freedom of association that is the right of every American? Possibly, by a small fraction, which may cause working journalists to advocate openly some desirable control over the credibility-destroying activity of many publishers, licensees, and media entrepreneurs.

The most important question of all is "Will these proposed practices go far to reduce the reputation for arrogance that is seriously weakening the credibility of all news media?" Definitely "Yes!"

The whole question of conflict of interest could fill an entire book. Julius Caesar's wife, Calpurnia, was required to be above suspicion, but the need for journalists' reputations to be quite that high is more problematic. In other words, the journalist must be credible—but not necessarily a eunuch, an abstainer, or a saint. Communicators are human beings, and enjoy the rights (including privacy) of other citizens so long as they not damage their essential credibility. So, the question is where one draws the line that determines which ethical and practical limitations need be placed on communicators that will enable them to retain their credibility—and do their jobs and live their lives at the same time.

It isn't either arrogant or destructive of credibility for a journalist to know a potential source socially, to vote, or to evaluate the truth of a source's assertion. But it takes very little to step across the line. As discussed in Chapter 2, somewhere in a list starting with voting, moving on to a small financial contribution to a political candidate and possibly winding up with serving anonymously on the candidate's staff while reporting on him or her, the line should be drawn beyond which credibility—and performance—suffers.

The other side of staying outside the fray is that a lot will happen that the reporter can't report. Once the idea is accepted that neutrality is, in practice, the same as ignorance or not caring, then only those who don't know anything about a subject will be acceptable reporters of the facts. This will be certainly as bad for the public as "know it all" arrogance.

References and Related Readings

Auletta, Ken. (1994). "Fee Speech." *The New Yorker*, September 12, pp. 40–47.

Knowlton, Steven R. (1997). *Moral Reasoning for Journalists: Cases and Commentary*. Westport, CT: Praeger.

15-F: CIVILITY, "DIRTY" LANGUAGE, AND RELIGION

KITTROSS: The right to swing one's fist ends where someone else's nose begins.

There are three topics I'm trying to discuss in this mini-chapter. They reflect some of what my non-media friends and relatives often ask—even hector—me about. These matters are amorphous enough that arguing them is difficult, and in any given case I'm not sure on which side I'd land. However, I believe they reflect some important principles that bring up questions that must be answered in any discussion of controversies in media ethics regardless of medium. Each of the topics listed in the title above—civility, language, and religion—has gratuitous injury, however major or minor, as a factor, and they are more related than they are separate. And, to live together on an ever-more-crowded world, civility and respect are the lubricants necessary to avoid friction.

The Civil Use of Honorifics

The road to hell can be paved with the best of intentions. For example, in an effort to end the prejudicial practice of using applicable titles and honorifics (Mrs., Mr., Ms., Rev., Dr., etc.) of whites but omitting them when reporting on members of other races (or sometimes, as in England, other classes), the stylebooks in U.S. newsrooms now suggest that all honorifics be omitted whenever possible. This has the further advantage of eliminating the need to ask every woman whether she uses Ms., Mrs., or Miss—a reflection of the discussion in Chapter 4.

But are all the results of this practice beneficial? Hardly! In the first place, even when it is an integral part of the story, the gender of an individual being reported on might be obscured because first names often are ambiguous.

Much more importantly, the omission of honorifics and titles is a further march down the road to increased daily *incivility*. Some titles are a function of gender, others are assumed, but many are granted only after major achievement. The paths to a professorship or to the privileges and responsibilities of a medical doctor or priest are long and difficult, and it is denigrating these achievements to ignore them. The style book of the *Chronicle of Higher Education*, which appends the title of "Doctor" only to medical doctors (even though the Ph.D. has a longer history) certainly doesn't improve the relationships at faculty gatherings. In some professions, such as the military, rank is the label for level of authority and responsibility. Why do the media now insult individuals of all classes, all occupations, and all conditions by omitting their earned titles and reducing legitimate individual accomplishments and status to naught?

Rudeness, whether on the part of a tough on the street or a reporter, should not be accepted. It makes the society in which we live a nastier one. It does not eliminate class barriers and promote equality, except at the meanest level. It reduces the impetus to excel in any field, particularly the traditional learned professions.

In a rip-roaring political debate, or a "the loudest gets the microphone" opinion and commentary program, or even in the British House of Commons, it is perfectly all right to insult your opponent, even if your opponent is the Prime Minister, the head of government. But, even in the House of Commons, the head of state—the Queen—would not be so insulted. In the United States, where the head of government and the head of state is the same person, in early September 2009, it was shocking to hear a member of the House of Representatives shout "You lie!" as President Obama gave a speech to a joint session of Congress. Regardless of how the shouter felt, this was unacceptably rude—with the Congress itself probably being the most injured.

Language

Here we deal with what our grandparents or great-grandparents might have called "filthy language." Of course, generally speaking, words—or pictures—by themselves can't cause harm. As children, we learned that "sticks and stones will break your bones, but words will never hurt you." But their denotations and connotations may harm people, intentionally or unintentionally.

The prudery of earlier times, which ignored the fact that every living animal excretes and has means to reproduce its species, gave rise to the use of euphemisms, many of which had excretory or sexual connotations. Social barriers have grown higher against using some of these common terms. "To pee" is no less useful a verb than "to urinate," and has been in English language use centuries longer. There no longer are any good reasons for not calling bullshit "bullshit," despite the fact that there are still regions of the United States where "cow brute" is said rather than "bull." We've come a long way since homosexuality was "the crime that had no name." Yet we—and the publishers of this book—still have some taboos in common with the major media, such as full frontal nudity and the common four-letter words for intercourse, penis, and vagina.

Is this because these banned words and pictures are inherently evil, or is it because there is no need to offend and disturb those who are bothered by such words—another aspect of civility? I believe that the second choice applies—or—as has occurred in some political campaigns, in both paid advertising and in public relations, does the public tune out when the language gets too rough?

It may have been clever to title what I think is the best book on how to start a radio station *Sex and Broadcasting* (Milam, 1975), but at what point does shock lose its value? Do pictures of nude women on page 3 of some popular British tabloid newspapers, or partially clothed models in the Victoria's Secret catalog, or gratuitous (not necessary to plot or character development) simulated or real sex acts in motion pictures really add to our understanding of the purposes or aesthetics of art, the human body, or human sexual or excretory functions? Do advertisers really sell more goods using ads with semi-nude models?

On the one hand, there was a saying in the Victorian era that one could do as one wished as long as one didn't disturb the horses. The best essay I know about censorship (Broun, 1927) reminds us that no woman was ever "ruined" by a book. Humans act—not books—and are responsible for their actions, regardless of whether they are moral or immoral.

On the other hand, to claim that sniggering titillation reflects the totality of human sexuality, or that a litany of four-letter words is a bold literary device, reflects at best laziness as well as a willingness to pander to what earlier generations would call our baser instincts. Those in the mass media are responsible for their actions, again regardless of whether they are moral or immoral.

Religion and the Media

Finally, there are the relationships of the media, public relations, and advertising to the traditional repository of morality: organized religion. These relationships are the most problematic of all because faith—the unreasoning suspension of disbelief—is something with which it is difficult to compromise, and what is perceived as an attack on one's religion often is considered an attack on one's very being.

Yet, the mass media are often faced with pragmatic ethical questions that involve religion. For example, with regard to content, is it ethical to publish something that others consider an attack on their religion, regardless of intent (such as Salman Rushdie's *Satanic Verses*)? Is an account of a real or fictional religious leader's peccadilloes justifiable (as in the 1960 movie *Elmer Gantry* or news accounts of pedophilic priests and other religious leaders)? How about religious practices that cause revulsion in those not of that religion (such as snake-handling by a sect in the American south)? Are ministers, priests, and rabbis fair game as butts for comedy programs or movies such as *Dogma* (1999)? Was the then Vice-President Dan Quayle right in attacking "Murphy Brown"—a fictional character in a television situation comedy!—for the moral lapse of bearing a child out of wedlock?

Religious sensibilities also can affect journalistic practice, as well as specific content. Should the media operate on religious holidays? (Journalists working on the Sabbath in Israel have been assaulted by Orthodox Jews throwing stones.) Are conflicts over succession, theology, and liturgy public or private matters? Should misbehavior involving sexual assaults on young people by priests be covered in the press, or should the church be allowed to deal with such matters in private? How, during the extended political campaigns leading up to the 2008 presidential election, should the media have dealt with religious facts and rumors about several of the candidates—including one with Muslim ancestors, another who was a Baptist minister, and a third who was a Mormon?

What ever happened to the "render unto Caesar the things that are Caesar's and unto God the things that are God's" instruction? More generally, should one's own moral standards be subject to any religious doctrinal discipline? Should all organized religion be sacrosanct—immune from coverage that might lead to criticism for its actions? What is blasphemy—and is it acceptable? And who decides? Is religion somehow different from all other societal institutions?

These aren't easy questions to answer. Not only do they have ethical and moral implications, but also there may be significant pragmatic consequences, no matter which course is chosen. Organized religion, in almost every nation or culture, can show wrath in many ways—from death threats (and sometimes death) and boycotts to diplomatic ruptures—for transgressions that might be deemed acceptable or unimportant in another country, at another time, by a different sect or faith, or by those for whom religion is relatively unimportant or who are truly open-minded. Following the attacks on the World Trade Center and Pentagon on 9/11/01, antagonism and suspicion in the United States against Muslims rose to extreme heights—as did Muslim antagonism and suspicion against Western countries following the invasions of Iraq and Afghanistan. Yet, in a country as culturally similar to the United States as Canada, a Canadian Broadcasting System situation comedy program, *Little Mosque on the Prairie*, became very popular.

The media always have been the target of religions that are arrogant enough to believe that they have the right to control what the entire citizenry—not just adherents to that faith—sees and hears. One can go back hundreds of years and find the same pattern: a rejection of lay-produced morality plays here, and a condemnation of the commercial theater there; an index of banned publications here, and a ceremonial burning of offending literature there.

Is this conflict, one-sided or not, real or imagined, to continue? I hope not, because religion is too important either to ignore or genuflect to without sound reason. Religion still plays a large part in domestic and international politics. The possibility of violent conflict between religions, on the order of Hindu versus Muslim in India after independence and partition—or between the Shiite and Sunni branches of Islam—is always with us. It isn't only in developing countries that such violence may occur; some fundamentalist sects in the United States are willing to fight for their Lord with clubs and guns as well as with words and political action. Sometimes, as in the former Yugoslavia, ethnic as well as religious issues are at stake. If the state becomes a religious one, the media will be subject to religious law, as in Iran. Fortunately for those living in the United States, the First Amendment to the Constitution prohibits both the establishment of religion as well as governmental barriers to its free exercise. It is where the law is silent that the conflicts between media and minister, between doctrine and entertainment, and between news and sin are most important.

Normally I believe that the separation between church and state should be reflected in separation between secular media and church doctrine because individual human beings are in their most vulnerable and limited condition when a monolithic body imposes its will—with sword, sacrament, or soundbite.

> individual human beings are in their most vulnerable and limited condition when a monolithic body imposes its will—with sword, sacrament, or soundbite.

When there are various countervailing forces—such as church and state—individual human beings can find ways to exist around the edges. When church and state (and, today, business) cooperate or conspire to control and profit from parishioners, subjects, and customers, then the media (until their suppression?) may be the only voices for freedom. Through their ability to stimulate public action or reaction, the media are the only major countervailing force in a world where multinational and even global firms control the economy, religions increasingly control government, and government claims the right to control movement and freedom, sanctions violence (all is fair in war) and often attempts to influence or control what we think, even in the United States.

As usual, easy answers are not good ones, and vice versa. The values of civility should make it incumbent on the media not to insult gratuitously the followers of any religion—not merely those regarded as "legitimate" by the consensus in a particular society, or by media employees. The 1993 mass deaths at the Branch Davidian compound in Waco, Texas, tell us what can happen if we do. After all, can anyone who accepts either Mill or Kant as a guide accept the forcible removal of someone's belief structure? Is brainwashing of any sort "good"? Is a middle course always the best fallback route? I don't think that the Golden

Mean is practical here. There are too many examples of terribly strong, but often-unreasoning or intolerant reactions on various sides to religiously oriented media content to be optimistic about ever developing a categorical rule for such content. Examples that would demonstrate this difficulty range from the so-called "Petition Against God" (Allworthy, 1976), the largest outpouring of mail on a single subject addressed to a single office—the FCC—in the history of the world, to the Fatwah (a legal opinion issued by a Muslim leader, that in its most extreme form might amount to a death warrant, as in the reaction to Salman Rushdie's novel, *Satanic Verses*). To show the sharp effect of such pressures, in 2008 Random House, the publisher, immediately withdrew a book because of a single warning that its publication might lead to violence by Islamic militants who could object to a non-Muslim writing, approvingly, about a member of Muhammad's family (Lacitis, 2008). Yale University Press's hasty censorship in 2009 of the pictures in a scholarly work dealing with the earlier European publication of cartoons depicting the Prophet Muhammad (which is considered a violation of Islamic religious doctrine), and the use of the copyright law by Scientology to prevent independent examination of its doctrine, illustrate the continuing presence of such rigid imposition of one religion upon all who get in its way.

The bare minimum of civility in a secular society dictates that the media in general should neither ignore nor be co-opted by any particular religion; they have obligations to everyone in their audience as well as to the truth (as argued in Chapter 4). An exception, however, might be the media now owned by religious organizations which, as long as competing secular media are available to the same audiences, should not adversely affect a diverse society.

Conclusion

Why do many of those in the mass media today take the easy way out in these three areas of civility, language, and religion? Laziness, arrogance, and immaturity are the only answers I can think of. Too much emphasis on and experience with the uncivil side of life—chicanery, scandal, disaster—may make it far too easy for the press to sneer at the rest of humanity. Repeated use can desensitize people's reaction to language. The institution of religion is certainly as important as, though different from, mass communication. The essential question is: are journalists part of society or separate from it? I believe that the media are a very important part of our society, and it would be sad if they enshrined laziness and arrogance as their goals.

GORDON: If "civility" is the concern, why are we ignoring the lack of it in cyberspace?

I don't disagree with much of what John Michael Kittross has written here—I just don't think he's zeroed in on what I think is *really* of concern.

Crude language or illustrations? Yes, an ethical concern, though as I said in Chapter 14, I'm far more worried about the effects of violence than of sex—or crude language about sexual functions—on even a prudish public. Ethics issues in the places where religion and the media intersect? Of course, and Kittross's discussion of them is quite good. The civil use of honorifics as an important ethics issue? Huh?

I believe it's much more important to discuss the tendency of many people to be rude (possibly unintentionally), crude and personally disrespectful when they are cloaked (or *think* they are cloaked) by the anonymity—or, more to the point, the sense of being *insulated* from others—that cyberspace in general, and e-mail in particular, seem to provide. A letter to the "Voice of the People" column in the Eau Claire (WI) *Leader-Telegram* stated the concern both well and succinctly. The author said he was a regular reader of the paper, but had

> become disheartened by the message boards that accompany each article. While the forums promote civic discussion and democratize the editorial page, the anonymous posts are frequently brazen—and sometimes hateful—attacks on groups or individuals in our community.
>
> To encourage a more productive dialog, posts should not be anonymous. Unbridled free speech has its place, but the anonymity of these posts enables readers to publish their most impulsive opinions and reactions, which rarely have lasting civic value. Perhaps if writers were accountable for their published thoughts, the Leader-Telegram website would cease being a forum for shameless arguments and mean-spirited opinions.
>
> (Blink, 2008)

Anonymity certainly compounds the feeling that the restraints are off. But think of how many times you've read signed postings online, or received signed e-mails, where the language has been disrespectful in some way. (I won't ask you to think of times when you might have done that yourself.) Have you ever reacted to this kind of disrespectful "flaming" with anger, or annoyance? And even if you haven't, did the lack of respect distract you from the message that someone wanted to get across to you?

Think a bit further—how do you start the e-mails you send? And is it the same way you'd start a snail mail letter (if anyone is still writing those any more)? Do you use a salutation of any sort ("Dear Bill," for example—which used to be the standard way of starting a snail mail letter)? Or is it just "Bill—"? Or do you even bother to use the person's name to lead off your communication?

In a way, this is an issue that parallels Kittross's concern with the civil use of honorifics, so I guess there's an ethics issue there after all. If each reader of this book were to decide to use some sort of salutation at the beginning of even half of her or his e-mails, I wonder what the ripple effect would be. At a minimum, some of us might be impressed enough to pay closer attention to what follows the salutation or to look more closely at the name of the person who signed the message. And I'd argue—as did the letter-writer quoted above—that using civil language in online forums or comment boards following online news stories would be highly likely to get a respectful hearing for the position you're putting forth. This is a concern that is being discussed increasingly among those responsible for comment boards, and it has no easy answers—in a time of reduced personnel budgets, few if any newsrooms can spare a person to moderate an online discussion or even to screen posts for civility (Singer, 2009). To make the situation even more complex, legal precedent as of 2010 indicates that only by taking a hands-off approach to online comments can the host news medium avoid potential liability for defamation or invasion of privacy—truly a situation where law trumps the possibility of ethics.

Given human nature, online civility is not likely to happen overnight, if at all. So, I'd urge that online forums of any kind should have a strict policy that communications *cannot* be posted anonymously, to eliminate at least one layer of the cyberspace insulation (a "security blanket," if you prefer) for people who might think twice about being hateful if they knew they would be identified as the source of that language. Some verification procedure (or technology) would be needed to sort out the pseudonyms that would undoubtedly be tried in place of real names, but I'd suggest that the effort to promote identity and therefore greater civility is worth it. It would make online life more pleasant—more "civil," if you will—and might even promote a more thoughtful and useful dialogue in the "public square" that cyberspace offers.

References and Related Readings

Allworthy, Pastor A. W. (pseud. of Lorenzo Milam). (1976). *The Petition Against God: The Full Story of the Lansman-Milam Petition (RM 2493)*. Los Gatos, CA: Christ, the Light Works.

Blink, Ben. (2008). "Web anonymity misused." Eau Claire, WI *Leader-Telegram*, August 18, p. 6A.

Broun, Heywood. (1927). "Censorship." In Heywood Broun and Margaret Leach, *Anthony Comstock: Roundsman of the Lord*. New York: Boni & Liveright.

Lacitis, Erik. (2008) "National publisher kills Spokane writer's book." *The Seattle Times*, August 20, p. B1.

Milam, Lorenzo. (1975). *Sex and Broadcasting*. Los Gatos, CA: Dildo Press.

Singer, Jane B. (2009). "Moderation in moderating comments." *Media Ethics* 20(2), pp. 1, 10–12.

15-G: HONESTY IN REPORTING

KITTROSS: To lie to get access to the news may be justified, especially if it is the only way the public can get the information it needs.

In the spring of 1997, a North Carolina jury verdict was rendered in the case of *Food Lion v. ABC*. ABC was on the losing side of a $5.5 million decision—not (according to jurors) because of what was said or shown in the program, or because of "hidden cameras" or investigative reporting per se. It was not a libel case. The basis for the punitive damages was that the two ABC producers who actually collected footage of unsanitary meat packaging conditions with hidden cameras had lied about their background in job applications, thus committing fraud. The jury also awarded Food Lion $1 for each of its claims that the ABC producers had trespassed on its property and had been disloyal to their ostensible employer.

Although the trial judge reduced the jury's punitive damages award to $315,000, the Fourth Circuit Court of Appeals threw out the claim of fraud entirely and, with it, any punitive damages. The appeals court left standing the two remaining claims—trespass and disloyalty to an employer. The case has caused many journalists to reconsider what had become fairly normal practice, that is, misleading sources as to the reporter's identity in order to get a story. This story was particularly interesting to journalists, because it followed directly in the tradition of Upton Sinclair, who had written on the terrible conditions of meat slaughter and packing houses a century before in his book, *The Jungle* (1906).

A vocal minority of members of the public, and some members of the journalistic profession (mostly print journalists, perhaps out of jealousy), hold that reporters should always identify themselves honestly. Ben Bradlee, *Washington Post* editor for many years, who fought so hard (and successfully) against giving a Pulitzer Prize to the *Chicago Sun-Times* after the newspaper and a civic group had bought the "Mirage Bar" and waited (with cameras) for city inspectors to ask for payoffs, still argues this way.

But is this really practical? And, in many instances, does it matter if the person interviewing you is John Jones, nosey neighbor, or Sally Smith, reporter?

David Gordon seems to have adopted this Kantian approach, and argues that it is *always* wrong for a reporter to pretend to be someone else. At the same time, as an example, he praises the "hard-nosed, tireless digging" of Woodward and Bernstein (and others) for the Watergate story—but apparently approves of the recruiting and use of "Deep Throat," their confidential source who provided direction and confirmed information that otherwise might have been available only through undercover work—or not available at all. But many would call recruiting an "insider" to do the snooping an act of suborning disloyalty to the source's employers. Sometimes, I'm afraid, "hard-nosed reporting" validates the injunction (variously credited to Otto von Bismarck, Mark Twain and others) that people who love sausage and respect the law should never watch them being made. It has been suggested that the reporting of news stories should be added to the list of things that one needs to have a strong stomach to observe.

Stealing documents or pieces of tainted food is one thing, but turning on a camera hidden on one's person is another. Our society's yearning for "security" leads to asking for "ID" more and more frequently, but almost anyone—mail carriers, fire inspectors, electricians, cleaners—could be coming through almost any commercial or governmental space at any time, which mitigates against any real expectation of privacy. In England, in 2007, there was one surveillance camera for every 14 people (and a single building at Yale University in New Haven had 74 such cameras)—today there also are millions of digital cameras and cell phones in the pockets of average citizens, just waiting to be used.

I've experienced too many examples—trespass (through my back yard), applications for graduate school or for jobs that played fast and loose with the truth, and disloyalty to the aims of the institution someone is asking to join—to think that ABC has been the only transgressor of note. I ignore the trespass, reject the dishonest applications, and try to instill loyalty in the disloyal.

As it happens, perhaps ABC should have looked harder for other ways to report the story. It might not have been necessary to hide a camera in a wig—Upton Sinclair didn't need one. Perhaps there were ways to fill out the job application that didn't lie or rhapsodize over the meat industry; they honestly (but deceptively) could have said they had been working for Disney, which then and now owns ABC.

But these are small points, less heinous than the rule that permits members of the Internal Revenue Service to use false identities when dealing with taxpayers. As Louis Hodges (1997) reminds us, the real issue, a utilitarian one, was tainted meat. The story and the potential benefits of that story to the public, and not what fibs may have been told to get it, is what is important: It isn't a game. For example, if ABC's undercover team had failed to do the job for which Food Lion had hired (and should have been supervising) them—to detect bad meat and get rid of it, rather than film it—then they are harming the public, and all appeals to the First Amendment will be of no avail if someone dies as a result of eating unhealthy meat.

What will be best for the public? A rigid rule that only allows every potential interviewee or subject of a story to be sure that he or she is not talking to a reporter? Or a flexible rule that permits the reporter to serve the public by covering something that needs to be covered—in this instance, the packaging and sale of tainted meat, and in other cases, "snake pit" mental hospitals, quack physicians, dishonest office holders, police officers "on the take," and others to whom we need to be alerted. This is a long—and honorable—tradition in journalism, providing the public with first-hand accounts of matters of public concern, as exemplified by the undercover work of 19th-century reporter Nellie Bly.

Unlike the police, who must gather evidence within the doctrine of the "fruit of the poisoned tree," which forbids the government to use illegally gathered evidence at trial, the reporter is not in a position to jail someone. If there is no penalty attached to using a nickname or a false identity in situations where there is no intent to defraud, then it is no big step to permitting reporters—when it is necessary to get the story—to omit their journalistic affiliation. Since the public—as represented by the Food Lion jury—disapproves of such practices, they should be used only when necessary and justifiable to a reasonable person.

The news media are a major part of the self-correcting mechanism of our society, and we should not allow Bradlee's iron-clad rule of "always identifying yourself" to make it impossible—in those few cases where concealing identity is necessary—to serve that function. If this is saying that "the end justifies the means"—so be it.

GORDON: I'm sorry, Mr. Machiavelli, but lying to get access to the news is a lazy excuse for not wanting to work very hard at the task, and is both unethical and unwise.

I'm unable to figure out exactly what John Michael Kittross is arguing here. He seems to conclude that concealing one's identity may be crucial to reporting a few stories, but it's really not a very good idea overall, probably, and he appears to suggest that this technique is appropriate only when it would be approved by "reasonable" members of the public—a vague guideline at best, and one that seems impossible to implement except in hindsight.

I'll argue for a much clearer Kantian standard for investigative newsgathering, one that requires reporters to avoid deceptive practices entirely, thus ruling out not only hidden cameras but also lying in order to secure a first-hand vantage point. Such a standard conceivably *might*, in a few instances, keep reporters from gleaning every last bit of the information that would round out their stories. But I doubt that this absolute rule would be more than an occasional hindrance, if news people do their job right. Even if it were to pose occasional obstacles, I believe that doing away with deceptive news-gathering practices will result in far more credibility for the media, which in turn will—at least in the long run— increase their news-gathering ability and the knowledge and protection they can offer to the society that they're covering.

Deception that the Internal Revenue Service may employ is hardly a justification for journalists acting the same way. And a utilitarian approach here is a very slippery slope. Where (and why) would you draw the line? If it's okay to mislead a source about your identity as a reporter, does it then become okay to steal a document that might otherwise be hard to confirm? If theft is okay, how much further would you go in the name of obtaining information to serve the "greater good"? Assault? Sexual favors? Murder, to make available information that would "save society"?

With regard to the Food Lion case, I agree with Kittross that ABC could well have looked for ways to report the story that would not have involved hidden cameras. It wouldn't have been as flashy a TV news story without the video, but the information would have been the same, and as effective in protecting the public. Kittross might argue that the reporters or videographers couldn't have gotten access to this information without going undercover, but there are so many examples of investigative journalists using confidential sources and other non-deceptive techniques to get information that this argument simply doesn't wash.

People with information about a story "that needs to be covered" have, time and again, provided that information to reporters (a form of whistleblowing) without the need for the reporters to stoop to dishonesty, or anything resembling "suborning disloyalty to the source's employers" or anyone else, to use Kittross's overstated phrase. To be sure, some of those sources have demanded that their identities be protected, often for various good reasons. Confidentiality, *properly used*, is a most important reportorial tool (see Chapter 15-D for discussion of the ethical dimensions of this topic). And it goes almost without saying that it often will require more effort for journalists to follow leads and talk with many potential sources than it would to assume a fake identity or steal documents and obtain information in other underhanded ways. Journalists who say that deception is the "only" way to get a story usually mean that they are unwilling or, in a short-staffed newsroom, unable to put in the time and effort to dig out the story properly. (See also pp. 339–340.)

But extra time and effort will pay off in both credibility and the likelihood of sleeping better at night. Whether it's in regard to tainted meat, mental hospital abuses, quack physicians, corrupt politicians and law enforcement officers, or something else that needs to see the light of day in order to protect the public, reporters who are willing to work hard at it should eventually be able—without dissembling—to find people who will give them, or guide them, or lead them, to the information that's needed to tell the story.

The Watergate investigation by *Washington Post* reporters Bob Woodward and Carl Bernstein, and many others—overseen, incidentally, by the same Ben Bradlee mentioned by

Kittross—remains a model of hard-nosed, tireless digging that eventually got the story. It gave the United States the information that was necessary, and it did so without stooping to unethical tactics that would have clouded both the public acceptance of those results and the news media's general credibility (see Woodward, 2005). Not every news organization has *The Washington Post*'s resources to throw at a difficult investigation, but almost all of them have the capability of cooperating with other news or civic organizations to increase the resources available to them. If it takes a loss of exclusivity (or of video images—the choice that ABC News was unwilling to make in the Food Lion case) to preserve this ethical standard for investigative journalism, that's a very small concession to make.

As Kittross conceded, there are relatively few situations where journalists should even consider that it might be "necessary" to conceal their identities, or otherwise act dishonestly in pursuit of a story. I believe that even in those few situations, there are other means to the desired end, and that Machiavelli must not become the model for news directors or managing editors.

References and Related Readings

Hodges, Louis W. (1997). "The real issue is tainted food." *Media Ethics* 8(2), p. 4. Hodges was an expert witness for the defense in the Food Lion case. This issue of *Media Ethics* contained several articles exploring *Food Lion* v. *ABC* from various viewpoints.

Merrill, John C. (1998). *The Princely Press: Machiavelli on American Journalism*. Lanham, MD: University Press of America.

Steele, Bob. (1997). "ABC and Food Lion: The ethics questions." *RTNDA Communicator*, April, p. 56. Retrieved from www.poynter.org/content/content_view.asp?id=5585 (September 6, 2009).

Sinclair, Upton. (1906). *The Jungle*. New York: Doubleday. (Many subsequent editions are also available.)

Woodward, Bob. (2005). *The Secret Man: The Story of Watergate's Deep Throat*. New York: Simon & Schuster.

15-H: PACK JOURNALISM

KITTROSS: The news media's current practice of "pack journalism" is both inefficient and unethical.

Any so-called "newsworthy" event draws so-called journalists as honey—or manure—draws flies. A visit by a potentate, a major political or sporting event, an airplane crash, a juicy court trial, the funeral or wedding of a celebrity all attract the pack: dozens or even hundreds of reporters whose words and pictures will be presented to readers and viewers as rapidly as modern technologies can carry them. When following the story in full bay, the very size of the pack often—in a travesty of what "news coverage" is all about—becomes a story in itself, or the subject of a *Doonesbury* or *Bloom County/Opus* comic strip.

Although one might blame the reporters, photographers, videographers, and sound recordists for the mob scenes that have cast disrepute on the news media and made public life much less attractive, the blame really should fall on the assignment or city editors who sent out these reporters and photographers. This process was disturbingly illustrated in the 1997 death of Diana, Princess of Wales. The paparazzi pursuing her were mostly freelance, but were nevertheless assured of cash rewards and promises of publication from both the tabloids and the mainstream press, for any pictures they could take of her. Trying to escape them contributed to her death in a Paris automobile crash. Despite general revulsion with the paparazzi in this case, leading to calls for stricter British privacy laws, some publishers showed no shame. Press magnate Rupert Murdoch was quoted on the BBC as saying that "privacy laws are for the protection of people already privileged" and that his only problem was that he had been paying too much to the paparazzi.

Why must each station or newspaper have its own people report an event that often is of very limited intrinsic importance? Why do editors, publishers, and news directors reject the possibilities of pool coverage or the use of wire services or freelancers (including the "citizen journalists" discussed in Chapter 15-C)? Why do we need to see dozens of ballpoint pens, throats, lenses, and microphones thrust at the accused, the victim, or the innocent bystander? For example, why was it necessary for any network to send its anchor to Los Angeles for the opening of the O. J. Simpson criminal trial? Did every photo outlet in New England have to get its own shot of the horror on the faces of Christa McAuliffe's young students when the spacecraft *Challenger*, with her aboard, exploded on live TV in 1986?

The usual argument is that only with their own staff reporting the story can newspapers or broadcasters be confident of the validity and reliability of their content. But when one thinks about the stories that *aren't* covered because the media's limited resources are devoted to being part of the pack, and of all media's frequent use of wire services, freelancers, CNN, or celebrity-seeking citizens, this excuse falls flat.

Indeed, it may well be that the worst result of pack journalism is the loss of independent reporting. Every newsroom has tales of reporters whose stories are killed by overly cautious editors because the competition carried a story with a different slant. At the reporter's level, as Timothy Crouse (1973) pointed out in his book about an election campaign, *The Boys on the Bus*, those on the scene keep asking one another what their—and the television networks'—leads were.

> it may well be that the worst result of pack journalism is the loss of independent reporting.

Stories are covered with the resources available. If a volcano erupts, it is covered by those fortunate enough (from a career point of view) to be on the scene; the carpetbaggers who swarm off the first available jets rarely add to the accounts that already have been made available, and it isn't inexpensive to send a staff correspondent to "parachute in" around the globe or take a helicopter directly to the scene. During wartime, pool coverage *is* used, ensuring that all members of the audience, regardless of what source they prefer, have access to the same important news. If news-gathering resources are left over, then human interest or sidebar stories are covered uniquely by each reporter—but this is merely frosting on the cake for most of the audience.

Remember, even though the same reportage is available to each media outlet, there is more than one way to present it; individual editors can place a particular spin or emphasis on any story. This is one reason why the copyright laws protect the *words* being used, and not the news event itself (with the exception of "exclusive" interviews).

The economic inefficiency of pack journalism is easy to demonstrate. If a substantial fraction of the nation's reporters are tied up covering a particularly juicy trial (and, to those who have read the U.S. Department of Labor's media employment statistics, "substantial fraction" isn't hyperbole), then other news—possibly of equal or greater importance and interest—doesn't get covered. If budgets are drawn down through the rental of aircraft or tying up of satellite trucks, then all news coverage for the rest of that fiscal year will be diminished.

But what about the ethics of the time-honored journalistic practice of making sure that the competition isn't given free access to a reporter's work on a story, story element, or angle? My opinion is that this practice results in both short-term and long-term harm to the public (see Bates, 1994). And if a news media practice harms readers and viewers, I believe that practice is unethical from all points of view. Desires for "scoops" or "beats" of competing media may energize reporters and editors, and sell the media product, but how can they help the public? Other fields face the same ethical dilemma, sometimes with life or death results, such as the medical business practice of considering new surgical techniques to be "trade secrets"—a practice that dates back at least to the invention of the obstetrical forceps. David Gordon claims that concern over reportorial "trade secrets" such as pack journalism is relatively unimportant: the practice will soon disappear because of economic trends. Although I doubt that this will happen as long as competition stimulates practitioners, he still overlooks the implications of current practices on the public at large, and further sets journalism firmly into the cement of commodification. His apparent belief in the disappearance of pack journalism is contradicted by the appearance of "the pack" whenever the story is big enough—such as the deaths of Michael Jackson and Senator Edward M. Kennedy.

In the short term, pack journalism uses scarce human, technological, and fiscal resources inefficiently. In the long term, pack journalism reduces all news values to "let's make sure the competition doesn't get too far ahead of us." The desirability of searching for stories to cover, or the benefits of uncovering something new and significant to the audience, are lost when the assignment editor is worried more about what the boss will say about falling behind than about the possibility of being out in front.

Furthermore, the constant badgering of people "in the news" that is the obvious corollary to pack journalism goes a long way toward reducing the number of people who are willing to put themselves in the public eye—a fact that may be reflected in the number of show biz celebrities who have entered politics, from Ronald Reagan to Al Franken. Not everyone is willing to have every action of every moment of their (and their family's) lives scrutinized by a horde of yapping journalists and hence lose the modicum of privacy to which everyone should be entitled.

If news is defined as "what everyone is chasing," then newsgathering becomes a sports event rather than an essential part of our social and political life. I don't think it should be.

GORDON: "Pack journalism" will largely disappear from the news media landscape within a decade, so why are we worrying about it?

For the sake of this argument, I'll concede that the so-called "pack journalism" of the 1970s and beyond was a poor way to cover news stories. But between the increasing news contributions from "citizen journalists"—which are *not* being rejected out-of-hand by many editors, John Michael Kittross to the contrary—and the emergence of a trend toward cooperation between sometimes bitter news media rivals, concerns about "pack journalism" are overblown. I'd suggest that we have far more important ethics issues to be concerned about.

The reason for my stance on this issue? Economics!

As newsroom staffs were cut back in 2008–09, the availability of journalists to become part of a "pack" almost ceased to exist. Editors found themselves increasingly unable to assign reporters to cover many events that had previously drawn individual coverage from competing newspapers, leading to the "pack journalism" phenomenon. Editors also came to understand that citizen journalists could fill in some of the news coverage gaps that resulted from the sharp drop in advertising revenues and the consequent staff cuts. Most important, though, was the realization that news media might well provide good coverage at far lower cost by cooperating rather than competing.

Three editors discussed their papers' participation in the early stages of such cooperative efforts at the 2009 convention of journalism and mass communication educators (J-Lab, 2009). Anders Gyllenhaal of *The Miami Herald* noted that while cooperation would be difficult in such areas as arts coverage or major investigative efforts, it was beneficial both in regard to breaking news stories and some beat coverage. His paper was already partnering with former competitors in Fort Lauderdale, Palm Beach and St. Petersburg, as well as with several English- and Spanish-language television stations and was hoping to bring some weekly papers into the mix. The cooperative coverage freed up the *Herald*'s resources for larger projects that would otherwise have been beyond the paper's capabilities, he noted.

Susan Goldberg of *The Plain Dealer* in Cleveland discussed cooperative news coverage by the eight largest dailies in Ohio, involving stories of statewide interest—including college and professional sports coverage, and a political poll in the fall of 2008 that went into more depth than any one paper could have afforded on its own, with the results localized for each area. This project allowed each of the eight papers to devote their available resources to better *local* news content for their readers, she said. Goldberg also noted that plans were being finalized for shared sports coverage nationwide, involving some 50 newspapers. If the cooperation on sports succeeds, it would decrease the papers' need for Associated Press sports coverage, a development that could save them considerable money. (Goldberg said her paper was paying the AP close to $1 million a year for its overall services.)

Rex Smith of the *Times Union* in Albany, New York reported on a consortium of three New York and two New Jersey papers, stretching from Buffalo through Albany to Newark and including *The Record* in Bergen County, New Jersey as well as the *New York Daily News*. (He noted that the two New Jersey papers had formerly competed bitterly with each other.) Smith said the arrangement drew strength from the various perspectives that each partner could provide (e.g., sports from Buffalo, state capital coverage from Albany, and the New York City focus of the *Daily News*). He noted that one potential problem—how to maintain standards—could be solved by exercising care in selecting one's partner news organizations, and acknowledged that such cooperative efforts had to be "sold" carefully to the newsroom staffs affected by them.

Smith said that, while some audience-generated content is both useful and inevitable, there is still a strong need for content generated by trained journalists. Goldberg noted that it is easier to collaborate with people who are operating on the same level that you're on, with regard to both resources and expertise.

Kittross is correct in noting that such off-the-scale newsworthy events as the deaths and funerals of Michael Jackson and Senator Edward Kennedy will continue to tempt "pack coverage." But even at that level, I'd argue that if papers nationwide begin to cooperate on sports coverage, as Goldberg suggests, then the same economic advantages will drive many of them to go with what is essentially "pool reporting" on events of extreme newsworthiness. After all, if Ohio newspapers are willing to rely on coverage of Ohio State football by sportswriters for the Columbus paper, almost any degree of cooperation is imaginable.

All three editors on the panel agreed that economics have ended the days of the "scoop mentality." And if—to use Ohio again as an example—one reporter is covering a statewide sports or other story for all eight (formerly competing) papers, the days of "pack journalism" are also over. So let's move on to more serious ethics concerns—like making sure the vestiges of the pack journalism mentality get stamped out, both in journalism programs and in newsrooms.

References and Related Readings

Bates, Stephen. (1994). "Who is the journalist's client?" *Media Ethics* 7(1), p. 3.

Crouse, Timothy. (1973). *The Boys on the Bus*. New York: Random House.

J-Lab. (2009). Comments by Susan Goldberg, editor, *The Plain Dealer*, Cleveland, Ohio; Anders Gyllenhaal, executive editor, *The Miami Herald*, Florida and Rex Smith, editor, the *Times Union*, Albany, New York. "Civic news networks: Collaboration vs. competition," panel discussion presented by J-Lab, American University, Washington, DC, at the annual convention of the Association for Education in Journalism and Mass Communication, Boston, MA, August 7.

15-I: INTERVIEWS

KITTROSS: The interview is an unreliable, often invalid, and even harmful way of obtaining information for the media.

There is an old—and sick—joke that has a reporter asking the widow of an assassinated president, "Apart from that, Mrs. Lincoln, how did you like the play?"

Such a stereotypical, vapid, and insensitive question may reflect the reporter's ineptitude or inability to focus on the real story, but it may also reflect an unreasoned faith in the efficacy and significance of journalistic interviewing—one of the most basic journalism tools.

Unfortunately, there are only a few ways through which reporters can gather news, and social scientists warn us about unreliability of eyewitness accounts—even when a trained reporter is the observer or the interviewer. It is my opinion that the best, if not the most common, reporting is in the form of reasoned essays providing an analysis of myriad documented as well as often-undocumented sources, including the reporter's own witness, rather than merely repeating another's words and others' data. Bernstein and Woodward (1974), in *All the President's Men*, illustrated the technique of using official and unofficial documents. But many reporters feel the need to validate their work by using someone else's statements rather than their own brains, and find it easier to allow someone else to filter the wheat from the chaff of complex documents.

It can be argued that interviews give people a chance to tell their own stories, that they are a more valid, more reliable, and even more ethical way of gathering information than using jaded, possibly biased reporters' or documentarians' direct observations or analyses. Certainly, one form of interview—the testimonial—has played a major role in the history of advertising. But I believe that the mass media's practices of interviewing actually are much *less* ethical than journalists, documentarians, advertising researchers, cultural anthropologists and others claim, and that the ethics of interviewing may be confused with often selfish and ineffective practices.

We really need to use the interview as a way of getting at the truth, not as a way of touching all bases or transferring the contents of the reporter's brain into someone else's mouth or vice versa. People can be mistaken, or they can lie or misspeak themselves, but you'd never know it from most of the media. In court, there is the opportunity to test the probity—the truthfulness and reliability—of testimony. In the media, perhaps due to reporter gratitude to the interviewee for allowing the interview to take place, almost every utterance is taken and presented to the audience at face value.

Certainly, there are a few interviewers—Ted Koppel when he anchored *Nightline*, for example, or the late Studs Terkel, or Terry Gross of NPR—who allow the audience to draw its own conclusions about whether to believe the questioned person.

More often, unfortunately, particularly in an "ambush" interview, the intent of a questioner is not to elicit answers, but to show the public how the interviewee reacted. It is inherently unfair. It is very easy to make someone look stupid or guilty—more so in television because the print media's willingness to clean up grammar and syntax disappears when a taped interview is broadcast. Back in the late 1980s, considerable criticism was leveled at CBS News' *60 Minutes* because of its heavy use of interviews in which the camera crew burst upon the interviewee with tape rolling and a reporter ready to pounce with questions. Was this technique necessary in all instances in which it was used? Would the criticism have been muted if CBS were not in sole and complete control of the interview situation—and the resulting editing? Even Don Hewitt—the producer of *60 Minutes*—came to believe that hidden cameras weren't necessary to tell a news or public affairs story, even though the public might have benefited from the stories in which ambush journalism *was* used.

I have three major objections to current standards of interviewing. First, much ambush and similar interviewing, particularly in the aftermath of a disaster, is an unconscionable invasion of well-deserved and much needed privacy. The media's habit of "doorstepping" the relatives of the recently deceased—asking how a person "felt" when a loved one is killed— is ghoulish and adds little to our understanding of the tragedy.

Second, the media have taken the Edward R. Murrow/Fred Friendly "law" ("there is no substitute for someone with a fire in the belly") and turned it from being a way of informing into a way of titillating the public with the juiciest soundbite.

Third, the media often use interviews—sometimes with mythical or invented "people on the street"—merely as a way of justifying preconceived (and often stereotypical) stories.

With respect to the last of these complaints, there also seems to be an unreasoning belief that just because someone is quoted as saying something, it necessarily is true or important. For example, a televised *vox populi* (Latin for "voice of the people") may provide significant insights once in a blue moon. But a trivial or obvious bit of information—for example, "It's the first warm day of spring"—doesn't need an interview to validate it.

Yet another belief of some editors (and readers, viewers, and listeners) is that all sins are forgiven if we merely present "both sides of the matter." Are there only two sides? Do we really need carefully balanced political opinions if one candidate really has something to say and the other doesn't? Must we balance every interview with a victim of a crime by an interview with the accused or the accused's attorney? Does the no-brainer triplet—soundbite interviews that say, "I like X," "I dislike X," and "What's X?"—tell us what the "person in the street" is thinking? (In a December 20, 2007 cartoon in—of all publications—*The Chronicle of Higher Education*, the first of three convicts in the exercise yard of a prison says, "I protected a source." The second says, "I exposed a source." And the third says, "I was a source." Some triplet jokes are timeless.)

For some reason, there are few separate college courses in journalistic interviewing, although sociologists, clinical psychologists, and anthropologists all accept the need for specialized training in this delicate skill. What little interviewing instruction embryonic journalists get tends to deal with topics—how to cover the courthouse, how to cover a fire— rather than with how valid and reliable our interviewing practices might be.

Because the editing of an interview—whether soundbite or lengthy discourse—is entirely in the hands of the media, there is no reason to expect that an interview is more valid than information garnered elsewhere or in other ways. The advertising testimonial, which can be considered a selective use of the interview form, certainly is susceptible to the same sort of manipulation even if it is regulated by the Federal Trade Commission or state agencies.

In general, I believe that the interviews and advertising testimonials we read and see and hear rarely give us useful information. The practice helps neither interviewer nor interviewee nor the ultimate user, the public. Hence, from a utilitarian point of view, they are ethically useless. Typically, interviews give the appearance of objectivity without the reality, and they take the reporter off the hook of having to justify her or his reportage.

Of course, I'm generalizing. And it has been justly said that all generalizations are false—including this one. But suppose you were Mrs. Lincoln? Or you were made to look foolish by an interviewer? Or you were misled because an interview was cut off in the editing room for dramatic, rather than informative, purposes?

Aren't there better, more utilitarian ways of procuring less-biased information?

15-J: CO-OPTION

KITTROSS: The media not only can be bought, but also are.

What makes this prostitution even worse is that the price often is set very, very low. Although reporters used to be taught that the only way to look at a politician is down their noses, those in the media are as susceptible to flattery and other ego-stroking as everyone else.

It is this that leads to "creampuff" interviews; maneuvering for social invitations; the proud wearing of a prestigious source's "freebies," from a lapel pin to a genuine sports team warm-up jacket, or, even better, one from Air Force One; a network anchor fawning over the president; acceptance of hospitality that might lead both parties to assume there is a reciprocal obligation to provide something in return. Often, this reflects the idea that the most important need of the reporter is to keep on the good side of sources, editors, publishers, advertisers and potential advertisers. These and many other instances where independent judgment is lacking or restricted can damage both the reporters' stories and the credibility of all the media.

For example, the White House Office of Media Affairs finds it easy to decide which stations or papers to target for political advantage (Garcia, 1994). The selected media will drop everything to be able to say pridefully "He chose us!" It is very rare, even in the most blatant cases of political maneuvering, for the media to turn down the opportunity to brag about being so important that they have been selected as a sounding board by the White House, regardless of what this might do to their credibility.

There are other examples of co-option that have been around for generations. Sometimes money or even a *quid pro quo* isn't involved. Although reporters are expected to be objective, particularly in political matters, neither columnists nor media executives are. There probably is a public benefit to having commentators of differing political persuasions—but, as mentioned in Chapter 3, which discusses truth and fairness—the idea that "he who pays the piper calls the tune" should not be used to justify leaning over backward to protect advertisers (or sources) from adverse reports. (Perhaps the common modification of the Golden Rule is appropriate here: "he who has the gold makes the rule.") Publishers and station owners feel free to impose their political views on the output of their media organization, even if such behavior is condemned when done by those in the lower ranks. There are many examples of this blatant exercise of power.

A more subtle manifestation was found in the results of the "embedding" of reporters with specific military units during the Iraq War. It would be a rare reporter indeed who wasn't affected by such close association with those on whom he or she was supposed to report—and, if dependent upon military transport to get to where the action was, the "free press" could find itself fettered.

Is this substitution of ego satisfaction or logistic convenience for journalistic judgment desirable? Is the co-option of network and studio chiefs, producers, and writers to concentrate on the "social ill of the year" (drug taking, spouse beating, etc.) through invitations to the seats of government power really the best way to set the agenda and enlarge public debate over major problems—or even to get original ideas for media content? Are all "public service" campaigns run by print and broadcast media really in the public interest?

If any of the answers to these questions is "No," and I think that is very likely, then perhaps, in a Kantian way, the media would best serve their own sense of self-esteem as well as the public interest by returning to the "looking down the nose" standard.

GORDON: The media do a better job of remaining independent than almost any other institution in society.

If John Michael Kittross is arguing that people in the mass media are human, and subject to human failings, then I have to agree. But when he generalizes about media "prostitution," I have to disagree strongly. It may be happening in the Middle East (see, e.g., Robertson, 2009) but it isn't—and isn't likely to become—a problem in U.S. journalism.

It is highly unrealistic to expect media people to live up to a Kantian standard that requires complete selflessness 100% of the time. Wearing a lapel pin or even an Air Force One warm-up jacket is not likely to influence news content very much.

There certainly are some potential dangers inherent in journalists becoming too cozy with sources or allowing themselves to be manipulated because the White House and other news sources can appeal to their egos. But by and large, journalists and their editors are aware of those dangers and do a pretty good job of either avoiding them or recognizing them soon enough to prevent the news coverage from becoming tainted. Most journalists, I suspect, try hard—and with considerable success—to follow the utilitarian prescription of having their work benefit the greatest number of people.

There will always be exceptions, because journalists are human and humans aren't perfect. But as advertisers have often learned, and as most public relations practitioners recognize, journalists are not all that easy to buy.

That doesn't mean that journalists and public relations people don't work together. They do, and they should, because at their best, these two fields are quite symbiotic. Public relations practitioners need to use the mass media to do what their clients hire them to do. Journalists can and do benefit from information, press and video releases, tips, suggestions, and guidance that public relations people or government press contacts provide.

Although a dash of skepticism is important for journalists, looking down one's nose, at politicians or anyone else, is definitely not the recipe for successful reporting! As long as journalists remember *why* public relations personnel are cooperating with them, and as long as PR people remember that the journalists must make the final decisions about whether and how to use the material provided to them, no one is being "bought" and their symbiosis will benefit the media's audience and the society as a whole.

References and Related Readings

Bernstein, Carl, and Bob Woodward. (1974). *All the President's Men*. New York: Simon & Schuster.

Garcia, Robert. (1994). "Hey Mom, the President's on the radio!" *Radio Reporting* (RTNDA newsletter) 1, November, p. 2.

Robertson, Campbell. (2009). "For Iraqi journalists, free press vs. free land." *The New York Times*, January 27. Retrieved from www.nytimes/2009/01/28/world/middleeast/28journalists.html?_r=2&ref=world (September 6, 2009).

Postscript

Some Questions without Answers and Answers without Questions

John C. Merrill

Each of the authors of Controversies in Media Ethics *has made sure that some of his or her own ideas have been incorporated. In particular, this volume has benefited from the thoughts of John C. Merrill, whose long service to journalism and the field of media ethics has showed no signs of slowing down. The "questions without answers" below are some of the thoughts that Merrill has had over the years, and they are presented without answers to give readers the opportunity to think about them at their own speed—and come up with answers they can live with. The "answers without questions" are the other side of the coin: a collection of aphorisms he has designed to be catalysts for thought and discussion—almost every one of which can be parlayed into a healthy discussion, in class, in the newsroom, or over a drink of some kind. We hope that those reading this book will enjoy trying to find answers to the questions and questions (or situations) for the aphorisms or answers.*

QUESTIONS WITHOUT ANSWERS

Any discussion of applied ethics usually resolves itself into a series of difficult questions. For the most part, the most important core question is this one: *who or what determines what is ethical?*

Many answers to this question have been given, in this book and elsewhere: the individual person, the peer group, religion, the government, society at large, and philosophers.

A companion—perhaps even more important—core question, and one I will deal with mainly in the following remarks, is: *what does it mean to be ethical?*

There are a myriad of sub-questions that spin off from these core ones. Here are a few:

■ Is what is ethical that which is believed by a large majority of the people? Or what the significant opinion leaders believe? Or—whatever the person feels is best for the human needs of a person or a group? Or—whatever conscience, instinct, or religious belief says is ethical?

- Is ethics purely subjective or is it rational or objective? If ethics has no monolithic meaning and is relative, then how can we come up with a definition that is absolute and universal? (If we cannot define it, then all we can say about ethics is that it is personal and that it is contextual or relative. And if this is true, then we should limit our ethical opinions to specific times, contexts, and cases, and never generalize.)
- Am I unethical if I, as a reporter, put my opinion in the story? (After all, I don't hesitate to insert other people's opinions.)
- If I am a conservative reporter, is it all right for me to quote only conservative sources in my story, or should I (to be ethical) balance the conservative sources with liberal ones?
- Is the following sentence ethical in a news story? "Right-wing conservative Ben Bosser will debate Democrat Hugh McGrath tomorrow at the Community Center."
- If my keeping a confidence results in permitting a guilty criminal to escape, is it ethical for me to keep it?
- If I work in a poor and less developed country and make very low wages, am I unethical to moonlight in another media job at night?
- Is it more ethical for a reporter to do what he or she is told to do—even if it is thought to be unethical—or to do what he or she thinks is the right thing to do? Which is more important, freedom or obedience to authority?
- Let's carry the preceding question further. If my family is starving, is it ethical for me to steal to feed them? How about slanting a story to serve the interests of my employer even if I haven't been instructed to do so?
- Is it ever right to think that one's own ethical decision is better than one coming from one's boss (e.g., an editor or the managing partner in an advertising agency)?
- Is something like a slight misquoting in a direct quote an unethical act—or simply sloppy reporting—or just clarifying the source's sloppy language?
- Is eliminating a word (perhaps one that's vulgar or racist) from a direct quotation always an unethical thing to do?
- What is plagiarism? Is it the theft of someone else's words without attribution, or could it be merely the usurping of someone else's idea and style? Suppose synonyms rather than specific words are used? Is it unethical to use a direct quote gathered by someone else?
- If a reporter knows that secret information held by a corporation or government is vital for the public's safety, is it ethical to try to get this information by any means possible?
- Is it unethical to use an indirect rather than a direct quotation in a story (with attribution) since the reporter's paraphrasing of the actual wording is subjectivizing the statement?
- Is it ethical for a reporter to falsify—even for laudable reasons—reality in a story? (See Chapter 15-A.)

ANSWERS WITHOUT QUESTIONS: SOME CATALYTIC APHORISMS ABOUT FREEDOM AND ETHICS

Freedom, if taken seriously, negates any kind of group-determined normative ethics. Freedom, if individually defined, will usually lead away from ethics. Freedom as libertinism is freedom for the insane. Ethical action is others doing what I would do. Freedom justifies all kinds of relativism. Ethics is one step away from authoritarianism.

Freedom leads to anxiety, ethics to peace. The seeker after ethics is a conservative, hoping to find safety in sheltered waters. Freedom found is security lost. Freedom and ethics are from different conceptual worlds. Who would seek freedom would shun ethics, and is open to all ideas blowing by. The only measure of goodness is success. Both freedom and ethics demand action, not words.

Character is superior to ethics; an immoral person can be ethical. The only thing that is certain is uncertainty. This I know—that I don't know. I sought freedom, got it, and now long for order. Ethics is a mask that the coward wears. Thank God I am free to shun freedom.

Freedom, like ethics, is no more than a shadow, consoling the lonely and the hopeful. The wise person runs from the voice of the people. The wisest person runs from every voice. The ethical person is one who looks in a fuzzy mirror.

The person who seeks the right path will forever wander. Why does Ethics (with an "s") seem plural, although used as if singular? Freedom implies confusion and encourages chaos, while also permitting the disciplined person to dominate and bring order. Ethics will never win over power and self-interest. The ethical person is a certain loser in worldly matters. Might does not make right, but it does lead to success.

Freedom is a kind of insurance against imposed equality. Ethics is human-made, not transcendental, therefore inferior in goodness. The soul grows with ethics; the ego grows with worldly success. Freedom allows the person to choose slavery and to succumb to immorality. Ethics is the attempt to fight the impossible fight, to confront the invincible windmill.

> Freedom opens the door to ethical frustration, and ethical certainty closes the door to freedom.

Freedom opens the door to ethical frustration, and ethical certainty closes the door to freedom. I had rather meet an ethical person than a free person, although they both may harm me. A "free" political society may be more corrupt and harmful than an autocratic one. There are no really free societies; they are all authoritarian; finding the locus of the authority is the problem.

Kant may be right in dismissing consequences as unimportant when determining ethical action, but he is only partially right. John Stuart Mill looked to possible consequences in making ethical decisions, but utilitarians can only speculate. (Relationships between the ideas of Kant and Mill about rules and consequences are complex, and are discussed more fully in Chapter 15-A.)

Societies are by nature composed of unfree people, but they—the societies—have considerable freedom. Codes of ethics are no more than public relations statements, resembling little more than "look at us, how good we are." Codes of ethics are good for hiding holes in the wall. Ethical codes must be internalized and normative, silently observed. Freedom *from* the press is a real problem. Ethics is what you do, not what you don't do.

Ethics rides on freedom's back, and will not be thrown off. Ethics, like a missile, sounds good before it lands. Freedom is a temporary respite from reality. Machiavelli used his freedom to win without ethics, believing success more important. Freedom to be secure is obtained by losing it. Egoism exalts freedom and ignores ethics.

Rousseau revered prehistoric man for his natural goodness. One wonders how many prehistoric men Rousseau knew. Voltaire would defend freedom even if it killed him.

Nietzsche would have us be beyond good and evil—in a kind of good-evil world of self-determination. If it works, embrace it, for it is ethical, say the pragmatists, reminding one of Machiavelli. Could John Dewey have been a Machiavellian? Christianity prescribes freedom while endowing it with norms. Hinduism enthrones inner-freedom that leads to total discipline. Ethical talk is like a flag waved to indicate good intentions—or a coming attack.

Ethics walks the walk; pseudo-ethics talks the talk. Freedom instills anxiety while ethics dissolves it—but is that true? The only road to freedom is death; but even then, you're trapped. How can I know myself when I am constantly changing? If one wants to find God, one needs to find one's self.

The fact that it is "the press" obviates its freedom by having a name. Freedom is a disjointed moment in reality, especially in social systems. Who can be "self-reliant," Mr. Emerson, except the person dying alone? The person who is, never is; the person who was, never was. The only truth is that there is no truth—at least in this world. Ethical freedom is the objective, but an impossible one. Expression can be free only for the hermit.

Cooperation is the gateway to mediocrity. Democracies assume ignorant governance. Individualists of the world should unite. Ethics, like news, is indefinable and is only personally relevant. When freedom and ethics sit at the peace table, societies cease to progress. A free society is an oxymoron. Libertarians are weak-willed anarchists, hobbled by caution. Conservatives want order while crying for freedom, and liberals want to conserve and increase their socialistic tendencies.

Arguments about ethics close minds rather than open them. What a person does is usually considered ethical—by him or her. Vulgarity is in the ear of the beholder. One must have words in order to think: how, then, were the first words formed? Political correctness is neither political nor correct. A funeral director is an undertaker who thinks language bestows status. An ethics discussion is like a wind in the trees. If God is dead, as Nietzsche said, there is no need for ethics. If Kant did not base his ethics on consequences, one wonders how his formal maxims came into being. John Dewey saw virtue, not in the successful results of action, but in the pragmatics of the attempt. If the existentialist worships freedom, ethics must not have much value.

Now it is your turn to have at these simplifications; I hope they will lead you to new ideas!

Glossary

Compiled by John A. Armstrong

Cross-references to other glossary terms are italicized. Terms related to forms of government and most legal concepts are omitted. John Armstrong wishes to thank those co-authors and others who provided suggestions for words to be defined, and—in a number of cases—the definitions themselves.

Accountability See *social responsibility theory.*

Agape ethics Ethics based on a God-inspired love and care for fellow humans. Agape ethics has a long history in the Christian religious tradition and draws on the Jewish ethical mandate to "love your neighbor as yourself" as well as such early thinkers as Mo Tzu in China. Unlike *divine command theory*, which often prescribes specific actions in specific situations, agape ethics calls for a more general application of love to all ethical questions, perhaps especially those dealing with social justice.

Agenda-setting The theory that by choosing what material to include, the mass media greatly determine the agenda for public discussion of issues. This idea can be applied to many aspects of the entertainment media, as well as to the news media. It is sometimes summarized as "the media tell us what to think *about* but do *not* tell us what to think." See also *gatekeeping.*

Airbrush An artist's instrument for spraying pigment on an illustration; frequently used to hide unwanted matter, such as a facial defect or a competitor's product. Largely replaced by computer programs such as Adobe Photoshop.

Altruism Placing the needs of others as paramount, often to the exclusion of one's own needs, and acting to meet the needs of others.

Anonymous source A source whom journalists promise not to name or otherwise specifically identify in their story, so he or she can provide information without fear of reprisal for doing so. It is sometimes used as synonymous with *confidential source*, although there is usually no ethically binding promise that a journalist will protect the identity of an anonymous source if required (especially in legal proceedings) to reveal it. There is overlap between the two categories, but anonymous sources lack the almost-certain protection given by journalists to confidential sources.

Aristotle (384–322 B.C.) Greek philosopher and tutor of Alexander the Great. Aristotle believed that ethics were tied to personal virtue and established harmonious relations between people. Aristotle argued that ethical behavior followed a middle ground between two extremes of vice. Unlike the *utilitarians*, who see moral behavior as a means to happiness, or *Kantians*, who connect moral behavior to duty, Aristotle perceived the exercise of virtue as central to human flourishing. See *Golden Mean, virtue ethics*.

Associated Press (AP) An American news cooperative that includes about 1,700 newspapers and 5,000 radio and television news organizations. Members share their news stories with this wire service and also receive stories that are reported by AP. Today, AP and its staff journalists and stringers (temporary reporters), and allied organizations abroad supply the majority of national and international news to U.S. media.

Banner ad An ad placed above, below or beside the other content of a Web page. It often links to a pop-up box or separate Web site containing more information about the advertised product. Sometimes, in order to make banner ads harder to ignore, they contain flashing or animated content or targeted solicitations.

Edward Bernays (1891–1995) American public relations practitioner who pioneered the application of social science to public relations. Bernays also advocated the professionalization of the public relations field; he argued that its practitioners should be credentialed and should follow codes of ethics.

Blog Short for "Web log," it is an informal, occasional, personal piece of writing posted on the World Wide Web that often invites readers to attach their responses to it—and perhaps get a response in turn from the initial author.

Sissela Bok (b. 1934) American philosopher. In her influential book *Lying: Moral Choice in Public and Private Life* she examines the various categories of lying, and the abstract and practical reasons for honesty. She concludes that lying is far too common in modern society and that even many apparently benign falsehoods are more damaging than is generally recognized.

Martin Buber (1878–1965) Jewish philosopher who was born in Austria and later emigrated to Palestine. Buber stressed the ethical importance of "I–thou" (subject to subject) as opposed to "I–it" (subject to object) relationships. He argued that when people engage in an I–thou dialogue, they embrace each other as holistic beings, not as "things," or as a collection of separate attributes.

Categorical imperative See *Kantian ethics*.

Checkbook journalism Using money (or something else of value) to buy information or visual images that one can publish or put on the air; or to buy access to a source of information. Such purchases usually are expected to be exclusive. Whether they are ethical is debated in Chapter 15-B.

Clifford G. Christians (b. 1939) American philosopher and communications author and educator. Christians has been a leader in bringing together media ethics and philosophy. A prolific scholar, he is noted as a speaker and is the author or co-author of more than a dozen books and more than 100 book chapters and journal articles. Christians spent most of his academic career at the University of Illinois, as director of the Institute for Communications Research, where he now is an emeritus professor. He has produced seminal work on many subjects in the field of media ethics, such as *communitarian ethics, protonorms*, the relationship of religion (primarily Christianity) to ethics, universal ethics and ethical humanism. Along with *John C. Merrill*, Christians was one of the first researchers to focus attention on the entire media ethics field.

Citizen journalism The concept and emerging trend that anyone with keen powers of observation, a little writing or audio-video skill and an Internet connection can collect, report, augment, fact-check, analyze and perhaps disseminate news and information—not just the trained professional reporters and editors who work for traditional news organizations. Dan Gillmor is one of the leading advocates and scholars of citizen journalism and founded the nonprofit Center for Citizen Media to promote it. It is at times confused with *civic journalism*. See also *crowdsourcing* and Chapter 15-C.

Civic journalism The movement that began in the 1990s, based on the idea that journalists and their media should be active participants in solving community problems, rather than serving only as detached observers. It fosters efforts to work with community members and to create opportunities for discussions of community issues, especially those of concern to ordinary citizens. Jay Rosen, a journalism professor at New York University, was one of the earliest proponents of, and writers about, civic journalism (also referred to as "public journalism"). It differs from *citizen journalism*, which shares some general goals although it developed a decade or so after civic journalism.

Classified material See *secrecy*.

Click-through data Statistics on the numbers and types of Web users who not only read a particular home page or a banner ad but also actually click on it to get more information from its underlying pages or pop-up boxes. Web site owners sometimes compile each visitor's click-through data, which show each of the other pages or ads the visitor clicked on within that site, along with the Web site visits preceding and following the visit to that site.

Codes of ethics/Guidelines for professional practice Guidelines for ethical and other good practices that typically are formulated by professional organizations. These guidelines are largely voluntary and the penalties for violating them are relatively mild. See Chapter 5.

Commercial culture A social value system in which people embrace consumption of material goods or products and services to the extent that material possessions are important cultural symbols that maintain a prominent place in everyday life. Sometimes called "materialism."

Commission on Freedom of the Press A committee of prominent American intellectuals formed with private funds (notably from Henry Luce of Time, Inc.) during World War II to assess the proper role of the news media in a democratic society. The committee is sometimes called the "Hutchins Commission" after its chair, Robert Hutchins, then the president of the University of Chicago. Its report, *A Free and Responsible Press*, issued in 1947 as one of a series of books produced by the Commission, was highly critical of the contemporary media for their failure to cultivate informed citizenship. The report is still considered by some to be an important guidepost for modern journalists. See *social responsibility theory*.

Common carrier A business that offers its services to the public at published non-discriminatory rates under the authority of a regulatory body. The term usually refers to transporters of people or goods, but in the United States it also refers to some telecommunications providers (e.g., telephone companies; see also *Net neutrality*). By law, however, over-the-air broadcasting is not considered a common carrier and is not regulated as such.

Communitarian ethics Communitarian thinkers stress the importance of community membership and participation; these lead to human fulfillment. Communitarians place cooperation and community values above individualism and competition. In journalism, this means that nurturing the community is more ethical than detachment, neutrality or individual autonomy.

Confidential source Someone who provides information with the explicit promise that she or he will not be identified by the reporter as the source of that information, regardless of legal proceedings or any other pressures. This is similar, but not identical, to an *anonymous source*. See Shield law and Chapter 15-D.

Conflict of interest When an individual compromises what is owed to another (e.g., an employer) by acting to benefit him/herself instead, or to benefit a competitor of one's employer. This could lead to a loss of credibility and perhaps revenue for all involved. Examples would be participation in a political caucus by a reporter who also covers politics; or a public relations professional who works for one company but consults with a competing company in his or her spare time, especially without disclosing this to either company. Generally, the ethical thing to do is give higher priority to one's duty to others than to his or her own interests. A perceived conflict of interest—when mass communicators potentially compromise what's good for their employer by taking an action that audience members might see as eroding the credibility of both parties (e.g., political participation of any sort by a reporter who does *not* cover politics)—raises many of the same concerns.

Confucius (551-479 B.C.) Chinese philosopher and government administrator. Confucius taught that moral principles should guide governmental action. Like Aristotle, Confucius used virtue as the basis for his ethics, and valued harmony and moderation. He stressed the importance of equilibrium and of respecting traditional roles and structures within society.

Conglomerate A firm made up of two or more companies that are engaged in unrelated businesses. Many major media outlets in the United States are owned by conglomerates. Critics argue that conglomerates that own media companies are more prone to ignore media ethics because media is only one subdivision of a larger company, or because the CEO or other decision-makers come from other fields and know little about media ethics.

Constitutional law The branch of law that deals with whether the actions of government (including the legislative branch), and decisions of courts and regulatory agencies are in accord with the basic document (the Constitution itself and any amendments thereto) that sets forth the powers and duties of the government and guarantees certain rights to the people living under that government.

Convergence The obliteration of distinctions between media, at the production level (e.g., using the same reporter to cover news for both a newspaper and a television station—which of course cuts operating costs—or using HDTV equipment to make a feature "film") or in the home (e.g., the use of a computer monitor to watch television programs or vice versa). As applied to journalism, the use of multiple media—such as print, photography, graphics, audio, and video— to tell journalistic stories in ways meant to be more encompassing and engrossing to the audience. Most of these stories are hosted on the Internet and use its interactive capabilities to let audience members provide feedback and access the stories as desired. Its multitechnology-toting practitioners are sometimes called backpack journalists, "mojos," or "cojos," short for mobile journalists and convergence journalists, respectively, or "one-man-bands."

Cookies "Byte-size" software programs that variously help track Internet usage and vary Web ads while also helping users navigate sites by remembering their paths and data they've entered. Users who don't want advertisers to know or manipulate their online histories can refuse to accept cookies, but most do not, because then they lose access to many of the features that Web sites and their advertisers offer.

Co-option When journalists surrender their independence in return for favors such as increased access to a news source—or the ego-satisfying status of being "in the know."

Crowdsourcing In a journalistic context, actively drawing on contributors from outside the newsroom to enhance a story. The underlying premise is that knowledge and expertise are dispersed among members of a community, constituting a valuable resource. Examples range from incorporating live reports from witnesses to a breaking news story to soliciting information from the public at large.

Cultural relativism The notion that various cultures have different but equally worthy values and that there are no grounds for claiming that one society's ethical practices are superior to another's.

Cybernetics A term coined by World War II-era technologist Norbert Wiener to describe any system that progressively uses continuous feedback to correct and refine its efficiency. The Internet, for example, allows Web site owners to gather data on the usage of their site and improve it based on those data.

Cyberspace A term that science fiction writer William Gibson coined in his novel *Neuromancer* (1984). It referred to a virtual world inhabited inside computer networks, but it has since come to mean the unseen, ethereal, timeless space where interactive communication takes place in any new media.

Dataveillance, or *data surveillance* The use of Web page tracking software by Web site owners and their clients, allowing them to compile and forecast the Web-surfing and online-purchasing patterns of the person logged in from any given computer's Internet address—along with all Internet users with similar patterns.

Defamation Communication that damages a person's reputation, for which the disseminator may be sued. The subcategory of *libel* today usually applies to both print or electronic media content, but in the past "libel" applied to defamatory printed material and "slander" to spoken material.

Deontological ethics Ethics in which right behavior is that which follows rules, regardless of the outcome. *Kantian ethics* are deontological, as is *divine command theory*. Deontological ethics stand in contrast to *teleological ethics*.

Deregulation Any removal (by Congress, the President or a governmental agency) of formal government rules or regulations, such as those affecting the behavior or size of a company, and substitution of reliance on market forces such as competition to control potential excesses. In regard to mass media, federal deregulation implemented primarily through the FCC has led since the early 1980s to an increase in the size of U.S. media companies and the elimination of many public service requirements for broadcasters. See *laissez-faire*.

Digital media Communication media for which information is transmitted, edited, and stored in the basic computer code of ones and zeroes. The fact that formerly disparate media such as video, audio, and print now use the same coding has helped erase barriers between these media: they are all available to audiences through a personal computer or other electronic device. Because of their coding, digitized sounds and images are easy to alter through computer programs such as Adobe Photoshop. See *convergence*; see also Chapter 7 in regard to the alteration of digital images.

Digital video recorders (DVRs) Computer hard drives with massive capacity used by viewers to record digitally various of the broadcast, cable or satellite TV shows they have access to. This allows viewers to replay any program at any later time, starting just a few seconds after it begins. Along with time shifting, the advantages of DVRs, such as *TiVo*, are that they let viewers pause, replay and zoom in on programs (including live events transmitted a few seconds earlier), just as they can do with DVDs. They can also skip most commercials at the touch of a button, but advertisers are likely to counteract that by increasing product placements within programs and using the viewing data that DVRs automatically collect in order to target ads, product placements, and their accompanying programs at consumers more efficiently.

Divine command theory The idea that certain laws of conduct were created by a deity and that followers of a particular religion—or, sometimes, all people—are obligated to obey them. Divine command ethics are deontological because virtue means following divine law, whether or not the outcome is beneficial. See *deontological ethics*.

Enlightenment values Beliefs that emerged from a period of European and American thought in the 17th and 18th centuries. Enlightenment thinkers (e.g., John Locke) valued human reason and were often suspicious of traditional authority, including organized religion. Many Enlightenment philosophers stressed individual autonomy and the natural rights of human beings; the opening passages of the United States' Declaration of Independence exemplify these beliefs.

Ethical egoism The idea that everyone should exclusively pursue his or her own interests. The most famous recent proponent of ethical egoism was the writer Ayn Rand. She believed that *altruism* (trying to help others) was ineffective and that each individual's pursuit of self-interest would lead to greater happiness and creativity in the world.

Ethics The study of concepts by which we determine what is good, right, and fair in our actions and in our treatment of others. Various philosophical systems define ethical behavior as a means to human happiness (see *utilitarian ethics* and *teleological ethics*); as a way to achieve personal virtue (see *Aristotle* and *virtue ethics*); as the fulfillment of our duty (see *Kantian ethics* and *deontological ethics*); or as the enactment of our inherently moral impulses (see *David Hume* and *personalist ethics*). See *moral/morality*.

Ethics of care The approach to ethics by contemporary feminist ethicists, following the lead of Nel Noddings (b. 1929), that stresses the importance of relationships rather than the justice-based approach to ethics put forth by Lawrence Kohlberg. Noddings' work followed the lead of Carol Gilligan and her emphasis on "ethical caring" but, unlike Gilligan, suggested that "caring" and "responsiveness" to others are preferable to "justice" as the basis for ethical behavior. See *moral development*.

Fairness Doctrine A series of decisions and regulations promulgated and enforced by the Federal Communications Commission from 1949 to 1987 that was often interpreted as not only requiring broadcast licensees to cover controversial issues of public importance, and to do so in an evenhanded manner, but also requiring that those individuals subjected to personal attack over the airways be given an opportunity for rebuttal. Sometimes confused with Sec. 315 of the Communications Act of 1934, which requires that equal opportunity for on-air appearances be afforded to all legally qualified candidates for a given political office. The FCC repealed the Fairness Doctrine on the grounds that it was unnecessary government intrusion into the broadcast marketplace. Some observers attribute the rise of talk radio to the elimination of the Fairness Doctrine.

Federal Communications Commission A U.S. federal independent regulatory agency, established in 1934, that oversees radio and television stations as well as all other radio transmissions (except those of the Department of Defense) as well as communications conducted over wires, such as telegraph, telephone and cable. It is responsible for ensuring that broadcast stations are granted licenses only if their issuance serves the "public interest, convenience and/or necessity" although this term has been vaguely and inconsistently defined over the decades. Because of the political strength of telephone and cable companies, as a practical matter the FCC exercises very little authority over wired and other telephonic communication.

Federal Trade Commission A U.S. federal independent regulatory agency, created in 1914, whose primary responsibilities are in preventing unfair competition between businesses and protecting consumers from fraud and misleading advertising.

First Amendment Added to the U.S. Constitution in 1791, the First Amendment protects the individual rights of freedom of speech, press, religion (both its establishment and freedom from it), and assembly, as well as the right to petition the government. It is often invoked in controversies over the rights, responsibilities, and ethics of the American *mass media*. (Note: The first 10 amendments to the U.S. Constitution are known as the "Bill of Rights.")

Fourth Estate A nickname for the news media that was probably first used in Britain as long as 300 years ago, and referred to the role of the press when Parliament consisted of three groups or estates: the Lords Spiritual, the Lords Temporal, and the Commons. In the United States, it usually refers to the media's First Amendment-enabled role as watchdog over the Congress and the other two branches of government, the judiciary and the executive.

Game theory A procedure for analysis and determination of strategies in situations in which the outcome of one participant's decisions is dependent on the actions of other rational, autonomous players. Game theory was introduced in 1944 in *Theory of Games and Economic Behavior* by John von Neumann and Oskar Morgenstern. It can be used to assess the possible outcomes of ethical decisions. See discussion in "Tools for Ethical Decision-Making" (pp. 199–201).

Gatekeeping The concept that journalists determine for their audiences what is news and what isn't, by metaphorically closing the newsroom gate on people, allegations, information and events that don't fit the journalists' definition of what's important or interesting. These journalistic "gatekeepers" are often editors or producers, who determine what stories will be published or broadcast; reporters also function in this role, particularly with regard to what information will be included in their reports. By extension, everyone who helps determine the information and ideas available to the public functions as a "gatekeeper." See *agenda-setting.*

Golden Mean The idea that ethical action is the mid-point between opposing poles of extreme behavior. In Western culture, its best known proponent is *Aristotle*, who equated ethical behavior with moderation. This should not to be confused with the *Golden Rule* of behavioral reciprocity.

Golden Rule The rule of behavioral reciprocity which appears in cultures around the world and is expressed in Christianity by Jesus' words "Do unto others as you would have them do unto you."

Greatest happiness principle For the utilitarian philosopher Jeremy Bentham (1748–1832), the "good" was no more and no less than human happiness. Thus his "greatest happiness principle" defines ethical behavior as that which "produces the greatest happiness (or pleasure) for the greatest number of people." More recently, in the media ethics field, this principle has been adapted to define ethical behavior as what produces the greatest good for the greatest number of people. See *utilitarian ethics* and *teleological ethics.*

Guerrilla marketing An unconventional way of executing promotions on a very low budget, e.g., street giveaways and displays, or other means of generating word-of-mouth marketing. The term was coined by Jay Conrad Levinson in his book *Guerrilla Marketing* (1984). These promotions are sometimes designed so that the target audience is left unaware they have been marketed to (also called stealth marketing). Guerrilla marketing tactics have been questioned ethically because of their tendency to be deceptive or misleading.

Guidelines for professional practice See *codes of ethics.*

Jürgen Habermas (b. 1929) German philosopher who came of age in the years following World War II. He stressed the importance of rational, mutual deliberation and saw this as a means to solve social problems and establish norms of behavior.

"Hate" speech Speech, writing, signs, gestures and works of art whose intent is to generate or stimulate public hatred of an individual, a group (such as adherents to a religion, a gender, an age cohort, a nationality, a race or ethnic group, supporters of a particular idea, etc.). Whether or not hate speech is under the protection of the First Amendment is a matter for debate. As beauty is in the eye of the beholder, hate speech typically is defined by those who object to it.

Hegemony A theory that Italian Marxist Antonio Gramsci developed to describe the circular process whereby people in power deepen their dominance by using culture to negotiate for the consent of those whom they control. Mass media are among the most powerful levers of hegemony and, according to Michael Dorsher's 1999 theory of hegemony online, the Internet is the most hegemonic medium of all, because it is the most cybernetic mass medium.

Humanistic stance An approach to ethics that emphasizes human welfare and dignity. See *professional stance.*

David Hume (1711–76) Scottish philosopher who stressed the preeminence of human emotion or "sentiment" over rationality in ethical behavior. See *personalist ethics.*

Information apartheid The notion that unequal access to media creates a disparity in the information available to citizens. In an information society, those citizens with less access to it will be economically, socially, and/or politically disadvantaged.

Infosphere See *cyberspace*.

Infotainment Media content that provides news and information but uses entertainment to attract audiences. The term is derived from the words "information" and "entertainment," reflecting the popularization (some would say "debasement") of information content. See Chapter 13.

Integrated marketing A management concept that is designed to make all aspects of marketing—advertising, sales promotion, public relations, and direct marketing—work together as a unified force. The goal is to create and sustain a single "look" or message in all elements of the marketing campaign, including packaging, positioning, promotions, pricing and distribution.

Intellectual property Ideas or information, products of the mind, that may be created or discovered and then bought, owned and sold. Intellectual property usually is distinguished from "real property" (land, etc.) or "personal property" ("things," including money, clothing, jewelry, furnishings, etc.). The right to intellectual property is inherent in Art. 1, Sec. 8, of the U.S. Constitution, which establishes a system of copyright (originally for written matter) and patents (for inventions). Musical compositions, trademarks, works of art in almost every medium and computer programs also are protected by copyright and patent as legal monopolies for a term of years, and it is even possible to patent living organisms. Although there is a legal exception called "fair use," it does not necessarily prevail against the rights of copyright owners, who now enjoy a very lengthy protection, particularly for written materials and items such as the cartoon character of Mickey Mouse, which Disney has been able to keep under copyright for nearly a century. Although there are international accords, there are substantial differences in the laws of various countries. Some, such as France, also recognize a moral right possessed by the creator of something, even though the commercial rights may have been sold.

Internet A worldwide network primarily for the interconnection of computers. Potentially, it is infinitely expandable. Any content that is convertible to digital form can be carried on the Internet—video, audio, e-mail, "one source to many receivers" shared data such as blogs, and social media. Content may be carried on any type of telecommunications device, from a copper wire to a space satellite circuit, and transmission can be two-way. While today the World Wide Web is commonly used for access to materials on the Internet (browsing), the evolution of the uses of this network has been very rapid, and—because it isn't under the control of a single entity—the Internet is perhaps the most free and flexible means of communication yet developed.

Intuitionism The idea that individual humans have a special instinct through which they can instantly and correctly resolve ethical questions. Critics say this is merely a cover for decisions based on prejudice or emotion.

Joint Operating Agreement (JOA) A contract authorized by the Newspaper Preservation Act of 1970, which exempts competing newspapers from anti-trust laws. It permits economies allowing both parties to continue to exist, even in a time of financial stress. Usually, all production (and sometimes classified sales, subscription fulfillment, etc.) is concentrated at one paper, but the newsrooms must be kept independent.

Kantian ethics An elaborate ethical system formulated by the Prussian philosopher Immanuel Kant (1724–1804). Kant believed that each person has an innate sense of Reason that he or she can apply to ethical questions. With this sense, we can discern a rule such as "do not steal," that must be applied in all situations and must be willed as universal law. Kant called this process the categorical imperative. In other words, we can act ethically by making our actions conform to a set of rules that we, as individuals, believe should be followed by everyone. Kant's ethics are *deontological* because he regarded ethical action as that which follows a categorical imperative or rule, regardless of the outcome. A central tenet of Kant's ethical system (often referred to as Kant's second categorical imperative) is that, as rational beings, people have intrinsic worth and dignity. For this reason, people must be treated as ends in themselves, never as the means to an end.

Laissez-faire Derived from the French phrase "let do," the economics term laissez-faire denotes a minimum of government involvement in the marketplace. Laissez-faire, neoclassical, and libertarian economic theories have been influential in the wave of media *deregulation* that began in the United States in the late 1970s.

Edmund Lambeth (b. 1932) American professor who argues that media ethics should be based on five principles: humaneness, truth, freedom, justice, and stewardship.

Harold Lasswell (1902–78) American scholar and political theorist who helped define the emerging field of mass communication. Lasswell defined propaganda as "the technique of influencing human action by the manipulation of representations." He believed that both advertising and publicity are propaganda.

Leak In media terms, this originally referred to someone within government or a corporation letting important (sometimes damning) inside information leak out to a reporter, often with the source demanding confidentiality to protect his or her job. More often now, however, government or corporate officials themselves leak information to favored reporters, while still demanding confidentiality to avoid embarrassment, in hope that the resulting story is favorable or to see how the public reacts to a proposal still under consideration—sometimes called a "trial balloon," a metaphor taken from weather forecasting experiments.

Lede The beginning of a news story—usually the first paragraph or two of a story (even if each is only a sentence long) but sometimes the first half dozen paragraphs of an in-depth story. Editors spell it that way to distinguish it from other things that are pronounced or spelled the same. It should contain the theme and other elements of a story.

Libel False statements that are broadcast or published that harm a person's reputation. See *defamation*.

John Locke (1632–1704) English philosopher who argued that governments have a "social contract" with the governed. The contract establishes the rights and responsibilities of the both the rulers and the ruled. This placed restraints on what were once believed to be the absolute powers of a monarch.

Logical positivism A form of rationalist philosophy that holds that valid knowledge about the world must be based on observable evidence.

Machiavellian ethics An approach to ethics based on the writings of the Florentine political philosopher Niccolò Machiavelli (1469–1527). In *The Prince*, he argued that, when necessary, rulers must skirt conventional morals to achieve the ends they desire. In other words, the end can justify the means. In contemporary media, this extreme form of *teleological ethics* justifies ignoring traditional and ethical standards to obtain information, create publicity, sell media products, or carry out other media functions that are deemed to be essential.

Market-driven journalism The integration of marketing values and journalism in a manner that journalism content reflects the interests of target audiences that advertisers wish to reach, and are willing to pay for the opportunity.

Mass media Although the earliest communications were interpersonal or point-to-point, when technologies (such as printing and radio) overcame the barriers of space, time, distance and need for multiple copies, today's mass media evolved. A *medium* becomes a mass medium when it reaches a large, typically undifferentiated audience (one whose members are not specifically selected by the originator of the message). There is no commonly accepted number of how many people a medium must reach to be considered "mass," but radio, television, newspapers, magazines, motion pictures, and Internet uses such as blogs are generally regarded as mass media. Occasionally, live performances—such as concerts—are so characterized. See *media/medium*.

Marketplace of ideas The notion of free, open, and healthy competition among diverse ideas. Adherents of the marketplace of ideas are optimistic that society will benefit from such competition because citizens will recognize superior ideas and be guided by them. This belief appears in the writings of John Milton and *John Stuart Mill*, and is a guiding principle in important 20th-century First Amendment decisions in the United States. The actual term "marketplace of ideas" did not appear in legal and philosophical discourse until the 1930s.

Media accountability systems (M*A*S) Approximately a dozen methods of holding *mass media* to account for their actions or inactions, often written about by Claude-Jean Bertrand. News councils, ombudsmen and codes of ethics are M*A*S, but so are such simple devices as publication of letters to the editor.

Media/Medium "Media" is the plural of "medium." A medium is something through which things travel. When applied to communication, it is most likely a channel of some sort (including the medium of print as well as a number of electronic media), or an environment, such as cyberspace, through which communication is transmitted or exchanged. See also *mass media*.

Media outlet A single station, newspaper or other mass media organization.

John C. Merrill (b. 1924) Professor Emeritus at the University of Missouri School of Journalism, former journalist, and an influential thinker on press freedom and journalistic ethics. He has authored or co-authored more than 30 books and 100 journal articles, traveled widely and received many honors. Merrill has contributed to this book in several ways (see Contents).

John Stuart Mill (1806–73) British philosopher and economist, and one of the best-known proponents of *utilitarian* philosophy. Unlike the utilitarian Jeremy Bentham, who regarded all forms of pleasure as equal, Mill distinguished between different forms of pleasure and argued that intellectual pleasure produces greater happiness than purely physical pleasure. Mill also figures prominently in media ethics because he was an influential advocate for free speech. He argued that society benefits from exposure to diverse and competing ideas and that even "wrong" ideas may contain a grain of truth.

Moral/morality Many philosophers and ethicists use the terms "morality" and "ethics" interchangeably. However, some thinkers use "morals" to denote a system of conduct practiced by a group or society, while using the term "ethics" to refer to the study or science of morals. Others apply "ethics" to the behavior of a group, and "morality" to individual standards. This confusion requires care in using any of these terms.

Moral development An approach to ethics which holds that individuals are capable of moving through a developmental process, from the lowest stage of ethics (based on instinct) to a middle level (based on custom) to the highest level (based on conscience). Lawrence Kohlberg (1927–87) refined this approach, drawing on the cognitive development theories of psychologist Jean Piaget (1896–1980) that children's moral judgment evolves through staged development. Kohlberg posited six stages of moral development, in three levels and with increasing emphasis on following rules and laws and seeking "justice," as the guide to ethical behavior. Carol Gilligan (b. 1936), an associate of Kohlberg, argued that his view of moral development—based on interviews only with males—ignores the female perspective, which considers interpersonal relationships, compassion and "caring" to be more important than rights and rules in defining ethical behavior. See *ethics of care*.

Natural law The belief that a natural order exists in the universe, independent of human action. According to some thinkers, including *John Locke* and Thomas Jefferson, humans can ascertain natural law and find that it contains basic human rights including the rights to life, liberty, and property.

Negative freedom Freedom from submitting to coercion. Negative freedom emphasizes that the individual possesses inviolable rights of autonomy and self-determination. Because these rights belong to everyone, it should be difficult for individuals to exert their will over others. Critics of extreme negative freedom argue that it undermines the possibility of concerted social action. The philosopher Isaiah Berlin contrasted negative freedom to *positive freedom*.

Net neutrality The idea that Internet service providers (ISPs) should make the Internet open and available to all users on a non-discriminatory basis (similar to being a *common carrier*). Advocates of this position argue that it is essential to provide for an open market for speech, ideas and commerce on the Internet and that failure to insure this would allow ISPs to discriminate against ideas or products they dislike—or against competitors for bandwidth.

Network An environment in which messages, message creators and multiple message recipients are interconnected. The contents of a network are neither finite, concrete or discrete. Everything in a network is fluid; it can be continually changed, expanded or combined with other material and other transmitters and receivers. In interpersonal communication, a network is a voluntary association of people; in broadcasting, it is a joining of a number of transmitters to provide the same programming to a wide audience.

New media Digital technologies that facilitate quick interactive feedback among many people alternately sending and receiving messages, such as the Internet, mobile telephones, cell phone cameras, and social media Web sites such as Facebook and Twitter. They are evolving in contrast to traditional, one-way *mass media* such as books, newspapers, magazines, radio, and television, where there is an elite set of message senders who offer few direct feedback opportunities to their many receivers. See *social media/social networking.*

Non-linear media Communication media that need not be viewed or used in one particular order, allowing users to pick and choose which pieces of content to access and when. The Web, mp3 players, and digital video recorders are more non-linear, for example, in contrast to linear media such as broadcast television, cassette tapes and videotapes where the ordering of content is determined by those in charge and is usually chronological.

Normative standard A standard that prescribes how things *ought* to be and how humans ought to behave. Normative standards can be contrasted with descriptive statements about the nature of reality.

Objectivity The practice of reporting the facts without the coloration of one's personal values. Despite many criticisms, including the inability of humans to be completely objective, objectivity remains the most influential model for professional journalists in the United States. See Chapter 15-A.

Obscenity In general discourse, obscenity refers to images, speech, or actions that offend due to their scatological, sexual, or blasphemous nature. But in United States law, "obscenity" specifically means material in which these characteristics are so extreme that it is beyond *First Amendment* protection. The currently controlling definition of obscenity in U.S. law comes from the Supreme Court's decision in *Miller* v. *California* (1973). To reach the level of obscenity, material must appeal to prurient interest; show patently offensive sexual conduct or excretory functions that are specifically defined by state law; and lack serious artistic, literary, political, or scientific value. "Indecency" is somewhat less offensive than obscenity; under the Communications Act of 1934, it applies only to broadcasting stations. "Blasphemy" is not against U.S. law.

Ombudsman Alternatively called a "reader's representative" or "public editor," ombudsmen (who may be women) act as a formal liaison between a media outlet's audience and its staff. According to the Web site of the Organization of News Ombudsmen, they receive and investigate audience complaints regarding "accuracy, fairness, balance and good taste in news coverage" and recommend "appropriate remedies or responses to correct or clarify news reports." Ombudsmen exist at both newspapers and broadcast stations, most commonly at newspapers. There, they frequently write a weekly column in which they summarize readers' complaints and staff members' responses about the ethics, accuracy and quality of the paper's journalism. Ombudsmen were once considered the conscience of good newspapers, but most owners now consider them a luxury, and fewer than 30 U.S. newspapers still have ombudsmen, though they are more plentiful in Western Europe. See *media accountability systems.*

Pack journalism When large numbers of journalists (reporters and/or photojournalists) swarm over the same story.

Pentagon Papers The United States Defense Department's secret history of U.S. involvement in Vietnam from 1945 to 1967. The papers were embarrassing for several U.S. administrations and when they were leaked to *The New York Times* and *The Washington Post*, President Richard Nixon sought an injunction to prevent publication. In *New York Times Co. v. U.S.* (1971), a major *First Amendment* case, the Supreme Court ruled in favor of the newspapers and against prior restraint of publication, at least in these circumstances.

Personalist ethics This broad category includes ethical practices that are based on intuitive, emotive, spiritual, non-rational and other highly personal moral factors. See *David Hume*.

Plato (428–347 B.C.) Greek philosopher, mathematician, and the author of *The Republic*, which presents his concept of the ideal state. Plato was a student of Socrates and a teacher of Aristotle, and founded the Academy in Athens (the Western world's first institution of higher education). He is perhaps best-known for his idea of the "philosopher-king" and for his Allegory of the Cave, in which chained prisoners are able to see "reality" only by watching the shadows on a wall of the cave.

Pop-up ad A Web ad that suddenly, without warning or request, appears on the computer monitor screen, obscuring the content the user was reading or viewing. In contrast to most Web sites, which are non-linear, pop-up ads are linear; as with TV commercials, Web users must wait for pop-up ads to finish loading before they can return to viewing their program or content.

Pop-up blockers Software programs that prevent ads from suddenly appearing and obscuring Web page content.

Positive freedom Freedom to accomplish. In this sense, one may exert one's will over others in order to achieve ends in the social or political sphere. In its extreme version, positive freedom for one person can mean coercion and dictatorship for others. See *negative freedom*.

Potter box A graphic representation of a process that allows one to work through various considerations in arriving at an ethical decision. The Potter Box is a rectangle, divided into four quadrants. In the order in which they are to be considered, the quadrants are: definition/facts; values; ethical principles; and loyalties. The box was conceived by Harvard theologian Ralph B. Potter, Jr. See "Tools for Ethical Decision-Making" (pp. 190–194).

Privacy Freedom from observation, intrusion, or the attention of others. Although people have long appreciated a general right to be left alone, the right to privacy received little legal recognition in the United States until the late 1800s. Since then, privacy law has developed into four distinct areas of protection: against intrusion into places where one has an expectation of privacy, such as the home; against the publication of private facts (even if true) that presumably offend the public; against publicity that portrays one in a false light; and against the appropriation of one's voice, image, or character for commercial purposes. With the intense attention paid to contemporary celebrities and with the information-gathering capabilities of modern media, the ethical and legal aspects of privacy present a complex challenge for media professionals.

Product placement When advertisers pay movie or television producers to use their product on camera—as an alternative to TV commercials, which consumers increasingly ignore, skip, or resent. A sub-species of this technique is the placement of billboards or other signs in range of cameras during sporting events. The Walt Disney Co. was one of the first to cultivate payment for product placement, in its films and television programs.

Professional stance   An approach to ethical problems that follows the rules and interests of the media worker, or the worker's organization or association, rather than broader concepts of human welfare and dignity. This stance can be contrasted with the *humanistic stance*.

Professionalism   Membership in a field of endeavor or an organization that has an organized body of knowledge; has control over entrance to its practice; expects its members to follow organizational codes despite external pressures; has the means to discipline those who violate the codes; and is imbued with the public interest.

Propaganda   A form of persuasive communication that attempts to influence human thoughts and actions by the manipulation of symbolic representations. The propagandist attempts to manipulate the audience, often deceitfully, in a way that benefits the propagandist's interests and ideas (or nation or political party), not necessarily for the audience's benefit.

Protonorm   A universal or generalized value, sometimes called a meta-tenet. In fields such as I.Q. testing, the development of protonorms has a technical statistical meaning. In less quantitative fields, such as communication ethics, typically a protonorm is global in scope and application, and self-evident regardless of culture or competing ideologies. *Clifford Christians*, who has written extensively on the use of protonorms in media ethics, has used "the primal sacredness of life" as an example of a protonorm. This field is early in its development, but may lead to global agreement on various truly basic aspects of communication ethics.

Public journalism   See *civic journalism*

Public Relations Society of America Code   The code of ethics formulated by the largest organization of public relations practitioners. The code states that PRSA members must uphold the highest standards of truth and accuracy.

Puffery   The writing technique advertisers use to try to manufacture "significant" distinctions in the mind of audience members between essentially identical products, such as aspirins or soaps. Empty or unsupported claims of a product being "the best" or "unbeaten" are examples of puffery, which essentially is meaningless.

RTDNA (Radio Television Digital News Association).   Before 2009, it was known as RTNDA (Radio-Television News Directors Association). An organization of news executives (and some in lower ranking positions) at American electronic media outlets. The organization strives to promote good journalistic and ethical practices among its members, and distributes its various *codes of ethics* widely, including one dealing with "Social media and blogging guidelines" issued in early 2010, ahead of other traditional news media organizations.

Rating   A measurement of the size of radio and television audiences. The rating is the percentage of all (including those with their sets turned off) radio or television households in a market that are tuned in to a particular program or station. A "ratings point" is 1% of all the radio or television households in that market (regardless of whether their sets are in use). Radio and television markets in the United States are both local (such as New York City or Los Angeles) and national. Commercial networks and stations use audience ratings and *shares* to set their advertising rates, since broadcasters are selling audiences ("eyeballs and eardrums") to advertisers. Other media use other means of audience measurement for the same purposes.

John Rawls (1921–2002) American philosopher who insisted that impartiality was a basic component of justice. To promote impartiality, Rawls proposed a thought experiment that he called "the original position." This meant that when choosing basic social arrangements, everyone should adopt a metaphorical *veil of ignorance* and act as if unaware of what his or her social position and interests would be in the future order. Rawls's philosophy thus emphasizes protecting the weakest party in any situation, since one could theoretically wind up as that weakest party.

Responsibility See *social responsibility theory.*

Secrecy Keeping information from others. It is the opposite of the concepts of *transparency* and openness. Secrecy can be and often is employed by individuals, groups, businesses or governments for their own purposes, using locked files, confidentiality oaths, and other formal or informal methods as well as legal restrictions. Because of the various exemptions contained in state open records (and open meetings) laws, it exists at all levels of state and local government. At the federal level, much information that the government keeps from the press and the public is "classified" as restricted, confidential, secret or top secret, with additions to this hierarchal list of classifications imposed by various agencies and by statute. There are a number of possible rationales for classifying information; the most common given in the United States is national security, which often is mirrored by secrecy intended to protect law enforcement activity. The disputed concept of executive privilege has been used by the President and others in the executive branch to keep internally distributed records and other papers secret. In the United States, Congress passed the Freedom of Information Act (FoIA) in 1966 to give greater access to government documents. However, FoIA contains nine major categories of exceptions which the government can still use to fend off the press and public.

Share Like the *rating*, the share is a common measure of radio and television audiences. It is the percentage of households with sets then in use that is tuned to a particular radio or television program, in a specific broadcast market and during a specific time period.

Shield law A law that protects a journalist"—in 39 states, as of early 2011—from being forced to reveal the identity of a *confidential source* to authorities. (Few shield laws provide absolute protection, either because they are written with some exemptions and/or because the courts jealously guard their right to everyone's testimony.)

Social contract See *John Locke*.

Social media/social networking Generally refers to applications that take advantage of the interactive attributes of a digital network to share quickly and easily content created by an individual with one or, more typically, many other individuals. More specifically, the term is used to describe such applications as Facebook, Twitter, YouTube and others, including some that will appear between the time this book goes to press and the time you're reading this entry.

Social responsibility theory The notion that the press (now taken to mean all news media) has an ethical responsibility to serve the welfare of society. In theory, this responsibility outweighs the obligation of both journalists and media executives to generate profits. Because it gives greater weight to the welfare of the general public than to the interests of media owners, the social responsibility theory reflects *utilitarian ethics*. In the United States, the social responsibility theory was prominently articulated by the *Commission on Freedom of the Press* in 1947, building on the thinking of other theorists of that time. Recent modifications of this theory have focused on the need for transparency, accountability and openness on the part of the press.

SPJ (Society of Professional Journalists) Although there are many trade organizations in the various media, SPJ (founded in 1909 as Sigma Delta Chi) is an association of individuals working in the news media, with a strong concern for ethics, free speech and press, diversity, and the free flow of information. Unlike many other such organizations, SPJ has both professional and student chapters.

Socrates (470-399 B.C.) Athenian-Greek philosopher known for his rigorous discussion of questions such as the nature of beauty and the nature of virtuous behavior. With his critical reflection on these earthly, human concerns, Socrates departed from the speculation about the unseen and the mystical that had dominated Greek philosophy. In Western societies, the tradition of critical examination of ethical questions may be said to have started with Socrates.

Spam Unsolicited e-mail advertisements sent in a bulk, scattershot approach. Even if fewer than 1% of the recipients respond by buying the product or service, it can be successful because there are no postage costs for e-mail and the number of potential customers reached is enormous. The name originally came from a homogenized canned meat product that was an often-unpopular staple in Army rations during World War II. (Today, its only connection to Hormel's spiced ham product SPAM® is metaphorical.)

I.F. Stone (1907-89) American journalist most famous for his self-published newspaper, *I.F. Stone's Weekly*. Stone was a master at finding obscure documents that revealed important—and often embarrassing—information about the government.

Cass Sunstein (b. 1954) Law professor and Obama Administration official who is concerned that online and specialized media enable people to insulate themselves from ideas that are new or which they might disagree with. Sunstein advocates the establishment of "deliberative domains" online where people are exposed to ideas from various points on the ideological and cultural spectrums.

Sweeps month Months when the surveys leading to radio and television ratings in all U.S. markets are taken, usually three times a year. The results of these ratings are used to set the rates charged advertisers by networks, stations and channels. (Ratings in large markets are taken more frequently.)

Targeted ad A *banner ad, pop-up ad* or other ad that is automatically customized for individual Web users, based on their particular history of online viewing and purchasing. To predict more accurately what goods and services individuals might buy online, each Web user's data are aggregated with those of people who have similar Web viewing and purchasing histories. Then each individual is automatically sent targeted ads for the same sorts of things their cohort was known to have bought.

Teleological ethics Also known as "consequentialist ethics." A concept based on the Greek word "telos" or "ends." The rightness of actions is judged on the outcomes they produce; an action that defies traditional rules can still be proper if it has a good outcome. Teleological ethical philosophies such as *utilitarianism* are often contrasted with *deontological* ethical systems such as *Kantian ethics*.

Time–place–manner The elements of a formula for determining whether *First Amendment* free speech rights may be curtailed. The courts have held that First Amendment protections for speech and press will prevail unless there would be unreasonable choices of timing, location and manner of presentation of that speech (e.g., using a bullhorn in a residential neighborhood at midnight).

Time-shifting When audience members record media programs and watch or listen at hours other than when they were originally broadcast. This practice became common among television viewers when home video cassette recorders gained popularity in the late 1970s. It has become even more pervasive with the emergence of *TiVo* and other *digital video recorders (DVRs)*.

TiVo A video recording device for the home that permits the owner to easily record programs for later playback as desired. It may also be used to remove and discard commercials automatically.

Tort A legal term, referring to an injury that leads to a civil lawsuit in which monetary damages may be sought.

Transparency This occurs when the workings of a person or organization are made visible to all. In media, it might mean that journalists are open about the processes through which stories are selected and information is gathered. (Professor Chris Roberts, now at the University of Alabama, delivered a paper at the 2007 AEJMC convention that contained a useful chart titled "Dimensions of Journalistic Message Transparency." The chart focused on 11 such dimensions such as evidence to support the story, error correction, etc., with a description and example of each in terms of whether it was "opaque," "translucent," or truly "transparent.") See *secrecy*.

Universal ethics A concept developed by ethicist *Clifford Christians* that respects both individual and collective rights, and focuses on the sacredness of life.

USA PATRIOT Act Acronym for the "Uniting and Strengthening America by Providing Appropriate Tools Required to Intercept and Obstruct Terrorism Act of 2001." Passed after the terrorist attacks of September 11, 2001, the Act increases the surveillance powers of law enforcement officials in the United States. Among the areas it opened to increased surveillance are telephone and e-mail communication, as well as financial and library records. Some sections of the law have been struck down as unconstitutional violations of privacy, and other aspects are still controversial.

Utilitarian ethics A system in which ethical behavior is described as that which maximizes happiness (a more tangible form of the vague concepts of "utility" or "good"). Its proponents generally agree that happiness should be accrued by as large a number of people as possible. However, they disagree on the equivalence of different forms of happiness. Utilitarian ethics is a *teleological* theory because it makes the attainment of human happiness more important than consistent adherence to rules. (As applied to media ethics, "happiness" is often equated with the less concrete concept of what might benefit identifiable individuals or groups.)

V-chip A device in television sets that allows adults to screen programs according to their ratings for sex and violence. The U.S. Congress mandated that, beginning in 2000, all new television sets 13 inches or longer must contain V-chips.

Veil of ignorance Philosopher *John Rawls* recommended that when members of a democratic society make decisions about its structure, they take an impartial stance. Rawls believed this could be done by adopting a "veil of ignorance": acting as if you are unaware of what position you will hold in society and what structure will best serve your personal interests.

Video news release (VNR) A video news or feature story that public relations practitioners produce for their employer or clients and send to the news media in hopes they will use it on their telecasts or Webcasts. It becomes unethical when neither the VNR producer nor the news channel identify the source as a PR professional rather than a journalist.

Virtue ethics Inspired by *Aristotle*, virtue ethics emphasizes personal virtue as the end to be achieved by ethical behavior. This is in contrast to utilitarian ethics, which defines ethical behavior as that which achieves the greatest human happiness, and to *Kantian ethics*, in which ethical behavior is defined by duty to rationally defined human rules.

Watergate The scandal that forced Richard Nixon to become the only U.S. president to resign the office, in 1974. It is named after the Watergate apartment and office complex in Washington that housed the Democratic National Committee office, site of a bungled burglary attempt by six Republican operatives. Two young *Washington Post* reporters, Bob Woodward and Carl Bernstein, traced the break-in to the White House. Woodward received crucial tips from an anonymous source nicknamed "Deep Throat." During this period, other media newsrooms also uncovered aspects of the story. President Nixon's resignation was a result of his "cover-up" of the Republican connection to the attempted burglary, and this demonstration of the power of the media led to a jump in the number of those who wished to join the profession. The "Deep Throat" mystery lasted until 2005, when ailing former FBI Associate Director Mark Felt said that he was the confidential source and Woodward and Bernstein—who originally had promised to keep the identity secret as long as "Deep Throat" was alive—confirmed it.

Fredric Wertham (1895-1981) German-born and educated American psychiatrist who claimed that images in comic books, television, and movies led to violence and sexual behavior among children. He was especially influential in the 1950s and his book *Seduction of the Innocent* (1954) led to a Senate investigation of the comic book industry.

Whistleblower Someone within an organization who alerts the media or government (or possibly shareholders or management) to misdeeds by that organization.

Bibliography

This limited bibliography includes the most important and widely useful sources of those appearing at the end of every chapter and overview. In addition, it provides a number of sources relevant to the issues discussed in this book but not specifically cited in any of the chapters. It usually shows the most recent edition of each standard work, even if an earlier edition was cited in the References and Related Readings at the end of a chapter. (Citations to online or periodical sources mostly are to be found at the ends of chapters, and some topics—such as game theory—are omitted from this bibliography. Mergers and acquisitions in the book publishing industry may make it difficult to locate a volume by the name of its publisher. For example, in this bibliography there are two different publishers with the name of Free Press, and Lawrence Erlbaum Associates is now part of Taylor & Francis.)

Altschull, J. Herbert. (1996). *From Milton to McLuhan: The Ideas Behind American Journalism*. New York: Longman.

Anderson, Kent. (1978). *Television Fraud: The History and Implications of the Quiz Show Scandals*. Westport, CT: Greenwood.

Andison, F. Scott. (1977). "TV violence and viewer aggression: A cumulation of study results 1956–1976." *Public Opinion Quarterly* 41(3), pp. 314–331.

Aristotle. (Many editions). *Nicomachean Ethics*.

Arnett, Ronald C., Janie M. Harden Fritz, and Leeanne M. Bell. (2009). *Communication Ethics Literacy: Dialogue and Difference*. Thousand Oaks, CA: Sage.

Arthur, John, and Steven Scalet, eds. (2009). *Morality and Moral Controversies: Readings in Moral, Social and Political Philosophy*, 8th ed. Upper Saddle River, NJ: Prentice Hall.

Auletta, Ken. (1991). *Three Blind Mice: How the TV Networks Lost Their Way*. New York: Random House.

——. (2009). *Googled: The End of the World as We Know It*. New York: Penguin.

Bagdikian, Ben H. (1989). "The Lords of the Global Village." *The Nation*, June 12, pp. 805–820.

——. (2004). *The New Media Monopoly*. Boston, MA: Beacon.

Baker, Lee W. (1993). *The Credibility Factor: Putting Ethics to Work in Public Relations*. Homewood, IL: Business One Irwin.

Barbour, William, ed. (1994). *Mass Media: Opposing Viewpoints*. San Diego, CA: Greenhaven.

Barron, Jerome A. (1973). *Freedom of the Press for Whom?* Bloomington, IN: Indiana University Press.

Benedict, Helen. (1992). *Virgin or Vamp: How the Press Covers Sex Crimes*. New York: Oxford University Press.

Bentham, Jeremy. (1823). *An Introduction to the Principles of Morals and Legislation*. Oxford: Clarendon Press.

Berger, Arthur Asa. (2007). *Ads, Fads, and Consumer Culture: Advertising's Impact on American Character and Society*, 3rd ed. Lanham, MD: Rowman & Littlefield.

Berry, David. (2008). *Journalism, Ethics and Society*. Farnham, UK: Ashgate.

Bertrand, Claude-Jean. (2000). *Media Ethics and Accountability Systems*. New Brunswick, NJ: Transaction.

——. (2003). *Accountability Systems*. Cresskill, NJ: Hampton.

Bivins, Thomas H. (2009). *Mixed Media: Moral Distinctions in Advertising, Public Relations, and Journalism*, 2nd ed. New York: Routledge.

Black, Jay. (1995). "Commentary: Rethinking the naming of sex crime victims." *Newspaper Research Journal* 16(3), pp. 96–112.

——, ed. (1997). *Mixed News: The Public/Civic/Communitarian Journalism Debate*. Mahwah, NJ: Lawrence Erlbaum Associates.

Black, Jay, and Ralph Barney. (1985–86). "The case against mass media codes of ethics." *Journal of Mass Media Ethics* 1(1), pp. 27–36.

Black, Jay, Bob Steele, and Ralph Barney. (1999). *Doing Ethics in Journalism: A Handbook with Case Studies*, 3rd ed. Boston, MA: Allyn & Bacon.

Black, Jay and Chris Roberts. (2011). *Doing Ethics in Media: Theories and Practical Applications*. New York: Routledge.

Boeyink, David. (1994). "How effective are codes of ethics? A look at three newsrooms." *Journalism Quarterly* 71(4), pp. 893–904.

Bogart, Leo. (1995). *Commercial Culture: The Media System and the Public Interest*. New York: Oxford University Press.

Bok, Sissela. (1982). *Secrets: On the Ethics of Concealment and Revelation*. New York: Pantheon.

——. (1999). *Lying: Moral Choice in Public and Private Life*, 3rd ed. New York: Vintage.

Boorstin, Daniel J. (1961). *The Image: A Guide to Pseudo-Events in America*. New York: Harper & Row. (Several editions).

Branscomb, Anne Wells. (1994). *Who Owns Information? From Privacy to Public Access*. New York: Basic Books.

Breed, Warren. (1955). "Social control in the newsroom." *Social Forces* 33(4), pp. 326–335.

Brewer, Marcus, and Maxwell McCombs. (1996). "Setting the community agenda." *Journalism & Mass Communication Quarterly* 73(1), pp. 7–16.

Broun, Heywood. (1927). "Censorship." In Heywood Broun and Margaret Leach, *Anthony Comstock: Roundsman of the Lord*. New York: Boni & Liveright.

Brown, Fred, ed. *Journalism Ethics: A Casebook of Professional Conduct for News Media*, 4th ed. Portland, OR: Marion Street Press.

Bryant, Jennings. (1993). "Will traditional media research paradigms be obsolete in the era of intelligent communication networks?" In Philip Gaunt, ed., *Beyond Agendas: New Directions in Communication Research*. Westport, CT: Greenwood, pp. 149–167.

Bugeja, Michael J. (1996). *Living Ethics: Developing Values in Mass Communication*. Boston, MA: Allyn & Bacon.

——. (2008). *Living Ethics: Across Media Platforms*. New York: Oxford University Press.

Byrd, Joann. (1992). "Fair's fair—Unless it isn't." *Media Studies Journal* Fall, pp. 103–112. (This entire issue is devoted to "The Fairness Factor.")

Cathcart, Thomas, and Daniel Klein. (2006). *Plato and a Platypus Walk into a Bar...: Understanding Philosophy through Jokes*. New York: Abrams Image.

Christians, Clifford G., John P. Ferré, and P. Mark Fackler. (1993). *Good News: Social Ethics and the Press*. New York: Oxford University Press.

Christians, Clifford G., Mark Fackler, Kathy Brittain McKee, Peggy J. Kreshel, and Robert H. Woods, Jr. (2009). *Media Ethics: Cases and Moral Reasoning*, 8th ed. Boston, MA: Pearson/Allyn & Bacon.

Commission on Freedom of the Press. (1947). *A Free and Responsible Press*. Chicago, IL: University of Chicago Press.

Compaine, Benjamin M., and Douglas Gomery, eds. (2000). *Who Owns the Media? Competition and Concentration in the Mass Media Industry*, 3rd ed. Mahwah, NJ: Lawrence Erlbaum Associates.

Comstock, George, Steven Chaffee, Natan Katzman, Maxwell McCombs, and Donald Roberts. (1978). *Television and Human Behavior*. New York: Columbia University Press.

Cooper, Thomas W., Clifford G. Christians, Frances Forde Plude, and Robert A. White. (1989). *Communication Ethics and Global Change*. White Plains, NY: Longman.

Cooper, Thomas W., Clifford G. Christians, and Anantha S. Babbili. (2008). *An Ethics Trajectory: Visions of Media Past, Present and Yet to Come*, edited by John Michael Kittross. Urbana, IL: Institute of Communications Research, University of Illinois.

Craig, David (2006). *The Ethics of the Story: Using Narrative Techniques Responsibly in Journalism*. Latham, MD: Rowman & Littlefield.

Crisp, Roger. (1977). *Mill on Utilitarianism*. London: Routledge.

Crossley, Nick and John Michael Roberts, eds. (2004). *After Habermas: New Perspectives on the Public Sphere*. Oxford, UK: Blackwell.

Dates, Jannette L., and William Barlow. (1990). *Split Image: African Americans in the Mass Media*. Washington, DC: Howard University Press.

Dawson, Miles M., ed. (1932). *The Wisdom of Confucius*. Boston, MA: International Pocket Library.

Day, Louis A. (2006). *Ethics in Modern Communications: Cases and Controversies*, 5th ed. Belmont, CA: Thomson Wadsworth.

Dennis, Everette E., and John C. Merrill. (1996). *Media Debates: Issues in Mass Communication*, 2nd ed. White Plains, NY: Longman.

Dennis, Everette E., Arnold H. Ismach, and Donald M. Gillmor, eds. (1978). *Enduring Issues in Mass Communication*. St. Paul, MN: West.

Dewey, John. (1927, reprinted 1991). *The Public and its Problems*. Athens, OH: Swallow Press.

Diamond, Edwin, and Robert A. Silverman. (1995). *White House to Your House: Media and Politics in Virtual America*. Cambridge, MA: MIT Press.

Downie, Leonard, Jr., and Michael Schudson (2009). "The reconstruction of American journalism." *Columbia Journalism Review* November–December, pp. 28–51.

Duska, Ronald, and Mariellen Whelan. (1975). *Moral Development: A Guide to Piaget and Kohlberg*. New York: Paulist Press.

Dworkin, Andrea, and Catharine A. MacKinnon. (1988). *Pornography and Civil Rights: A New Day for Women's Equality*. Minneapolis, MN: Organizing Against Pornography.

Edwards, Audrey. (1993). "From Aunt Jemima to Anita Hill: Media's split image of black women." *Media Studies Journal* 7(2), pp. 215–222.

Elliott, Deni, ed. (1986). *Responsible Journalism*. Newbury Park, CA: Sage.

——. (1987). "Creating conditions for ethical journalism." *Mass Communication Review* 14(3), pp. 6–10.

Entman, Robert M., and Andrew Rojecki. (2000). *The Black Image in the White Mind: Media and Race in America*. Chicago, IL: University of Chicago Press.

Ernst, Morris L., and Alan U. Schwartz. (1962). *Privacy: The Right to be Let Alone*. New York: Macmillan.

Etzioni, Amitai. (1993). *The Spirit of Community: Rights, Responsibilities, and the Communitarian Agenda*. New York: Crown.

Federal Communications Commission. (1965). "Memorandum opinion and order in re-application of Pacifica Foundation for Renewal of Licenses of Station KPFA-FM and KPFB (January 2, 1964)," reprinted as "The 'Pacifica' Decision: Broadcasting and Free Expression." *Journal of Broadcasting* 9(2), pp. 177–182.

Fink, Conrad C. (1988). *Media Ethics: In the Newsroom and Beyond*. New York: McGraw-Hill.

Fletcher, Joseph. (1966). *Situation Ethics: The New Morality*. Philadelphia, PA: Westminster Press.

Free Press. (2009). *Changing Media: Public Interest Policies for the Digital Age*. Northampton, MA: Free Press Action Fund.

Friend, Cecilia, and Jane B. Singer. (2007). *Online Journalism Ethics: Traditions and Transitions*. Armonk, NY: M. E. Sharpe.

Gant, Scott. (2007). *We're All Journalists Now: The Transformation of the Press and Reshaping of the Law in [the] Internet Age*. New York: Free Press.

Gardner, Howard, Mihaly Csikszentmihalyi, and William Damon. (2001). *Good Work: When Excellence and Ethics Meet*. New York: Basic Books.

Gilligan, Carol. (1982). *In a Different Voice*. Cambridge, MA: Harvard University Press.

Gillmor, Dan. (2004). *We the Media: Grassroots Journalism by the People, for the People*. Sebastopol, CA: O'Reilly Media.

Glazer, Nathan, and Daniel Patrick Moynihan. (1963). *Beyond the Melting Pot*. Cambridge, MA: MIT Press.

Good, Howard, ed. (2008). *Journalism Ethics Goes to the Movies*. Lanham, MD: Rowman & Littlefield.

Goodwin, H. E., and Ron F. Smith. (1996). *Groping for Ethics in Journalism*, 3rd ed. Ames, IA: Iowa State University Press. (See Smith, Ron F. (2009) for 6th ed.)

Greenberg, Karen Joy, ed. (1991). *Conversations on Communication Ethics*. Norwood, NJ: Ablex.

Habermas, Jürgen. (1989). *The Structural Transformation of the Public Sphere*, translated by T. Burger and F. Lawrence. Cambridge, MA: MIT Press. (German ed., 1962.)

Hatley, Donald W., and Paula Furr, eds. (2007). *Freedom Fighter: A Festschrift Honoring John C. Merrill on His Six Decades of Service to Journalism Education*. Natchitoches, LA: Northwestern State University Press.

Hausman, Carl. (1992). *Crisis of Conscience: Perspectives on Journalism Ethics*. New York: HarperCollins.

Hazlitt, Henry. (1972). *The Foundations of Morality*. Los Angeles, CA: Nash.

Henry, William A., III. (1994). *In Defense of Elitism*. New York: Doubleday.

Hilliard, Robert. (2009). *Hollywood Speaks Out: Pictures that Dared to Protest Real World Issues*. Chichester, UK: Wiley-Blackwell.

Hobbes, Thomas. (1950). *Leviathan*. New York: E. P. Dutton.

Hodges, Louis. (1994). "The journalist and privacy." *Journal of Mass Media Ethics* 9(4), pp. 235–242.

Huff, Darryl. (1954). *How to Lie with Statistics*. New York: Norton.

Hulteng, John L. (1985). *The Messenger's Motives*. Englewood Cliffs, NJ: Prentice-Hall.

Iggers, Jeremy. (1998). *Good News, Bad News: Journalism Ethics and the Public Interest*. Boulder, CO: Westview.

Jaksa, James, and Michael S. Pritchard. (2004). *Communication Ethics: Methods of Analysis*. Belmont, CA: Wadsworth.

Jaspers, Karl. (1957). *Socrates, Buddha, Confucius, Jesus: The Paradigmatic Individuals*, edited by Hannah Arendt. San Diego, CA: Harcourt Brace Jovanovich.

Johannesen, Richard L., Kathleen S. Valde, and Karen E. Whedbee. (2008). *Ethics in Human Communication*, 6th ed. Long Grove, IL: Waveland.

Johnstone, J. W. C., E. J. Slawski, and W. W. Bowman. (1976). *The News People: A Sociological Portrait of American Journalists*. Urbana, IL: University of Illinois Press.

Jones, J. Clement. (1980). *Mass Media Codes of Ethics and Councils*. Paris: Unesco Press.

Journal of Mass Media Ethics. (1985–86). 1(1). (The entire issue is devoted to discussions of media ethics codes.)

Kant, Immanuel. (1998). *Groundwork of the Metaphysics of Morals*, trans. Mary J. Gregor. Cambridge, UK: Cambridge University Press. (Original German ed., 1785.)

Kapor, Mitchell. (1993). "Where is the digital highway really heading?" *Wired* July–August, pp. 53–59.

Keeble, Richard, ed. (2008). *Communication Ethics Now*. London: Troubador.

Kidder, Rushworth. (1995). *How Good People Make Tough Choices*. New York: William Morrow.

Kieran, Matthew. (1997). *Media Ethics: A Philosophical Approach*. Westport, CT: Praeger.

Knowlton, Steven R. (1997). *Moral Reasoning for Journalists: Cases and Comments*. Westport, CT: Praeger.

Knowlton, Steven R., and Patrick R. Parsons. (1995). *The Journalist's Moral Compass: Basic Principles*. Westport, CT: Praeger.

Kohlberg, Lawrence. (1981). *The Philosophy of Moral Development: Moral Stages and the Idea of Justice*. New York: Harper & Row.

Korzybski, Alfred. (1933). *Science and Sanity: An Introduction to Non-Aristotelian Systems and General Semantics*. Lancaster, PA: Science Press.

Kovach, Bill, and Tom Rosenstiel. (2001). *The Elements of Journalism: What Newspeople Should Know and the Public Should Expect*. New York: Three Rivers Press.

Krasnow, Erwin G., Lawrence D. Longley, and Herbert A. Terry. (1982). *The Politics of Broadcast Regulation*, 3rd ed. New York: St. Martin's Press.

Kubey, Robert, ed. (1997). *Media Literacy in the Information Age: Current Perspectives*. New Brunswick, NJ: Transaction.

Kuttner, Robert. (1997). *Everything for Sale: The Virtues and Limits of Markets*. New York: Knopf.

Lacy, Stephen, Esther Thorson and John Russial, guest editors. (2004). *Newspaper Research Journal: Special Issue—Good Journalism, Good Business*. 25(1), pp. 1–109.

Lambeth, Edmund B. (1992). *Committed Journalism: An Ethic for the Profession*, 2nd ed. Bloomington and Indianapolis, IN: Indiana University Press.

Lambeth, Edmund B., Philip E. Meyer, and Esther Thorson, eds. (1998). *Assessing Public Journalism*. Columbia, MO: University of Missouri Press.

Land, Mitchell, and Bill Hornaday, eds. (2006). *Contemporary Media Ethics: A Practical Guide for Students, Scholars and Professionals*. Spokane, WA: Marquette.

Lashner, Marilyn A. (1984). *The Chilling Effect in TV News: Intimidation by the Nixon White House*. New York: Praeger.

Lebacqz, Karen. (1985). *Professional Ethics: Power and Paradox*. Nashville, TN: Abingdon Press.

Lester, Paul Martin, ed. (1991). *Photojournalism: An Ethical Approach*. Mahwah, NJ: Lawrence Erlbaum Associates.

——. (1996). *Images that Injure: Pictorial Stereotypes in the Media*. Westport, CT: Praeger.

Levitt, Theodore. (1970). "The morality (?) of advertising." *Harvard Business Review* July–August, pp. 84–92.

Liebling, A. J. (1961). *The Press*. New York: Ballantine.

Limburg, Val E. (1994). *Electronic Media Ethics*. Boston, MA: Focal Press.

Lippmann, Walter. (1922). *Public Opinion*. New York: Macmillan.

Locke, John. (1690, reprinted 1980). *Second Treatise of Government*. Indianapolis, IN: Hackett.

Loevinger, Lee. (1968). "The ambiguous mirror: The reflective-projective theory of broadcasting and mass communication." *Journal of Broadcasting* 12(2), pp. 97–116.

Lowrey, Wilson and Peter J. Gade, eds. (2011). *Changing the News: The Forces Shaping Journalism in Uncertain Times*. New York: Routledge.

MacBride, Sean. (1980). *Many Voices, One World: Towards a New More Just and More Efficient World Information and Communication Order*. London: Kogan Page; New York: Unipub; Paris: UNESCO.

Machiavelli, Niccolò. (Many editions). *The Prince*.

MacIntyre, Alasdair. (1966). *A Short History of Ethics*. New York: Random House.

MacKinnon, Catharine A. (1993). *Only Words*. Cambridge, MA: Harvard University Press.

Makau, Josina M., and Ronald C. Arnett, eds. (1997). *Communication Ethics in an Age of Diversity*. Urbana, IL: University of Illinois Press.

Marks, Jeffrey. (1989). "New improved RTNDA ethics code!" *Media Ethics Update* 2(1), p. 6. See also Kittross, John M. (1988). "New, improved RTNDA ethics code?" *Media Ethics Update* 1(1), pp. 5, 10; Kittross, John M. (1989). "Round three: Response to Marks." *Media Ethics Update* 2(1), pp. 7, 16–17.

Matelski, Marilyn. (1991). *TV News Ethics*. Boston, MA: Focal Press.

McChesney, Robert W. (2004). *The Problem of the Media: U.S. Communication Politics in the 21st Century*. New York: Monthly Review Press.

———. (2007). *Communication Revolution: Critical Junctures and the Future of Media*. New York: New Press.

McChesney, Robert W., and John Nichols. (2004). *Our Media, Not Theirs: The Democratic Struggle Against Corporate Media*. New York: Seven Stories Press.

———. (2010). *The Death and Life of American Journalism: The Media Revolution that Will Begin the World Again*. New York: Nation Books.

McCord, Richard. (1996). *The Chain Gang: One Newspaper versus the Gannett Empire*. Columbia, MO: University of Missouri Press.

McCulloch, Frank, ed. (1984). *Drawing the Line: How 31 Editors Solved Their Toughest Ethics Dilemmas*. Washington, DC: American Society of Newspaper Editors Foundation.

McElreath, Mark P. (1993). *Managing Systematic and Ethical Public Relations*. Dubuque, IA: Brown & Benchmark.

Merrill, John C. (1974). *The Imperative of Freedom: A Philosophy of Journalistic Autonomy*. New York: Hastings House.

———. (1993). *The Dialectic in Journalism: Toward a Responsible Use of Press Freedom*. Baton Rouge, LA: Louisiana State University Press.

———. (1994). *Legacy of Wisdom: Great Thinkers and Journalism*. Ames, IA: Iowa State University Press.

———. (1995). *Existential Journalism*, rev. ed. Ames, IA: Iowa State University Press.

———. (1997). *Journalism Ethics: Philosophical Foundations for News Media*. New York: St. Martin's Press.

———. (1998). *The Princely Press: Machiavelli on American Journalism*. Lanham, MD: University Press of America.

———. (2010). *Farewell to Freedom: Impact of Communitarianism on Individual Rights in the 21st Century*. Spokane, WA: Marquette Books.

Merrill, John C., Peter J. Gade, and Frederick P. Blevins. (2001). *Twilight of Press Freedom: The Rise of People's Journalism*. Mahwah, NJ: Lawrence Erlbaum Associates.

Meyer, Philip. (1983). *Editors, Publishers, and Newspaper Ethics*. Washington, DC: American Society of Newspaper Editors.

———. (1991). *Ethical Journalism: A Guide for Students, Practitioners, and Consumers*. Lanham, MD: University Press of America.

———. (2006). *Newspaper Ethics in the New Century*. Reston, VA: American Society of Newspaper Editors.

Mill, John Stuart. (Many editions). *On Liberty*.

———. (Many editions). *Utilitarianism*.

Miller, Arthur. (1971). *The Assault on Privacy: Computers, Data Banks, and Dossiers*. Ann Arbor, MI: University of Michigan Press.

Mitchell, William J. (1992). *The Reconfigured Eye: Visual Truth in the Post-Photographic Era*. Cambridge, MA: MIT Press.

Moore, Roy L., and Michael D. Murray. (2007). *Media Law and Ethics*, 3rd ed. New York: Routledge.

Newman, Jay. (1989). *The Journalist in Plato's Cave*. Cranbury, NJ: Associated University Presses.

Newton, Julianne H. (2000). *The Burden of Visual Truth: The Role of Photojournalism in Mediating Reality*. New York: Routledge.

Nietzsche, Freiderich. (Many editions). *Beyond Good and Evil*.

Noddings, Nel. (2002). *Educating Moral People: A Caring Alternative to Character Education*. New York: Teachers College Press.

Nordenstreng, Kaarle, ed. (1995). *Reports on Media Ethics in Europe*. Tampere, Finland: Department of Journalism and Mass Communication, University of Tampere (Series B 41). Or see special issue of the *European Journal of Communication* (4/1995, pp. 435–558), edited by Kaarle Nordenstreng.

Packard, Vance. (1981). *The Hidden Persuaders*. New York: Pocket Books.

Parenti, Michael. (1992). *Make-Believe Media: The Politics of Entertainment*. New York: St. Martin's Press.

Patterson, Philip, and Lee Wilkins. (2005). *Media Ethics: Issues and Cases*, 5th ed. New York: McGraw-Hill.

Paul, Ellen Frankel, Fred D. Miller, Jr., and Jeffrey Paul, eds. (2000). *The Right to Privacy*. Cambridge, UK: Cambridge University Press.

Pavlik, John V., and Shawn McIntosh. (2003). *Converging Media: Introduction to Mass Communication in the Digital Age*. Boston, MA: Allyn & Bacon.

Peck, Robert S. (2002). *Libraries, the First Amendment, and Cyberspace*. Chicago, IL: American Library Association.

Peikoff, Leonard. (1983). *Ominous Parallels*. Briarcliff Manor, NY: Stein & Day.

Pember, Don. (1972). *Privacy and the Press*. Seattle, WA: University of Washington Press.

Perebinossoff, Philippe. (2008). *Real-World Media Ethics*. Burlington, MA: Focal Press.

Piaget, Jean. (1932). *The Moral Judgment of the Child*. Glencoe, IL: Free Press.

Pickard, Victor, John Stearns, and Craig Aarons. (2009). *Saving the News: Toward a National Journalism Strategy*. New York: Free Press.

Plaisance, Patrick Lee. (2009). *Media Ethics: Key Principles for Responsible Practice*. Thousand Oaks, CA: Sage.

Postman, Neil. (1985). *Amusing Ourselves to Death*. New York: Viking.

Postman, Neil, and Steve Powers. (2008). *How to Watch TV News*. New York: Penguin.

Preston, Ivan L. (1996). *The Great American Blowup: Puffery in Advertising and Selling*. Madison, WI: University of Wisconsin Press.

Rachels, James. (1986). *The Elements of Moral Philosophy*. New York: Random House.

Radio Television Digital News Association. (2010). "Social media and blogging guidelines." February 6.

Radio-Television News Directors Association. (2008). "Guidelines for avoiding conflict of interest." October 10, 2008. Reprinted in *Media Ethics* 2009, 20(2), pp. 8–9.

Rand, Ayn. (1964). *The Virtue of Selfishness*. New York: New American Library.

Rawls, John. (1971). *A Theory of Justice*. Cambridge, MA: Belknap. (Republished by Harvard University Press, 2005.)

Reaves, Shiela. (1992–93). "What's wrong with this picture? Daily newspaper photo editors' attitudes and their tolerance toward digital manipulation." *Newspaper Research Journal* 13(4)–14(1), pp. 131–155.

Rest, James. (1979). *Development in Judging Moral Issues*. Minneapolis, MN: University of Minnesota Press.

Ritchin, Fred. (1990). *In Our Own Image: The Coming Revolution in Photography*. New York: Aperture Foundation.

Rivers, William L., and Cleve Mathews. (1988). *Ethics for the Media*. Englewood Cliffs, NJ: Prentice Hall.

Rosen, Jay. (1999). *What Are Journalists For?* New Haven, CT: Yale University Press.

Rosen, Jay, and Davis Merritt, Jr. (1994). "Public journalism: Theory and practice." Occasional paper of the Kettering Foundation, Dayton, OH.

Rubin, Bernard, ed. (1978). *Questioning Media Ethics*. New York: Praeger.

Sanders, Willemien. (2010). "Documentary filmmaking and ethics: Concepts, responsibilities, and the need for empirical research." *Mass Communication and Society* 13(5), pp. 528–553.

Sartre, Jean-Paul. (1957). *Existentialism and Human Emotions*. New York: Philosophical Library.

Sauter, Van Gordon. (1989). "In defense of tabloid TV." *TV Guide*, August 5, pp. 2–4.

Schramm, Wilbur. (1949). "The nature of news." *Journalism Quarterly* 26(3), pp. 259-269.

Schudson, Michael. (1984). *Advertising, The Uneasy Persuasion: Its Dubious Impact on American Society*. New York: Basic Books.

Seib, Philip. (1994). *Campaigns and Conscience: The Ethics of Political Journalism*. Westport, CT: Praeger.

Serafini, Anthony. (1989). *Ethics and Social Concern*. New York: Paragon.

Sheehan, Kim Bartel. (2004). *Controversies in Contemporary Advertising*. Thousand Oaks, CA: Sage.

Shepard, Alicia C. (1994). "Legislating ethics." *American Journalism Review*, January–February, pp. 37–41.

Siebert, Fred S., Theodore Peterson, and Wilbur Schramm. (1956). *Four Theories of the Press*. Urbana, IL: University of Illinois Press.

Silha Center for the Study of Media Ethics and Law. (1998). *Media Ethics and Law Conference Book*. Minneapolis, MN: Silha Center, University of Minnesota.

Sinclair, Upton. (2003). *The Brass Check: A Study of American Journalism*. Urbana, IL: University of Illinois Press. (Reprint of 9th ed., published 1928 in Long Beach, CA, by the author.)

Smith, Adam. (1759). *The Theory of Moral Sentiments*. Oxford, UK: Clarendon Press.

Smith, Anthony. (1980). *The Geopolitics of Information*. New York: Oxford University Press.

Smith, Robert E. (1969). "They still write it white." *Columbia Journalism Review* Spring, pp. 36–38.

Smith, Ron F. (2009). *Ethics in Journalism*, 6th ed. Malden, MA: Blackwell.

Solove, Daniel J., Marc Rotenberg, and Paul M. Schwartz. (2006). *Privacy, Information and Technology*. New York: Aspen.

Squires, James D. (1993). *Read All About It!:The Corporate Takeover of America's Newspapers*. New York: Times Books.

Strossen, Nadine. (2000). *Defending Pornography: Free Speech, Sex, and the Fight for Women's Rights*. New York: New York University Press.

Surgeon General's Scientific Advisory Committee on Television and Social Behavior. (1972). *Television and Growing Up: The Impact of Televised Violence*. Washington, DC: U.S. Government Printing Office.

Tannenbaum, Percy, and Mervin Lynch. (1960). "Sensationalism: The content and its measurement." *Journalism Quarterly* 37(2), pp. 381–392.

Tuchman, Gaye. (1978). *Making News: A Study in the Construction of Journalism*. New York: Free Press.

Turow, Joseph. (1992). *Media Systems in Society*. New York: Longman.

——. (2010). *Media Today: An Introduction to Mass Communication*. New York: Routledge.

Twitchell, James B. (1989). *Preposterous Violence: Fables of Aggression in Modern Culture*. New York: Oxford University Press.

Ward, Stephen J. A. (2004). *The Invention of Journalism Ethics: The Path to Objectivity and Beyond*. Montreal: McGill-Queens' University Press.

——. (2010).*Global Journalism Ethics*. Montreal: McGill-Queens' University Press.

Ward, Stephen J. A. and Herman Wasserman, eds. (2010). *Media Ethics Beyond Borders: A Global Perspective*. New York: Routledge.

Warren, Samuel D., and Louis D. Brandeis. (1890). "The right to privacy." *Harvard Law Review* 4(5), pp. 193–220.

Weaver, David H., Randal A. Beam, Bonnie J. Brownlee, Paul S. Voakes, and G. Cleveland Wilhoit. (2006). *The American Journalist in the 21st Century: U.S. News People at the Dawn of a New Millennium*. Mahwah, NJ: Lawrence Erlbaum Associates.

Wheeler, Tom. (2002). *Phototruth or Photofiction: Ethics and Media Imagery in the Digital Age*. Mahwah, NJ: Lawrence Erlbaum Associates.

Wicker, Tom. (1971). "The greening of the press." *Columbia Journalism Review*, May–June, pp. 7–12.

Wilkins, Lee, and Clifford G. Christians, eds. (2009). *The Handbook of Mass Media Ethics*. New York: Routledge.

Wilkins, Lee and Renita Coleman. (2005). The Moral Media: How Journalists Reason About Ethics. Mahwah, NJ: Lawrence Erlbaum Associates.

Williams, Frederick, and John V. Pavlik, eds. (1994). *The People's Right to Know: Media, Democracy and the Information Highway*. Hillsdale, NJ: Lawrence Erlbaum Associates.

Willis, W. J. (Jim). (1991). *The Shadow World: Life Between the News Media and Reality*. New York: Praeger.

Wilson, James Q. (1993). *The Moral Sense*. New York: Free Press.

Wong, David B. (2004). *Confucian Ethics: A Comparative Study of Self, Autonomy and Community*, edited by Kwong-loi Shun and David B Wong. Cambridge, UK: Cambridge University Press.

PERIODICALS FOCUSING ON MEDIA ETHICS

American Journalism Review, 0222 Tawes Hall, University of Maryland, College Park, MD 20742-7111, USA.

Columbia Journalism Review, 700 Journalism Building, Columbia University, 2950 Broadway, New York, NY 10027, USA.

Ethical Space, International Journal of Communication Ethics, Abramis Academic, ASK House, Northgate Avenue, Bury St. Edmunds, Suffolk IP32 6BB, UK.

Extra! The Magazine of FAIR (Fairness and Accuracy in Reporting), Suite 10B,104 W. 27th Street, New York, NY 10001-6210, USA.

Index on Censorship, Free Word Centre, 60 Farringdon Road, London EC1R 3GA, UK.

Journal of Mass Media Ethics, Taylor & Francis Group, 325 Chestnut Street, Suite 800, Philadelphia, PA 19106 USA.

Media Development, World Association for Christian Communication, 308 Main Street, Toronto, Ontario M4C 4X7, Canada.

Media Ethics, Institute of Communications Research, College of Communications, University of Illinois, 810 S. Wright Street, Suite 228, Urbana, IL 61801 USA. (Available online at www.mediaethicsmagazine.com.)

The News Media and The Law, Reporters Committee for Freedom of the Press, Suite 1100, 1101 Wilson Boulevard, Arlington, VA 22209, USA.

Quill, Society of Professional Journalists, Eugene S. Pulliam National Journalism Center, 3909 N. Meridian Street, Indianapolis, IN 48208, USA.

RTDNA Communicator, Radio Television Digital News Association, Suite 425, 529 14th Street, NW, Washington, DC 20045 USA (Until 2009, Radio-Television News Directors Association, RTNDA.)

Silha Center Bulletin, Silha Center for the Study of Media Ethics and Law, School of Journalism and Mass Communication, University of Minnesota, 111 Murphy Hall, 206 Church Street NE, Minneapolis, MN 55455, USA.

Student Press Law Center Report, Student Press Law Center, 1101 Wilson Boulevard, Suite 1100, Arlington, VA 22209-2211, USA.

In addition to the preceding periodicals, many organizations or parts of organizations active in the field of mass media ethics (such as the Media Ethics Division of the Association for Education in Journalism and Mass Communications) publish newsletters. A list of some of them may be found in *Media Ethics* 1996, 8(1), pp. 24–25.

Index

(In addition to the specific pages noted in each entry below, we suggest using the corresponding entries in the Glossary (pp. 536–554) whenever they are listed for an item in the Index. Although they serve different functions, both the Glossary and the Index can be useful in helping the reader to understand the meanings of the concepts and topics found in Controversies in Media Ethics.*)*